CO-CCD-524

INDIRA GANDHI

INDIRA GANDHI

Revolution in Restraint

UMA VASUDEV

VIKAS PUBLISHING HOUSE PVT LTD
DELHI BOMBAY BANGALORE KANPUR LONDON

VIKAS PUBLISHING HOUSE PVT LTD
5 Daryaganj, Ansari Road, Delhi-110006
Savoy Chambers, 5 Wallace Street, Bombay-400001
10 First Main Road, Gandhi Nagar, Bangalore-560009
80 Canning Road, Kanpur-208001
17-19 High Street, Harlesden, London NW 10

ISBN 0 7069 0294 7

PRINTED IN INDIA
AT INDRAPRASTHA PRESS, BAHADURSHAH ZAFAR MARG, NEW DELHI-110001,
AND PUBLISHED BY MRS SHARDA CHAWLA, VIKAS PUBLISHING HOUSE PVT LTD,
5 DARYAGANJ, ANSARI ROAD, DELHI-110006

To my parents

PREFACE

This book is not a judgment. It is an attempt at analysis. I have sought to trace the development of a personality: the conclusions are implicit. Though the book ends at a certain point, which it must for new events keep taking place while Indira Gandhi remains in power, the interpretation should be valid for any future that she may seek, in politics or outside. The epilogue, which contains Mrs Gandhi's very comprehensive answers to a series of questions I put to her on current issues that concern the national mind, brings the book up to date.

The writing of contemporary history has its hazards. In India there is no tradition of the biography. A probe into the personal is taken to be an affront to the private life of an individual even if he or she happens to be a public figure. To write of a living prime minister is even more difficult. Those who are too close to the center of authority are inhibited about talking freely because of the fear of being misunderstood or misrepresented. Prejudice very often colors interpretation, and one must sift the possible from the probable.

The personal interview nevertheless remains a significant source. I have therefore based my study on interviews with the prime minister herself, and several of her colleagues, relatives, and friends apart from the considerable material that one finds accumulated on Mrs Gandhi over the years. I have also drawn upon unpublished correspondence from the Nehru Papers.

I wish to express my deep gratitude to the prime minister for granting me interviews on several occasions and answering questions in a manner which set an example in forthrightness and spontaneity.

The prime minister's secretariat arranged for me to accompany Mrs Gandhi on two election tours, and were always cooperative and ready in providing the relevant material.

I am grateful to B.R. Nanda, Director, Nehru Memorial Museum and Library, New Delhi, and his staff for permitting me the use of the Nehru Papers and enabling me to choose some rare and unpublished photographs, particularly from the personal collection of Mohammad Yunus which has been obtained by them. The Press Information Bureau of the Government of India provided some material and the opportunity to make a selection from a wide range of photographs, including some exclusive ones of Mrs Gandhi and her family; others I got from *Socialist India, Link* newsmagazine, and the *Times of India.*

I owe special thanks to K. Natwar Singh.

I am grateful to Satish Gujral; to Inder Malhotra for helping me meet the politicians involved in the hectic drama of the 1967 leadership contest; to Y.P.R. Kapoor for personal sidelights on the Nehrus and the graphic account of the pre-election scene; to Sudarshan K. Seth for getting some of the photographs and other details; to numerous friends and colleagues who provided insights with incisive comments; and to that peculiar Indian trait which involves an entire family in one person's effort—to "L.K." Malhotra for the invaluable help with the references, the interview with Coonverbai Vakil, and the incidental difficulties that arise in the course of writing a book over a period of seven years, to Raka and Kamia for bearing up with a mother too often closeted in a room with paper and pencil, and to Aruna Vasudev Ploman for unfailing moral support.

Above all, I must acknowledge my deep debt to my parents, without whom the book just would not have been possible.

New Delhi   UMA VASUDEV
December 3, 1973

CONTENTS

PART IV
IMAGE

PART I

LIFE

1. AFFLUENCE

The story of Indira Nehru Gandhi is the story of a family, a tradition, and a country in travail. It is not the story of the growth of a political party but of a movement for freedom. It is not the story of one person but of a family that stood as a symbol. It is not even the story of a country as the term is normally understood but rather of a colorful, varied, warring, hating, loving subcontinent in revolt. Nowhere in its society or in its individuals could modern thought and political fearlessness be taken for granted. The fight, not only for freedom from British rule but for the form it should take, was hard, continuous, and bitter.   In the forefront of it all was the Nehru family into which Indira was born on November 19, 1917.

The tone for the Nehrus was set by the dominating Motilal Nehru, Indira's grandfather and head of their joint family household.   A proud patriarch and rebel, he was a lawyer of means and a man of great generosity.   His flashes of temper vied with his roars of laughter.   If the former overawed his colleagues, friends, and immediate family, the latter drew their fascinated loyalty.   Motilal was a self-made man who in his thirties had reached a point of professional success, material affluence, and personal magnetism that made his home, his personality, and his way of life the subject of envy and admiration in the quiet northern city of Allahabad.   He was a handsome man with a determined chin, piercing eyes, large mustache, and a complexion that glowed with good health and good humor.   He took an epicurean delight in dressing well, eating well, and talking well.   His suits were made in Savile Row, and his cellar had the choicest wines.   Often in the evenings the walls of his house resounded with the wit and repartee of the elite—men of taste, intelligence, and attainment, over whom Motilal towered in match-less form.   He had that "exquisiteness of attire which symbolized the clean fighter and the great gentleman and that impressive face, deeply lined and careworn, on which character and intellect were so deeply imprinted.... Eminent as a lawyer, eminent as a speaker, and in the first rank as a political leader, he could not but take the foremost place wherever he might be...."[1]

A colleague recalls seeing him for the first time one October evening, and the image stamped itself forever on his memory: "The green carpet of a well-kept lawn under his feet, seated in a wicker easy chair, smoking an Abdulla cigarette, there he was scanning the day's paper at Anand Bhawan. It was the picture of a man of many victories, with one leg crossed over its fellow, enjoying the good things of life."[2]   Anand Bhawan or "the abode of happiness," was the palatial house which Motilal had bought in 1900. He had completely remodeled it to accord with his style of entertainment and his personal taste.   He was the first man in Allahabad to have running water and electricity, to build an indoor swimming pool, the first to import a car in 1904, the first with the latest gadgets, bought on successive trips to Europe.   Added to this were the rich carpets, the finest china, the most sparkling crystal. He also endowed Anand Bhawan with great Danes, fine stables, and sprawling orchards. He had a large family of wife, sister-in-law, nephews, and daughters over whom he held protective sway.   "In the days of affluence or in days of hardship, the household was sternly governed by my grandfather—his awe-inspiring temper softened by quick forgiveness and infectious laughter, his strict discipline tempered by his love for his family and his enormous zest for life," says Mrs Gandhi now.[3]

The Nehrus trace their descent from the pure Brahmin lineage of Kashmiri Brahmins. Motilal's great-great-grandfather, Pandit Raj Kaul, was a renowned Sanskrit and Persian scholar.   The emperor Farrukh Siyyer was so impressed by him on one of his visits to Kashmir that he brought the family to Delhi in 1716 and granted them lands, villages, and a house as *jagir*. Because the house was situated on the *nahar* which then ran through the city of Delhi, the pandit came to be known as Kaul Nehru and gradually Nehru itself came to be used as the surname.   By the time of Motilal's grandfather, Pandit Lachhminarain Nehru, the family fortune had gone through many ups and downs and he became the first *vakil* of the Sarkar Company at the imperial court.   Motilal's father, Pandit Ganga Dhar Nehru, was *kotwal* of Delhi for a while before the revolt of 1857 but died at 34, three months before Motilal was born on May 6, 1861.   On his mother's side, Motilal's great-grandfather was the *diwan* of "Shamru Ki Begum" (the Begum of Dyce Sombre), and his grandfather, Pandit Shankar Nath Zutshi, was a famous literary figure of his time.

Motilal grew up under the generous protection of his elder brother, Pandit Nandlal Nehru, who for ten years was the hard-working Diwan of Khetri State.   When the raja died, Nandlal shifted to Allahabad, qualified as a vakil of the Allahabad high court, and soon made a name for himself.   When he died in 1887 Motilal was only 26 years old. Impelled by the sudden responsibility not only for his own but his brother's large family of eight children, he threw himself into the same profession with such perseverance, industry, and dogged determination that he soon gained fame and financial prosperity. He never looked back.

On one occasion years later a young colleague of his, Chaman Lal, recalls sipping tea with him at a round table covered with papers. When the postman brought the morning mail, Motilal opened a few letters, chuckled, and threw them toward Chaman Lal.   There were three letters containing checks totaling Rs 90,000 in payment for Motilal's advice which was given on the basis of records submitted to him.   Typical was the lusty humor with which he remarked, "I do not know any more law than you do but it seems that I have done a lot better in my previous life," and the hearty laugh that followed.[4] Obviously he did not completely accept the theory of reincarnation but the levity with which he referred to it was not necessarily an indication of his disbelief.   He simply valued human endeavor more than religious injunction and his confidence came from the knowledge that he had made his life what it was.

Once, after attending a condolence meeting on the death of Hakim Ajmal Khan, a prominent political figure, he became a little pensive and later told a friend that he did not want anyone to pray for him after his death.   When he was asked the reason, Motilal replied gravely, "Throughout this life I have fought my way by myself and I propose to do the same after death. I do not want any props from this side."[5] He would not let himself be drawn into the more orthodox vortex of Hinduism.   He preferred its spirit to its ritual.

"Who do you think is the ideal Hindu?" he once asked his secretary Shiv Dutt Upadhyaya.

"Malaviyaji, of course," replied the poor man, thinking of the high praise that Motilal lavished on his great contemporary, for his spotless character and steadfastness of purpose.

"No," Motilal said categorically. "I am the true Hindu! A good Hindu does not practice untouchability and sectarianism. When the Hindus lost their capacity for assimilation, they began to assume their habitual narrowness and small-mindedness. The ideal Hindu must be able to absorb and digest everything."[6]

The Hindu in the north of India certainly had to. From the time of the earliest Aryans through the Greeks, the Ghaznavites, and the Muslims, it was the north that first braved the invading hordes and then assimilated them. The result was a blending of races, languages, looks, and customs which created a rich tradition of mutual dependence. It was only religion that drew a demarcation line, but so inextricable was the confluence, for instance, of Hindu and Muslim cultures that in the heyday of unity there was an underlying tolerance for the idiosyncrasies of the other which prevented any overt conflict. Allahabad, like Delhi, was one of the centers of this common culture where Urdu was spoken with ease, and a background of training in Sanskrit among the educated Hindus vied with Persian and Arabic. Even Motilal's wife, the delicate Swarup Rani, reared in the orthodox Hindu milieu, spoke Urdu, as her daughter Vijayalaxmi Pandit later wrote, with the "polished elegance of the high society of the times and could cap Persian quotations and recite Sanskrit verses with anyone."[7] Representing the more traditional aspects of Hindu society, religious-minded, believing in the stars, in regular visits to the temple, in purification fasts, and daily worship at home, Swarup Rani had to contend with the westernization of her husband's outlook that increased with each trip to Europe. She had to part with her only son, Jawahar, when Motilal decided to send the fifteen-year-old to Harrow for his education. Her daughters, Swarup[8] and Krishna, were dressed in the height of European fashion and they were brought up under the overall supervision of an English governess. They were allowed a freedom by their father she found difficult to approve. But, like a true Hindu wife, she submitted to his will, even to the point of adopting the hideous European coiffeur of the day when she accompanied him to take their son to Harrow.

"Put your foot down and do what you like for once," the spirited Swarup would say to her impatiently at times, only to get the irrevocable answer, "My dear, I do like what your father likes and, anyway, he knows best."[9] Swarup Rani could always find a congenial spirit in her widowed sister, Bibima, who lived with them and seemed to have taken it upon herself to dedicate her life to her care. As a young widow, she had had no place in the society of nineteenth-century India. Remarriage was impossible and it was a measure of progress that at least she was not shunned as widows were in the past. In fact, Bibima was dearly loved by Indira and her cousins. At lunch time on Sundays they would eagerly troop into her living quarters, where she would serve piping hot *puris* and delicious vegetable dishes from copper and brass vessels. She lived a short distance from the main house, where she had a separate kitchen with a scrupulously clean floor, earthen stoves, and little bamboo mats to sit on. She preferred to do her own cooking because she did not eat meat and would not touch anything from the two big kitchens where European and meat dishes were made. In the afternoons she would sit beside the children under a tree in the garden or under a fan inside if it was too hot. While chopping areca-nuts and peeling cardamoms she would dig into her enormous store of mythology from the *Mahabharata* and the *Ramayana* and relate the glorious tales of bravery, dramas, and morals that form the substance of these epics and the ethical base of Hindu belief. Together with Bibima and later Kamala, Indira's mother, who too was schooled in the older traditions, the imperious little Swarup Rani, with her daily *puja* and her sedulous regard for the ritual ceremony, represented the traditional religious belief that ran parallel to the agnosticism of Motilal and Jawahar. It was to the credit of both that neither really interfered with the other.

There were thus two marked styles of living. There were two kitchens, one in which meat was cooked and the other which was strictly vegetarian. The separate kitchens were not due to Swarup Rani alone but to the friends and colleagues with varying tastes, backgrounds, and commitments that Motilal entertained. If they were vegetarians they sat at the table with him and were served in round silver *thalis* and *katoris* all the choice fare of vegetarian food while he dipped with relish into aromatic meat or chicken curries cooked in the spicy Kashmiri way or in the European fashion. Once when he was served some eggs, Sri Prakasa, then a young aspiring politician, later governor of a state in free India, said with shocked surprise, "Why, Panditji, you eat eggs!" Motilal reacted by confiding to him heartily, "The mother is also soon arriving," whereupon a succulent dish of chicken did indeed appear.[10]

There were evening parties when Englishmen who were to become political enemies but were good personal friends at the time, like the lieutenant-governor of the United Provinces, Sir Harcourt Butler, would come, and "rivers of champagne" would flow. There were also tennis parties, garden parties, and swimming parties. Motilal even started a private European club in his house where Europeans and Indians could mix freely. But always at the end of every party there would be a family dinner in the Western style or in the Indian manner, for Motilal's ties with his family were strong, possessive, and abiding although he was not a demonstrative man.

"You are living for your family, I envy you," wrote Mohandas Gandhi to him later with sharp awareness; once when he was asked what he thought was Motilal's greatest quality, he said, "Love of his son,"

"Was it not love of India?"

"No," replied Gandhi. "Motilal's love for India is derived from his love for Jawaharlal."[11]

"Exceedingly foolish stories about his Western habits were spread widely over the north of India," recalled C.F. Andrews, an Englishman who was a great friend of Gandhi, Tagore, the Nehrus, and the Indian cause, and who spent long years in India, "which were ridiculous to those who knew him in his own house, for whatever he did in this direction, as events proved, was merely on the surface, and could be thrown off at a moment's notice.... All through his life he was far too deeply wedded to his own country and its traditions to make him ever forget his birthright."[12]

Perhaps it was this fierce throwback to the core within him that made Motilal utter the Gayatri *mantra* just before he died, a prayer that Jawaharlal recalled he had not heard him say for nearly 40 years.[13] This Hindu prayer does not describe God as an "irate father or a stern judge" but as *jyotisam jyotih,* the light of lights, the spirit of light shining in the future." It seemed typical that Motilal, a passionate believer in reason, intellect, and the human will, should invoke a prayer that centered on the concept of enlightenment rather than on mercy.

Such, then, was the man whose overpowering presence defined the standards of his family, and especially for Indira during all her impressionable years until she was thirteen. A change in his life meant a change in the life of the entire family.

Motilal's involvement in Indian nationalist politics, and subsequently, his family's, was rather vague in the early years partly due to his intense preoccupation with advancing his career and the family fortune, and partly due to the feeling that his countrymen had fallen low and deserved what they got. There was a "trace of contempt in his mind," wrote Jawaharlal in a powerful portrait of his father later, "for the politicians who talked and talked without doing anything, though he had no idea at all as to what they could do. Also, there was the thought born in the pride of his own success, that many—certainly not all—of those who took to politics had been failures in life."[14] He had attended the fourth session of the newly formed Indian National Congress at Allahabad in 1888. It was started by an Englishman, Allan Octavian Hume in 1885, as a forum for the discussion of social and political questions and as a means of educating the British raj to the responsibilities of enlightened government and bringing the people of India to a new awareness of their constitutional rights. It soon attracted the cream of the Indian intelligentsia. It also became evident that if it had not been started by an Englishman it would have been conveniently snuffed out at its inception, for the clash between official prejudice and public demand was immediate and incontrovertible.

At the fifth session of the Congress in 1889 at Bombay, Motilal was elected to the Subjects Committee. This position brought him into intimate contact with the leading figures of the day—men such as Surendra Nath Banerjee, Gopal Krishna Gokhale, and Madan Mohan Malaviya. At the Nagpur session two years later, he again found himself a member of the Subjects Committee and at Allahabad in 1892, he was secretary of the Reception Committee. Then came a period during which he confined his attention to his profession and his family and his son's education at Harrow. However, in 1905 when Lord Curzon's scheme to partition Bengal triggered nationwide anger, Motilal found a challenge that his pride as an Indian could hardly resist. He went as a delegate to the Congress session at Benares in 1905, and then to Calcutta in 1906. For the next few years he saw a pattern of agitation, repression, and conflict, which ultimately won the day for Indian nationalism when the notorious partition was repealed in 1911.

Anti-British protest in the Congress during those years consisted of constitutional agitation by the moderates, whose aim was self-government within the empire, and by the extremists, whose aim was immediate reforms that would transfer authority from the British to the Indians. The moderates were led by Gopal Krishna Gokhale and the extremists by Bal Gangadhar Tilak, known as *Lokmanya*, "the beloved of the people." Gokhale was a clever strategist, Tilak a fiery idealist. Both were brilliant orators, firm patriots, and Congressmen of unimpeachable loyalty. But a series of repressive measures culminating in Lord Curzon's dictatorial decision to partition Bengal, the utter disregard shown for Indian feeling, and the ruthlessness with which the protests were met, broke the back of Indian patience. The extremists felt that they had a stronger case for using coercion and other aggressive methods of obtaining redress for their grievances from a government that had repeatedly shown itself to be intractable. Speeches, petitions, and pleas had failed where pressure, force, and anger must win. Gokhale realized that the Englishmen's own fight for liberty had been achieved through parliamentary victories doggedly won over the years and believed that the Indians could win freedom by the same means. Tilak believed that a different principle must apply to a dependency which could think in terms of developing precedents only after achieving independence and not before. When Mahatma Gandhi first met Tilak and Gokhale in 1896, he felt that Tilak towered like the Himalayas in his grandeur and aloofness while Gokhale seemed like the Holy Ganges, inviting a confident plunge. Yet it was Tilak who drew his inspiration from the common people and Gokhale who depended upon the educated elite.

Gokhale's plan was to improve the existing constitution, Tilak's was to reconstruct it. Gokhale had necessarily to work with the bureaucracy, Tilak had necessarily to fight it. Gokhale stood for cooperation wherever possible and opposition wherever necessary; Tilak inclined toward a policy of obstruction....Gokhale's methods sought to win the foreigner,

Tilak's to replace him....Gokhale looked to the classes and the intelligentsia; Tilak to the masses and the millions. Gokhale's arena was the
council chamber; Tilak's forum was the village *mandap*. Gokhale's
medium of expression was English; Tilak's was Marathi; Gokhale's
objective was self-government for which the people had to fit themselves
by answering the tests prescribed by the English; Tilak's objective was
swaraj....Gokhale was on a level with his age; Tilak was in advance
of his times.[15]

For Motilal, whose training as a lawyer was to win an argument step by
step, whose sophisticated, westernized background, and luxurious habits
ensured him friendships among like-minded men of the Indian elite, the
choice, if it was to be a political one, had to be for the rule of law and the
patient patriotism epitomized by Gokhale rather than for the inflammatory,
anti-institutional nationalism of Tilak. A slogan for the boycott of British
goods he could understand. But a boycott of British institutions with all
the concomitants of constitutional progress? That seemed anathema.
At the Calcutta Congress, Motilal found an atmosphere of intense excitement in which a struggle for supremacy seemed imminent between the two
wings of the party. But an open split was avoided by a last-minute compromise on the part of everyone. Unexpectedly, however, the very person
whom the moderates had thought they could rely upon for conducting the
Congress along their lines, the doughty eighty-year-old leader, Dadabhai
Naoroji whom they called all the way from England to preside, presented
the stirring and revolutionary slogan of swaraj in addition to the slogans
of *swadeshi*, boycott, and national education defined at Benares the year
before. But in spite of the joyous reaction of the extremists, who thought they
had won a point, national aspiration as it was defined in the Congress
resolution at the time was still very limited. Self-government did not imply
more than a demand for simultaneous examinations in England and India,
appointment to high posts through competitive examinations, adequate
representation of Indians in the councils of the governors of Madras and
Bombay, a more effective representation of the people in the supreme and
legislative councils which were sought to be expanded correspondingly and
more power for local and municipal bodies with only minimum official control.
The meaning of swaraj then and the meaning of swaraj twenty-three years
later when Jawaharlal Nehru gave a clarion call for complete independence
was separated by a period of internal conflict within the party, turmoil within the country, a resurgence of national consciousness inspired by Mahatma
Gandhi, and the personal tribulations of the Nehrus that were to be sharpened
by politics and invite them to stand the most supreme tests of patriotism.
The first of many meetings held to hammer out a political strategy took
place at Anand Bhawan soon after the Calcutta session. There was a unanimous demand that Motilal preside over a provincial conference of the

United Provinces. This conference was to be part of a series of congresses held throughout India to introduce the public to the moderate view. Two such conferences had already been held at Bombay and Raipur. Motilal immediately wrote about the proposed presidency to his son at Harrow as it had become his habit to confide his innermost thoughts to him in a lengthy weekly letter. "I have been compelled to accept it....It is entirely a new line for me and I have very grave doubts of being able to justify the expectations of my friends...."[16]

Jawaharlal had been following events in India with intense concern. He felt a rising commitment in his heart to the extremists and was pleased that his father was to be more actively associated with the political struggle even though on the moderate side. "I am sure," he wrote back, "you will be as successful in the new line as you have been in other fields." But he reserved judgment about the good faith of the British. "I personally like to see the government blamed and censured as much as possible," he said, adding pointedly, "As regards John Bull's good faith, I have not so much confidence in him as you have."[17]

Nonetheless, at the Congress session in December 1907 the efforts of the extremists to have their own president in the person of Lala Lajpat Rai or Tilak were thwarted and the moderates gained control of the party. The following years—even though they saw the introduction of the Morley-Minto Reforms, which left a large section of Indians quite dissatisfied—were quiet ones. Gokhale's sedate attempts to bring change overruled Tilak's tempestuous advocation of liberty, which finally landed Tilak in prison. One of the reasons Motilal stood by the moderates was his suspicion that for all their patriotic fervor the extremists embraced a reactionary Hindu revivalism, something which his good-natured agnosticism could not brook. Jawahar, by then in Trinity College, Cambridge, reacted with the same disgust.

In fact, in social matters Motilal was uncompromising and showed a progressive spirit that was to pass down to his son and from his son to the granddaughter. In April 1909, as president of the third United Provinces Social Conference at Agra, he made a hardhitting and forceful address in favor of social reform:

Imagine for a moment that there was no caste system in India, that Hindus and Musalmans, and the numerous sub-divisions of these two great communities sank their differences and met together as children of a common mother, that the ladies of India instead of being shut behind the prison walls of the *zenana* were properly educated, that there were no longer in the population of India the children of premature mothers and underdeveloped fathers. Suppose we reached such a social, moral and physical perfection, could any power on earth keep us from obtaining the fullest political privileges enjoyed by the most advanced

nations of the world? ...Let us, therefore, begin at once, and in all earnestness, to remove the two ugliest blots on our social system—caste and
purdah. These are the two evils which have dragged us down the social
scale and made us the laughing stock of modern civilization.[18]

Again his son realized that the characteristic frankness had overcome whatever diffidence his father might have felt about the feelings of the conservatives in his audience. "I do not think that you are such a slow and steady sort
of person as you make yourself out to be,"[19] he had once written to his father,
and it was natural that when Motilal's tremendous energy later united with
Gandhi's stirring idealism, the result should be cataclysmic not only for him,
but for his entire family. In the interim, although his ardor for the moderates
began to fade under the impact of their continual compromise and the bad
faith of the Morley-Minto Reforms, Motilal contested and won a seat on
the enlarged provincial council under the so-called "reformed" constitution.
What had begun as a tentative brush with politics promised to turn into a
full-fledged role, for Motilal could not help but bring to the provincial and
central assemblies later the same personal magnetism, incisive argument,
and brilliant repartee that had made him a legendary figure at the bar.
Yet there was time enough for other things. In 1912, Jawaharlal
returned to India. Motilal had already ordered two additional rooms
for the first floor of Anand Bhawan. He had had an interesting exchange of correspondence with his son about his marriage as he was eager
that a choice be made quickly due to the limited number of eligible girls in
the Kashmiri community. But although Jawaharlal returned with a grounding
in liberal thought it did not extend to rejecting one of the oldest Indian
customs—the arranged marriage. Perhaps the Europe of 1912 could not give
a very forward example either, for the revolutionary social changes were
essentially an aftermath of World War I. Nevertheless, while in England
he had refused to have his father arrange his engagement in his absence.

It was only after Jawaharlal had been back three years that Motilal found
a girl who he thought would be a fitting companion for his son. Kamala
Kaul was sixteen, tall, slim, lovely and, what was to Motilal most important, healthy. As his own wife became a semi-invalid after the birth of a
second son (who lived only a month) he was anxious that Jawahar should
be spared the worry of a sickly wife. Seeing Kamala then, no one
imagined she could ever be the cause of worry on such an account."She was
one of the most beautiful women I knew or ever have known," recalled her
sister-in-law Krishna.[20] She was very, very Indian, outwardly gentle, inwardly steel. She was later to prove that she could match the daring
patriotism of her husband with a no less courageous one of her own. She
was also capable of invoking the most fierce loyalties from those who were
won over by her instant sympathy and deep consideration for others. But
at the time, although she was the daughter of a wealthy Kashmiri business-

man of Delhi, her background, upbringing, and outlook were totally different from that of the Nehrus. She was unfamiliar with the entire range of Western living that characterized the Nehru household. Motilal immediately sought a way to provide her with the necessary confidence. He suggested that she come and stay at Allahabad, visit Anand Bhawan often, and spend a year under the supervision of the English governess of his daughters. For as his daughter-in-law she would be responsible for entertaining high society with the same ease as the Nehrus themselves.

Kamala was uncomfortable at first with her limited knowledge of English and her confrontation with the equally beautiful but much more confident Swarup, who was of the same age and therefore superior and intolerant. In fact, there was a clash that was later to result in simmering resentments. Swarup, apparently could not bear her place as the idol of her father and brother to be even partially shared by another. "Apart from their temperamental differences, this was the first time Swarup had to contend with a rival," stated a member of the family. "She was everybody's darling. Nobody would refuse her anything."[21] Meanwhile, Jawahar and Kamala were thrown together at informal gatherings arranged with care. The shy but mutual attraction that both seemed to feel was marked with satisfaction by the rest of the family. Jawahar was not in love with Kamala, but he was not in love with anyone else. It was more a deference to the norm than passion that led finally to their marriage on February 8, 1916, the auspicious day of *Basant Panchami,* the herald of spring. But he was handsome and she was beautiful and Motilal's pride as a father, his love of style, and his great wealth combined to make the wedding the most elaborate social event of the decade. The bridegroom's party of nearly a hundred people traveled to Delhi in a specially decorated train. At Delhi they were joined by hundreds of other guests and as it was obviously impossible to accommodate them all at the houses of friends or elsewhere, Motilal settled them on the outskirts of the old city in a group of splendid tents, which was dubbed the Nehru Wedding Camp. The tents had wooden floors covered with beautiful carpets and were furnished with wall hangings. There were separate bed room, dining room, drawing room, and kitchen tents. A retinue of servants waited on the guests and there was even an orchestra to add to the gaiety.[22] Motilal's Western habits in no way diminished his love of Indian rituals and the marriage ceremony was conducted with the pomp, gravity, and glitter of the ancient Vedic rites. In this matter Jawaharlal seems to have given himself up to his father's wishes and both of them, although fundamentally devoted to social reform, happily embraced certain aspects of Indian orthodoxy.

For the wedding ceremony Kamala wore, according to Kashmiri custom, bracelets, necklaces, earrings, and bangles made of flowers. Her sari was pink and sumptuous as was the beige brocade *sherwani* of her husband, with which he wore tight white trousers and a pink turban. As was the romantic custom, he came to her house riding a white horse. The day after her wedding (when the bride is supposed to wear the clothes and the jewelry given by her in-laws), Kamala was arrayed in a fabulous collection of diamonds, emeralds, pearls, and other precious stones, over a pink sari studded with real pearls. It was characteristic that Motilal himself had supervised the making of Kamala's jewelry by jewelers who had sat working for months in the verandas of Anand Bhawan. It seemed significant that Kamala, shy and hesitant, was not paled by the brilliance of the ornaments she wore. "Her beauty," remarked her sister-in-law, "triumphed over this ostentatious display, not overwhelmed but enhanced by the glittering jewels."[23] But if Motilal was an eager participant in that ostentation, it was only a few years later that he showed that he could give up his possessions with the same grandeur with which he had acquired them—horses, carriages, carpets, crystal, great Danes, servants, the beautiful house he lived in, his law practice, in fact, his very way of life. Later, his son would sell Kamala's carefully wrought jewels at a time when sentiment had to be sacrificed in the cause that was to obsess them all: freedom for their people and freedom for their country.

On November 19, 1917, Kamala and Jawaharlal had their first and only child, Indira Priyadarshini. Priyadarshni means "dear to the sight." To Jawahar's mother, who wanted a grandson to carry on the family line, the birth of a girl was a disappointment. To Motilal, any child of his beloved son was precious. Nothing was too good for the little girl and two years later, Motilal ordered a pram for her from Whiteaways Laidlaw in Calcutta and wrote to his son: "I am always thinking of Indira, the very thought of a personification of innocence is soothing. By a very easy slip it justifies idol worship and many other things which modern civilization sets down for senseless superstition...."[24] Sentiment was such that an old family retainer, Munshi Mubarak Ali, who was in charge of the servants and lived in a cottage on the grounds of Anand Bhawan, defied the wracking finale of cancer to linger and behold for a moment Jawahar's newborn child. Mubarak Ali, a Muslim from an aristocratic and wealthy family that suffered reverses of fortune during the Indian revolt of 1857, with his dignity, benevolence, and utter loyalty earned the absolute confidence of Motilal and his wife who trusted him with numerous supervisory tasks. He was a favorite mentor of the Nehru children, to whom he would relate, like Bibima, but in a different style, all the tales of history and mythology that could hold imagination spellbound. Loyalty on his part had obviously turned to great love and, waiting determinedly on his deathbed, it was only when the infant Indira was brought wrapped up to him and he blessed her with tears in his eyes that he breathed a sigh of contentment and let the end come peacefully.

"You were the proudest looking baby I've ever seen,"[25] the irrepressible, poet and politician Sarojini Naidu said to Indira of the first time she saw

her.   And well she might have been as she lay, six months old, in her grandmother's arms while Swarup Rani stood on the marble steps of Anand
Bhawan to welcome Sarojini Naidu.   When Jawahar was born, Motilal
had been only ordinarily well off.   At the birth of Swarup twelve years later
he was prosperous.   When Krishna followed six years after Swarup he was
extremely rich.   In this house of great wealth Indira was to find great
love.   In addition she had a proud and spirited mother and a father who
valued the larger dimensions of the intellect.   These personal qualities, together with wealth and fierce patriotism, made a combination that was to
prove irresistible in creating a living legend of the Nehru name.   When
there was so much to the foundation, the future did seem indeed to rise with
promise.

2. PLUNGE

Meanwhile, Jawaharlal was impatient. In his autobiography written seventeen years later, he mentions his marriage in three lines and the birth of his daughter not at all, and later only in the context of some political event or the other. It shows that his mind was far from being preoccupied with domesticity. He had come home from England in 1912 after passing his science examination in Cambridge and then taking his bar examination at the Inner Temple with "neither glory nor ignominy" as he called it. Back in India, he described himself "a bit of a prig," though the remark shows that discontent was beginning to simmer as soon as he joined the high court and became his father's junior. He had accepted without question the pattern of joint family living set by his father and although he and Kamala had a separate suite, the utter security with which he could leave his wife and child in the care of the large household relieved him of routine domestic responsibility. The social round of parties and club-going did not interest him, and there was in his heart, a faint but recurrent dissatisfaction with his possible future role of a "mere lawyer."[1] He had attended the Bankipore Congress in 1912 with his father and found essentially "a social gathering with no political excitement or tension" where the British upper class appeared dressed in the height of European fashion. He was impressed by Gokhale, but no one else. His own politics had already acquired an extremist tinge, much to the chagrin of his father and his own peace of mind; but any positive activity seemed to hang in abeyance as World War I took the form of the restrictive Defence of India Act, which was a repressive act passed for the undeclared purpose of enrolling recruits from the Punjab. Jawaharlal began to feel more and more intensely that "both individual and national honour demanded a more aggressive and fighting attitude to foreign rule." He did what he could. He became a member of the Congress, attended some of its meetings, took part in the agitation against the oppression of Indian workers in Fiji, and the treatment of Indians in South Africa. He met Gandhi at the Lucknow Congress of 1916 and though filled with admiration for his brave stand for the Indians in South Africa, found him "distant," "different," and almost "unpolitical."

It was also about the time of the Irish uprising and Roger Casement's stirringly nationalistic speeches which seemed to find an echo in Jawahar's heart. His absolute nationalism so dominated his mind that it overrode his vague preoccupation, lingering on from his Cambridge days, with modern creeds like "socialism." "I felt more and more," he realized, "that it was not possible to reconcile public work, especially of the aggressive type which appealed to me, with the lawyer's job."[2] Though the war drew only surface loyalty from the Indians for the British, the Nehrus were drawn into active discussion of the news and the battles of the day. While Swarup Rani joined the European and Indian women of Allahabad in knitting and collecting clothes for the soldiers, the younger Nehru girls formed the Kumari Sabha, a patriotic society whose spirited proceedings, consisting of debates, national songs, and plays, began to resound against the walls of Anand Bhawan. And so did the argument, the one basic argument, between father and son. Motilal stuck to his belief that there was no satisfactory alternative to constitutional agitation and Jawaharlal felt that more fervent measures were necessary. Tension would mount and any insignificant topic would take on a political hue. Motilal was afraid that Jawaharlal might be veering towards the dangerous attitudes of the terrorists while Jawahar chafed under his father's divergent stand and his own inability to find a way out.

During 1915 and 1916, Tilak had been trying hard to strengthen his party through magnetic leadership, a rallying point, and a war cry. These he thought could be provided by (1) the Congress compromise, a reconciliation between his Nationalist party and the moderates who controlled the Congress; (2) the reorganization of the Nationalist party; and (3) a strong movement for home rule. The moderates, however, would not admit Tilak and the Nationalists back into the Congress because they feared he would employ obstructionist methods and start a "boycott the government" move. Mrs Annie Besant, the theosophist leader, who was soon to play such a dominant part not only in the politics of the country but in the lives and decisions of the Nehrus, tried her best to effect this reconciliation to no avail. At its Bombay session, the Congress decided to readmit the Nationalists in an indirect way, but set a limit of one year for Tilak before allowing him to exercise his influence on the organization. In 1916, at Lucknow, the seeds of communalism sown by the separate electorates provided for under the Morley-Minto Reforms were buried for a time under the Muslim League-Congress concordat and their joint formulation of a scheme for self-government.

The details of the League-Congress agreement had been hammered out at a meeting in 1916 of the All India Congress Committee at Anand Bhawan on April 22, 23, and 24. This was only the beginning. It was yet another barrier which fell to make Motilal's commitment to active politics imperative. He had been holding back on the ground that lack of unity between Muslims and Hindus made a demand for the substitution of Indian for British power useless, and while he appreciated the weakness of the moderate stand he saw no alternative.

On April 23, Tilak, prevented from exercising control over the Congress by the one-year time limit, decided to carry out one part of his program alone. He formed the Home Rule League, with headquarters at Poona. But always under suspicion by the government, he was soon bound over for "good behavior" for a year and prohibited from entering Delhi or the Punjab. Each repressive government act, however, boomeranged by making Tilak more and more popular with the people. Although he was only 60, he was physically weak and unable to take advantage of the rising tide of national consciousness by sponsoring his home rule idea with the broad-based propaganda and energy it demanded. On the other hand Mrs Besant, a friend of India and spurred by her sense of justice and dedication, felt that the Congress was proving too slow. The heroic contribution of Indian soldiers to the winter battles of 1914 in Flanders had not only evoked admiration from the West but led Indian nationalists like Surendra Nath Banerjee to think in terms of a "reward" by the British in the form of concessions to Indian aspirations. But Mrs Besant thought differently. "There had been talk of a reward due to India's loyalty," she cried then, "but India does not chaffer with the blood of her sons and the proud tears of her daughters in exchange for so much liberty, so much right. India claims the right as a nation, to justice among the peoples of the Empire. India will ask for it after the war; but not as a reward, but as a right does she ask for it. On that there must be no mistake."[3] It was a spirited reaffirmation of Tilak's famous cry: "Swaraj is my birthright, and I shall have it." In fact, Tilak and Mrs Besant soon formed a team that carried the idea of home rule like a war cry throughout the length and breadth of India.

Mrs Besant first formed an auxiliary Home Rule League in London on June 12, 1916, as a more dynamic substitute for the British Committee of the Indian National Congress which contented itself with merely holding "a watching brief," according to its own admittance. In India she opened her campaign in Madras in September that year by founding the All India Home Rule League, so termed to distinguish it from Tilak's first Home Rule League in Poona. Thereafter, Home Rule Leagues were established all over the country and both Tilak and Mrs Besant worked in conjunction to see that their work did not overlap. Mrs Besant, though older than Tilak, was in the happier position of having better health, demonic energy, tireless organizing capacity, and a world reputation that ensured her immediate attention. In India, the spectacle of a foreigner, and especially an Englishwoman, devoting herself to the Indian cause proved cataclysmic. Enthusiasm spread like wildfire and the year 1917, the year of Indira's birth, was one of magic discontent. The British government became alarmed, lost their heads, and the Madras governor, Lord Pentland, clapped Mrs Besant and her followers into jail.

As a visitor to the Nehru home Mrs Besant had been a familiar figure. Jawaharlal's childhood tutor, part Irishman, Ferdinand T. Brooks, had been employed by Motilal on Mrs Besant's recommendation and, under his influence and attracted to the weekly meetings of theosophists in his room, Jawahar began to be inducted into theosophical phraseology and ideas. "I did not understand much that was said but it all sounded very mysterious and fascinating and I felt that here was the key to the secrets of the universe,"[4] he recalled later. For the first time he became conscious of religion and particularly of Hinduism and its philosophical treatises. But when he heard Mrs Besant deliver some of her frequent speeches on theosophy in Allahabad at the time, he returned "deeply moved by her oratory—dazed .... and as in a dream."[5] Years later, when his thoughts turned to politics rather than religion and he found that Mrs Besant's great gift in moving the masses was allied to the cause closest to his heart, he lost no time in joining her Home Rule League and pressed his father to do the same. For Motilal it was a period of severe mental conflict, for change for him had to come from deep intellectual conviction and once adopted followed through. He was already dissatisfied with moderate philosophy but still not ready to reject it.

Meanwhile, talk of forming an Indian defense force on the lines of the

European defense forces in India was prevalent.   Indians were not allowed
to possess arms and although Jawahar was not eager to cooperate with the
scheme because of the humiliating conditions it imposed, he and others decided that some sort of military training would be better than nothing.   Not
only did he send in his application to join the force but formed a committee
with his father, Sir Tej Bahadur Sapru, and C.Y. Chintamani, and other
moderate leaders to help the scheme achieve wider approbation.   It was at
this point that the news of Mrs Besant's imprisonment came like a thunder-
clap to sensitive nationalist ears.   It seemed to be far too logical a consequence to the long series of measures that the British had taken to deny
India its right to self-government.   Besides, it seemed unthinkable that a
frail old foreigner should fight their battles and for the sake of their liberty
forgo her own.

It is understandable in the light of Motilal's temperament and his code of
honor and ethics that the event should have had a profound impact on him.
He had successfully resisted Jawahar's blandishments. He found he did not care
to resist the indirect though imperative one posed by Mrs Besant's trial.
He joined her Home Rule League as did several of his moderate colleagues,
Sir Tej Bahadur Sapru, Munshi Narayan Prasad Asthana, C. Y. Chintamani,
and others, but while some of them would turn back from the extremist aftermath of this decision, for Motilal it was going to be a straight and narrow
path toward total involvement and total sacrifice.   "There's nothing moderate about Motilal except his politics," someone had said.   This was soon
to change to "everything being moderate about Motilal except his politics ,"
with the restraint in personal style that this implied.

Within a week Motilal had made a stirring presidential address at a meeting
of the citizens of Allahabad and the next day, June 23, the Allahabad Home
Rule League elected him its president and his son its secretary.   In a
month's time he and Jawahar infused a new determination in the League and
on August 10 Motilal was selected to preside over a special conference of the
Provincial Congress at Lucknow, where he mixed his criticism of British
bureaucracy with admiration for British democracy, and so dominated the
proceedings that "not a word was breathed in defiance or disagreement
while he was on his legs...."   In fact, there was a move to adopt passive
resistance as a means of applying pressure on the government, but Motilal
preferred to restrict the conference to exercising its original purpose: to
protest against the treatment meted out to Mrs Besant, and to call for political reforms.

On July 28 the All India Congress Committee and the Council of the Muslim League met at Bombay to consider the question of starting a mass campaign of passive resistance throughout the country to secure the release of the
internees.   It decided to ask the Provincial Congress committees and the
Council of the League to submit their views in six weeks.   But within that
period the situation changed rapidly.   In England, a raging debate took place

in Parliament.   Edwin Montagu, a brilliant young politician of 36, already an
under secretary for India, made such a scathing attack on Austen Chamberlain, then secretary of state for India, for the indifferent supply of men and
materials from India resulting in the notorious "Mesopotamian muddle"
that Chamberlain was forced to resign and Montagu appointed in his place.
It was Montagu who referred then to His Majesty's Government in India
as "far too wooden, far too iron, far too inelastic and far too antediluvian
to subserve its purpose in modern times,"[6] and his appointment was seen as
portending a possible change of policy.   This soon became evident.   On
August 20 Montagu made his famous declaration promising on behalf of
His Majesty's Government and the Government of India, "the increasing
association of Indians in every branch of administration and the gradual
development of self-governing institutions with a view to the progressive
realization of responsible government in India as an integral part of the
British Empire.... I would add that progress in this policy can only be
achieved by successive stages.   The British government and the government
of India on whom the responsibility lies for the advancement of the Indian
people, must be the judges of the time and the measure of each advance
and they must be guided by the cooperation received from those on whom
new opportunities of service will thus be conferred, and by the extent
to which it is found that confidence can be reposed in their sense of
responsibility...."[7]

On September 16, Mrs Besant and her companions were released.   On
October 5, Mrs Besant was given a rousing reception when she visited Allahabad.   The next day, a joint session of the All India Congress Committee
and the Council of the Muslim League held at Allahabad agreed to drop the
idea of passive resistance, but decided to press upon Lord Chelmsford and
Montagu (who was scheduled to visit India in November) the merits
of the Congress-League scheme.   At the Calcutta session of the Congress
later in the year, Mrs Besant was elected president, the first woman to be so
honored.   What she said in her presidential address at Calcutta seemed to
signify the future trend of Indian political participation.   "The strength of
the Home Rule movement was rendered tenfold greater," she announced,
"by the adhesion to it of a large number of women who brought to its helping
the uncalculating heroism, the endurance, the self-sacrifice of the feminine
nature.   Our League's best recruits and recruiters are amongst the women of
India."[8] The religious overtones were concomitant.   "The women of
Madras," she added, "boast that they marched in procession when the men
were stopped and that their prayers in the temples set the internal captive
free...."

"The atmosphere became electric," Jawahar remembered later, "and most
of us young men felt exhilarated and expected big things in the future."[9]

For Kamala, the atmosphere in the house as far as she was concerned only
added cruelty to her husband's "casual and semi-forgetful attitude."[10] Full of

regrets later, Jawahar realized that even an outright unkindness might have
been better and that "she must have suffered and felt a little neglected."
What he probably did not care to realize was that she also had to cope with
an almost alien world.   In spite of the "training" by Cecilia Hooper, the
Nehru girls' governess, in the arts of Western living, she felt out of place,
especially when Swarup made no effort to conceal the fact that she considered her sister-in-law gauche and plebeian, and carried her jealous taunts
and complaints to Swarup Rani, and to Jawahar.   Jawaharlal refused to
take sides and affected or felt a total indifference to these domestic bickerings.
In any case, his mind was too full of politics.   But his mother was no saint
in spite of her delicate, Dresden doll beauty, and the love she bore her son
in no way softened her attitude toward his wife when the occasion arose.
Krishna, the younger sister, was only nine and hardly as active int hese
family tensions, which was probably the reason why, when Indira grew up,
she preferred her younger aunt to her more famous one.

    "Kamala was an unsophisticated, quiet person, while the Nehru family
was very sophisticated.   She was very Indian, they were very Western, and
she was made to feel that she was not 'in,' " recalls a member of the family.
"My sympathy for her was the sympathy for the underdog," he added.[11]
Jawaharlal, apart from the interest in politics he had at the time, was engrossed in law, and often sat late at night over his books.   The resultant loneliness for his wife "caused her to draw herself within herself," remarks the
same member of the family, while her pride and sensitivity prevented her
from making any complaints.

    "I think Swarup's nastiness to Kamala has been played up too much,"
states another younger member of the Nehru clan.[12] According to her, Swarup also confided most of her teenage woes in Kamala and when it came to
needing support for going out somewhere or meeting someone the father
would not like, it was Kamala who came to her rescue and was prepared to
brave his fury.

    It was an odd challenge for the young bride.   On the one hand, she had to
meet the modern imperatives posed by the Nehrus and on the other to
cope with their recurrent throwbacks to convention.   She soon acquired the
outward trappings of the former, and became ardently feminist as a reaction
to the latter, but without losing her restraint or decorum on both counts.

    "She was much more militant than my father," recalls Mrs Gandhi of the
time when they were all involved in the freedom struggle later. "Everywhere
my father went he received letters of complaint that 'Kamalaji' had been
inciting the women.   Otherwise she was very gentle.   I never heard her
raise her voice against anybody."

    "Your father did?"

    "Oh yes, he did!"

    "How else did she influence you more than him as you've said she did?"

    "Well, about the women," she said referring to the whole question of rights, freedom and prejudice, and her own subsequent work for women's uplift, "I would have taken it for granted and not done anything. I had been born in freedom. But she had come from a more orthodox background so she knew what it could be."

According to Indira, Kamala was also responsible for giving a new dimension to the inspiration that her husband drew from his Indian background.

"You mean she made him more nationalistic. . .?"

"Not that, in a different way—the concept that he put forward later about science and spirituality was due to her. He believed in science but she made him realize that there was something more."

"Was she religious?"

"Oh, no, not at all, she never went to a temple."

"But you?"

"No, no, never."[13]

The Montford Report, published in June 1918, embodying the Montagu-Chelmsford Reforms, came as an anticlimax to Indian expectations. Both Chelmsford and Montagu referred to the earlier Morley-Minto Reforms as having "ceased to satisfy Indian opinion," and that its continuance could "only lead to a further cleavage between the Indian members and the government and a further cultivation of criticism unchecked by responsibility." They therefore almost rooted out the Morley-Minto system. A bicameral division made the Indian legislature into the upper house, or Council of State, and the lower house, or Legislative Assembly. The Congress-League concordat on representation arrived at in Lucknow was accepted and incorporated en bloc while the issue of communal representation initiated by the Morley-Minto Reforms became an elaborate design including several other minorities. Elections, both provincial and central, became direct, and the franchise determined on community interest. But it overlooked the Congress-League scheme for responsible self-government in favor of the introduction of a system of dyarchy. Under this, administrative spheres were divided between the central and provincial governments, into reserved and transferred. The reserved spheres were under the control of the governor and his executive council and the transferred in charge of the governor acting with ministers. While the Congress-League scheme stressed fixed executives responsible to the legislature, the Montagu-Chelmsford suggestions went further and provided for "replaceable cabinets possessing corporate responsibility and subject to the vote of the legislatures"; on the face of it, a blameless example of parliamentary functioning.

However, as Motilal said in his speech in the provincial council when he opposed the resolution welcoming the proposals, there were so many reservations and safeguards, guaranteeing the ultimate freedom of the governor-general and the governors to act over and above the legislative will that the concessions toward self-government became meaningless. If the scheme provided a constitutional stepping stone to eventual federalism, it also rested on the assumption that though the British government had declared itself in favor of granting self-government, it was not prepared to risk authority in the hands of the Indians altogether until, as it felt, the Indian people had some experience of what it meant to have self-government. Nothing could be calculated to infuriate the political sensibility of the educated Indians more.

"We cannot learn to walk," said Motilal Nehru, "unless you give us the opportunity to exercise the function. If we keep lying down all the time, then good-bye to all benefits of the exercise."[14]

Motilal, presiding over a political conference at Lucknow, found himself at variance with most of his moderate colleagues over the new proposals. At a special session of the Congress called at Bombay immediately to discuss the Montford report, the moderates were not present at all. The moderates in fact broke away completely and formed a separate organization called the National Liberation Federation. Thus at the age of 57, Motilal found himself facing the challenge of a revolution in his own make-up. He had become a militant advocate of rapid reform and although the transformation seemed strange to his friends and colleagues it was a logical consequence of a nature that mixed the qualities of arrogance and sensitivity in proportions that could not tolerate passive submission to a personal or political imposition.

With the end of war, India's excitement grew. The war had been fought for the principles of self-determination, President Woodrow Wilson's Fourteen Points had provided a new vision, and it seemed reasonable to think that Britain would rise to the occasion with an appropriate gesture. "The dominant note all over India," wrote Jawahar, "was one of waiting and expectation, full of hope and fear and yet tinged with fear and anxiety."[15] It was the anxiety that seemed justified after all. At the thirty-third session of the Congress, which was attended by 4,865 delegates, the resolutions of the special Congress of Bombay were reiterated with greater earnestness. A call for the recognition of India as "one of the progressive nations to whom the principle of self-determination should be applied" came again in the light of another review of the Montagu-Chelmsford scheme, a demand for an act of Parliament that would guarantee complete responsible self-government, with a status equal to that of the other self-governing Dominions within the British Empire. A total break with Britain was not even visualized and what seemed revolutionary then was to emerge as a pallid prologue to later developments. However, it was in view of the Congress concern with "the immediate repeal of all laws, regulations, and ordinances restricting the free discussion of political questions, and conferring on the executive the power to arrest, detain, intern, extern, or imprison any British subject in India outside the processes of ordinary civil or criminal law," that the next phase of imperial repression came as a shock. Instead of the expected concessions to Indian national feeling, came the Rowlatt bills in February 1919.

The year before a committee had been appointed by the government under the presidency of Sir Sidney Rowlatt, with two Indian members, to enquire into the possibilities of evolving legislation to deal effectively with the difficulties that had arisen in relation to the "criminal conspiracies connected with the revolutionary movement." The report of this committee was published at the time of the special session of the Congress at Bombay, and even then the Congress had warned that if the recommendations of the Rowlatt committee were put into effect they would "interfere with the fundamental rights of the Indian people and impede the healthy growth of public opinion." The government, however, was not detered from introducing the bills into the imperial council and having them passed in spite of the vehement opposition of the Indian members.

"To me the bills are the aggravated symptom of the deep-seated disease," wrote Gandhi to Srinivasa Sastri, the liberal leader who was known as a silver-tongued orator. "They are a striking demonstration of the determination of the civil service to retain its grip of our necks. I consider the bills to be an open challenge to us."[16] On February 24 he announced his intention of inaugurating *satyagraha*, a movement of passive resistance, if the bills were passed. On March 3 the Rowlatt Act was passed in the Supreme Legislative Council. On March 18 Gandhi published his satyagraha pledge. "Being conscientiously of the opinion that the bills known as the Indian Criminal Law Amendment Bill No. 1 of 1919, and the Criminal Law Emergency Powers Bill No. 2 of 1919, are unjust, subversive of the principles of liberty and justice and destructive of the elementary rights of an individual on which the safety of India as a whole and the state itself is based, we solemnly affirm that in the event of these bills becoming law and until they are withdrawn, we shall refuse civilly to obey these laws and such other laws as the committee, hereafter to be appointed, may think fit, and we further affirm that in the struggle we will faithfully follow truth and refrain from violence to life, person or property."

Gandhi also formed an organization called the Satyagraha Sabha to enable him to carry his movement forward. He visualized it shrewdly yet naturally in terms of a deep-rooted traditional reference point for the majority of Indians—that of penance, prayer, and self-purification. He inaugurated satyagraha therefore with a fast, and fixed March 30 for a day of hartal. The government's apprehensions were mixed with a clear appraisal of the man and his motivation.

At Anand Bhawan there was a crisis. For Jawahar the Satyagraha Sabha presaged the positive political action he had been looking for and he decided to join it immediately. For Motilal extra-constitutional agitation was still anathema. He also thought the whole idea was impractical, unfeasible, and illogical. The deliberate breaking of the law would automatically land thousands in jail and he could not see the British government in India succumbing to pressure. To visualize his son in jail seemed especially preposterous, for the "trek to jail," as Jawahar put it later, "had not begun and the idea was most repulsive." However, the love that each bore the other and the respect they had for each other's will prevented them from risking a precipitate decision that might ruin their relationship. So Jawahar, knowing his father's feelings, wandering about alone night after night in the grounds of his father's spacious house, tortured in mind and trying to find a way out, postponed taking the final plunge. And Motilal, knowing in his inner heart that he would respect his son's wishes, tried sleeping on the hard floor to see what his son would have to suffer in the cold discomfort of His Majesty's prisons.

The women silently bore the burden of the intensely strained atmosphere in the house. There is no indication that Jawahar consulted Kamala or let her share the agony of his conflict. Swarup Rani could hardly interfere in an intellectual clash of this dimension between father and son, and the two-year-old Indira played happily, unaware in the guava orchards and among the great Danes that roamed at will through the house. It was a measure of how much the situation affected even the eleven-year-old Krishna that when Motilal invited Gandhi to visit Anand Bhawan and resolve this domestic crisis, she thought resentfully that he had come to "drag" them all into the movement. Gandhi had no such intention. His entire philosophy was based on drawing such participation that would enrich the giver and certainly not at the cost of jeopardizing valuable human relationships. He told the unhappy Jawahar that he must not do anything to upset his father, and the crisis seemed temporarily to blow over.

Within a few weeks the country was in turmoil, not so much because of Gandhi's Satyagraha Sabha but because of the inexplicable panic, the rash cruelty, and lack of policy on the part of the government. First, it chose to introduce the Rowlatt bills when what the people had been waiting for was the fruition of the Montagu-Chelmsford scheme. Second, it embarked upon a virtual reign of terror in the Punjab. It did so out of fear that the soldiery of the Punjab, which had shown prowess and courage in the war, had presumably returned with a new awareness of its potential and might give substance to the freedom movement if it began nourishing political ambitions. To prevent such a contingency, the combustible governor of the Punjab, Sir Michael O'Dwyer, decided that he would not let the Congress meet at Amritsar, where it had been invited to do so. He pounced upon two well-known Congress workers who had been sent there to organize the session and had them spirited away to an unknown place. This caused a furor among the local population. Crowds gathered to demand information as to their whereabouts, there was firing on government orders, there were some casualties, and the mob reacted with violence then and later. Five Englishmen were killed, Amritsar was handed over to the military authorities, and Gandhi was arrested and turned back to Bombay when he set out for the Punjab. The arrest of Gandhi caused even more disturbances, which spread throughout the country—more firings took place, more people were killed, and Gandhi, for whom all this was absolutely contrary to the spirit of his

movement, issued a statement suspending satyagraha. The government was
not moved by such considerations and on April 13, 1919, the Hindu New
Year, General Dyer perpetrated the notorious Jallianwalla Bagh massacre
in Amritsar.

The incident was nefarious not only for the innocence of the victims
involved but for the hard-heartedness with which the crime was perpetrated.
Twenty thousand man, women, and children had gathered in the large open
ground within the city of Amritsar called the Jallianwala Bagh. The place
was encircled on all sides by walls of houses and it had only one entrance,
a bottleneck, which would barely allow the passage of three people abreast.
The crowd was peaceful and unarmed. But General Dyer arrived upon
the scene, ordered the people to disperse and, according to his own testimony, within two minutes ordered his troops to fire into the crowd. The
firing stopped only after sixteen hundred rounds, when the ammunition was
exhausted, and as he surveyed the dead, maimed, and helpless his dominating
feeling was, according to the evidence he gave later before the Hunter
Committee of Enquiry: "I thought that I should shoot well and shoot
strong, so that I or anybody else should not have to shoot again. I think
it is quite possible I could have dispersed the crowd without firing, but they
would have come back again and laughed, and I should have made what I
consider to be a fool of myself."[17]

An obstinate empire attempted to secure its nervous confidence by setting
in motion a chain of humiliations after declaring martial law, which was
intended "to teach the people a lesson." So strong was the censorship that
nobody knew either the sequence of events or the extent of the atrocity, and
it was as late as July 1919 before the All India Congress Committee meeting
at Calcutta learnt what had happened in the Punjab. Motilal's belief in the
efficacy of constitutional reform was completely shaken and he and Jawaharlal
waited for scraps of information with bitterness in their hearts. As soon as
martial law was lifted, Motilal offered his services for relief and enquiry
work,[18] and it was for the latter that he and C.R. Das combined to work with
the close cooperation of Gandhi. It was during this period that Motilal came
to appreciate the incisive logic, the patient exposition, and the determined
resolve of the Gandhian approach. At the end of the year a triumphant
session of the Congress was held at the same place, Amritsar. Motilal
was elected president. But when he made a fervent appeal to his moderate
colleagues to join in unity with the Congress for the sake of "the lacerated
heart of the Punjab" they still refused. The Amritsar Congress was the
first "Gandhi Congress" and Motilal chose to break with his old stand
completely.

3. CATALYST

Motilal's decision made Indira's first memory political: "The burning of foreign clothes," she said. It was 1921, the high tide of Gandhi's call for noncooperation, a non-violent boycott of the machinery of government. Her grandfather had taken the plunge. He had not only resigned his seat in the United Provinces Council, but had even given up his fabulous law practice because noncooperation, according to Gandhi's unswerving concept, meant noncooperation with everything British—administration, education, and economic imposition. No practice meant less money and practical common sense dictated a change in the sumptuous pattern of old. So Anand Bhawan underwent a soul-searing metamorphosis. The great Danes, the carriages, the horses, the beautiful china, and sparkling crystal were sold. The two kitchens were reduced to one, the large number of servants was decreased, the style of dressing changed from European to Indian and, whereas earlier, recalls a Nehru cousin, "we were hauled up for talking in Hindustani, from then on we were hauled up for talking in English."[1]

For Motilal it meant giving up at one stroke the habits, tastes, and commitments of a lifetime at an age when he had been hoping to settle back to enjoy the fruits of his labors. But his decisions were never small. There were no regrets, and after a while the sacrifices seemed as enjoyable as the achievements had been. This was greatly due to the great moral strength that both he and Jawahar drew from their family, and the willingness with which the women undertook this dramatic transformation in their lives. The comfort of the house, of a settled routine, and of familiar things perhaps meant more to them, because they were not yet part of the political fever that gripped the men. But both Swarup Rani and Kamala were made basically of traditional stoic stuff; they shed their fine Parisian chiffons, velvets, satins, and silks to wear the coarse, handspun *khadi* that was the only cloth the British permitted to be manufactured in India. The thirteen-year-old Krishna was also called upon to contribute her share. She had to give up her beloved school, and revert to being taught by private tutors at home, an arrangement against which she had won a battle with Motilal only a short while before. And Indira? There was the drama of that grand gesture that the whole of India made of consigning Western materials to public and private bonfires.

"I can still feel the excitement of the day and see the large terrace covered with piles of clothes," Mrs Gandhi recalled later, "and what rich materials, what lovely colors! That was the day, too, when I discovered my power over my parents. Everybody was going to the bonfire [the public one], but I was considered too small and was being put to bed. I appealed to my grandfather, who then as always later, took my side."[2] But like any other normal child, the excitement proved too much, she grew tired and sleepy, and she saw only the burning wood being thrown on the mountain of clothes and the fire leaping upward in a joyous first flame.

Nothing was going to be normal thenceforth and the tests that for her father, mother, and grandparents came at least when they understood what it was all about came for Indira at the age of pure, unknowing innocence when instinct was the only guide and the precepts for right or wrong came garbed in political hue. One evening when only a little older she was playing by herself near her mother, and a relative who had just returned from Paris came to visit them. She brought a lovely embroidered frock for Indira but when she gave it to her mother, Kamala smiled and returned it. "We now wear only handspun and handwoven material," she said. She seemed oblivious of the coarse sack cloth which was the only khadi then being made, which she was wearing as a saree and her delicate skin unused to the rough texture had become red and sore wherever the cloth rubbed against it.

"I think you've all gone mad," burst out the visitor, "but you are adult and if you want to be ill, I suppose that is your business. But you have certainly no right to make the child suffer, and it is for her that I have brought this gift."

"Come here, Indu," Kamala called her daughter and said softly, "Auntie has brought you a foreign frock. It is very pretty and you can wear it if you like, but first think of the big fire where we burnt our foreign things. Would you like to wear this dainty thing when the rest of us are wearing khadi?"

It was a cruel choice to put before so small a child but Kamala was the first to see that training in fortitude should come early to her daughter. There was no attempt to spare her the unpleasant vicissitudes of an insecure political life. Later, even Motilal proudly sat his four-year-old granddaughter on his knee while he was indicted in court the first time for implied disloyalty to His Brittanic Majesty.

That evening Indira looked longingly at the frock. It was of such delicate and lovely material that she longed to touch it. But she shook her head and exclaimed: "Take it away—I shan't ever wear it," and while Kamala no doubt wore a satisfied look, the visitor provoked her further.

"But why not," she insisted. "Don't you like nice things...?"

"I do, I do," said the little girl, "but—" and out came trembling in half remembered form all the arguments she had overheard from her elders.

"All right, Miss Saint," the woman pursued her relentlessly, "how is it that you have a foreign doll?"

It was an idle remark, but to the child cataclysmic.

"For days on end," later recalled Mrs Gandhi, "or was it weeks? Does it matter? It was eternity to the child, overwhelmed by the burden of decision....Never fond of food, at this time it became even more irksome and sleep came only out of exhaustion. My mother thought I was worried sick over something and so I was. At last the decision was made and quivering with tension I took the doll up on the roof terrace and set fire to her. Then the tears came as if they would never stop." But after that the doll's place was taken by an occupation that was expressive of the milieu. She began to collect as many servants as she could, stand on a table and deliver speeches, "repeating disjointed phrases, that I had picked up from the grown-ups' talk."[3]

"She was a child of the Home Rule movement, a war baby," says Shyam Kumari, her cousin. "It is important to remember that though she was doted upon, she had nobody to play with. We have become conscious of children's needs now. Previously we saw only to their diet and left them alone... she was and is the loneliest woman, I still say that. She told me once after she was married, 'I'm going to limit my family, but I'm not going to have an only child.' She said that from the beginning."[4]

Obviously the scars remained.

If Indira's memory was political so was her vocabulary; all the activity around her made her precocious. Even as a three-year-old, when the Nehrus' increasing stature in nationalistic politics drew upon her young father the first act of wrath from the British, she had been used willy-nilly as the "symbol" of controversy. Both her mother and grandmother had been ill and Jawahar had taken them all to Mussoorie. They stayed at the Savoy Hotel, where the Afghan delegation was also ensconced. This was the aftermath of a short Indo-Afghan war and the delegation had come for negotiations. Jawahar never met or saw any Afghan member, but the government, presumably suspicious that some sort of conspiracy might be hatched, promptly served him with a notice to quit the hill station as the mountain resorts were called. Civil disobedience not having begun, Jawahar saw no option but to leave. Motilal of course took up the issue immediately with Sir Harcourt Butler and questioned the propriety of such an act, both on personal and political grounds. Sir Harcourt thought the order harmless, apologised for any inconvenience caused to the ladies of the family for being left alone, but did not rescind the order. Jawahar and Motilal, both in Allahabad, decided to disregard the externment order when they learned that Swarup Rani's condition had deteriorated. Just before they left for Mussoorie they got a telegram withdrawing the restriction on Jawahar. When they reached the hotel the next morning the first thing Jawahar saw in the courtyard of the Savoy was Indira in the arms of a member of the Afghan delegation! The Afghans' chivalry had been aroused when they realised that their presence had indirectly caused the Nehrus inconvenience and the leader of their delegation sent a basket of fruit and flowers to Swarup Rani every day, while Indira became a special object of attention and sympathy.

Jawaharlal had given up his law practice by 1919 in favor of politics and he was so busy that in spite of the strength of his family bonds, as he wrote, he "almost forgot" his family, his wife, his daughter. It was only long afterward that he realised, he said, "what a burden and a trial I must have been to them in those days, and what amazing patience and tolerance my wife had shown toward me."[5] Motilal was elected member of the working committee toward the end of 1920 and one of three general secretaries of the Congress party for 1921. Moreover, the office of the All India Congress Committee shifted to his house in Allahabad and Anand Bhawan not only for him but for his family acquired all the constant tempo, flurry, and temper of a political headquarters. Politicians and intellectuals replaced as visitors the fashionable, western-dressed elite of before. Although the lack of privacy affected Swarup Rani and Kamala most of all, it was they who felt

more relaxed in the new circumstances. Kamala no longer felt at a disadvantage for her lack of proficiency in English and Swarup Rani no longer
felt apologetic for her religious bent as the whole movement was guided by
Gandhi's spiritualizing influence. In fact, both Swarup Rani and Kamala
became vegetarians and even Jawahar admitted that he was closer to a
religious frame of mind in 1921 than at any other time since his boyhood.
"Even so," he wrote irrepressibly, "I did not come very near," because it was
the moral and ethical side that attracted him more. It was, nevertheless,
"an extraordinary year [with] a strange mixture of nationalism and politics
and religion and mysticism."[6]

Even a happy event like the young Swarup's wedding the same year did
not escape the growing pressure of conflict between Congress defiance and
government suspicion. Because the date fixed for it, May 10, was also the
anniversary of what was then called the Mutiny of 1857 at Meerut and the
leading congressmen, including Gandhi, were invited to attend a meeting of
the Working Committee arranged at the same time, the government suspected
a conspiracy might be brewing, and the English residents of Allahabad went
about with revolvers in their pockets as they no longer trusted their Indian
servants. On the day of the wedding police were detailed around the house
to keep watch!

For Indira the pattern of abnormality spread further with the arrest of her
father and grandfather. Both took it in characteristic fashion. Motilal
knew it would come one day and he had decided that if there was to be any
imprisonment it would be for the two of them, and not Jawahar alone. The
extremist turn that his own politics took was due in great measure to the
realization that it would be the inevitable direction in which his son would
go and it would be better, he decided, if he went the same way.

"Spiritually Motilalji regards Jawaharlal as his father, as you know,"[7]
wrote the office secretary of the All India Congress Committee, M. S. Godbole,
to Gandhi from Anand Bhawan, describing the arrest.

It seems that Godbole was showing Motilal some papers when the police
officer was announced. Motilal was a well-known figure and the officer
was nervous. After an exchange of greetings in typical U.P. style, the officer
presented Motilal with a search warrant. Motilal remarked good-humoredly
that he should go ahead but that to do justice to Anand Bhawan it would
take him at least six months. The officer still fidgeted and shuffled, not
daring to tell Motilal that he had orders to arrest him. But Motilal guessed
something was wrong and on getting it out of the shamefaced man merely
quipped, "Oh, I am ready for it, but why did you not produce it [the warrant]
all at once?"[8]

The officer still found himself in a quandary, for he could barely muster
the courage to say that he had also a warrant for Jawahar's arrest.

Jawaharlal was occupied in the Congress office away from Anand Bhawan
when an excited clerk came running to him and informed him that the police

had come to search the building. Jawahar's pulses quickened but the desire to show off was strong and he wished to appear "cool and collected, unaffected by the comings and goings of the police."[9]   So he decided to show complete indifference, told the clerk to take the police around, and continued writing a letter, even when a colleague was arrested and stood before him waiting to say good-bye. "I treated my colleague in a most unfeeling manner," he wrote regretfully later.[10]   But when news came of other arrests, he rushed home to find that he and his father had to go to prison, too.

Soon both of them were being sped away in a police van while Swarup Rani and Kamala looked wanly after them, the older woman proud of "the great privilege of sending my dear husband and my only son to jail" as she told a correspondent later, but at that time on the verge of collapse, and the younger one quiet and determined to restrain her tears. The big house suddenly felt empty and for the next forty-five years it was to be the scene of heartrending separations on the one hand and joyous reunions on the other, and in between a witness to the suspense and loneliness of those who waited.

"Do not think that because they were deeply involved in high politics and tragic events," wrote Krishna of the period just before this, "Father and *Bhai* became glum and solemn. On the contrary their irrepressible spirits and high humor burst out at the least relaxation of tension and the old house still echoed with their happy laughter . . . [but] the shadow on our lives was Kamala's failing health. Ever since Indira's birth she had seemed frail and easily tired, now she began running a low temperature and feeling miserable."[11]   The emotional strain had indeed proved too much for the young bride, but after 1921 her own growing participation in politics gave her a new sense of comradeship with her husband, and while the strenuous activity proved disastrous for her health, it rejuvenated her spirits and brought husband and wife closer.

On December 7, the day after their arrest, both Motilal and Jawahar were sentenced to six month's imprisonment and a fine of Rs 500 each. In accordance with the policy of civil disobedience they refused to pay even this small fine, but the result of this refusal was the steady denudation of Anand Bhawan by the police of its valuable carpets and furniture. Everything familiar seemed to be slipping away. At the trial of her grandfather Indira had "sat very still with her enormous dark eyes fixed intently on the judge, taking in far more of the proceedings," recalled Krishna, "than we believed possible."[12]   When she saw the police vulgarly snatching away the things she knew belonged to her "mommy and Papu and Dadu," she went like a fury after them, particularly the police inspectors, and cried and stamped her feet while the others looked on grimly and then tried to pull her away. "I protested to the police indicating my strong displeasure in every way I could," recollects Mrs Gandhi herself, and once nearly chopped off an officer's thumb with a bread slicing gadget. "I am afraid those early impressions are likely to color her future views about the police force generally," wryly reflected her father when he heard of the incident.[13] He was right.

"The police, for instance," said Mrs Gandhi as Prime Minister significantly when I asked her in 1967 what changes she would encourage to make the working of her government more efficient, "they treat people as a potential enemy. You can see it at once if there's an exception—it's so rare. At times, the people come forward in love and affection (this was with reference to unruly election crowds) ... it is when they are treated tactlessly that they revolt." She elaborated upon the different context in which the role of the police should be viewed now, "it being a system then for keeping law and order, and not building a nation," but her basic antipathy to police methods sprang no doubt from that dim consciousness of old.

Soon after the arrest, Swarup Rani, Kamala, and Krishna were invited by Gandhi to attend the Congress session at Ahmedabad. Kamala took Indira along to this first of many sessions of the Congress party. They travelled third class, following the precedent set by Gandhi to move on the level of the common man. Their aristocratic upbringing hardly suited them for the discomfort of the journey, but material deprivation was submerged under the weight of the adulation of the crowds on the way, who came with garlands at almost every stop to show their oneness with the family of Motilal and Jawahar and their appreciation of the fact that they were going to meet Gandhi. They stayed at Sabarmati Ashram which conisted of a cluster of small cottages on the banks of the Sabarmati. In the central cottage lived Gandhi and Kasturba, or "Ba," his wife. Swarup Rani was allotted a cottage for herself and a little boy to act as a servant. But Kamala, Krishna and Indira, and some of their relatives slept on the floor in a kind of student's hostel. The routine was austere. They had to be up at dawn even though it was the bitterly cold month of December, to attend Gandhi's prayer meetings. They had to do their own washing and cleaning. They were required to eat food that was unseasoned and tasteless. The emphasis was on things of the spirit, introspection, analysis, concentration, devotion, and self-realization. Even on the eleven-year-old Krishna the impact was great, while Swarup Rani and Kamala were already converted.

Indira Gandhi does not remember the details of her Sabarmati stay.

"It is difficult to say when I first came into contact with Gandhi," she ruminates. "He forms part of my earliest memories. I regarded him not as a great leader but more as an elder of the family to whom I went with difficulties and problems which he treated with the grave seriousness which was due to the large-eyed and solemn child I was. Later I disagreed with many of his ideas and had long discussions with the usual dogmatism of the very young—even as I was thus arguing with him I was amazed at his patience, his interest in and awareness of minute details and the real pain he felt at any wrong doing."[14]

"Would you say you were influenced by him"? I asked her.

"It's difficult to say", she repeated. "He influenced the family and the family influenced me, so how—?"

"You mean there was nothing particular?"

"No, I suppose there wasn't."[15]

She was aware, nevertheless, as she wrote once, that "Gandhism, like all great religions in the lifetime of their founders, had a dynamic quality. It was living, growing, and evolving. There was no set line to be followed, no question of interpretation. Each policy was formulated according to the circumstances."[16] She believed that while he was there, her father followed a path based on Gandhi's ideals which perpetuated the image of the "father of the nation" as he was later called. The outer forms of Gandhism like the stress on khadi and prohibition, she thought, were irrelevant in free India to the "fundamental thought of the man," his tolerance, vision, and lack of religious dogmatism. Jawaharlal meant presumably the same thing when he recalled how he and other Congress workers discussed Gandhi's "fads and peculiarities" and said half-humorously that "when swaraj came these fads must not be encouraged" while at the same time feeling that he was "a great and unique man and a glorious leader" in whom they could safely repose the country's trust.

For Motilal, too, it was Gandhi's qualities as a man and not as a religious leader that mattered. "Evidently," commented Jawahar about his father's relationship with Gandhi, "he wanted to stress the fact that he did not admire Gandhiji as a saint or a mahatma, but as a man. Strong and unbending himself, he admired the strength of spirit in him."[17]

With such a legacy of attitudes Indira could hardly regard him as an awesome figure. He was first a friend of the family, then a politician who guided her country to independence. "As I grew up," she says, "I learned to understand him better and to realize how intimately he was in contact with the masses of our country, their thoughts, their ideals and aspirations." For her this contributed "in no small measure to his greatness," and when she really came into contact with him as an adult in 1947 it was as a political force rather than as a religious figure, when he urged her to work in the riot torn areas of Delhi after partition. Her political pragmatism as prime minister was compounded as much of her grandfather's hard common sense as Gandhi's preference for tackling one concrete issue at a time, but it was the latter's insistence on absolute political integrity that gave personal participation in the struggle for independence a kind of religious fervor. Only in that sense was Gandhi, for the Nehrus, a religious hero and only in that sense were they his willing and most outstanding disciples.

It was the occasion of the Prince of Wales's visit to India in November 1921 that was used by the Congress and the Khilafat party—with which the Congress had made common cause on the issue of Muslim grievances against the British betrayal of Turkey—to consolidate Indian disaffection with the government. Hartals were organized, bonfires were made of foreign

cloth, and a boycott undertaken of all functions. When he landed in
Bombay the resentment exploded into violent clashes in spite of Gandhi's
exhortations. He was so disgusted that he exclaimed that swaraj
"stank in [his] nostrils" and promptly undertook a fast of five days
as penance for the misdeeds of the people. The Bombay incidents were used
by the government to declare the Congress volunteers and the Khilafat
volunteers, who had joined to become civil resisters, illegal. It was under
the Criminal Law Amendment Act that thousands of arrests were made
including that of the Nehrus at Allahabad. But the government still was
afraid to touch Gandhi. It was Motilal who had organized the boycott of the
prince's visit to Allahabad and it must have buoyed his spirits greatly to
learn that its execution was so complete and so successful that the prince
saw Allahabad only as a dead and silent city.

In fact, with such massive cooperation from the people, the movement
seemed to be building to a pressure which its leaders thought the government
might find difficult to withstand. Hopes were not only high, but exalted.
The Ahmedabad congress at the end of the year placed on record "the fixed
determination of the Congress to continue the program of non-violent
cooperation with greater vigor than hitherto in such manner as each province
may determine, till the Punjab and the Khilafat wrongs are redressed and
swarajya is established and the control of the Government of India passes
into the hands of the people from that of an irresponsible corporation."[18]
It was characteristic of the temper of the period that even Muslim divines
took a significant part in the political decisions of the Congress and, as
Jawahar wrote, "it was Hindu-Muslim *ki jai* all over." Within a short
period, of the large numbers who willingly courted jail, the government had
clamped down upon 30,000 people and Gandhi announced on February 1,
1922 that he had decided to start the first civil disobedience campaign in the
form of a no-tax movement from Bardoli in Gujarat under his personal
guidance.

But there was, as Sitaramayya says, "a fatality hanging over the Congress."[19] On February 5, 1922, when the spirit of noncooperation was at
its height, a Congress procession apparently ran amuck in a place called
Chauri Chaura in the U.P. The mob trapped twenty-one policemen and a
sub-inspector in the police station and set the building and the men on fire.
Gandhi, who had been so upset with the show of violence at Bombay and
Madras during the Prince of Wales's visit took the Chauri Chaura incident as
a sign that the population was not mature enough to follow his brand of
nonviolent political agitation. At a moment when it seemed that the country was poised to strike at its chains, he suspended the entire program of
mass civil disobedience and on February 22 made this shattering declaration
at the Congress working committee meeting at Bardoli itself.

"Our mounting hopes tumbled to the ground," Jawahar wrote of
their feeling in jail.[20] His father was shocked and angry. The general re-

action was that if a whole movement had to be based on disciplining all
the 300 million people of India then its culmination would always be
at the mercy of any wilful deviation, perhaps even a deliberately incited
violence by those wishing to destroy the movement. Jawahar's faith in
Gandhi alternated with his inability to accept the logic of his stand.

"I do believe," Gandhi had clarified, "that when there is only a choice
between cowardice and violence, I would advise violence . . . . I would rather
have India resort to arms in order to defend her honor than that she should in
a cowardly manner become or remain a helpless victim to her own dishonor.
But I believe that nonviolence is infinitely superior to violence, forgiveness is
more manly than punishment. . . ."[21] He was not a visionary however,
but, as he himself claimed to be, "a practical idealist." So when Jawahar
wrote of his and his father's total disenchantment with the ultimate outcome
of the movement Gandhi answered on the level that made practical sense.

"I must tell," he said, "that this Chauri Chaura incident was the last straw.
I received letters both from Hindus and Mohammedans from Calcutta,
Allahabad, and the Punjab, all these telling me that the wrong was not all
on the government's side, that our people were becoming aggressive, defiant,
and threatening, that they were getting out of hand. I assure you that if the
thing had not been suspended we would have been leading not a nonviolent
struggle but essentially a violent struggle. . . . The cause will prosper by this
retreat."[22]

Jawahar realized that more than anything else it was Gandhi's instinctive
appreciation of the mood of the masses that had led to his decision. For
despite the apparent public zeal, the organization of the movement was going
to pieces. Almost all the leaders were in jail and there had not been time
enough to train the masses to act with independent force. His decision,
however, marked a low point in his popularity with those who had keyed
themselves up to a direct confrontation, and the government, which had
hesitated to risk the reaction to Gandhi's arrest, now felt the opportunity
ripe to take him into custody. His trial, remarked Jawahar, was "a memo-
rable occasion and those of us who were present are not likely to forget it."[23]
He himself had been released three months earlier than scheduled because of
an error that the authorities discovered in their charge. He was sorry
to leave his father behind, but he rushed to see Gandhi at Ahmedabad,
where he had already been arrested. "A convict and a criminal in the eye
of the law . . . a frail, serene, indomitable figure in a coarse and scanty loin
cloth," described Sarojini Naidu later, "nevertheless the entire court rose
in an act of spontaneous homage when Mahatma Gandhi entered."[24] He
made no defense but a statement in which he presented reasons for his transformation from a "staunch loyalist and cooperator" to "an uncompromising
disaffectionist and noncooperator"; his lack of personal ill-will; his charge,
apart from the disillusioning moves of the British government in the preceding two years that "India was less manly under the British rule than she ever

was before," his opinion that "noncooperation with evil is as much a duty
as is cooperation with good," his faith in nonvioence, and his challenge
to the judge to act only according to the dictates of his conscience.

Judge Robert Broomfield admitted that Gandhi was in a different category
than any person he had ever tried or was likely to try and that "even those
who differ from you in politics look upon you as a man of high ideals and of
noble and even saintly life"[25] but the imperatives of law and governance
were harsh and the sentence severe—six years' imprisonment.

"We came away ... emotionally stirred and with the impress of his
[Gandhi's] vivid phrases and striking images in our mind,"[26] commented
Jawahar and there were many who had tears in their eyes.

Jawahar's own reprieve was short-lived. Back in Allahabad he thought
he would reorganize the faltering organization of the Congress and interested
himself particularly in the boycott of foreign cloth, an item on which individual satyagraha was allowed under the AICC resolution of Delhi of February
24 and 25. Even a hint of picketing was enough to bring some of the recalcitrant cloth merchants of Allahabad to heel, but two days later
Jawaharlal was charged with "criminal intimidation and extortion" and
sentenced to imprisonment for a year and nine months.

The Lucknow jail was no longer the same. Motilal had been transferred
to Nainital prison, conditions were much more stringent, and there was no
privacy. But together with the discipline Jawaharlal decided to maintain
over both mind and body by catching up with his reading and doing hard
exercise, he was in for a long enough period to begin worrying about his little
daughter. Barrack No. 4 was not a bad place, but it could hardly guarantee
him the facility for supervising his daughter's growing needs, especially when
she was far from being a sturdy child. On one of her visits he found her
"pale and weak" and for three months he never saw her at all. He began
to be concerned about her education. "I wish some arrangements were
made for Indira's lessons. I am confident that I could have managed her
easily but I am in Barrack No. 4,"[27] he wrote helplessly from prison on August
18 after his father had been released. He heard that Motilal had presented
Indira a new spinning wheel, so he wrote to her in Hindi asking her to
send him some of her yarn. "You must get well quickly, learn to write
letters and come and see me in jail," he said, adding wistfully, "I am longing
to see you."[28] For a while at the end of 1921 Kamala had managed to put
her in Delhi. But she had the first taste of the constant traveling and the
unsettlement that was to mark the rest of her life, for soon she was in
Calcutta, where she heard from her father:

"Love to dear daughter Indira from her Papu. Did you like Calcutta?
Is it better than Bombay? Did you see the Calcutta zoo? What animals did
you see? Have you seen a huge tree there? You must get strong and plump
before you return to Allahabad."

In one of his letters he asked her significantly, "Do you join mother in prayers every day?"[29]

"We used to read the *Gita* every morning," recalled Mrs Gandhi, as prime minister years later, "Some of the *shlokas* are beautiful."

"The whole family?" I couldn't help interjecting.

"No," she said quietly, "the three of us."

She had come to believe that the characteristics of the Indian tradition were tolerance and nonviolence but also, in the deepest sense, a realistic approach to life. To see that, she said "one must separate superstition from what is of real value to our thought." But so strong was the political reference in her makeup that even the illustration she drew for this came from her role as a politician and her contact with the uneducated rural communities among whom regard for tradition took the shape of superstition.

"I put it to them like this," she said, "suppose there is your grandfather's house, and it is very beautiful, well, you keep it clean, clean it up occasionally otherwise it will get dirty and dusty and there will be cobwebs. What happens today—the Hindu's adulation of the cow, or the position of women—has nothing to do with religion."

She referred to the old Hindu injunction to take a bath before one's meal.

"The priests made it a religious thing and people began to accept it as such. But actually its origin was as a sanitary and hygienic custom . . ."

But when I suggested that an attempt should be made to shed ritual and superstition she protested vehemently.

"No, ritual has meaning and value for some people. It depends how it is used. The idea was to induce concentration. Take Zen. The tea ceremony; the purpose is to disengage yourself, you have to concentrate and a ritual . . . helps you to do that. You can do it without ritual too," she added. "I can concentrate anywhere and anytime now. I used to meditate —I can do it now. I almost go into a trance. . . . It's very relaxing."

She leaned forward earnestly, her dark eyes, searching for a formulation of her thought, drawn into an abstract inward gaze. I could see the light freckles on her pale translucent skin come sharply into view as the sun, which she does not like, caught her face.

"I do believe . . . in this question of being detached. Being passionately interested and still be able . . . to be detached," she said.

"What about the concept of God then?"

She went back to the *Gita* again for that, to its basic tenet that the essence of godhood is in everything, even in inanimate things.

"I am the brilliance in the sun," she quoted in the original Sanskrit from Krishna's profound exposition. "I am the good and the evil. I think this is what Hinduism has, this acceptance of evil also, of the total being, or reality. It's not negative, you know, like the immaculate conception . . . or the idea of sin. So we don't have a, a . . ."

"A guilt complex?"

"Yes, that's right."

"If you believe that it is some sort of inner power."

"Yes, Gandhi said truth is God, Tagore said beauty is God . . . it allows
each person to find his level. For some it's the abstract or the level of idol
worship, but I . . . am on a different level, not higher or lower, but different.
It is something within you. Whatever makes you better, I suppose . . ."

"Is God?"

"No, not God. Well, how would you put it? I have never really thought
about it." She began to laugh, a little helplessly.

"Let's leave God alone!" exclaimed the prime minister.

With the decline of civil disobedience, the controversy over joining government began. Gandhi's arrest left a vacuum that made it impossible to
conduct civil disobedience as he had envisaged it. June of 1922 became the
month for a "re-examination of fundamentals." The AICC met at Lucknow
and it became evident immediately that there were many congressmen like
Motilal Nehru, C.R.Das, and Vithalbhai Patel who felt that the circumstances
warranted a shift in method. Noncooperation, they felt, should be extended
to the heart of the bureaucratic machinery by standing for elections, entering, and then obstructing the running of the provincial governments themselves. But a decision as to whether civil disobedience in some form or other
should be adopted at all was shelved to a later meeting and meanwhile a
civil disobedience committee was appointed to gauge public opinion.
Motilal, of course, was one of the prominent members of the committee.

After a detailed tour to assess the mood of the people and the possibilities
of further action, the committee published its report. It revealed a schism
in approach which threatened a party split as serious as the one at Surat
in 1907. Apart from unanimously recommending that limited mass civil
disobedience be undertaken by provincial committees on their own responsibility, Motilal, Hakim Ajmal Khan, and V.J. Patel were firmly for entering
the legislatives councils, against the recommendation of Dr M.A. Ansari,
C. Rajagopalachari, and S. Kasturi Ranga Iyengar that there should be no
change in the existing Congress program of boycott. The AICC discussed
the report in a mammoth session at Calcutta, but on the burning question of
council entry deferred a decision to the Congress session at Gaya, where the
historic confrontation between logic and sentiment took place.

Das was elected president, but while making his presidential speech, carried
a letter of resignation and the constitution of a new Swaraj party in his pocket.
"Noncooperation" was the common aim of the "pro-changers" and the
"no-changers," but whereas the former merely wanted to extend the idea
to the legislative field, the later stuck stoically to the policy initiated by
Gandhi and felt that change implied "disloyalty" to his leadership. The
pro-changers were defeated by a vote of 1,840 to 890 against council entry.
As a result, they immediately formed the Congress Khilafat Swaraj Party.
The manifesto declared that it was to be "a party within the party." It would

have the identical creed and noncooperation program as the Congress, but would make its own decision on elections for the councils. Das was to try to gain control of the Bengal council while Motilal would concentrate on the center.

It was clear that not even the spell of Gandhi could prevent Motilal from breaking with him on a political issue when time, necessity, and his own judgment dictated that it should be so. It was an act of dissent that Jawahar in later years would always hesitate committing. At that moment, however, Jawahar could view events only from jail, and although his own inclination was wholly against council entry he realized that direct action had to yield for the time being to parliamentary activity. Gandhi, on the other hand, believed as he had in 1920 that there could be no compromise. Either you entered the legislature to work on what constructive programs you could or you kept out and opposed the government. But he had far too much respect for Motilal and Das to conclude that they were guided by anything but intense patriotism. A month after the Swaraj party was formed, Jawahar was released from jail, and in 1924, after an appendectomy which made the entire nation anxious, Gandhi was released after having served two years of his sentence. During the next three years Motilal made an earnest effort to win Gandhi to the Swarajist point of view, Jawahar acting as a mediator to bring the two sides together, and Gandhi relenting in the end. The no-changers were asked to desist from carrying on propaganda against the Swarajists and by the end of 1925 the Swaraj party became the sole political arm of the Congress.

Personally, the relations of the "Father, Son, and Holy Ghost," as the trinity of Motilal, Jawahar, and Gandhi was referred to by the foreign press, remained close and intimate. Along with the destiny of the nation they had a running concern about the future of Indira. Already, Jawahar was showing an interest in the quality of her development which unconsciously but inevitably guided her toward a role other than that of a doll in the drawing room which he despised so much. He was angry when Motilal withdrew Indira from a "national" school in Allahabad and admitted her instead to St. Cecilia's, run by three European sisters, the Misses Cameron. The national schools had been started as part of the boycott against government-run or government-aided schools, and it was at one of those schools, the Modern School, that Indira had been enroled in 1923. But as no system had evolved there of dividing the children into age groups, Indira was thrown among boys and girls of all ages. St. Cecilia's was a privately run institution and "solely prompted by desire to give Indira companionship of children of her age regardless of instruction," as Motilal wrote to Gandhi, he put her there instead.

"It was very difficult in Allahabad those days," Mrs Gandhi later recalled, "they used to beat us in school there because we took part in these political activities—I was beaten up the first time when I was only five or six."[30]

For the little girl she was then, there was a brief period of certainty. There was a lull in the political storm, and although her father was soon involved in Congress and municipal work, he was at least there. "I realized, with some shame at my own unworthiness in this respect," wrote Jawahar later, "how much I owed to my wife for her splendid behavior since 1920. Proud and sensitive as she was, she had not only put up with my vagaries but brought me comfort and solace when I needed them most."[31] The one thing that worried him was his financial dependence on his father. He knew he could find a job if he wanted to but it would mean giving up or at least curtailing the time that he could give to politics. When he broached the subject to his father, Motilal pointed out calmly that it would be foolish to sacrifice the work he was doing for the sake of a little money, especially as he could earn in three days what Jawahar and his wife would require for a year.

But soon he also had cause to worry about Kamala. She had never been robust and frequently suffered from headaches and minor ailments. In 1919 she had begun to run a persistent temperature. The problem was first diagnosed as tuberculosis, but subsequent diagnosis indicated some other internal trouble. Early in 1925 she conceived, and the eight-year-old Indira must have looked forward to having a little baby sister or brother to relieve her loneliness. But this was not to be. After seven months of an apparently healthy pregnancy, a premature baby boy was born who died two days later. "God's will be done" telegraphed Gandhi from Sabarmati consolingly, but Indira now saw her mother's health failing before her eyes. According to Jawahar, the trouble lay deep. In a case history on her written meticulously in his own hand in 1935 with the detail that showed his intense concern, he concluded with rare objectivity: "It will be noted that the patient has had an emotionally and psychologically troubled life for the last sixteen years, chiefly due to political reasons, which have repeatedly caused domestic upsets. She has herself been keenly interested in these political developments and her desire to take part in them has exceeded her physical ability to do so, and this maladjustment has been a cause of great regret and anxiety to her. She is definitely neurotic, probably due to some repressions and maladjustments during her early years. Subsequent happenings, political upsets, and excitements have added to this. When she had herself taken an active part in public affairs she had been mentally far happier and the neurotic element has faded into the background. But her continued illness always brings it to the fore."[32]

In the autumn of 1925 Kamala fell seriously ill and was taken to a hospital in Lucknow for several months. Jawaharlal as general secretary of the Congress shuttled distractedly between Lucknow, Allahabad, and Cawnpore, where the Congress was held that year. Indira was again plunged into loneliness. The next year tore her away completely from the familiar surroundings of Anand Bhawan, for her mother was advised to seek further treatment abroad, and she sailed with Kamala and Jawahar to Switzerland.

"I had long nourished a secret grievance at not having any brothers or sisters when everybody else seemed to have them," wrote Jawaharlal when recalling the occasion of the birth of Vijayalaxmi, 12 years his junior, "and the prospect of having at least a baby brother or sister all to myself was exhilarating.... I remember waiting anxiously in the verandah for the event. One of the doctors came and told me of it and added, presumably as a joke, that I must be glad that it was not a boy, who would have taken a share in my patrimony. I felt bitter and angry at the thought that any one should imagine that I could harbor such a vile notion."[33]

But it is odd to think that the history of India might have been different if Indira's little baby brother had lived or had Indira herself been a boy.

"The fact that you were a daughter and not a son makes it . . . more interesting, because had you been a son, I wonder how many fewer difficulties you think you might have encountered in being a colleague [of Jawaharlal's]?" asked historian and writer Arnold Michaelis of Mrs Gandhi years later when she was Minister of Information and Broadcasting.

"Or more," she retorted.

"Or more, that's true."

"I think," she elaborated, "there probably would have been more difficulties because, first, I could not have really remained with him and helped him in the way that I have; I would have had to make a living, or something like that. That would have created an entirely new situation. I think the political world also would have been much more sensitive to the situation and wary of it."

"In terms of a male successor?"

"Yes."

While Motilal led the Swarajist attack on the government through the legislatures of India, Jawahar welcomed the idea of leaving India to be able to see things in better perspective. For Indira, her first trip to Europe became one of many in which academic training alternated with the wide education that life with her father automatically entailed. In fact, school work invariably ran second to the varied experience of coming into direct contact with men and women of history, instead of merely reading about them. This had been true of her experience in India, where history was more often than not made on the lawns of Anand Bhawan. It also became true in Europe, where her country's struggle and her family's pre-eminent part in it brought her face to face with the sources of power and policy, and leaders of the literary world. The attention she got was indirect, but she could draw upon it with advantage and confirm it in her own right when the time came for an independent stake in the affairs of her country. On arriving in Switzerland, the family settled in Geneva, and she was immediately admitted to the International School. Within a month she became the subject of an assurance to her father by Romain Rolland.

"Is it not your little daughter who is in the International School at

Geneva?" asked the eminent writer of Jawahar in a letter inviting him and Kamala to visit him. "Her teacher, Miss Hartoch, is an excellent friend of ours. She is the best and the most devoted woman. You can be sure that your little daughter could not be in wiser and more affectionate hands . . . ."[34]

So while her father gazed as a distant onlooker at the happenings in India and absorbed the atmosphere of postwar Europe, and her mother steadily fought for her health, Indira began anew the process of making friends and learning a new language. "She always had a good mind," states Krishna, "and that intense, unchildlike concentration that enables her to master any subject and make the best of what each school had to offer."[35] And within a year Sarojini Naidu was guessing rightly in a letter that she supposed "Indu's a young Ma'mselle by now, jabbering in French with a real Swiss accent."[36]

"It was a quiet and restful period," Jawahar later wrote, and for both Indira and Kamala it was a rare occasion to have Jawahar all to themselves. He made periodic visits to another places, but never for long. In the summer of 1926, Krishna came to keep house and help Kamala, who went out for treatment but stayed at their little flat otherwise. But shortly after there was another wrench for Indira. Jawaharlal arranged for her to be admitted to a good but distant boarding school at Bex, called Ecole Nouvelle, for when Kamala's health did not improve they all went up to nearby Montana, where Kamala entered the sanatorium.

For Jawaharlal it meant a spell of deliberation in which he did a lot of reading and found "the vast political, economic, and cultural changes going on in Europe and America a fascinating study." Despite certain unpleasant aspects of its regime he thought the Soviet Union held a message of hope for the world. He began to be convinced that the Indian fight for political freedom must be enlarged to include social freedom as well. Nationalism began to appear insufficient in view of the need for a socialist structure of society and the lifting of imperialist oppression from the colonial worlds. In Geneva, he had been interested in the activities of the League of Nations and the International Labour Office. News of the general strike in England soon after they arrived in Switzerland excited him greatly and months later his visit to England during a miner's strike opened his eyes to class injustice there. In February 1927 he enthusiastically attended a congress of Oppressed Nationalities at Brussels, and got the Congress at home officially interested. The idea behind the Congress was that colonial and dependent countries form a common front against the imperialist powers, ensuring joint deliberation, and, if possible, joint action. Composed of the labor left-wing and progressive elements, the gathering was not communist or near-communist, but certainly had a lot of goodwill for them. Jawaharlal was elected a member of the League Against Imperialism, the nine-man permanent organization set up by the Brussels' Congress. His association with the League, which had patrons as distinguished as Albert Einstein and Madame

Sun Yat-sen, proved to be an invaluable experience for Jawahar. It enabled him to view with sympathetic understanding the problems of the colonial countries and gave flesh and substance to his theoretical knowledge of the inner conflicts of Western labor. It formed the base for his subsequent leanings toward an international interpretation of the role of politics in India.

From home at the time came echoes of controversy. The Swarajists, led by Motilal and Das, had won a series of legislative victories in the three years they were in power but their value was mostly psychological as a result of the viceroy's veto. A permanent opposition faced an irremovable executive, and Motilal was beginning to feel the impossibility of the situation. There were dissensions within the Swaraj party, or the official Congress party in the legislature as it had become. The party had been a vigorous, aggressive force in the legislatures. But a breakaway group, allying itself with other independents and nationalists, formed a more moderate Indian National party which claimed the liberty to resort to responsive cooperation with the legislature.

According to Lajpat Rai, the Punjab nationalist leader who ultimately joined with Pandit Madan Mohan Malaviya in bolstering this alternate nationalist group in the legislatures, Motilal's noncooperative methods were hurting the Hindu cause. The communal temper of the country was already up. The Khilafat issue on which the Hindus and Muslims had eagerly joined was unexpectedly resolved in 1922, and a series of riots brought the Hindu-Muslim unity, so assiduously cultivated by Gandhi and the enlightened leadership of the Congress, tumbling down. How politics could intermix with personal loyalties and how the principles by which the Nehrus stood affected fellow workers is glimpsed in a touching letter by a young Muslim colleague, Syed Mahmud, to Jawaharlal in November 1923.

"Your letter from Amritsar reached me at Ajmer... where I was busy in trying to reconcile the irreconciliable—the Hindus and the Muslims," wrote Mahmud. "I had given it up as a hopeless task but your charming letter spurred me up and brought back new hopes. I thought when I could love a Hindu and he too could not dislike me why then the Hindus and Mussalmans could not tolerate each other?... Sri Krishna's or [the] Hindu ideal of life always appealed to me but I never had the fortune of meeting a Hindu before I met you who had appealed to me in actual life. Now I try to see and realize that ideal through you."[37]

By 1926 the situation had crystalized into Muslim fears of a Hindu majority and Hindu resentment at being "bullied" by the Muslims. "Many a Hindu," analyzed Jawaharlal later, "felt that there was too much of an attempt to extort special privileges with the threat of going over to the other side. Because of this, the Hindu Mahasabha rose to some importance .... The aggressive activities of the Mahasabha acted on and stimulated still further this Muslim communalism and so action and interaction went on."[38]

The Swaraj party suffered in consequence. Some of its Muslim adherents left it, and the fanatic fringe among the Hindus went over to the Nationalist party. When the time came for the triennial elections to the councils and the legislatures, Motilal found he had to brave the storm alone. Das had died, his own party was disunited, and the opposition was strong. That was precisely the set of circumstances that could provoke his great energies for he enjoyed a fight. He won a fair victory in most provinces: in the Punjab he lost, "thanks to Lajpat Rai's lies," as he wrote to his son, but a debacle in his home province due largely to false and bitter propaganda carried on against him by his ex-colleagues left him disgusted. "It was simply beyond me to meet the kind of propaganda started against me under the auspices of the Malaviya-Lala gang. Publicly I was denounced as an anti-Hindu and pro-Mohammedan but privately almost every individual voter was told that I was a beef-eater in league with the Mohammedans to legalize cow slaughter in public places at all times."[39]

But in the midst of all this, two weeks later he was apologizing, "Dear little Indu has had do go without a birthday present from us due to my pre-occupation with the elections and the absence of imagination in others. I am sorry."[40]

The Congress met at Gauhati that year under the strain of conflict between non-cooperation and cooperation in the legislature and the devious blandishments of the government by which, as Congress historian Sitaramayya put it, "wavering minds and timid hearts are won over." But even while the session was on, there came the tragic news of the assassination of a leading Arya Samajist leader called Swami Shradhanand. He had been stabbed in bed by a Muslim called Abdul Rashid. Only eight years before the Swami's calls for Hindu-Muslim unity had resounded from the pulpit of Delhi's Jama Masjid, and the crowds had reacted with shouts of Hindu-Muslim ki jai. "I do not even regard him [Abdul Rashid] as guilty of Swami's murder," declared Gandhi at Gauhati in an address expounding the tenets of true religion. "Guilty indeed are those who excited feelings of hatred against one another."[41]

In Europe, Jawaharlal was again getting impatient. "Kamala has been tolerably well in spite of this fatigue of living in a great city," he wrote to Gandhi from London. "But she is tired out. We are all tired of staying in foreign parts and want to go home. It was my intention to return in September but now father is coming here."[42]

"I remember celebrating my tenth birthday in London," says Indira.[43] But in September 1927, Motilal joined the family in Europe and for the next three months, while Indira stayed in school, her mother, father, aunt, and grandfather traveled all over Italy, Britain, France, Germany, and attended, on Jawahar's suggestion, the tenth anniversary celebrations of the Russian Revolution at Moscow. After that it was good to be going home again although for Indira it meant another break in what had become the even tenor of school in Switzerland.

Back in Allahabad, she went to a new school, St. Mary's Convent, while a tutor was appointed to teach her Hindi at home. With Kamala feeling slightly better, Jawahar felt relieved. He had come back with two strong convictions: that the political aim of India should be independence and not the vague and confusing question of dominion status within the empire, and that there must be a parallel social goal. Gandhi, he found, was keeping on the periphery of Congress politics since the Swaraj party had begun to dominate it. He did not attend the working committee meetings, of which he was a member, and took no part in the shaping of policy. But he was very much the power behind the throne for nothing was done without consulting him.

In November of 1927, the Secretary of State for India announced the formation of the Simon Commission, led by Sir John Simon, whose purported aim was an inquiry into "the working of the system of government, the growth of education and the development of representative institutions in British India, and reporting whether and to what extent it is desirable to establish the principle of responsible government."[44] There was not a single Indian member on the commission, and the reaction was sharply resentful. Motilal, in England, commented that the commission was only an eyewash. "The only honest course is to declare what government wants to do and then to appoint a commission to draft a scheme giving effect to that declaration."[45]

At the Congress meeting at Madras in December, it was decided to conduct a total boycott of the commission, and Jawahar's resolution defining "Complete National Independence" as the goal of the Indian people was passed without protest to his considerable surprise. Its validity, however, was offset by a plea for an All Parties Conference to draw up a constitution for India on the basis of dominion status. It was manifest to Jawahar that the moderate groups, with whom cooperation was sought, could never think in terms of independence and "the very utmost they could go to was some form of dominion status." But he stepped back into his former post of Congress secretary under the new president, Dr M.A. Ansari, and for two months there was quiet, politically as well as domestically. Kamala again spent long evenings in the first floor suite at Anand Bhawan, while her young daughter kept her company. B.K. Nehru, Jawaharlal's cousin, who lived at Anand Bhawan during 1927-29, remembers that Kamala was very fond of classical novels, especially the Russian ones and on a number of occasions he used to sit and read out loud to her. He felt sorry for her because she was still an "outsider." "She was very frail, tall for an Indian girl and supposed to be very beautiful but I don't think she was beautiful. She had begun to wear spectacles which detracted from her beauty." Indu he recalls only vaguely as a little girl, "always very quiet."[46]

"Until a few years ago, children [in India] were treated as miniature grownups," Mrs Gandhi later wrote in an article in 1956. "Even now we see them at political gatherings and other adult activities, sitting passively with large solemn eyes."[47] She might have been describing her own predicament for she herself admits that her childhood was "an abnormal one, full of loneliness and insecurity."[48] Even the sharing of that loneliness, her mother's and her own, in 1927-28, and the sense of oneness induced by it, was soon to be sacrificed to her mother's growing preoccupation with political work, so that years later when she was asked if she saw more of her mother than her father in that period she could only recall regretfully:

"Hardly. Because she was also very busy in politics."[49]

But beneath the pathos was a hard discipline that kept personal unhappiness subordinate to public obligation and the high idealism of the times. When she was herself asked at what time she could say that she first became involved in politics, she answered simply, "It is impossible to say. I do not remember any time when I was not involved."[50]

Nevertheless at the time she did resent the fact that her parents could not be with her like those of other children. But she was proud of them, and could not envisage any other life. Unlike her father whose childhood and adolescence were sustained by Motilal's immense capacity to earn, live and spend grandiosely, she knew, from the age of four, the comparatively Spartan standards enjoined by the freedom movement. Even when she learnt, as she grew up, how bountiful had been the luxuries of the Nehru household, she felt no regret. Perhaps it was a "defence mechanism" as she puts it, but she developed the feeling that not to lead a luxurious life was the right thing.

"All the difficulties of that life were brought into your home, so that you, at an early age, had to live with them?"

"Yes, that's the only world I remember."[51]

The one year old Indira, with mother, Kamala and father, Jawaharlal

Grandfather Motilal Nehru, driving the first family car

Indira, at the age of seven, with Mahatma Gandhi during his fast in 1924

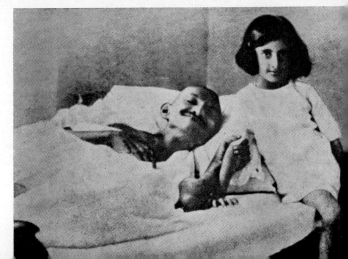

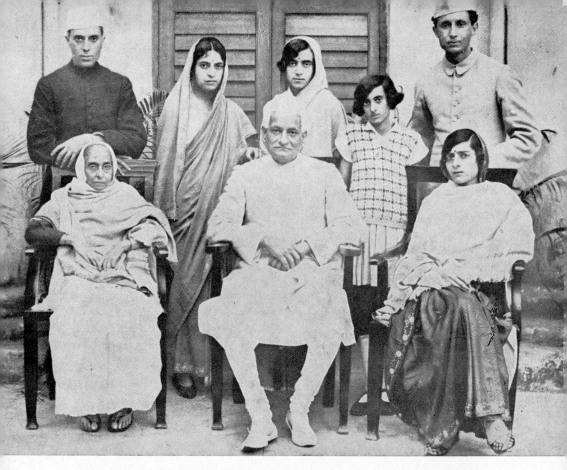

Jawaharlal Nehru, Swarup Rani (Vijayalaxmi Pandit), Krishna, Indira, Ranjit Pandit
(sitting) Swarup Rani Nehru, Motilal Nehru, Kamala Nehru

The ten year old Indira

Indira with mother

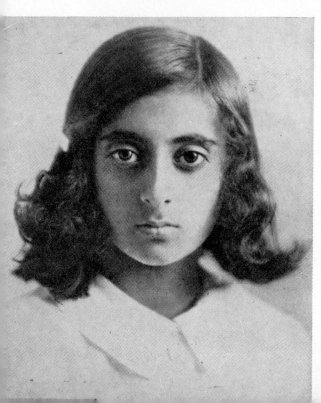

Indira, in Badenweiller, 1935

Indira, in Vanar Sena uniform, with
father and mother

Indira with Jawaharlal Nehru and friends in Europe

Indira with parents

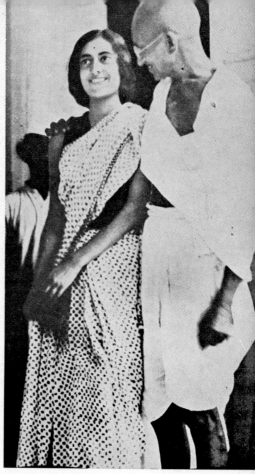

Indira with Mahatma Gandhi

Indira, with Mahatma
Gandhi, and Khan Abdul
Ghaffar Khan, Wardha, 1941

With mother before Kamala's
arrest in 1931

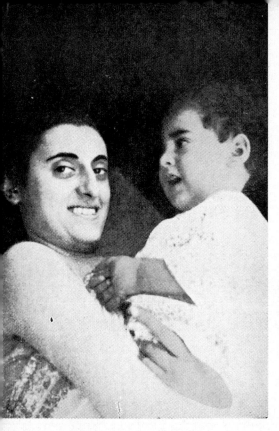

With Rajiv, Pahalgaum, 1945

With Rajiv

Wi h son Rajiv, Pahalgaum, 1945

Indira, in Singapore, 1937

With Jawaharlal and sons Rajiv and Sanjay at breakfast in Tin Murti house
With father and Nahas Pasha during a visit to Egypt in 1938

With Jawaharlal and sons Rajiv and Sanjay on the deck of INS Delhi, 1949

Mohammad Yunus, Indira, and Jawaharlal Nehru at Wardha, 1941

With father, the artist Roerich and son, Yunus, and others in Nagar Kulu, 1942

Indira with Jawaharlal in Kashmir, 1951

With father Jawaharlal and President Soekarno, Indonesia, 1949

Indira in Zurich, 1939

Indira on horseback, accompanying Jawaharlal

Indira, Fatima Jinnah, and Jawaharlal, 1946

Indira with I. K. Gujral and Satish Gujral

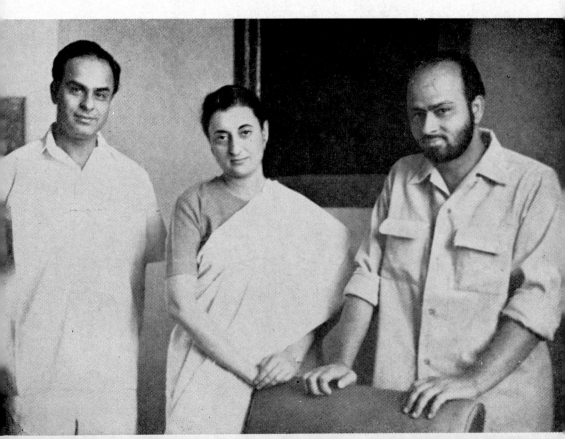

Indira with
father

With Feroze,
sons, and
others in the
lawns of Tin
Murti house,
1956

With father

The marriage ceremony of Indira and Feroze Gandhi, being conducted by Lachmi Dhar Shastri, in the verandah of Anand Bhavan, 1942

Feroze and Indira, during the ceremony

With father, Jawaharlal Nehru, during the ceremony

Feroze and Indira at Tin Murti house, 1957

Feroze, Srinagar, 1942

Feroze, with a friend, Mohammad Yunus,
at Tin Murti house, 1956

Indira, with son Rajiv, father, and relatives celebrating Rajiv's first birthday, Srinagar, 1945

Indira, with father and Khan Abdul Ghaffar
Khan, holding Rajiv, Srinagar, 1945

Indira, holding Rajiv, with
Jawaharlal, Srinagar, 1945

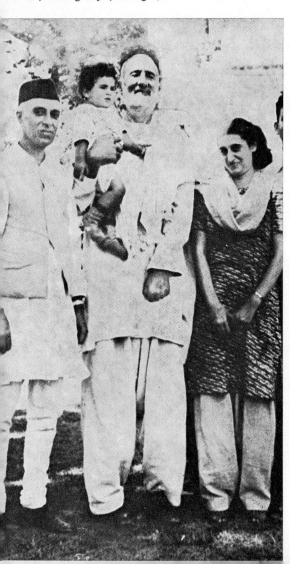

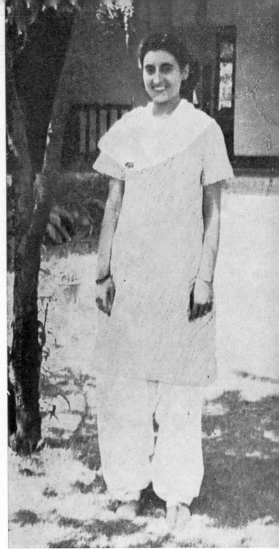

Indira, in Punjabi dress, Srinagar, 1945

Indira, with Rajiv in lap, and Jawaharlal
Indira, with father at a women's conference

With father, in Pahalgaum, 1946

4. PRECEPT

It was a world of political excitement and personal sacrifice. In 1925, Indira hardly saw her father. In 1926 when they had left for Europe their country had been subdued, still brooding over the events of 1919-22. But back in India two years later it seemed to Jawaharlal "fresh, active, and full of suppressed energy."[1]

On February 3, 1928, the Simon Commission arrived in Bombay. It met with almost total boycott. In Madras, the crowds were threateningly fierce and the police opened fire. In Calcutta, the students and the police clashed. In Delhi, there was again blank hostility. In fact, so consistent was the refrain of "Go back, Simon," wherever the commission went, that its members began to hear the slogan even where it was not uttered. An apocryphal story began to go the round that the members of the commission while staying at the Western Court in Delhi complained that the crowds were shouting "Go back, Simon" when it was actually the jackals who were howling in the wooded areas around the city! However, the success of the boycott provoked the government to a show of belligerence. In Punjab, it ordered a *lathi* charge in which the veteran hero, Lajpat Rai, was severly assaulted. An enraged India argued that his death a few weeks later was hastened by this dastardly attack on him, and a deep anger spread throughout North India particularly. It was in this mood that Jawaharlal organized a procession of protest against the Simon Commission in Lucknow and felt for the first time the blow of police batons on his body. "I thought how easy it would be to pull down the police officer in front of me from his horse and to mount up myself," recalled Jawaharlal later, "but long training and discipline held and I did not raise a hand except to protect my face from a blow."[2] The Gandhian way was not an easy one, but Jawaharlal felt tremendously exhilarated that he had gone through this ordeal with dignity and fearlessness. He was only chagrined to find that as the blows rained down upon him his colleagues, thinking that he was a special target, carried him off bodily from the field.

Motilal had rushed to Lucknow the evening before when his son had a preliminary skirmish with the police, but it hurt him deeply to see him injured though he could not nor did he want to prevent it from happening, such was the logic of the political stake then. Gandhi wrote admiringly, "My dear Jawahar, my love to you. It was all done bravely. You have braver things to do. May God spare you for many a long year to come, and make you His chosen instrument for freeing India from the yoke."[3] No wonder the little girl, his daughter, thought that it was worth having such a parent even at the cost of those cosy routines that make the life of the average child so secure.

"Once when Sanjay was quite small," related Mrs Gandhi when she herself became the mother of two sons, "a nursery school friend of his came to our house with his mother. The mother, a society lady of means, commenting upon my public work remarked that I could not be spending much time with my sons. This hurt Sanjay and before I could think of a reply he rushed to my rescue with the words: 'My mother does lots of important work yet she plays with me more than you do with your little boy.' It seemed his little friend had complained about his mother's bridge playing!"[4]

"However," she added, "it is not the amount of time spent with the children that matters as much as the manner of spending it. When one has only a limited period at one's command one naturally makes the most of it. No matter how busy I have been, or how tired or even unwell, I have taken time out to play or read with my sons."

She had a marvellous precept to follow. Her father may not have had the time to read or play with her, but he could write. And all through the long summer of 1928, while she was away in the cool hills at Mussoorie and he remained in Allahabad under the shadow of imminent arrest, he wrote her beautifully simple, instructive letters which not only gave a clue to his own make-up but presaged what hers would become. He wrote to her about the origin of the universe based on the theory of evolution in simple and eloquent terms. But more important, he encouraged an understanding of the world through rational analysis unfettered by religious sentiment but tempered by a strongly humanistic approach.

"Your letters to Indu are excellent and should be published," commented Gandhi. "Your treatment of the subject is quite orthodox. The origin of man is now a debatable subject. The origin of religion is still more a debatable matter. But these differences do not detract from the value of the letters. They have a value derived not from the truth of your conclusions but from the manner of treatment and from the fact that you have tried to reach Indu's heart and open the eyes of her understanding in the midst of your external activities."[5]

Jawaharlal had seen to it that Indira's "patchy and interrupted" education was bolstered by wide interests. While she was at school in Switzerland for a year and nine months, he had taken her with him on visits to neighbouring countries, and arranged for her to attend an American camp at Annexy in France during a summer vacation. He took her to the museum in Geneva and the South Kensington Museum in London. They strolled in Kew Gardens, and he pointed out, to quicken her interest in natual history, the orchids and pitcher plants that actually eat flies.[6] In Geneva they were paid a visit by the famous scientist Sir Jagadish Bose, who had proved by experiment that plants had life, and Indira met him as she did so many of her father's well-known friends. Jawaharlal again took her with him when they went to see a professor at Heidelberg and she saw his small museum full of fossils and the skull of the Heidelberg man, which he took out of a carefully locked safe. She also had a gradually increasing interest in art, music, and poetry. But above all her father encouraged in her a sense of purpose. "Not to work oneself and to live on the work of others is nothing to be proud of,"[7] he told her in one of his letters, sowing the seeds of independence in his child as much as he wanted to in the hearts of his countrymen.

In February 1928, three months after Jawahar and the others, Motilal had returned from Europe, cutting short his holiday because of a medical check-up that made him feel that it was "the beginning of the end." He was already asthmatic and was now warned that the traces of albumin and of glucoma found in his blood could have disastrous consequences. But the existing political developments of the year soon had him exercising his legal brilliance on one hand and his paternal fortitude on the other. The All Parties Conference met in twenty-five sittings in Delhi during the months of February and March and voted for settling on a constitution for India on the basis of full responsible government and solving the question of communal representation. In May a subcommittee with Motilal as chairman was appointed to draft the principles of the constitution. Because Jawaharlal as general secretary of the Congress also had to act as secretary of this subcommittee it came to be called the Nehru Committee. The task it faced was challenging: to frame a constitution that would fulfil the aspirations and meet the claims of the three major communities of India— the Hindus, Muslims, and Sikhs—and even, more important, allay Muslim fears of Hindu domination. Over the years the separate electorates established by the Morley-Minto Reforms of 1907 had caused communal division to deepen. In 1916, the Congress had willy-nilly accepted the principle in the famous pact at Lucknow, in 1919, the Montagu-Chelmsford scheme had extended it further, and by 1928 the uneasy tensions and communalistic rivalry of the two major communities had resulted in a further polarization of views aggravated by the interested presence of Britain which saw in the conflict a means of maintaining its own status quo.

"It is difficult to stand against the foreigner without offering him a united front," said Motilal. "It is not easy to offer him a united front while the foreigner is in our midst domineering over us."[8]

Motilal had to overcome the hurdle of seemingly irreconcilable demands. Although the Congress and the Muslim League at least agreed that there should be reservation of seats for the majorities and the minorities, the Sikhs wanted no reservation at all, and the Hindu Mahasabha only for the minorities. At one point he was so discouraged about the prospect of finding unanimity in the committee that he felt he could do nothing further for the country. In addition, the fact that the draft constitution was to be envisaged within the framework of dominion status and not complete independence, provoked violent opposition from his son. To Jawahar, who had had the resolution on independence passed only a few months earlier at the Madras Congress, any come down was betrayal. To Motilal dominion status meant another step toward the goal; to Jawaharlal it seemed an unfruitful compromise.

But by July 11, Motilal was confidently writing to Gandhi that the committee had arrived at a unanimous decision and he and Jawaharlal were busy drafting the report. By July 21, the sixty pages of typed matter evoked the enthusiasm of hard-headed Sir Tej Bahadur Sapru, and at the end of August the draft constitution it outlined was accepted with few reservations by the All Parties Conference at Lucknow. Indian leaders as a whole were in a buoyant mood. The challenge of the British government to Indian nationalists to find an agreed constitution had been met, and the significance of it was not lost on the discerning. At Lucknow, Jawaharlal and Subhas

Chandra Bose suggested that the communal act should be accepted but the question of independence versus dominion status left open. But when the conference declared itself in favor of dominion self-government, they refused to support the resolution but agreed not to obstruct the work of the conference.

Jawaharlal formed the India for Independence League as a separate pressure group which was to propagate for complete independence within the Congress, with the additional aim of the "reconstruction of society on a new basis." Motilal was determined to have the report accepted at the Congress session to be held on December 31 at Calcutta. Jawaharlal was equally adamant that there could be no compromise on the issue of independence. The relations between father and son became tense as at no time before, and mingled with Motilal's exacerbation was a nagging worry that Jawaharlal's extreme views would result in his return to prison.

The Calcutta session was historic. At Motilal's behest Gandhi forsook his self-imposed exile from active Congress politics, and came to Calcutta to his support. When the conflict over dominion status threatened a serious split between the young radicals and the old guard, Gandhi suggested a compromise resolution: the Congress would accept the Nehru report in its entirety but if the government did not act upon it within two years, the Congress would fight for complete independence resorting again to the effective method of mass civil disobedience. Jawaharlal's amendment approved the Nehru Committee's recommendations for communal settlement but would not agree to the time limit. Ultimately, Gandhi settled for a year's grace for the British government and the resolution which was passed in the open Congress declared: "Subject to the exigencies of the political situation, this Congress will adopt the constitution if it is accepted in its entirety by the British Parliament on or before the 31st December, 1929, but in the event of its non-acceptance by the date or its earlier rejection, the Congress will organize a campaign of non-violent non-cooperation...."

The die was cast, and though Jawaharlal vacillated uneasily between his conviction and this commitment, the fact was that he had won the day for total independence, even if its active expression was delayed by a year. It was clear that a challenge had been prevented for nobody believed that the British government would accept the constitution within a year, if at all.

But the irony and the tragedy was that the unanimity of the decision at the All Parties Conference, which was held almost simultaneously with the Congress at Calcutta, again came under question when a supplementary report was submitted for approval. Mohammed Ali Jinnah, a member of the committee who had recently returned from England, had been chaffing against the Nehru Report from the beginning and at the Calcutta convention decided to voice his dissent. He joined the faction led by Aga Khan and the Ali brothers in the Muslim League and condemned the Nehru Report outright. The quarrel was over the question of separate

electorates, reservation of one-third of the seats for the Muslims in the
central legislature, and the residuary powers of the provinces. It was a
long way for a pre-1921 nationalist and "the ambassador of Hindu-Muslim
unity" as Sarojini Naidu had once called him, to have come. Jawaharlal's
reading was that Jinnah veered away from the Congress after 1921 not so
much on political grounds as on feeling temperamentally ill at ease with
its Gandhian look.

"He felt completely out of [his] element in the khadi-clad crowd demanding speeches in Hindustani," said Jawaharlal. "The enthusiasm of the
people outside struck him as mob hysteria. There was as much difference
between him and the Indian masses as between Savile Row and Bond Street
and the Indian village with its mud huts."[9]

But whereas in Motilal a deep aristocracy of outlook transmuted itself
into a sensitivity to the nation's needs, Jinnah became "a rather solitary
figure in Indian politics," turning eventually to reactionary alignment with
the forces of communalism that took him along the road to the country's
dismemberment in 1947. In 1928, when he repudiated the Nehru Report
it was evident that it could not be because of any suspicions about the motivations of its sponsors, the enlightened, fair-minded, utterly non-communal
Motilal and the co-author Sir Tej Bahadur Sapru. It was basically a clash
of vision between the claims of community and the claims of nationhood;
between those like the Nehrus who visualized India as a cultural entity and
those like Jinnah who would prize sectional ambition above country; and
between those who would, through joint electorates, encourage a "common
citizenship" and a "national spirit" and those who would, through separate
electorates, ensure a permanent cleavage in stake. There was hardly any
meeting ground and Motilal made no secret of his contempt for the alleged
grievance on Jinnah's part that Motilal had been cold to him. "If the cold
reception of an individual, however great in one place, and a rather hot
reception of the same individual in another place," related Motilal to a
colleague, "is to affect the solution of a great national problem we had better
say goodbye to it. What Mr Jinnah said on the occasion left me cold and
I could not work up an artificial warmth to please him."[10] It was left to
Gandhi to administer the death dose to the dying convention. He suggested
that it should adjourn *sine die* and the motion was passed.

Behind the drama of these political events was the drama of personal
relations: the apex of Motilal's political authority and Jawahar's rising one.
In 1927, while Jawaharlal was away in Europe, Motilal had written to him
about two young contemporaries of his from Cambridge who were members
of the central assembly. "What I feel on seeing these men is that you
should have been in my place. This would have been more in the fitness
of things than my being here...."[11]

Later that year when the question of choosing the Congress president
for the Madras session came up, ironically, Jinnah, along with Sarojini

Naidu, suggested the candidature of the elder Nehru. Gandhi thought the circumstances unpropitious and Motilal, while declining the offer, suggested Jawahar instead. Gandhi thought the idea had an "irresistible appeal" but wondered if it would be fair to Jawahar to make him come in when the organization was in the grip of "anarchy and a growing hooliganism." He expressed his doubts when he wrote to him:

> There is some talk of your being chosen president for the coming Congress. I am in correspondence with your father about it. The outlook here is not at all happy in spite of the unanimous resolution of the AICC on the Hindu-Muslim question . . . we have lost hold upon the masses, and it seems to me that if you become president, you will be lost for one year at any rate to the masses. I know you are capable of taking a detached view and you will say quite unselfishly, 'put the crown on my head' and I have no doubt that it will be so put. I do not myself see the way so clear as to make me force the crown on you and plead with you to wear it.[12]

Jawahar in any case was unwilling and the selection turned to M.A. Ansari. In 1928, for the momentous session at Calcutta, Bengal was determined to have Motilal as president but again he suggested Jawahar's name. "The hero of the hour is Vallabhbhai Patel," he wrote to Gandhi, "and the least we can do to appreciate his public services is to offer him the crown, failing which under all the circumstances Jawahar would be the next best choice. He has no doubt frightened many of our goody goodies with his plain talk. But the time has come when the more energetic and determined workers should have their own way of guiding the political activities of the country. Our race is fast dying out and the struggle will sooner or later have to be continued by men of Jawahar's type. The sooner they begin the better."[13]

"We must have you," wrote J.M. Sen Gupta, one of the leading congressmen of Bengal, to Motilal, "You must come and lead us in this political crisis. . . . I can well understand the feelings of a father when his son is also in the field. But most of us are in the position of your sons. . . ."[14]

"There is no question of sentiment about father and son," replied Motilal, "or of the son requiring any persuasion to retire in favor of the father. The only question which weighs both with the father and the son is how to serve the country best . . . my idea of putting him in the presidential chair of the Congress is an old one and has nothing to do with the fact that he is my son. The reason why I recommended Jawahar was that among the younger set I believed he was most likely to command the confidence of the majority. This has since been proved to be true, as is evident by the fact that he and I are being mentioned almost in the same breath. . . ."[15]

It was Motilal who finally presided over the Calcutta session and was in charge of organization in 1929. It was a year of preparation. As events moved toward a showdown with the government, "barbarous" methods of repression began to be used by the authorities; there were numerous arrests of labor and political workers who in turn organized strikes inside and outside prison. By July the Congress realized that it would be advantageous for the coming movement if Congress members of all the legislatures were to resign. Motilal and others were by then disenchanted with the functioning of the councils and its members, Gandhi was back on the scene, and the next logical step seemed to be civil disobedience.

Accordingly, the presidency of the Congress scheduled to be held at Lahore on December 31, 1929, when the time limit given to the British would be up, became one of intense significance. Motilal was not shy of again declaring that the "need of the hour is the head of Gandhi and the voice of Jawahar," and that the "revolt of youth" necessitated a younger man at the helm of affairs while Gandhi of course would be "the real power, whether on the throne or behind it."[16]

Jawaharlal was less sure and begged Gandhi not to "press his name for presidentship." "I represent nobody but myself," he observed, trying to be as objective as possible. "I have not the politician's flair for forming groups and parties. If I have the misfortune to be the president, you will see that the very people who put me there will be prepared to cast me to the wolves."[17]

Gandhi proved still to be the obvious choice of most provinces, but he wanted it otherwise and at his insistence Jawaharlal was voted the next president by the AICC on September 28, 1929. "About the crown no one else can wear it," Gandhi reassured Jawaharlal when he expressed doubts as to whether he could carry the Congress his way. "It never was to be a crown of roses. Let it be all thorns now."[18]

By October, Lord Irwin, the current viceroy, made a pronouncement on his return from England that it was "implicit in the declaration of 1917 that the natural issue of India's constitutional progress ... is the attainment of dominion status," and that a conference be set up of representatives of British India and the states and His Majesty's Government "for the purpose of seeking the greatest possible measure of agreement for the final proposals."[19]

"We understand, however," stated the Delhi manifesto as a reply from leading Indian statesmen and the Congress working committee, "that the conference is to meet not to discuss when dominion status is to be established, but to frame a scheme of dominion constitution for India."[20]

"I can wait for a dominion constitution if I can get real dominion status in action," Gandhi assured his liberal friends in England, "that is to say, if there is a real change of heart, a real desire on the part of the British people to see India a free and self-respecting nation. My conception of dominion status," he added, "implies present ability to sever the British connection if I wish to."[21]

Jawaharlal signed the manifesto unhappily because it meant a retreat from his oft-repeated demand for complete independence. Two days later, on November 4, he wrote to Gandhi, "Something seems to have snapped inside me evening before last and I am unable to piece it together. I am myself a believer in discipline. And yet I suppose there can be too much of discipline. I am afraid we differ fundamentally on that issue and I am not likely to convert you. I shall only say that I believe the statement to have been injurious and a wholly inadequate reply to the Labour government's declaration."[22] He felt he should resign as general secretary of the Congress, as he was then, while his position as the next president was also untenable. "You were the only possible president for the occasion and the year," he told Gandhi. "I cannot be president if the policy of the Congress is what might be described as that of Malaviyaji...."[23] Jawaharlal's instinctive stand was invariably opposed to Gandhi's, but the result was mostly a compromise.

"There were great differences between them," points out Mrs Gandhi, "But I think my father . . . went to the heart of the man and picked out what he thought were the essentials." What is revealing of her own attitude is the added comment: "There is only one thing about which my father and I quarreled, and that was about this... because there were many things about Mr Gandhi which I simply could not accept."

"But there were some things that your father couldn't and wouldn't accept."

"Yes, but I was more vocal about it, perhaps," says Mrs Gandhi, "and he thought that meant showing disrespect."[24]

The December confrontation with the viceroy by Gandhi and Motilal on the one hand, and Jinnah, Sapru, and Vithalbhai Patel on the other, proved abortive. Gandhi wanted an assurance that the Round Table Conference would spell out the scheme of full dominion status. The viceroy was unable to comply. With a week left for the Lahore session it became evident that a grim struggle would have to be launched and "everyone to his place and all for his life,"[25] thought the nationalists. All the roads led to Lahore where a transfer of power from the father to the son, Congress president-elect Jawaharlal Nehru, was soon to take place.

Indira had seen the tremendous reception accorded to her grandfather the year before, when he had been driven through the streets of Calcutta in a carriage drawn by thirty-six horses in a great and ceremonial presidential cavalcade. At Lahore she saw how the people showered rose petals on her father, as the crowds surged and swelled in the streets of the city. There were people everywhere, in windows, on trees, and on the roofs to see "the most popular young politician of the hour." The people she was to see in increasing numbers always hovered around her father in awe, adoration, and enthusiasm to the day he died when they broke all bounds and swamped the city, hundreds and thousands of them, in an unforgettable homage. This was only the beginning. This was the first time in the history of the Congress that a father was going to hand over charge to a son, and in the whole of India that day, as Sarojini Naidu had written to Jawahar on his nomination, there could not have been a prouder heart than the father's.[26] What Motilal said on the occasion followed naturally from "the great and brilliant future" he had predicted for his son as a young boy. *"Herche ke pidar, natawanad pesar tamam shud,"* he recited with moving confidence the Persian couplet that means, "What the father could not achieve, the son will accomplish." But whereas Motilal did not hesitate to openly sponsor his son's future in politics, Jawahar was never to be so obvious about his confidence in his daughter. "You must be a brave little soldier in India's service," was the theme of his instruction to her. But thirty years later, when he was prime minister and she became the third Nehru to serve as Congress party president, he disowned any attempts on his part to help her along. He had a horror of the dynastic order. He had written of the rajas and maharajas of the day as an anachronism in a modern society and he was certainly not inclined to establish a pattern of privileged family status, even if it were a justifiable one. But he did think that Indira deserved the honor because he had a high opinion of her. He may not have groomed her for a particular office, but he certainly groomed her to be dissatisfied with the ordinary routines of living. He left the shape of the outcome to circumstances and her own predilection, but it was obvious that it could only be politics: both the atmosphere and the precedent were inalienable.

"What I want to point out is the fact," Nehru affirmed later, "that I did not choose her or groom her for that high post, probably the highest in the country. The people chose her. I remained neutral. In fact for sometime I was mentally opposed to the idea ..." He made it clear however, "I am neither preparing her for anything, nor do I propose to prevent her from taking any responsibilities the country or the people may desire of her."[27]

To correspondents on February 7, 1959 after her election he said: "Nobody had mentioned it to me before and it came rather as a surprise. I gave a good deal of thought to this matter and I came to the conclusion that I should firmly keep apart from this business and not try to influence it in any way except rather generally and broadly to say that it has its disadvantages." He however could not help adding that it also had its advantages. Minoo Masani, a leading member of the Swatantra party and one-time congressman, related to me the instance of an influential Congress friend who told him that although Nehru really never officially sponsored his daughter's name his advice, which was sought automatically, that the choice should be of a younger person and that it could even be a woman was hint enough as to what he wanted.

It is difficult to reconcile this with Nehru's impulsive straightforwardness, even if in 1959, after twelve years in power as prime minister, he could be presumed to have acquired some circumspection of approach

"Normally speaking," he said, "it is not a good thing for my daughter to come in as Congress president when I am prime minister."

He pointed out however that the election indicated a desire on the part of the organization to "get out of the rut" of old leadership and that some Congress leaders definitely wanted a younger person.

Mrs Gandhi herself was emphatic later in stating that her father had not encouraged her to take a more active role in politics.

"Why?" I insisted, and for a woman for whom politics has opened a world of power and glory, her reply was astonishing.

"No man," she said, "who has some concern for his child would let him take up this field. That is why I have seen to it that my sons have nothing to do with politics, that they come nowhere near it. I have kept them away."

"But then why did you yourself come into it?"

"I was in it from the beginning."

"But as you were in it was your father in favour of your taking up the post of Congress president?"

"Absolutely not" she declared. "It was Pandit Pant who ultimately persuaded him to agree. Then I wouldn't agree. Panditji kept telling my father to persuade me, but he said it must be left to me to make up my mind. I remember he [Pant] was very angry and banged the phone down once because I wouldn't agree."[28]

Indira's attitude to politics was certainly not hostile when she was a young girl. Merely being "in it from the beginning" does not explain the positive initiative with which she undertook public and even semi-political work when other girls of her age were probably thinking of looking pretty. But the times were unusual and there were many girls and boys who were afire with the nationalistic spirit of their parents with whom she could feel a common bond. Until she turned sixteen when, as she says, "the delight of being a woman began to unfold itself," she had wanted to be a boy and looked, according to her own description, like "a long-legged tomboy in frocks."[29] She was thin, scrawny and pale, her long nose and large eyes swamped her face, and the obligation to wear thick, coarse, and shapeless khadi dresses was not conducive to any assumptions of vanity. She was a child herself when she started the children's section of Gandhi's Charkha Sangh (Spinning Association), and while at Allahabad she used to cycle out to a leper home to work among the unfortunate inmates. Her ideal was Joan of Arc, according to her father, who wrote once reminding her of it. She herself has no vivid recollection of this as such. But Krishna says in her book about the family: "I remember one evening, when she was eight or nine years old, I saw her standing on the railing of our house clutching a pillar with one hand, the other raised high. She seemed to be muttering something, so I went up to her and asked, 'What in the world are you trying to do?' She looked at me solemnly with her round little face ringed by jet-black hair and her dark eyes burning, and said, 'I'm practising being Joan of Arc. I have just been reading about her, and some day I am going to lead my people to freedom just as Joan of Arc did'."30

Apparently she was not a mere dreamer. As early as 1929, when the country was seething with suppressed excitement and talk of civil disobedience was in the air, she wanted to become a member of the Congress party. But being only twelve, her request was turned down and she was advised to wait until she was eighteen or twenty-one. Young as she was, she was infuriated and vowed that she would have an organization of her own instead. So she initiated the famous Vanar Sena, or the Monkey Army, in Allahabad, a sort of a children's army of Congress helpers, which ultimately had a membership of six thousand children and branches in Calcutta and Bombay. They had a regular uniform with narrow trousers, a loose *kurta,* and a khadi cap. She could even then turn a disadvantage into practical count. Being a child, she naturally had a small voice and as there were no loudspeakers in India, she used an ingenious method for reaching the thousands of children that came to the first meeting of the Vanar Sena. She would say something, another boy or girl would take it up a little farther down the line and bellow it forth and then another and another and a chain of human loudspeakers would thus be formed till the last line of young volunteers got their instructions. The idea behind the organization was simple. Its purpose was to relieve the Congress members of time-consuming but ordinary tasks like writing notices, putting up posters, addressing envelopes, making flags, cooking, giving first aid, and carrying messages, thus freeing them to do more important work.

"The functions were according to age groups," recalled Mrs Gandhi. "We functioned a bit like women do in war-time. We tried to take over every possible job from the older people so that they were free to do other things."31

On occasions they succeeded where an adult might have failed.

"Sometimes," described Mrs Gandhi, "a house might be surrounded by the police, and you couldn't send out a message. But nobody bothered about an urchin hopping in and out of the police lines. Nobody thought that he could be doing anything. Well, the boy would memorize the message and go to the person concerned and say 'You know, this is what has to be done, or not done. All the police are there. So-and-so is going to be arrested,' or whatever the news was. In a similar way, we also acted as an intelligence group, because frequently the policemen, sitting in front of the police station, would talk about what was going on—who was to be arrested, where there would be a raid, and so on. And four or five children playing hopscotch outside would attract no one's attention. And they would deliver the news to the people in the movement."[32] It was impossible to conceive of a time when as Minister of Information and Broadcasting in a free India she would be concerned with such activities on a high official level. But at that time even her father did not know of the project until she had completed all the preliminaries.

After that the ramifications spread. Upadhyaya, who was secretary to Motilal then and remained with the family for a long time, relates that one day a few months later, a bright little ten-year-old girl from a far off village turned up at Anand Bhawan. She had been reading Gandhi's *Young India* in Hindi and had been thrilled by the Congress call for action. She had run off from home to Malacca jail where by then even Kamala Nehru was in prison. Kamala advised her to go to Anand Bhawan. "Her clothes were torn and ragged but she had such bright eyes that I thought she could become Induji's Secretary for the Vanar Sena," recalls Upadhyaya. So he sent her to Indira who immediately took charge, gave her a bath and a set of new clothes and was all prepared to make her a permanent member of her little army. Shortly after the girl's family turned up in search of her, but nothing would persuade her to return till her father asked her sadly, 'Who'll feed your little baby brother?' and the little girl burst into tears, and went off home, and the Vanar Sena leader lost a potential personal assistant.[33]

"What is your position in the Monkey Army?" Indira's grandfather teased her in a letter from jail on July 16, 1930. "I suggest the wearing of a tail by every member of it, the length of which should be in proportion to the rank of the wearer."[34]

"The people had looked upon us condescendingly when the whole idea was mooted," says Mrs Gandhi now, "but after a while they weren't so condescending because we really did quite a tough job."[35]

She could say that of almost every period in her life when she undertook any significant job, for she had always to fight the same condescension of attitude bred by two disadvantages: that she was merely her father's daughter, and that she had a delicate, feminine manner that in no way indicated her capacity for taking hard knocks and making hard decisions.

"We're obstinate mules in our family," says a Nehru cousin, "the more you're thrashed the more you rise up."[36]

The Congress at Lahore was like a spark that set the fires of civil disobedience burning. The year's grace in the ultimatum to the British government being up, complete independence was declared to be the goal, and the AICC was authorized to launch a program of civil disobedience whenever it deemed fit. The main resolution was declared carried, by a curious coincidence, on the stroke of midnight on the thirty-first and the scene was unforgettable for those who were present, especially Indira. The flag of independence was unfurled on the banks of the Ravi river and her father danced round the flagstaff, while the entire Congress camp succumbed to wild enthusiasm. Soon after the session, Motilal called upon his Congress colleagues in the councils and legislatures to resign their seats, and on January 26, Gandhi decided to ask the nation to observe Independence Day and take the pledge of independence both as a start to the campaign and a test of its popularity.

Indira, too, took the oath, as did her family and the people in public meetings all over the country. "We believe," Jawahar said, "that it is the inalienable right of the Indian people, as of any other people, to have freedom and enjoy the fruits of their toil and have the necessities of life, so that they may have full opportunities of growth. We believe also that if the government deprives a people of these rights and oppresses them, the people have a further right to alter it or abolish it. The British government in India has not only deprived the Indian people of their freedom but has based itself on the exploitation of the masses, and has ruined India economically, politically, culturally, and spiritually. We believe therefore that India must sever the British connection and attain *purna swaraj* or complete independence. We hold it to be a crime against man and God to submit any longer to a rule that has caused this disaster to our country."[37]

Gandhi showed that he was prepared to settle for details when he made an eleven-point offer, but the British government remained adamant. The question was now only of picking a major tactic, and no one but Gandhi imagined that the breaking of the salt laws could be an efficacious one. The state salt monopoly forbade the collection of salt from sea water. Motilal reacted with the same amusement, even anger, he had shown before when Gandhi had insisted upon so many spinning hours as a condition for Congress membership, and the government itself tended to look upon the idea as portending only a "kindergarten stage of revolution." But on March 11, Gandhi led a small band of volunteers on a 241-mile trek from Sabarmati to Dandi on the west coast with the purpose of making salt out of sea water. The journey became historic. Wherever Gandhi went the people rose up with him, and the temperature of the country shot up too.

"The air is thick with rumor that I'll be arrested during the night," wrote Gandhi to Jawaharlal from his march, but he was optimistic. "Things are developing extraordinarily well. Offers of volunteers are pouring in."[38] On the thirteenth, he was saying, "We have reached the second stage safely," and on the thirty-first, "Unless you hear from me to the contrary, please take April 6 as the date for simultaneous beginning [of the salt satyagraha]."[39] At the AICC meeting at Ahmedabad, a plan of action was mapped out, a devolution of authority settled upon in case of mass arrests, in which a "dictator" in each region would carry on the work till he or she was arrested and another could take his place, and the president was given all powers to function on behalf of the committee. "We hastened back to our posts," recalled Jawaharlal "and as Sarojini Naidu said to pack up our toothbrushes for the journey back to prison." On the way they met Gandhi at Jambusar, and Motilal took the opportunity to hand over his beloved Anand Bhawan to the nation. He bequeathed it to the Congress in a moving ceremony in which again the son was the official recipient, and Anand Bhawan was renamed Swaraj Bhawan, the Abode of Freedom. The family meanwhile moved to a more compact house that Motilal had built in the compound and this was named Anand Bhawan. "I hope you will give me the credit of fully realizing what it means to me and mine to throw in my lot with Gandhiji in the coming struggle," wrote Motilal to a friend and colleague. "Nothing but a deep conviction that the time for the greatest effort and the greatest sacrifice has come would have induced me to expose myself at my age and with my physical disabilities and my family obligations to the tremendous risks I am incurring. I hear the clarion call of the country and I obey."[40]

For Indira there was no time to feel unhappy even though it had been a wrench parting with the familiar memories of the old house. She had left St. Mary's Convent because she disliked it and was now studying at home. There was so much continued excitement that the whole family was caught up in it, and she was further involved with the Vanar Sena. For months the Congress had been drilling its volunteers to make them efficient and capable of handling large crowds. Her mother and Aunt Krishna had joined them, of course, and to the utter consternation of Swarup Rani they had begun to wear men's clothes for the purpose. On April 6, Gandhi broke the salt laws at Dandi by making his own salt and three days later, as salt-making spread like a prairie fire round the country, "we felt a little abashed and ashamed for having questioned the efficacy of the method when it was first proposed by Gandhiji," said Jawahar. It had become a powerful symbol of revolt, and a symbol that the poorest and the most ignorant could understand. Salt was made anyhow, anywhere, and anytime, and people danced about in the streets and waved fistfuls of it in triumph.

"Let the fist be broken," said Gandhi, "but let there be no surrender of salt."[41]

The government soon realized the dangerous potentialities of the movement. On April 14, Jawaharlal was arrested. On May 5, Gandhi was taken to Yeravada jail near Poona, and on June 30, Motilal joined his son in the barrack at Naini central prison. The entire working committee was declared an unlawful body, and because this meant that it could be arrested en bloc if in session, the acting presidents were authorized to add a list of substitute members who could keep stepping in as the arrests took place. Kamala, too, became a substitute member.

In fact, most significant of all, like a tidal wave, the women of India came out of their seclusion, and everywhere there were overwhelming number of them, picketing foreign cloth shops, shouting slogans, braving lathi charges, storming shop depots, and winding their way in procession through the streets of the cities and villages. All the Nehru women were in the forefront, even the delicate Swarup Rani, who not only went about regardless of the scorching heat of the sun but even made a fiery speech. For Kamala it was like a release from bondage. All her pent-up emotions found expression in the work. She was never so fit again as she was in 1930 and she not only drove herself hard but won the admiration of both her husband and her father-in-law for the great organizing capacity that she showed. She had been elected president of the Allahabad district Congress committee and practically ran the movement from there. Her kindness which was already proverbial—no one came away from seeing her without being won over by her hospitality—was now directed toward being mother to all the Congress orphans. She turned one wing of the house into a hospital to treat victims of lathi-charges and firings, and had Indira help her nurse them. But Indira did more. She made it a point of faith to make the impossible possible. There was one boy who came in with such a severe injury that even the doctors gave up.

"But he was my first patient," recalled Mrs Gandhi, "and I was determined to see him through. I almost staked my faith in God on his pulling through,"[42] and he did pull through!

Most of the Congress workers, who were either going to jail or who were released from jail, on their way home were fed and looked after by Kamala at Anand Bhawan first. She even gave them money to help them get back to their villages. She found one very persistent eighteen-year-old admirer who followed her everywhere with devoted attention, even to carrying her tea, coffee, and sandwiches when she journeyed to the villages for her work since she was on a strict diet.[43] This was Feroze Gandhi, a Parsi, who thought Jawaharlal was a hero, Kamala the sweetest of women, and who later wooed their daughter Indira with a single-mindedness that was to make him their son-in-law. A boy called Deshbandhu whom Kamala had helped with money, a political worker who later used to sell books, mentioned at the time that Kamala used to say laughingly then that Feroze and Indira would make a good match.[44] There was no doubt that Kamala had a soft corner in her heart for her young Parsi devotee, but it is doubtful if she seriously entertained any idea of him as her future son-in-law. She was against all thoughts of marriage, for when three years later Feroze proposed she told him that Indira was too young to marry, and when Indira's grandmother tried to get her engaged otherwise, "this hazard was avoided," says Mrs Gandhi now, "thanks to mummy's staunch support."

Kamala's activities and the role of the women pleased Jawaharlal thoroughly. "By the time I come out," he wrote from jail, "I expect to find the womenfolk running everything."

But Kamala was impatient that the utmost had not been demanded of her. "How I wish I could be arrested before you come out," she cried in a letter to him.[45]

"One often wondered whether she was ever meant for home life. When the call came she and her husband jumped into the field, regardless of health, comfort, convenience," said Bidhan Chandra Roy, a family friend, eminent doctor, and later free India's Chief Minister of West Bengal. "There is no doubt that her inspiration came from her great father-in-law and the encouragement came from her husband. So great was her conviction in the future of Indian politics that she induced her mother to join her in the movement and suffer imprisonment. She was a firm believer in the dictum that a woman has her place in the fight for freedom of the country and in this matter she was not only an aid [to Jawahar] but perhaps his inspirer also."[46] Roy remembered particularly the morning of August 26, 1930, when he was in the crowd waiting to receive Kamala Nehru at the Delhi station, when she was to come for a meeting of the working committee. In spite of being ill—she was again living on fruit and milk—she wore her customary smile when she met the crowd. Rumor was strong that the working committee members would be arrested when they met at 3 o'clock in the afternoon. At 11 o'clock when they gathered together informally to discuss the items on the agenda, it was suggested that the two women members, Mrs Nehru and Mrs Hansa Mehta, should not offer themselves for arrest. Both of them protested strongly.

"Mrs Kamala Nehru said that it was not possible for her to avoid taking the risk of arrest as she shared the responsibility of a member of the working committee along with her colleagues," recalled B.C. Roy. "The other members had to agree to the position and she and Mrs Mehta were present at the formal meeting of the working committee held at Dr Ansari's house. When the superintendent of police came with the warrant of arrest, Mrs Nehru was disappointed that her name did not appear in the list. She persisted in maintaining that as a member of the working committee she was entitled to share the fate of other members."[47]

On November 11, Kamala, Indira, her two aunts, and a cousin Shammi (Shyam Kumari Khan) went to watch the trial of some young nationalist colleagues and there Krishna and Shammi were suddenly arrested.

"They are now enjoying each other's company in Malacca jail," wrote Motilal in irrepressible vein to Jawahar in prison. "Clothes, food, etc., were being sent to them. So far as I have been able to ascertain the only part Betty [Krishna's pet name] and Shammi took was to lead the music while the rest of the company was squatting on the road and singing."[48]

On November 16, which Motilal as acting president had decreed should be observed as Jawaharlal Day as a protest against "the savage sentence of two and a half years passed on the Congress president," the passages from Jawaharlal's speech for which he had been convicted were read at hundreds of meetings all over the country. At Allahabad, all the Nehru women, including Indira, joined a procession in the city and, at the public meeting, it was Kamala, among others, who proudly read out the whole of her husband's speech.

On January 1, 1931, Kamala was arrested. When a correspondent asked her how she felt, she answered characteristically, "I am happy beyond measure and proud to follow in my husband's footsteps. I hope the people will keep the flag flying."[49]

"It was a pleasant new year's gift for me," wrote Jawarharlal to Indira from Naini prison. "It had so long been expected and I have no doubt that Mummie is thoroughly happy and contented."[50] But he could not help taking a gentle dig at Kamala. "Probably she wouldn't have said just that (to the newspaperman)," he wrote in his autobiography, "if she had thought over the matter, for she considers herself a champion of women's rights against the tyranny of man. But at that moment the Hindu wife in her came uppermost and even man's tyranny was forgotten."[51]

In the midst of all this the family had to cope with an extraordinary situation. Allahabad attracted a constant stream of pilgrims because of the holy confluence of the three rivers, Jamuna, Ganga, and the invisible Saraswati, and because of a place called Bharadwaj, where in ancient times a sage of the same name had started an informal university sanctified by associations with the *Ramayana*. Anand Bhawan was situated very near this spot and in the course of their tour, the pilgrims also came streaming in to see the legendary Nehrus.

Jawaharlal thought the whole thing not only embarrassing but irritating, but as always the love of these hero-worshipping crowds "looking up with shining eyes full of affection, with generations of poverty and suffering behind them," overwhelmed him and the sense of irritation yielded to humility and awe. He realized that only a saint or an inhuman monster could survive the adulation unscathed and unaffected, and he did not place himself in either of the categories. But not only his own sense of humor but his entire family's helped him in maintaining his equilibrium and theirs. The pompous, flowery language of public speeches and the pious tongue, the extravagant titles of his extreme popularity like Bharat Bhushan (jewel of India) and Tyagamurti (emodiment of sacrifice) were used for him in light-hearted and constant raillery at home by his wife and sisters. "Even my little daughter joined in the game," he said.[52]

It made Indira look upon crowds as a friendly part of the environment thereafter and explains her absolute rapport with them when it came to dealing with them on her own. Like her father, she felt quite at home with them. Once, later, when she was asked if she always spoke impromptu, her answer gave the clue to one of the main considerations that guided the party's choice of her as prime minister. "Yes, yes, of course," she said. "Once I wrote a prepared speech and when I saw the audience I just tore it all up and said what I liked instead. It is natural and from the heart that way. I always size up an audience the minute I see it. It is not difficult really, for I grew up in crowds.   I like crowds."[53]

"You are fortunate in being a witness to this great struggle for freedom
that is going on in our country," Indira had read in her father's letter
to her from prison, on her thirteenth birthday. "You are also fortunate,"
he added, "in having a very brave and wonderful little woman for your
Mummie, and if you are ever in doubt or in trouble you cannot have a
better friend."[54]

Well, she thought forlornly, it was hardly much use when they were all
in jail and she was left pretty much to her own resources.   In fact, she had
to give solace to both, visiting her father in jail just across the Jamuna once
a fortnight and her mother in Lucknow jail also once a fortnight and carrying messages from one to the other.   There was not even Aunt Krishna,
who otherwise tried to fill their place.   "Indu and I would sit in the lovely
garden full of the scent of flowers and the song of birds," Krishna recalls
of Indira's vacations from school "and I would read the classics with her
as Nan [pet name of Vijayalaxmi] had read with me."[55]   This time she was
away with Motilal who had gone to Calcutta to recuperate after he had
been released early from jail on account of illness.

Generally it was not all scent and song.   Vijayalaxmi had come from
Calcutta with her husband, Ranjit Pandit, to take part in the movement and
family tension mounted.   The old resentments rose to the surface and drew
Indira into their vortex.   According to Upadhyaya, Kamala, before going
to jail, had arranged for an old and trusted maid servant to take care of
Indira because she was worried at her being left on her own, even though
Swarup Rani and Bibima were there.   Vijayalaxmi and Krishna, he said,
took it upon themselves to turn Indira against the maid servant and succeeded
to the extent that when Indira went on her fortnightly visit to Kamala she
urged her to dismiss the maid servant.   Motilal, who rushed back to Allahabad from Calcutta when he heard of Kamala's arrest—after sending Krishna
first—and was also present at that meeting, perhaps sensed that Kamala
was being unduly harassed, and fond as he was of her, he even lashed out
at his granddaughter.

"Perhaps Induji was a bit rude," remembers Upadhyaya, who was also
there, "but that was a rare occasion when Motilal really got angry with
her."[56]

It seems likely that this incident took place while Kamala was still in
Malacca jail in Allahabad.   After that she was shifted to Lucknow jail
and Motilal by then had become quite ill.   A scheduled interview with
Jawahar on January 10, 1931 was postponed as a result and for his son the
precious *mulaquat ka din* turned into a blank day.   Two days later when
Motilal did turn up for the interview Jawahar was shocked to see how
swollen his face was and how weak and ill he looked.   On the twentieth,
Motilal wrote to Jawahar that they had heard that Kamala was being well
looked after in jail in Lucknow, and that their first interview with her had

been fixed there for the twenty-fifth. "I am afraid I shall have to deny myself the pleasure of seeing her," he added, "as I do not expect to be fit enough to undertake the journey on the 24th. Your mother, Betty and Indu will go." In the same letter he told his son that Indu was quite happy. "She has fitted up the old wooden house in which the deer was kept as a sort of summer house, and Betty and she both spend some time in the middle of the day in it."[57]

In fact, apart from spending leisurely afternoons in conversation, Indira was reading voraciously from the Nehrus' well-stocked library and periodically asking her father what new book he would recommend. She was apparently reading so fast that it provoked a mild and indirect rebuke from him. "You do not tell me what you have read. It is a good habit to read books, but I rather suspect those who read too many books quickly." But he added benevolently, "Well, read on, and I shall give you such help as I can."[58]

A few days later, Motilal's illness took a serious turn which coincided with the decision of the government to release all members of the working committee in an effort to make the conditions propitious for negotiations. On January 26, Kamala was released from Lucknow after only twenty-six days. Jawahar was released from Naini, and Gandhi from Yeravda. Two days later, Gandhi arrived at Allahabad to see Motilal and gradually congressmen began to gather at Anand Bhawan until almost the entire working committee was there, to pay their last respects to the man who had towered among them in largeness of intellect and generosity of heart. The nation knew he was dying, but Motilal mustered up the last reserves of his energy to crack his usual jokes and jibe at ritual belief. He challenged the Mahatma to a race to Heaven if they were to die at the same time: the Mahatma, he said, would probably walk alone across the River of Death or hang on to the tail of a cow while he, Motilal, would come in from behind and speed across in a motorboat and shoot past to the gates of Heaven. Whether he would be allowed into Heaven he said was another matter! Chronic asthma was taking its toll and the swelling on his face obliterated the classic Roman contours. It made him remark that he was now properly qualified to enter a beauty competition. His superb confidence never failed him to the end. He was happy that all his family was near him, and the Mahatma's presence was soothing. As it had been decided to hold a working committee meeting at Swaraj Bhawan, to coincide with the wish of the members to come to Allahabad to see Motilal, he had the satisfaction of knowing until the last that history was being made in his old house as a last requiem. "I am going soon," he told Gandhi, "and I shall not be here to see swaraj, but I know that you have won it and will soon have it."[59] On February 6, even as Jawaharlal looked and thought that sleep had relieved the tension on his father's face, it was death which had cleared the shadows over his countenance and his form was still.

For Indira it was the end of a phase. As her father wrote to Krishna, "His [Motilal's] amazing love for his children enveloped us and protected us, and we lived freed in a large measure from the care and anxiety which most people have to face. We have to do without him now and a terrible loneliness takes hold of me."[60] Indira could not formulate it exactly but she knew that her grandfather had been the most decisive influence on her until then, even more than her father. He was so strong, she thought, and he had a vigorous zest for life which her father developed only later.

"I was tremendously impressed with my grandfather's bigness," said Mrs Gandhi years later. "I don't mean physically—but you know, he seemed to embrace the whole world. I loved the way he laughed."[61]

Three months later, in April, she was in Ceylon with Jawahar and Kamala on a holiday to remember, for it was the first time the three of them had been alone together and it was to be the last time. During the previous ten years there had been very few occasions when all the Anand Bhawan clan had been together, but being only with her father and mother was special. She remembered only once before that all of them had managed to be in Mussoorie in a spirit of complete relaxation. That was when Motilal was undergoing treatment there and she had gone up with him and Dolamma (her grandmother), her two aunts, and Vijayalaxmi's three daughters and Jawahar and Kamala had joined them for three days, during a brief week's respite that Jawahar got from prison. Jawahar had joined in playing games with her and her little cousins, though even then the overtones had been political for they would make Rita (Vijayalaxmi's youngest daughter) lead them in a march around the house with flags in their hands, singing *jhanda uncha rahe hamara*.

Ceylon was different. She felt more grown up. She had been given her first sari on her thirteenth birthday and when she wore it she looked exactly like her mother. Kamala had so retained her "girlish and virginal appearance," according to Jawahar, that in later years when they visited strange places she was often mistaken, embarrassingly for him, as his daughter. "She and Indira looked like two sisters,"[62] he said. In Allahabad once when both Kamala and Indira sat in the audience listening to a speech by Jawahar, a person, who was a student then, recalls that it was difficult to make out the difference. "Next day it appeared in the papers that Kamala had been hurt and her finger damaged," he described, "and it was then that the students talking amongst themselves exclaimed 'See, so that was Kamala and not Indira'."

"History, if we are to learn anything from it," Nehru had told Indira, "must be a succession of vivid images in our mind,"[63] and he himself had seen to it that those images should come alive in her mind. In continuation of the letters he had written to her at Mussoorie, he had started a fascinating record of world history in the form of further letters to her during periods of enforced rest in prison between October 1930 and August 1933. It was

an attempt both to fill in any gaps in her education that he thought might
be there because of lack of parental supervision and to occupy time when
the days and the nights stretched bleakly and endlessly in front of him within
the confines of prison. For him history was not a dry study of dates and
eras but of the progress of man and the men and women who provided its
"flesh and bone." He let no opportunity slip to initiate his daughter into
this magic world. He had taken her to museums wherever and whenever he
could, he showed her illustrations of works of art and famous monuments,
and he wrote her unfailingly almost every day while he was in prison,
giving her "glimpses into world history" with which no textbook could
compare, for it was imbued with a father's love and an intellectual's
concern for the proper unfolding of his daughter's mind. Impressionable,
sensitive, and serious as she was, it was indoctrination of the most
civilized kind, for her father's life made an invaluable precept and her
country's predicament the reference point against which controversial
economic policies and the principles of war came alive.

A visit to a country with her father was like reading a page out of historical
romance, so wide-ranging was the play of his instruction. But if credit for
effective instruction must be given to an imaginative father, credit must
also be given to a daughter who proved receptive. His ideas took root in
fertile soil, but he tempered his tutoring with the repeated warning: "One
can learn much from others, but everything worthwhile one has to find out
or experience oneself ... do not be in a hurry to decide. Before you can decide
anything big or vital you will have to train yourself and educate yourself..."[64]
The assumption was implicit in his argument that she must make herself
a worthwhile person. "To read history is good," he said to her, "but
even more interesting and fascinating is to help in making history."[65]
Where could there be a clearer injunction to tread the paths of individual
courage?

So even in a comparatively familiar country like Ceylon, their private
holiday turned into an occasion for public adulation. It was her first visit
to the tropics, so both the lushness of the landscape and the hospitality of
the people were overwhelming. At Nuwara Eliya during a comparatively
peaceful two weeks, the people still came, all classes of them, visiting them,
plying them with presents, which her parents would pass on to hospitals and
orphanages, and just smiling through the barriers of language. There were
of course the trips to the monuments and her father's infectious enthusiasm.
On their way back to Allahabad, they toured some of the princely states of
southern India and visited the "White Jews" quarter in Cochin, the Syrian
Christian town, and found, to Jawahar's surprise, a colony of Nestorians,
a sect, he thought, had long since disappeared. Indira had already had a
chance to see the various peoples of Europe, but the diversity that she now
saw in India she was to find fascinating ever after. At Hyderabad, the most
"feudal relic" of all, they stopped to visit Sarojini Naidu and her two

daughters, Padmaja and Leilamani. Kamala's presence tempted even the veiled women to come out to meet her, and at an all-women's gathering at Sarojini's house, Kamala apparently gave them a good talking to.

"Probably she spoke of women's struggle for freedom against man-made laws and customs [a favorite topic of hers]," mused Jawaharlal with ironic good humor, "and urged the women not to be too submissive to their menfolk."[66] But what happened as a sequel was symptomatic of the "wave of unrest" that was tearing India's women from their hothouse seclusion. Kamala already had to her credit the responsibility for having persuaded, among others, as staunch an orthodox matron as Pandit Madan Mohan Malaviya's wife to shed her purdah. But it must have buoyed her spirits to find a letter a few weeks later from the husband of one of those women who had listened to her at Hyderabad. He complained distractedly that since her visit his wife had behaved most strangely. She would not do what he said any more, and she would not only argue with him but had even become quite aggressive. It was amusing yet satisfying. It was good to be young as Kamala was, only thirty-one, a Nehru at that, and it seemed natural to be giving a lead. Shy, reserved, and insular, she, too, had been drawn into the activism of the Nehrus, and for Indira her mother was yet another example to be added to that of her grandfather and father before her.

5. INDIRA DIDI

The day Motilal died (February 6), with Jawaharlal stunned and Gandhi suffering deeply from a sense of bereavement—"My position is worse than a widow's," he said, "what I have lost through Motilalji's death is a loss for ever"—the twenty-six independent delegates to the Round Table Conference landed at Bombay and made an immediate appeal to the Congress that the scheme they had arrived at represented only a bare outline and that they hoped the Congress would contribute toward its completion. Events were thus set

in motion for a meeting between Gandhi and Irwin, and the result, after fluctuations that dashed the hopes for an agreement to the ground at one moment
and raised them skyhigh at another, was the Gandhi-Irwin Pact signed on
March 5, 1931.

On each of the points some member or the other of the working committee was disappointed, but what upset Jawaharlal above all was Clause 2
which stated that federation was essential to the scheme outlined, as was
Indian responsibility and reservations or safeguards in the interests of India,
for such matters as defense, external affairs, the position of minorities, the
financial credit of India, and the discharge of obligations. The provision
of "reservations or safeguards" seemed to Jawaharlal to jeopardize their
objective of complete independence while Gandhi argued that the phrase
"in the interests of India" allowed for an interpretation more in line with
Congress thinking. This was another occasion when Jawahar felt that he
could not reconcile himself to Gandhi's penchant for compromise and, yet
again, he was moved to consent by two considerations that invariably prevented a break with the older leader: Jawaharlal's sense of disciplined loyalty
to the Congress and his admiration for the personality of Gandhi.

"We had the feeling," wrote Jawaharlal, "that while we might be more logical, Gandhiji knew India far better than we did, and a man who could command such tremendous devotion and loyalty must have something in him
that corresponded to the needs and aspirations of the masses," though he
added, "his way of springing surprises upon us frightened me; there was
something unknown about him which . . . I could not understand and which
filled me with apprehension."[1]

At the Congress session at Karachi that followed, Gandhi asked Jawaharlal
particularly to move the resolution in the open Congress accepting the
Delhi pact; Jawaharlal, who had not reconciled himself to it, did so at the
last minute. He was motivated by the feeling that it was "not proper to
prevaricate" and leave people guessing at his attitude and that he might as
well declare himself in favor of it. He was pleased, however, at being
able to get his own resolution on civil rights and economic policy approved
at this session. He had long felt that a political program must also include
an economic plan, and the Congress so far had not thought along these
lines. His socialistic beliefs were at variance with Gandhi's theories about
trusteeship, in which the rich were expected to hold their property in trust
for the less affluent and behave with a sense of responsible honor. Nonetheless, Gandhi's ability to convince his colleagues of the rightness of a
course of action made them overlook their disagreements with his philosophy.
It was also at this time that he spelled out his conception of the future role
of the Congress. Contrary to Jawaharlal's view that after independence
the Congress should be transformed into a political party capable of weilding
executive authority and changing the economic or political fabric, Gandhi
thought it should remain outside the realm of power as a self-denying moral

force. Jawaharlal thought that to do so would be to positively invite the machinations of vested interests. But the later monolithic structure of the Congress and its lack of polarization, which enabled it to exercise a constant influence on fundamental policy, sprang from this unresolved Gandhi-Nehru conflict.

Though civil disobedience had been called off with the Gandhi-Irwin agreement, the Karachi congress was held under the shadow of the executions of the three terrorists whose names had become a legend in the north, Bhagat Singh, Sukhdev, and Raj Guru. Though the Congress made it clear that it dissociated itself and disapproved of political violence "in any shape or form" it placed on record "its admiration of the bravery and sacrifice of the three revolutionaries and expressed the opinion that the triple execution was an act of wanton vengeance and . . . a deliberate flouting [by the British Government in India] of the unanimous demand of the nation [for] commutation." And while the Congress was in session a renewal of communal riots in Cawnpore (Kanpur), in which a well-known, devoted young worker of U.P. was murdered by a frenzied mob, spread further gloom. The government itself seemed discomfited with the exuberant welcome being given to released prisoners throughout the country, and there was no certainty that the political situation would remain stable.

Perhaps foreseeing that they might again be sent to prison, Kamala and Jawaharlal decided to make more secure arrangements for Indira. In fact, immediately after Motilal's death they had realized that life at Anand Bhawan could no longer be as carefree for Indira as before. She had been thoroughly miserable at the convent and they had been toying with the idea of sending her to Shantiniketan. This institution, founded by the Nobel prize-winning poet Rabindranath Tagore, was based on his concept of combining India's ancient systems of learning with a modern, scientific but humanitarian outlook.

Jawaharlal had written to Bidhan Chandra Roy in Calcutta to inquire about the school. Roy replied: "I asked Basanti Devi about the school at Shantiniketan. She told me that she had no specific objections to Indu's going there, only she feared that the influence of the masterful personality of Tagore tended to create in the minds of the pupils a habit of dependence which gives little chance for the individuality of the pupil to have full play. That is of course inevitable in case of such personages."[2]

Mrs Gandhi says that her father then wrote to a man called Jehangir Jivaji Vakil. He had been at Oxford, was a brilliant student, and a poet himself who instead of following his father's suggestion to join the Indian Civil Service preferred to go with Tagore and become a teacher. After a few years at Shantiniketan, and then with his wife, Coonverbai, he had opened a similar institute at Poona, near Bombay. Inaugurated by Tagore himself it was called the Children's Own School. Vakil wrote to Jawaharlal that Shantiniketan was not aimed at the elementary level. He suggested that if Jawaharlal liked, Indira could stay with them and they would personally look after her education until her matriculation.

"Once Jawaharlal visited Shantiniketan with Mahatmaji," recounted Mrs Vakil, an 80-year-old bustling tornado of energy and interests. "He came for a few hours and met my husband. From that day they began corresponding because my husband too had the same idea. So, then Motilal expired and . . . Jawaharlal began to wonder what he should do about Indu. . . . Jawaharlal wrote to my husband to ask what he thought of his sending Indira to Shantiniketan. He said he should send her, have a little hut built for her and if some relative were there, it would be fine for her. At that time, you see, Shantiniketan was also a small unit. There was a small school at Vishwabharati, meaning the college. It had just started. Then the boarding, you see, we used to think about it. . . . Whether it would suit her or not. So just incidentally my husband told Jawahar that he had a small school here [Poona] but it was not a boarding school. 'My two girls are with me and if you want her to be with us she can come and stay here and she can study in the school.' So Bapu, who knew us very well, said: 'This is the opportunity you must not lose, Jawahar, send her there'."[3]

Thus when Kamala and Jawaharlal found that the Vakils were in Karachi for the congress they thought it would be ideal to send Indira with them at the end of it.

"She [Indira] said 'no no, I am not going now'," described Mrs Vakil in her homespun but vivid way. "So Jawahar said, 'not just now. You do not have to be in school, you go with them, stay with them, try to find out whether you like the place . . . the town, the school. First you go there and try to find out.' And then she came with us."[4]

Indira stayed in Poona with the Vakils for about fifteen days while in school recess, familiarizing herself with the surroundings. The Vakils were unusual enough for her to feel at home. They were staunch nationalists, were not overly religious, and combined a sense of humor with a variety of interests. Furthermore, Vakil's socialist views reminded her strongly of her father. She liked what she saw and decided to return. In May 1931 Indira was formally admitted to the Children's Own School. It was like no other school she had attended. Physically, it did not resemble a school as it was just a big bungalow and classes were held in the garden. It was almost like being at home although she did not have a room to herself, like her lovely yellow room at Anand Bhawan. She shared a large bedroom with Mrs Vakil and one of her daughters. One bedroom was always kept vacant in case some of the children fell ill. She was the only boarder of the school's forty or so pupils.

"At that time," reminisced Mrs Gandhi, "they ran only a kindergarten and the school as a school started afterwards, for soon the city of Poona fell upon it because of my being there!"[5] She did not mean it as an indication of her appeal, but as an example which a number of nationalists, who were in the same predicament as her parents, drew upon to rush their own children there. She found that the unusual still dogged her footsteps. "Most of the children were younger than I was," she says, "so I did the housekeeping and looked after them."

The atmosphere at the school was not only extremely informal but conducive to developing in the students a habit of intellectual freedom. The bungalow at 3, Stapeley Road, Poona, in which the school was run, was a large, rambling structure set in wide grounds into which the noises of the city never penetrated. After the crowds at Anand Bhawan, this was a soothing silence. There was a happy routine in the program of the day but no routine about the method of teaching. Classes were conducted outside under the trees; there was no timetable and no bell.

"We taught . . . by the Dalton Plan," explained Raghubhai Naik,[6] who taught history and Sanskrit. "There were no examinations, only periodic tests. We gave the students assignments and guidance about books, so that they could study themselves. When we finished teaching a subject [for the day] we would ask them to write about it . . . and check the papers there itself. After that, we would ask them to go to another teacher, whoever was free to take them . . . we religiously avoided religion there." The Vakils themselves were Parsis and while the majority of the students were Hindu, some were Muslim. This heterogeneous base was further strengthened by the fact that the school was coeducational so that Indira, who came from an environment in which boys were treated as political comrades rather than as marriage-and-sex symbols for the average Indian girl, was further encouraged to regard herself as "a person with a task" rather than as a girl with a traditional future. The school was also art-oriented, which not only compensated for the intensely political atmosphere that she had lived with until then, but also suited her own unacademic inclinations.

Naik recalls: "Temperamentally, she was a keen learner but in formal academic learning she wasn't good. She was a good reader, read for hours on a subject she liked . . . she didn't talk much, but when she disagreed she'd argue quite vehemently. Wouldn't take anything for granted . . . and appeared to be quite obstinate, wouldn't accept an idea but once she accepted it she would stick to it and apply it most devotedly. She had a very high sense of duty. At times she didn't like to do what she was told—you can see that on the faces of children—but she never refused. If she believed in a thing, she'd go out of her way to do it, so we believed that wherever she'd be, she'd work her way up. She never gave up."[7]

She would not give up on the issue of Sanskrit for one thing. Her father was determined that she should develop a wide outlook, and continually sent her books he thought she should read. His instruction was biased in favor of the modern approach, but his own lack of knowledge of Sanskrit and his inability to go directly to the sources of the Indian tradition made

him urge her to learn it. She argued that it was a dead language and would
not help her in the future. Besides she just did not like doing the grammar.
There was nothing her father could say to that: it was like hearing himself
speak, for he admitted later that grammar had never held any attraction for
him. A compromise was arrived at by Indira's agreeing to learn only
Sanskrit literature. In this she soon proved herself proficient and began
to recite Sanskrit verses fluently. Her flair for languages was evident. She
already knew Hindi, she began to learn Sanskrit, and soon could read and
speak Gujarati, the language of most of her fellow students and the Vakils.
She took up French again and, because there was no provision for French
classes at the school, the Vakils arranged for her to be tutored by a French-
woman who lived nearby.

It is amazing how Indira's aptitudes in school foreshadowed her aptitudes
in politics later. Although she was reserved, withdrawn, and shy of
debates—a poor precedent for her performance in Parliament later—she
showed two qualities that can be said to have earned her the prime ministership of free India thirty-five years later: a capacity to organize, and sensitivity to human relations. She became the secretary of the literary society of
the school, but because she would hesitate to participate in the debates, she
was not as much in the limelight as her more eloquent counterparts, and
then, as later, this habit of doing sound, hard work in the background gave
the impression to the unwary that she could be disregarded, though not to
those who knew. "I never saw her take a major part in anything," commented one who knew her then.[8] But it seems such a dramatic coincidence
in the light of later events that even in school, when it came to the test it was
she who was chosen *Mahamantri* of the *Samanya Sabha* and not any of
the others.

Indira's position as Indira *didi* among the schoolchildren gave her a
privileged status, but her sense of duty led her to vindicate it. She had "an
organizing temperament," as Mrs Vakil describes it, and everything from
picnics, debates, meetings, excursions, games, and sports fell under the
purview of Indira's tireless management. Her role of "housekeeping" as
she herself has called it, included helping the smaller children to dress, comb
their hair, and help them in their lessons and after school hours take time off
from her voracious reading to make her own bed, clean the room, help
the others with their chores, and even go out in the garden to look after the
flower beds. For a girl who came from the comparatively subdued but
still affluent atmosphere of Anand Bhawan, she was remarkably free from
any prejudice about working with her hands. "She never grudged any
menial work," Mrs Vakil confided. "When her father was [to come] to the
school to visit her, I always asked the children to prepare a room for him.
They used to wipe the floor, make the bed, change the curtains and the linen.
They used to do all this. In my school, you see, we did not use any servants.
The children were running the school. Indu used to participate in all this."[9]

The credit must also go to her family's astonishing power of adjustment, her father's strong precepts, the atmosphere of self-help generated by the Gandhian influence, and her own development as a dedicated, but practical person.

"She was immaculate, meticulous, and methodical," recalls a school friend of hers, "and very particular about how she behaved. Some of us would be outspoken or definitely disobedient but I never saw her impolite, never disobedient."[10]

"It was difficult for me to teach her Sanskrit because I knew she didn't want to learn," says Naik, "but she was a cooperative student. She was outstanding in discussions on history and politics and at table, during meals, got very intense."[11]

Her love of detail found expression in making the place beautiful. It was she who was called upon when the need arose for any interior decoration. "She excelled in that," claimed her school companion. But what she loved most was arranging excursions which involved mountain climbing and visiting the art caves and monuments that abounded in the region nearby. She had learned mountain climbing from her father and now his interest was her own. It made her give special encouragement years afterward as prime minister to teams that seemed to carry her hobby to the point of high adventure. "How good of you to keep me in touch with your climbing plans," she once wrote to one of them. "I share my father's great love of the high mountains and am naturally interested in the attempts and achievements of Indian mountaineers." She added that to her the challenge of the Himalayas seemed an unending one, and any attempt to scale its peaks only another path towards "the pursuit of adventure and knowledge."[12] In Switzerland, she had done a lot of skating, skiing, and mountain climbing with her father. She had inherited his fondness for swimming and his facility in riding. He had even taught her how to sprint.

"I had a very good style," recalls Mrs Gandhi without a trace of self-consciousness while describing her father's training of her. "He used to make me run a mile every morning in Allahabad and see to it that my feet fell right and that I did it gracefully."[13]

The result was that she easily won in sprinting races over the girls and most of the boys. She was naturally interested in games, but of the Western type the school provided facilities only for badminton. For the most part they concentrated on vigorous Indian games.

"Then again we used to go out for small trips," recalls Mrs Vakil. "The children used to play games but she [Indira] was very keen on winning the game and"—here Mrs Vakil let out a huge chuckle—"sometimes they used to have a good fight between them. Oh, yes, it is in her to want to achieve so many things . . . even now."[14]

Largely because of Mrs Vakil, whose amazing amalgam of talents included being a good singer and sitar player, the young Indira began to like

music.   "Mrs Vakil had learned under Vishnu Digambar," says Mrs
Gandhi, "so I was initiated into Indian music then."[15]

"Do you like Western or Indian music now?" I asked her.

"Both," she said, adding characteristically. "It depends on the mood."

"Fine buildings, fine pictures, and books and everything that is beautiful
are certainly signs of civilization," Jawaharlal had told Indira, "but an even
better sign is a fine man who is unselfish and works with others for the good
of all."[16] Young as she was, she had been able to act accordingly.   But when
in trying to define culture and civilization he had said that among other
things culture includes "restraint on oneself and consideration for others,"
she did not have to try, as she had these qualities already. She was a good
learner, but everything in her was not necessarily a concretization of her
father's ideas. She was restrained, not because she thought it was good,
but because it came naturally from the circumstances of her growth. She
was hesitant of confiding in anyone, she felt terribly lonely, she missed her
parents intensely and, as she admitted later, she was all bottled up, too
proud to show it, and when she wanted to cry in that school, nine hundred
miles from home, she would draw up the bedclothes to smother her sobs
at night or stand behind a tree quietly and stoically and let the tears trickle
down her face. What saved her personality from being imbalanced was
the realization that her emotions were the result of a great and stirring cause.
If she suffered because of her parents' involvement in politics, it was because
of them that she also felt worthwhile.

It was a period of fantastic idealism anyway, and Gandhi's methods of
winning political rights were calculated to bring out the best, not the worst
in human nature. The revolution had to be nonviolent, the spirit was of
service, and the enemy had to be won by love, not pressure. It created a brand
of people in the pre-independence era in India that could not be simulated
again, for life and politics became just one and the highest values of the
former had to govern the latter. Not that they always did, but you were
always conscious of it. Even the dastardly firings on innocent people—
like that boy with the stomach wound she had nursed in the Anand Bhawan
hospital—moved one to awe at their forbearance rather than anger at their
victimizers, for there was no outlet for fury. You could not get hold of a
rifle and shoot back, there were no rifles anyway, but you were told that to
teach them a lesson, you must learn to take it.

She had learned early to spring to the defense of the weak. There was
always before her the example of her mother, who was so loving, so humane,
and so considerate of others that she earned the lifelong devotion of utter
strangers. Indira herself felt an instinctive sympathy for the underdog, and
in school it took the form of preventing the natural cruelty of children from
fastening upon some unfortunate. Like the girl who was so fat from some
glandular trouble that they all made fun of her and she would try her best
to stop them. Or those girls who came from rich but culturally backward

families, at whom Indira's arty friends would turn up their noses with a stricture. At table where she sat with the Vakils, their two daughters, and the other teachers, the subject would come up after the meal. Naik recalls an occasion when Jai, the Vakil's elder daughter who was in Indira's group, referred disparagingly to a girl's "terrible accent" and Indira immediately retorted, "Well, so what? She hasn't had a change to know a different accent." She showed a lot of concern for the servants, too, and whenever the cook fell ill, she would go regularly to the servants' quarters to inquire about his progress.[17]

But Indira's feeling did not spring from pure philanthropy and trusting concern, it was mixed with a sharp perception which resulted from her precocious knowledge of people and events and which sometimes led to a biting analysis. One of the girls, a day scholar who was enjoined by her orthodox family to stick sedulously to vegetarianism, who wore her hair long and used on her forehead the vermilion powder mark called the *bindi*, would be overly critical of short hair and meat eating. Indira, who had perhaps seen the girl looking longingly at her own short hair in an unwary moment or casting a curious look at the egg and meat dishes which were served to others at the school lunch or perhaps suspicious as she was wont to be of anyone who protested too much, made the pithy observation, "This girl wants all the other things . . . but argues against them because she can't have them." She had no illusions either about a wealthy young man of Poona who used to invite their whole school group to his house for meals or picnics and sent his huge car to pick them up. Indira apparently realized that this was all a cover for his interest in her, but apart from that divined him to be "shallow" and "superficial" and urged them all not to accept his invitations.[18]

She was quick to sense another's predicament and could be helpful without necessarily becoming familiar, so that a basic warmth was always at war with the desire to remain aloof, and the sensitivity in both cases was due to having been thrown into situations where she was persistently lonely. A newcomer to the school found that, on her very first day, as she stood forlornly not knowing what a teacher meant by instructing her to do *alpana* in a room in which a debate was scheduled to be held the next morning, it was Indira who came to her rescue with a gentle tap on the shoulder and a warm offer of help. She and the girl Shanta Gandhi became friends. Years later, one sunny morning as she was walking along Connaught Place in New Delhi, she found that a ministerial car came to a halt near her, Indira Gandhi peered out, asked her if she was doing anything for lunch that day and on her saying no, carried her off to reminisce over old times. Power was not to dull spontaneity, provided the person who provoked it was someone Indira could trust—and that, especially later, she was never sure of.

While Indira was finding her way in her new environment, the country was trying to find a way out of an impasse. The dominant question was whether Gandhi should attend the second Round Table Conference. When Lord Willingdon succeeded Lord Irwin as viceroy immediately after the Delhi pact, the Indians were apprehensive that his sterner personality would lead to a hardening of the British attitude. The realization that British policy was not affected by the people who executed it came gradually. In another way it took the form of Congress insistence that Indians must differentiate between the "people" and the "system." The fight had to be against "British imperialism," not against the British "people." It gave to hatred a curiouly vapid air. As it is much easier to hate people than to hate concepts, this intellectual emphasis robbed the fight for freedom of its fanatic emotionalism. It explains the lack of bitterness that helped a free republic of India years later to choose to remain within the British Commonwealth. Only a highly sophisticated national mentality could match up to such restraint. But India was poor, downtrodden, and illiterate and Gandhi had to tap the hidden reserves of a 5,000-year-old history implicit in the people to call forth their requisite response. Perhaps therefore Gandhi's invocation to ancient scriptures, ancient ideals, and a philosophy were not so "reactionary" as Jawaharlal thought but only another way to revive an ancient pride dulled by 200 years of subjectivity. The essence of satyagraha, according to him, lay in strength, not in weakness, but a strength expressed in nonviolent terms. It was like urging a horse to gallop and drawing in the reins at the same time. Energy remained taut, controlled, and unreleased. It was very civilized but it never let India go on a warring spree, and there was no other outlet provided. Some of India's persistent ills became the ills of psychological repression, and when it could not resist its own energy anymore, instead of turning on the British, it turned upon itself and cut off its own limb.

But had it not been for the notorious stake of British policy to "divide and rule," the victory of the Congress might yet have been total instead of being conditioned by the ultimate partition of the land. The bogey of Muslim opposition to the Congress was set up early and as far back as October 1885, when Sir Aucland Calvin, the lieutenant governor of the North-West Province, had sown the seeds of communal bitterness by challenging "the representative character of the Congress, stressing the divergent needs and aspirations of the Muslims, and pointing to the hazards of premature and aggressive propaganda among the literate population."[19] It is curious to note that three years later Sheikh Raza Hussain Khan produced at the fourth session in Allahabad a *fatwa* from the leader of the Sunni community in Lucknow supporting the Congress, and declared perceptively, "It is not the Muslims, but their official masters who are opposed to the Congress."[20]

Forty-two years later, the same forces were at work. The working committee, meeting immediately after the Karachi congress, had resolved that Gandhi should attend the Round Table Conference on the understand-

ing that his purpose would not be "to hammer out the details of a constitution but to negotiate the fundamentals of a treaty."[21] The real question
was how much power the British would be prepared to transfer to a democratic India, but Gandhi felt, with his usual acumen, that to go to London
without a Hindu-Muslim agreement in his hands would be to fall into a
trap. So he was reluctant, but the working committee met again on
June 9, 10 and 11 at Bombay and reiterated that "in order to avoid any
possibility of the Congress attitude being misunderstood in any shape
or form . . . Gandhi should represent the Congress at the RTC for the
presentation of the Congress position."[22] It met again on July 20,
and midst initiating activity based on the assumption that there would be
an agreement with the British, it took a far-reaching stand on the issue of
minorities. Though it envisioned a strictly nationalistic solution of the
communal problem in a free India, it suggested for adoption, in the circumstances obtaining then, a solution which in its opinion "though communal in
appearance," was "yet as nearly national as possible and generally acceptable to the communities."[23] This was a guarantee to be added to the article
on fundamental rights safeguarding the rights of the minorities concerning their culture, language, practice of religion, etc., making the protection
of their political and other rights a federal concern, joint electorates, but
reservation of seats for the minorities in the provincial and federal legislatures
wherever their population would be less than 25 per cent, with the right
to contest extra seats, the rights of the minorities to be recognized by convention in the formation of federal and provincial cabinets, an impartial
public service commission ensuring the principle of equal opportunity to all
communities, etc. It repeated: "The future constitution of the country
shall be federal. The residuary powers shall vest in the federating units
unless"—and this was the phrase added perceptively by Gandhi—"on
further examination, it is found to be against the best interests of India."[24]

A month later the situation had changed radically. The agrarian crisis
in the United Provinces took an appalling turn in which the government
would not help to alleviate the distress of the tenants. Jawaharlal, who
spent most of his time, after his return from Ceylon, in the area, carried on
an unremitting fight for economic justice for the tenants, trying to make the
Congress organization there function as a kind of temporary peasants' union.
Their argument for remission of rent for the tenants in view of the fall of
prices was meant to be an economic one quite separate from a campaign of
political civil disobedience. But official intransigence remained blind to
this suffering and the Congress began to feel that such an attitude was hardly
conducive to a propitious climate for negotiations. Reports of breaches
of the Delhi pact poured in a steady stream from most of the provinces,
including Bengal, Bombay, and Madras and it became clear that items like
"peaceful picketing" allowed under the agreement were, in actual circumstances, inviting the full wrath of repression from the civilian authorities

who had from the beginning taken the signing of the Gandhi-Irwin agreement as a blow to imperial prestige. In fact, expression of national sentiment was squashed with brutal disregard. Political prisoners were kept under detention, even those for whose release there was a specific understanding in the Delhi agreement, inoffensive processions were lathi-charged, political meetings banned, students and lawyers made to swear allegiance or pay security, and a general policy of intimidation, repression, and individual or group punishment continued. The culminating irritant to Congress sensitivity came with Bardoli, where Vallabhbhai Patel had conducted such a successful no-tax campaign in 1929. Contrary to the terms of the Delhi agreement, the government began to try to collect through coercive processes, and police pressure, fines, current dues and arrears in cases where the peasantry had already suffered heavy losses.

"Inability [to pay] must be proved and not merely pleaded,"[25] was the government rejoinder to a plea for humane consideration made by Gandhi. Matters came to a head when the government rejected Gandhi's suggestion for setting up a permanent board of arbitration in conjunction with the Congress to decide the questions of interpretation of the Delhi pact in each case and the terms on which it was carried out by one party or the other. The government took the strictly legal view that Congress representatives could not be allowed to come in as official arbiters of the merits of one case or another at the expense of the authority of the courts and the police.

If these breaches of the Delhi pact induced Gandhi to have second thoughts about attending the Round Table Conference another more blatant breach of faith on the part of the British government made him resolve not to go at all. Lord Irwin, the previous viceroy, had indicated that apart from others, three persons would definitely be nominated for the conference, Pandit Madan Mohan Malaviya, Sarojini Naidu (as the representative of Indian womanhood), and Dr M.A. Ansari. Dr Ansari was a congressman and a nationalist Muslim representing the Nationalist Mussalman party and a staunch adherent of purna swaraj for India. Cleverly but surely, the government retained Pandit Malaviya and Sarojini Naidu, but dropped Dr Ansari in favor of an almost total weightage of communalistic Muslims. To Gandhi it became obvious that the British were again out to paralyze the Hindu-Muslim formula prepared by the Congress by ensuring that only those Muslims should attend the conference who would be hostile to it. Therefore on August 13 Gandhi telegraphed the viceroy his decision, which had been endorsed by the working committee, not to attend the Round Table Conference. Malaviya and Sarojini Naidu canceled their passages on the S.S. *Mooltan* though the liberal leaders Sapru, Jayakar, and Iyengar sailed and the country was plunged into gloom.

Matters might have ended there—or, rather, begun again in the form of satyagraha—when a renewal of correspondence between the viceroy and Gandhi led to a meeting and an agreement in which the government promised "to secure the observance of the specific provisions of the settlement in those cases, if any, in which a breach is established."[26] It also agreed to hold an inquiry into the complaints regarding Bardoli, while Gandhi on his side offered "to avoid direct action and to gain relief by discussion, persuasion, and the like" but reserved the right to "defensive direct action in other cases where it might become the paramount duty of the Congress to seek relief in the absence of an inquiry."[27] The way to the Round Table Conference was thus made clear and special arrangements were made to enable the frail but indomitable man of sixty-two to catch the *Mooltan* at Bombay.

It was obvious that Gandhi's continuing reluctance to go—until the last minute he worried about the situation in the United Provinces, Bengal, and the Frontier Province—was in proportion to the government's determination to have him in London. It soon became clear why. They wanted the conference to spend itself out on the communal issue and its failure to redound, in the person of Gandhi as the only and most eminent representative of the Congress. The Congress had escaped the stigma of the first abortive Round Table by not attending it; this time its participation involved the risk that the communal tactics of the rulers would leave some of the mud clinging to it in case of failure. Friends of India were worried on another score. "Gandhi's personal representation of a whole people, coupled with the wide discretion given to him," wrote Roger Baldwin to Jawaharlal, "and his record of compromise looks at this distance like another Wilson at Paris . . . . Beyond that," he added warningly, "is the capacity of the English to dress up nefarious purposes in moral language, to cajole, coerce, hoodwink even the best intentioned and most courageous of men. If Gandhi will stick, and you back home push him hard, we may get some effective backfire here."[28]

The question hardly arose. The British government would not accept the Congress as the representative organization of Indian opinion, and the field was taken over by sectional interests all of which demanded a solution which would best suit them. Gandhi was the lone figure arguing for a constitution-building emphasis: the rest was, as Jawaharlal remarked, "all jobbery—big jobs, little jobs, jobs and seats for the Hindus, for the Muslims, for the Sikhs, for the Anglo-Indians, for the Europeans, but all jobs for the upper classes, the masses had no look-in."

The leader of the British Indian delegation was the Aga Khan, who might as well have represented imperialist England instead of an India with which he was not even familiar or sympathetic. It was learned later that he had demanded of the British government that they make him a ruling prince of some part of India as reward for his cooperation with them at the Round Table Conference.[29]

The general elections were due to take place in England at the time the Conservatives were expected to win, and Lord Irwin, who it was thought would probably be in the future cabinet, tried to persuade Gandhi that the future held promise and that he would try his best to see that most of the Congress demands were made acceptable. But Gandhi, contrary to Baldwin's fears, was "speaking out his mind anywhere and everywhere." He had tried to go along with some demands of the communal Muslims in the hope that he could get them to agree on independence, but when even that was turned down, it proved that the issue was not even communal, but opportunistic.

"The talks with the Mussalmans are at a standstill and Bapu will not trouble to seek them unless they want him," wrote Mahadev Desai to Jawaharlal on October 23 from London. He added an irresistible account of what could be presumed to be Jinnah's private feelings. "Datta [Dr S.K.] told us a story," wrote Desai, "which is sure to amuse you. He was dining with Jinnah the other day at an English friend's—Campbell Rhodes. Jinnah had been through his third bottle of champagne when the minorities question was being discussed. Mr Rhodes said, 'why don't you give an agreed solution and compel government to yield?' Jinnah under the sobering effects of champagne replied: 'That is exactly where you are mistaken. It is impossible to have an agreed solution until we know what we are going to get, and government are putting the cart before the horse.' Exactly the thing Bapu has been saying and the Mussalmans denying."

To Gandhi the government's own minority scheme nowhere touched upon the realities of responsible government for Indians and the proposals were such under which according to him "the hardy tree of freedom" could never grow: he would rather, he said, that the Congress remain in the wilderness "no matter how many years." He was also bitterly incensed by the treacherous attempt to drive a wedge into the Hindu social structure by defining the "untouchables" as a separate class, and made his most famous speech on the issue that was to have repercussions on Hindu society in the years to come.

"I can understand the claims advanced on behalf of other communities, but the claims advanced on behalf of the 'untouchables' are to me the unkindest of all," he said feelingly. "It means a perpetual bar sinister. . . . Sikhs may remain such in perpetuity, so may Muslims and Christians. Will the untouchables remain untouchables in perpetuity? I would far rather that Hinduism died than that untouchability lived. Those who speak of the political rights of the untouchables do not know India and do not know how Indian society is constructed. Therefore, I want to say with all the emphasis I can command that if I were the only person to resist this thing, I would resist it with my life."[30]

By November 18, 1931, the British were tired of the conference and decided to kill it. In a confidential circular Benthall, who had gone to the RTC as India's commercial representative, wrote that "after the general elections, the right wing of the government made up its mind to break up the conference and to fight the conference and to fight the Congress . . .

we had made up our minds that the fight with the Congress was inevitable, we felt and said that the sooner it came the better but we made up our minds that for a crushing success we should have all possible friends on our side. The Muslims were all right, the Minorities Pact and the government's general attitude showed that. so were the princes and the minorities." The unfortunate fact was that even some of the non-Congress Hindu leaders fell into the trap, while the Congress itself, the largest body of political opinion, was left with empty hands. Gandhi, as thoroughly disenchanted as he had expected to be, hoped that some day the Englishman would become aware of his duty and declared with a peculiar mixture of naïveté and firmness, "We must infect the British with [that] love for India. If the British people think that we shall require a century before that can be done, then for that century the Congress will wander through that terrible fiery ordeal; it must go through that storm of distress, of misrepresentation, and if it becomes necessary and if it is God's will—a shower of bullets."[31] He returned to India on the morning of December 28, 1931 to find the country in tumult and Indira waiting for him with a letter from Jawahar, excited at her role as an intermediary in high events, but depressed that her father was again in jail and her mother was again in hospital, in Bombay.

While Gandhi had been away in England, the agrarian revolt in the U.P. took an even more serious turn, Bengal was afire with two incidents—the Hijli detention camp, where prisoners were fired upon, and the Chittagong affair, where the killing of a Muslim police inspector was deliberately given a communal coloring, and the result was communal rioting and the suspicious involvement of certain groups. In the Frontier Province the Khan brothers' *Khudai Khitmatgars*, a nonviolent volunteer corps that had been incorporated into the Congress that year, immediately earned the wrath of the government. By December, special ordinances had been promulgated in Bengal, U.P., and the Frontier Province. The Khan brothers were arrested on December 25, and Jawaharlal on the next day as he was en route to see Gandhi in Bombay.

Jawaharlal had been touring a great deal. He visited Bengal, and when Kamala's health had again broken down he had taken her for treatment to Bombay before going on to the Karnataka. He was back in Bombay by the twentieth of December and might have stayed on another week to see Gandhi if he had not thought it imperative to rush back to Allahabad, where some of his colleagues had already been arrested, and to attend a provincial conference. He left Kamala bedridden in Bombay, thinking he would be returning soon. He had seen Indira both times he was in Bombay —Poona is only 120 miles away—and she was soon to have her winter holiday from school. But with her mother ill and the news of her father's arrest Indira could not even have the consolation of being at Anand Bhawan. She had been at school in Poona barely six months and already she felt uprooted. She wanted to run away from it all and also join the movement. They would not let her, specially Bapu (Gandhi) telling her to wait, she was too young, and she must study and he would give her work to do when she grew up. It seemed such a mess, and she felt forlorn, lonely, and bereft. She told her school friends how proud she was of her parents, but the tears invariably lurked threateningly close to her eyes.

"When her parents used to come she used to get very upset," recalls Mrs Vakil, "they would come for a few hours, a day or so. But then when they used to go away she would be all right. She used to feel it most of the time that Jawaharlal was in jail . . . she used to speak very little. She didn't want to come to school. Then Bapu said, 'no' you, have to go to school . . . you cannot do any work just now . . . you are too young to do anything . . . go, study, then you come to me and then I will give you some work!' She was very anxious to be with her parents."[32]

The parents it seemed were not unduly worried. "You see," continued Mrs Vakil with a great big confident laugh, "supposing she was upset and began to cry, they [Jawaharlal and Kamala] would say: 'Why do you cry, when you want anything, you can ask Aunty, she will do everything for you.' That's all, and everything used to be all right."

"In school, were you conscious of being Nehru's daughter?" I asked Mrs Gandhi. Perhaps it was an unfair question. Perhaps memory could not go back to visualizing herself as having any of the attributes her father was always warning her against, particularly false vanity.

"No, never," replied Mrs Gandhi vehemently.

"What about the others' reactions?"

"They all knew, of course, but it was never made obvious."[33]

But she was human after all, and if her reserve precluded any show of pomposity, it fed on a sense of pride nevertheless.

"The school atmosphere was such as to make her forget this," observed Mrs Vakil. "It is of course natural for a child of thirteen because when she first came she was very conscious. Afterwards," she added understandingly, "she was not, but of course she knew she was the daughter of a very big man, a very important man."[34]

Had she been a different sort of person, her pride in her parents alone might have been sufficient to keep her happy. But she found it galling that all along she had been part of everything, in all the political arguments, battles and victories around her parents, and now she was out of it, cut off completely in a remote corner, in a school. She was an avid reader of the newspapers. That was one sure way of getting news about her parents when letters from jail could not be relied upon, and in any case came only once in a fortnight. It stirred her even more to find that the entire country was in a ferment.

Soon after his arrival, Gandhi was greeted by tales of woe from every province. He himself related his unpleasant experiences of the moderates'

validity, the communal Muslims' and Hindus' reactionary tactics, and the
utter implacability of the British government at the Round Table Conference.
The signs were of war, and when he found that Lord Willingdon was not
even prepared to consider the complaints, he gave the final call. On December 31 the Congress working committee resolved that the nation should
resume civil disobedience.

"No province or district or *tehsil* or village," it said mightily, "is bound
to take up civil disobedience unless the people . . . are ready to undergo suffering of loss of life and property," adding, the source ancillary, "nonviolence
must be observed in thought, word and deed in the face of the gravest provocation."

The government retaliated with force. On January 4, 1932, it arrested
Gandhi and Vallabhbhai Patel, then president of the Congress, and issued four
new ordinances which put almost the entire country in a state of siege. The
all-India body and all the provincial committees of the Congress were
declared illegal, most leading congressmen were put in jail, official and
personal properties were confiscated, and all civil liberties put at the mercy
of the new laws. The country rose up in defiance and as each law was
deliberately broken, the jails filled up and spilled over and overflowed.
Within ten months an unprecedented 90,000 men, women, and children
were behind bars. Except for the very few, most of the political prisoners
were lumped together with hardened convicts and criminals, and the same
brutal rules applied to all. The lathi-charge which came later in the movement in 1930 was used first in the movement in 1932. When government
gaols could not accommodate the stream of non-cooperators, temporary
camps were set up, and when they too became overcrowded, the government began to discriminate between those it could accept in jail and those
it could paralyze into inactivity with threats, beatings, and a "cat and mouse"
policy of arrest and release and again arrest. Unspeakable tortures were
perpetrated in an effort to secure the lists of organizers, volunteers, and
Congress offices. There was the horrific case of an advocate of the High
Court whose pubic hair were plucked out one by one because he would
not divulge the information police asked for.[36]
But the system of survival devised by the Congress worked out beautifully,
as in 1930. All the powers of the working committee had been vested in
the Congress president, he in turn left a list of names of persons who could
take this place, so that as one was arrested, another immediately stepped in.
It was the same with the provincial presidents. The result was that the
organization remained intact to a great extent, to the point that it triumphed
over restrictions on press, mail, and telegraphs, publicity, and even travel by
publishing its own leaflets, bulletins, and news sheets in unnamed presses or
stenciling and typing them and distributing them to remote villages. The
government found it difficult to locate these centers of authority and even
when it did another one sprang up immediately. This at least was a familiar

aspect of any revolutionary movement, but the amazing part was that except for sporadic acts of violence the large bulk of the people followed Gandhi's stern precepts for political behavior. They suffered with dignity, but they defied with nonviolence.

As before, the women joined in, expecting no quarter from the government and getting none. Prison for the male prisoners was generally conditioned by the severest hard labor and punishment by whipping became frequent. A confidential circular to the prison officials from the inspector general of prisons stipulated that there was "no justification for preferential treatment of civil disobedience movement prisoners as such," and that they were "to be kept in their places and dealt with grimly." For women the torture was refined. As Jawaharlal observed:

> They were mostly middle class women, accustomed to a sheltered life, and suffering chiefly from the many repressions and customs produced by a society dominated to his own advantage, by man. The call of freedom had always a double meaning for them, and the enthusiasm and energy with which they threw themselves into the struggle had no doubt their springs in the vague and hardly conscious but nevertheless intense, desire to rid themselves of domestic slavery also. Excepting a very few they were classed as ordinary prisoners and placed with the most degraded of companions and often under horrid conditions.[37]

He recalled an experience which disturbed him deeply. He was once lodged in a jail which was separated from the women's enclosure by a wall. The women political prisoners had to live with their lowest and most criminal counterparts in the same enclosure and he discovered that he had been the house guest of one of them. Over the wall he heard with horror the vulgar language and the curses that these women suffered from the women convict wardens. He might have felt worse had he realized that his own sisters were soon to suffer similar indignities.

Kamala was no longer bedridden but she was still not well and remained confined in Bombay. While her daughter chafed under the restraints imposed by her extreme youth Kamala felt helpless on her side. "She is brave and has the heart of a lioness," Jawaharlal had written worriedly to his daughter when Kamala went to jail in 1931, "but she has a weak body and I would not like her to become weaker. What can we do, however stout-hearted we may be, if our bodies fail us?"[38] Well, she had taxed herself too hard in her enthusiasm in 1930 although things had eased a bit after the Delhi pact the year after. But the threat of imminent arrest hanging over Jawahar during the whole of that summer because of his no-rent campaign had been too much to bear. And even Indu had been away. Previously it was she who had taken a more active part in the movement, now it was Nan and Betty who were in the forefront. Even her mother-in-law, aged and frail as she was, went about addressing meetings in the towns and the adjoining villages! "She was a constant source of nursing to us," remarked Krishna of Swarup Rani. "All her life she had been more or less an invalid, unable to lead a normal active life, but suddenly she seemed to have gained strength and great determination ... and became quite as energetic as we were, sometimes more." Two weeks before Independence Day, January 26, 1932, both Vijayalaxmi and Krishna were served notices stating that they should refrain from attending meetings, organising hartals, or participating in processions. Vijayalaxmi quickly packed off her three little girls Chandralekha, Nayantara, and Rita to Indira's school at Poona. On the twenty-sixth she and Krishna attended one of the largest meetings seen in Allahabad which was presided over by Swarup Rani. She made a fiery speech, there was a lathi charge, and the next morning Vijayalaxmi and Krishna found themselves in jail. Ranjit Pandit, Vijayalaxmi's husband, had already joined his brother-in-law in Naini prison, and to Swarup Rani, left alone except for her sister, their huge house must have seemed like a vast empty cavern.

But the fever had got her too. In April, during celebrations of national week—a remembrance of Jallianwala—she also joined a procession. When it was halted by the police those who were looking after her in the procession brought her a chair to sit on, but soon they were arrested and taken away. The police then made a lathi-charge, and to the horror of Indira, and the others who were in prison, Jawahar, Vijayalaxmi and Krishna, they learnt that she had been knocked down from the chair, hit repeatedly on the head with canes till an open wound smothered her with blood and she fainted. She lay there alone while the street was cleared of the others and only sometime later she was taken by a police officer in his car to Anand Bhawan. Motilal could scarely have imagined, when he drove along the same streets of Allahabad in the 1890s in his magnificent carriage drawn by a matched pair of horses and drew sighs of envy and admiration from both his English and Indian friends, that his plunge into politics and his family's fight for cherished human freedom would bring things to such a pass. His son lay helpless in jail and wondered, as the image of his wounded mother obsessed him how far, if he had been at the spot, Gandhi's nonviolence would have taken him. He took care not to let Indira know how agonized he felt. "I have been disturbed and thrilled by news from Allahabad," he wrote to her, "and above all, by news of Dol Amma, your old grandmother. And I have chafed a little at my comparative comfort in gaol when my mother, frail and weak, has had to face and receive the lathi blows of the police."[40]

Meanwhile in Poona, the coming of Indira's cousins to the school was like a breath of home. They were small; they, too, had been torn away from their parents and, nearing a sober fourteen, she felt quite responsible. Rita, the youngest, was only two and a half. Mrs Gandhi relates with great zest how when all of them were once taken for a treat by some friends in Bombay, they ate their ice creams and all, but how regretfully Rita, who was used to spoonfuls of the stuff, exclaimed when they got back, "But we never got any cod liver oil!"

"She [Indu] made friends very well with little children," remembers Mrs Vakil. "She had no special friends as such. My girls used to be with her all the time. Once, she was chairman of our council and one small child, of whom Indu was very fond, became naughty. The children said: 'Now come on Indira it is your turn to punish the child.' She said: 'I will . . . ' She just took the child and placed him on top of a cupboard."[41]

There were no dancing classes in the school at that time, but Indira even then became fond of participating in the folk dances held on festival days. Later, as prime minister she would happily take a turn with each of the folk dancing groups that would collect in Delhi on Republic Day but she was too shy to be really good at dancing then though she enjoyed doing the *Garba* and was "all right in that," as Mrs Vakil says.

When it was time to go home for vacation she confidently carried with her the school report on her little cousins to show it to their parents. Both Vijayalaxmi and Ranjit Pandit were in prison, of course, but so was her father and communication would take place in those awful twenty-minute interviews which left her feeling sometimes worse than before, it was so frustrating. But she did not bargain with the incivility of the jail authorities. She went to see her Uncle Ranjit in the Allahabad district jail on May 27 with her mother and grandmother and she told him all about his daughters, read out the report, and then handed it over to him to see for himself. The jailer began to object and became generally offensive to her uncle as well as to her mother and grandmother. Three days later she traveled with her mother and grandmother to Bareilly to see her father, who had been tran-ferred there. They told him what had happened and he was so angry he thought the jail officials should express their regrets for what happened. Instead they became vindictive. On June 6, Jawaharlal was taken to yet another jail, this time 200 miles away, at Dehra Dun, near Mussoorie. This presumably was done as a gesture of consideration to enable him to escape the intense heat of Bareilly, but when Kamala and his mother traveled all the way to see him for the fortnightly interview, they were told that no interviews would be allowed for a month. While they waited and fumed Jawahar wrote an acid letter to the superintendent of jails to find out from the authorities concerned what the nature of his offense was supposed to be for which this "punishment" had been devised. He was informed on July 8 that it was as a result of his mother having used "insulting language" to the jailer and being "impertinent."

"For the inspector general to say that my mother 'used insulting language' to the jailer and was 'impertinent' shows that he is strangely lacking in a sense of proportion, knows little of Indian society, and is not happy in the use of language,"[42] wrote back the furious prisoner, and after giving them a true account of what had happened, told them that he would not have any interviews at all in the future. Kamala and Swarup Rani returned disappointed to Allahabad, and Indira could not see her father for at least another few months. *o* *more* *her* *condition*, *she* *thought*.

But back in school the comfortable routine of prayer in the morning, a little talk, classes, lunch, and classes again until four in the afternoon—and after that music and dancing or a film or those little excursions to historical monuments that she was so fond of—was broken dramatically by an event outside the school but which the nationalistic minded students of the Child ren's Own School, particularly Indira, made very much their own. On August 17, 1932, the British premier Ramsay MacDonald announced his decision about communal representation called the Communal Award in which the untouchables were treated as a separate entity from the Hindus. Not only was the scheme of communal electorates in which each community could vote only for a member of its own community reiterated with regard to the major communities, but a new group of the Hindus, the so-called untouch ables, were to be drawn into the orbit of separatism, at the instigation, no doubt, of the leaders of the untouchables and orthodox Hindus, but very much with the active support of the government. This is what Gandhi had said at the Round Table Conference he would fight against with his life. On August 18, he wrote to MacDonald that he had decided to undergo "a fast unto death" which would cease only if "the British government of its own volition or under pressure of public opinion, reverses its decision and withdraws its scheme of communal electorates for the depressed classes, whose representatives should be elected by the general electorate under the common franchise."[43]

"I regret the decision I have taken," added Gandhi, "but as a man of religion that I hold myself to be, I have no other course left open to me."[44]

"I am afraid," wrote back MacDonald on September 8, "that . . . the government's decision stands and that only agreement of the communities themselves can substitute other electoral arrangements."[45]

On September 15, Gandhi affirmed that "the fast was resolved upon in the name of God, for His work and as I believe in all humility, at His call." He, however, added, "The contemplated fast is no appeal to mere emotion. By the fast I want to throw the whole of my weight [such as it is] in the scales of justice, pure and simple."[46]

Jawaharlal, sitting in virtually solitary confinement in Dehra Dun jail, was not convinced. The religious approach to what he could regard only as a political question seemed to him to set a terrible example. But his personal anguish at the thought of Bapu's possible death threw him into despair. On September 20, Gandhi began his fast. But the result was nothing that Jawaharlal could have foreseen. The whole country groaned with remorse, then bubbled with enthusiasm, and finally threw itself into a reformist endeavor to show that the great man's agony was not in vain.

He was like a magician, thought Jawaharlal.

Free of her father's complex intellectuality, Indira reacted with pure emotion. She, too, went on a fast, but a sympathetic one for September 20 only, as countless people did throughout the land that day. Even the buoyant Mrs Vakil was drawn into this exalted scheme for self-expiation and decided to fast along with Indira, while a plan of partial fasting was drawn up for the rest of the school's eager ones. The smallest omitted breakfast, the slightly older ones omitted breakfast and lunch, but Indira and Mrs Vakil did without food the whole day though late at night poor Mrs Vakil felt a little sick.

The principal himself, Jehangir Vakil, though loftily tolerant of the others, denied himself a wholehearted take his doing full justice to his meals that day. He was all for more practical schemes, and the same day, the school as a whole "adopted" a little Harijan girl. They got clothes ready for her and she began to attend the class every day when she came," says Mrs Vakil, "it was Indu's charge to give her a bath and do her hair and bring her to the class. Then she used to have lunch with us, stay with us whole day, and go back home in the evenings."[47]

"We also worked in the area of the untouchables in the city," recalls Mrs Gandhi now. "There was a cooperative store, part of the swadeshi movement. We helped in the preparation activities, buying of things, arranging them, etc. When the shop was established it was managed by people who were paid for it."[48]

With Gandhi's fast, Indira's fretting that she was cut off from political excitement came to an end. The entire Hindu leadership of India converged upon Poona to find a solution to the problem that had made Gandhi risk his life, and the center of activity was again right where she was. She gathered her little cousins and went off to see Gandhi. He had been anxious about Jawahar's reaction so he took the occasion to send him a telegram in prison: "During all these days of agony you have been before my mind's eye. I am most anxious to know your opinion.... Saw Indu [and] Swarup's children. Indu looked happy and in possession of more flesh..."[49]

By September 25, the Hindu leaders reached an agreement which rehabilitated the "depressed classes" within the general Hindu electoral fold but provided certain safeguards like reservation of seats. On the twenty-sixth, at 5.15 P.M., Gandhi broke his fast after prayer and the singing of hymns. He had made his position clear earlier that "the satisfactory ending of the depressed classes question ... should in no way mean that [he] would be committed to the acceptance of His Majesty's Government's decision on the other parts of the communal question."[50] He left that as a purely political aspect to be determined by the Congress party, but the result of his staking his life at that particular juncture on what he called "a matter of pure religion"[51] shifted the emphasis in the whole country from civil disobedience to social reform. Though Jawaharlal and the others, including Gandhi

himself remained in jail, those outside renewed themselves in anti-untouch-
ability work with an eagerness that seemed to show that they were glad to be
on this safer, nonpolitical ground. The movement had begun to labor under
a growing need for positive methods to overcome the government's stringent
measures, this not only contributed to an increasing tension and flux among
the members but went against the open methods advocated by Gandhian
satyagraha. In April 1933, a mammoth session of the Congress was held
in Calcutta in spite of the government ban. Although 2,200 delegates were
elected only 1,100 succeeded in reaching Calcutta from all parts of the
country. Spirits were buoyed even more as the result of Swarup Rani Nehru's
decision to attend in spite of her age and worsening health, an aftermath
in some ways of the horrible lathi charge she had suffered the year before.
But Indira was again horrified to learn that even she had not been spared,
and that the thousand delegates arrested on the way to Calcutta included
her frail old grandmother.

In May 1933, Gandhi undertook another fast, but this time a personal,
self-purificatory one for twenty-one days only. "A heart prayer," as he
called it, "of purification for myself and my associates for greater vigilance
and watchfulness in connection with the Harijan cause."[52] Taking into
account the nature of the fast, the government released him. But Gandhi
felt morally bound not to take advantage of this release to pursue any
political work, and recommended instead the suspension of civil disobedience
for six weeks. Jawaharlal pondered in jail:

> Again I watched the emotional upheaval of the country during the fast
> and I wondered more and more if this was the right method in politics.
> It seemed to me to be sheer revivalism, and clear thinking had not a ghost
> of a chance against it. All India, or most of it, stared reverently at the
> Mahatma and expected him to perform miracle after miracle and put an
> end to untouchability and get swaraj and so on, and did precious little
> itself! And Gandhiji did not encourage others to think; his insistence
> was only on purity and sacrifice. I felt that I was drifting further and
> further away from him mentally in spite of my strong emotional attach-
> ment to him.[53]

From far-off Vienna came evidence of a more practical revolt. Both
V. J. Patel, the great Swarajist figure of the legislatures in the 1920s, and
Subhas Chandra Bose, a fiery young nationalist, who were abroad because
of ill health, argued that this latest action of Gandhi's in suspending civil
disobedience was "a confession of failure," and for the first time the suggestion for the formation of a new party of radical breakaways from the
Congress was made.

In July, Poona again became the scene of hectic activity. Gandhi called
an informal conference of congressmen and it was decided that mass civil

disobedience should be further suspended, and only individual satyagraha be offered. As a start for himself, Gandhi disbanded his well-loved Sabarmati Ashram and tore himself from the last of his material links. On August 1, 1933, he was again arrested before he could start on a scheduled march to the village of Ras. The president of the Congress, Jawaharlal, was already in jail. But the acting presidents one after the other had been arrested and the last of them, Sirdar Sardul Singh Caveeshar, decided this time to terminate the office itself as well as the line of "dictators" in districts and provinces so that the movement would become one of pure individual responsibility. From August 1933 to March 1934, the jails kept filling up with a courageous stream of "civil resisters."

Soon after his arrest, however, when Gandhi was denied facilities to carry on his Harijan work from jail as he had been allowed to do before, he went on another fast and this time the government's obduracy seemed to be in proportion to Gandhi's own desperate state of mind. After five days his condition became serious and he was removed to the hospital. By August 23, when it was realized that he might not survive, he was released. Again, embarrassed at his predicament, not wishing to take political advantage of a situation that had arisen because of a fight on another principle, he decided to treat himself as a prisoner until his sentence for political activity had expired, and concentrate instead on the Harijan movement. To all apparent purposes, India was again facing a stalemate.

All through these months in school, as Indira looked upon political events being shaped by Gandhi from Poona, and as she grew toward maturity, she harbored a nagging anxiety about her mother. In 1932 it was again suspected that Kamala might have tuberculosis and toward the end of the year she began to get what are called heart attacks, shortness of breath, and feeling of suffocation which brought on fainting. She was examined by B. C. Roy in Calcutta, who wrote to Jawaharlal in jail that "there is no organic disease of the heart. The attacks were due to the heart muscle being weak and the worry and anxiety she is passing through."[54]

In July Indira herself fell ill. It was a wonder she could continue to concentrate on her studies and her father fretted with helplessness.

He wrote forlornly on July 22, 1932:

So you have been ill, my dear, and, for ought I know, may still be laid up. It takes time for news to reach the inside of a jail. I can do very little to help you, and you will have to look after yourself. Strange how we are all spread out—you, far away in Poona; Mummie, unwell in Allahabad; and the rest of us in various prisons! I thought of you lying ill in Poona, and I wondered when I would see you again, how many more months or years would pass before we met; and how you would have grown during the interval.[55]

But when she went home for her winter vacation she traveled farther north with her mother and grandmother to see her father, for he had by then lifted his self-imposed restriction on interviews. Soon both her aunts were released and when she was back in school, they came down to Poona because Swarup was eager to see her little daughters after so long. They all saw Bapu again a number of times, which made Gandhi inform Jawaharlal promptly that "Indu was in excellent health and seemed to be quite happy." In August Indira learnt that Swarup Rani had become seriously ill and that Jawaharlal had been released thirteen days before the expiry of his two-year sentence so as to be able to attend her. But as soon as his mother was better, Jawaharlal, feeling the shock of being out in the world after his long and wondering how long he would remain so, rushed to Poona to see Gandhi and Indira.

It was a mark of hardly pleasure as far as Indira was concerned because Jawahar stayed with the Vakils. It was she he had come to see, but the whole school clustered round him and he became like a child with them. He was interested and curious about everything. Once he took a history class and at another time gave practical advice on a lesson in photography. As a result of his visit the police were stationed around the school and Indira was the only one of the children who viewed them with the equanimity of old acquaintanceship.

In October, Krishna married a sensitive young Oxonian, Raja Hutheesing. They settled permanently in Bombay and it was good to know that one at least of the family would be so near her. Toward the end of the year, there was terrific excitement which moved her to Bombay also. An outbreak of plague necessitated the Vakils moving lock, stock, and barrel to a resort near Poona called Panchgani and from there the school was shifted to Bombay, where it reopened as the Pupils' Own School. Because of the shift, she and another girl had to prepare for their examination within one term and soon she was wrapped up in studies. She heard from her parents that they were planning to go to Calcutta to consult doctors about Kamala, but on January 15, 1933, there were earthquake tremors in various parts of India including Bombay. Indira dashed off a very typical, schoolgirlish letter to her mother.

Mummie darling,   17th Jan.

You must be back from Calcutta by now. What did the doctors say? Do let me know. Did you go to Shantiniketan? How did you like it? Did you feel the earthquake in Allahabad? I read in the papers that the cathedral was so shaken up that the Bishop thought the statues on top would fall. There was also one in Bombay but not where we live.

Is it cold in Allahabad or is it raining? I hear it is raining all over the U.P. There is no rain here, but a cold current passed over. It was very cold on Saturday, Sunday and Monday. But I was brave and bathed with cold water throughout. Today it is much warmer.

What's the news about Dolamma? You people might write oftener.

Mr Vakil has received Papu's letter with the lecture on swimming. He was amused but gave me permission to go for a bath. Shall I ask Psyche or someone to accompany me though I suppose she must be busy.

I have met Fi and told her about the ring.

Chand and Tara spent the day here on Saturday and I went to this place on Sunday. Poor Rita has to wear specs now. Her lovely eyes will be hidden. But I hope she'll soon not need them.

Phupi has given me the book you sent. I have just read somewhere that you intend staying on in Calcutta. For how long?

I am quite fit. Our papers are over but we have not got the results yet. I feel so worried—there is less than a month left for the preliminary examination!

Give my love to Papu, Dolamma and keep lots of it for yourself.

Your ever loving,
Indu

I saw Mrs Naidu on Sunday.[56]

For Indira it was a consolation and a great joy to receive her father's letters that he began to write from March 26, 1932, after stopping them temporarily in January 1931 when he was released at the time of Motilal's death. "They are," he himself wrote to her expressively, "or at least I please myself by imagining them to be—little talks *entre nous,* which we might have had if 1,000 miles and many solid walls did not separate us."[57]

"I enjoyed them," Mrs Gandhi said years later, "and they served as a link between us at a time when there was no other communication. They helped me to know my father better as well as the subjects which he covered."[58]

He certainly covered a lot, for he was not interested in dry descriptions of a king's conquests and a nation's losses, but in human history; history as the struggle of man for a living, of the people who make up a nation, their work, their reactions to each other, and their achievements. Jawaharlal chose a challenging canvas for his interpretation of men and events, the major civilizations of the world, and he involved his growing daughter in his own search for conclusions. If Indira was cheered by getting these letters, she was again filled with pride, because most times Mrs Vakil or one of the other teachers would read them out to the whole class as a fascinating lesson. But invariably there was a reference which made her feel that they belonged to her alone.

"You are a lucky girl," wrote her father at the end of a long letter in which he elaborated his view on what "real history" was. "Born in the month and year of the great revolution which ushered in a new era in Russia, you are now witness to a revolution in your own country, and soon you may be an actor in it."[59]

Jawaharlal wrote the last letter of this historical series on August 9, 1933, with the injunction to his daughter not to take what he had written as "the final authority on any subject." Nevertheless they were an invaluable interpretation of world history in capsule, but a curious corollary makes it doubtful if she received the letters as regularly as is normally thought. "One has moods in prison—as indeed one has in the world outside too—and lately I have felt little inclined to write these letters which no one sees but myself," wrote Jawahar on August 4, 1932. "They are pinned together and put away to await the time, months or years hence," he added pessimistically, "when perhaps you may see them. Months or years hence! When we meet again and have a good look at each other, and I am surprised to find how you have grown and changed ... there will be quite a mountain of them by that time and how many hundreds of hours of my prison life will be locked up in them!"[60]

He had denied himself all interviews in jail for a period, but there was no bar on correspondence and the letters as such had no need to pile up. But apart from that so much industry, feeling, and creativity had gone into the writing of them that Nehru, being as particular as he was, would never risk losing them because of the uncertain state of postage for a political prisoner then and the certain event of the inevitable slashings of the censor. He could not have made copies with the thick swadeshi paper he was using for them. He might have handed his daughter chunks of these letters when he had an opportunity to meet her in interviews. He certainly must have shown her all of them when he came out of prison finally in September and spent that week in Poona.

But whether Indira was receiving copies of the historical series or separately written letters, altogether she was subject, for those two years while her father was in jail and she in school in Poona, very much to the persuasions of his beliefs through either. Even in an intensely personal letter the processes of his thought, caught up as they were in the interpretation of history, would automatically be revealed, for Jawaharlal was not one to separate the discoveries of the intellect from the emotions of the heart and he would have liked to share both with his daughter. The two major strains of these letters were a feeling for the downtrodden in all centuries, and a questioning of authority and rigid assertion, in politics as well as in religion. If, on the one hand, he could point out the validity of a Marxian theory he would bring in a quotation by Lenin himself at the same time which said that "in no sense do we regard Marxist theory as something complete and unassailable."[61] And if he wished to emphasize certain of the values of tradition and the ancient scriptures of India or religion in general, he was quick to instil doubts in her, the same doubts he felt himself, the same doubts in fact which

assailed Prince Siddhartha twenty-five hundred years ago before he became
the Buddha and whose own cry Jawaharlal used:

> How can it be that Brahma
> would make a world and keep it miserable.
> Since if all powerful, he leaves it so,
> He is not good, and if not powerful,
> He is not God?

So, taught to see both sides of a question or the myriad angles of a question,
Indira would have long arguments with Vakil, her principal, who would
plumb for the superiorities of the communist philosophy and reject the
mystic search with a diehardism that made her tell him that it would not
last.

"She used to argue in the proper way," says Mrs Vakil. "She would try
to understand and argue. My general impression of her remains that she
did everything in the correct manner."[62]

Indira's correctness, luckily just falling short of the prim, prevented those
extremes of passion and prejudice which could cloud judgment—and even
gave her instinctive prognostications, like the one about Vakil's future
intellectual direction—a balance which belied her years but which seemed to
be the natural outcome of a childhood influenced by adult interest.

By 1936, in fact only two or three years after those spirited discussions,
Vakil was writing to Jawaharlal in terms which were incompatible with his
earlier stand:

I have passed through a spiritual revolution so stupendous that I am
filled with wonder when I think of it. As a consequence of it, I have
come not only to feel, but to know, that into Mahatmaji's hands have been
given the reins of India's destiny, under God. Strange language for an
ex-communist (even a parlor-communist!) to use. The instinct that
has made you cleave to Mahatmaji, in spite of your serious differences
is an instinct that has come from what is highest and best in you....In the
old days I used to wonder how you could manage to work with the
Mahatma—and not break off and form and lead your own group. I
used to think it your weakness. I see I was wrong, quite wrong....[63]

Jawaharlal's reply was characteristic of the flexible norms that he had
instilled in his daughter also.

My dear Jehangir,

I find it a little difficult to write to you on the subject of spiritualism
because my own way of looking at it is very different from yours.

You mention your experience. If some such experience comes to me I suppose I shall change my outlook also. Till then I must carry on in my own way. The only safe way for any person is the way he feels impelled by his own inner being to go. I am not vain enough to deny the truth that may be in someone else but I must see it for myself before I can act upon it.

"He [Vakil] is a queer fellow now I might tell you," recalled Indira in a conversation years later. "He used to be a terrific atheist then—not that I was a believer or anything but I always maintained that you can't be so rigid in your views—that there can always be another side to the picture. We used to have terrific arguments and I told him then that whenever somebody is so dogmatic and extreme there's always the danger of his swinging completely to the other extreme. That is what hapened." She laughed delightedly, obviously pleased that she had turned out to be right. "He lives now in some ashram near Bombay!"

6. SHANTINIKETAN

When Jawaharlal was released from prison in September 1933, he took
the opportunity to settle long-pending domestic affairs. With Motilal no
longer there it seemed like a burden to him which he would have willingly
overcome by getting rid of all his possessions once and for all. It was better
not to have anything, he argued to himself, than labor under the constant
apprehension that the government could confiscate it at any time.
"Neither my wife nor I had any special need for money," he wrote loftily,

but his lack of illusion made him add, "or so we thought, being unused to the lack of it."[1] He was worried on two counts, that his mother, bedridden and ill, should not have to suffer any "marked lowering of the standard of living" that she had been used to, and that there should be money enough to send Indira to Europe to continue her education there. Since Motilal gave up his law practice in the noncooperation movement, they had been living on what was already there: politics had been too demanding for Jawaharlal to add any new sources of income. Consequently, he decided to sell cartloads of odds and ends together with, alas, those jewels of Kamala's the making of which had been so preciously supervised by Motilal in the halcyon days of old. Even Kamala's heart suffered a pang when it came to that. She had not worn any of her jewels for the past twelve years, but she had visualized more normal times when she could have given them to her daughter to wear. But then normalcy and happiness and gaiety were a distant vision while the altar of political freedom demanded immediate sacrifices. So the jewels went, and with them perhaps her link with the beautiful, teenaged bride who might have lived a happy, carefree life had not the mantle of the Nehru name fallen so challengingly on her and had she herself not wished to carry it with such spirit.

Basically, anyway, there was too much to do and with Jawahar around, no time to brood or even to think of her illness. It was uncertain how long she would remain out of prison and she did not want to waste this precious period consulting doctors and undergoing new treatment. She felt ill, but she was not going to reveal it until she collapsed. Jawaharlal did decide, however, to go to Calcutta. He wanted to get Bidhan Roy's and some of the other doctors' advice on Kamala and also felt he must express his sympathy for the people of Bengal in their extraordinary suffering under the ordinance and other oppressions by the government. Before they left Allahabad on January 15, the town felt a minor tremor, but only when they reached Calcutta did they discover that the earthquake had wrought havoc in Bihar. Before anything could be done about that they had to fulfil their commitments in Calcutta, as Jawaharlal was scheduled to address three public meetings. At the meetings he argued against employing terrorism as a means of political redress, but he could not help decrying the government for its inhuman suppression of nationalistic feeling.

Three and a half days later, Jawaharlal and Kamala went to Shantiniketan. Indira was to sit for her matriculation shortly and they thought that the best place for her to go, if Europe did not work out, would be Tagore's university. At least it would be an escape, thought Jawaharlal, from the dead hand of the other usual "official, oppressive, and authoritarian" centers of learning. He had great admiration personally for Tagore. The seventy-three-year old poet, dramatist, musician, painter, educationist, and humanist was the supreme literary figure in India at the time. He had won the Nobel Prize for Literature in 1913 for his prose poem, *Gitanjali*, but international acclaim merely set the seal on what was already an amazing reputation in India. He had been knighted by the British but he had surrendered his title on May 29, 1919, as a protest against the massacre at Jallianwala and though he did not take an active role in Indian politics after the twenties, he was a staunch nationalist and friend of Gandhi and Jawaharlal. It was a song written by him which later became the national anthem of India.

Tagore had been one of the handsomest young men of his time: with slim, clear eyes, chiseled features, a beautiful head, an aristocratic background and bearing, and a sensitive intelligence that shone on the face. He seemed as an old man with long wavy hair, a flowing white beard, and loose robes—the epitome of graciousness.

If Gandhi represented the ascetic strain in Indian tradition, Tagore embodied its great aesthetic ideal and that the two could subsist side by side seemed to Jawaharlal another indication of "the richness of India's cultural genius which could throw up in the same generation two such master types, typical of her in every way, yet representing different aspects of her many-sided personality."[2] Indira was already familiar with the Gandhian influence. Jawaharlal was not particularly worried that the poet's personality would prove to be too overwhelming for her. She was older now, the years in school had given her poise and self-confidence, and she could be expected to derive some benefits from it rather than succumb to awe. He hoped, on the contrary, that "she would imbibe something of the atmosphere of the place and more particularly, profit by the presence of and contact with *Gurudev*."[3] Kamala wanted to see Shantiniketan and the environment in which her daughter might find herself, and as it was always a pleasure to meet the poet himself, they went.

Tagore, in fact, found himself facing a minor dilemma about the reception that Shantiniketan should give the eminent young couple. It was their normal custom to have a ceremony in which Vedic mantras were recited but Jawaharlal was generally known to be impatient with anything that he thought smacked of religious cant. Tagore decided however that they would stick to their custom. So the "keeper of their Sanskritic lore," Pandit Kshiti Mohan Sen, dug hastily into all the old scriptures to select the most appropriate verses though "Gurudev till the last," remembers Anil Chanda, who was acting as Tagore's private secretary then, "had doubts as to how the recipients of the honor would act."[4]

The ceremony itself was intensely moving. Shantiniketan was like a garden university, and the green grounds and lofty trees created an enchanting vista of peace and quiet. The mystic light of sundown added to the effect evoked by the romantic figure of the poet and the sonorous verses of welcome that he himself intoned:

Come thou who bringest delight
Come thou with thy magnanimous mind
We offer this seat to thee.
Thou art a hero
Waken us today into a perfect well being.
Thou are friendliest of all friends
Thou art the messenger with thy forward moving mind.
Dispel all hatred and fear.
Be thou great among all men
But thou harbinger of good to all men and be their friend.
Thou art the leader of men, we welcome thee;
Thou art our richest treasure, we welcome thee;
Let all thy paths be propitious and all men
And all thy desires and deeds.

Tagore need not have had his doubts. Though Jawaharlal did not understand Sanskrit, he was too susceptible not to catch the spirit. He was thrilled, and later wrote to Chanda asking for an English translation of the verse.

Kamala and Jawaharlal stayed in Tagore's own cottage called Uttarayan. Anil Chanda, a teacher at Shantiniketan, had a cottage close by and was asked specially to look after them. He remembers one evening after dinner when Jawaharlal had a long discussion with him and Krishna Kripalani, a teacher who was married to Tagore's granddaughter, and elaborated on his ideas about the sort of education that he wanted Indira to have. He mentioned that he might send Indira to Shantiniketan, but he could not thrust the idea of Europe completely from his mind.

Events soon made a decision in favor of Shantiniketan inevitable. On their way back to Allahabad, Kamala and Jawaharlal visited Patna and some other areas of Bihar and were horrified by the damage done by the earthquake. Back in Allahabad, collection of funds and supplies was immediately organized, and soon Jawaharlal returned to Bihar to conduct relief operations. He spent a gruelling ten days in the "torn and ruined territories" and probably because it was a mission of mercy the government stayed its hand. But no sooner had he returned to Allahabad than the summons to prison came on February 12. He had been expecting it, but this time, as it was for his speeches in Calcutta, he was taken first to Presidency jail, and then to Alipore central jail in Calcutta. He was sentenced to another two years, and began his seventh conviction. It was perhaps fortuitous that Jawaharlal was in Calcutta jail for Kamala's treatment had been fixed there and he hoped that with him in a prison nearby she could give all her mind to getting well.

Just before leaving Allahabad, Jawaharlal had sent off a telegram to Indira with irrepressible good humor: "Going to other home." For Indira, the news was hardly conducive to study. She became troubled and anxious

also about her mother, but she finished her exam somehow and even took
part in Vakil's Gujarati translation of Tagore's *Ritu Raj*, a drama they
enacted at Bombay's Capital Theater to help collect funds for the school.
She had been busy with dance practice before the performance and rather
enjoyed "her brief appearance for the only time on the stage of a regular
theater."[5]

In April, Indira went straight to Calcutta. Most of the students and
some of the parents had come with her to Victoria Terminus to see her off
on the express train to Calcutta. They had sung and laughed and cried in a
touching farewell. Suddenly school was behind her, and she was now a
"sari-clad young lady" of sixteen and a half. Life, however, did not seem
to promise much change. Her mother was again ill, her father again in
jail, and it was a sad homecoming. But there was the consolation of being
with her mother and being able "to share with her," as she recalls now, "the
unsatisfactory but greatly treasured twenty-minute fortnightly interviews
with my father."[6]

It was a different world from the one of song and dance and youthful
chatter that she had come from, but Kamala's strong spiritual instincts
and Indira's nascent ones joined in strange amusement for a teenager.

"Mummy and I spent much time in the Ramakrishna Mission," Mrs
Gandhi recalled years later. "Sitting peacefully by the riverside, a new
world of thought and experience opened out to me."[7]

It was to be a long time before she could define happiness with the equanimity of perfect detachment which she did when she became prime minister
as "not the absence of sorrow or hardship but rather when in spite of them
one is at peace with onself and one with nature. It is the radiance within one
which shows through and spills over the others."[8] The "new world of
thought and experience" which she realized then in silent companionship
with her mother came perhaps from watching the flow of the river toward
its inevitable goal or from the effect of her mother's own heightened sensitivity
to thoughts of eternity because of her illness, but if her later detachment
had its beginnings then in her mind, she was too young to forget that life
beckoned in a thousand different ways.

As soon as her mother was slightly better they returned to Allahabad,
where Indira received her first proposal. The twenty-one-year-old Feroze
Gandhi, a veteran, as he considered himself then, of three imprisonments in
the freedom struggle, felt that he certainly qualified for the hand of even one
of the most eligible girls in India. He was apparently not overawed by the
fact that she was the granddaughter of the legendary Motilal, and daughter
of India's beloved Jawahar. He had worked enthusiastically for the Allahabad
Congress as an assistant to K.D. Malavia, the secretary of the Allahabad
city Congress committee. On more than one occasion he had shown
that he possessed the attributes of future leadership: tact, humor, and
authority. That politics had scotched his college education, that he had

not qualified for earning a livelihood, and that he came from a very ordinary middle-class family, which might compare unfavorably with the Nehrus, did not dim his ambition. The mundane was not the standard of judgment those days. He felt confident enough of his future capacities. He was short, five feet six, a little stocky, but extremely good-looking with a wide forehead, large light-colored eyes, sharp nose, chiseled lips upturned at the corners, and a firm, well-rounded cleft chin.

Familiarity with the Nehrus had probably taken the edge off any awe Feroze might have felt, for he was a frequent visitor at Anand Bhawan and had been sympathetically treated by Kamala. Possibly it was her attitude that gave him the courage to propose; although some answering light in Indira's eyes must have helped to bring his feelings to the point of expression. He had seen Indira very rarely since she had been at the Vakils' school, but there had been the short vacations in which he had seen her gradually growing from childhood into adolescence. And now at sixteen, although thin and scrawny and still a mere girl really, she was, in his eyes, beautiful.

"He proposed almost straightway—told my mother he wanted to marry me," says Mrs Gandhi now, without elaborating on what her own reaction was. "She just said that I was too young then."[9]

Swarup Rani had a bagful of other formal proposals on the customary level of interfamily connections, but Kamala's answer was the same to those as well, and in fact there was one from a particular stranger, recalls Mrs Gandhi, "which had us laughing for days!"[10] She did not guess then that Feroze was not the type to accept defeat quickly. Perhaps she even hoped that he was not, as she left soon after with her mother for a holiday in Kashmir. Mummie she could depend upon to understand in the final analysis, if it came to that.

"Her father spent so many years in jail away from his family . . . [so] she was much closer to her mother in those early years," is the interpretation given by Fory Nehru.[11]

Indira's father at the same time was going through another anti-spiritual phase. An effort on the part of those outside to find a way out of the political stalemate facing nationalist aspirations had resulted in a move for a revival of the Swaraj party and arguments in favor of Congress participation in the coming elections to the Legislative Assembly. The White Paper presented earlier by the British was a document which, as Jawaharlal wrote, "left one gasping for breath."[12] It gave the representatives of the Indian states dominance in the federation, left India tied hand and foot to the economy of Britain, and as before whatever autonomy was ceded was surrounded "with all the safeguards the wit of man could devise"[13] to ensure the ultimate authority of the governors and the viceroy. At a conference of Congress leaders at Delhi on March 31, 1934, presided over by Dr Ansari, it was not only decided that the Congress should fight the elections but also seek the repeal of all repressive laws and reject the White Paper proposals in favor of the Gandhian stand at the Round Table Conference. On April 5 Gandhi wrote to Ansari that although his views on the utility of the legislatures remained what they had been in 1920 he felt that "it was not only the right but the duty of every congressman who, for some reason or other, does not want to or cannot take part in civil resistance and who has faith in entry into the legislatures, to seek entry and form combinations in order to prosecute the program which he or they believe to be in the interest of the country."[14] Two days later, he issued a statement that he had drawn up earlier, advising congressmen to suspend even the individual civil resistance allowed earlier and leave it to him alone.

Here again, the logical course of action was obviously suspension of satyagraha. The workers were tired, the average man and woman wanted safer avenues of political expression. It was psychologically impossible for a mass movement to retain a high pitch for so long. There are high points and low points, and this was a low point. Unpleasant as the truth was, Jawaharlal forced himself to face it, and once again acknowledged Gandhi's unique ability to interpret the mood of the country. But what brought all his own rational instincts to the fore was the reason that Gandhi gave for suspending the political fight. This was his disenchantment with a particular colleague who he said had failed to live up to the true spirit of satyagraha by preferring his private studies to his full allotted task in prison. "More than the imperfection of the friend whom I love, more than ever it brought home to me my own imperfections," said Gandhi. "The friend said he had thought that I was aware of his weakness. I was blind. Blindness in a leader is unpardonable. I saw at once that I must for the time being remain the sole representative of civil resistance in action."[15]

"He was perfectly entitled to treat his ashram inmates in any manner he liked, they had taken all kinds of pledges and accepted a certain regime," fumed Jawaharlal angrily to himself in prison. "But the Congress had not done so; I had not done so. Why should we be tossed hither and thither for, what seemed to me, metaphysical and mystical reasons in which I was not interested?"[16]

Compared with Gandhi, he thought himself a practical politician and even though he had willingly and daringly staked his entire life in following Gandhi's lead, his reaction seemed justified. But on the same practical, rational level which he prized above all, he did not seem to realize that not everything was metaphysical in Gandhi's arguments. It was, as he had himself pointed out, only a trivial lapse on the part of the unhappy colleague that was the cause of Gandhi's pronouncement. But for Gandhi this one example probably signified the indifference that was creeping into the entire movement, and he chose that example as being representative. At the same time he had said in a statement during the Bihar earthquake that the calamity was the result of the sin of untouchability. Nothing could be calculated to change cruel and ignorant prejudice than this concept, but its appeal was obviously to superstition rather than to reason. It made Jawaharlal argue acidly that if an earthquake was a punishment for sin then the loss that the Maharaja of Darbhanga, "an owner of enormous estates," suffered could be taken to be a judgment on the *zamindari* system.[17] His whole being during these desolate days in Alipore jail was torn between his recognition for and love of Gandhi's supreme qualities and their clash of ideas. Perhaps it was his reaction against all vagueness during this period that gave an almost absurdly practical edge to his ideas about education, especially the education of his daughter.

"Personally, if I had the chance," he wrote rebelliously to Anil Chanda in connection with Indira's studies, "I would like to have my daughter work in a factory for a year, just as any other worker, as a part of her education." But the letter otherwise was a model of restrained interest on the part of a father. "When we were in Shantiniketan, my wife and I, last January," wrote Jawaharlal, "I mentioned to Gurudev the possibility of my daughter Indira joining Shantiniketan. Since then I have not had the chance of meeting Indira. She has now just come from Bombay after appearing for the matriculation examination and I hope to see her soon. We have now to decide about her future education. We have no desire whatsoever to send her to the official universities. I dislike them greatly. I had intended sending her to Europe, probably Switzerland, but events have a way of taking the initiative out of our hands and for the last many years we have lived in many ways, a hand-to-mouth existence, finding it difficult to plan the future. My repeated and frequent visits to prison disturb domestic arrangements. There is much to be said for this, of course, as it prevents our falling into grooves!"

He wrote that he wished Indira to join Shantiniketan, but added, "I shall discuss this with her when I see her for, of course, decisions must not be imposed on the modern girl!"

Even with regard to the subjects she could take, he thought, he could tell only after he had had a talk with her. "She must choose," he affirmed. "She may even choose them after she goes there. My own ideas of education are rather peculiar. I dislike the education which prepares a girl to play a part in the drawing room and nowhere else."[18]

When he met his daughter and talked to her it was apparently decided that she would go to Shantiniketan. She was somewhat familiar with Tagore because he had visited the Children's Own School whenever he came to Poona, and she was confident of having at least one friend there, Abdul Ghani, the son of Abdul Ghaffar Khan, one of the two Khan brothers and the "Frontier Gandhi," as he was called. Ghaffar Khan was still languishing in jail and had asked Jawaharlal to do something about Ghani who, he feared after a sojourn he had had in the United States, might find it difficult to adjust himself to the spartan standards of nationalist India.

Jawaharlal had promptly arranged for him to be admitted to Shantiniketan, which he thought would provide an ideal amalgam of Indian ways and Western thought, and tone down the habits of Western affluence to the requirements of Indian simplicity.

On May 7 Jawaharlal was again considerately taken to Dehra Dun jail at the foothills of Mussoorie, to be away from the oppressive heat of Calcutta, where he had begun to lose weight and health generally. So while Kamala and Indira went to Kashmir he looked longingly over the 15-foot wall for at least a glimpse of the mountains he loved, and saw only a few tree tops. But he was happy that the question of Indira's education had been resolved. He had received the copy of the application form from Shantiniketan for her admission, and on May 20, he sent it along with a note on "Indira Priyadarshini Nehru" for the benefit of her teachers which, in Jawaharlal's meticulous fashion, reads like her early biography in capsule.

From her earliest childhood Indu has had to put up with national political troubles and domestic upheavals caused by them. Her education has suffered because of these and there has been no continuity in it. For long periods there has been no peace or quiet in her home atmosphere owing to her parents' and other relatives' preoccupation with public affairs, and often because of their absence in prison. These events naturally left a strong impression on her mind.

After giving the details of her schooling, he said that the result of her Bombay university matriculation examination had not yet come in.

This matriculation examination was taken by her as most of the boys and girls in her school were taking that course. Her parents attached little importance to the examination as such as they had no intention of following it up by sending her to the Bombay or any other official university in India. It was their intention to send her later to a foreign university, probably in Switzerland. But circumstances do not permit her leaving India for a considerable period. It is hoped, however, that some time or other, she may be able to continue her education on the continent of Europe.

Then comes a paragraph that shows that with the ideas Jawaharlal and Kamala held, it was inconceivable that their daughter's life would not be comparatively unconventional, given her own predilictions.

Her parents would like her later to specialize in some subject or subjects which would enable her to do some socially useful work in [after] life efficiently, and at the same time enable her to be economically independent, so long as the present structure of society lasts. She is not likely to have an unearned income and it is not considered desirable by her parents that she should depend for her subsistence on a husband or others. For the present these questions hardly arise but I am mentioning them to indicate what her parents have in view. They would not like her merely to possess a literary or other culture which does not help her shift for herself in the years to come.

As to her tastes, he wrote:

We have tried to find out what her own inclinations were but so far we have not succeeded in bringing out any marked bent. Unfortunately during the last four years I have been mostly in prison and thus cut off from her and unable to watch her development. She has a vague desire to do social or public work, probably because she has a certain admiration for her parents' activities. This is no doubt good but it does not take one far, and special knowledge is necessary in a special subject. She will have to choose this later.

Again, weighing carefully her own desires with what he thought she should do, he said:

Apart from the other compulsory subjects (such as English, history and civics, social service, etc.) I would suggest that she might take Hindi as one of the Indian languages and French as a modern language. Although Hindi is our mother tongue (our spoken home language is more Urdu than Hindi) Indira is rather backward in it. She did some Hindi and a little Sanskrit some years ago but she did not take kindly to Sanskrit and I did not want her to continue with a subject for which she did not have a liking.

She is fairly good at French. This was one of her subjects for the Bombay matriculation. This will be useful for her in case she goes to Europe later on.

Of the optional subjects in the intermediate course I should like her to choose for herself the subject she likes. I believe she has some liking for natural sciences and, if so, I shall be glad if she takes chemistry or physics or botany. She has so far had little chance of indulging in the fine arts or music and I cannot say if she has any particular bent that way.

Obviously he did not place much significance on her dabbling in music and dancing at the Vakils' school, nor even on the very strong interest she showed, according to Mrs Vakil, in embroidery. "But if she wants to I shall welcome her taking fine arts," went on Jawaharlal, "especially as there are such excellent arrangements for teaching them at Visva Bharati."
Then he gives an account of her health which, contrary to later reports

of her frailty—one of the reasons given, for instance, for not having her as prime minister by those opposed to her—was neither particularly good nor bad.

Indira is fairly healthy and has grown well. Occasionally she has little troubles which are not important. Her throat is especially troublesome at times. When she was a child, about ten years ago, her tonsils were removed but lately there has again been throat trouble. Her eyes also give her a little pain occasionally and she was advised last year to wear glasses when reading, but she has seldom followed this advice. These troubles usually depend on her general health. When she is otherwise fit, the troubles disappear, when she is below par they appear. At present, and for some time past, she has been fit. Absence of physical exercise usually makes her languid and seedy.

She can ride, is very fond of swimming, and was a good runner as a child. In Switzerland she went in for winter sports.[19]

Shortly after, Indira's matriculation results came in. She had barely managed to get pass marks.

"You see," Mrs Vakil tried to explain loyally, "she did a four years' course in three years and it was a bit difficult for her to get the class. It was a very small school when we shifted from Poona to Bombay, the children had to prepare for their examination in one term. She did very well in English."[20]

On July 2, when Indira and her mother were back in Anand Bhawan, Kamala wrote a rather imperious little note to Chanda.

"I am accompanying Indira to Shantiniketan," she informed him. "We shall reach there on the sixth. I would like to stay there for two or three days. Please make the necessary arrangements."[21]

"During my mother's brief stay at Shantiniketan," recapitulates Mrs Gandhi, "we both lived at Uttarayan, Gurudev's own house. Trying to find my way around, meeting my teachers, left hardly any time to spend with Gurudev. During our rare meetings I remained tongue tied and inarticulate. . . from earliest childhood I had regarded Gandhiji and other eminent people not as great men or leaders but as members of my family. Even important foreign personages who visited our home seemed to get absorbed in the family circle; such was the tempo and informality of our life in Anand Bhawan. So in a way, Tagore was the first person whom I consciously regarded as a great man and, being painfully shy with strangers, I was completely overawed by his magnificent presence."[22]

It was also a far cry from Gujarati-speaking Poona and suburban Bombay. Shantiniketan was a haven of rural seclusion and the language was Bengali.

"I seemed suddenly to have landed in another world," Mrs Gandhi remembers, adding a typical humorous parenthesis, "in pre-Gagarin days this had quite a different meaning!"[23]

"She was a sickly child, all bones and very frail,"[24] says Chanda of Indira as she looked then, but on the question of whether they were all conscious of having to treat her in any special way because she was Nehru's daughter, he asserted that even though Nehru was a prominent man he was still just one of many nationalist leaders in 1934, and the question of paying undue attention to his child did not arise. The privileges, however, were implicit. Kamala and Indira were received at the station by Chanda himself, and not every student or his parents could stay at Gurudev's house.

"But Indira herself was a model student that way," says Chanda, who later taught her civics. "She was very correct in her studies and in her behavior. She mixed with all and sundry and merged her life into the institution."[25]

"You were conscious that she was Nehru's daughter," says Krishna Kripalani, who taught her English composition, "but not so much that she was like him, as how much she was unlike him!"[26]

The comparisons were implicit either way. She was too young to think of them then, but they were to shadow her throughout her life until she became prime minister, and more obviously after that. She did not have her father's exuberance, nor did she fly into the mercurial rages that made his behavior afterward all the more warm hearted. Much as she had admired the gusto for life and the great guffaws of laughter of her grandfather and the zest of her father, she herself developed over the years a cool sense of humor.

"She was intelligent, very attentive, serious. Too serious at the time," remarks Chanda. "She looked sad, and not very happy . . . ."[27]

It was almost as if there were no time to take off for happiness. She had barely been settled when within a month of her coming to Shantiniketan she had to rush back to Anand Bhawan. Her mother had fallen seriously ill, and in a few days her condition became so critical that the government released Jawaharlal to enable him to be with his wife. It was more than Indira or her father could bear to see Kamala frail and utterly weak, a shadow of herself, while her illness, now definitely diagnosed as tuberculosis, almost conquered her valiant spirit.

To Jawaharlal the entire span of eighteen years of marriage spread across his mind; all the early maladjustments, the petty quarrels over trivialities, "boy-and-girl affairs which did not last long," as he called them, ending in a quick reconciliation, his neglect of her because of his preoccupation with politics, Kamala's own advent into the political field and their growing nearer to each other, and then the imprisonment which made their rare meetings so precious, they would count the intervening days. It was a romance that flowered late, and now, just as they had begun to understand each other, surely she was not going to leave him, he thought, not now, when he needed her most.

For Indira too, her "brave little mummie," with "a heart of a lioness," as Jawaharlal termed it, was not just mummie but a friend. They not only looked alike but were enough of an age to be companions to one another. It was already August and in another three months Indira would be seventeen. Kamala was only thirty-five, in the prime of her womanhood. They were such a small family unit that mother, father, and daughter were extremely close. It could not break. But as Indira watched the cluster of friends and relatives around her mother's bedside, the tranquility of Shantiniketan seemed a dream and her heart contracted with a rising sense of desolation.

On August 18, Jawaharlal found time to reply to Chanda, who had made inquiries. "My wife's illness is giving us all a great deal of anxiety. She is, I am glad to say, just a little better but her condition continues to be serious. She is likely to remain bedridden for many months. I am glad Indira is getting on well at Shantiniketan," he added. "It is a pity she had to come away in the middle of term. Perhaps she may be able to go after a week or so. I am likely to return to prison in a day or two "[28]

Because Kamala had rallied slightly, Jawaharlal was indeed rearrested four days later but kept in Naini prison in Allahabad itself, and shortly thereafter, Indira returned to Shantiniketan. But in the minds of both father and daughter there remained the fearful question of Kamala's future condition. While Jawaharlal spent "the most damnable thirty days" in prison wondering how Kamala was because they would not take him to see her, Indira was worrying and fretting five hundred miles away during the renewal of her brief acquaintance with Shantiniketan. She forced herself back into the routine. After her mother had left in July, she had shifted to Shree Bhawan, the girls' hostel. They had to wake up every morning at 4 A.M. Each girl had a cot, a table, and a rack for clothes. She would make her bed, clean the room, have a bath, and join in the early morning drill with everyone else before classes began. The pattern of self-help was the same as in the Pupils' Own School, and so was the system of learning. There were two academic courses, the regular one after which the students could take the Calcutta intermediate examination and the Viswabharati one, Tagore's own, for which official recognition had been obtained. Indira naturally chose the more unorthodox Viswabharati course.

"There were very few buildings," says Krishna Kripalani, "no money, no government support—anyway, we believed in the open air; we all carried a two-foot square assan, taught fifteen students at a time and never marked any papers." It was a question, as he added, of "learn what you like, teach what you like."[29]

The students were encouraged in expression through craft and activity, and were also asked to maintain periods of meditative silence. There was emphasis on the performing arts. Indira gave herself up to the heady intoxication of these predominantly aesthetic ranges of experience in Shantiniketan.

At Tagore's suggestion she began to learn the Manipuri, one of the four main classical forms of Indian dance which has a shy, evanescent delicacy she found appropriate to her own form of expression. She would eagerly join her tall gangling friend Ghani at the Kala Bhawan, the art school building and spend happy hours drawing or painting. She was thrilled at having people of her own age around her; for the first time, she felt normal and free from the premature sense of responsibility that had plagued her younger years. She felt as if the load of resentment and bitterness had been lifted from her heart and her soft, hesitant smile turned more often to laughter.

But the habits of political conditioning and the activist itch of the founder of the Vanar Sena were strong. The soft breezes, the warm leisurely days, the songs in the air, the sound of dancing rhythms tapping the earth, the great sensuous environment of Shantiniketan as a whole could not divert her mind from a "political" course of action when a cause arose. The cause was to teach a visiting European professor of art a lesson. It was the custom at Shantiniketan to take off the shoes at the door of the classroom for the students squatted on the floor when inside a building or on the lawns or on little square carpets or mats when in the open. Even for painting lessons, the canvas or drawing book was placed directly on the floor in front of the student or on small slanting desks.

The fetish that the ancient Indian made of personal cleanliness made him turn this rather expedient habit of leaving shoes outside into a sanctified custom especially in places of learning and worship. The professor did not understand this custom or did not care to. He would invariably come into class with his shoes on. Indira decided that a "nonviolent agitation" would solve the problem. The next time the professor came, she and Ghani calmly led all the students out. When this happened repeatedly, the professor admitted defeat and thenceforth left his shoes at the door.

He was a Hungarian, Dr Charles Fabri, who in time became more Indian than the Indians themselves in his appreciation of Indian sculpture and art. In fact, he ultimately settled down in India, married an Indian girl, and almost ruled the art world of Delhi till his death in 1968. According to him, Indira was more sensitive than her father. "He had a great respect for art, but no feeling. Everybody knows that she was the 'eyes of Nehru.' She knows more than many of our art critics," he said. When they happened to be at an exhibition together he could see that she could spot a fake easily, although only the merest smile or a slight lifting of the eyebrows would indicate what she thought of a painting.[30]

When she first came to Shantiniketan, her growing interest in art together with her academic studies seemed to take place in spite of Gurudev rather than because of him. She stood in such awe of him that she did not have the courage to approach him. Once, however, chatting gaily, she and her friends were going past Uttarayan when they became aware of the poet watching them intently from his garden.

"We fell silent and shy wondering whether to stop or hurry past," recalls Mrs Gandhi. " 'Why do you stop laughing? Are you afraid of me? Why don't you come to see me sometime? Perhaps you will be bored, visiting an old man?' he questioned. We were horrified at the interpretation of our shyness and hastened to assure him that we had not wished to disturb him or waste his time. 'But what is time for?' he asked. 'I like young people.' After this complaint of negligence," she continued, "we saw quite a lot of him."[31]

In fact, since the ice was broken, she began eagerly to go with others to spend evenings at his feet listening to him talk, read out, or recite poetry. Sometimes they would just sit and watch him paint while on other occasions he would insist that their dancing lessons be conducted at Uttarayan itself so that he could see their progress for himself and make comments. Indira found that these evenings particularly opened her mind to the concept of the integrated personality, the "whole man" that Gurudev cherished. Jawaharlal had tried his best to instil in her an appreciation of the artistic wealth of the world, but her environment had previously been all political. Through Gurudev and his university she felt for the first time the arts warm her being. On the intellectual level, she found herself treading in the footsteps of Tagore, a familiar ground outlined by her father; cosmopolitanism of outlook in national and international affairs, a universality of spirit, and a breadth of vision that rejected all orthodox compartmentalization of values. "The complete man must never be sacrificed to the patriotic man, or even to the merely moral man," Tagore had once written to Charles F. Andrews. "To me humanity is rich and large and many-sided."

"These friendly meetings," Mrs Gandhi says now, "influenced me profoundly."

Her father had chosen well. Though Vakil had extemporized greatly on the theories of socialism, his school was a practical example of self-help, community living, and cooperative organization and in its art activities presaged what Shantiniketan would be. With Tagore she got a further dose of her father's internationalism, but together with that, a definition of her artistic sensibilities. All through, her father's influence did not wane. The historical series of letters were over, for he was engaged at that period in writing his autobiography, but there were, of course, the purely personal letters. Primarily, there were always the books he wanted her to read, and the consistency of her political discipline is revealed in an incident that took place toward the end of her stay at Shantiniketan.

It was February 6, 1935. As part of the country's recurrent clash with the British, even Shantiniketan found itself in trouble with the district authorities, who wanted to take away two or three students under one of the Detention Acts. However, the governor of Bengal, Sir John Anderson, decided to inspect the place himself and forestal any unpleasantness. But the institution was emptied and a general picnic was arranged for the students and most of the staff to be away. When the governor arrived he was taken around the girls' hostel also. In one of the rooms on a table he spied John Strachey's books on socialism and George Bernard Shaw's *An Intelligent Woman's Guide to Socialism.*

"Ah, that seems to be a Red lady's table!" exclaimed the governor.

It was pointed out to him that the table belonged to Nehru's daughter.

"Ah, that accounts for it," he commented dryly.[32]

On the first day of the Hindu New Year, April 13, which Shantiniketan traditionally celebrated with songs, dances and plays, Indira was excitedly preparing for her first solo appearance on the stage in a Manipuri number. She had shown such promise that Tagore had told her he would take her in his troupe which was to tour India later in the year to collect funds. She had already tried on the exquisite dance costume with its glass-studded, embroidered skirt, its matching *choli*, and its delicate transparent veil. She had always loved wearing costumes and this one was beautiful. It softened her sharp features and set off her fair skin, black hair, and slim body so that she looked really quite lovely. All Shantiniketan was alive with expectation of the evening festivities. And then the blow fell. She was summoned by Tagore and shown a telegram from her father saying that Kamala was seriously ill and that Indira should come immediately to be with her and take care of her. She took it stoically, though a flame of pain shot up through her body. She forgot her dance, the gay, comparatively untroubled months, the new found friends. It must be really bad for her father to have telegraphed her and she wanted desperately and immediately to be with her mother.

She left the same evening. A few days later Tagore, on learning that Indira was to accompany Kamala for treatment abroad, wrote to Jawaharlal, "It was with a heavy heart that we bade farewell to Indira for she was such an asset in our place. I have watched her very closely and have felt admiration for the way you have brought her up. Her teachers, all in one voice, praise her and I know she is extremely popular with the students. I only hope things will turn for the better and she will soon return here and get back to her studies."[33]

But for Indira there was hardly ever any turning back and the anchors kept slipping away.

7. OXFORD

Toward the end of August the year before when Kamala survived the crisis
that had brought Indira from Shantiniketan and Jawahar from prison rushing
to her bedside it had been decided that when she got a little better she should
be sent to the sanatorium at Bhowali, a tiny hill station in the United Provinces. Her condition, however, got steadily worse. The government suggested to Jawaharlal that if he would give even an informal assurance that
he would keep himself aloof from politics during the remainder of his term

they would release him so that he could look after Kamala. This was a gruesome predicament for Jawaharlal. To give the assurance meant a betrayal of his cause, his pledges, his colleagues, and "almost everything [he] held sacred!"[1] Not to give the assurance meant risking Kamala's life; there was no doubt that his presence made a lot of difference. But brave as she was, she resolved his dilemma. When he was taken to see her in early October, she had a high temperature and was almost in a daze. But before he left she asked him to bend down, and whispered, "What is this about your giving an assurance to government? Do not give it!"[2]

When she left for Bhowali she looked much better and he felt considerably relieved. Three weeks later he was transfered to Almora jail so that he could be nearer her. In the King Edward VII Sanatorium, where she was admitted, Kamala gradually improved and what had been an acute stage turned into a chronic one. Her "heart attacks," or the paroxysms of breathlessness, ceased, her temperature rose occasionally, but she gained about 16 pounds in six months, the maximum weight she ever had.[3] She did not sleep well, but she could sit up for her meals although she had to remain in bed otherwise. Jawaharlal would be taken to see her from time to time. Another devoted visitor she had was Feroze who traveled all the way from Allahabad whenever he could. Although he could not in the circumstances press his suit regarding Indira, the concern and solicitude he showed for Kamala must have softened her attitude toward him even more. It seems doubtful that Jawaharlal knew anything of Feroze's proposal to Indira at the time.

In March Kamala began a two-month course of Nordalin treatment. Soon her condition grew so bad that Indira had to be called. Krishna and Raja came from Bombay with their six-week-old son, whom both Jawaharlal and Kamala wanted to see. When Krishna took the baby to Kamala's room, she instinctively stretched out her arms to hold him but then drew back and said with tears in her eyes, "No. I do not want him to catch my disease."

"I couldn't care less," exclaimed the sorrowing Krishna, and wanted to thrust the big, fat, healthy baby into Kamala's arms. She refused to touch him and just lay there, "beaming and smiling all the time in her joy for me and delight in my son."[4]

By April it was decided that Kamala should go for treatment to Berlin. Her departure was fixed; she was to sail on the *Gange*, which would leave Bombay on May 23. Indira and a cousin of Kamala, Dr Madan Atal, would accompany her. But a third person who was trying desperately to work out a trip abroad at the same time was Feroze. He persuaded his family that conditions for his education would be more propitious outside politically torn India. Untouched by the stream of nationalist politics themselves, they viewed with relief the prospect of Feroze even wasting his time in Europe rather than serving repeated jail sentences and bringing official retribution down on the family in India. Nobody except Kamala and Indira knew that he was not prompted by academic interests alone. He was too attached to Kamala not to want to be with her during her illness, but that Indira was going along was an irresistible factor which made his decision imperative.

The day before Kamala left Bhowali, Jawaharlal was brought from jail to bid her good-bye. "To watch his face was heartbreaking," remembered Krishna as she and Swarup Rani stood close by. "His eyes held all the sorrow which he tried in vain to hide by a stern expression."[5] He watched the car take Kamala and his daughter away and as he walked toward his own, "he seemed suddenly to have lost the spring in his walk and the energy he always had."[6] The price of patriotism seemed heavy.

Indira was naturally disturbed and upset but that she did not let the situation daunt her was proved by the capable way she dealt with everything in Bombay.

"Kamala on the whole kept really well in Bombay in spite of the fatigue of the journey and the usual visits," a friend wrote to Jawaharlal on May 25, after their departure. "She was very happy that she had a long talk with Bapu. Dear little Indu," added this friend Psyche, "was decidedly the 'business heart' of the party."

And then, after Berlin, there was Badenweiller tucked away in the Black Forest in Germany, and in spite of her fortitude and her mother's, the daily fluctuations in health, in which hope and despair fought a long drawn-out battle. Feroze, who had gone to London to wait for admission to the London School of Economics, visited frequently and nothing could have been calculated to cement the relationship between him and Indira more. There were their existing feelings for each other; definite and decisive as Indira was, Feroze could not have proposed if he had not found a certain degree of reciprocity. There was the love they shared for Kamala; Feroze was so solicitious, gentle, and meticulous in his nursing of Kamala that Indira could not help but be drawn toward him. Kamala on her part, seeing the fair, stocky youth of 23 with his tenderness and his cheery good humor displaying such qualities of dedication, must have felt confident in his ability to look after her slender, pale wisp of a daughter. All three of them were so young. Kamala herself was only 37 and it was not difficult for Indira and Feroze to confide in her and seek her encouragement for their future plans. And then, for the first time both Indira and Feroze were away from the inhibiting environment of politics-dominated India and Allahabad, where others, if they themselves were not conscious of it, would seek to point out the differences in their families, their backgrounds, and their styles of living which could mar if not destroy their discovery of each other. Together with this, Badenweiller was beautiful, quiet, aloof, made for a romance to flourish even if it grew out of shared sorrow and the times were not happy.

Not all their devoted nursing and the efforts of the doctors, however, could stop the inroads that the disease was making on Kamala, and toward the end of August Indira sent off a desperate cable to her father to come. As early as October 1934 Tagore had issued an appeal to the government to release Jawaharlal so that he could be with his ailing wife. In reply the governor of the United Provinces had informed him that as Jawaharlal had been convicted for his speeches in Calcutta, the government of Bengal was the relevant authority and his letter would be forwarded to them. Nothing happened. On September 2, 1935, Tagore again appealed, this time in a telegram to the viceroy: "Have alarming news of Mrs Jawaharlal Nehru's condition. Doctors desire her husband's presence by her side. In name of humanity I appeal to your excellency to release Pandit Nehru immediately, enabling him to proceed Europe next air mail."[7] On September 3, the viceroy's secretary informed Tagore that he had received a similar wire from the chief medical officer of the Badenweiller Sanatorium and that Nehru would be released shortly. On September 4, Jawaharlal was told that his sentence was suspended and he was released. By September 9, he was with Kamala.

He found her bravely smiling but full of pain. By September 25 he was writing with a mixture of confidence and nervousness to Agatha Harrison, an English Quaker friend of the family, who worked hard for the cause of India's freedom: "Kamala is much the same. Yesterday there was another operation followed by a fairly thorough cleaning up and some disinfecting stuff put in. The job was a painful one but the patient bore it well. I'm inclined to think, perhaps it is my imagination, that she is just slightly better since I came but one cannot count on this much and the way her temperature shoots up to extraordinary heights frightens me."[8]

As he watched the mists steal up the valley or brooded in those lonely autumnal evenings in his room at the Pension Erhardt, where he and Indira stayed, his twenty years of marriage passed before his eyes in a vivid kaleidoscope of hundreds of images of Kamala—Kamala as a dear, lovable mystery which he had not been able to fathom; Kamala, "sensitive and proud, childlike and grown-up, foolish and wise."[9] Kamala, with her bright eyes and vital being, quick in judgment, instinctive in her likes and dislikes and her transparent sincerity. Kamala, in a rich and varied aspect as woman, and as an eager comrade-in-arms; Kamala, whom he had neglected in the beginning for his obsession with politics but to whom he had always returned as a sure haven; Kamala, torn from him by illness and by jail just when both had begun to realize how much they meant to each other.

Even now they could not converse very much with each other for Kamala would tire easily, but Jawaharlal would sometimes read to her a little at a time from Pearl Buck's *The Good Earth* which Kamala liked particularly, and several other books. So much, however, was unsaid. He remembered that in their brief periods together when he came out of jail he had sensed that she was "greatly troubled and distressed over many things,"[10] but they had tried to avoid discussing anything unpleasant so as not to mar the relief of being together. He wondered when they would ever have the chance again.

"I see that Kamala is putting forth a very brave effort," wrote Gandhi consolingly from India. "It will be rewarded. You know my partiality for nature cure methods. There are in Germany itself many nature cure establishments. Kamala's case may be past that stage. But one never knows."[11]

Politics, however, had followed Jawharlal within three weeks of his arrival in Badenweiller, for in the same letter, Gandhi wrote about the possibility of Jawaharlal's becoming the next president of the Congress. "Your letter about the wearing of the next year's crown was delightful. I was glad to have your consent."[12] With Gandhi's support it was already obvious that Jawaharlal's election as president of the Congress for the second time for the coming session at Lucknow in April 1936 would be more or less ensured.

A correspondent of the *Amrita Bazar Patrika,* giving an account around this time of a visit to Kamala, seemed to have caught the conflict this induced in her. "Mrs Nehru keeps up her cheerful spirit well and continues taking lively interest in affairs at home and abroad; but one has the impression that mentally she is worried, with many anxious thoughts...."[13]

It must have irked her proud spirit that she should have needed her husband so much at a time when the country needed him. If it had been possible to cure herself by will alone she would have done it.

"I earnestly hope that the amazing strength of mind which she has shown through all the vicissitudes of her life will help her," wrote Tagore anxiously from Shantiniketan. He did not forget her daughter. "Kindly remember me to dear Indira," he added. "I hope some day or other she will find the opportunity to revisit our ashram and revise her memory of those few months which she had spent here making us happy."[14]

Both Jawaharlal and Kamala were worried about Indira's education. Her intermediate course had been cut off midway at Shantiniketan. There was no question of sending her back. Jawaharlal had wanted her to go to Europe in the first place and now that she was there he began to wonder what to do. With the crisis of Kamala's illness at least temporarily over he began to plan a short visit to London with Indira and wrote immediately to Charles Andrews, who was in Cambridge at the time, about the possibilities of Indira's being admitted to Cambridge or Oxford. Indira herself indicated a preference for Oxford.

"Will you think over whether Indira would like to go to Cambridge, or has she set her heart on Oxford?" asked Andrews in a prompt reply. "If her mind is interested in science or mathematics, then Cambridge is best. But if she loves literature and history then undoubtedly Oxford."[15]

She evidently loved literature and history more, for Jawharlal wrote back to say that he would go up to Oxford himself and fix her admission there.

"The one person whom you must see," suggested Andrews, "is the Master of Balliol who is vice-chancellor and can tell you all about Somerville because his daughter was there. Then Bharati, Ambalal's daughter, will be there and Shahid is at Balliol and Amiya Chakravarti. If it is possible to see you in London I will do so but I can be of much more use to Indira if I run over to Oxford and see . . . the head of Somerville (whom I know fairly well) before you go up."[16]

Andrews was as good as his word. He went to Oxford and did his bit for Indira. He wrote again to Jawaharlal:

Bharati is eagerly looking out for Indu's arrival, and will help you in every possible way. I saw Mrs Lindsay, who is on the council and an intimate friend of Miss Darbyshire. Then I saw Miss Darbyshire. Everyone speaks so highly of her and she told me she would like so much to take Indu if she could qualify. Usually, the college, which is an Honors College only, requires a previous university course in India for Indian students in order to ensure their being up to honors standard. I told her the circumstances which had made that impossible with Indu and she would be ready to take that into account, but 'wouldn't it be best for her to take a year (or less) at an English school and be sent up from there?' I spoke of the importance of her being near to her mother if possible, but suggested that this could be talked over when you come to Oxford. She promised to give you full time for a talk if you could bring Indu with you.

The Nehrus concluded that the best course would be to take up Miss Darbyshire's suggestion and that Indira should be admitted to her old school at Bex in Switzerland to prepare for her entrance examination to Oxford. Kamala had improved considerably in health and was even out of danger.

Back in Badenweiller, Jawaharlal found the landscape white with snow. He took up the same routine, saw Kamala twice a day, and wrote and received a number of letters. Sometimes friends in Europe would drop by to see Kamala and be misled, as Jawaharlal wrote, "by those bright eyes and that smiling face" into thinking that she was better than she was.

In December something went wrong again; her condition became critical and to her despairing husband the calm winter scene began to appear like "the peace of cold death" itself. Somehow Kamala pulled through that also. She began to look and feel more cheerful, but wanted to go away from Badenweiller where the death of a young Irish boy in the same sanatorium was too depressing for her to bear. She also wanted a change. So they shifted her to Lausanne, and it seemed then that she was making slow but sure progress.

On December 19, Jawaharlal had heard from Rajendra Prasad, then Congress president, saying that the chances were that he (Jawaharlal) would be elected the next president and that there were important matters to be discussed. In January he went for a short visit to Paris and London and learned there that he had been elected. Meanwhile letters were pouring in from India anxiously questioning him on two counts: How was Kamala and when could he return?

Congress politics were in a state of crisis. A momentous thing had happened in October 1934 while he had been in prison. Gandhi had resigned from the Congress to devote himself to his social and economic programs, although his advice was sought at every stage of a major formulation of policy. Officially thereafter the Congress was committed to fighting to win in the elections. In 1935 it got a splendid response from the voters and the brilliance of Bhulabhai Desai as leader of the opposition in the assembly evoked nostalgic memories of the great Motilal and contributed in the same way toward dealing a series of defeats to the government.

Jinnah, who had struck a lofty but lonely attitude at the Round Table Conference in 1931 and almost cut himself off from Indian politics by settling down in England, returned, assumed the leadership of the Muslim League, and gained only 5 per cent of the Muslim vote in his bid in the elections. But he was to become a force to reckon with. A series of talks between him and Rajendra Prasad to devise a more acceptable alternative to the Communal Award resulted in failure, but in the teeth of almost universal Indian condemnation of the Joint Parliamentary Committee Report, the proposals of which were considered by the Congress to be even worse than those contained in the earlier White Paper, the new constitution was enacted in the English Parliament in 1935. "A charter of slavery," Jawahar called it, but British Conservative opinion, led by Churchill, viewed even such measures for self-government as a betrayal of the British Empire. To palliate both forms of opposition in India and at home, the government found itself in the awkward position of having to make the constitution seem like 'self-government to the Indians and like British raj to their own countrymen!' The Congress itself at the time was riven by dissenting opinions. There were those who had come in to seize leadership when the parliamentary programs had made politics safe; there was the strictly Gandhian group, and there were the socialists who had banded together to give a more revolutionary impetus to the urge for constitutional and economic reforms. Jawaharlal had been cut off from any active participation since his arrest and the setback while he was in Switzerland was considerable. He was, as he admitted, very much a political animal and it was difficult to perceive things going wrong and not be able to do anything about them. Jawaharlal consulted Kamala and the doctors at Lausanne and decided to fly back to India on February 28.

The choice was cruel—to leave Kamala as she was, or to resign. She herself would not hear of the latter course and said bravely that he should go and come back later. A few days before he was to leave, Indira came from Bex to be with her parents. She found the situation full of the tragic conflict that had bedevilled normal relations between her father and mother: the consciousness of political duty warring with personal need and, always, the latter was sacrificed to the former. It was clear that Kamala did not want her husband to leave her, but she would not say so. She knew he was needed in India, she knew that he needed to be there, and she would feel guilty if he had to change his plans. But she could not help wanting him to remain with her. In Jawahar, too, reason and feeling were locked in confusing agony. He wanted to go but he did not want to leave Kamala. There was nothing that Indira could do to solve her parents' dilemma except feel miserable herself. But then a strange change seemed to come over Kamala. She seemed to lose the will to live. Nothing else could explain the fact of her continuing physical well-being but her increasing alienation from her physical environment. She began to have hallucinations and the feeling that someone was calling to her. Jawaharlal gave up the idea of leaving on the twenty-eighth, but on that very day Kamala died. It was an uncanny coincidence and, given her hypersensitive nature, it seemed almost as though she had not just given up the will to live but had even willed herself to die so that her husband would be free to go.

Kamala was cremated at Lausanne.

India reacted to Kamala's death with a great burst of emotion. In Bengal the Congress committee decided that national flags should fly at half-staff for ten days. In Calcutta, a silent procession carried an oil painting of Kamala on a bier decorated with flowers, wreaths, and national flags, to Loha Ghat, where the flowers and wreaths were immersed in the holy Ganga amidst shouts of "Bande Matram" and "Kamala Nehru-ki-Jai." In Lahore and Bombay Indian businesses were closed. The Allahabad municipal board decided, "In commemoration of her great services to the cause of the country to denominate the city road as Kamala Nehru Road."[17]

Dr Rajendra Prasad declared: "In the passing away of Kamalaji the country loses a brave fighter in the cause of her freedom and a devoted helpmate to the idol of the nation....In order that the nation may have an opportunity of giving public expression to its sense of grief over this tragedy, I announce that Sunday, March 8th, which will be the tenth day of Kamalaji's death, be observed throughout India as a day of mourning."[18]

And over Anand Bhawan there lay a shadow. "Mrs Pandit was the only person in the family who showed remarkable presence of mind and was able to attend to numerous calls and phone inquiries and send necessary messages."[19] Kamala's mother had rushed to Anand Bhawan to meet Jawaharlal, but returned to Delhi sadly when she learned that he had postponed his departure from Europe.

Those were black days for Jawaharlal and his daughter. They went away to Montreux to be quietly together but the sharing of the blow softened it only a little. From Bapu a letter to Indira showed how perceptive was his confidence in her.

Dear Indu,

With Kamala gone, your responsibilities increase even more, but I am not worried for you. You have become mature and understand your duty well. Kamala had qualities which are generally not there in other women, and I am firm in my hope that these very qualities will find expression in you in the same measure. May God give you fortitude and the courage to make the graces of your mother, your own....[20]

For both Indira and Jawaharlal it meant a new orientation of attitudes. For Jawaharlal it would be a total commitment to politics and for Indira it would be a total commitment to a lonely father. Inextricably linked with both commitments would be the fortunes of their country.

"My one relief is to know that you were not compelled to leave her [Kamala] and then find that you could not be with her at the end," wrote Charles Andrews sympathetically to Jawaharlal. "That must be a consolation even in the midst of all you have suffered. I am wondering most of all," he continued, "whether you will be able to leave Indu behind, preparing for Oxford, or whether she will return with you. That must be a very difficult choice."[21]

Indira decided to stay in Europe. There was nothing to draw her to India at the time. Her father would be plunged immediately on his return into the whirlpool of politics. Anand Bhawan would hold only heart-breaking associations, and there was no one else with whom she could share her grief other than Feroze, who would be nearby, in England. She returned to Bex. It was difficult to concentrate on studies with that awful feeling of emptiness inside but that she managed to adjust herself well was revealed in the impressions that the Princess Aristarchie carried of her shortly after. The princess was an ardent follower of Gandhi and an admirer of Jawaharlal. In a letter to the latter after a visit to Indira, she wrote on April 2, 1936:

I have just returned from Switzerland where I was able to combine a visit to Indira last Sunday. She prepared for me a loving welcome, and we had lunch together at her school where I spent several dear hours with her, speaking of what [was] dear and sacred to us and Kamala was between us all along. It was a joy to see her in those beautiful surroundings, and working so bravely for her coming exam. God has blessed her with a heritage of will and of courage she has from both her parents—so you can be quiet about her. She is working for your sake, and that is giving her the necessary strength.[22]

Indira was even planning to go to Italy, for the princess mentioned that "her trip to Italy will surely do her good and be a help to her, all the more so, as Kamala had made her promise to go. That will mean her mother's special blessing accompanying her."

Not only did Indira keep her promise to her mother to go to Italy, but she seems to have reacted sharply to the political situation and shared with the princess at a subsequent meeting her disgust at Italy's role in Abyssinia and in the incipient war which was beginning to threaten Europe.

Indira kept herself in touch with events at home also because on Jawaharlal's request the princess began to pass on to Indira copies of the *Bombay Chronicle* that he sent her. But an observation she made in another letter to Jawaharlal about the trouble that Indira had taken, in the midst of her studies for her exam, in procuring a copy of her father's autobiography which the princess wanted, showed the respect she had for Indira's ingenuity. "I knew she would, if necessary, overcome any 'hitch'," wrote Princess Aristarchie.[23]

Soon after that, Indira appeared for her exam, and then left for London.

"I had to do Latin and European History for Oxford," she says now, "and it wouldn't have been possible to do it from the Swiss school. So I went to London to find out what to do."[24] When she rang up Agatha Harrison, who was really her guardian in Europe, she immediately asked her to join her for a lunch which she was having with Miss Baker, who was the principal of the Badminton School.

"'Miss Baker would be able to tell you,' said Agatha," recollects Mrs Gandhi, "so I went for the lunch and immediately after we finished Miss Baker suggested that I go with her straightaway. 'I'm catching the train in forty minutes,' she said. I had no clothes with me or anything, so I rushed and brought two dresses for ten shillings each—those days nothing would fit me, I was so thin!" And off she went to Badminton.

Her father was getting worried on a different count.

"I'm afraid all of you are rather spoiling Indira," he wrote to Agatha Harrison. "She has had a good deal of this kind of thing at home and the treatment continues abroad. It must be very pleasant for her but I hope that she will not succumb to it."[25]

Indira wrote and told her father that she liked Miss Baker's school, but whatever inflation her vanity might have suffered from the spoiling that her father was afraid of was flattened soon enough when she got the results of her examination. She had failed in her bid to enter Oxford. That she was upset was proved by the fact that she did not write for some time even to her father, and the circumstances in which she had had to study so soon after her mother's death did not seem to mitigate a sense of inadequacy. The only consolation perhaps was that she had had to make the attempt after her matriculation whereas other Indian students usually did so after their graduation from an Indian university.

"I was very sorry to have missed seeing Indira," wrote Sheila Grant Duff, a journalist friend of Nehru's to him after Indira had spent a few days at her home in August. "My mother praised her very highly to me . . . I am sorry about her exam but I'm sure it will be all right if only she has good tutors in the autumn. I think the Oxford exams are rather difficult for anybody who has not had an English education, but a good tutor would soon teach her what she lacks and once she is there," added Miss Duff significantly, "she will certainly find that she has a wider and better education than most of her contemporaries."[26]

"I was disappointed of course that Indira had failed in her examination," wrote Jawaharlal to Agatha Harrison, but though his views on academic rigidity had not changed, he realized what Indira might be feeling. "I do not attach too much value to examinations," he added, "but a sense of failure is depressing. I do not wish Indira to be depressed in that way and yet if she has any stuff in her, as I hope she has, it will no doubt do her good."[27]

It made her more determined certainly and, disregarding the initial setback, she plunged back into study. She remained at the Badminton School, where, like Shantiniketan, she found companionship with girls of her own age a pleasant experience. Early in 1937 she sat again for her entrance examination and this time she had the satisfaction of getting admission to Oxford, beginning with the October term.

She decided, on her father's suggestion, to spend the intervening months with him back in India. Meanwhile she had grown into a staunch antifascist. Her father had refused to meet Mussolini on his way back to India in 1936 in spite of persistent attempts at persuasion by the Duce's officials, but Indira would not even tolerate traveling by Italian ocean liners and told her father that she would far rather suffer the lengthy and complicated journey on a French boat sailing via Colombo![28]

If Indira and her father had hoped that her staying in Europe would ensure an uninterrupted academic spell, those hopes were dashed. The politically conscious young Indian students in London at the time were moved to participate in international politics because the passion for freedom had an immediate relevance to their own struggle for independence. The India League run by Krishna Menon gathered the scattered energies of Indians in Britain into an effective propaganda force, and was a sensitive organ of world reaction. Jawaharlal and Menon had got along well together when they met in London in 1935 during Jawaharlal's brief visit. Jawaharlal found in Menon the same tendency to place national aspirations in the context of world trends, the same emphasis on socialist belief combined with the same rejection of its totalitarian methods and the same unswerving faith in the parliamentary procedures of constitutional democracy.

But Menon's irascibility and Jawaharlal's peace-making impulses became evident even then for Jawaharlal found that a number of Indians, presumably incensed by Menon's attitude, had formed a rival to the India League called the Friends of India Society. But when he suggested that there should be unification, Menon staunchly stood his ground. It was obvious that Menon's gruffness was proportionate to his distrust of those whose motives were impure and to his own dedication to India's cause. It was this dedication that drew an ardent group of young students around him, which included Feroze Gandhi and Indira, and the elite of free India's future leadership: Bhupesh Gupta, Minoo Masani, Jyoti Basu, Mohan Kumaramangalam, Parvati Subroyan, Renuka Roy, and Nikhil Chakravarty. Menon was only forty years old but it was his recognition of the role that the youth of a country could play in its destinies that spurred the students to enthusiasm. They worked not only for the India League but for all the causes that sprang up then—Spain, China, the persecution of the Jews.

"I saw a lot of him [Menon] or, rather, a lot of his office," Mrs Gandhi remembers, "because I worked for the India League in the afternoons and evenings. In the evenings he was usually away organizing meetings. He was very good at that. Menon gave you the feeling there was something worthwhile to do for India. Otherwise there was no outlet at the time."[29]

Bhupesh Gupta, now one of the principal leaders of the Communist Party of India, who was then a great friend of Feroze and Indira, recalls that between 1936 and 1940 she was very much under the influence of Nehru's ideas. "She was broadly progressive and forward-looking. She had sympathies for the Spanish resistance; the working-class movement, especially the People's Front in France worked favourably on her mind. She was anti-fascist in outlook. She got interested in socialism, but very vaguely at the time."[30]

"I felt then," Mrs Gandhi herself says, "that it was not isolated whatever was happening. I was mostly bothered about Hitler. In the China-Japan war I was on the Chinese side—I helped in the publicity. I was for China because Japan had committed aggression."[31]

Typically, she worked in administration. As she herself says, she was good at it and at the detailed attention it required. The result was she kept busy being "secretary of this and treasures of that."[32] She was even secretary of a committee set up to condemn atrocities against the Jews. It again meant her intense interest found expression in work in the background. She managed to make occasional speeches in connection with the Spanish Aid Committee while others more creatively inclined would raise funds through cultural shows. But a gesture more in line with her impulsive enthusiasm was made when she offered a lovely bracelet of hers in an auction for the Spanish cause and had the satisfaction of seeing it fetch fifty pounds. She even helped in enrolling volunteers for the International Brigade for Spain, though it must have given her a hard jolt when Feroze himself decided to fight for Republican Spain. He was, however, prevented from doing so when British intelligence stepped in and impounded his passport. Throughout it was the sympathy for the underdog coming to the fore. Nations, she must have thought like her father, were very much like individuals after all.

If Feroze can be said to have influenced the future prime minister of India it was during those years in England when they were both evolving a personal equation to each other and to a political one outside of themselves. He was the more ebullient of the two. He took his bachelor of science degree from the London School of Economics in international law and diplomatic relations. He worked with the Royal Institute of International Affairs at Chatham House and as an apprentice in public administration with the London County Council, but he participated in the political issues of the day with a verve that matched that of the Nehrus. He could give a sharper edge to analysis of current affairs than Indira, according to those who knew them then, but he was also five years older. His leftism was marked and he was on more equal terms with Krishna Menon. "He was the radical type and a genuine anti-imperialist at that time," says Bhupesh Gupta.[33]

But he, too, looked for guidance to Jawaharlal and attempted throughout his stay in London to maintain some sort of intimate touch.

"I wonder if you would like me to send you cuttings from the *Times* and other papers referring to you," he wrote to Jawaharlal on June 3, 1936. "I am enclosing one which appeared yesterday. Every few days something appears either about you or Bapu. The other day London had an opportunity of seeing you in the news theater. It was the Movietone News but the editing was so bad that someone else was referred to as Jawaharlal Nehru. The film was probably shot at a Bombay meeting."

"I am going to Paris on the fifteenth and intend to stay there for two or three months," he confided to him further. "My next exam is at the end of September. The news from India is so disheartening that apart from getting excited I do not know what to do. I do remember word by word the conversations we've had and I am striving toward a better understanding of things in order to be of greater use than hitherto."[34]

Jawaharlal, without guessing that this was to be his future son-in-law, was considerate, sympathetic, and interested as he always was in younger men. Feroze was half his age, but he took him seriously.

"Congress work and the coming elections keep me so terribly busy that it is becoming increasingly difficult to read or write," he wrote back apologetically a few months later. "I have had no news about you but someone told me that you have been ill. I am sorry to learn this and I hope that you have recovered. Write to me how you are and how you are faring in your university college."

"It is not a bad thing," he advised, probably in answer to Feroze's doubts about his future career, "to have to decide for one's self. The point is that whatever one takes up one should do well. We have far too many second and third-rate people about. Any person really knowing his job is always welcome, whatever that job might be."[35]

Unlike Indira, Feroze was expressive, full of violent extrovert energy that dazzled her but was to lead to trouble later, while his enthusiastic plunge into the more active side of politics in contrast to her participation on the organizational side added zest to interest. He could not join the International Brigade, but he did go to Spain as well as Russia. He went to France to cover the general strike for the *National Herald* of Lucknow and the story of his trip that he later told his friends had the exaggerated risque humor which was to become his trade mark. It was a highly colored account of his camera being snatched away, the film being destroyed, and a night spent in a French prison cell. He added to this a fanciful detail in which he said he was stripped naked, made to stand on a revolving stool while the official photographer clicked away with his own camera. He was then ordered to stand still and the thought that he might find himself the subject of a pornographic series in French cards made him dissolve into guffaws of laughter. This was perhaps one of the earliest instances when the temptation to add spice to an anecdote proved too strong for truth, for Feroze would always warn his listeners in later years after relating a highly dramatic version of something: "*Aré bhai, discount kat dena*" (Friends, do allow a discount on this!). The style of humor was not likely to appeal to Indira's finicky sophistication, but the overflowing vitality, the cracking of jokes, the love of good food, and the *joie de vivre* that she found in Feroze were constant reminders of her grandfather. The incident made him a minor hero and she was too much in love with him by then to find reasons for disapprobation. A letter about this incident to Nehru by one young man of Menon's group, Rajni Patel, struck of course, a very high-minded note.

"You must have read in the Indian papers about the expulsion of Feroze and Kabadi [another journalist] from France . . . the sphere of liberty seems to be contracting everywhere."[36]

A year later, Feroze was urging Jawaharlal to lend them his moral support.

"My colleague Rajni Patel has already informed you that a committee has been set up in London for the purpose of sending medical aid to China. I am one of the secretaries of that committee. Perhaps you'd like to know that Krishna Menon was present at our first meeting but declined to serve on the committee as he says he has too many other things on hand at the present moment. Uday Shankar is giving a performance in aid of China under the auspices of the committee on the 30th October." He told Jawaharlal that the Chinese ambassador and Sir Francis Younghusband had agreed to be patrons and that at the end of November they proposed to hold a public meeting at Friends House. "I wish you would send us a message which we might read at the meeting," Feroze added hopefully.[37]

Rajni Patel and H. L. Haraon were also joint honorary secretaries of the

China-India Committee along with Feroze and in July 1938 a rather lofty
note in typical socialist terminology went out to the man who was hero
to them all.

"Dear Comrade Nehru," the note said. "The China-India Committee
has asked us to inform you that it welcomes the formation of the Congress
China Committee to send a medical unit to China." "Comrade" Nehru
must have been taken quite by surprise by this form of address, but the
enthusiasm of these youngsters was genuine and vital and as far as Feroze's
political impact on Indira was concerned, she admits now, "Feroze's being
there kept me focused."

She on her side drew him into the cultural world that she had become
so alive to when she was at Shantiniketan. They did not have very much
money between them. Feroze got an occasional allowance from his sister
and brother in Allahabad while Indira could draw upon her father's account
which consisted mostly of the royalties from his book and the sum that he
had set apart for her. He was concerned that she should not feel any lack,
but there was obviously no occasion for the extravagance that Motilal could
have afforded in his day for himself and for his son. Besides, Indira was
careful with money, as Shanta Gandhi recalls, and not prone to willful
spending at all. But tickets for an opera, ballet, or the theater were a must,
and if political involvement could make them stand for hours in the rain
just to catch a glimpse of the heroine of the Spanish Revolution,
La Passionaria, when she came on a visit to Britain, their love for the arts
could make them patiently stand in queue for the cheapest seats in the gallery
so that they could afford to see everything they wanted to. It was for an
evening at the theater that Indira one day told Shanta that she would bring
somebody "special" for her to meet. And so she introduced her to Feroze.
All her initial reserve had been dissolved with the torrid campaign to win
her that Feroze had conducted since they had been in Europe, but this
affirmation of her love to a third person seemed to set the seal on their
relationship.

But young, susceptible, full of love and admiration for him, at the very
height of their feelings for each other, Indira had a life apart from Feroze
which he could not share then or ever—her life with her father. In England
this took the form of opportunities for friendships with leading writers and
politicians that he could not share with her. Except for a few close friends
nobody knew Indira's and Feroze's feelings for each other and the question
of making it official would not arise until Jawaharlal himself could be told.
So Indira saw these people alone. In England she was acquainted with
H.N. Brailsford, Aneurin Bevan and Jennie Lee, Ellen Wilkinson, Sir
Stafford Cripps, the Dean of Canterbury, John Strachey and had as
friends Edward Thompson and his wife, C.F. Andrews, Ernst and Christianne
Toller, Paul Robeson and his vibrant wife. Eslanda Goode Robeson. In
Switzerland she had come to know many famous people, including those

who were special like Romain Rolland. It was a happy advantage even
if it meant an experience apart from Feroze. He was too young and
too busy to mind at the time, but it was a pattern which was to have a definite
effect on their later life for the feeling of being left out ultimately did begin
to play upon his mind.

Ironically, in England, Indira was not really happy with her environment.
She evidently told her father this in a letter in which she nostalgically mentioned Tagore. So when Jawaharlal in turn told Tagore, he said in his
reply, "I am indeed deeply touched by Indira's affectionate reference to me
in her letter. She is a charming child who has left behind a very pleasant
memory in the minds of her teachers and fellow students. She has your
strength of character as well as your ideas and I am not surprised she finds
herself rather alien to the complacent English society."[38]

And yet when her father suggested that Indira return to India for the
summer of 1937, the inherent conflict again presaged the pattern of the
future. Jawaharlal asked her in all innocence for he felt that Swarup
Rani who had had a paralytic stroke would like to see Indira. But it
was not easy for her at that stage to tear herself away from Feroze.
Nevertheless, the thought of her father, lonely and companionless, returning after a gruelling day's electioneering—for the Congress had
decided to fight the elections under the new constitution—to an Anand
Bhawan without Kamala, made the choice, as it always would in the
future, an inevitable one. She left for India on March 31 and less
than three weeks later found herself at Anand Bhawan, fighting back her
tears at everything that reminded her of her mother, but happy to see her
father and grandmother and excited at the ferment, this time of a constitutional nature, in which she found the country.

The results of the elections had come in. The Congress had won a splendid
victory. It secured an absolute majority in the legislative assemblies of the
five provinces of Madras, United Provinces, the Central Provinces, Bihar,
and Orissa. It was the biggest single party in four others—Bombay, Bengal,
Assam, and the North-West Frontier Province. The enfranchisement of
35 million men and women, even though that comprised one-tenth of the
population, caused a revolutionary stir. Thousands and thousands of
women made what they were asked to regard as virtually a pilgrimage to
Congress polling booths and so did men who could barely sign their names.
Fierce patriotic propaganda penetrated even their illiteracy and the result
was a silent revolution in political awakening. It had seemed anomalous
to fight an election under a constitution they were sworn to destroy, but
the Congress argued that this would give them a chance for a direct contact
with the masses and also enable them to know what sort of a mandate they
would get from them. It was a tumultuous victory.

There was a purely personal one for the Nehrus. Vijayalaxmi Pandit,
in the first of many achievements that was to set a record in women's parti-

cipation in the political world, sent off an exultant telegram to her three suspense-filled daughters waiting at Anand Bhawan. "Yes for Mummie." Only for a brief moment did they look at one another, puzzled, until Chandralekha shrieked. "Yeah for Mummie, it means "yeah for Mummie. Mummie's won the election!"

"Resigned to our use of American slang," recalls Nayantara, "Mummie had obviously thought 'Yeah' would be the most apt way to announce her victory to us and the telegraph office had of course changed the word thinking it was a mistake. We dropped our forks and joined in a wild dance round the dining table. We whirled into our grandmother's room where she and Bibima sat on the floor reading the *Ramayana* and sang out the good news."[39] Shortly afterward they celebrated again when they learned that their father, Ranjit Pandit, had defeated a wealthy and powerful local landowner!

But for Jawaharlal, as Indira found, it was not a period of unmixed joy. He was Congress president and in the past year his comparatively radical views had repeatedly clashed with the conservative wing of the Congress. Only his stern regard for party unity had prevented him from stepping down. A legacy she was to inherit many years later were the two streams of thought which always ran parallel in the party which, in 1936 during the Faizpur session for choice of president, found obvious representation on the one hand through Vallabhbhai Patel, who was to become free India's home minister, and on the other through her father, who was to become India's first prime minister. Together with his declared belief in the efficiency of a socialist policy, Jawaharlal vehemently opposed the idea of the Congress taking office if the eventuality even arose. It would imply, he said "an association to some extent with British imperialism in the hateful task of the repression of our advanced elements."[40] He thought the Government of India Act of 1935, as did most of India, "reactionary" in structure and with "no seeds of self-growth," but contrary to those who thought it could be combated from within he felt that nothing short of some kind of revolutionary action would do.[41]

Patel while opting out of the presidential election stated:

My withdrawal should not be taken to mean that I endorse all the views Jawaharlalji stands for. Indeed congressmen know that on some vital matters my views are in conflict with those held by Jawaharlalji. For instance, I do not believe that it is impossible to purge capitalism of its hideousness. While the Congress holds to nonviolence and truth as indispensable means for the attainment of independence, congressmen, to be logical and true to their profession, must believe in the possibility of weaning those who are mercilessly exploiting the masses from what is a crime against humanity. I believe that when the masses awake to the sense of their terrible condition they will know how to deal with it.

There is again no difference of opinion about the objective. All of us want to destroy the imposed constitution. How to destroy it from within the legislatures is the question, but on the issue of holding office if it came to that we know Jawaharlalji to be too loyal to the Congress to disregard the decision of the majority, assuming that the latter lays down a policy repugnant to him.[42]

On March 17, the All-India Congress Committee did in fact decide in favor of the Congress forming ministries wherever it had the majority provided, it insisted, "the Congress party in the legislature was satisfied and was able to state publicly that the governor would not use his special powers of interference or set aside the advice of ministers in regard to constitutional activities." This set off a constitutional wrangle that began to exercise the legal brains of both India and Britain. Could such an assurance by each governor be given within the provisions of the act? While the debate raged, the governors refused to give the assurances and the country went through the odd experience of the majority party refusing to touch office; the administration of the provinces was conducted by interim ministers. After three months the viceroy issued a statement in an attempt to clear the air of misunderstanding. Its basic tenet was that while the governor was called upon to exercise his special powers in extreme contingencies, this did not mean that such contingencies should turn into realities, and that in the everyday administration of the provinces the governor was bound to go by the advice of his ministers.

The Congress accepted office in July 1937 and one of the ministers appointed in U.P. was the beauteous Vijayalaxmi, the second woman in the Commonwealth to acquire such status. There were happy instances here and there of cooperation between the civil service and the nationalists-turned-ministers whom they had fought before, but nothing altered the strict injunctions under which Congress legislators were to function. Congress policy declared:

The Congress has entered the legislatures not to cooperate with the new constitution of the government but to combat the act.

The objective of the Congress is *purna swaraj,* or complete independence, and to that end all its activities are directed.

The immediate objective of the Congress in the legislatures is to fight the new constitution, to resist the introduction and working of the federal part of the act, and to lay stress on the nation's demand for a constituent assembly.

Congress members of the legislatures must remember the Congress policy of not assisting or cooperating with any function or activity, calculated to enhance the power or prestige of British imperialism in India.

No Congress members of the legislatures may accept a title given by the British government.[43]

There were other conditions and it was Gandhi's idea that the Congress should seize the opportunity to effect its constructive economic program. His advice was characterized by the subtlety that had made politics under him a strange and unusual instrument indeed. He thought that Congress representatives could thwart "the assumed intention of the framers of the act" by "lawfully using the act in a manner not expected of them and by refraining from using it in the way intended by them."

The tension, however, was so great during and after the elections that Jawaharlal suffered one of his rare lapses from good health. He fell ill and within a few days of Indira's arrival in India she was called upon to play, for the first time in her adulthood, a role that was to become familiar, that of her father's unofficial deputy. Jawaharlal had been invited by Tagore to inaugurate the China wing of Viswabharati. The ceremony was to acknowledge a magnificent donation of Rs 50,000 and a huge library made by the people of China to India. Tagore was anxious that the work of the Sino-India Cultural Society, which included as one of its organizers Marshal Chiang Kai-shek, should get off to a good start with a "beautiful gesture."[44]

"I cannot think of anybody better fitted than you for the opening ceremony," Tagore had written feelingly to Jawaharlal, and added, "Do not forget to bring Indira along with you."

"I shall be with you in spirit," Jawaharlal wrote back regretfully but he sent Indira "to pay her respects [to you] and to meet old friends,"[45] and she also dutifully carried his speech to be read there.

The next month, for the second time since Ceylon, she found how exciting it could be to go on an official trip abroad with her father, for in May, they went to Burma and Malaya. Had she been a different sort of person she might have wanted to relax at home after a year of studying, scrimping on money, and lacking the comforts of home. But in spite of her shyness she found travel "fascinating," and "loved meeting new people and getting to know about their customs and food."[46] She was never to lose her taste for it. This was also the first time she had a chance to be with her father as an adult. But close as she came to him she still was not as close to him as she had been to her mother, and she could not yet mention Feroze.

By June Jawaharlal was beginning to get worried. Indira had lost weight. Perhaps, he thought, it was because of the hot weather she had had to face after two years of a cooler climate. Partly, as the doctors said, it was due to her tonsils, which they decided should be removed. But in some part it was certainly due to the tension within her. Like her mother her physical condition and mental state were liable to be far too closely interlinked.

"Meanwhile she has suddenly been reminded by the Somerville people," wrote Jawahar anxiously to Agatha, "that the Latin test has still to take place. Also she must read up a large number of fairly heavy books in English, French and Latin to prepare for the coming term at Oxford."[47]

At the end of July she had her tonsillectomy and a month later she began to pay her farewell visits.   On September 11 it was good-bye to Papu.   She took the P & O liner, *Viceroy of India*,[48] and in less than three weeks again, it was Paris for a few days, London, Feroze—and in October, at last, Oxford.

Oxford was beautiful, with its narrow streets, its spired university buildings and its air of quiet ferment.   This was no sylvan retreat like Shantiniketan, where the days were like a lazy stream finding its inevitable direction with hidden insistence.   Here there were tempo, competition, and challenge, and the mind had to be alive to every human and intellectual provocation.   Here, too, was a onymity which prevented her from being overconscious of being Nehru's daughter.   In fact, she felt terribly shy and only some of her fellow Indian students could have thought of attributing her apparent aloofness to   "Nehru exclusiveness." She had a dreadful evening when as a new and "painfully shy undergraduate," as she herself puts it now, she received her first invitation to eat at the high table.

"I found myself sitting next to a tall, gaunt woman with sinister dark hollows under her eyes who was our Dean," she recollects.   "She turned to me and with an air of putting me at ease, asked 'What are your views on music, art and literature?' "[49]

She does not say what sort of an answer she managed to give to that, but as a public speaker she remained a disaster.   Not that she spoke badly but she did not speak at all.   At the meetings of the union or the debates organized by the Majlis, the Indian Students' Society of Cambridge, she proved to be remarkably like her father.   Jawaharlal had been so shy in his youth that he frequently had to pay the fine imposed by his college debating society, the Magpie and the Stump, on members who did not speak for a whole term.   Indira, too, listened avidly, but remained silent.

"She was a quiet, shy, modest girl who liked to keep in the background,"[50] one of her contemporaries said, but a more cruel judgment was one which describe l her as "basically inadequate intellectually."[51]   There was worse to come. She herself described the occasion when she attended a big meeting on China for which she had gone from Oxford to London, and where she had been asked to speak.   When one of the organizers got up and announced, "Miss Nehru will now speak," she got so nervous she did not know what to do.   "I could not speak a word," she recalls.   "Someone even got up and said, 'She does not speak, she squeaks.' "[52]

She did not have a chance to develop according to her own tempo because willy-nilly she was expected to meet the great expectations people had of her because she was Jawaharlal's daughter.   If this pushed her into situations which she might not have otherwise invited upon herself, like that attempt to speak at the China meeting, it also made her withdraw safely into herself so that there should be no question of argument about the qualities that she had or had not inherited from her father. Nobody could guess then, as they had not been able to from Jawaharlal's years at Cambridge, that this embarrassed reticence marked an ability that in time would enable her to address hundreds of thousands of people at an average of twenty-five public election meetings a day without batting an eye. But as a nineteen-year-old at Oxford, she had to feel her way carefully.

Indira veered naturally toward the leftist group in Oxford. The atmosphere made some sort of political alignment almost a necessity, even in British nationalist politics, and she naturally chose Labour over Conservative and began to work for the Labour party', student wing. She enthusiastically attended mass political rallies, for if she was not vociferous, she was very intense. She became a member of the Left Book Club but, according to Nikhil Chakravarty, there was an Indian bookshop owned by a Sinha who had standing instructions from Jawaharlal Nehru to supply her with the books she wanted. All her quietness, however, did not still strong convictions. She not only loved but admired—even hero-worshipped— her father, but she could be critical when the occasion demanded and she was not afraid to show it. She once attended a debate organized by the Majlis which centered on the proposition that the "Congress leadership should be more revolutionary." Among the speakers were Nikhil Chakravarty from Oxford and Yusuf Meherally from the socialist group in India, who was visiting Britain, and in the course of the debate a lot of broadsides were fired at the Congress and even Jawaharlal. Indira just listened, but when it came to the votes being taken at the end, she firmly raised her hand in favor of the proposition. Bhupesh Gupta, who is one of the severest political critics of Indira's government now, talks of her with a personal regard that dates from their student days together and recalls that he once wrote an article for the magazine of the Federation of Indian Students in London called *The Student* of which Parvati Subroyan (now Parvati Krishnan, prominent in the Communist party) was the editor. "It was a strongly critical article on Nehru," claimed Bhupesh. "I showed her [Indira] the article, and had the feeling that she agreed with some of the things."[53]

But Bhupesh Gupta went wrong in his assessment of what Indira is like now, as prime minister. In talking about their years in England, he mentioned that she had once been invited to speak at the annual convention of the British Communist party and that she got a standing ovation. The party in those days, he made haste to point out, strongly supported the Indian cause for independence, but he doubted if, in view of her stand against communism now, she would like to admit having associated in any way with the activities of the British party or would like to have it written about. But when I asked Mrs Gandhi whether she had spoken at this meeting she did not show the slightest hint of embarrassment. She was quite casual and forthright. She shrugged her shoulders. "I may have. In those days, for anybody who gave a platform, I was prepared to speak. The idea was to propagate Indian freedom."

Before the Tollers migrated to America where later the brilliant young

Ernst committed suicide in despair against the rising tide of Nazism and his inability to go back to his beloved Germany, Indira had met his wife Christianne for lunch in London. As a playwright and political agitator and leader of social revolutionary movements in Germany, Toller was sentenced to one year imprisonment in 1919 and deported in 1933. Of her meeting with Indira on August 26, 1936, Christanne wrote to Jawaharlal: "I only want to tell you how delighted I was to have met her. Not only that she is so beautiful, but so pure which makes one feel very happy...she seemed to me like a little flower which the wind might blow away so easily, but I think she is not afraid of the wind."[54]

Two years later Jawaharlal himself realized that it was not so easy to "blow" his daughter in any direction even in the matter of his political engagements about which he could have been presumed to exercise competent judgment. Not that she attempted to prevent him from meeting certain people, but she reserved the right not to accompany him, even when she was particularly invited, if she did not approve of their politics. This happened in the matter of Lord Lothian. He had very much wanted to meet Jawaharlal during his stay in Europe in 1936 but it had not been possible. In 1938, Jawaharlal decided to go to Europe for the summer.

"It is true that the position here is getting extraordinarily complicated," he wrote to Agatha from India, "and one does not like to shirk responsibility at the time of difficulty. But I feel stale and it seems a little difficult even to carry on till the next Congress. I should in any case like to see Indu. To ask her to come to India in summer would mean that she would have the worst time of the year in India."[55]

But a trip to England meant a spate of personal and public engagements and one of the first persons to invite him and Indira for a weekend at Blickling Hall, "one of the most beautiful houses and gardens in England,"[56] as he had himself described it, was Lord Lothian. Jawaharlal had exchanged exhaustive correspondence with Lothian and was quite anxious to meet him. He immediately wrote to Indira about it, but as he described it to Agatha later, "her [Indira's] personal reaction to it was not favorable as she objects to Lothian's pro-fascist politics."[57] In fact, she pleaded a prior engagement. But that Indira had begun to play a part in her father's affairs was revealed by Jawaharlal's reply to Lothian in which he said he would like to visit him but pointed out at the same time that his engagements were being fixed at the London end.

"Mr Krishna Menon of the India League . . . is in charge of my program and I believe he is drawing it up in consultation with my daughter, Indira. If you could kindly get in touch with my daughter (Somerville College, Oxford) or Mr Menon, this would prevent overlapping."[58] Lothian in fact issued another invitation to Indira, asking her if she could not possibly cancel her other engagement, and when Jawaharlal reached London, he argued with her on the merits of always listening to what the other side had to say even if it put one in a rage. So eventually she did go but, as she says, in a very aggressive frame of mind. It turned out to be highly interesting because some of the other guests included Lady Astor, General Ironside, "one of the best soldiers in England,"[59] as Lothian said, Thomas Jones, who was Baldwin's adviser when he was prime minister and, of course, Lord Lothian himself. Even if she merely listened to the discussions that took place it was an apprenticeship in participation for the twenty-year-old girl that was difficult to rival; the pattern for her political training as in childhood in India was direct. She did not have to read in books what she could see happening in front of her. Largely because of her father which gave her an advantage over others and also because she herself wanted to be, she was invariably at the heart of events.

Later in the summer of 1938, Indira accompanied Jawaharlal to Europe— the Europe "with Mr Neville Chamberlain's appeasement in full swing and marching over the bodies of nations, betrayed and crushed, to the final scene that was staged at Munich."[60] Both Indira and Jawaharlal went to Czechoslovakia and watched at close quarters,[61] how subtly political hypo- crisy found a way to break faith with friends and principles on the most moral grounds. They then followed events leading up to the Munich crisis from Paris, Geneva, and London. In Munich Jawaharlal took time off from his own sense of political despair to indulge in a favorite activity: he took his daughter on conducted tours of the famous Munich museum. They found Indira's teacher from the Pupils' Own School, Raghubhai Naik, living in Munich, and sometimes the three of them would go to the museum together. They stayed in the best hotel in Munich, the Vier Jahreszeiten, recalls Naik. He also remembers that the German government was very insistent that Jawaharlal be their state guest, but he was as resolute about having nothing to do with Hitler as he had been about Mussolini. But oddly enough, what impressed Naik most about their stay in Munich was Jawahar- lal's infectious enthusiasm about the museum and his desire that Indira should derive the most from it.

"Those days, the Munich museum was the only one of its kind in the world," says Naik. "There was a literature section, an art section, but more of science. You could X-ray your own hand, and if you pressed a button an artificial coal mine would start functioning. Jawaharlal was very keen that Indira should see the whole of it, and what was especially interesting was that during their stay there he would take her to the museum everyday."[62]

This was an enjoyable interlude, but soon after, back in London, Indira fell ill with pleurisy. Vijayalaxmi who was visiting England at the time also fell ill and Jawaharlal was left with the familiar task of looking after two ailing Nehru women. Letters of concern poured in from India, in- cluding a cable from Bapu. Indira's full term at Oxford was nearing and when she improved a little both she and her father settled down to discuss what subjects she should take.   They eventually decided that she should take the public and social administration diploma, the French group and subjects needed for Moderations, "the first public examination, after passing which," as Helen Darbyshire, her principal at Somerville confirmed, "she will have qualified for the B.A. degree."[63]

"I will make application next term," promised Miss Darbyshire in a letter to Jawaharlal about Latin which seemed as "dead" to Indira as Sanskrit, "to get her exempted from Latin," but that she had been fairly impressed by Indira even during the short period of less than a year that she had been at Somerville seemed evident in the remark she made in conclusion.   "I am very glad," she wrote warmly, "that we are to have Indira back."

A week later it became evident that Indira's Oxford sojourn would have to be interrupted, like her studies at Shantiniketan, if not given up altogether. She was too weak to brave the cold of an Oxford winter and the doctors advised a better climate.   Jawaharlal decided to take her back with him to India.

"I will of course keep a vacancy for her for the next academic year, from October 1939," assured the cooperative principal of Somerville in a rare gesture.   "At the same time it is very likely that if she is well enough and the doctors recommend it, we might have a place for her for the summer term."[64]

For Indira it meant parting from Feroze again, yet not be able to tell her father about him and the frustration of leaving Somerville just when she was getting used to it.   The winter of 1938 was not likely to be like the winter of 1937, she must have thought mournfully, when she and Shanta had gone off for the holidays to south Germany for the winter sports and had had a marvelous time skating, skiing and mountain climbing.   It is likely that Feroze accompanied them although from his letters to Jawaharlal it appears that he was busily engaged with the affairs of the China India Committee.

Sensitive as Jawaharlal was, he had the same blind spot of any father, for he could not still see Feroze as anything more than one of those who had frequented Anand Bhawan so often that he had been accepted as part of a devoted circle of friends, and because he was young, it was natural to accept him as a companion of Indira.   For her the pleasant prospects of rest and comfort at home had a heartbreaking corollary: to leave her relationship with Feroze unresolved.

But on October 11 Jawaharlal wrote to Moustapha El Nahas, the leader of the Wafd party, that he hoped to break the journey back to India in Egypt.

"My daughter is accompanying me back," he said.   "We expect to sail from Marseilles on the S.S. *El Nil* on October 26, reaching Alexandria on the afternoon of October 31.   We have to catch our boat to India from Port Said in the early morning of November 9 so we shall have eight clear days in Egypt."[65]

The regard, affection, and welcome Jawaharlal and Indira got in Egypt was to predispose them even more in the future toward a common Indo-

Egyptian "fight against imperialism while safeguarding our respective independence,"[66] which Jawaharlal already held dear. But it was perhaps the intimacy with which Jawaharlal and the Egyptian leader discussed affairs of state that led to a rumor that they were planning even closer bonds, like the marriage of Indira with the Pasha's son. Indira's name at this time was being linked with some of the young bachelors from suitable families by hopeful elder relatives, but like the proposal that had come when she was sixteen which had "the family laughing for days," the story of the Pasha's son now provided as much mirth especially when people realized that El Nahas did not have a son!

Back home in Allahabad, Anand Bhawan yawned emptily. Both Swarup Rani and Bibima had died the year before, three months after Indira had left for Oxford, and the house felt lonelier than ever. Almost the first thing she now did was to march into Swaraj Bhawan opposite, where the AICC office was and enroll herself as a fullfledged member of the Congress party. She had realized with satisfaction that as she was now twenty-one they could not turn her back as they had done nine years ago. But the time to vindicate that incident was still to come. For the present the immediate problem was to get back to England and Feroze and to complete her studies. Within a few days of their arrival she told her father that she must go back.

On January 4, Jawaharlal wrote to Madan Atal: "Indu went to Almora three weeks ago. She is fairly well but does not pick up strength as she should. She wants to go back to Oxford for the summer term but I fear she will not be strong enough to do so."[67]

On February 3, he wrote again. "Indu has come back with me from Almora. She is certainly better but she has not put on much weight and is still liable to get tired easily. I do not quite see," he added, slightly worried, because the war cries in Europe were beginning to acquire volume, "how she can go back to Europe this summer. My own view is that she should not. But she seems rather keen on it."[68]

Two months later, he admitted defeat.

"Indira is returning to England next week," he wrote on April 6 to Madan, who was by then in Yenan as leader of the Indian medical unit. "She is not going to Oxford for the summer. I hope she will go to Switzerland for some time, but as you know, Europe hovers on the brink of an abyss."[69]

It did not make him feel any better when he heard from friends who reiterated his fears: "War looks more imminent than ever before," wrote Rajkumari Amrit Kaur. "I am sorry Indu has gone back to that atmosphere."[70]

Why, one wonders, did he yield to her pressure against his better judgment? She was not even going back to Oxford and she could have recuperated in Kashmir as well as in Switzerland. Jawaharlal's attitude toward his daughter at this time provides the key to their future relationship when the increasingly significant role that Indira was to play along with her father in the political affairs of her country began to invite speculative theories that she was her father's shadow. This did not do justice to either of them. Jawaharlal, as later correspondence shows, was careful almost to the point of obsession not to impose his will on his daughter. Second, he did not like his decisions to be governed by thoughts of physical danger and he probably wished her to develop the same fearlessness. Third, it seems that he had begun to realize that her heart was in Europe and that there were problems that she might like to resolve on her own. So, as he always would in the last analysis, he let her go her own way.

It turned out differently from what Indira had imagined. She got to England, and soon after left for Switzerland. It was probably on the trip to Switzerland that Feroze accompanied Indira, for he took a number of photographs which he later sent to Jawaharlal. The tone of the letter reveals a greater intimacy than before with his prospective father-in-law.

"The photographs are in technicolor," wrote Feroze. "To view them just hold them against the light with a white paper in between the picture and the source of light. It is also possible to project them on the screen. As these are negatives," he advises Nehru with the concern of a man fond of photography, "will you kindly put them away someplace where we can get at them later."

The photographs were meticulously listed as having been taken at "the river at Stanstaad," "the hotel lawn," "outside the hotel at Bergenstock," "the lake at Stanstaad" and "at Luzern," the "Jochpass" and so on. One is particularly arresting.

"Luzern at night from Indu's window at Bergenstock," it says. To this Feroze adds an interesting bit of information. "As a fellow amateur," he says to Jawaharlal, "it might interest you to know that the exposure for this was five and a half hours."

"Some days back when I was in Bombay your friend who had come back from England gave me the technicolor photographs," wrote back Jawaharlal. "They are remarkably fine pictures," he added with perhaps the stirrings of awareness of what was going on, "and, if you have taken them, as I presume you have, I must congratulate you."

By August 8, Agatha Harrison was informing Jawaharlal from London, "Indira has come back looking, I think, distinctly better. It was so wet in Switzerland that she lost all interest in being there. At present she is staying with Nan Adams till she sees Dr Bhandari. I hope she will decide to go off to the sea somewhere and not stay in London. She thinks she will do this."

On September 3, 1939, World War II began.

Indira stuck to her plan to go to Oxford for the fall term.

Jawaharlal had told her before she left in April, when they had discussed the possibility of war, that she should remain at Oxford for a while and later if she felt like it she could go to the United States. Even if she thought of returning to India, he argued, the better way would be by way of the States. She could spend a few months or a year in some college or institute there, but he left it to her to decide what she wanted to do.

"It is not the actual physical danger that troubles me," he wrote to Agatha, "but the nervous tension which must necessarily exist all over England ... we cannot think in terms of a long course of study during these changing times." After giving Agatha some details of the college that Indira could go to in America or the many friends who could help her if she decided to go there, he repeated, "So far as I am concerned I shall agree to any decision taken in this matter by Indu. I cannot wish her to feel in the least that I am imposing any decision on her."

On August 26, Kailash Kaul, Indira's maternal uncle who was also in London at the time, informed Jawaharlal that she looked much better after her stay in Switzerland. "For a few days she stayed here," he adds, "but now she has gone out to a place called Penn."

"I had a cablegram from Indu a few days back telling me that she was at Penn and well," wrote Madan Atal all the way from Yenan in China. This was on September 27. "She will probably be at Oxford in the next few days," he added, then remarked consolingly, "I daresay Oxford is as safe a place in England to be [in] as any other."

Penn proved to be her undoing, however. She was caught in the rain, got a chill, and developed pleurisy of the kind she had had the year before. This time it was Jawaharlal who told Madan sorrowfully, "She was unable to go to Oxford and instead went to a hospital."

In a London hospital during wartime. It was not a situation calculated to put one in one's best mood. There was Feroze, solicitous and full of humor, but who must have worried like Jawaharlal in India and perhaps like Indira herself deep down in her heart, that her health would follow Kamala's unhappy example. However, Indira showed the resilience that Jawaharlal had hoped she would have in tackling difficult circumstances.

One day while she lay in the hospital, Mrs Gandhi remembers, there was a false air raid alarm.

"The siren went off wrongly," she says, "and there was absolute panic. The nurses began to shout nervously 'Shall we put you under the bed?' 'For God's sake, let me alone, you do your work,' I said. It didn't frighten me."[71]

But the value she places upon ritual became apparent again when she pointed out the efficacy of the method used by the hospital to control that sudden and utter confusion. It was a kind of ritualism according to her which decreed a disciplined adherence to a particular activity in the midst of danger. "For instance," she says, "it was decided that each person should go on doing a job. One nurse must make tea, the other must talk to the patients, and so on." For herself, it was obvious, the panic was stilled by standing by her duty as a patient, to stay in bed.

Indira's illness in London cut off at one stroke the possibility of her return to Oxford. When she improved the doctors suggested she should go to Devon. After that the choice was strictly limited.

"England during winter and during wartime is hardly a suitable place for an invalid," wrote Jawaharlal worriedly from India. "I do not suppose Switzerland is a desirable place to go to under present circumstances and there is no other place on the continent." There was the United States, but only if she were strong enough. And of course there was India. "In this matter, however," repeated Jawaharlal, "Indu's wishes must decide. I do not want her to do anything against her own inclination. Therefore decisions should be made in England in consultation with the doctors and Indu."[72]

Agatha Harrison and Indira decided that she should go to Switzerland and the kindly Agatha offered to accompany her there.

"What a lot of trouble you are taking about Indu," wrote a grateful Jawaharlal. "I do not propose to say much about her future program." Again he added, "This must be decided at the other end . . . as to the place in Switzerland, this also can be decided by Indu and Bhandari, her doctor." Like his father, especially in this case, he was unconcerned about the expenses that the treatment entailed.

"This is obviously investment for the future," he agreed with Agatha, "and it would be folly to avoid a course of action which is indicated because of the expenses involved in it. This present expense is not only necessary now but may save us a great deal of trouble and expense later. So in no event must that come in the way."[73]

On December 15, Indira and Agatha left for Leysin.

Indira liked the place immediately and it was even more cheering when, as she wrote to her father, the doctor promised to "transform her into a Diana in the course of three months."[74]

The quiet and the peace there also gave her an opportunity to discuss her own state of mind at length with the understanding older woman. Jawaharlal apparently guessed at the period of emotional tension that Indira was passing through and in a letter to Agatha revealed an attitude that was well-nigh exemplary: it contained that mixture of concern, love, reserve, and understanding that was gradually to draw the most willing dedication from his daughter over the years.

He wrote to Agatha:

I quite agree with what you say about Indu. She is going through a very difficult period of her life. None of us can be of very mnch help to her. She will have to find her way out herself. All we can do, and that is very little, is to enable her to find herself. I am terribly afraid of interfering in any way and thus add to the difficulties of the situation.

When she wrote to me that she was very anxious to come to India I was put in a difficulty. To discourage her seemed to me wrong. To encourage her was also not very desirable. I was convinced in my mind that she had really no desire to come to India but her affection for me and her wish to be of some help to me were forcing her to want to return to India. This was not a sufficient reason and it would have led to an intensification of the conflict within her. In a sense this conflict would have taken the shape of what she considered to be her duty overriding her own clear wishes. I do not want her to have that conflict. She should come back to India not because of me but because of herself when she feels that way. I wish she could realize this and put away any sense of obligation from her. That in itself would relieve the tension in her mind.[75]

The changing war scene was constantly imposing the necessity for new decisions on father and daughter, but Jawaharlal in each case left it to his daughter to decide what to do. In the same letter to Agatha he added: "Recent developments have raised new questions and I have cabled to Bhandari accordingly. I hope he has been able to go to Leysin. There is obviously a possibility of Indu not being able to stay on in Switzerland. What she should do then is for her and the doctors to decide. Many of our friends here grow excited and ask me to arrange for her to fly back to India. I am going to do no such thing."[76]

In May Dr Bhandari went to Leysin and in consultations with the other doctors decided that Indira should stay on there until the winter. She had improved in health during the four months she had been there.

"Indu was anxious to come back to India," Jawaharlal confided to Madan Atal, "but it was felt by the doctors that her treatment would be seriously interfered with if she returned now. I left the decision to Bhandari and Indira herself."[77]

"My daughter is caught up in Switzerland," two months later he wrote to Esse Robeson. "Now it is not possible for her to go out apparently till the war ends and no one knows when that will be. I cannot even correspond with her. Only cables can be sent."

By then, Leysin was considered to be one of the safest places even if Switzerland became involved in the war. England was more dangerous than before while the route back to India was also fraught with risk. But while Indira was compelled to wait she began to feel unhappy and restless, and even Leysin began to seem quite "uncongenial." By November she thought she had had enough rest, she had derived whatever benefits she could from the clinic and she decided she should go home to India for good. At first she thought she would take the "first available plane,"[78] but on the way London beckoned, war-torn, war-damaged but brave and exciting. London was also where Feroze was. She decided to go there.

It was not an ordinary choice. How many people would leave the security of a beautiful mountain resort for a bomb-riven city where she, as an Indian, would still be considered an outsider? Jawaharlal was hardly in a position to say anything. He had himself dared the dangers of the Spanish war by going to Barcelona with Krishna Menon, who had met him at Marseilles, on his way to England in 1938. He could not tell his daughter to avoid an experience that he had welcomed. On the contrary, when Krishna, his sister, expressed her alarm at Indira's decision to return home in the circumstances, he told her, "I am glad she has decided to return. There are all manners of risks and dangers, of course, but it is better to face them than to feel isolated and miserable. If she wants to return then she must do so or take the consequences. Life grows harder for all of us and the soft days of the past already belong to an age that is gone."[79]

Even the route to London was a tortuous one. She had to go by Antibes from Geneva to Marseilles or beyond. Then by air to Barcelona, Lisbon, and London. She reached Lisbon, but then got stuck. She could not get a passage to London. Her personality, in spite of its quiet exterior, was so activity-oriented that she could not wait there, doing nothing. Lisbon was strange and unfamiliar, but she began to work for the Red Cross, and then among the refugees. She even gave lessons in English and French "to earn a little money to help them."[80] When she eventually reached London, she had to wait again before getting a sea passage to India. Here, too, she joined the Red Cross and volunteered to drive an ambulance through the air raids.

Bhupesh Gupta, who was also still in London, remembers a hair raising experience. "Indira, Feroze, and I emerged out of Piccadilly tube station once to find that a bomb had fallen there only a short while before."[81] Indira still keeps as a trophy of the blitz the air-raid warden's helmet which she borrowed to help put out the fires raging round them.

The three of them decided to go back to India together and soon after they got their passage on a ship called the *City of Paris*. To avoid German submarines in the Mediterranean, the ship had to travel by the Cape of Good Hope. Indira was given a special cabin by the captain because she was still not well, but that was the only concession she allowed herself. Bhupesh Gupta recalls that they had terrific quarrels with some of the Englishmen on the ship who were going to British Burma, among them Governor General Dorman Smith, who cast aspersions on the stand of the Indian nationalists. The ship stopped at Cape Town for a day, but when they touched Durban, Indira found that she was to be honored as Jawaharlal's daughter. The wealthy Indian business community had obtained special permission from the racist South African government for Indira to stay in an exclusive sea front residence. The segregationist principle underlying this privilege was too humiliating. She refused to be their guest there. But she agreed naturally to attend a big meeting which they had arranged in a cinema hall at Durban. On the question of making a speech, even a two-minute one, she was polite but adamant. She felt far too shy. She did not want her China meeting scene to be repeated here, although it was certain that not one of the polite and respectable Indians that she would meet in Durban would have the temerity to get up and call her possible attempts "squeaks." She had partly got over her nervousness in London, where everything had gradually begun to seem familiar and less intimidating, especially when it came to talking about a subject that she felt as strongly about as India's fight for freedom. But here, in apartheid South Africa, what should she say to these well-to-do Indian settlers with their memories of Gandhi?

Indira knew what conditions were like and how the Indians and the Negroes lived compared with the whites. But it turned out to be different to see for herself. Before the meeting, Feroze, Bhupesh, and she visited the "black" areas. She was shocked, affronted, and humiliated and by the time they reached the meeting she was so full of anger that she could not wait to speak. The organizers were just beginning to make her excuses because she had said she would not make a speech, but Indira cut them short and stood up and poured out her anger. She condemned the Indians bitterly for not fighting against such offensive divisions of society on the basis of color and race, and for what she had found to be their own non-cooperative attitude toward the black Africans. She had obviously not the soft-spoken but steel-like humility of the Mahatma which had enabled him to knit the South African Indian community in the late 1890's and in the early 1900's into an effective force for change: she was tense, forthright, and blunt and the result was that even though the three of them stayed in Durban for a few more days, there were no more invitations for them.

It was, however, a personal triumph for Indira. She lost her embarrassment about public speaking. She knew henceforth that if she felt strongly enough about something the words would come somehow, enough to make her audiences angry, like this one, or receptive as numerous other occasions would prove. Invariably though, and that remained a weakness or her strength, depending on how you looked at it, she had to be personally stirred before she could be publicly effective. Luckily, the challenges were always forthcoming.

Indira could, in fact, look back on her four turbulent years in England and on the continent as an experience that sharpened her perceptions and helped her, as her father had hoped, to find herself. For one thing she had decided she would marry Feroze. For another she had no academic degree to display but the worthwhile people she had met on the level that demanded intelligent participation rather than a mere social response had given her the poise, confidence, and judgment that a routine four years of book learning, even at Oxford, might not have done. Finally, her politics had had a chance to acquire an international edge.

She had come into close contact in this regard with Krishna Menon because of the India League, because he was her father's friend and because Feroze also admired him. But she was not overawed. She respected his intellectuality, but she had reservations. Minoo Masani, who was a member of the Congress socialist group at the time and therefore close to Menon, is reported to have said many years later when his own politics had taken him into the opposite camp of the Swatantra party, that "both Indira and Feroze were taken in tow by Menon in England."[82] It is interesting to see in the light of that remark, in the light of Menon's subsequent role in Indian politics as Nehru's friend and defense minister, and in the light of the contradictions attributed to Indira's own attitude toward this controversial man when she became prime minister, what opinion she had of him as a young woman of twenty-two when she had just returned to India and presumably was most vulnerable to his influence. She gave her opinion in a conversation she had with Purnima Banerji, a beautiful and clever nationalist woman who admired Jawaharlal greatly.

"I met Indu for a short while," related Purnima to Jawaharlal after Indira was back in Allahabad. "I feel so grown up and old and parental and played out that I cannot enter into any discussions with bright people just returned from Europe. [But] I asked about Krishna Menon. Indu says he is as 'shaky' as ever."[83]

8. FOCUS

Although the Congress ministers, when they took office on July 13, 1937, were pledged to "combat the constitution from within," routine affairs of state conducted jointly with the administration soon created a working bonhomie. There were some human episodes which cut across the cold barriers between a bureaucracy conditioned to rule and those who now aspired to rule over it. Vijayalaxmi Pandit remembers an occasion when, "never having learned sufficient arithmetic in spite of the best masters," the trying preparation for the first budget threw her into despair and she appealed for help to her parliamentary secretary who was a young Englishman. "These figures alarm me," she wrote on the file. "Will P.S. kindly explain?"

"Figures alarm you?" came back the disbelieving rejoinder. "I cannot believe it. I know H. M. [Honorable Minister] is prepared to face battalions and mold the destiny of nations. I can only take her note as an encouragement to me in my work." But an explanatory note was attached, after which she says, "the figures certainly seemed less alarming."[1]

It was a brief honeymoon. Personal relations could hardly carry the burden of an autocratic system. The Congress had agreed to work the provincial autonomy aspect of the act but the government of India was impervious to any responsibility to the Indian legislature, to Indian opinion, or to the Indian people. The conflict was inherent and most of the provincial legislatures passed resolutions formalizing the demand for a constituent assembly to draw up a constitution for India. The Congress ministries were committed to work for constructive reforms and they did achieve substantial measures in agrarian relief, in introducing prohibition, educational reorganization, development of industries and home crafts, uplift of backward communities, enactment of labor laws, and in encouraging reorientation of attitudes toward a cultural resurgence. The ramifications of the Congress organization spread so wide that it began to be said that a village without a Congress committee was like a village without a temple. When the Congress formed the ministries its membership got a tremendous boost for it soon became evident to the more ambitious that the four-anna membership fee was a key which could open the door to a possible chief ministership of a province. It was illusory glamor. The greatest drawback for the Congress was that it was in office, but not in power. It suffered the disadvantages of the former and none of the benefits of the latter.

"I am greatly distressed at the turn events are taking all over in India, insofar as the Congress ministries are concerned," wrote Jawaharlal disgustedly to Govind Ballabh Pant toward the end of 1937. "If I may put it in technical language, the Congress ministries are tending to become counterrevolutionary. Apart from this the general attitude is static. We dare not be static for that means that we are merely carrying on the traditions [with minor variations] of the previous government."[2] But the task of the ministries was superhuman. The leadership of the Congress in those days lay in the hands of a comparatively affluent intellectual elite and thus while the ministries were manned by enlightened people, they came fresh from the agitational methods of a political movement to find in the intricacy of the administration an unfamiliar challenge. At one point the Congress ministries flourished in actuality or in the influence they wielded in as many as nine out of eleven provinces. The semblance of power gave a sharper edge to political ambition which resulted in a certain amount of in-fighting. The expectations rose skyhigh and their demands became imperative. British raj had been replaced by Congress raj and they thought the millennium must be just around the corner. The jealous machinations of the Muslim League began to look for lapses in the functioning of the Congress ministries to prove that Jinnah was right in having arrived at his extraordinary theory that the differences between Indian Muslims and Indian Hindus were not religious, but national. The seeds of partition were plowed into the ground but they needed to be watered and nourished and that could only be done by emphasizing tendencies toward separation rather than those toward unity.

The differences were there, no doubt, but they were aggravated by the economic ones. The Muslims were comparatively backward. Part of the Muslim upper class had been broken by early British rule, the remainder was landowning and feudal. The Muslim majority, consisting of converts from the deprived sections of Hindu society, retained the burdens of its past. There was almost no competition to Hindu domination in commerce, industry, and scientific training. To allay Muslim fears of this domination becoming total in the event of an independent India, the Hindus obviously were required to make a gesture which had to be out of proportion to the merits of the situation in respect of reservation of seats and percentage in appointments to office for the major minority. Maulana Abul Kalam Azad, a leading Muslim congressman and later India's education minister under Nehru, points out in his *India Wins Freedom* that C. R. Das, the great Swarajist colleague of Motilal, made just such a gesture in the late twenties when he promised the educationally and politically backward Muslim majority in Bengal 60 per cent of all new appointments in the event of Congress achieving power, and 80 per cent of all new appointments to the Calcutta Corporation until such time as inequalities disappeared and made reservation unnecessary. It meant a period of deprivation for the educationally advanced Hindus and struck at the concept of merit getting its due award.

It is arguable how far the rights of one section can be disregarded to palliate another section, but it shows that some part of the Congress leadership was prepared to balance one against the other for the sake of ultimate unity. This is not to say that there was not a fanatical Hindu fringe even within the Congress. In fact, Das's declaration was repudiated by some of his followers after his death, but in its resolutions, in principle, and in the last analysis, the Congress continued to argue from the secular premise. Had the Muslim League proceeded from the same stand, the resolving of the economic disparities and the fight for political equability would not have been difficult. But the clash, as I said earlier, was one of vision. Once Jinnah chose to label the Muslims a separate nation, denying altogether the language, customs, and a history held in common with the Hindus, the dialogue between the Congress and the League had to be fruitless. On

December 25, 1937, Jinnah threw out a challenge. In a speech in Calcutta
to the Muslim Students' Federation, he declared, "The Congress high command must be brought to their senses." Thereafter, the communal temper
of the country was stepped up and the Congress ministries were made the
target of repeated criticism.

"Things are almost normal now in Allahabad and Benares but communal
frenzy may burst at any time," Govind Ballabh Pant described the situation
to Jawaharlal on March 23, 1938. "The propaganda carried on during the
last few months by the Muslim League under the cloak of politics is primarily
responsible for this state of affairs. It is so easy to rouse feelings in the
name of religion and when a party has to stoop to this in order to secure
its political ends it cannot have any reasonable grievance against the existing
order."[3] As regards the League charge about the Congress ministries, even
the viceroy and the British governors were compelled to refute its claims
that the Congress ministries had tried to victimize the minorities. Maulana
Azad, who was a member of the Congress Parliamentary Board which had
been constituted to supervise and establish guidelines for the ministries,
declared from "personal knowledge and with a full sense of responsibility"
that "the charges leveled by Mr Jinnah and the Muslim League . . . were
absolutely false."[4]

"If there had been an iota of truth in any of these charges," he said, "I
would have seen to it that the injustice was rectified. I was even prepared to
resign, if necessary, on an issue like this."[5]

But what were the League's political ends? Jawaharlal wished Jinnah to
pin his organization to specific demands. "It may be that I am dense or
not sufficiently acquainted with the intricacies of the problem. If so, I
deserve to be enlightened."[6]

"Perhaps you have heard of the Fourteen Points," was Jinnah's sarcastic
rejoinder. But further in the same letter Jinnah refers to articles and statements by others and says that "various suggestions that have been made or
are likely to be made, or are expected to be made, will have to be analyzed
and ultimately I consider it the duty of every true nationalist to whichever party
or community he may belong, to make it his business and examine the situation and bring about a pact between the Mussalmans and the Hindus and
create a real united front. But if you desire," he continued contrarily, "that
I should collect all these suggestions and submit to you as a petitioner for you
and your colleagues to consider, I am afraid I can't do it."[7] It was obvious
that Jinnah preferred to keep what he had in mind to himself. Subhas
Chandra Bose, who became Congress president in 1938, was forced to
declare in a statement on the eve of the Haripura session that though the
Congress was anxious to solve the communal question it regretted that no
concrete demands had been set forth on behalf of the Muslim minority.
Jinnah in fact made the extraordinary plea that his only basis for negotiations
with the Congress was that the League be accepted as the sole representative

body of the Muslims, and the Congress that of the Hindus.

"To admit Mr Jinnah's claim meant in effect to push out our old Muslim colleagues from the Congress and declare that the Congress was not open to them. It was to change the fundamental character of the Congress, and from a national organization, open to all, convert it into a communal body. That was inconceivable for us," commented Jawaharlal harshly. "If the Congress had not already been there, we would have had to build up a new national organization open to every Indian."[8]

On December 16, 1938, at the end of another attempt at negotiations with the League, President Bose was compelled to inform Jinnah that the working committee of the Congress found it impossible to agree with the council of the League on the basis stipulated by it; any further dialogue therefore would be abortive.

But at the same Haripura session, the Congress was beginning to worry about the role that the British might give India in the event of a world war. The signs were ominous. War preparations had begun. The Congress made it clear that any attempt to involve the country without the consent of its people would not be tolerated. But Gandhi pronounced gravely to the working committee at Delhi in September 1938 that he would not be a party to wresting political advantage out of such a situation. This seemingly lofty sense of loyalty to the ruling enemy arose from Gandhi's code of moral political behavior and also from the realization that it was not possible to create a mass civil disobedience movement out of unresponsive people. But a combination of circumstances was soon to result in a disenchantment which would make him lead the last and the most awesome of those movements that corroded the structure of British power in India.

In the months before war was actually declared the Congress found that its disapproval did nothing to stop the British from sending Indian troops to Egypt and Singapore. The Central Legislative Assembly insisted vainly that any such decision must have the consent of the members. Indian troops had been sent as mercenaries to Burma, China, Iran, the Middle East, and Africa. "I remember the bitter remark of an Egyptian," recalled Jawaharlal himself somewhat bitterly. " 'You have not only lost your freedom but you help the British to enslave others'."[9] Even the 1935 act with its reluctant concessions to provincial autonomy was being amended by the British Parliament to enable the central government to function more authoritatively in the event of war. On September 3 war was declared. On the same night that King George VI broadcast his message that this was to be a war to fight the concept of might is right, the viceroy in India declared India to be a belligerent without consulting her people.

"One man, and he a foreigner and a representative of a hated system, could plunge four hundred million of human beings into war without the slightest reference to them. There was something fundamentally wrong and rotten in a system under which the fate of these millions could be decided in this way. In the dominions the decision was taken by popular representatives after full debate and consideration of various points of view. Not so in India, and it hurt," Jawaharlal summed up the reaction in his country which was to lead to the events of 1942.[10]

For Gandhi, the fundamental issue was one of pacification as opposed to force. He could not advance a Congress alignment with violence when it had a chance to project its national image for the first time into the international sphere. He was against Congress participation in the war regardless of any conditions that the British were prepared to make. But for one section of congressmen led by Jawaharlal the dilemma was heartrending. They wanted India on principle to fight on the side of France and Britain against fascist domination, because they recognized its greater dangers, but Britain's pugnacious policies made it impossible to do so with honor. Purely from the nationalistic point of view, there seemed to be no choice between one kind of imperialism and another, and when a subject nation was forced to participate in a war for the sake of a ruler who was intent on keeping it subject, the line between first principle and national self-respect tended to become hazy.

The question for the Congress, as historian Sitaramayya says, was if it got what it wanted from the British, what help it would give them and, if it did not get what it wanted, what action it would take.[11] On September 11, the king sent a message to India. "Britain is fighting for a principle vital to the future of mankind." How did he expect the support from India that he said he hoped to be able to count upon when that vital principle did not apply to her at all? In a historic sitting from September 9 to 15 the working committee made its decision to support the war effort contingent upon a declaration of war aims by Britain. The draft was prepared by Jawaharlal. "The author of the statement is an artist," said Gandhi, and though he was all for giving unconditional but only *moral* support to the British, he could not help seeing the reasons that had prompted Jawaharlal to promise full aid in exchange for an admittance by Britain of the validity of the democratic aspirations of a subject people and a promise of total independence.

On September 26, Lord Zetland, the secretary of state for India, made a statement in the House of Lords which patronizingly questioned the discretion of the Congress in choosing an "ill time" for a reiteration of its claims.

"I suggest that the Congress has done nothing strange or less than honorable in asking for such a declaration," Gandhi said in a gentle but firm rejoinder. "Only a free India's help is of value. And the Congress has every right to know that it can go to the people and tell them that at the end of the war India's status as an independent country is as much assured as that of Great Britain."[12]

Jawaharlal was much more caustic. "Lord Zetland speaks in terms of yesterdays—he might have delivered his speech twenty years ago." His frustration was evident. "Because we feel that a large number of British people have the same world ideals as many of us possess," he added disappointedly, "we have offered them our cooperation in the realization of these ideals. But if these ideals are not there what do we fight for? Only a free and consenting India can throw her weight for ideals that are openly proclaimed and acted upon."[13]

The viceroy meanwhile began to interview a variety of people with what seemed to be the latent purpose of finding a safely impossible "agreed solution." India was too vast and varied not to throw up contentious opinion and on October 18 in his declaration about British policy in India the viceroy took the expected plea of having found "marked differences of outlook, markedly different demands, and markedly different solutions for the problems that lie before us" to maintain the status quo. A review of the situation was all that was promised after the war.[14]

"The old policy of divide and rule is to continue. The Congress has asked for bread and it got stone," remarked Gandhi.

The viceroy had also specified that His Majesty's Government had not themselves "defined with any ultimate precision their detailed objective in the prosecution of the war," and that these objectives would be conditioned by the campaign of war and the shape of the outcome.

The working committee soon after declared that in the circumstances no support could be given to Great Britain for "it would amount to an endorsement of the imperialist policy which the Congress has always sought to end."[15]

By October 31 the Congress ministries in all eight provinces resigned

It became clear as more meetings took place between Gandhi and the viceroy, between Gandhi and Jinnah, between Jawaharlal and Jinnah, that the issue had again been thrown into the communal fire. The Congress reiterated that given a constituent assembly it would be the Indians' responsibility to find an acceptable constitution, that communal differences were used by the British as an excuse not to give India her rights, and that the presence of a third party was exploited by the Muslim League to strengthen its bargaining position with the Congress.

But Gandhi was implacable. Though he had dissociated himself from negotiations with the British at a time when he thought that unconditional moral support should be offered, and the working committee had differed, they both knew that when the time came for leading what could only be a nonviolent movement against their immediate oppressors, it was Gandhi they would call upon. He made it clear that the timing had to be his.

"There can be no civil resistance so long as, first, the viceroy is exploring the possibilities of a settlement, second, the Muslim League blocks the way, and third, there is indiscipline and disunity in the Congress." He added a few days later: "A stage may be reached when direct action may become the necessary prelude to the constituent assembly. That stage is not yet."[16]

By the end of the year, the Congress executive was constrained to call upon the people to get ready and to take the Independence Day pledge on January 26, 1940, with the reiteration of the "national will to freedom." The viceroy's repeated promise to expand his executive council by including a small number of political leaders added insult to injury. At the end of yet another abortive series of talks with the viceroy, Gandhi pinpointed the difference. Britain wanted to impose its own determination of India's destiny, but what India wanted was self-determination. Feelings again ran high and the clash between British and Indian interests seemed inevitable.

"As we stand today," declared President Maulana Azad at the momentous Ramgarh session of 1940, "we have to decide whether we should march forward in this direction [toward noncooperation] or go backward. To cry halt is to go back and we refuse to go back. I am sure that the voice of every one of you joins mine when I proclaim that we must and will go forward."[17]

And Gandhi, who had been attending the meetings of the working committee only off and on since his withdrawal from the Congress in 1934, this time addressed the Subjects Committee and the open session of the organization. He was adamant that the only adequate preparation for satyagraha was a disciplined fulfillment of the constructive program by congressmen, the wearing of khadi, the attempt to establish communal harmony, and the effort to remove untouchability. If there was no such discipline in the Congress he could not lead it, he said.

> You must allow me to tell you that if you do not fulfill these conditions it will not be possible for me to launch a struggle. You will have to find another general. You cannot compel me to lead you against my will. . . . Because my only sanction is love, I argue with you, for love must be characterized by patience . . . . Every Congress committee must therefore become a unit of satyagraha. I may have to lay down my life for preserving the power that has accrued to India. You may not be able to analyze that power but it is there. It is the power of ahimsa.[18]

At that period the clash within the Congress was between those who thought that civil disobedience would automatically integrate all dissenting forces and Gandhi, who said that discipline must come first. A few months later, the issue became a different one altogether. The fall of France and the possible invasion of England precipitated an immediate concern with the role that India should play in her own defense. The Congress had to give a lead for there was a feeling that it could not let events shape its efforts any more. The question was: How would India meet an attack? For Gandhi it seemed an ideal occasion for the Congress to declare a policy of nonviolence for all times and all situations. Not only should the internal fight of the Congress against the British be based on nonviolence, according to him, but also its external defense. He wished this principle to be decreed as the future state policy of free India. This was impossible for his colleagues to accept. Gandhi was arguing like a prophet. They were politicians.

"For me, nonviolence was a matter of policy, not of creed," affirmed Maulana Azad.[19]

But Gandhi visualized nonviolence as a weapon of the strong, not merely of the weak. Complete nonviolent resistance to an aggressor implied the ability to pay the supreme penalty, that of the life of every man, woman, and child so that an obstinate enemy would have to have the nerves to march over the bodies of the people it wished to conquer, only to get the hollow satisfaction of capturing an empty country. In the final analysis, it would work. But what people in any country could be stirred to the extent of making death without a fight their greatest fight?

At Wardha in June 1940, therefore, the Congress decided regretfully to let Gandhi "be free to pursue his great ideal in his own way and therefore absolve him from responsibility for the program and activity which the Congress has to pursue, under the conditions at present prevailing in India."[20] It meant that Gandhi would not be responsible for any decisions of the Congress regarding military and police matters although its affirmation of faith in nonviolence as such provided the loophole for both to come together in the possible struggle of satyagraha.

Jawaharlal said:

Every one of us was convinced that we must adhere to our policy of nonviolence, as we had so far done, in our struggle. But to commit the future state was another and more difficult matter, and it was not easy to see how anyone moving on the plane of politics could do it. Mr Gandhi felt, and probably rightly, that he could not give up or tone down a message which he had for the world. He must have freedom to give it as he liked and must not be kept back by political exigencies. So for the first time, he went one way and the working committee another. There was no break for him, for the bond was too strong, and he will no doubt continue to advise in many ways and often to lead. Yet it is perhaps true that by his partial withdrawal a definite period in the history of our national movement has come to an end.[21]

At a meeting of the working committee at Delhi only a fortnight later Gandhi was interested enough from the outside to point out that the earlier stand had confused congressmen and needed clarification. But the precise demand was for a provisional national government responsible to the central assembly as a prelude to full national government later. The Congress promised the British it could "then throw its full weight in ... the effective organization of the defense of the country." The resolution, framed by C.R. Rajagopalachari, was ratified by the AICC at Poona a fortnight later.

The conflict within the Congress on this issue was intense.

"Perhaps you all appreciate that Rajaji's resolution sounds the death knell of the Congress," wrote Jayaprakash Narayan just before this despairingly from prison to Jawaharlal. He urged him to lead the opposition in the AICC and even leave the Congress if a settlement came about and form another party. "Will you hesitate to fulfill your obvious historic task?" he argued. "I do not know how much you will achieve. But, in any case you will have blazoned out a glorious path for those who will come after you."[22]

Gandhi was not present at Poona, but a group of congressmen was staunchly behind him in his stand of unconditional moral cooperation with the British, another behind Jawaharlal who stood for conditional moral cooperation but only on the basis of a promise of complete independence for India, another section behind M. N. Roy, who argued for unconditional cooperation which included moral and military help, and those led by C. R. Rajagopalachari, who had managed to amass the majority in favor of conditional cooperation, again both moral and military.

Jawaharlal did not take up Jayaprakash's challenge; the shape of Indian history might have been different otherwise. He preferred a patched-up front which would lead the organization somewhere instead of a divided one which would lead it nowhere. For Gandhi himself, there was considerable reassurance to be found in that part of the Congress resolution at Poona in July 1940 which affirmed the desirability of nonviolence for India's internal struggle.

"In a telegram of congratulation he sent me," recalled Maulana Azad, "he said he was particularly pleased that I had pleaded the cause of nonviolence in the internal struggle. He had felt that in the present temper of the country the AICC would readily accept my proposal that India should participate in the war if her freedom was recognized. In view of this he had doubts if I could persuade the AICC to pass the resolution on nonviolence in respect of our internal struggle."[23]

Nevertheless, Gandhi made it clear that he thought that those who really believed in nonviolence should leave the Congress and "serve it better" from outside. An obvious split was averted when Azad tactfully suggested to the purists that Congress participation in the war was contingent upon a settlement with the British and that was nowhere in sight. In fact, the viceroy's offer of August 8 came as such an anticlimax to the Congress demand for equal partnership that Azad rejected it without bothering to consult his colleagues. The principle of Indian responsibility for the framing of a new constitution was conceded, but with the reservation that this was not the time for it. Britain's long association with India was used as an excuse for wanting to see differences settled before relinquishing hold and the preposterous statement was made that no transfer of power could be contemplated "to any system of government whose authority is directly denied by large and powerful elements by Indian life . . . nor could they be parties to the coercion of such elements to such a government." For the moment, therefore, the British said they could only invite Indians to join the executive council and form a war advisory council to help in the war effort. It was a slap in the face that denied the minimum Congress demands and implied placing the fate of the country in the hands of any vested minority group like the League and the princes whose interests clashed with the majority will.

All along the government had been carrying out its policy of arrests and intimidation, but it chose this period to step it up because of the congressmen who had opposed the resolution for conditional war support made in Poona. People began to have the feeling that the government was taking advantage of the extraordinary restraint employed by the Congress party in not launching any aggressive movement during Britain's difficulties. "If that suspicion is proved to be well grounded," declared Gandhi ominously even from the outside, "nothing on earth can deter me from adopting some form of satyagraha."[24] On August 14 the secretary of state made a pronouncement in the House of Commons that followed the same line as that of the viceroy. Indian national opinion was stung into reaction and the impulse was to rush back into Gandhi's arms. Britain's summary dismissal of the Congress offer and the fact that even in its gravest crisis it was not prepared to come to terms with nationalist India made an active struggle imperative. And in an active struggle which could only be nonviolent, Gandhi was the savior, who alone possessed the magic formula. In the last analysis, when it came to a fight, the Congress knew it had to depend upon him alone.

By the end of August Jawaharlal was affirming that as the Poona resolution was dead, the path had to be the Ramgarh one of "suffering and sacrifice" and nonviolence had to be both creed and faith if Gandhi were to lead. On September 15 at Bombay the AICC in turn rejected the British offer and the same time officially declared its Poona decisions to have lapsed. Gandhi decided that the fight should be on the basis of a demand for civil liberty for the moment and not independence. Secondly, its form in the circumstances must be that of individual civil disobedience. He chose one person, Vinoba Bhave, who on October 17, 1940, initiated the movement with an antiwar speech and the satyagrah pledge: "It is wrong to help this British war effort with men or money. The only remedy to war is to resist all wars by nonviolent resistance."[25]

Jawaharlal was to be the second person to offer satyagraha on November 7. But on October 31 he was arrested and sentenced to four years' imprisonment for a speech he had already made. The sentence was so severe that it left the country gasping and shocked liberal opinion even in Britain. By the second week of November, "representative satyagrahis" had been selected from the official bodies of the Congress like the working committee and the AICC and from Congress members of central and provincial legislatures. The year 1940 closed with about 400 Congress legislators, 29 of whom were ex-ministers, in jail. The year 1941 opened with another group of satyagrahis, drawn up by local Congress committees and approved by Gandhi, courting arrest. By April 1941, the "rank and file" fourth stage of the campaign was reached, which involved the recruitment of ordinary members of the Congress. By May 1941, 25,069 convictions had been made for individual civil disobedience: a slow, snowballing symbolic protest that seemed to "proceed languidly and without much interest"[26] but which prepared the ground, the mood, and the atmosphere within the year for the dynamic demand of 1942: "Quit India."

For Indira, when she returned in March 1941, her country provided no straight answers. In Europe the issues had been simple. She was on the side of the Allies, and she had decided to marry the man she loved. In India, she was on the side of the Allies but had to fight the British at the same time, while the question of being able to marry Feroze became a family problem. She told a sharply perceptive school friend who met her at Bombay that there was something between her and Feroze, but mentioned it to no one else. Her father was in jail again. She had become very close to him in the years since her mother had died, but she was not sure how he would react to her final decision regarding Feroze, even if he had anticipated it all along. His objections would not be on grounds of religion. That was certain. A pattern of unorthodoxy had already been set in their family. Vijayalaxmi, after going through a harrowing experience with her first love, had married a fellow Brahmin, but Ranjit Pandit was a Maharashtrian, not a Kashmiri. Krishna had married outside her caste as well as the region—Raja Hutheesing was a Gujarati, like Gandhi, and a non-Brahmin. Further, he was a follower of Jainism, a faith only allied to Hinduism. Shyam Kumari, their cousin, had married a Muslim, while another cousin, Braj Kumar Nehru, who was to become free India's Ambassador to Washington, had even crossed national lines and had married a Hungarian girl. In writing about British Indian law, existing at the time of Krishna's marriage under which two limited civil marriage acts made the validity of inter-caste and inter-religious marriage possible under certain conditions, Nehru had said, "Personally I should like to encourage inter-caste marriages but whether they are encouraged or not, it is very necessary to have a permissive general civil marriage act applicable to persons of all religions permitting them to marry without any denunciation or change of faith."[27] There was no reason to believe that he had changed his opinion since then. The fact that Feroze was a Parsi was not going to be the determining factor in her father's attitude, Indira was sure. But whereas both Ranjit Pandit and Raja Hutheesing were Oxonians who had come back from England as qualified lawyers and had family wealth and background to support them,

Feroze had only promise and very little background.

Feroze's father, Jehangir Fardoonji Gandhi, was the first Parsi marine engineer to be appointed warrant engineer by the king's commission in World War I. His aunt, Dr. S. A. Commissariat, was the first Parsi woman to become a fellow of the Royal College of Surgeons and she was a respected staff member of the Lady Dufferin Hospital at Allahabad. When World War I broke out in 1914 and Jehangir Gandhi had to travel with his ship from place to place, he sent the tiny two-year-old Feroze and his four older sisters and brothers and their mother Rathibai to their aunt in Allahabad. Even though little Feroze had his elder sister Tehmina and brother Faredun to look after him besides his mother it was a traumatic experience at that age to be deprived of both home and father and this orphaned feeling made his childhood difficult, emotionally dry, and in a sense alienated. It took the form of a revolt against the middle class, conformist environment of his own family and a fascination for both the warm clannishness of the Nehrus and the mixture of daring and dedication with which they approached the political scene. He became a special favorite of Uma Nehru, the wife of Jawaharlal's cousin, to whom he ran for solace whenever he fell victim to the tyranny of his bewildered brother and sister, who felt unable to deal with either his overbrimming energy as a mere four-year-old or his defiance as a political initiate at sixteen. They could not understand why he spurned a secure future for a nebulous adventure in politics. But his first en- counter with the police committed him totally to the other side. It was in 1928; the demonstrations against the Simon Commission at first attracted him as an interested spectator, but he soon found the police attacked participants and bystanders indiscriminately. He was caught, thrashed, and handcuffed. He was released only when they learned that he was the redoubtable Dr Commissariat's nephew.

Feroze never forgave the police, but it was much more than that. His schooling at an ordinary institution like the Anglo-Vernacular School gave him a popular base. At twelve he became a junior scout in the troop of city scouts and came under the influence of Scoutmaster K. D. Malaviya, whose political predilections were strong enough to make him general secretary of the Allahabad City Congress only a few years later. "He joined my troop along with my younger brother," describes Malaviya. "It did not occur to me then that Feroze Gandhi would, in later years, become a political comrade working shoulder to shoulder with me in our struggle for indepen- dence."[28]   In fact, Feroze helped him as an active worker in the City Cong- ress till Kamala Nehru's benevolent presence further drew him along what his family considered to be a fatal course. He remained immune to the effect that his "subversive" activities might have on his aunt, who was in the service of the government, his brother Faredun, who was studying for his law degree, and his sister Tehmina who was finishing her master's degree in education. His family gave up when even hiding his clothes and shoes did not deter him from running away to join a demonstration, picket a shop, or participate in a rally. By 1934 he had had a full taste of British wrath and been jailed four times in the cause of freedom.

"Well, it couldn't have been love of country," argues his brother Faredun now. "Patriotism and sacrifice are adult impulses, and Feroze was just a teenage kid. I think it was circumstances and personalities. He was wronged by the police, and Feroze, being a very determined sort of fellow, was out to defy them. Then, of course, he had this extraordinary fascination for the Nehrus. He hero-worshipped them."[29]

Typically, he did not let his awe of the Nehrus intimidate him. He had the courage to ask for Indira when he was only twenty-one. Swarup Rani Nehru was still alive; Motilal Nehru's name even after his death cast a majestic shadow over Allahabad society, and the Nehru home, Anand Bhawan, formed the focal point of national activity. By 1941, things had in a sense become even more difficult. Jawaharlal was a national hero, beloved of millions. It made his family a further subject of public curiosity. Indira was the personable young daughter of the family upon whom the limelight would fasten with increasing glare. Feroze had humor, determination, and confidence in his own future. But that would be cold comfort to the members of what was fast becoming the first family of the nation while the rest would no doubt see him merely as an impecunious young suitor in the Nehru clan. "You must give Indira the credit for seeing the promise in him," now observes Chalapathi Rau, editor, journalist, and friend who was close to Jawaharlal and Feroze a little later.[30]

Perhaps that is what made Indira as quietly determined as ever. Coming from the environment that she did, her love had to be built on respect. But she was also tactful and then, as later, very careful in her way of handling a situation. Both she and Feroze resolved to keep their momentous decision to themselves for a while. In fact, there was hardly any occasion for people to see them together that summer. There were the trips up to the district jail at Dehra Dun to see her father. And in June, she suddenly went off to Calcutta.

"I have been dissatisfied with her health," wrote Jawaharlal worriedly from prison to Krishna. "Madan Atal going to Calcutta consulted Bidhan Roy who, as was to be expected, said bring her here and we shall overhaul her. So . . . in the middle of this heat, she has departed. It all seems rather crazy but I hope she will be back soon."[31]

He had made arrangements for a small house called the St. Clair Cottage, to be engaged for Indira for the season at Mussoorie.

"It is a tiny affair—two bedrooms and two other rooms," he wrote in the same letter to Krishna. "If at any time you would care to come up there with the children," he suggested hopefully, apparently thinking that his daughter might be lonely, "I am sure Indu would be glad." But characteristically not wishing to impose even upon his own sister, he could not help adding, "You need not come because of Indu. I think a month or so of full quiet and rest will be good for her. But later if the children require a change or you feel like it yourself, you can think this over. It is just possible that in August or thereabouts Indu might like to go to Kashmir. But that is too far off yet."

"It was evident to me that *bhai* was terribly worried about Indu, as well he might be after his tragic experience with Kamala," observed Krishna later, so in August she went up to be with her niece. "We had a cook and two servants and a nursemaid for my two sons, so we were very comfortable," she describes. "I stayed nearly three months with Indira, getting to know her all over again and seeing how she had grown and developed during her final years in Europe. We had a very quiet time, living more or less cut off from the world, which was just what Indu needed. As September gave way to October and the chilly winds of the Himalayas' eternal winter blew down the valley her health improved and her dark eyes sparkled with vitality."[32]

But so strong was Indira's resolve not to divulge what was actually nearest her heart until she had talked to her father about it that even this cosy interlude with her aunt did not tempt her to tell her about Feroze. They used to go for interviews with Jawaharlal every fortnight, but it was only when her aunt went back to Bombay and she was alone once again that, in one of these interviews, she took the plunge and told her father that she wanted to marry Feroze. When I asked Mrs Gandhi when was the exact occasion when she broached the subject with her father, she made the revealing rejoinder, "I...I don't remember. I think it was always understood that I would marry Feroze." According to Krishna, Jawaharlal's immediate reaction was to get greatly "upset." He suggested that Indira should allow herself to meet more Indian boys before making a final choice. But he found his daughter, as usual, adamant. "In his distress," says Krishna, he fell back on ancient tradition. He told Indira that since he was in prison and her mother was dead she must ask permission to marry from her aunts, Nan and me."[33] Predictably, what concerned her forward-looking family was not the difference in religion between her and Feroze but the practical aspects of compatibility. But when Vijayalaxmi coolly gave the same advice to her as her father, and Krishna repeated it when she went to stay with her at Bombay, she came out with the indignant retort in what Krishna describes as "a flash of Nehru temper." "It took you only ten days," Indira apparently said to her, "to make up your mind about Raja Bhai, and I have known Feroze for years. So why should I have to wait, and why should I have to meet other young men?"[34]

"Darling, if you think he is the right person, go ahead and marry him," Krishna says she finally told her. She also says that Jawaharlal, when he found he could not bend his daughter to his will, took refuge in the plea that she could get married after his release. Considering that he had three years yet to serve of his four-year sentence, it seemed a clever enough delaying tactic on the part of an unwilling father. But circumstances played into the hands of Indira rather than Jawaharlal. In a surprise move for conciliation the British government freed Jawaharlal along with a number of political *detenus* almost immediately after, on December 4, 1941. He found he had to face the issue sooner than he expected.

Feroze's own relatives had no objections, only reservations. His aunt, Dr Commissariat, disapproved, although it is not clear on what grounds. The rest of them, including his mother, sister Tehmina, and brother Fared-un, thought that he would not be able to match the standards Indira was used to, however diminished they might have become since Motilal's bold sacrifices. The orthodox were incensed on both sides, but Feroze himself was warned teasingly by some to be careful, the Nehru girls they said had a tendency to ultimately draw their men to their own home. Vijayalaxmi was the most glaring example. She was far too politically inclined to tear herself away from her home base and had managed to persuade Ranjit to leave Bombay and settle in Allahabad. While Krishna remained dutifully in Bombay with Raja, she was nevertheless embittered by conflict.

But in spite of everyone's objections in this first major confrontation of will with her father, Indira won, although in one sense the victory was also Jawaharlal's. His exhortations to maintain a modern outlook free from religious prejudice had taken hold in his own daughter to the extent that she was able to disregard the religious factor altogether in one of the most crucial decisions of her life. It placed her on the side of those who are not bound by cultural inhibitions and helped give her a progressive image which later earned her, a non-religious national loyalty. She was of the highest caste in the jealous hierarchy of Hinduism but she had dared, in spite of public opinion and the certain censure of the conventional majority, to choose a Parsi for her future husband. The minorities were always to feel comparatively secure with her.

The religious aspect was not what troubled Jawaharlal then. He simply felt strongly that Feroze was not the right person for Indira, and in his despair he turned for advice, as usual, to his beloved Bapu—Mahatma Gandhi, who went about it in his characteristic way. He sent for Indira and Feroze, had long interviews with them separately, and asked them searching questions about love and sex. He had rigid ideas about the role of sex in life, he had had no qualms about analyzing his own sexual experience in his autobiography and he could be disconcertingly blunt on the subject. He wanted to be sure that the basis of their relationship was something more than mere sexual attraction. He was obviously convinced that this was so for he told Jawaharlal that the match would have his blessing. Although nothing was declared officially close friends soon knew the question was settled. As early as January 25, 1942, Syed Mahmud, that long time devotee and fellow worker of Jawaharlal, wrote to inquire about the wedding.

The possible complications of the actual ceremony were already beginning to be a matter of concern. "I think it should be done according to Hindu rites," advised Mahmud, adding apologetically, "you will probably accuse me of being a reactionary at this suggestion but it is not the form I care [for]. You will I am sure understand my point of view."[35]

Jawaharlal may have understood, but he could not have approved. The two civil marriage acts he had criticized at the time of Krishna's wedding were the only ones in force. The one under which Krishna was married allowed a union between Hindus and members of allied faiths. But in the case of inter-religious unions the act required what Jawaharlal called an "unnecessary denunciation" of faith on the part of one or the other, or a "patently superficial conversion to get within the law." The problem had come up earlier when B. K. Nehru, his nephew, had wanted to marry Magdalena Friedman, a Hungarian Jew. The Nehrus had been very daring. They had decided to beat the legal tangle by resorting to an unorthodox Hindu marriage ceremony devised by Lachmi Dhar Shastri, a professor of Sanskrit. In a work on the Vedas Shastri had drawn upon ancient Hindu sacrament and rituals to formulate Hindu marriage rites which he claimed could be used with impunity even by those belonging to different faiths.

"We consulted lawyers and supreme court judgments," recalled B. K. Nehru. Among them was the family friend and political luminary, Sir Tej Bahadur Sapru, who declared unequivocally that the ceremony would not be able to stand the test of a court. "But it was Gandhiji's suggestion," B. K. Nehru recalled further, "[that] we observe the Hindu form. Whether it was legal or not did not matter. In the eyes of God it would be fine. The pandit had invented a form of marriage called Vedic and observed some sort of form. There was a strange innovation. He had a sword put into the hands of the bride, and made her vow that she would safeguard the rights of the country. [This was] not done by the man."[36] Obviously the tenor of the times had deeply affected the learned professor for not only was there this nationalistic tinge to the ritual, but also, as one sees, an emphatic pride of place for the woman. The Nehrus had decided in favour of the pandit's version then, regardless of the niceties of the legal question, and now twelve years later, it seemed that it would be the only way out for Indira and Feroze. If Sir Tej Bahadur had been unequivocal about the legality, Jawaharlal was now equally unequivocal about the morality of the issue: no "conversion" or "denunciation."

"I don't want my daughter to begin her life with a lie," he said.

But while these matters formed a turbulent undercurrent to discussions among the family and close friends, in the outside world, rumor fed on speculation. For Jawaharlal politics was at its most demanding with the fluctuations of World War II causing serious repercussions at home. Toward the end of February Generalissimo Chiang Kai-shek and his wife paid a return goodwill visit to India, and Jawaharlal took them to Shanti-

niketan where a China wing had been established by Tagore with such
enthusiasm a few years back. But on February 21, when they were in a
meeting with Gandhi in Calcutta, Jawaharlal was told that the news of his
daughter's impending marriage to Feroze had leaked out to the *The Leader*
of Allahabad which that day carried the announcement on its front page.

MISS INDIRA NEHRU'S ENGAGEMENT

The marriage of Miss Indira Nehru, daughter of Pandit Jawaharlal Nehru,
has been settled, it is understood, with Mr Feroze Gandhy, brother of
Mrs Tehmina K. Gandhy, personal assistant to the Chief Inspectress of
Schools, United Provinces.

The wedding may take place shortly. A date for the ceremony will
be fixed on Mr Nehru's return to Allahabad.

There was no immediate denial or affirmation of the announcement by the
Nehrus. But Ansar Harvani, now a veteran congressman, seems to remember the actual occasion when the question came up. Mrs Uma
Nehru, the United Press correspondent, S. P. Bhattacharjee, and Indira
and he were sitting in the room of Rafi Ahmed Kidwai, another Congress
leader who later became one of Nehru's most trusted colleagues and who remembered Feroze as a young boy from their days together in Faizabad jail
in 1930 and thought very well of him. In fact, Feroze modelled his political
personality to a large extent later on that of "Rafi Sahib."

"Rafi asked Indira whether she wanted to marry Feroze," describes
Harvani, "Indira said 'yes,' so he asked the U.P. correspondent to flash
the news as a *fait accompli*."[37]

From Calcutta Jawaharlal was due to go to Lucknow to inaugurate an
Indo-Soviet conference, but his train was late and he came straight from the
station to the dais. Sarojini Naidu, who was presiding, had already begun
her speech, and Harvani argues that when he saw Chandralekha Pandit,
Vijayalaxmi's daughter, go up agitatedly to her uncle on the platform and whi-
sper in his ear, it must have been to reassure him about this personal problem.

The family took another five days to adjust to the finality of Indira's
decision. On February 26, Jawaharlal issued a statement which sought to
set the public at rest. It also provided a clue to the principles that had made
Indira's decision possible and his own acceptance of it inevitable. He had
advised her long ago, when she was only thirteen to "make friends with the
sun and work in the light and do nothing secretly or furtively."[38] She had
indeed grown up "a child of the light" as he wanted for she had had
the courage to openly affirm a decision in face of almost the whole country's
disapproval because she thought it was right. She had sought her father's
consent and in spite of his strong reservations, he believed that ultimately
he must give it. It must have irked him to have to justify publicly what
was purely a private matter. But he was too much a public man to resent it.

"A marriage is a personal and domestic matter, affecting chiefly the two parties concerned and partly their families," he said in a statement. "Yet I recognize that in view of my association with public affairs, I should take my many friends and colleagues and the public generally into my confidence." He went on, "I have long held the view that though parents may and should advise in the matter, the choice and the ultimate decision must be with the two parties concerned. The decision, if arrived at after mature deliberation, must be given effect to, and it is no business of parents or others to come in the way. When I was assured that Indira and Feroze wanted to marry one another I accepted willingly their decision and told them that it had my blessing."

He could not help a reference to Bapu. "Mahatma Gandhi," he stated, "whose opinion I value not only in public affairs but in private matters also, gave his blessing to the proposal. The members of my family as well as the members of my wife's family also gave their willing consent."[39]

The next day telegrams and letters went off to the Nehrus and Kauls. One to Kamala's mother, Mrs Rajpati Kaul, from Jawaharlal stated, "Fixing Indu's wedding for twenty-sixth March. Hope you will come here early and help in the arrangements."[40]

The die was cast.

Mahatma Gandhi reacted with touching solicitude. "I have seen your views about Indu," he wrote to Jawaharlal. "I liked it [the statement]." [41]

But that orthodox opinion in the country reacted with a vengeance was revealed in what he said further. "I receive letters concerning her marriage every day. Some are dreadful, I have destroyed all of them. Since yesterday letters from Muslims have started pouring in." Here, the original letter, which is in Hindi, adds in the context of the teenaged Vijayalaxmi's involvement with a young Muslim and how it was prevented from materializing into marriage: "*Usme hamle ka mudda Swarup wala kisa hai. Aisa to chalta hi rahega.*" (The target of attack is the incident about Swarup. This, of of course, is bound to go on.)"[42]

The occasion revealed such sharp prejudice in communal groups that Gandhi was provoked to discuss the implications publicly and incidentally recapitulate the remarkable breadth of his religious conception.

He wrote in *The Harijan*, in the March 8, 1942 issue:

I have received several angry and abusive letters and some professing to reason about Indira's engagement with Feroze Gandhi. Not a single correspondent has anything against Feroze Gandhi as a man. His only crime in their estimation is that he happens to be a Parsi. I have been and I am still, as strong an opponent of either party changing religion for the sake of marriage. Religion is not a garment to be cast off at will. In the present case there is no question of change of religion. Feroze Gandhi has been for years an intimate [friend] of the Nehru family.

He nursed Kamala Nehru in her sickness. He was like a son to her. During Indira's illness in Europe he was of great help to her. A natural intimacy grew up between them.

He took pains to emphasize the "purity" of the relationship. "The friendship has been perfectly honorable. It has ripened into mutual attraction. But neither party would think of marriage without the consent and blessing of Jawaharlal. This was given only after he was satisfied that the attraction had a solid basis. The public knows my connection with the Nehrus. I had also talks with both the parties. It would have been cruelty to refuse consent to this engagement."

Not only did he put this particular question on a rational, humanistic level, but calmly stated that society as a whole must move in a similar direction. "As time advances, such unions are bound to multiply with benefit to society. At present we have not reached the stage of mutual toleration, but as toleration grows into mutual respect for religions, such unions will be welcomed. No religion which is narrow and which cannot satisfy the test of reason will survive the coming reconstruction of society in which the values will have changed and character, not possession of wealth, title or birth will be the sole test of merit."

Then there was the implied rebuke to those without vision.

"The Hinduism of my conception is no narrow creed. It is a grand, evolutionary process as ancient as time, and embraces the teachings of Zoroaster, Moses, Christ, Mohammad, Nanak, and other prophets that I could name. It is thus defined:

विद्वद्भि सेवित: सद्भिनित्यमद्वेषरागिभि:
हृदयेनाभ्यनुज्ञातो यो धर्मस्तं निबोधत:

(Know that to be true religion which the wise and the good and those
who are ever free from passion and hate follow, and which appeals
to the heart.)

"If it is not that it will perish. My correspondents will pardon me for not acknowledging their letters. I invite them to shed their wrath and bless the forthcoming marriage. Their letters betray ignorance, intolerance, and prejudice—a species of untouchability dangerous because not easily classified."[43]

Indira was indeed lucky to have Gandhi's stirring conscience on her side. However she might have questioned the apparent whimsicality of some of the social causes he pursued, she was as much under the influence of his high-minded criteria and the subtle power of his personality as her grandfather Motilal had been and as her father was. Concurrent with the intellectual rebellion from time to time of three generations of Nehrus was their subservience like the rest of India to the passionate sway of his vision. Indira tore herself free to an extent later on, but the reference point at that period certainly was a kind of Gandhian ethos. But the courage was her own and she was under terrific pressure. Public hysteria victimized her with the same barrage of unnerving correspondence.

"I was getting hundreds of letters every day threatening, abusing, all kinds of things." Mrs Gandhi recalls now. "Of course, [there were] a very few encouraging, saying, 'good for you.'"

But when it was put to her that that must have "tightened her resolve," she gave an answer that showed that her own reactions were rarely hysterical. "Well, I don't think—you know, I am rather balanced in this way," she concluded. "If I know what I want, it doesn't bother me if somebody opposes it. It neither tightens nor loosens, you see. I go my way. And once I had made up my mind, there it was."[44]

"Now, talk of Indu's wedding sent a wave of interest through India and presents began to arrive from all over the country," recalls Nayantara, remembering also how she and Rita were "awkward and gangly" worshipful young cousins, who followed Indira around the house imitating her in every way they could. "Her room became a cloud of rustling tissue paper and satin ribbon from which emerged gifts of silver and crystal, lovely saris, and occasionally a velvet-lined casket containing a jeweled ornament. Most of these presents had to be carefully rewrapped and returned to the senders, for in many cases they were from people whom the family did not know."

"Is the entire orthodox ceremony going to take place?" they excitedly asked their father, Ranjit Pandit.

"No," he said. "Mamu is in favor of a simplified version, so we shall have only the essential ceremony which is really all that is necessary and meaningful. It should not last longer than an hour and a half."[45]

In fact, Gandhi had originally suggested something austere.

"I hold a firm opinion," he had told Jawaharlal, "that no one from outside need be invited. A few persons who are at Allahabad may, however, be called as witnesses. You can send *Lagna Patrika* to as many people as you like. Ask for blessings from everybody but make it clear that no one in particular need take the trouble of coming. If any person is asked to come, no one can be left out."

"It has to be considered whether Indu likes to go to this extent of simplicity or not," he added doubtfully. "If perhaps you also do not like to go to this extent, you can rule out my suggestion."[46]

Both father and daughter wished it to be the same but intense public involvement in the matter made Gandhi himself suggest a more elaborate affair later on. In fact, Indira felt that she almost had to be made to "give in" on that point.

"We had thought that we would have a very quiet affair and not invite anybody," she recollected. "But Mahatma Gandhi rightly pointed out ... that with a wedding as controversial as this, people would think that my father didn't want to do anything for my husband and me, and this, he said, would not be fair to my father or to us. So that's why we had a wedding—I won't say in the 'grand manner,' because compared to Indian weddings, it was still very, very simple—but nevertheless a lot of people turned up from all over India."[47]

It was a sunny March morning of the twenty-sixth, the auspicious Hindu day of *Ram Naumi*. By selecting that particular day so much at least had been allowed by the Nehrus to their basic Hinduism. No matter how progressive their ideas, they clung to certain forms of ancient belief with, indeed, deep feeling. Motilal, the fiery social rebel, had had a horoscope of Indira drawn up when she was born. Jawaharlal suggested the same later when Indira had her son and Indira herself, contrary to her grandfather and father who did not indulge in personal ceremonial prayer, developed a strong mystical feeling which could not be subdued by an almost equally strong sense of rationality. Their rebellion was invariably influenced by a sense of cultural continuity and they were not prepared to be iconoclasts. Even in her marriage ceremony Indira's mixture of attitudes was evident. She was prepared to pay full reverence to the chanting of Sanskrit verses on the one hand, but insisted that a translation in Hindi should also be given so that she would know exactly what she was saying "yes" to.

The ceremony devised by Lachmi Dhar Shastri was divided into two parts, the *Prag Homa* and the *Vivaha*. The Prag Homa, or the prelude opened with homage to the law of righteousness, virtue, and truth and a desire for the spread of goodwill among mankind. This was followed by *Atmodvaha*, the bride's consent to the marriage, in which the bride is alone with the priest and can answer his questions freely. Indira herself later commented that she thought this had great practical significance in the context of arranged marriages in India for it provided an opportunity for the girl to reject an imposed match. She herself was proud to give happy affirmation. After Atmodvaha came the controversial inclusion B. K. Nehru had talked about. This was *Jaya Homa* which, according to Professor Shastri, was an ancient ceremony symbolizing the love of freedom and the determination to preserve it. The sword, *Khadga*, mentioned in the verses, is the "symbol of strength." And the verses that Indira had to repeat were natural to her political consciousness.

"If there are any people in the four quarters of the earth, who venture to deprive us of our freedom, mark! Here I am, sword in hand, prepared to resist them to the last! I pray for the spreading light of freedom; may it envelop us on all sides!"

The *Shanti Patha,* or the closing verses of this part, contained a benediction for universal peace, praise for *abhaya, jagrivi,* and the cultivation of social virtues in life.

Krishna later recollected:

The setting was typical. The wedding day dawned bright and beautiful. From early morning people were busy seeing that all was in readiness for the marriage ceremony. Many cousins and friends flocked to the bride's room to tease her and joke with her as young girls do, and to be with her while she was dressed in her bridal clothes. . . . Slightly flushed and a little excited, though pretending to be quite calm, the bride sat surrounded by people and by the hundreds of presents which kept streaming into her room. Lovely to look at, on this special occasion she looked lovelier than ever, frail and almost ethereal. She laughed and talked to those around her but sometimes her big black eyes would darken and hold a distant sorrowful look. What dark cloud could mar the joy of this happy day? Was it due to a longing for the young mother who was no more, by whose absence a void had been created which even on this day remained unfulfilled? Or was it the thought of parting from the father, a father whose very life she had been? The eyes became darker for a fleeting moment, then they regained their natural look and were unfathomable.[48]

Guests, friends, relatives and eager gate-crashers spilled over as Indira, Feroze, and Jawaharlal sat around the fire in the traditionally decorated veranda in front of the rooms that used to be Swarup Rani's for the second part, the Vivaha, or the actual wedding rites. Indira was dressed in a shell-pink khadi sari made out of delicate yarn spun by her father in prison. It was edged with a silver border. Like her mother on her wedding day Indira, too, wore flower jewelry, painstakingly created by Mrs Vakil who had come all the way from Bombay. Feroze wore a simple *achkan, churidar* trousers, and a Gandhi cap. Vijayalaxmi watched nostalgically from the side of a pillar with unexpected tears glistening in her eyes, while the empty mat beside Jawaharlal seemed like a forlorn invocation to Kamala's presence. No Indian wedding is an occasion for unadulterated joy: the burdens of relinquishing the past, the change, and the finality sit heavily on the emotions. Tradition sanctifies an air of sadness on the parting of a daughter from her parents, and sentiment turns to recapitulation. For the Nehrus particularly, with the whole clan gathered together in a rare moment between dramatic interludes, the walls of the old Anand Bhawan just across the way rose like shadows of the glittering past, of other weddings, other times, while politics now beckoned to an uncertain future. Only a few of them could rely on the easier paths to happiness.

Professor Shastri's text for the second part again imbued the wedding ritual with a political emphasis. While the incense spiraled upward and the ghee was dropped in sizzling rhythm on the fire and the photographers sweated to get the right angles, the sonorous chanting urged Indira and Feroze to "maintain inviolate the sovereignty of the people."

swaraj asi . . . rashtre cha jagrihi
ma no rashtram adhibhrashat

ojaswat, kshatram, ajaram
no astu.

After the *Kanya Dan*, Jawaharlal got up and stood sadly apart, and a poignantly beautiful rite was performed on behalf of Kamala, who should have been there. Flower garlands representing eight virtues were offered to Indira with the words: "Please adorn yourself with the grace of divine character and accept this offering of the first flower, that of non-violence: this second flower of self-control; this third of compassion for all living beings, this fourth of forbearance; this fifth of enlightenment; this sixth of purity; this seventh of profound meditation; and this eighth that is the flower of truth."

Indira and Feroze then repeated passages from the *Saraswati Anuvak* after which Feroze read alone: "Love created this universe, love encompasses it. Love divine that reaches the heavens has taken for me a form in thee, my wife, so gentle and graceful. Under thy shelter, O love, may I attain the highest purpose of life."

That last was a prophetic sentence, though the inspiration was not to be quite that conventional.

The rest of Professor Shastri's ceremony followed the usual pattern. Indira and Feroze went round the sacred fire, they took the *Sapta Padi*, the seven steps, and with each step the husband promised to provide the bride with all the comforts and to make her happy. They then ate a symbolic meal together and afterward were showered with flower petals by friends and relatives to the accompaniment of appropriate verses. The last and concluding verses were then chanted, among them the one from the *Rig Veda*, which brought the theme back to social sacrament.

Samanah mantrah, samitih samani
Samanam manah sahachittam esham
(May our projects be common
And common the assembly of our people
May our people be
Of like mind and purpose.)

"Once I had made up my mind that was that," Indira had said. So they were married in spite of the fact that "the whole nation was against [their] wedding," and in spite of the reluctance of the family itself.

"They didn't really approve of your marrying Feroze, did they?" I asked Mrs Gandhi.

She was silent. "Well, no, not really," she said at last. "Mummie wasn't there then—she had died. My father thought we would not be compatible. That was true. We were not compatible." After a pause, she laughed. "But he was the most compatible person I knew, so it was all right!"

"In what way would you say you were not compatible?"

"Oh, I don't know—you have to pay for everything, I suppose. You can't have everything. He wouldn't have become what he did if he hadn't married me. If I had been a sweet little wife like anybody else he wouldn't have wanted to prove himself somehow. Perhaps I, too, would have been content to live a very domestic life and not even turned to politics."[49]

But the point is that she turned to politics long before the challenges of incompatibility with her husband could drive her toward it. The challenge, if any, lay in her own character. Any other young woman might have been content to bask in the glory of being Motilal's granddaughter and Jawaharlal's daughter, but Indira wanted to prove herself worthy of them. She could not have been content to derive, like Vallabhbhai Patel's daughter, Maniben, could or Jinnah's sister Fatima, enough satisfaction in wielding a strong influence within the restricted family orbit. For Indira there was a search for identity apart from that given her by her father or her family and it led her along a path that Maniben could not dream of and Fatima could not achieve.

"She used to be so skinny that we used to feel sorry for her. She looked so innocent. She was never flashy and talkative. She was very grave but very active," states Uma Agarwal, the daughter of Congressman Jamnalal Bajaj, who remembers attending almost every Congress session with Indira. "But the confidence and the ambition," she adds, "were always there."[50]

Mrs Gandhi herself feels that she rarely had the time to sit back and plan out a role for herself. She just moved, she says "from job to job," but the fact remains that the impulse to participate never flagged. She feels she would have liked to have been an archaeologist, an interior decorator, or even a writer: the conflict remained but the urge for a private commitment did not triumph over one for a more public calling. At each stage in her life this was evident, as a child, as a teenager, as a student in England, as a young woman in love, as a bride, and of course almost totally so thereafter. Each of these occasions could have been used as a reason for not participating, but personal circumstances never won over a sense of duty to a public cause. Even her attachment to Feroze grew from a common political commitment, and whatever the incompatibilities it is easier to see her as the wife of a man like Feroze, free-minded, politically conscious, and with a fluid future—than of any bureaucrat, executive or diplomat, howsoever brilliant, whose careers must run according to pattern.

In fact, as soon as they came back from England, both Indira and Feroze had begun to interest themselves in the student movement, although one of her first public appearances in India was like the China meeting in London and brought back all the inhibitions that had temporarily been scotched. A meeting to welcome her back was held in Lucknow at the Ganga Prasad Memorial Hall. There were huge crowds, composed of young and old alike, although the meeting was actually held under the aupices of the Congress dominated Youth League. "She stood up," relates a person who was there. "She was very nervous and fumbled and said she was finding it difficult to speak in Hindi. So the crowd urged her to switch to English. She began by saying, 'These are days of storm and stress . . . .' It was a typical Nehru sentence. In fact, people remarked that it was a copy of Nehru. Suddenly she said she wasn't feeling well and sat down."[51]

The All India Students Federation at the time had two wings, the Gandhian right wing, led by Rajkumari Amrit Kaur, who acted on behalf of Gandhi as students' adviser, and the communist wing. There was a split in the All India body after Germany attacked Russia in June 1941 and the communists were forced to do a lot of soul-searching on the character of the war, but even after the session at Nagpur in February 1942, when the two wings formally broke apart, they both continued to hold the same name. The Gandhian wing got the official backing of the Congress at the same time while the practical effect of the split made itself most evident in the opposition of the communist wing to the Quit India movement and their plea for strenuous Indian participation in the war.

In the winter of 1941, Indira was in indifferent health and she went to Lucknow to have some X-rays done by a cousin of her father's, Dr Nehru, who was superintendent of the hospital there. People who came to know her then found her very unassuming and friendly. At the beginning of December, when Jawaharlal was released from prison, he went to Lucknow, Indira was there, and by then, along with Feroze, she had allied herself with the communist wing of the students' body. She had been invited by them to address a meeting of their Students Federation at Cawnpore. S. K. Kitchlu, a young Kashmiri student who later became the representative of the *Hindustan Times* in Lucknow, remembers that while he was walking up the staircase with her to the place where Jawaharlal was to hold his press conference after his release, they were followed by Jagdish Chandar Dikshit, who later became president of the Indian National Trade Union Congress and member of the legislative council. The split had already taken place in the federation. Dikshit was urging Indira then not to side with the communist faction of the federation but give her support to the Gandhian group instead. She did not answer.

Later in December Feroze arranged an exhibition of photographs and slides of the Soviet war effort, in a room in the office of the *National Herald* at Lucknow and in February 1942 he had a big hand in helping to organize the Indo-Soviet Congress that Jawaharlal inaugurated. "Feroze, fresh from London, had a bagful of enthusiasms, including enthusiasm for the Soviet Union and machines," recalls Chalapathi Rau, who met him at that time.[52] The greatest story about him those days, recalls another, was that he *was* indeed fresh from London. But this was the period when Feroze was the more active of the two and seemed to be reaching towards a tangible political future of his own.

But what is significant is that in spite of their strong socialist bent both Indira and Feroze were not prepared to toe the communist line as such. In August 1942 their choice was clear. They were unequivocally with Gandhi, the Congress, and the Quit India movement rather than with the communists. What was significant then remained so as far as Indira was concerned, and it is quite astonishing to find how consistent she has been in the balance she struck between dogma and doctrine, arriving eventually at a kind of mellowed socialistic idealism.

Politics, however, had even been the refrain to their wedding. Instead of the yearning notes of the *shehnai* that define the mood of a traditional Indian wedding, there were the discussions on a new set of British proposals brought by Sir Stafford Cripps, who had landed in Delhi on March 22, only four days before the wedding. Against the highly charged political atmosphere, even the customary aplomb of Indira tottered, and at dinner one evening for Sir Stafford who came to Allahabad she offered him "potato cripps" instead of "potato chips."[53] To one person at least she gave the impression of being, for a change, in a private dream world of her own. This was Teji Bachchan, wife of one of India's most eminent Hindi poets, and later the prime minister's close friend. Teji was from the Punjab but married in Allahabad, and Allahabad at the time meant the Nehrus. When she was introduced to the Nehru household at the time by Sarojini Naidu, she met Indira. "She had a very shy, misty look," recalls Mrs Bachchan, "and being newly married and very much in love myself, I was sensitive to another's state of being."[54]

Yet while the discussions raged between Indian leaders and Sir Stafford Cripps, and the Congress working committee went into one of its most extended sessions on record from March 29 to April 11, Indira and Feroze chose to stay on at Allahabad. Even afterwards, Indira accompanied her father to Manali and Feroze remained behind to look out for a house. It was only after Indira had also visited Lahore on a personal errand that she and Feroze finally escaped for a prolonged honeymoon to the mountains of Kashmir.

"Wish we could send you some cool breezes from here," they wired commiseratingly to Jawaharlal from Gulmarg. And Jawaharlal, not to be outdone, telegraphed back with characteristic humor: "Thanks. But you have no mangoes."[55]

But the deep bond between father and daughter impinged subtly even on Indira's honeymoon, for Jawaharlal was anxious that the plans she was making to go to the North-West Frontier Province should work out conveniently, and in the process dashed off a number of telegrams to her, sometime addressed, rather significantly, to Indira Nehru Gandhi.[56] Here indeed was a touch of unconscious arrogance for certainly up to that time, Indira had not achieved the sort of independent reputation that might have merited the retention of her maiden name and Women's Lib had not arrived! Feroze's admiration for Jawaharlal was at its peak and only later when

the logic of being a son-in-law began to raise issues of a more personal
nature did he realize that he had to pay a price for having dared to become so. It was not merely a question of Jawaharlal's stature; it was
a question of Indira's natural love for her widowed father sharpened by
her sense of his greatness and her need to give him the extra care to conserve his energies for his momentous role. The January session of the
AICC had already proved to be exhilarating. Gandhi had scotched all
rumors of any fundamental split between him and Jawaharlal by pointing
out a more fundamental sense of oneness.

"It will require much more than differences of opinion to estrange us.
We have had differences from the moment we became co-workers, and yet I
have said for some years and say now," he added in a statement which itself
became historic, "that not Rajaji but Jawaharlal will be my successor. He
says he does not understand my language, and that he speaks a language
foreign to me. This may or may not be true. But language is no bar to a
union of hearts."

And then the prophetic utterance: "And I know this, that when I am
gone he will speak my language."

There are varying accounts of what Indira and Feroze did to give Professor
Shastri's unorthodox Hinduism and the marriage rites he had evolved a
cover of law. But according to one interpretation, on their way back from
Kashmir, Feroze and Indira stopped at a princely state where Feroze had
found a marriage act permitting a civil ceremony between two people of
different faiths without their having to renounce their religion. Sir Tej
Bahadur's opinion that Shastri's marriage rites were illegal evidently wrankled
in their minds and they went through another ceremony just to be on the
safe side.[57]

According to another account they underwent a civil marriage ceremony
in the court of a magistrate in Allahabad, just before the ritualistic one of
Shastri's which was attended by friends, relatives, and an adoring Nehru
public.

When I asked Mrs Gandhi if she and Feroze did indeed stop in a state
and go through a second ceremony she looked quite startled.

"Certainly not," she exclaimed.

"But at Allahabad, then?" I asked. "I understand that the marriage
was registered before the other ceremony took place."

"No, no, not at all."

"I understand that you were worried that Shastri's rites may not have
been legal," I insisted, trying to prod her memory, "and that's how the
question arose of ensuring that one legal ceremony should be undergone
in any case."

The prime minister's denial was not only categorical, but defiant.

"Nothing of the kind. It just didn't bother me, whether it was legal or
not."

In Allahabad, they took a small house at 4 Fort Road in what was then called George Town, but it was near enough to Anand Bhawan for them to feel that they were still part of that hectic center. Feroze had no job. He began to make use of his collection of photographs for illustrated articles for magazines and papers, substantiated by odd insurance work. His hobbies, apart from photography, were carpentry and gardening, and soon the little house had furniture in excellent taste and a garden that bloomed under his tender care. It was a short interlude of adjustment and happiness. The political portents were ominous. By August the country was in turmoil and Indira and Feroze were caught in the vortex of political demands, agitations and subsequent imprisonment. But for them as well as for thousands of their countrymen, led by Gandhi and Nehru, it was a willing plunge.

9. JAIL

The events that led to the 1942 movement were the war crisis that brought
the Cripps mission to India and the Indian crisis that followed its failure.
Churchill declared scathingly in the summer of 1941 that he had not become
"His Majesty's first minister to preside over the liquidation of the British
Empire" and had excluded India from the provisions of the Atlantic Charter
he had himself been a signatory to—"the right of all peoples to choose the
form of government under which they will live."   He had refused to consider

the Congress offer of conditional cooperation that it had arrived upon at
its January meeting at the cost of Gandhi's valuable support. But when
the Japanese army entered Rangoon on March 8 and the route to India lay
wide open Churchill was forced to seek a workable arrangement with
nationalist India. "If the effective defense of India was to be organized,"
he wrote later, "it seemed to most of my colleagues important to make
effort to break the political deadlock."[1] India, however, had reason to
be satisfied with the choice of negotiator.

Sir Stafford Cripps had long been a perceptive spokesman for the Indian
cause. He had extremely good personal relations with Nehru and Gandhi.
He had also the authority of being a member of the war cabinet, the leader
of the House of Commons, and after his brilliant stint as British ambassador
to Russia, was at a prestigious peak in his political career. But what Cripps
brought proved to be only a dressed-up version of Britain's terms of August
1940, while his conflicting personal advocacy made Jawaharlal comment
later that he was "surprised at his woodenness and insensitiveness, in spite of
his public smiles," and that "he was all the time the formal representative of
the war cabinet, in fact he was the war cabinet speaking to us with a take it
or leave it attitude." Gandhi's reported reaction when he saw the proposals
was to suggest to Cripps that he take the first plane back home.

"I felt this was due more to his aversion to war than to his objection to
the proposal as such. In fact, his judgment of the merits of the proposal
was colored by his inherent and unchangeable aversion to anything which
might involve India in war," declared Maulana Azad years later in a rather
one-sided interpretation of Gandhi's motives.[2]

Azad as president was the official spokesman of the Congress, but his
own initial sense of optimism was soon dissipated. There were snags all
the way. There was the promise of dominion status for India and the
right to elect its constitutent assembly and frame a new constitution for
itself. Not only was this promise conditional on the end of the war, but
also the right was given to "any province of British India that was not
prepared to accept the new constitution to retain its present constitutional
position, provision being made for its subsequent accession if it so decides. . . .
With such non-acceding provinces, should they so desire, His Majesty's
Government would be prepared to agree upon a new constitution giving
them the same full status as the Indian Union." Here was the culmination
of the steady policy of separatism that British interests had pursued over the
years. A stamp of reality was given to the League demand for partition[3]
which until then, as Jawaharlal said, "few had taken seriously."

"The introduction of separate religious electorates a generation or more
earlier had played enough mischief; now the door was opened to every
obscurantist group giving trouble . . . and the possibility of an indefinite
number of partitions,"[4] he commented. Secondly, the actual composition
of the proposed constituent assembly envisaged a parity between the

elected representatives from British India and persons from the Indian states nominated by the rulers, with the implied option that they would have to withdraw from the responsibilities of their own decisions if they ultimately decided to remain outside the purview of the union. He was present with the Maulana at almost every interview with Cripps and the more he examined the implications of the proposals the more acute grew his sense of "profound depression."

The Congress concluded that although it was impossible for it to accept the long-term aspect of these proposals, it was prepared to cooperate along the lines of a provisional national government to meet the perils of the war. For this the Cripps draft declaration declared that "until the new constitution can be framed, His Majesty's Government must inevitably bear the responsibility for and retain the control and direction of the defense of India as part of their world war effort but the task of organizing to the full the military, moral, and material resources of India must be the responsibility of the Government of India with the cooperation of the peoples of India." This seemed to suggest that barring defense all other subjects would be transferred to Indian hands and in the place of the British members of the executive council there would henceforth be only Indians. In his first interview with the Congress president, Cripps indicated that the council would function like a cabinet and the viceroy would be in the position of a constitutional head and bound by the decisions of this cabinet. This gave considerable scope for agreement. But it slipped again on the vital matter of defense. Subsequently, Cripps went back on his assurances about the powers of the council even otherwise, and all that emerged from the apparent *volte face* was that the viceroy would retain supreme veto over everything.

Whether he had painted everything too rosily in the beginning to win over Indian opinion and then regretted it, or whether he genuinely thought that within the general framework of the proposals there was a possibility of a convention of democratic function emerging and therefore urged their acceptance, the fact that he also could not depend on total support from home for any interpretation that he gave to the proposals led Cripps into a pattern of conflict, mistrust and misunderstanding in his dealing with Indian leaders which left a pall of bitterness over the failure of the talks. There was a personal disenchantment with Cripps, from whom something of more substance had been expected. But there was also a fateful realization that the British had never meant to part with power and that this was a temporary device to win cooperation for the war effort. Even so, Churchill had never thought much of Congress support. "Bringing hostile elements into the war machine will paralyze action,"[5] he had said in January 1941 and it was only the stern urgency of the Japanese advance that made him opt for a political palliative in the form of the Cripps proposals. Under no circumstances was he willing that a national government be set up in India in the foreseeable future and there was a note of tremendous relief in his reaction when President Franklin Roosevelt, posted with the latest on the Indian situation through his personal envoy in Delhi, urged him toward a more radical approach, and to do for India during the war what they seemed to be willing to do afterward. "I was thankful that events had made such an act of madness impossible," Churchill confessed for Cripps had left for India by then.[6]

With their sympathies naturally lying on the side of the democracies, Indian leaders found themselves in a dilemma. Nothing, they thought, seemed to have stirred conscienceless Britain into an honorable settlement, neither the Congress policy of "nonembarrassment" in 1939-40, nor the one of restrained, symbolic protest through the limited campaign of individual civil disobedience in 1940-41. The reaction to the Cripps fiasco had been as intense and unanimously hostile as to the Simon Commission in 1928, and nationalist leaders feared that the strong anti-British feeling that was generated thereby might lead to a passive acceptance of the Japanese advance.

"I have no desire to exchange the British for any other rule. Better the enemy I know than the one I do not. I have never attached the slightest importance or weight to the friendly professions of the Axis powers,"[7] declared Gandhi categorically. He was convinced that it was "the British presence which was the incentive for the Japanese attack" on the one hand and on the other that effective, nonviolent resistance—he would not visualize any other—on a national basis could only be organized by an independent India. He had always held the view that British withdrawal from India was imperative for the solution of the communal problem. In April 1941 he said, "Why do not British statesmen admit that it is after all a domestic quarrel? Let them withdraw from India and I promise that the League and all other parties will find it to their interest to come together."[8] A year later he realized that the same precondition was necessary to enable the Indians to feel a stake in the defense of their country. "The time has come for the British and the Indians to be reconciled to complete separation from each other."[9] This mild understatement took on dramatic emphasis with his spirited cry, "Leave India to God and if that be too much, leave her to anarchy."[10]

"In the first week of July, there was a meeting of the working committee at Wardha. I reached Wardha on 5th July," recalled Azad, "and Gandhiji spoke to me for the first time about the Quit India movement."[11] Gandhi indicated that he was "thinking aloud," and in fact, on July 7, incidentally revealing how flexible were the processes of his thought, he wrote: "I had not given expression to the whole idea in my mind. It is not my nature to work out and produce a finished thing all at once."[12] Nevertheless, the resolution of the working committee which sat in session at Wardha from July 6 to 14 was able to spell out the actual details. The British must withdraw from India, it said, so that first it could transform the existing illwill against Britain into goodwill and make India "a willing partner in a joint enterprise of securing freedom for the nations and peoples of the world" and second, so that it could be left free to solve its communal problem by the formation of a provisional government represented by all sections of the people who could devise an appropriate scheme to call a constituent assembly for the purpose of preparing a constitution which, in turn, would be acceptable to all those sections of the people. India would then cooperate with Britain on an equal basis as an ally to meet aggression, and on the condition of obtaining its freedom, and this was the operative clause sanctioned by Gandhi himself, "the Congress [would be] agreeable to the stationing of the armed forces of the Allies in India, should they so desire, in order to ward off and resist Japanese or other aggression, and to protect and help China."[13]

"For him this was a remarkable and astonishing change involving suffering of the mind and pain of the spirit," Jawaharlal analyzed later. "In the conflict between that principle of nonviolence which had become his very lifeblood and meaning of existence, and India's freedom, which was a dominating and consuming passion for him, the scales inclined towards the latter. That did not mean, of course, that he weakened in his faith in nonviolence.... But it did mean that he was prepared to agree to the Congress not applying it in this war. The practical statesman took precedence over the uncompromising prophet."[14]

One basic concept, however, was never to be sacrificed. The fight, whether against the British or the Japanese, was not to be against the people but against the systems or the stand they represented. Unlike Stalin, whose exhortation to his people on May Day the same year had been that to fight the enemy you must hate him thoroughly, Gandhi believed that you must be detached from all personal rancor. It was the political compulsion of having to carry one's colleagues in a decision that made him yield on the issue of violent resistance to the Japanese. Left on his own he believed that love or moral pressure could win all. Even when it came to demanding British withdrawal from India he was quick to point out that this did not mean "the physical withdrawal of all Britons and certainly not of those who would make India their home and live there as citizens and equals." This point was thought important enough to find its way into the main resolution at Wardha as an indication of India's willingness to remain on terms of goodwill with Britain in the future.

"Even at the height of the struggle," according to Mrs Gandhi, "the British were always welcome in our homes."[15]

This was revolution framed by rationality. It was an extraordinary criterion. Even while feeling that Gandhi demanded too much of human nature, those who were close to him could not help but be elevated by the sheer idealism of the man and were drawn into the orbit of his unconscious but powerful magic.

But human nature could not be denied, nor the logic of governance.

"Events were not waiting for a Congress decision or resolution, they had been pushed forward by Gandhiji's utterances and now they were moving onwards with their own momentum,"[16] recorded Jawaharlal later. By August 1942, when the AICC met at Bombay to consider the working committee's resolution, emotions across the country were stretched tight. The temper of the people as well as of the government was high. There was no indication that His Majesty's Government in India was in any mood to listen to the Congress appeal. On the contrary, Congress leaders had evidence that it was poised to strike. The AICC sat long in session that evening on August 8 and then in a stirring reiteration of the Wardha resolution sanctioned "the vindication of India's inalienable right to freedom and independence, the starting of a mass struggle on nonviolent lines on the widest possible scale ... such a struggle," it added, "must inevitably be under the leadership of Gandhiji."[17]

Gandhi believed that in the last resort the British would recognize the justice of India's demand. He had not spelled out what form the movement which was bound to follow the British rejection would take. He was quite taken up, according to the Maulana's version, with Jawaharlal's phrase of an "open rebellion" or an "open nonviolent revolution" as he himself began to term it in early July. He was convinced, however, that the British would comes to terms as soon as the movement was launched or that he would have the time and opportunity to guide it along the right lines and evolve, as before, a staged manifestation of protest. But his address to his colleagues after the resolution was an inspiring one.

"It is going to be a mass struggle," he said. "There is nothing secret about our plans ... I have pledged the Congress and the Congress will do or die."[18]

He made it clear that before launching the movement he would issue another appeal to the viceroy and wait for the answer. But the British, under the threat of an imminent attack by the Japanese on the Indian front, preferred, paradoxically, to immobilize India's leaders rather than obtain their cooperation. In a dramatic simultaneous swoop in the early hours of August 9, the government arrested all the members of the working committee, including Gandhi, the Congress president and Jawaharlal, as well as leading local congressmen in all the major cities.

Indira and Feroze were there to witness not only the rousing proceedings of this historic Congress, but the heart-rending corollary at home. They were staying with Jawaharlal at Krishna's flat in Carmichael Road. It was a fairly spacious three-bedroom flat, but Krishna and Raja had moved in with a friend across the road to make more room available for "the chaos that always erupted" when Jawaharlal stayed with them. There was a constant stream of known and unknown politicians who came to argue, confabulate, and talk endlessly and with passion. For that one whole week that preceded the final decision, the Carmichael Road flat was bristling with excitement and it seemed that wherever Jawaharlal was would henceforth be like a miniature Anand Bhawan, recalling the familiar atmosphere of people, noise, discussion, and the making of history. But on the evening of August 8, when they returned with some of the other leaders from the Congress session with Gandhi's words ringing in their ears, they were elated but exhausted. Their nervous exuberance kept them talking until after midnight so that by the time Jawaharlal got to bed he was dead tired. At five in the morning, the doorbell rang; the street below swarmed with police. Krishna and Raja rushed from across the street to see lights blazing in their apartment. Indira looked calm and grave but no doubt felt forlorn as her father was asked to accompany the British officials again to prison. This was his ninth conviction and already he had spent eight years and twenty-two days of his life in jail. This time they would not even indicate where they were taking him, so fearful was the government of possible public outcry.

Raja was also arrested, and Indira, Feroze, and Krishna followed the police to the railway station in a friend's car to see what they could find out. But there was a group of policemen at the gates of the railway station and they were not allowed to enter. Indira and Krishna took the desperate but in the circumstances hardly noticeable action of scaling the walls to see what was happening inside, but when they found nothing but policemen there they jumped back. So they stood at the gates and watched with sinking hearts a succession of police cars carrying the leaders of the Congress party and the lesser known but ardent second line. When they saw a car with Gandhiji in it, recalls Krishna, they felt that this was the very end. The news of the arrests had spread and suddenly the streets were filled with masses shorn of all their leaders but angry, resentful, and in no mood for quiet submission. Indira, Feroze, and Krishna went straight to Birla House, where Gandhi had been staying and where they hoped to find Kasturba, his wife, and others to determine what they should do. There was the same atmosphere of uncertainty and confusion. Gandhi had said that this time the people should not willingly court arrest but resist the autocracy of the government. But he had also said that there should be no "subterranean activity." According to Krishna, however, at Birla House, in a meeting that lasted forty-five minutes, they decided not to defy the government openly, but to start an underground movement.[19]

Feroze perhaps had been waiting for something just like this to gather his energies together, for the zeal with which he plunged into the role of an underground worker suggests that he was certainly not content to bask in the glory of the Nehru sacrifice. On August 10 both Indira and Feroze left Bombay for Allahabad. But because Feroze had decided to go "underground" he began to grow a mustache and donned a khaki uniform.

"Because of his complexion, which was fair and ruddy," says Mrs Gandhi, "he passed as an Anglo-Indian soldier. On his journey from Bombay he got off at a small wayside station, thinking that he was too well-known in Allahabad to risk being seen at the station, even in disguise." His dare-devilry combined with his irrepressible sense of fun led to a mocking encounter with the enemy. "Because no conveyance was available," Mrs Gandhi relates further, "he hitched a ride from a truck full of British and Anglo-Indian soldiers, who were scared stiff and almost refused to let him get off again, saying that the damned natives would hack him to pieces if they found him alone and unarmed!"[20]

At Allahabad Feroze went off to a loyal locality called Yehiapur, an ancient and picturesque place with winding lanes and bylanes where it was easy to hide in the houses of friends. Indira had gone straight to Anand Bhawan. She found that not only was Swaraj Bhawan occupied by the military, but a row of guns was trained toward Anand Bhawan from across the garden. The servants were nervous and confused. Simple people who were unfamiliar with English, they were terrified of the curt warning that came each time they happened to go near the wall: "Halt, who goes there?" Her aunt was there with her three daughters. She learned that they had gone through a fearful experience earlier during the day. The police had fired on a procession of students and Vijayalaxmi and the two elder girls had spent time helping the wounded young men to hospital.

"I was utterly weary in mind and body and more than a little dazed," recorded Vijayalaxmi later. "Both Lekha and Tara . . . had seen sights which would not easily be effaced from their memory and were bewildered and unhappy."[21]

The police came for her at 2 A.M. She was not expecting to be arrested. She had made no arrangements for her daughters. But this was a price that had to be paid. She was thoroughly angry, however, when she saw that armed police were swarming even up to the porch of the house. "Why is it necessary for so many armed men to come to arrest one unarmed woman at this amazing hour?" she expostulated as the city magistrate shuffled with unease. Indira was fast asleep in her room on the first floor—the room that remained hers even after her marriage—when her aunt rushed up, gave her a few hasty instructions to look after the girls, and kissed her good-bye. The girls put up a brave front, and it was pathetic to watch little Rita cling to her mother yet say firmly, "Mummie, darling, take care of yourself. We shall be fighting the British outside while you are in."[22]

So Indira, barely five months married, was left in sole charge of a sprawling mansion and three young cousins. She could meet her husband only briefly in utter secrecy at carefully arranged times at the houses of sympathetic but nonpolitical friends. There was no saying when or how they, too, might be arrested. It was a dramatic backdrop to a new marriage and the hazards they shared served to bind them closer together. Feroze had to be constantly on the move even within Yehiapur. The police and the intelligence were on the lookout for him but the people of Yehiapur guarded him so well that he could freely meet Congress workers and give them instructions. Congress volunteers would station themselves at vantage points wherever Feroze happened to be. "The moment any policeman or intelligence man was seen, Feroze was at once informed. This would enable him to disappear in the nearest house in the twinkling of an eye. All houses were open for him," says Kamla Prasad Mohiley, who knew Feroze as a student and worked with him in the underground movement.[23]

Indira was hiding Lal Bahadur Shastri in a room at Anand Bhawan. "Shastriji," as she was always to call him, had taken a gamble that nobody would imagine he would dare stay at the Nehru home and therefore would not look for him there. That is precisely what happened. Indira, the Pandit girls, and the faithful servants pretended that they had an ailing relative staying with them. So food was sent up to Shastri's room and he came out only after dark. People met him and messages were given and the work of the movement carried on in this manner until the risk became too great and Shastri had to move out. He was arrested shortly after. Indira was trying to remain as inconspicuous as possible so that she could help as much she could.

"We were hedged in on all sides," she says now, "and it was well-nigh impossible for workers to get together. My husband became one of the links through whom I could pass on money and political literature to other underground workers."[24] She soon had her first experience of a lathi attack. She was invited by students of the Ewing Christian College to attend a function at which they were to hoist the national tricolor in the compound of their college. She knew she might be arrested. But what she found when she reached there horrified her. The police had already arrived and the boy who held the flag was being beaten. He soon fell so she rushed up and took the flag. The students took heart and began to sing the popular patriotic song: *"Jhanda Ooncha Rahe Hamara"* (May Our Flag Forever Fly High).

Then a policeman struck her on her back with his baton. Another blow and a push sent her sprawling on the ground, and as images of her father and grandmother, who had suffered similarly, went flashing across her mind, the policeman trod deliberately on her body with his nailed boots as he stepped across.

"I felt pain, but only later on when I went home," she recalls now. "At that moment I felt only anger—an enormous anger, a passionate anger."[25]

The government soon realized that Nehru's daughter could hardly be a political innocent, and Indira got news that she was to be arrested. She did not feel like going to jail tamely, she says, so she packed up some clothes and—like her father, the inevitable books—and disappeared from Anand Bhawan. The idea was to arrange a meeting and at the last moment emerge and address the crowd. News was spread by word of mouth from worker to worker, and though the police got an inkling that something was brewing they could not discover where the meeting was to be held. On September 11 the police began to swarm all over the city. At the scheduled time of 5 P.M., Indira suddenly appeared at the previously arranged venue and with her came crowds of her ardent countrymen spilling over from all sides, the cinema, the houses nearby, and the streets where they had been gathering quietly for hours.

Mrs Gandhi's own description is vivid.

I had hardly spoken for ten minutes when truckloads of armed British military drove up and formed a cordon around us. My husband had decided not to get involved and was looking down at us through the shutters of a first-floor window. However, at the sight of a gun barrel just a yard away from my head, excitement and anxiety got the better of him and he came charging down, yelling at the sergeant to shoot or to lower his gun. The sergeant made the mistake of touching my arm to lead me to the prison van. It was like a signal, the crowd surged forth— my other arm was grabbed by some Congress women and I thought I would be torn asunder. Somehow we all survived. There was no firing though rifle butts were used and many were hurt. A large number of us, men and women, including my husband, were arrested. The ride to the jail was rather an extraordinary one, for police in my van were apparently so moved by my talking to them that they apologized, put their turbans at my feet and wept their sorrow because of what their job compelled them to do.[26]

An eyewitness describes Indira's manner as impeccably dignified, but he seemed to think that Feroze was rather flamboyant.[27] Feroze in fact had done an extraordinary thing. In the melee that followed the scuffle around Indira he somehow got onto the roof of the van, and began to address the crowd from there. It was only when Indira was put into the van that the police realized where Feroze was and hastily caught him, too. Meanwhile "the audience," recalls Mohiley, "was electrified by his heroism and determination."[28]

And so, as Jawaharlal would have said, to prison.

There was terrific excitement that evening at Naini central prison. At 6.30 Indira found herself at the high arched gate she had entered so many times to visit her father and others, but this time she was a prisoner herself. It was half an hour after lockup and a tremendous knocking at the outer gate ushered them in. The matron apparently was a little overawed that Jawaharlal's daughter had been arrested for she burst into Vijayalaxmi's barrack with an excited "Mrs Indira is here." It was almost like an announcement preceding the appearance of a distinguished guest at a banquet or ball. But what actually greeted Indira, apart from the welcome sight of Vijayalaxmi and Lekha, who meantime had also been arrested, was a rectangular room with gratings at short distances all along each side, mud-colored walls, broken roof tiles, and the depressing light from a lantern that cast weird shadows on the walls. On one side of the barrack, four steps up there was a tiny latrine for use during the night, and one of the gratings formed a door which was bolted at "lockup time." Indira had been arrested with five other women and after the initial eager chatter about what had happened there was the raucous noise of the prison night when forty-four women criminals in an adjoining yard erupted into abuse every now and then and the frogs croaked, while the callous goings-on of jail officialism soon overwhelmed the new arrivals.

"What a world of difference there is between hearing and seeing from the outside and the actual experience. No one who has not been in prison for any length of time," describes Mrs Gandhi, "can even visualize the numbness of spirit that can creep over one ... when day after day is wrapped in sameness and in spite and deliberate humiliation ... herded together like animals devoid of dignity or privacy, debarred not only from outside company or news but from all beauty and color, softness and grace. The grounds, the walls, everything around us was mud-colored and so became our jail-washed clothes, even our food tasted gritty. Through the barred apertures we were exposed to the dust storms, the monsoon downpour, and the winter cold."[29]

At the time she was arrested, it was hot, flies swarmed all over, ants got into their sugar ration, and the jail cat drank up all the milk. The lack of privacy was insufferable, for the women liked to talk most of the time, and although Indira was determined to suffer all with fortitude and a capacity for aloofness, her physique rebelled and she developed a temperature within two days of her incarceration. She had no news of her father and although Feroze was in the men's section in the same prison she was not allowed to see him. Another morbid factor in their prison life was the discovery that a young woman called Vidyavati, who had been arrested along with Indira, was pregnant and the youngest prisoner, Govindi, was only twelve years old! There was no limit, it seemed, to the harsh follies of an alien rule.

Indira found that the wardresses, too, were a mixed lot. Mrs Pandit, who wrote a lively prison diary of the time, gives a fascinating picture of these women:

Zohra is a deadly female. Incredibly dirty in her person and in her habits she is a born cringer and looks unreliable. Zainab is a fat, placid woman, very talkative and full of anecdotes of her past. Service in a prison has not warped her and her sense of humor is quite delicious. Vishnudei is tall and strapping. In size and physique she is the ideal wardress and looks imposing in her uniform. She is reticent and does not speak. Shyama is a negative person altogether, the type one hardly notices. Mrs Solomon seems the nicest of the lot—as a human being she is superior to the rest and is gentle in manner. A Christian, she looks upon herself as being in a different class to the others and, in the way of Christian converts in India, her standard has been raised beyond her status in life and she is in constant difficulties.

Only a door separated the yard in which their barracks were from the yard of the "habituals," the convict women in for abduction, theft, and murder. They were not allowed to come into their side, but occasionally when the door between was opened, they would smile at each other and exchange stories. There was Sharbati, with her beautiful name, but her disease-ridden body, and Naraini, in for her eleventh conviction, with her bony skin, broken teeth, and close cropped hair, a hideous sight, hysterical, full of threats and possessor of a furious temper. Once she had climbed up a tree, taken a sheet from somewhere, knotted it up, and threatened to commit suicide if her sentence was not reduced! When the superintendent persuaded her not to kill herself, she agreed but jumped down the tree and fractured her arm and broke a rib.[30]

There was a rigid social hierarchy. The women in for abduction were looked down upon by the counterfeiters of coin, and the latter by those in for theft. Murder brought the highest status. "It is usual when a quarrel takes place for a woman to say—'Don't dare treat me as if I were a common thief—won't stand for it—I am in for murder'," records Vijayalaxmi Pandit. One of the murderers was the twenty-six-year-old Durgi, a girl with pleasant manners and good features who was caught for killing her husband. She had been appointed by the matron to come over to the "politicals' yard" and help Vijayalaxmi with cleaning and cooking. Durgi had reason enough to hate her husband because he had been indifferent to her, beaten her, and not even given her enough to eat. But the evident satisfaction with which she described the gruesome details of her act to Vijayalaxmi was not for weak stomachs. On the whole, they were a vulgar, abusive lot. Given to terrible quarrels and unruly behavior even in prison, they certainly did not make for the atmosphere of intellectual fecundity that Jawaharlal had managed to create for himself in prison. Though Indira was not aware of it at the time, and the world was to profit by it later, Jawaharlal was in Ahmednagar Fort with eleven companions among whom were Maulana Azad, Govind Vallabh Pant, Narendra Deva, and Asaf Ali, who represented a cross-section of Indian scholarship in the classical as well as the various living Indian languages and whose talk, erudition, and scholarship were stimulating him toward another valuable addition to literary history, his *Discovery of India*.

Indira it appears was not then in a frame of mind in which she could sit back and write of what she was experiencing. Perhaps she felt that she would only be repeating what her aunt was recording in her prison diary. She said later that she almost "sealed in her mind" while in prison with the result that while some others hankered longingly for a certain type of food or the amenities of the outside world, she did not miss anything. The result was as she discovered when she came out, that she had actually lived only on a "surface level." It was a deliberately induced state of detachment which led more toward a stoic discipline than to thoughts of writing like her father. She had to suffer the additional nuisance of being placed in the extraordinary category of X as a prisoner. There were prisoners' cards of three established categories in the Naini jail, A, B, and C, allowing different privileges, but the magistrate had drawn an engimatic X on her card, and the prison superintendent concluded that this meant that she was to have no privileges at all, such as being allowed interviews or receiving or sending mail. From his "unknown destination"—for the government would still not reveal where they had jailed Jawaharlal and his companions—Jawaharlal wrote to Krishna. He was upset although he tried to cover it with an air of casualness.

> For nearly a month I waited for an answer from her [Indu] to my first letter. Finally I decided to write again. Hardly had I done so when I learned from your letters that Indu was not allowed to receive any communications or to write letters. We have been told that we may only write to certain near relatives—father, mother, brothers, sisters, wife, sons, daughters, and a few others. Having no father or mother or brothers or wife or son, the burden of writing is therefore lessened for me. It appears to be limited to my daughter and two sisters. As the daughter and one of the sisters are in a prison in UP where they may not get letters, the list is further reduced and only you ultimately find a place in it. Of course, you are a host by yourself and it is very delightful to hear from you and to write to you. But being so made, I do not take easily to writing under these conditions.[31]

Moreover, they were all *detenus*, which meant that they had to remain in prison at His Majesty's pleasure. On September 19, Indira and Vijayalaxmi learned that Feroze had been sentenced to a one-year imprisonment and fined Rs 200 which made Vijayalaxmi remark that it was better than being suspended in midair, as they were. Five days later they heard that Feroze had also been brought to Naini and had been placed in the low-privileged C class.

"There was no yearning for the outside world," Mrs Gandhi wrote later, "because no one worthwhile was there. Besides, we had convinced ourselves that we were in for seven years. I was determined to bear all privations and insults smilingly." There was the galling occasion when Jawaharlal, knowing how fond she was of mangoes, arranged for a friend to send her a basket. The next day the superintendent, who seems to have been quite unpleasant, calmly thanked her for the delicious fruit. "And he didn't

even have the grace to give us one small piece!" Mrs Gandhi recollects
wryly.[32]

There were some considerations shown, nevertheless. Because of her
temperature in the beginning she was allowed to sleep outside even though
it turned out to be a mistake for the wind at night came from the opposite
direction and she slept badly. On September 27, when her temperature
persisted, they heard in prison that recommendation had been made for her
release, although nothing happened for about a month. On October 22 the
civil surgeon was asked to examine her and report to the government on her
health. "He prescribed a tonic and a special diet including delicacies such
as Ovaltine," Mrs Gandhi adds. "But hardly was his back turned when the
superintendent tore up the list and tossed the pieces on the floor. 'If you
think you are getting any of this,' he said, 'you are mistaken!' This was
surprising for I had not asked for anything—even the surgeon's visit was
unexpected."[33] On October 4 the Nehru women were informed that they had
been placed in A class and would be entitled to draw 12 annas a day as ration
money. But Vijayalaxmi decided to find out the grounds for this privilege
before accepting it.

Meanwhile Indira managed to remain characteristically concerned with
practical activities. There were the purely mundane areas of routine.
She and Lekha decided that they would cook the dinner, while Vijayalaxmi
would fix the lunch. Indira decided to help Lekha with her French if she
were allowed the books. They planned to do a considerable amount of
reading. She also began to give lessons to some of the convict women,
but her major achievement in jail was the future she gave to the young
prisoner Kalavati Mishra, who was brought to their barrack on October 1.
Kalavati had been arrested because she had been carrying the Congress flag
while her husband had been arrested earlier for distributing Congress leaflets.
"She is the vaguest person I have ever seen,"[34] observed Vijayalaxmi, but they
were all thrilled with Kalavati's little daughter, Sarla. The mother, as
Vijayalaxmi thought, was "sublimely unconscious" of what went on around
her and was "unable even to look after her baby." So Indira, perfectionist
as she was having promptly read up on baby care after her marriage, decided
to take the infant in hand and try out her knowledge. She bathed, cleaned,
and fed her, with occasional help from Lekha and Vijayalaxmi, who sewed
clothes for her. In a few days the "political baby," as they started calling
her, not only began to thrive in jail but became very much a part of their
lives, so much so that ultimately Indira had to be dissuaded from adopting
the child legally as her own. But it was Indira's effort with Kalavati that
bore fruit. It is almost fantastic to realize that Kalavati, who knew nothing
when she came to jail, so profited by Indira's guidance that she was able to
take on a teaching job when she left jail. Indira kept in touch with her
through the years. When little Sarla grew up and got married Indira made
her a wedding present of Rs 500.

For personal amusement in the evening, Indira and Lekha would read plays and each take a part. Vijayalaxmi made rather a tolerent audience for she found it all quite amusing. Indira's distinct talent to tell a story dramatically, though in intimate, private conversation, seems to have taken shape in those mud barracks in Naini. "Indu and Lekha are both gifted with imagination and the evenings are seldom dull,"[35] her aunt acknowledged gratefully, and admitted that they were a source of great moral support. In fact, the days sped by quite fast because the gap between illusion and reality was bridged lightheartedly by the two young women. Indira said later that she did not miss anything in the outside world. But the point is that she did attempt to dress up the drabness of jail with all the little graces that make life otherwise charming; pretense had a lot to do with acceptability. They began to decorate their corner of the barrack and give it various names to personalize it. Lekha's side was called "Bien Venue" which she had taken over from her mother where a slight view of the main gate was available, and when, if inadvertently the door was left ajar, you could also get a tantalizing glimpse of grass and trees. Vijaya-laxmi, a true sacrificing mother, had to be content with "Wall View" while Indira gave her area the strange and exotic name of "Chimborazo." Even the beds and the table had names, the jail lantern was "Lucifer," and a bottle of hair oil which had lost its top was "Rupert, the Headless Earle."[36] Indu chose the musical name of "Mehitabel" for the jail cat. The happy accident of having brought an old blue rug along with her bedding and which Vijayalaxmi had placed in the center of the space enclosed by their beds resulted in the area being given the exalted title of the "Blue Drawing Room," where Indira and Lekha even planned to have a little party and toyed with the idea of writing out the menu in French. They had invited the other barrack for lunch on the Dussehra festival and it had been a resounding success. On November 7, Purnima presented the whole barrack with red bangles and they all looked bright and gay. On the eighth it was Diwali and they lit a few lights in the barracks and outside. On the twentieth Purnima invited them for tea on her side. But for New Year's Eve they asked only Purnima over from the other side of their barrack for supper in the "Blue Room"!

Though this surface gaiety contrasted sharply with Jawaharlal's rather intense experience in jail, there were some lighter occupations which most political prisoners shared. One of them was gardening. While some like Feroze and Ranjit—the latter had also joined them in Naini—made an art out of it, others sought to obviate some part of the monotony through it. Indira and Lekha tried hard with larkspurs and other flower seeds given them by Ranjit in an interview, but apart from gardening being one more way of getting through the days they could not make anything out of it.

There were some dramatic diversions, however. One night the horrible Zohra, their most unpopular wardress, screamed with fear and woke them up at 2 A.M. when she found a snake coiled up in the yard. The way Mrs Gandhi describes it the whole thing acquires an episodic quality. Vijaya-laxmi's impression recorded in a diary straightaway is perhaps the more accurate account, but it is worth giving in full Indira's own description of the same incident recollected in tranquillity thirteen years later as an indi-cation that she can not only liven up a story in the telling of it but also in the writing of it.

One night we were startled out of sleep by a blood-curdling shriek. Al-though Zohra was the nastiest and the most unpopular of our wardresses, we could sympathize with her terror and agitation, for there was an enormous cobra only a yard away from our bars, coiled under one of the clocks which the wardress had to punch on her rounds. So, apart from the imminent danger of snakebite there was the legitimate fear of losing her job. We were locked inside the barrack and she within the outer wall. These was no stick or other weapon. Zohra's shouts, now fright-ened, now exasperated, now bullying, now entreating, did nothing to shake the calm of the sentry outside, who wanted detailed information regard-ing the exact location of the snake, specifications of its length and breadth and so on. '*Are Kambakht!*' [O, you unfortunate one!] shouted Zohra. 'Have I got a tailor's tape to measure it from head to tail?' It was several hours before the sentry could be persuaded to call the matron. Her house was three furlongs away and she in turn had to walk to the superin-tendent's house to awaken him before they could go together to the main office to fetch the key to the women's prison. By the time this little procession entered our enclosure, we had long since fallen philosophically asleep and the snake had glided away.[37]

On October 31, Indira was allowed to meet Feroze for the first time since they had been arrested and it buoyed her spirits. Two days later the un-cooperative superintendent had to give the pleasant news that thenceforth a fortnightly interview would be allowed between all husbands and wives in the same prison. In fact, a clandestine traffic was established between the men's and the women's sections. The men managed to get the daily papers with devious ingenuity. According to one of the inmates, Feroze persuaded an old man who used to supply food to the prison to bring a newspaper for them every day rolled up in the hollow of his bamboo stick. And it was also Feroze, in whom imagination and high spirits mingled with a basic consideration, who hit upon the idea of passing them on to the women. He made a fellow prisoner, who happened to have the requisite agility, climb up the drainpipe, hold the parapet wall separating them from the women's section, and throw the newspaper into their yard! After a while the men tired of this one-sided generosity and demanded a home-cooked meal from the women in return! For Indira, happily, there was an added incentive, for the daily paper sometimes enclosed a surprise note from Feroze. Her second interview with Feroze on November 19 came as a birthday gift. She was twenty-five years old, young enough to be frivolous and old enough to be purposeful. It is not fair to compare the use Jawaharlal made of his nine-year total of "enforced leisure," as he called it, and the economic, political, and social theories that took shape in his mind with Indira's activities during her nine months tenure. She had neither the solitude, nor the sort of companionship, nor the depth of maturity to evolve an intellectual pattern of thought. He was fifty-five and certain of his vision. She was half his age, and certain only of her direction. To gain the solitude that she, too, prized, she asked her companions to accept her decision not to talk or be talked to everyday until 5 P.M. She read a lot, but she was as full of formless uncertainties as he had been at the same age, although she felt that her months in prison helped in developing the character that later led to years of meaningful political companionship with her father.

Jawaharlal certainly spared no effort to see that Indira's intellectual development did not suffer under any circumstances. In the difficult situation of both of them not only being in prison at the same time but also in different prisons and cut off totally from each other, he showed his concern to the only person he could, his sister Krishna. "I should like you to send books from time to time to Indu,"[38] he instructed her, although the actual choice he had perforce to leave to Krishna. He certainly communicated his love of books to his daughter.

On New Year's Day, 1943—the government had a feel for the occasion, it seems—Vijayalaxmi and Indira were informed that the government of India had given permission for members of the Congress Working Committee to correspond with their families. This meant that they could hear from Jawaharlal. But typically he was not informed of this permission. "Some two months ago I read in a newspaper that Indu had been given permission to write to me, or rather to write to her relations," Jawaharlal wrote disgustedly to Krishna on February 16. "This was a message of a Delhi correspondent. Some days later a further message appeared to the effect that I had been allowed to write to her. As a matter of fact I had not heard anything about it. Now you inform me that the U.P. government has written to you officially on the subject. I have been expecting to hear from her all the time but no letter has come."[39]

A month later he was more optimistic. Thus, on March 5, again to Krishna: "Today I am also writing to Indu and sending the letters [through the Bombay government, of course] to Naini Prison. I understand she is there. I have not heard from her yet."[40]

And then, on March 21: "At last I have found out about correspondence with Indu and Nan. It really is extraordinary that the U.P. government should come to this decision and not inform me of it, for the whole thing

depended on my knowing and acting accordingly.   For over two months
I wanted to get a letter from Indu."[41]

Even the mango fiasco was righted ultimately. Jawaharlal had earlier
asked Krishna to arrange to have a large basket of fresh fruit to be sent to
Indira, together with "such things as jam, honey, marmalade," and money
to be deposited in her jail account. But the churlish superintendent and
government rules had remained an effective barrier to the implementation
of this solicitude.   When Indira eventually received the luscious Alphonso
mangoes her reaction was not so stoical as she had imagined she had taught
herself to be.

"She was quite excited about the Alphonsos," recounted Jawaharlal to
Krishna when he heard from Indira, "and smelt them and touched them
and almost hugged them. She loves mangoes and getting good fruit and
especially good mangoes, after long being deprived of them, was an exhilarating experience."[42]

Being put in category A had some other benefits. You could sleep
outside, have a fan in the barrack, have money deposited in the office, buy
newspapers and, of course, write and receive one letter a month, with the
rather curious stipulation that it should consist of only 500 words. But
Indira and Purnima kept on sleeping inside the stifling barrack in the growing heat of a north Indian April because of Vimla, another companion who
was only in the second-class category. "I thought it foolish to make a
martyr of myself," commented Vijayalaxmi. "It makes a tremendous difference.   The space, the fresh air and above all the stars help one to retain
one's sense of values and there is a feeling of calmness which I at least never
attain inside the barrack."[43]

The next few days were even hotter, but Indira remained obstinately
inside. "I wish Indu would sleep out," her aunt wrote again with apparent
concern, but she could not change her niece's mind.[44]

On March 21, Vijayalaxmi went home on parole for a month. "I hate
leaving Indu and Lekha but it can't be helped," she had put in her diary,
but she could not help seeing the humor of the situation and added, "They
will have to cook for themselves when I go and will benefit by the experience."[45]
But even while Vijayalaxmi was away, Lekha was released and Indu was
left alone to act as high priestess in the Blue Drawing Room. When Vijayalaxmi returned, Lekha and Tara were on their way to the United States
and "the education in a free country" that their parents thought they
deserved. On May 5 both Indira and her aunt were called to the office
and told that they would be released on the condition that they proceed
to Almora and stay at Khali, Vijayalaxmi's home in the hills. There they
were told they would be under the surveillance of the deputy commissioner.

"If government wants to give us the benefit of a cooler climate, the correct
procedure is either to release us and let us go to any hill station we
please or to send us wherever they please as *detenus*. I have no desire to

go to a cooler place while my colleagues are here," argued Vijayalaxmi loftily.[46]

Both she and Indira refused to give any promise. They were released, nevertheless, on May 13. Within a week Vijayalaxmi was back at Naini, for the externment order was served upon them and they had refused to comply. Surprisingly, there was no warrant of rearrest for Indira. She was left again in solitary command at Anand Bhawan, this time with a fever and a virulent cold. It was later that she realized the joy of her unexpected release, and her reaction, like that to the mangoes, was almost sensuous. She could not even see a color without feeling, as she puts it dramatically, "the shock of it."[47]

"I was dazzled with the rush of life, the many hues and textures, the scale of sounds and the range of ideas. Just to touch and listen was a disturbing experience...."[48]

Although the "admixture of happiness and sorrow," as Mrs Gandhi describes the natural pattern of any life, was to continue to govern hers, too, and she finds it difficult to isolate any event or occasion or phase as the "happiest," she does say that "the most peaceful period of my life was the one during which my two sons were born."[49] Even this period was not without shadow, however, because her father was in prison, the world was at war, and India was devastated by a famine of unimaginable magnitude. The supply lines of rice cut off with the fall of Burma due to inefficiency on the part of the British who remained immune to the plight of the people too long led to death from hunger of an unbelievable 3,500,000 persons. The burden of this gruesome tragedy was borne by Bengal. Both Vijayalaxmi, who was released in June, and Krishna rushed to Calcutta. "I never saw so many people die, hopelessly, uncomplainingly, just lie down in the street and die .... After a month I could stand no more and went back to Bombay,"[50] recounted Krishna. Vijayalaxmi had to rush back when Ranjit was released in October seriously ill. The appalling conditions in the Bareilly jail had sapped the last reserves of his weak constitution. He was not meant, as Vijayalaxmi had written while he was in prison, for the "rough and tumble of politics. With his wealth and learning and fastidious scholarship, his love of art and of all those finer aspects of life which are understood by so few people...[prison] is breaking him down physically. It is a slow daily sacrifice which can be so much more deadly than some big heroic gesture made in a moment of emotional upheaval."[51] Asthma combined with pleurisy turned into pneumonia and he died on January 14, 1944, at Lucknow. Raja, Krishna's husband, was released in November. He, too, was suffering acutely from asthma and it was almost a year before he recovered fully. It is odd to think that the husbands of both these politically active young Nehru sisters should have been basically so unpolitical, while Feroze, with whom Indira was supposed to have made such an incompatible match, was ideally attuned to the same political pitch as

Indira, if not more. In August, when he, too, was released, he was all set, though there was nowhere yet for him to go.

It was a period of domesticity. They had been married only a few months when they were thrown into prison. Now it was a question of rediscovering the sense of companionship. They stayed on at Anand Bhawan. Indira worked on the periphery of politics only. She helped to collect funds for the Bengal famine while Feroze looked for a job. But they could savor to the full the joy of being alone and jointly concerned about the things that mattered. In January, of course, they went to Lucknow and felt the tragic loss of Ranjit in the family. But in January Indira discovered that she was pregnant. She had been carrying on a chatty correspondence with her father all through, but the news about her now made him nervous. She wrote to Krishna that she would like to go to Bombay for a check-up, but Jawaharlal apparently suggested that she should stay on there because of better medical facilities. Feroze accompanied her to Bombay. They stayed with Krishna, but Feroze returned shortly afterward while Indira stayed on. She was as thorough, conscientious, and scientific as ever and apparently followed the precepts for easy childbirth so well that she did not suffer at all. Rajiv, a son, was born on August 20, 1944.

"I was happy to get the news," wrote back Jawaharlal to Krishna's excited telegram. "I was particularly pleased to learn of the easy delivery Indu had."[52]

But Indira's way of putting it was, as usual, more picturesque. Uma Shankar Dixit, a friend and colleague, describes the occasion when she told them about it and how impressive her lack of squeamishness was compared with the basic inhibition that he had found in even the most enlightened women politicians he had known.

"I remember one evening," he says, "when we got back to Anand Bhawan after a long hard day of electioneering. Mrs Gandhi just dropped on to the carpet and reclined against the sofa. A maid servant came in to massage her tired feet to which Mrs Gandhi agreed reluctantly. There were three of us men with her, and the conversation drifted from one subject to another till we came to childbirth. As we men listened dumbfounded, she explained to us all there is about childbirth just as if it were one other natural function— like breathing or blowing your nose, for instance, which of course it might well be. As a man I wouldn't know. But that isn't how Indian women, or even men regard it. 'It's really nothing!' she had exclaimed. She had gone on to describe how hungry she was feeling just before Rajiv was born and had even asked for a piece of toast, and then concluded. 'I was so sorry I couldn't finish my toast'."[53]

The peculiar combination of fearless modernity and a nostalgia for tradition, which marked the Nehrus from Motilal to Indira, came to the surface on this occasion in the mind of Jawaharlal. Just as Motilal had had a pandit waiting to make a horoscope when Indira was born, his son now wrote to her to get one done for her son. He tried to put it rationally.

"Such permanent records of the date and time of birth are desirable," he told Krishna, but it was evident that a horoscope meant more than just that for he went on to say, "As for the time, I suppose the proper solar time should be mentioned and not the artificial time which is being used outside now. Wartime is at least an hour ahead of the normal time."[54] When it was left to him to settle a name for the boy, sentimentally he chose Rajiv, which means lotus, the meaning of which is the same as Kamala and Indira. He had said that he was not so excited about the news of Rajiv's birth as Krishna must have been because "excitement is less in my line" but it made him reminiscent of the time Indira herself had been born and her whole growth swept before his eyes. "Nature goes on repeating itself," he wrote with a wonder that had its own excitement, "but there is no end to its infinite variety and every spring is a resurrection, every birth a new beginning. Especially when that new birth is intimately connected with us, it becomes a revival of ourselves and our old hopes center round it."[55]

By October, Indira was back at Anand Bhawan and although life fell into some sort of routine, there was always the unhappy thought that she could not meet her father. Though they knew by now that he was at Ahmednagar Fort along with other leading congressmen, the government was not allowing any interviews and the prisoners were not asking for any.

"It struck me as an odd and arresting fact," ruminated Jawaharlal in a letter to his sister, "that for nearly 26 months—for 785 days to be exact— I had not seen a woman even from a distance. And I began to wonder, what are women like? How do they look, how do they talk and sit and walk?"

And further, with a touch of sadness: "The private worlds each one of us lives in, worlds of fancy and feeling and imagination, have so long lain apart that they are apt to become strangers to each other, separate circles overlapping less than they used to. Partly that happens as we grow older, but the process is accelerated by the abnormal conditions we have been living in."[56]

In January there was a family wedding which drew the clan together at Allahabad and had Jawaharlal recapturing the happy environs of other times and the faces of those who must have changed. Even when at last the government decided to allow interviews, Jawaharlal felt that the conditions under which they were likely to take place did not "fit in with my conception of my dignity or the dignity of my dear ones." He refused to accept the privilege, and for Indira one part of her being remained closed and anchorless.

It was a strangely unpolitical period for Indira, but her use of the word "peaceful" in describing it is quite significant. One of her friends maintains that years later, if she had not lost Feroze, she would never have accepted the prime ministership of India. "She would have been willing to live in a small house and help him achieve his political ambitions. In her heart of hearts, I think, she would have been happiest as a housewife."

When I suggested that the conflict was nevertheless there, she argued, "No, there was no conflict. That is a wrong word. If there had been a conflict she would not have accepted these positions of power. She had this feeling that if she is called upon to take responsibility she must discharge it to the full."[57]

This is a naive interpretation of a nature which seems to have plunged with quiet but passionate intensity rather than a mere sense of duty into the world of politics. Indira herself has eulogized the "gentle thread of domesticity"[58] that she says has run through her life, but if it had been totally fulfilling she would have called her quiet years from 1943 to 1947 "happy" rather than just "peaceful," and she is particular enough about her choice of language to discriminate between such nuances. However, even this peaceful phase was just an interlude. After that, as she says, she "got involved once again in public life." By May 8, 1945, the war with Germany was over and on August 14, 1945, the war with Japan ended. On June 15 Jawaharlal was released, and the whole of India was rapturous with joy and eager to welcome him.

Indira, who happened to be in Ranchi, sent him a wire worded in characteristically vivid fashion, which also revealed the depth of her feelings: "Welcome home, darling. World has been dark without you."[59]

The resignation of Winston Churchill on May 23, 1945; the advent of a Labour Government in Britain on July 26, 1945; the selection of Clement Attlee as prime minister; and the rising tide of liberal opinion in favor of a free India in Britain and America were four factors which ultimately precipitated a subtle shift in postwar British-Indian relations. But it was a slow beginning. The day after his release Jawaharlal rushed to Bombay for a meeting of the working committee and immediately after to Simla for what proved to be abortive negotiations with the viceroy, Lord Wavell. The Muslim League's claim to be the sole representative body of all Indian Muslims proved a grave stumbling block and Wavell's unimaginativeness an effective bar to any progress toward a solution though the first thing that Attlee did was to advise that elections to the central and provincial Indian legislatures, postponed due to the war, should be held immediately and a constitution making body be convened. India was disappointed because there was no immediate declaration of independence and in some respects the proposals put forward seemed even less fruitful than those outlined in the Cripps offer. In spite of its dissatisfaction even with the preparation of the electoral rolls, the Congress decided to contest the election full force; although it felt, as the Congress general secretary cynically wrote in a party circular: "There is little difference between Conservative Churchill and Labourite Attlee. The present elections were devised merely to gain time."

The same sentiment was evoked by the British parliamentary delegation which came to India in January 1946 on a fact-finding or, as Sitaramayya says, a fault-finding tour. "We know," liberal leader Shastri told Gandhi when the latter went to visit him on his death bed, "Labour or Conservative, so far as India is concerned, they are all one and the same."[60]

But impelled either by the political climate in Britian, the critical state of national sentiment in India, a measure of idealism, or a combination of all three, Attlee was determined to break the deadlock. In March 1946, he sent a powerful three-man cabinet delegation to India, composed of Lord Pethick-Lawrence, the new secretary of state for India, Sir Stafford Cripps, who was now president of the Board of Trade, to maintain the continuity with earlier negotiations, and A.V. Alexander, the first Lord of the Admiralty. For the first time Indian leaders felt that the British were serious about their intention to hand over power.

But the unfortunate part was that as a political solution seemed nearer on the one hand the communal problem assumed draconian proportions. Persistent British effort at exploiting the divisiveness between communities to make it easier to rule had now resulted in a polarization of separateness between Hindu and Muslim which spelled doom to the dreams of a free, united India. Jinnah's fanatic stake in a Muslim nation-state was paying dividends. In 1937 Jinnah had received a mere five per cent of the Muslim vote for his Muslim League. In 1946 he emerged with 80 per cent of the Muslim vote. Steady exploitation of the communal angle aided by Britain had swung the pendulum in his favor with the "paralyzation"—consequently of no possible progressive counteraction—and the resignation of Congress ministries in 1939 and Congress suppression in jail from 1942 to 1945. Those three years particularly were to cost the country dear. Now that Britain was prepared to accept any solution put forward by Indian leadership or to give power to any acceptable central or provincial authorities and quit India, the damage that had already been done was seen to be almost irreparable. In 1940 when the Muslim League passed its Lahore resolution in favor of Pakistan, it had seemed too ridiculous a claim to be taken seriously.

By 1942 the Congress was forced to admit, although in a tragic vein and in language which bore the hallmark of Jawaharlal's feelings: "The Congress has been wedded to Indian freedom and unity and any break in that unity, especially in the modern world when people's minds inevitably think in terms of even larger federations, would be injurious to all concerned and exceedingly painful to contemplate. Nevertheless, the committee cannot think in terms of compelling the people in any territorial unit to remain in an Indian union against their declared and established will."[61]

In 1944, a month before Gandhi was released early on account of ill health, Rajagopalachari made Jinnah an offer endorsed by Gandhi which admitted the desperate measures of separation for the sake of a joint stake in obtaining Indian independence. If the Muslim League agreed to press the demand for independence jointly with the Congress and cooperated with the Congress in the formation of a provisional interim government, stated the "Rajaji formula," as it came to be known, the Congress on its part would be agreeable that "after the termination of the war a commission shall be appointed for demarcating contiguous districts in the northwest and east of India wherein the Muslim population is in absolute majority.   In the areas thus demarcated, a plebiscite of all the inhabitants, held on the basis of adult franchise or other practicable franchise, shall ultimately decide the issue of separation from Hindustan."

Even in the event of separation, however, such significant matters as defense and communications were visualized to be the subject of common arrangements between the two states.   To accept the principle that the two "sister" communities of the beloved country could not live together was a source of unutterable anguish to Gandhi, who had already spent a lifetime in the attempt to bridge all gaps between them. It was like the anguish of a father who has to see his sons become estranged with each other.   He had cried out painfully soon after the Lahore resolution, "I know no nonviolent method of compelling the obedience of eight crores [80 million] of Muslims to the will of the rest of India, however powerful the majority the rest may represent.   The Muslims must have the same rights of self-determination that the rest of India has.   We are at present a joint family.   Any member may claim a division."[62]   But he believed genuinely that if the British were out of the way and the Indians were left to themselves they would be able to work out an arrangement that would not lead to dismemberment.

When Jinnah reacted coldly to Rajagopalachari's scheme on the ground that only the Muslim population of the Muslim majority areas should vote on the question of separation, Gandhi made what protagonists of unity think was a blunder. He sought out Jinnah for talks on the issue.   They met from September 9 to 27, 1944 and what Gandhi got was, as he said when he was asked about their first confrontation, "only flowers."[63]

That Gandhi should have gone out of his way to seek a rapprochement with Jinnah raised the latter's prestige unduly at a time when he was nowhere close to being the alter ego of the Indian Muslim conscience. Further, it impressed even the nationalist Muslim into thinking that Jinnah was being taken as the spokesman for all Muslims. By 1946 the League, as one has seen, captured the imagination of the majority of the Muslims although the reasons, on analysis, were various. Some looked to a separate Muslim state for the promised Islamic millenia, some to a less competitive society free from the economic hold of the better organized Hindu commercial class, while the feudal elements sought escape from the rising influence of progressive modern thought in which again the Hindus carried more voice. Finally, for all of this closed society of a future theocratic state, there were the prospects of a short cut to success because of fewer numbers. What they forgot was, as Maulana Azad argued as a fellow Muslim, that this would solve no problems for the Muslims who would be left behind. Jinnah, of course, had scotched all suggestions for a common defense, communications, and foreign affairs arrangement as implying an infringement of each other's sovereignty, so that what remained as the genesis of Pakistan was that a part of the Indian Muslim community should stake its hold on one part of Indian territory and stand forever in awkward belligerence with the rest of the Muslims in the rest of India. Intellectually, it was an inadequate idea. But Jinnah had both the genius and the fanaticism, first, to deliberately let the outlines remain blurred and allow his demands to take an arbitrary jump ahead each time and second, to make the absurd real.

Even so, at the Simla conference in June 1945, called by Lord Wavell, the stand against the purely communal ideal represented by Jinnah's two-nation theory was strong enough for a large body of Muslims led by Khizar Hayat Tiwana to submit a separate list from that of the Muslim League for nomination to the viceroy's council, while the Ahrars, the nationalist Muslims, the Momin community, the Shias, and the Jamait-ul-Ulema jointly sponsored Maulvi Hussain Ahmad Madani to negotiate with both the Congress and the viceroy on Muslim representation. Jinnah's insistence even then that only the Muslim League should be considered the true representative of Muslim opinion verged on the farcical. Within a year the situation had changed to the extent that the League drew even the recalcitrant into its orbit when it seemed to prove through sheer dogmatic persistence that its voice was the one that was heard above the multitude by both the British and the Congress. In fact, the Congress attitude to it was compounded of the same mixture of severity, laxness, indignation, and frustration that an understanding but hapless parent might employ, albeit ineffectively, with a child that has got out of hand. Nowhere was this more truly reflected than in the critical vicissitudes of reaction to the cabinet mission plan.

The scheme as ultimately elaborated and presented on May 16 by Pethick-Lawrence, Cripps, and Alexander envisaged a three level structure in which the central authority comprising British India and the princely states would deal with communications, defense, and foreign affairs. The rest of the subjects would be vested in the provinces and the states, but the provinces could form a third governmental authority by grouping together on the basis of certain subjects held in common. This was substantially the solution that Maulana Azad maintains he was the first to suggest to the cabinet threesome. "If a constitution were to be framed," he said, "which embodied this principle [division of subjects], it would ensure that in the Muslim majority provinces, all subjects except three could be administered by the province itself. This would eliminate from the minds of the Muslims all fears of domination by the Hindus."[64] Although the controversy between the Congress and the League over the compulsory or voluntary grouping of Hindu and Muslim majority provinces and the formation of the interim government was bitter and intense, Jinnah was drawn into unwilling acceptance of the long-term constitutional scheme because he realized that the mission wished to devise a solution within the framework of unity and that the Congress was willing to agree to complete autonomy for the provinces, but not to the actual partition of the country. It was, however, only a facade of agreement for both sides for although the Congress could rely on the semblance of unity, it had to see Pakistan come in from the back door through the provision for the compulsory grouping of six Muslim majority provinces. The compromise was essential and it might have been a workable arrangement given continuing goodwill on the part of both. Gandhi was against the terms for the interim government as well as the constitutional structure and advised rejection but the working committee decided to work at least the constitutional angle.

The British delegation left India at the end of June. Jawaharlal was chosen to succeed Azad as Congress president for the year 1946-47 in a momentous party election.

It was to be a historic choice not only for the future trends in free India, but a critical one for the time. The accumulated frustration of largely unsatisfactory negotiations, the complex ramifications of the plan itself, and Jinnah's communal politics resulted in Jawaharlal making a speech at the AICC meeting at Bombay in which, though he made a farsighted analysis of the plan, he could not conceal his misgivings nor his anger. Although the AICC officially endorsed the plan, Jawaharlal made the bitter observation that the grouping scheme would be physically and psychologically impractical. He was also provoked into asserting: "There is a good deal of talk of the cabinet mission's long-term plan and short-term plan. So far as I can see, it is not a question of our accepting any plan—long or short. It is only a question of our agreeing to go into the constituent assembly . . ."[65]

Jinnah was alarmed into instant reaction. He had accepted the plan on sufferance as it was. He interpreted in Jawaharlal's statement to mean that the plan was to be regarded flexible, and that this would enable the Congress to sabotage the privileges he had won for the Muslims through its dominance in the constituent assembly later. It is certain that Jawaharlal was not impelled by communal considerations to comment upon the unworkability of the entire plan. But Jinnah needed an excuse and unfortunately he was given it. He cried out that the Congress president's views had altered the whole situation. He called a meeting of the Muslim League Council immediately. On July 30, 1946 the League passed a resolution rejecting the plan. The Congress saw its carefully sought compromise vanishing. The working committee sat again, and tactfully evading the issue of its president's remarks that had precipitated the crisis, reiterated its intention to work the plan *in toto*. But Jinnah was set on a path of hostile confrontation. It became a question of Pakistan or nothing, and then or never. The sequence of events that followed was impelled by two considerations: to repudiate the common stake of the Hindus and the Muslims and to show that complete separation was the only solution.

He called for a Direct Action Day on August 16 to achieve the goal of
Pakistan. He did not recommend violence, but did not denounce it. His
inspiration was fanatic. "Today we bid good-bye to constitutional methods,"
he told his League council, "we have forged a pistol and are in a position
to use it."

Naturally enough, the eruption was horrific. From 16 to 19 August,
there was a crazed communal uprising in Calcutta that became known as
the "Great Calcutta Killing." There was no evidence of a direct incitement
on the part of the League ministry which was then in power in Bengal. But
as August 16 was declared a public holiday, thousands were able to gather
at the Muslim League rally. Instead of the usual resort to hartals or demonstrations which "direct action" in Indian political jargon had meant
until then, the Muslim supporters of the League went on a raping, murdering,
looting rampage. After a stunned interval, the Hindu majority was provoked into furious retaliation. It was a gruesome example of the clever
maneuvering of susceptible masses that irresponsible leadership can indulge
in, for it was evident that the Bengali Muslim had more in common with
a Bengali Hindu than with a fellow Muslim from any other part of India,
so acute were the regional rather than the religious differences. But once
religious differences were evoked they acquired nothing less than a lunatic
edge. The events in Calcutta set off a chain of reprisals between the two
communities. In Noakhali the Muslim majority retaliated against the
Hindu retaliation in Calcutta and the nature of it left the country gasping
in horror. For added to killing were abduction, forcible marriage, and
conversion and an attempt to wipe out entire families. A similar holocaust
in Bihar followed soon.

The remaining incidents in the intervening months leading up to partition
became almost irrelevant. Jinnah's strategy had paid off. Bitterness
between the Hindus and the Muslims became so acute that it threatened
to explode into actual civil war, while it corroded the idea of a unified India
although the Congress hung on to the concept gamely until the end.

Alarmed at the spreading chaos and unable to break the League's intransigence, Lord Wavell invited the Congress alone to form the interim government. On September 2, it was formally installed and Jawaharlal became
vice-president of the viceroy's executive council and member for external
affairs and commonwealth relations. On October 15 the League decided
to enter the government but only, as one of its nominees Ghazanfar
Ali Khan remarked, "to get a foothold to fight for our cherished goal of
Pakistan." It was obvious that the League was intent on sabotage rather
than cooperation. Here again, Jinnah's idea seems to have been to counteract the possible perpetuation of Congress power if it were left to itself and
second, to illustrate again that the two communities could not function together even on the executive level. Whether or not there was "mental alliance
between the League and senior British officials," as Jawaharlal charged in

rising frustration, conditions reached such an impasse that Attlee invited party representatives to meet in London to find a way out. He assured Jawaharlal, who had misgivings, that the constitutional question settled by the cabinet mission would not be opened. The conference ended in deadlock after four days but Attlee issued a statement on December 6 which militated against the plan and almost gave official sanction to Pakistan. "There has never been any prospect of success for the constituent assembly," he stated, "in which a large section of the Indian population had not been represented [i.e., the Muslim League]. His Majesty's Government could not of course contemplate—as the Congress have stated they would not contemplate—forcing such a constitution upon any unwilling parts of the country."

The constituent assembly was convened in Delhi three days later, marking a historic culmination of years of Congress struggle, but the League was absent. On December 21, Jinnah demanded his terms for the grouping scheme as a condition to participate in the assembly. The Congress refused, but in January 1947 it passed a resolution accepting the grouping of the Muslim majority provinces but allowing the dissidents involved, like the Sikhs, the Muslim but Congress-dominated North-West Frontier Province, and the province of Assam to settle their own fate. On January 20, the assembly reconvened, but the League refused to join. At the end of January it declared that it would accept nothing but Pakistan. In February, the Congress rejoined with the demand that the League should resign from the interim government if it was to continue its boycott of the constituent assembly. And on February 20, 1947, Prime Minister Attlee made his famous declaration that the British government definitely intended "to take the necessary steps to effect the transfer of power into responsible Indian hands by a date not later than June 1948." But there was a rider. "His Majesty's Government will have to consider," Attlee elaborated ominously, "to whom the powers of the central government of British India should be handed over on the due date, whether as a whole to some form of central government for British India or in some areas to the existing provincial governments, or in such other way as may seem most reasonable and in the best interests of the Indian people."

Jawaharlal was elated at this categorical promise of certain independence. Gandhi saw the danger. "This may lead to Pakistan for those provinces or portions which may want it. No one will be forced one way or the other," he warned his exuberant heir. The deadline made decisions imperative. The very clause that spelled danger to Congress ideals held a future for Jinnah's divisive politics. He decided to make the League secure for the time of the handing over of power in the three provinces which he claimed as part of Pakistan but which eluded him officially: the North-West Frontier Province and Assam, in which the Congress was in power, and the prized Punjab, "the granary of India" in which a unionist ministry of a Hindu,

Muslim, and Sikh coalition had obtained a working majority against the dominant League. In January the League launched, ironically, a movement on the lines of Gandhi's methods of mass civil disobedience against the unionist ministry. On March 2, the unionist premier Khizar Hayat resigned, and the League's Khan of Mamdot took over. The unbearable tension broke with a Sikh call to "finish the Muslim League." By March 4, riots broke out in endemic form and were to develop to such an extent as to scar for years the conscience of the Hindus, Muslims, and Sikhs who had thus far lived in comparative camaraderie. On March 8, the Congress working committee was forced to propose the partition of the Punjab in an effort to save the non-Muslim areas, which in effect meant they had further reaffirmed the principle of separation.

On March 26, Attlee's historic announcement was followed by a historic choice. Lord Louis Mountbatten arrived in India to replace the unsuccessful Wavell. Few other men could have done what Mountbatten then did; he cajoled, bullied, argued, persuaded, and won from both the Congress and the League decisions which they did not like. Yet he retained for his country a fund of goodwill. It was superb salesmanship of the highest caliber and so hectic was the pace of executive finalities that by August 15, 1947, the transfer of power was effected to two successor states, India and Pakistan. The Congress saw its long-cherished dream of independence come full flower when the Union Jack came down and the Tricolor went up on the ramparts of the Red Fort in Delhi. It had had to yield on Pakistan, but it had some satisfaction in having yielded only the basic minimum and not the large chunks that Jinnah had demanded. Jinnah got the impossible. A separate country for himself, even though it was, as he called it, a "motheaten one," and appointed himself its first governor general.

"Mr Nehru, I want you to regard me not as the last viceroy winding up the British raj, but as the first to lead the way to the new India," Mountbatten said disarmingly to Jawaharlal at the end of their first interview in India.

Nehru smiled and replied, "Now I know what they mean when they speak of your charm as being so dangerous."[66]

India thereafter not only elected to remain within the Commonwealth with certain provisions accorded to her rights as a fully independent country, but asked Mountbatten to stay on as her first governor general. It was an unprecedented expression of the lack of bitterness with which her statesmen could take a decision, and the credit went equally to the gallant equation that Mountbatten had been able to establish.

"No power in history," commented K. M. Munshi in a profound and deeply felt analysis, "but Great Britain would have conceded independence with such grace and no power but India would have so gracefully acknowledged the debt."[67]

"It helped considerably that we had a family like the Mountbattens at the helm of our affairs because they were exceedingly perceptive," comments

Indira Gandhi now. "They were very friendly to us—as a family personally, but to India as a country too. And I think it was very much due to this gracious approach that things could go smoothly."[68]

But there was one man who thought that it was not enough compensation that things should have gone smoothly. The hatred, the violence, and the partition were factors which militated against his very soul. Gandhi in August 1947 was like Christ in the wilderness.

"I am unable to discover the truth," he cried at the communal holocaust. "There is a terrible mutual distrust. Oldest friendships have snapped. Truth and Ahimsa, by which I swear and which have, to my knowledge, sustained me for sixty years, seem to fail to show the attributes I have ascribed to them."[69]

He went to the extent of suggesting that Jinnah should lead the interim cabinet with an all Muslim administration if that would help avert Pakistan. He was convinced as late as April that after the British left, adjustment would become possible. But if the British policy of divide and rule had resulted in a situation where their presence was necessary to maintain law and order, he told Mountbatten, he would still rather they went and India be left to face a "bloodbath" if necessary, so strong were his feelings on the principle of separation. When he realized that the Congress was not prepared to accept the plan on Jinnah and that even his staunch lieutenants, Jawaharlal and Vallabhbhai, were so overwhelmed by the possibility of civil war that they were prepared to relent on the issue of Pakistan, he committed the greatest act of self-abnegation of his remarkable life. He handed over all future negotiations to the working committee and for all practical purposes withdrew from the events leading up to partition. He was to remain the revered "Father of the Nation," but his action presaged the close of an epoch in Indian political history. It marked the end of the Gandhian age, and the beginning of the Nehru era.

For Indira, these events marked the gradual fading of a domestic dream. With Jawaharlal's release in June 1945 the tempo in their life had again quickened with politics, but it was still Feroze who led. He became an office-holder of the Legal Aid Committee sponsored by the League of Released Congressmen for the redress of grievances of those who were still in captivity on charges of sabotage in the 1942 movement. The committee's task was to arrange for financial and legal aid. Feroze threw himself into the work with an enthusiasm that characterized most of his endeavors. Indira, with a tiny son, was content to look on.

In July, when the British Labour premier made his inaugural pronouncement on the Indian situation and it was advised that elections be held that winter, Feroze was put in charge of the Congress election machinery in the United Provinces by his friend and mentor, Rafi Ahmad Kidwai, presumably with the consent and perhaps encouragement of Nehru himself. His trips to Lucknow, necessitated by his work for the Legal Aid Committee, now became more frequent and more prolonged and routine domesticity was disrupted. In March 1946, when the cabinet mission came to India, the Congress party opened a small publicity office in the Imperial Hotel and Feroze again held charge. He had to deal primarily with the foreign correspondents posted there, but it was his first opportunity to establish the general rapport with the press for which he later was noted. He had done some coverage for the *National Herald* when in England and he probably realized that in addition to politics he would fit in best in the newspaper world, for a few months after the mission left he went to Madras to train with a reputable daily, *The Hindu*.

Later, Feroze and Indira went with Jawaharlal to Delhi. Jawaharlal became *de facto* prime minister of the interim government on September 2, 1946, and they were all housed in a modest little bungalow at 17 York Road. The constituent assembly officially came into being on December 9, 1946, and Indira's excitement at this partial fulfillment of India's —and her father's —dream would not allow her to remain away in what now seemed the staid confines of provincial Allahabad. Besides, she was to have her second child, and while Feroze was away in Madras, it seemed only right that she should be with her father. By December, however, Feroze was back. Also in Delhi were Krishna and Raja, who were scheduled to go on a lecture tour in the United States. It was a merry family gathering although her child was due in three weeks. Indira wished that her aunt could stay on somehow. On the evening of December 14, she was feeling faint and a little nervous for Krishna and Raja were to leave the next day. But the same evening Lady Cripps dropped in and asked Indira to go shopping with her to help her choose a Kashmiri shawl.

"There isn't anyone who knows just what's right for me the way you do," exclaimed Lady Cripps in a comment similar to those many others had made and were to make in acknowledgment of Indira's impeccable taste.

Indira could not resist the compliment and so she went.[70]

Later the same evening her doctor came to examine her and though he confirmed that there was still time, he told Krishna that he thought Indira was "so keyed up that anything might happen."[71]

"That night my second son was born prematurely," recalls Mrs Gandhi. "We put up a tent, and my husband was put out in that, and the nanny and baby and I stayed in the bedroom, as we couldn't risk the outdoor chill."[72]

They named him Sanjay, after the philosopher in the *Mahabharat* who relates the epic story that forms the great substance of the *Bhagavad Gita*.

Now the father of two sons, but still exuberant at thirty-five, Feroze took over as managing director of the *National Herald* in Lucknow. It was a family paper, similar to the Allahabad dailies, *The Leader,* with which Motilal had been associated, and *The Independent*, which had been directly owned by him and effectively expressed the voice of national resurgence in the early twenties. Jawaharlal had started the *National Herald* in 1937. With its influential backing and its stirring idealism it managed to obtain standing in India before independence. In 1946 when Jawaharlal joined the interim government he decided to resign from the chairmanship of the board of directors of the *National Herald.* M. Chalapathi Rau, a fearless and accomplished man, was its editor. When the directors insisted that Nehru should not resign because the company was a nonprofit-making one and legally he was not bound to do so, Jawaharlal said, "I do not want to embarrass Chalapathi Rau and I do not want to be embarrassed by him."[73]

When Feroze joined the paper on the managerial side the idea was that he should reorganize it in order to start a Delhi edition. Indira and the children moved to Lucknow. Indira was not able to settle down in Lucknow as she felt that they were not there for good and that Feroze would ultimately return to the capital with the new edition. Although she needed time to look after her newborn child and Lucknow offered the necessary peace and quiet, she hated the thought of leaving her father alone at a time when he was anguished by the turn events had taken. The independence of his beloved country was in sight, but so was its possible partition. The League had joined the interim government but its effective sabotage of any constructive work made it a daily hell for the sensitive man who was prime minister. His official position also made it incumbent upon him to do at least a minimum of entertaining on a scale that required assistance. He had only his official staff. When Madame Chiang Kai-shek paid another visit to India and he felt he must contribute to her welcome as an old friend, even though she was staying with the viceroy, he was forced to call upon his sisters for help. Both Krishna and Vijayalaxmi dutifully escorted Madame Chiang on a sightseeing trip to Agra and elsewhere.

But for some of the time Vijayalaxmi did act as hostess, and even when Indira happened to be in Delhi she was seen to remain in the background on formal occasions. Had Vijayalaxmi been less ambitious politically and therefore content to remain by her brother's side, and had Indira been a more conventional wife content to remain by her husband's side, the historical outcome might have been radically different.

For a while when he went to Lucknow Feroze stayed with an old friend, Raja Bakshi. Later he took a house at 8 La Place on Oliver Road: a compact affair with two bedrooms, a dining-sitting room, and a little nursery. Because there was ample space, and Indira was only briefly at Lucknow in the early months of 1947, Feroze invited Kitchlu, who was by then with the *Hindustan Times,* to stay with him. Whenever Indira was absent, there were regular letters from her to Feroze and whenever they were together, recalls Kitchlu, there was ease and a healthy banter between the two and none of the strain that was to mar their relationship later.

Indira was in Delhi on March 22 when the Mountbattens arrived to play their momentous role in the affairs of the nation. The next day there was the Asian Relations Conference at which Nehru made his formal debut

on the world stage with his inspiring call to Asian solidarity. Indira felt
again the excitement at seeing India's destiny take shape. Such was the
terrific pressure of decisions set by Mountbatten, that each day, from March 22
until power was actually handed over on August 15, became one of feverish
activity. She was not at the crucial meetings, obviously, but she was certainly one of the first of the outsiders to hear what happened. She was
invited to lunch by the Mountbattens the very morning, for instance, that
the viceroy had his first meeting with Jinnah on April 5. She had had ample training in dealing with the world of greatness, and socially, she could not
have been more at ease. She chatted happily with Alan Campbell-Johnson,
Mountbatten's publicity aide who has given such a graphic account of those
feverish, impassioned days, about the time in London when she was in some of
the worst blitzes in London and the trophy she kept of "the air raid warden's
hat which was lent her one evening while she was trying to put out incendia-
ries in Piccadilly,"[74] mentioned earlier. Campbell-Johnson records how, on
one occasion when he went to have tea with the Nehru household, Indira
and Krishna Menon recalled the origins of the Muslim League and its leadership, pointing out, probably in an effort to emphasize the paradox of his
intensely communal stance, that Jinnah himself was a Hindu by birth. She
attended some of the other frequent lunches, teas, and dinners either hosted
by Mountbatten or attended by him as part of his high-powered campaign
of "diplomacy by discussion" and bolstering the political with a maximum of
personal goodwill. But so hectic was the pace that when he left for London
in the middle of May for consultations, even the energetic Nehru felt the
need for some breathing time.

Indira had left by then for Mussoorie with the children and on May 17,
Nehru was writing to Krishna who had returned from her American tour.
"The viceroy is going away to London tomorrow for ten days or so and this
means some relief. I am thinking of going to Mussoorie to see Indu and the
children and for a brief rest. I am not quite sure how long I shall stay there
as this depends on Bapu's movements."[75]

The heartbroken Mahatma was in Bihar trying to assuage the madness
that had overtaken his people. Since October 1946 when the "Great Calcutta
Killing" had torn the fabric of Indian unity, he had spent his time in recreating
a sense of proportion, but he was so tormented in spirit that when he was
congratulated on his birthday, he countered with: "Where do your congratulations come in? Would condolences not be more appropriate?"[76] In Calcutta early in August 1947 when the League ministry was no longer in power,
the mass migrations between India and what was to be Pakistan had already
assumed terrifying proportions, and the Bengali Hindus began to feel that now
that they had the upper hand they could fully retaliate for the horror perpetrated the year before, Gandhi effected the most miraculous of his cures.
He went on a fast when he found the savagery unabated and such was the
impact of the possible suffering of this frail, seventy-eight-year-old man

that Independence Day, at least in Calcutta, was ushered in with scenes reminiscent of the great Khilafat get-togethers of the two communities in the 1920's.

However, Gandhi could be in only one place at a time, and in the far north the situation was almost out of control. The Punjab migrations hit Delhi with shattering force. As the Hindu refugees crowded in with tales of suffering and horror, of loot, murder, rape and loss of entire families, their wrath turned upon the Muslim residents and the machinery of government reeled under the sheer magnitude of maintaining law and order and salvaging some administrative sanity out of the chaos. Delhi became a city of refugees, of those who came pouring in, and those waiting helplessly to go out.

Nehru's house in York Road teemed with people who looked to him for succor. Feroze had come in from Lucknow to help, but when Indira wrote desperately from Mussoorie that she, too, wished to be there, he thought it was too risky for her to come.

"We couldn't dream how serious the situation was—he'd say it was too dangerous and so on. I even got suspicious," confessed Mrs Gandhi. "You know how a woman might feel in such circumstances. I felt there might be another reason for his saying no." So she telephoned. "He told me then that they didn't even have anything to eat, all the rations were exhausted because there were so many refugees living in the house itself. They had had only tinned stuff for lunch that day. So I told him I'd go anyhow. I told him that if I had to die I'd rather we all died together. I took whatever I could with me, sacks full of potatoes and vegetables."[77]

On the way she got a macabre hint of what the situation was like. When the train was about to stop at Shahdara, just one station before Delhi, she heard shouts as she was dressing. Looking out of the compartment window she saw that a man of about sixty or seventy was being pursued by about 200 armed people on the platform. She was so horrified that she impulsively jumped out of the slowing train to prevent what she thought was going to be a certain murder, and pushed the old man behind her.

"What do you think you are doing, who are you?" shouted the crowd.

"It doesn't matter what my name is, but I want to know what you are doing? I know what I am doing. I am saving this man. What are you doing?" she retorted angrily.

"You can't save him. We are going to kill him and if you stand there we will kill you, too."

"Well, if you want to kill me," she stated calmly, "you may do so. But I don't think you have the courage—not one of you two hundred people has the courage to lift his hand here."

"And it was true," she commented later, "they did not have the courage. Because there is nothing that frightens a bullying mob more than anybody not being afraid. No weapon is needed and nothing is needed except the fact of genuinely not being afraid. There was nothing to prevent them [from killing the old man or her]. I had nothing in my hands, I was barefoot. I just ran out of the [train] car without thinking [of] any kind of action or not."[78]

"I told them that it just can't be done. And the time in which he would have been killed was spent in arguing, and then the train was leaving, so the whole thing was settled."[79]

This was courage under fire indeed. "Courage—this sort of courage more especially," a correspondent was to record in admiration years later, when she was prime minister, "is one thing that she shares with her late father, whose physical interventions at points of disturbance made something of a legend."[80]

But there were fiercer trials ahead of her in Delhi in 1947. By September 8 Gandhi was in Delhi lodged in Birla House because the Harijan Colony, where he normally stayed, was overcrowded with refugees. He had intended to go on to the Punjab, but seeing that the capital itself was riven by riots he halted there. Indira was not feeling particularly well. But one day he sent for her.

"Why didn't you tell me what happened at Shahdara?" he remonstrated with her.

"Well, there's nothing to tell about it." She was matter of fact, and a little embarrassed. "It was not anything that I had thought out in advance. But if such a thing happened again I would probably do the same."

"And what are you doing now?"

"Working in a refugee camp, but it's not very satisfactory."

"Why is it unsatisfactory?"

"Anybody can do it, and lots of people want to. I feel I want to take some part in stopping what's happening, not merely in cleaning up after it."[81]

Gandhi thought for a moment, then said, "I know you are not well, but I want you to do a job of work. I want you to go into the Muslim *mohallas* of Delhi and report and let me know whether they have food, how they are faring, and what is the general condition of health, and so on."

She was a bit taken aback. "Bapuji, I don't know Delhi. I have not lived here and I don't know which are the Muslim areas and Hindu areas. I don't know the roads. I don't know people here. Who will go with me?"

She could never forget his answer.

"If I had one person who could go with you," he said, "I would not ask you to do this. I trust you to see this work through. I have asked several others and they have replied 'yes, Bapu,' but I know they are still hesitating."[82]

So she went alone. She went the next day to the town hall, where a control room had been established to deal with reports of rioting. She saw a girl there in a white khadi sari whom she did not know, but she walked up to her and asked her if she lived in Delhi.

"Yes," replied the girl.

"Do you know Delhi? Have you been working here?"

"Yes, I have been working in the labor areas and I know the areas quite well."

"Do you know where the Muslims live?"

"Yes, of course."

"I want to go into the Muslim areas and I want somebody to go with me. Will you come with me?"

"Yes," answered the girl simply.

They still did not know each other's name, although the other might have recognized Indira.

"My name is Indira Gandhi, what is yours?"

"My name is Subhadra Joshi."[83]

That is how they met, and for a tense period in India's history they formed a redoubtable team.

"Every morning she used to pick me up from Pusa Road to go to these mohallas," recalls Subhadra. "At first she used to say she must get back early because of her little son—but soon she was spending long hours outside. Crowds used to gather when they found that she was Nehru's daughter, but in those days, they used to gather anyhow wherever there were two people."

Emotions were on edge and could flare up against the innocent and the guilty alike. It was "dangerous work and calculated to bring the utmost unpopularity," as Indira herself realized. They were abused by both communities—by the Muslims for belonging to the community responsible for their plight, and by the Hindus for trying to give succor to the community that had made them flee their homes in terror and given them no quarter in Pakistan. They were caught in the crossfire. Propaganda by the more fanatic elements played up the danger to each of the communities from the other. The first mohalla they went to, the Bara Hindi Rao area in Delhi, they were told that the Muslims were gathering arms and were on a killing rampage. What they actually found was pathetic. The Muslim families were herded together in fear, the ration shops were empty, there was no sign of any arms, and the wounded had no doctors to tend to them. All the same, they did not meet with any warmth.

"The minute we entered that quarter we were abused, and bricks were thrown at us, and all kinds of nasty words, and so on," Mrs Gandhi remembers.

Some of the areas were full of water and there were the additional hazards of stepping on live wires. Nevertheless, they managed to write down lists of needs, and Indira did her best to convince these unfortunate countrymen of hers that the madness would pass and that they should remain in Delhi.

"We thought that part of the job was finished and we could get on with other things," she says. "But it was not finished. In spite of our report we found the rations were not supplied. So we had to get hold of a truck, go to the depots, measure out the rations ourselves, take them in, dole them out, and see to all the details."[84]

"When the Hindus used to see her going into the Muslim areas," describes Mrs Joshi, "and see her carrying *atta* and eatables, they used to feel irritated and angry. Once when we were looking into a Muslim area, we had to pass through a Hindu lane. They immediately surrounded us. 'Who looked after us in Pakistan?' they cried, 'Why do you look after them!' She told them she would get them whatever they wanted also, but soon from offering economic consolation it turned into a lecture on communalism itself."[85]

But memories were too sharp and recent for those who had suffered, to forget. Nehru began to get letters threatening his daughter. "Do you think we can't kill her? Our daughters have been raped and we can do the same."[86]

Once she and Subhadra left their car at the turn into a lane and began to walk toward a particular mohalla. In front of Indira there erupted a nightmare repetition of the scene she had witnessed at the Shahdara platform. A man was being chased by a raging mob intent on killing him. Again, she ran forward and stood in front of the man, and again she dared them to come forward. But this time the crowd was in an uglier mood and she knew she had to be wary.

"I told the man to remain behind me and I went out backward—I wasn't going to let them see my back. When we came out through the crowd I found that the car was missing! For a moment I thought they had left us and run away. But it was parked farther on." The irony of it was that when they dropped the man at the hospital, he began to abuse her. "He said all we Hindus were alike, that we were going to destroy the Muslims and so on!"[87]

On another occasion they found a Hindu woman on the verge of hysteria. She had been separated from her family and she was too frightened to look for them alone. So they provided her accommodation and set about tracing the rest of the family members. But for Indira these "rescues" were not acts of kindness generated by the drama of the moment. Years later, the same woman, called Vidyavati, came to Indira again. She had developed tuberculosis in both lungs and the same family with which she had so desperately sought to be united was unwilling to look after her. It was Indira, again, who came to her aid, sent her off to a sanatorium, and paid for her treatment.

It was true, however, that soon this pattern of individual prevention, help, or punishment by having the guilty arrested began to appear inadequate to them, and characteristically Indira began to ponder introspectively.

We found after a little while that our whole contact was with all these bad people who were doing bad deeds and suddenly we stopped and we looked at each other and said what are we becoming? All our time is spent with these awful people. Let those who want to look out for these people, well, do it, we will try and look out for good people. And from that day we started a new strategy. We went into a Muslim mohalla and said: now, you live with the Hindus as your neighbors. Can you give us one or two or three or four names of Hindus who throughout this dreadful period have not done anything wrong, who have not indulged in bad actions, who have not said anything that has hurt. Is there any single person? And the reply came: of course there are. There are so and so and Pandit so and so and so and so and two and three names were given. We then went to the Hindu mohallas and then we said: do you know of any such Muslim name? And they equally readily said, we know, these are the people. Then we said, well, now, we know these are good people. Will you meet together? Oh, no, they said, we can't meet these people.

You know, it took us days going back and forth from one house to another to persuade the first five of one religion to meet the five of the other religion. But once that first step was taken, and afterward it became... it was very much easier and I think it was only within about ten days that we were able to have a tea party [of] over five hundred people and by that time we had stopped counting who was which religion. And once we got on to that step, the communal rioting stopped. So I think, this is the track, this is the path we must follow, to try and see how to give more courage to those who are sensitive, who are of our way of thinking, that is, who believe that this country cannot exist unless all the different religions, the people of different thoughts, can live peacefully together.[88]

"We never had any policemen or guards or anything," Mrs Joshi says of this period, "[but] she [Indira] was not afraid. Neither Panditji nor she . . . lost her temper. Nehru changed when he was older, she's had to assume responsibility earlier. But she was very human and sympathetic. I don't know whether she inherited this, this *insaniyat* [humanitarianism]. Once I had gone to a village called Tihar where there was a Muslim camp. I stayed back because they were very panicky and there was danger of their being surrounded. I sent her a note. The next day she rushed there herself with food and other stuff. She's very considerate. When my husband was ill with cold, she insisted that I stay back and look after him. She's very simple too. When all the mohallas were closed we'd bring tea or sweets—she'd eat anything, even make the tea for all of us and pass around the cups, if I was doing the talking. Later we formed an organization called the Shanti Dal, a big volunteer corps with her as patron. When she began to work so much, people began to go to her direct. She was in political life all right though I don't think she ever tried. This was the period when she established mass contacts."[89]

"Whenever possible," says Mrs Gandhi, "I went to Bapu to report and these visits gave me fresh strength but on many days there just wasn't the time. On these occasions he would send a message or a flower." When at last the crisis surely but slowly ebbed, Gandhi, she says, "packed me off to Lucknow for a rest" with the words, "Now I know your education and your years abroad have not been wasted."[90]

But if the immediate crisis was over, a shattering aftermath was to follow. On January 30, 1948, she was again in Delhi. In the afternoon, she and Nayantara, Vijayalaxmi's daughter, who had returned to India after three years of college in the United States, received a message from Gandhi saying he was free and would like to see them. Indira took the three-and-a-half-year-old Rajiv with her and Krishna, and Padmaja, Sarojini's daughter, who happened to have arrived in Delhi, also went along. Just before she got into the car their gardener brought her a jasmine garland for her hair, but it looked so fresh and lovely that she kept it to give to Bapu. When they arrived at Birla House she placed it on a table beside him.

"Well, well," said the irrepressible Mahatma when he saw them. "Have all these princesses come to see me?"

Rajiv took the garland and began to play, sometimes slipping it over Bapu's feet like an anklet, sometimes hanging it on his big toe. At other times he chased butterflies on the big lawn, where the sun rivaled the brightness of the winter flowers spread around them.

"Bapu was in a remarkably relaxed mood," Mrs Gandhi recollects, "and we talked of many things and of the film which he had not allowed his Ashram girls to see. He had not found it a very pleasant experience and Gandhi told us that he had known what it would be like because of the person who made it. He explained how each person was being subtly molded and formed by his own thoughts and actions day by day and how these affected the quality of his work. He laughed and joked and was full of fun."[91]

The next evening, when they were having tea, they got an urgent call from Birla House. Bapu had been shot. They rushed there, stunned and unbelieving. He had been ten minutes late for his customary prayer meeting. He had just raised his hands in *namaskar* to the congregation of about five hundred, apologizing for being late when a man came out of the crowd, bent down as if to prostrate himself at Gandhi's feet, but instead whipped out a revolver and fired three shots into him.

"*He Ram*," [Oh, God] were the only two words that the Mahatma said as he fell.

He had once described his desire for a violent death in what appeared to be masochistic terms but was really a desire to put his theory of Ahimsa to the supreme test. "How noble that death will be, a dagger attack on me from one side, an axe blow from another, a lathi wound administered from yet another direction and kicks and abuses from all sides and if in the midst of these I could rise to the occasion and remain nonviolent and peaceful and could ask others to act and behave likewise, and finally I could die with cheer on my face and [a] smile on my lips, then and then alone my Ahimsa will be perfect and true."[92]

"The light has gone out of our lives and there is darkness everywhere," Nehru broadcast to the nation the same night in what was perhaps one of the most moving statements of his life. But Sarojini Naidu, who came from U.P. where she had become India's first woman governor of a state, with her face "haggard and her eyes glassy with unshed tears but with a spirit as indomitable as ever," as Nayantara Sahgal puts it, placed the happening in the context of a personal poetic logic: "What is all the sniveling about?" she asked. "Would you rather he had died of decrepit old age or indigestion? This was the only death great enough for him."[93]

Even the national connotations of the act somehow answered the same logic. The killer was a Hindu, Nathuram Godse. The fury of Hindu communalists who felt that Gandhi was selling them to the Muslims was fused into the murder and, paradoxically, it caused a cathartic release of the poison that had bred so much hate. It was such a terrifying act that the consciences of fanatic Hindus and Muslims were shaken and they sank into remorse. The drama was over. The time for realization had come.

And for a young woman of 31, who was to inherit the future, it was a time for some thoughts of her own. What had Gandhi lived and died for? And what was her father going to do? Years later she spelled it out.

Well, there was something in our midst [in ourselves], some idealism ... something which was spread throughout our country and it was this which is the basis, the foundation of Hinduism and I think it was to strengthen this that both Gandhiji, who was known as a man of religion, and my father, who was not known as a man of religion [lived] ... I think he [Nehru] was an Indian in the real sense of the word. He was not a Hindu nor was he a Muslim. And yet I think he was more Hindu than any Hindu that I have met. He was deeply versed in the Vedanta and kept for it a deep concern too, and because he kept for it [this concern] he kept for the thought behind it not the routine of going to a temple or worshipping before an idol, but the fundamentals for which Hinduism has stood, the fundamental truths which have kept our people going through centuries of oppression and hardship and suffering. It was for this they fought. Because they knew that without this India would be nothing. And with this India would not only live but perhaps be the greatest thing that ever was.[94]

At midnight on August 14, 1947, free India's first prime minister addressed the jubilant constituent assembly in words which caused exaltation in those who heard him there and the millions of his countrymen who listened over the radio.

Long years ago we made a tryst with destiny and now the time comes
when we shall redeem our pledge, not wholly or in full measure, but very
substantially.   At the stroke of the midnight hour, when the world sleeps,
India will awake to life and freedom.   A moment comes, which comes
but rarely in history, when we step out from the old to the new, when
an age ends, and when the soul of a nation, long suppressed, finds utterance.
It is fitting that at this solemn moment we take the pledge of dedication
to the service of India and her people and to the still larger cause of
humanity.   The achievement we celebrate today is but a step, an opening
of opportunity, to the greater triumphs and achievements that await
us....Peace has been said to be indivisible.   So is freedom, so is prosperity now, and so also is disaster in this One World that can no longer
be split into isolated fragments.

He showed the way above rancor with the concluding exhortation: "This
is no time for petty and destructive criticism, no time for illwill or blaming
others.   We have to build the noble mansion of free India where all her
children may dwell."[95]
"I was so excited and proud," says Mrs Gandhi with almost schoolgirlish emotion, "that I really thought I would burst."[96]
She realized, of course, that the facing of danger and the sense of comradeship that marked the pre-independence period was quite different from
the solving of day-to-day difficulties and problems which would characterize
political commitment in the post-independence one.   The first phase had
certainly been more exciting, she thought, especially for the impressionable
young, but "for a mature mind the second would be the more challenging."
At the same time the memory of her own lonely childhood made her want
to devote herself fully to her children at least for a while.   Had the passage
to freedom been a smooth one, and her father left to deal with the routine
challenges of his new task, she might have done just that.   But freedom
came with the partition of India and added to Nehru's anguish at this dis-
torted fulfillment of a dream was the enormous burden of dealing with the
fearful suffering of riot beaten multitudes of his people.
In 1947, primarily to save her father's time, Indira began to hold regular
morning meetings with people who thronged the prime minister's house.
She sat "solidly and patiently," as she says, between 8 A.M. and 1.30 P.M.
and sometimes again in the afternoons, interviewing group after group.
"For the majority there wasn't much one could do except listen to their
tale of woe, but even this apparently gave peace of mind and there were
always just enough cases which were within one's power to help to keep
up hope.   I did it both in my own right," she says, "and sometimes as representing my father to keep in touch with people and their problems
directly."[97]
Jawaharlal's first item in his day's program would still be to listen to

these homeless refugees, but the swarms of other people who also wanted to meet him made lunch a late and hurried meal.   Quite often some of them would even stay on to eat and on such occasions, says Nayantara, "Indira and I would have to wind up with omeletes in the kitchen."[98] Later in the year Vijayalaxmi became India's ambassador to the Soviet Union and Indira made a compromise.   She decided to divide her time between her husband in Lucknow and her father in Delhi.

"I was constantly commuting.   Whenever father had to arrange a big dinner or reception I'd go and then come back."[99]

On the occasions when she had to be away she would depute Nayantara, who was around and devoted to her *mamu*, to look after him.   Nayantara tried all kinds of ruses to distract her uncle from his long hours of work, and deliberately drew him out on her own problems when she saw him wrapped up in files after midnight. He had his sprightly but faithful valet, Hari, who had been with Motilal and worshipped the ground his son trod on, but that was only a consolation for the lack of family warmth.   If Nayantara in Delhi could feel for him so deeply, Indira in Lucknow could hardly forget it for the sake of a total involvement in her own life.

The conflict aggravated the differences that now gradually began to emerge in her and her husband's way of doing things. She tended to be reserved, aloof, quiet, standoffish with strangers.   She had a keen sense of proper behavior. Being the prime minister's daughter made her conscious, in spite of herself, of people who began to seek her out for the advantages they could get, and of situations that could cast a reflection on the Nehru name.   Feroze was free, easy, jovial, fond of people, eager for friends, and uninhibited about situations.   He was extremely fastidious in his person and his style of living and was as proper as Indira might have desired.   But at 35 he was tending to develop a paunch and gave the impression of being rather a fun-loving congressman.   He developed a reputation for having an eye for beauty and its concomitant diversions; he thought nothing of spending time in the Lucknow coffee house in the impeccable company, however, of journalists and intellectuls, including Chalapathi Rau, and his jokes verged on the ribald. But for all that he was fiercely independent, very much in love with his wife and liable to chafe against the dubious distinction of being the son-in-law. Beneath the facade of his lightheartedness, as Chalapathi says, there was "a belief in sound purpose and a sustained love of the underdog.   His energy was terrific.   I have seen few other people plunge themselves into some activity with such abandon as Feroze."   It was a combination that made a political calling imperative, and indeed, at that time he was enmeshed in U.P. politics along with his job at the *Herald*.   This was the formative period when he probably felt he also needed his wife, but her frequent absences gave an edge to the obsession with which he tackled his work.   He controlled the finance at the *Herald* and had the imagination to let it be used well.   Between him and Rau, the *Herald* came out with lavish, spaciously planned supplements, the Independence Day one inviting a telegram of congratulations from Nehru himself. Feroze was at the press day and night, mingling with the men and machines with that "common touch" which endeared him to the workers. For all practical purposes his was also a career that was set upon great heights.

In October 1948, the prime minister's household was shifted to the elaborate Tin Murti residence of the former commanders-in-chief of India. It was a huge, twenty-bedroom mansion with towering ceilings and sprawling lawns and vast public rooms in which life-size portraits of stern members of the imperial army stared down from the walls. When Indira went to look over the place, the first thing she did was to order the portraits to be dispatched to the store rooms of the Defense Ministry. Anticipating Jacqueline Kennedy twelve years later in the White House, Indira initiated a minor revolution in decor in the prime minister's house in India. Works of contemporary Indian art went up on the walls and along the long corridors that swept beside the rooms. The dull, somber shades of the draperies and furnishings were banished back to a past era and bright yet sober Indian raw silks began to throw a subtle sheen. A minor war of rights also took place. Vijayalaxmi was in Delhi for a brief spell. Mridula Sarabhai, a congresswoman who had tried hard to be close to the Nehrus, was also in town and conflicting orders about the colors and the textures of the new fabrics began to be placed, and overt hostility almost erupted. Years later, on the same matter, a similar tussle took place when Jacqueline Kennedy was to visit India. The issue was an insignificant one, but the results were significant, for it was Indira who emerged as the final and sole arbiter, as she always would in the last analysis.

This inflexibility of purpose was not limited to matters affecting her personal stakes. Just before the shift to Tin Murti she was told of a certain amount of in-fighting amongst the staff which resulted in an effort by one of them to prevent the then receptionist-cum-secretary from shifting along with them. When Mrs Gandhi was told of these jealous machinations, she listened quietly but did not promise anything. But the next day orders were given that "we don't shift till Vimla does." From then onwards, the man who tried to create the trouble, kept quiet.[100] The staff also describes how accommodating Mrs Gandhi was in the comparatively small house at York Road. On one occasion, Nehru went to Kurukshetra and was so moved by the story of a woman who had lost her husband in the riots that he brought her and her children to his house in Delhi. After that, it was left to Indira to look after them and make space available!

Whether it was the nature of the political grounding she got, with Gandhi's criteria of simplicity and discipline, or whether it was the precept set by her own parents that "either you don't do a thing but if you do it then you should enjoy doing it," the lack of comfort at a particular time or the lack of anything at any time did not upset her as much as it would someone who was geared fundamentally to wants. She herself related once, with that ironic questioning and the sharp humour that fills her eyes when she talks of those whose actions belie their protestations, an incident when she and another woman were travelling together in a third class compartment, the mode of travel that had been set by Gandhi. The woman had been living in *ashrams* and prided herself on her stoicism. But when she felt the hard, wooden bench that comprises a third class berth she was unnerved by the prospect of sleeping on it.

"At night," said Mrs Gandhi, "when I spread out a sheet on the berth she began to exclaim that it would be impossible to sleep like that! But I lay down, and I slept very well indeed."

The lady in question could not.

"I think," Mrs Gandhi remarked ruminatively at this point, "It depends on how you are brought up. If you've always had something you don't hanker for it...."[101]

One sensed vaguely that by then she was not thinking of comfort so much as of power. She smiled, and I smiled back.

10. INFLUENCE

As the prime minister's official hostess at Tin Murti, Indira's social responsibilities grew to such extent that her sojourns in Delhi became lengthier and her trips back to Lucknow less frequent. She got the Pandit girls' old Danish governess back from Denmark to look after Rajiv and Sanjay. Anna Ornsholt, "a tall, slim, erect Dane, with iron-gray hair, blue eyes, a smooth, unlined rose-and-tan complexion and a swinging stride,"[1] as Nayantara recalls, was a veritable tartar who believed in self-help, nature, and discipline and had so much energy herself that her repeated exhortation to her charges to "sit up!" or "walk straight!" was one way of saying that only a virile people are worth their freedom. Indira believed that "a child's need of a mother's love and care is as urgent and fundamental as that of a plant for sunshine and water,"[2] but that it is not the time a mother spends with her children that matters but the way she spends it. Consequently, she spaced her increasingly varied activities in such a way that her children would not feel deprived. With Anna around, however, she had the consolation of knowing that they were in the hands of a warm-hearted if stern disciplinarian.

The family had always kept dogs—"the good kind with long pedigrees and others rescued off the streets"—together with parrots, pigeons, and squirrels. Sanjay once went to a fete and brought home two ducks, which were also assimilated into the spreading menagerie. In fact, the vast silences of Tin Murti were soon filled with the healthy noise and mischief of two growing boys, and home for them became the grand house of their grandfather, much as Anand Bhawan had once been for Indira. Perhaps she wanted them to feel this way while they had the chance. Whenever Indira could not go to Lucknow, Feroze would come to Delhi on weekends, and on several mornings he gave up everything else to "play trains" or other games with his sons. It was an impossible situation for a marriage. Although Feroze accepted the necessity of Indira's being with her father, who was not only prime minister but a hero to him as well as to India's millions, resentment as a husband was bound to set in.

Indira's energies in the period between 1947 and 1959 when she was her father's aide and confidante and between 1959 and 1964 when she assumed the stature of a colleague were absorbed by three demands: state entertainment, social welfare, and political influence. She was an ideal hostess who mixed personal warmth with an attention to detail that ranged from seeing whether the faucets were running properly to remembering the gastronomic idiosyncrasies of both the most unassuming and the most exalted guests. She would even see that the shorter guests were provided with footrests and the taller ones with straight backed chairs. She inspected the menus herself and it was a task that had connotations unique to India.

"Even such simple problems are made more complicated in India by the peculiar fads of our people," she herself pointed out with typical humor. "Apart from the main taboos of Hindus not eating beef and Muslims not eating pork there are endless combinations and permutations! There are meat-eaters who are vegetarians on certain days of the week, there are vegetarians who eat eggs, others eat fish as well, and one distinguished guest who declared himself a vegetarian, ended up by eating everything except chicken!"[3] She was extremely particular about seating arrangements at formal lunches or a banquet, as well as on more informal occasions.

"It is like walking on a tightrope to adhere close enough to the formal side of protocol so as not to offend even the most particular of dignitaries, and yet manage not to stifle the human element and to keep the function interesting, and homely," she said then.[4]

But the constant concern with the human side of political relationships, to see who to put next to whom and who gets on with whom, so as to make hospitality scintillating provided an invaluable initiation into what makes politics tick also. The tact, discretion, and clever maneuverability she acquired as "first lady" then was to stand her in good stead when she became first lady in the absolute sense. As for national leaders, she not only got to know them on an individual basis but perceived over 17 long years their personal vulnerabilities. Her success in effecting an intricate balance of support when some of them became members of her own cabinet was due not a little to that experience, an experience which hardly any of the more actively involved in politics over the same span of time could match.

There were the lighter challenges of her role. As a concession to the prohibitionist sights of Congress policy, newly independent India in the first year zealously had its official receptions at the "in-between hour," as Mrs Gandhi says, of 6.30 P.M., that is, after tea and before cocktails which are generally at 7.30 P.M. With sophisticated guests like diplomats she found that very few *hors d'oeuvres* served with drinks were consumed. But on one occasion the guests were of a different type and the experience proved to be one which she thought could occur only in nightmares. Like meteorological departments the world over the Indian one had its own reasons for deducing that the weather would be bright that day. The party was arranged out of doors. When the guests began arriving, the clouds began to gather and soon a thunderstorm made it necessary to accommodate everyone inside where it was so hot that a couple even fainted. But the heat apparently did not dull their appetites, for when the *hors d'oeuvres* appeared they helped themselves not to one or two from each but at times relieved the bearers of the entire tray.

"To our mounting dismay and horror," Mrs Gandhi remembers, "we saw the food being exhausted even before all the invitees had arrived. That sturdy standby, the *pakora*, saved the day, alongwith dried fruit and nuts. Strange as it may seem neither my father nor the guests noticed anything out of the way." But since that dreadful day she took good care to have "extra stuff available, and to make duplicate arrangements outside and inside, even if there [was] a speck of cloud."[5]

There were last-minute adjustments made at other unnerving times, but of a different nature. Once when the Dalai Lama and other venerable monks who had come to attend the Buddhist conference were invited for lunch by Nehru, Indira realized that the monks had to eat their last meal before noon while the other guests would not be free till 1.30 P.M. So lunch was served twice, once at 11.30 for seventy-five monks and the second time at 1.30 for a hundred other people.

There were also the whimsical hazards of living with her father, "a being so versatile and calm, politician and poet,"[6] who each time he went abroad found himself so enchanted with something new that he would want to adapt it to life at Tin Murti. He liked the custom at Buckingham Palace of serving the milk and sugar before the coffee so much that he decided they should do the same at Tin Murti, with bewildering results. Each time it happened the guests would look around furtively, says Mrs Gandhi, to see if they had "somehow mislaid, or forgotten to take the coffee." Another time his stay at a country house found him reacting favorably to the custom of everyone serving himself with breakfast.

Indira, too, thought it a good thing because each of them was caught up in separate activities and breakfast was usually a hurried meal. "But again it is a habit," she saw ruefully, "to which guests could not accommodate themselves and it ended in our having to serve them ourselves."[7] From Sweden, however, came a charming custom. After every meal the children go up to their parents and thank them for the food. Poor Rajiv and Sanjay had to do the same, though their mother thought they looked rather sweet and shy. One does not know how long they maintained this "unaccustomed rite!"

But there was always the joy that they all shared of getting to know a wide range of the animal world. In Assam they got "a little bundle of fur" and thinking it would grow to be a huge bear, they called it Bhima, after the great Pandava fighter Bhima in the *Mahabharata*. It was a red Himalayan bear as they found later and it became a job to housetrain him. "He always climbed on to the towel-rack to do his business, besides racing all over the house,"[8] Mrs Gandhi put it bluntly, while they all raced after him. Ultimately, when he grew too big they put him in a wire netting enclosure outside and even got him a wife, Pema, which is Sikkimese for the lotus, the derivatives of which were such a favorite with the Nehrus. Bhima and Pema produced an adorable little family of baby pandas upon whom Nehru called every morning and evening and once when he was ill, they took Bhima to see him in his bedroom!

Then came the tiger cubs, and one, also called Bhima, used to frighten quite a few guests with his ferocious baby roar. Once when Bhima fell seriously ill, Indira took turns with one of their dedicated reception officers to sit up all through the night so that he could be given the prescribed dose of saline injections at the proper time. For four nights she would sedulously get up at 2 A.M. and relieve the other person till the fifth morning when Bhima raised his head and they could relax. "My own children had got used to playing with the cubs and did not care how boisterous they got," Mrs Gandhi describes wryly, "but for other children and visitors it was a boon to have Bhima still dazed and docile from his illness, and many who ordinarily would not come within ten yards felt courageous enough to stroke him!"[9]

There were times of pure fun when Nehru would become as boyish as his grandsons. Once they all happened to be visiting the Mandu fort near

Indore. The main cluster of monuments there is separated by a road and a deep depression from the other monuments and a guide of long standing there made full use of the myth that the buildings "answered" each other, while of course what happened was that as he shouted a sentence from a particular point the last word would come echoing back. He tried to impress Nehru with the call, "Is Kashmir Pakistan's or ours?"

"Ours," came back the resounding answer.

Nehru realized immediately what the trick was so he jumped to the spot from which the echo was evoked and shouted "Is Rajiv a clever boy or a fool?"

"Fo-o-o-ol," replied the echo, and they roared with laughter.

But the guide was a retired anthropologist, a cunning fellow and with a humor not to be outdone. He called again, "Does grandpa tell the truth or lies?"

"Li-e-e-es," reaffirmed the echo, and this time it was Rajiv's turn to relish the joke.[10]

From 1948 onwards when she began accompanying her father abroad, the great world opened up to Indira: the tensions, the chicanery, the sordidness, the tragedy, and conflict, but above all the fierce excitement of the world of international politics; the subterranean rivalries, the outward poise, the wit, the glamor of high society. She enjoyed international politics—it was her natural element—but she was bored by high society. She is snob enough to enjoy, but only for a short time, the experience of banqueting with kings, queens, presidents, and prime ministers. But as she was not then one of their company it meant, as she says, the submerging of her personality and playing the unfamiliar role of society lady, of which she says, "I must confess I find this more difficult and tiring than doing almost any other kind of work."[11]

As she used her role at home as hostess to sharpen her political awareness she used her role abroad to observe the unfolding and strengthening of Nehru's foreign policy which in the 1950s earned him the stature of a world figure and made India the voice of resurgent Asia. When she went with him to London for his first Commonwealth Prime Ministers' Conference the whole question of India's relationship with the Commonwealth had become a vital one. India's decision to become a sovereign independent republic was incompatible with a "common allegiance" to the crown. In 1936 Nehru had defined complete independence as "the separation of India from Britain," but he had always drawn a distinction between the British as rulers and as equals and had added, "Personally, I can conceive and welcome the idea of a close association between India and England on terms other than those of imperialism."[12] The whole tenor of the Gandhian struggle, the view of Nehru as well as Patel on the desirability of Indo-British understanding, the goodwill generated by Mountbatten's skillful and sympathetic handling of the transfer of power, and Krishna Menon's strenuous efforts to find a formula were the prelude to the Prime Ministers' Conference that Nehru attended in London in October 1948. In an *aide-memoire* for the British secretary of state for commonwealth relations, Mountbatten had gone so far as to advise that there was "room for a republic within the Commonwealth." At the conference Attlee and Nehru agreed informally on this concept that was to change the nature of the Commonwealth and bring it more in line with the aspiring freedoms of the times.

From London, Indira went with her father to Paris, where he made his international debut as prime minister of India with his first address to the United Nations General Assembly. His speech was a Gandhian exposition in which he emphasized the priority of means over ends and economic solutions over the political ones, called for the recognition of Asia, the ending of colonialism and racial inequality, pledged for peace and an end to the vicious psychosis of war. He presented the core of his policy for a revolution of minds, and the audience was quite moved. "Many people in the West knew him as Gandhi's aide in the struggle for freedom and as an author of renown [but now] he became a name to remember."[13]

Barely six months later Indira was again traveling with Nehru, this time on an official tour of the United States, his first "voyage of discovery," and hers, too, of the country that had stood by India in her quest for freedom, but now seemed to falter in her need for progress.

India was hit by famine, and Nehru needed two million tons of wheat and capital to bestir the economy. The United States, then in the throes of the cold war, was prepared to help if India was willing to "stand up and be counted."[14] For a man who had just managed to throw off the yoke of British imperialism, this seemed to portend another form of slavery. Perhaps he was too naive or too new to international politics, but Nehru saw governmental relations in terms of human values. He was too proud to accept the United States Congress terms for aid with strings, and came away empty handed. Eighteen months later, the wheat arrived in India, but by that time thousands of people had died of starvation. It was a disenchanting first encounter and his subsequent misgiving about Western vested interests was partially derived from that initial disillusionment.

The next year they went to the People's Republic of China. It was Indira's first experience of the fanaticism of Chinese communist society, and although she was impressed by its progress she was sceptical of its direction. But Nehru had a grand design of drawing China into the orbit of an Asian political morality, which was to find expression at Bandung the following year. Meanwhile Indira created her own impact in Peking.

"When Indira Gandhi entered the clinically furnished room there [at a reception given by a Chinese communist women's group] among the massed blue boiler suits of ideological orthodoxy and the square bobs of liberation," noted a correspondent, "she resembled in some way a lotus flower that had been planted in a bed of broccoli."[15] But it was not only as a decorative flower that she struck the Chinese themselves, one of them who had seen her function at closer quarters being provoked to exclaim, "It's remarkable, she has a lot of the West in her but, dear me, how intelligent!"[16]

At the Bandung Conference in April 1955, Indira was again with her father, where his sponsorship of the wider acceptance of *Panchsheel*— the five principles of peaceful coexistence—sprang from his belief that they symbolized a "new code for international relations as against the old school of Clausewitz diplomacy which believed in war and intervention as legitimate instruments of political solution."[17] He thought that it reflected the spirit of the present and projected "the creative and cooperative urges of modern science and technology," and that the inability of political ideas to keep pace with the great technological and military revolutions resulted in the big powers "being locked up in their communist and anti-communist crusades." Ultimately both America and Soviet Russia were to see it that way, but at that period it was Nehru who led with this logic of peace.

"This led us to organize what is called the nonaligned group, which has been developing into the biggest association of independent nations both in terms of population and territory," he explained, "We want to make it a third area, an area of peace and cooperation, some sort of a no-war land, or link, between the power blocs . . . it was to be our workshop of peace, the world's workshop of peace."[18]

It was not an easy concept to develop, and at Bandung there were stormy arguments which taxed the thin reserves of his patience. After a particularly heated session, he stalked out in a temper while the rest of the Indian delegation cowered nervously, only to find Indira waiting quietly outside and chastising him gently but firmly: "Papu, control yourself."[19]

There were occasions, however, when Nehru had state business that was not tense and serious. London in May 1953 was delirious with enthusiasm over the coronation, and the atmosphere that both she and her father found when they were invited to attend the big event was gay and sentimental. Although the British had tucked away their monarchy on a safe and harmless pedestal, their ritual obeisance to it brought forth all the pageantry of their past. Indira's encounter with Sir Winston Churchill emerged as the high point of the visit for her. Here was the man who had vowed to retain India as the "brightest jewel of the British Crown" for as long as possible even if it meant slavery for her people. At the coronation they happened to be sitting together and began to chat away in the most friendly manner. Suddenly he said, "Isn't it strange that we should be talking as friends when we hated each other such a short while ago?"

"Sir Winston," replied Indira quietly, "we didn't hate you."

"But I did," he expostulated, and then after a pause, "but I don't now."[20]

After London she decided to take a holiday. She left the prime minister's party and went on to Moscow alone. K.P.S. Menon, ebullient, suave, and a writer, was India's ambassador there, and she stayed with him and his wife, Anujee. With good friends, as always, her reserves fell away.

"Of all the states in the Soviet Union the one which Indira was most anxious to see was Georgia, because she had heard that Georgian men were the handsomest in the world," recollected K.P.S. Menon irrepressibly. "And I decided to accompany her because Georgian women were the most beautiful. Overhearing our talk, Anujee thought that it was not safe to leave us both at large in Georgia and decided to come with us!"[21]

Indira could not escape from being who she was. When they arrived in Tbilisi on an afternoon in June, they got "an effusively warm reception" as Menon says, because Indira was in their party. For the rest, it was a holiday to remember. The Georgians did not disappoint them. The men were handsome, the women ravishing, and Tbilisi at night was "like a bride decked in all her jewels, ready to receive the bridegroom," according to Menon's enchanted eyes. The view from their balcony was so lovely that he kept gazing at it long after midnight. He found out in the morning that Indira, who had a balcony adjacent to theirs, had felt so intoxicated by the sight that she had stayed awake until three in the morning. Her comment was warmly sensuous. "I do not get drunk on wine," she told him. "I get drunk on other things."[22]

On the last night of their stay, the Georgians entertained them at dinner. There were poets, professors, musicians, historians, and film stars and distinguished artists. In the long gaps between courses they would dance and sing and play. The wine and the food and the gaiety dispelled all language barriers, and the dinner which began at 9 ended at 1.30 A.M. The hosts presented Indira and Anujee with gorgeous Georgian costumes, and to suit the mood of the occasion, they decided to change into them immediately. So they went off with their hostesses and when they reappeared in that colorful finery there was a burst of applause from everyone! To the Georgians Indira, with her black hair, sharp features, and light complexion, doubtless appeared one of them, while her name with its trailing vowels was similar to their own women's names and caught their imagination. After this trip and on subsequent trips when she accompanied Nehru to the USSR there were several new-born baby girls who were named Indira.

"I am delighted to learn that you have named your daughter after me," she wrote in reply to one of her admirers who had decided to call her daughter Indiratchka. "In our language, Indira is one of the names of the lotus, which is our national flower," she explained patiently. "It grows in lakes but rises well above the water and is very beautiful. The root and the seeds are delicious to eat. Commonly it is pink in color but there is also a white variety. Indiratchka is rather long. My own family have always called me Indu, which means moon. Perhaps you could call your daughter Indutchka, which is easier to say."[23]

There were "golden moments," as Mrs Gandhi puts it feelingly, in that period of her life. But the witchery of art and abstract concept, of beautiful cities and novel experiences could still not compare with the human commitment in her thinking: "I love birds and mountains and music and pictures and yet all these cannot vie with the deep joy of bringing happiness to a human being."[24]

The human condition, she should have said. Her absorption began to rise above the personal.

"She felt almost this physical ache about poverty," Mrs Bachchan reveals. Sometimes when they would go for long drives outside Delhi toward the villages or for a casual family picnic when Indira's time was not so pressured, and she saw the hungry naked little village children appear like distortions in the beauty of the countryside, she would burst out, "Oh, when will the time come when they'll have all the facilities, can eat well and be clothed and study!"[25]

It was not an idle reaction. She could not bear to see anything wrong without wanting to put it right. Child welfare became the work nearest her heart. Her life in Delhi, which started by making a home for her father, turned gradually from "circumstances" and her "own intense interest in the path that the country was trying to follow," as she says, "to a deeper involvement in public affairs."[26] Whereas the afternoons and evenings were given over to her responsibilities as official hostess—more often than not there were guests even for lunch—her mornings were devoted to her own work. After breakfast, which the family usually had together—Feroze if he was in town, the boys, Nehru and herself—she would go to the office she had set up in Tin Murti to dictate letters and attend meetings in connection with her growing welfare activities. One day when she was at Connaught Place, New Delhi's fashionable shopping center, a little boy with a tray of combs began to urge her to buy one. When she refused he pestered her from shop to shop until she had to take one. By then she had become interested enough to ask him about himself. "He was a beautiful child," she says. "We talked and I asked when he went to school. He worked all day, didn't go to school and made two rupees a day."[27] It made her think it might be a good idea to have a children's cooperative. She gathered some more little boys, got a building for them, and started the Bal Sahyog, a project in which the boys employed their talents for carpentry, tailoring, woodwork, canework, and even gardening in a cooperative venture toward self-sustenance.

When kindergartens—the Bal Wadis—were opened in the rural areas and small towns as part of the community development block, she found that the women teachers were not trained. "While I was working I realized what a difference there was between those who had studied under a trained teacher and those who had not," she says. "Also that something was better than nothing. The ones who attended school even under an untrained teacher, in small habits ... of cleanliness and manners... were far ahead of those who had no schooling at all."[28] But she fought for the regulation to have trained teachers, and initiated a scheme for their training. She began to visit several centers all over India to see personally how they were progressing.

When in Europe or the United States with her father, she would look forward to salvaging some free time from official engagements in order to visit various children's homes. In 1956, for example, it was only after the Commonwealth conference was over and her father went to Ireland that she found she could spare the several hours at a stretch necessary to indulge her own interest. Her work in India was concerned with children who were "deprived" of a normal home life, either through poverty or lack of parents. She was eager to see how the problem was tackled elsewhere. In London what impressed her most was the effort that was made in the better centers to provide a homelike atmosphere. In Bonn, she made a point of seeing the German institutions. On her return to India, as she relates, "although we were barely 24 hours in Cairo I snatched the chance of motoring out to the Tahsin El Seha city at the foot of the Pyramids."[29] Here over 300 boys and girls were looked after by a women's committee which ran the institute. She found a pattern identical to the one she had initiated for the Bal Sahyog. The children made beautiful things which found a ready market and brought funds for the institute and also helped to establish a means of livelihood for them later on.

She saw that the problem of the delinquent child was closely allied to the "deprived" one. She visited the children's court in London and the remand homes for boys and girls, and although she felt that juvenile delinquency was growing in the West, it was serious enough in India to merit preventive measures. "Prevention is much more difficult to plan and to organize," she affirmed, "and may at first seem more expensive but who can doubt that the results will be well worthwhile. The main cause of many of our young boys roaming the streets is economic. Our experiment in the Bal Sahyog in Delhi has shown that sympathetic care and training will soon put them on the path of good citizenship. However, there is far too little of this work being done in India." She urged some imaginative attention. "I hope the government as well as the various agencies interested in the care of children will give greater thought to the development of such necessary services."[30]

In Washington later the same year, she told an interviewer that she was interested in practically everything. "Of course my pet hobby is the study of children. I'm most interested in projects dealing with delinquent or handicapped children, but in India every kind of thing has to be developed now... India today is really like a garden. When you have a garden you can't say this year I will water the roses and next year I will water the lilies. You must do everything now. There's so much to be done."[31]

She took the opportunity while there to discuss the question of coordinating childwelfare activities, and to visit, between a crowded schedule of official luncheons, dinners, and receptions, the Goodwill Industries in Washington, a private self-help institution emphasizing vocational rehabilitation of the severely handicapped. At the District of Columbia Health

School she was intensely moved to see corridors lined with wheel chairs, classrooms where young children learned their lessons with their crutches beside them, and psychotherapy units for health treatment. At the famous Institute of Physical Medicine and Rehabilitation in New York, she was conducted around by Dr Howard A. Rusk, who told her: "Nowhere in the world will you see more severely disabled persons, and yet nowhere perhaps will you find more hope."

She saw amputees learning to walk with artificial limbs and the handicapped learning different trades to support themselves. There was an amazing range of equipment, from elaborate hydrotherapy machinery and prosthetic devices to a simple potato peeler designed for housewives who had lost the use of one hand. But it was when she saw a young man of 21, who had lost both arms, playing checkers with his nurse by moving the pieces with a stick held in his mouth, that she realized what Rusk meant. "I was impressed with the spirit of acceptance," she said. "There is no atmosphere of charity or pity. I think that helps the patient to become more self-reliant."

It made her think of Satya. A youthful 20, but her body misshapen and ugly from an accident at childbirth which had cut off her legs at the thighs. She had come dragging herself on her hands among the crowd of other refugees in 1947 to the prime minister's house when her father, a railway level crossing guard, had been cruelly murdered. What could she do to help her, Indira had wondered. The only possible way was to provide her with artificial limbs, but the Artificial Limb Center at Poona, the only institution in the whole of India at the time which could provide this facility, was reserved exclusively for military personnel. It had taken her months to persuade Sardar Baldev Singh, the defense minister, to make an exception and to allow Satya to be fitted with new legs there. There had been several visits to Poona thereafter for Satya, all arranged by Indira. There had been moments of terrible depression when Satya had sought out her determined benefactor for reassurance. But the results had been rewarding. That pathetic twisted body had been coaxed into normal shape, and Satya not only found a pair of good legs to stand on, but soon learned how to drive a car. Later in Delhi, she had come to show off a little and to announce her engagement, "her face transformed," remembered Indira, "glowing, positively scattering the gold dust of her happiness on all who happened near."[32] But this was a solitary triumph. Indira saw to it that the Poona center was eventually opened to all civilians.

In fact, what usually began with a concern for one individual ended up with an institution for that category of suffering. It happened again in 1962, when she went on a lecture tour to the United States. Gopala Menon, who had been India's consul general in New York and was then resident director of the Indian Investment Center there, had a son who suffered from cerebral palsy and had been admitted under the care of a famous specialist, Dr Martin F. Palmer at the Institute of Logopedics at Wichita, Kansas. Indira had heard about the Menon's son earlier and felt immediately drawn to the problem. Wichita was on the schedule of her tour. She went and stayed with the Palmers for two days and addressed their internationally known speech and rehabilitation center.

She spent a long time touring the institute and examining the details of its work. She became determined to fill the gap in India where this type of work was practically non-existent. Although the government at home was hard pressed to meet the demands of priority diseases and had limited means, Indira eventually initiated a move to have a logopedics center at Mysore on the basis of a generous offer from the maharaja of Mysore.

"Although Mrs Gandhi modestly disavows all credit for it, she has actually been its moving spirit," says Gopala Menon. "She discussed the whole project with the institute in Wichita, cleared the hurdles back home and has gone over practically every minute detail."[33]

Certainly Indira likes to go to the root of a problem. As vice-president of the Indian Council for Child Welfare she encouraged both the mental and the physical aspects of child care, but she always was aware and wished others to be also that if a country is to develop it must begin with the young. "When we want to build a new India, it is important that its people be free of superstition and receptive to new ideas. We won't necessarily succeed with grown ups. But I feel it is very important now that our children are dealt with at this stage. We must work with the children now. There can be no delay."[34]

She stressed the need for children's literature and pointed out to Indian publishers that they were lagging far behind Britain, America, Russia, and other countries in this respect. She urged a library service for children, which would not only include children's sections in libraries but a children's librarian.

"The subject of books is a fascinating one," she told an audience at the opening of an exhibition of juvenile literature during the National Congress of Child Welfare in 1956. "My father has taught me to love books, not only the reading of them but looking at them and handling them. I should like the children of India to share in this joy. I should like them to cultivate the art of reading which should lead them not toward bookishness, but toward greater vitality." She quoted Anatole France: " 'What is a book? A series of little printed signs, essentially only that. It is for the reader to supply himself the forms and colors and sentiments to which these signs correspond. It will depend on him whether the book be dull or brilliant.' "

But it was in relation to her association with the Youth Congress which came into being in 1952 and her strong feeling that nation-building must involve the young in general that she began to formulate her socio-political philosophy. Her address at the Youth Congress at Baroda on November 21, 1958, coalesced her beliefs, compounded of that mixture of revolutionary fervor and restraint that was to mark her politically like her father, as an implacable democrat, and personally, again like her father, as an unconventional and imaginative human being. There was certainly no stuffiness about the advice she gave.

"Youth should be a positive force for bringing in social reform, creating a new outlook and accelerating the pace of change," she said. "Reform, like charity, begins at home. Anyone who allows himself to be bullied into acquiescing in barbarous customs in his own family circle will not command respect if he sets out to preach to others."[35]

Here was an open call to rebellion against all the anachronisms of traditional Indian society, but it is only when it is realized how deeply ingrained is the habit in India to turn respect for age into virtual subservience that her remarks acquire significance.

"Our young people are too dependent, too eager for advice and guidance at an age when they should be striking out for themselves. Don't wait for someone else to find opportunities for you but make them yourself. Learn to work so competently that you cannot be ignored."[36]

She was 41 at the time and it was apparent that she was full of the future. "Sometimes I cannot comprehend why youth should have any difficulty in finding a direction. There is so much to be achieved, so many laurels to win." She was clear what that direction should be. "In education and in our work we must cultivate the modern outlook and the scientific spirit—the inquiring mind, the search for truth regardless of personal gain or loss, the search for better and more efficient ways of functioning.... Original thinking is the need of the day. To forge a new path, to invest something requires the capacity of thinking straight ahead without getting entangled in previous conceptions, it requires the strength for making mistakes and of accepting failure before you can achieve success."[37]

It was the creed of a rebel but of a rebel with a cause. She was no iconoclast for she perceived that "the will to destroy arises only when the will to create cannot be satisfied." She did not believe in empty sermons. She did not believe in sermons at all. She was prepared to offer workable goals and what she spelled out as a course of action for the Youth Congress contained the organizational sense, the practical sweep, and the imaginative emphasis that was to mark her attitudes in power. She had the right ideas. It remained to be seen how well she could execute them herself.

She suggested that the Youth Congress be broadbased so as to include the young from industrial as well as rural areas. She suggested it establish contact with professors and others constantly dealing with young people and become a forum for translating ideas into action. "There is no meaning in having academic discussion," she stated at the Baroda meeting on November 21, "which cannot show practical results." She suggested that the Youth Congress be regarded as a testing ground for future leadership, and that coordinated functioning should be established at *Mandal* Congress level.

But it was in her advocacy of "decentralized and specialized group responsibilities" in the social welfare work of the Youth Congress and her belief that a little job well done is better than ten well imagined that she anticipated the essential pragmatism of her prime ministership. She thought that the lack of progress in this area was due to the fact that "we tend toward grandiose schemes, and in attempting too much achieve too little." She thought that it would be only through imaginatively conceived and homogeneous local units that the people at various levels could be made conscious of the varied needs of our times.

"Work must therefore be planned," she reiterated sharply, "on a small and practical scale, each person undertaking to do a particular job in a given area within a specified period of time." She suggested job counseling, learning to think along new lines, willingness to undertake any job that needs to be done, better inducements for young people to work in remote areas and, at a time when the "student revolution" was nowhere in the offing, a plea for the setting up of a machinery for ventilating students' complaints. "There could be a panel within the college or university premises for the arbitration of disputes, or for the redress of their grievances," she urged. She thought that India's system of education needed to be reoriented. "It does not help them to attain integrated personalities, to develop their latent talents and to bring out their social consciousness," and she quoted India's prophet-reformer Swami Vivekananda, " 'We must have life-building, man-making, character-making assimilation of ideas.' "

She persuaded the education ministry that it was essential to have a central body to coordinate the efforts of social welfare agencies spread throughout the country. The Central Social Welfare Board that came into being was her "brain-child," and she not only inspired its birth but actively worked towards its implementation. She toured India, and sent in valuable and meticulously detailed reports and suggestions for courses of action. She was also the founder of the Bharat Sewak Samaj, which required members to donate part of their professional time free, or if they were not technical people, to personally help in other ways.

Throughout, she remained an optimist.

"By nature I am a forward-looking person," she confesses, and she began to see that the men and women with a spirit of service and adventure, even if a few, were like "tiny *deepaks* twinkling in the darkness of Diwali night opening the doors to Lakshmi [Hindu goddess of wealth], beckoning to good luck and prosperity."[38]

It was her quiet buoyancy that affected the women. Gandhi had flung open the doors of their consciousness by calling them to engage in the fight for national freedom. Backward, illiterate, ignorant, and vulnerable, they came surging out of seclusion to fight on an equal basis with the men. Not only did the resistance of men collapse in face of the risks the women shared with them, but they became ready to acknowledge them as partners outside the home. The spirit with which the women were inspired was indicated by the presidential address of the first Indian woman president of the Congress as early as 1925. Sarojini Naidu exhorted men and women alike. "In the battle of liberty fear is the one unforgivable treachery, and despair the one unforgivable sin." The most remarkable aspect of the emancipation of Indian women was its lack of controversy. Perhaps this was because the Congress organization stipulated social reform as the necessary adjunct of the political struggle, but the credit must go to the men in it for being enlightened.

"If we have no distinctions of class and creed," declared Gandhi, "we have no distinctions of sex either."[39]

A group of women led by Sarojini Naidu met Montagu when he came to India in November 1917 to seek assurance of equal rights, but how readily their demand was underwritten by Indian leadership became evident when the Calcutta Congress of 1917 expressed the hope that "the same tests be applied to women as to men in regard to the franchise and the eligibility to all elective bodies concerned with local government and education." Annie Besant was the president then, but the fact remained that the whole organization, composed largely of men, was with her. The Congress deputation that went to England in 1919 to put the claims of India before the British public was all male. Yet when the question of women's suffrage arose, and Montagu wished to leave the decision to local legislatures, the deputation asked for a guarantee of its acceptance to be incorporated in the promised act (of 1919). The Congress of 1918 reiterated that with regard to representation to the legislatures, "women should not be disqualified on account of sex." Thereafter almost every official resolution of the Congress saw to it that equality for women was one of the major policy demands.

With independence, when they had time to take stock of themselves after the consuming passion of the struggle, women literally awoke to freedom in more ways than one. Free India's constitution granted them absolute social equality, equal opportunities for education, the right to vote, to seek election, and the right to hold any public office. It was like inheriting lush fields from which only the harvest had to be gathered. There was no need to strike a feminist posture, to redress the balance with strident suffragetism. The Indian woman could afford to remain feminine, smile quietly, draw the flowing folds of the sari even to cover her face in purdah and yet know that when it came to the point, she was free to achieve anything. And because there were no residues of bitterness from a prolonged and direct confrontation between the sexes as in the West, the men could more readily accept, when the issue arose, a woman as prime minister.

The improvement of the status of women, the area in which Indira did her most strenuous work in the years before she achieved power, therefore did not involve a fight for the recognition of the rights of women but for a transformation of society, for a reconditioning of values, and for the seemingly simple but incredibly difficult leap away from the habits of poverty. India's social legislation for women always remained ahead of social reality, and the effort was to fit them for the opportunities that were already provided.

She thought that the partition of India in this sense yielded some good. The butchering of families was horrific, but where all the earning members perished in the riots and girls from "good and respectable families" had to begin to support the less capable members it gave a "last firm kick to the taboo against women" and helped them take the second stride forward. By 1956 the passing of the Hindu Code Bill covered 85 per cent of India's women. It recognized the inheritance rights of the daughter and raised women's "limited estate" to one of absolute control over property. It enforced monogamy, and in granting equal rights of divorce to men and women, it included one of the most lenient divorce clauses in the world, the option to divorce by mutual consent.

Oddly enough, though the Congress had had three women presidents, itself a singular mark of its progressivism, it had no women's section. It was in 1940 that a scheme was prepared for its inception by Mridula Sarabhai, who wrote to tell Jawaharlal that "Smt. Vijayalaxmi Behn" had given her approval and that it had gone to President Maulana Azad and been circulated among women workers in the provinces for their support.[40] But it was only as late as March 3, 1942, that the Maulana could tell Jawaharlal, "We have created a women's branch in the AICC office, but it is not enough. We have to do something more to create practical enthusiasm in the work. I wish to appoint an advisory committee the members of which may devote their time [to] this work."[41] He proposed Vijayalaxmi Pandit, Mridula Sarabhai, Aruna Asaf Ali, Ismat Iftikharuddin, and Sucheta Kripalani.

It was Jawaharlal's reply two days later which confirmed how valiantly the fighting on behalf of the women was being done by their men.

"My own conception of the women's branch of the AICC," wrote Jawaharlal, "is that it should collect all material relating to women's activities in India, it should keep in touch with all women's organizations in India, it should particularly keep in touch with such women's work as is being done by Congress women, and through Congress organizations it should send such suggestions as may be desirable for the coordination of these various activities and it should issue special directions to provincial Congress committees in this behalf." This was the period of the 1941-42 crisis and Jawaharlal showed particular concern that attention be paid to women's work because he recognized that "public morale depends greatly on how women feel and act."

"My own little experience has been," he added in a significant affirmation of his belief in women's role, "that women are anxious to know what they can do at present and any lead given to them will yield results. I am all against treating women as helpless human beings who cannot look after themselves and who must run away from the danger zone. At any time this is bad policy and makes them even more helpless than they are. In present circumstances it is completely pointless as you cannot limit the danger zone. Any and every place may become the danger zone and even the privacy of a house will not be outside this zone. So the only way to tackle the problem is to make women realize that they have to and can face it and to prepare them mentally and otherwise for this."[42]

The women could hardly find a more ardent protagonist among themselves. For the next five years they were so actively involved in the political excitement of the times that "schemes" for work became unnecessary. When Indira settled down to work after independence, the women's section was in need of guidance. Indira with her infallible sense of timing, dictated by luck or wisdom or both, was naturally and obviously on the scene. The original names were quietly and effectively out of the picture. By 1953 Vijayalaxmi, for instance, was riding the crest of the wave of international politics, much to her chagrin later for it robbed her of a home base, and Mridula Sarabhai and Sucheta Kripalani were only in the background. Indira put a bright-faced young Bengali woman, Mukul Mukherjee, in actual charge of the section but remained in effectual control behind the scene. "She didn't work in an official capacity, but I accepted her as head of the women's department," says Mukul (now Banerjee). "I worked as her secretary, arranged all her tours and everything. And the budget proposals drawn up by me had to have Indiraji's signature also."[43] This was only the first of many instances which showed that Indira preferred influence to office. It left her free of mundane responsibilities, and it helped her avoid becoming a subject of controversy. She could concentrate on evolving a policy rather than functioning as its executive, but she agreed to become chief editor of the section's monthly magazine, *Women on the March*.

She again showed the organizational grasp, indefatigable energy and humanity which earned her the loyalty of nearly half of the country's population. In fact, with her involvement in the women's department of the Congress, Indira in spite of her lack of an official office, stepped forth irrevocably into active politics. For it was at this time that she traveled extensively to almost every remote village where women could be galvanized into a force for constructive work, and made her own discovery of India. And this is when she established that enormous mass contact with the rank and file of the Congress party as a whole, for invariably when she went to address the women workers in a district or small town or village, the state Congress committees or the district Congress committees would hold a meeting for her. So she got to know the average mind. She was not bound like those standing for elections by one constituency or the need to secure regional support. Her concern was all women, therefore all India.

The whole of 1954 was taken up by convening the women leaders in each state, while it was under Indira's guidance that the first All-India Congress

Women Conveners' camp was held in Delhi in 1955. This was followed up by four zonal training camps in 1956 held regionally at Patiala, Ranchi, Andheri, and Madurai. The idea was to train women Congress organizers, and after the elections in 1957 they went one step further and divided India into seven zones and held camps to train the newly elected women legislators "to counter the reactionary male argument," as Mukul Banerjee says, "that getting women elected was a national loss!"[44]

The department had a hand in screening all the women candidates, and on a number of occasions was instrumental in getting women adequate representation by putting pressure on the Central Election Committee to include more women than the number suggested by the district Congress committees which had the initial power to sponsor.

"Those of us who were in the districts on polling day during the last general elections...will remember the gay groups dressed up in their festival finery, singing as they walked to the booths. However, for many of them it was too new and strange a procedure to grasp," Mrs Gandhi pointed out this reason for sponsoring a pamphlet, *Women and Elections,* one of the many that came pouring out of the women's department to educate the women in their new responsibilities.[45] She encouraged women to take to kitchen gardening as not only a worthwhile element of home economy but in the context of India's situation as a matter of national urgency in the Grow More Food campaign. She thought the women had a key role to play in the National Savings Campaign. She put it to them in that mixture of literary references and homely phrases that was to become a style of her speech making.

"Mercy had been poetically described as twice-blessed. Shakespeare writes that 'it blesseth him that gives and him that takes.' In the context of our present-day social and economic conditions, thrift which leads to small saving, may well be described in similar ethical terms. The giver here is the same as in the case of mercy—the individual or the family. The taker, however, is the state. In the ultimate analysis the taker, too, is the individual or the family. The state, after all, is an impersonal but organized agency which works for the welfare of the entire community and the individuals who constitute it."[46]

She was conscious, like her father, that she had to frame her thoughts in a way that could be understood by a largely uneducated populace. She actively pursued and fought in the vanguard for legislation to impart dignity to the role of women. In fact, she says that her influence over Nehru was predominant on the status of women and on child development. But she believed that the awakening must come from women themselves. She was conscious of the need to activize the Congress women workers at the lowest level of the *Mahila Vibhags* and the Mandal Congress committees, and the method she advocated was uncompromising. "'Freedom is not the right to do as you like, but the liberty to do as you ought'," she quoted. "The emotional approach is not enough. The appeal to emotion must be based on reason, which in turn is nursed by accurate and thorough knowledge."[47]

But her voice in the background and her lack of flamboyance in public affairs made some of those who were with her in her London days think that she had failed her promise. Parvati Krishnan, who had become a Member of Parliament in 1952, is said to have remarked in surprise, "Why, is Indu now left to produce children only!"[48]

Indira's public face was nearly always deceptive. But to those who worked closely with her, she was near goddess, and yet very human. Mukul Banerjee remembers the occasion when Indira came rushing to her rescue in what threatened to be a nightmarish predicament. Mukul had asked Nehru to come and speak at the Conveners' Conference in 1955. He had agreed. "But I was immature then and forgot to tell his secretary and have it put in his diary," she says. "So on that day, knowing that the security guards came an hour before, and when they didn't turn up and we waited and watched, I rang up and they said 'no,' the prime minister would not be able to come. I ran up to Indiraji and said that only she could save the situation. She was presiding at the time, so she asked Manibehn to take her place and ran down immediately *without her sandals* and went and brought Panditji. She didn't even scold me," added Mukul Banerjee gratefully.[49]

At the Nagpur session in 1959 they were all gathered together and found to their horror that some fundamental facilities had been overlooked. Indira did not lose her sense of humor.

"What have you got for bathroom arrangements?" she asked Mukul.

"We have to suffer the same thing," came the unhappy reply.

"What?"

"Well, we have no doors also!"

India told her that she would make Krishna (another worker) stand outside and they could take turns! The reception committee ultimately put up some curtains.

On another occasion when she came back from a visit to Japan, and the women's department arranged a meeting, the first thing Indira burst out laughingly with was, "Do I look like an elephant?" The elephant presented by India to Japanese children she had found was called Indira and she confessed that at first it made her most unhappy till she realized what fun the elephant was providing the children!

Fun was something she rarely missed out on herself. She somehow gleaned it out of the severe protocol of her days as hostess—to be as gay and informal as possible. Once she asked the women who had gathered for a women's conference in India to come to her house dressed in their own provincial costumes, while she herself wore an Assamese one. The food was served in an unorthodox way as in a fete and consisted of delicious, peppery *hors d'oeuvres* preparations that are especially popular with India's women. She was not a heavy eater or fussy about food, but she liked tasting all kinds of varieties, and in her visits to the different Indian states, she would always have indigenous dishes. There were times when a frantic message would go to "Om" [Bajaj] Agarwal, for instance, asking for a recipe for a Gujarati dish that she wished to serve at her own house. With the women she could let her domestic fancies and her love for decoration run free. At times she would have a massive peacock made of flowers contribute to the gaiety of the gathering, and at others have a baby elephant decorated beautifully as part of the fun. She loved to mimic, but only when it did not hurt and her ability to pick up languages and imitate each accent allowed her to range playfully over the regional speech patterns of India. At home at a small but informal party on one occasion she appeared wearing a Moghul dress, and "once when I went for breakfast," recollects Om Agarwal, "she was wearing a *lehnga* and *chuni*," and she remembers also, at the Indore Congress years back, how excitedly Indira ran up to her reveling with delight in the new gossamer cottons that promised such relief from the khadi. "Om, Om," exclaimed Indira, "here's a Chanderi! Have you seen it?"[50]

She insists, nevertheless, that she is the wrong kind of person to talk about fashion. "My clothes never tear. I still have my first saris . . . and nobody believes they are so old."

But when she was asked how she appeared to be so well groomed, she answered simply, "I hate doing what everybody else does," while occasionally one can detect a sharp look of appraisal in her eyes when she is looking at another well-dressed woman.

She has good taste, that's all. It's as simple as that. And as in other things her decisions are quick. "I don't take long to select what I want. I know exactly what I want. We were in Paris once for half a day. It was a very crowded program. I told the wife of an embassy official that I had to buy myself a coat. She said we couldn't possibly do it. I looked at the program and found a half-hour between engagements. We went to a shop. The woman there showed me a number of coats. But I was sure," emphasized Mrs Gandhi, with the imperious vanity of the knowing, "that I wanted something . . . that said 'Paris' the minute you looked at it."

The sales woman then brought out two more coats from inside, and Indira immediately selected one.

"We had done it within that half-hour!"[51]

But unlike a truly vain woman, she can have a bath and get dressed in five minutes which, as she says, "very few men can do."

She had acquired a reputation for being frail, but her energy flowed in all directions. She was interested in everything, as she once remarked. She says she does not know much about art, but she likes "new paintings, old paintings and old sculpture." She is especially appreciative of the immense variety of India's cultural lore. She likes the folk music of the different regions, and it was she who suggested to Nehru that the Republic Day Parade on January 26 each year be enlivened by a pageant of India's colorful folk dances. She is sharp and responsive to her environment, "instantly noting the colors, the placement of the furniture, and the objects in a room." She is a fine horsewoman, and loves swimming and hiking. She is interested enough in Western music to have become at one time vice-president of the Delhi Music Society. She found time to indulge in a favorite pastime, that of bird watching, with the then British High Commissioner, Sir Malcolm MacDonald. In fact, she promptly founded a Bird Watching Society. She loves doing the *Times of India* crossword puzzles, and likes to play Scrabble, and always, when there is time and even if there is no time, there are the books she likes to read.

In all of this she never forgot the personal touch. When Mukul finally decided to get married Indira apparently realized that a woman who had lived and worked so independently would not have an easy time adjusting to a new pattern. The day of the marriage she telephoned first thing in the morning and spoke soothingly of the future to Mukul and told her to take it calmly. "I wondered," says Mukul now, "how she could, in spite of her other great preoccupations, think of my strange predicament ... and attempt to put me in the proper frame of mind."

According to Mukul, "Indiraji" does not harbor ill feelings for long against anybody. She gives the instance of a woman M.P. with whom Indira was greatly annoyed because she had spoken badly of India when abroad. She told her never to see her again. The woman came and cried on Mukul's shoulder, who, in turn, went to Indira to persuade her to forgive the person. Indira immediately relented. "All right, send her tomorrow," she agreed, and a few days later, Mukul found that she had gone off happily to a meeting with the same woman.

Fory Nehru, B.K. Nehru's wife, says that she is a woman of great integrity. "If she doesn't like some one, she lets them know it. She never sweet-talks you to your face and then talks about you behind your back."[52] But one certainly has the impression that there is a core of finality about her reactions. She may not harbor ill feelings, but once a compact is broken, she is not able to feel the same again.

"At first glance there is something forbiddingly regal about this child of the Indian revolution. Her long, thin face and Roman features are severe in repose. I am somehow reminded of a Hapsburg empress when I see her slender sari-draped figure sweeping through the carpeted halls of the prime minister's residence," remarked Welles Hangen. "But her imperial aura and my confusion soon vanish as soon as she greets me in a voice so soft that I must strain to hear."[53]

The "imperial aura" no doubt resulted from her preference for aloofness. In 1949, for example, when she fell ill, the old family friend, doctor, and politician, Dr. B. C. Roy, advised her to go to Kashmir for a rest. Both he and Nehru were sitting in the room when a young woman, who had newly joined the Nehru staff, was called in to be told to accompany her. Nehru gave her some advice which was indicative of how well he understood his daughter, at the same time revealing what he thought others should understand of her.

"About Indu," he advised the person, "you must understand one thing—you'll get by—be available, but don't go near her. Don't intrude."[54]

Indira also had her moods. As hostess in the prime minister's house she set a trend toward warmth. She was charming, informal, and chatty. At a party once at home she found that the women had collected in one corner and the men in another. She decided to break the pattern and urged the then young deputy minister of health, Raju, to be the first to come over to the ladies' side. When he seemed to hesitate, she laughed, "Nobody will eat you. Come here."[55] But she presented a different picture at a comparatively formal party outside. First of all, the awe about Nehru had begun to rub off on her, too. She did not invite familiarity and guests hesitated to go up to her. She moved in a little circle of glacial air. But on one occasion two women at a party decided to brave that icy calm and went and sat next to her. The conversation turned to Japanese women and the male ego which thrived on the sort of loyal subservience that they could offer. Suddenly, Indira, with a habit she has of exploding into an abruptly frank statement, said flatly. "I do a lot for my husband, I even type for him, but that doesn't seem to help ..." and the air closed around all three in sudden warmth.[56]

She was half serious. Her personal life was subject to other compulsions. Feroze had again preceded her in giving a more tangible political stamp to his life. He had run for Parliament from Rai Bareli in the first general election in 1952. She had helped him by touring the constituency with him, and he had come out with flying colors. He had a sense of achievement. But his apprehension that everything might be because he was Nehru's son-in-law or Indira's husband began to alternate with the determination to prove his worth.

"He was egotistical. Any lesser man would have enjoyed the role [of being connected with the P.M.] but he had a very deep-seated grouse against himself for being in that situation," comments one of his friends.[57]

Indira was tactful, discreet, protective, and loving, but helpless. He was resentful, hurt, proud, in love with her, but rebellious. Their growing activities took different forms. Yet they were unusual enough to defy the usual strains, to hold together a common duty, common interests, and a common goal. In 1953 he left Lucknow and the *National Herald,* and became general manager of the *Indian Express* in Delhi. "He had given the impression of being a playboy with a light heart in the coffee houses [of Lucknow] which call only for light heartedness," recalls Chalapathi Rau, "but behind that false facade, I could see an engine of energy."[58] For three years more it lay almost dormant. He retained his bantering manner, but brooded over his predicament, and sat quietly in Parliament, absorbing with decep-

tive casualness the details of procedure with which he would fire salvo after
salvo in the future. He was also unsure of his independence in one sense.
He stayed at Tin Murti with his wife and children, in a separate suite on one
side of that impressive residence, but it was still the prime minister's house
and he was hesitant to entertain the assortment of people that would come
to him from his constituency and elsewhere, sometimes even telling him facts
that could militate against his father-in-law's government. Perhaps he was
also not certain in some cases whether they would come to him in his own
individual capacity or because—that painful thought—he could be a pipe-
line to the prime minister. He wanted to be sure of that and avoid embarrassing Nehru. As an M.P., he was officially allotted a house in Queen Victoria
Road, so he began to spend his working hours there. He would have
breakfast with all his family and return only in the late evening. He did
not feel at home in that entire milieu of formal entertainment that
sometimes awaited him, so if there was a dinner or a function which
required his presence yet off stage as it were, he felt cold and indifferent. It
was not a pleasant experience to be invited with Nehru and Indira and then
because of protocol to be seated far back at the end of the table. Or
sometimes, go on sufferance. Indira went officially as the Prime Minister's hostess. Feroze was only a Member of Parliament. He would laugh
it off a number of times. Very often he and Mohammad Yunus, an old
family friend and political colleague (now a senior government official),
would be together and Feroze would exclaim, "Indu has to be out there.
Let us eat here in the room. We will enjoy it more," and he and Yunus
would sit down happily with the boys.[59]

Indira's frequent trips abroad opened a whole new range of experience
to her and also left them less time to be with each other. In fact, he
reacted violently by never stirring out of the country, although he did
accompany Nehru and Indira on tours in India. But at a public meeting
or function he would prefer to lose himself in the background. Once at a
meeting in Assam where they had gone together he kept sitting at the back
of the dais on the stairs. When a staff member of the Prime Minister's
party urged him to go up he shrugged nonchalantly. *"Are Bhai,* I'm all
right. You don't want me to imprison myself up there, do you? Thank
you. I am enjoying my smoke."[60]

There was a pattern of privilege which applied automatically to Indira
from which he was shut out. Being the sort of person he was, proud,
aggressive, and sensitive, it was not the lack of privilege as such which upset
him but that the male ego naturally suffered. There was the occasion, for
instance, when at the civic reception for Khrushchev and Bulganin at Delhi's
Ram Lila grounds, Nehru and Indira were escorted swiftly through the
milling crowds while Feroze and a score of fellow M.P.s were stopped outside by the security police. Feroze took up the issue angrily at a meeting of
the Congress parliamentary party and argued for the safeguarding of the

dignity of Members of Parliament. Though the subject had a general relevance, it had a personal sting for Feroze because colleagues, acquaintances, and even friends were not above throwing out an occasional taunt about the circumstances of being a *ghar jamai*.

These were crucial years for the practical equations between Indira and Feroze, and between Feroze and Nehru. Three things had upset the more ardent of Nehru's leftist group of followers of whom Feroze was one when India gained freedom: Nehru's acceptance, even though temporary, of dominion status; his first major enunciation of industrial policy which did not fall upon big business as hard as they expected; and the strong pro-British current set in motion by what they concluded to be Nehru's "weakness" for the Mountbattens and his consequent vulnerability to their advice. Feroze, it seems, in a fit of disenchantment, dashed off a letter to Nehru saying he was resigning from the Congress because he had expected a more democratic, socialistic direction. One of his friends remembers reading through this letter and says that it ended with these famous lines from "The Lost Leader" by Robert Browning on disillusioned faith:

> *Just for a handful of silver he left us*
> *Just for a riband to stick in his coat.*

When he asked Feroze what happened to the letter, he said he had given it to Indu. Whether she passed it on to her father or not no action followed. Feroze remained very much in the Congress, but as an angry young rebel. Nehru on his part remained largely indifferent to Feroze. He had accepted him mainly because of Indira, but Feroze's career up to 1955 was not so distinguished as to make Nehru admire what seemed till then to be his rather facetious extremism. Feroze had been elected to Parliament but for three years from 1952 to 1955 he did not utter a word. He was imbibing the atmosphere, studying the procedures, planning a course of action, but none of this appeared on the surface to offset the impression given by his light-hearted air and casual bonhomie.

But suddenly in 1955 he made his debut with a maiden speech that was a *tour de force*. It hit out with facts, statistics, and controlled eloquence at one of India's three leading industrial magnates, Ram Krishna Dalmia. Not only did Feroze's logic expose the corrupt working of the insurance companies controlled by Dalmia, but did it with such a marshaling of detail that it led not only to Dalmia's arrest but prepared the way for the ultimate nationalization of the life insurance business as such.

"As I saw him speak with ease and conviction and logic," recalls Chalapathi Rau, "I knew he was on the way to becoming a fine parliamentarian. His interventions became dramatic and historic and were looked for."[61] In 1956 he helped pass the Parliamentary Proceedings Act of 1956 which gave the press the hitherto denied right to publish accurate reports of parliamentary proceedings without being subject to the risk of being held up for contempt of Parliament and to the proceedings of the courts of law. It was an important enactment and Feroze with his long and intimate association with the press became even more popular with the capital's newspaper world.

In 1957 after he was re-elected, but toward the end of the year, he created a furore not only in Parliament but in the entire country. Life insurance had indeed been nationalized but it was the corruption in the Life Insurance Corporation of India that he revealed, in a brilliantly argued speech in Parliament. He cited a pattern of orders, counter orders, relaxation of rules, or their enforcement which made its dealing with a young businessman called Haridas Mundhra suspect. His opening sentences gave only an inkling of what was to follow.

"Mr Speaker, sir, a mutiny in my mind has compelled me to raise this debate. When things of such magnitude, as I shall describe to you later, occur, silence becomes a crime. That public expenditure shall be subject to the severest public debate is a healthy tradition especially so in an era of growing public enterprise."[62]

Feroze had worked in the utmost secrecy and those who had chosen to help him research the case had done so in strict confidence, visiting him at his house in Queen Victoria Road late at night and sometimes entering from the back. His conclusions were startling. He thought there was a deliberate effort to help the fortunes of Mundhra by manipulating the funds of the corporation. His analysis in Parliament seemed irrefutable. He asked pointed questions of the finance minister, T. T. Krishnamachari.

"I hope I have established collusion between the Life Insurance Corporation of India and Mundhra," he concluded dramatically. "I have, I hope, established a conspiracy in which public funds were wrongfully employed for financing the interest of an individual at the cost of the insured."[63]

Parliament was stunned. The repercussions were serious. Nehru was persuaded by Feroze to set up a Commission of Enquiry. Its hearings began to be followed by the country with an interest matching that in a murder trial. There was an unseemly attempt on the part of officials to apportion blame on each other. The principal secretary of finance to the government of India, H. M. Patel, declared that he had acted under orders from the minister. Krishnamachari denied this. The governor of the state bank, H. V. R. Iyengar, and the chairman and managing director of the corporation were equivocal. Krishnamachari ultimately gave conflicting reasons for the transaction by which the LIC purchased 15 million rupees worth of poor-rise stock in six corporations controlled by Mundhra. The net result was that the secretary of finance was severely "reprimanded" by the one-man commission (M. C. Chagla, chief justice of Bombay), and the minister of finance was held "constitutionally responsible" for bad judgment although exonerated of any corruption. Krishnamachari was obliged to resign. It

was "the scandal of the decade" and some mud was left clinging to all three—
the government, the civil services, and the public sector. The one redeeming
feature was that Nehru had had an inquiry instituted fearlessly and immediately.

Feroze himself had started with trepidation. He had brought the matter
to the notice of the prime minister, who in turn had confronted TTK with
it. Krishnamachari had actually pleaded with Nehru that Feroze should
be allowed to bring the question into the open in Parliament. That, he
said, would clear the atmosphere and scuttle all rumors. After a few days
Feroze had again gone to Nehru and said that there would be serious
repercussions. But TTK was sanguine about his innocence and adamant
that the subject should be raised on the floor of the house. The third time
Feroze went, TTK literally begged him to go ahead. In the intervening
days Feroze had been able to gather more information and the conclusions
proved damning. Nehru had drafted the resolution of the Congress in
1951, in which the tendency toward indiscipline had been decried and he
had emphasized the need for confining criticism of party matters to party
meetings alone. But here it was an exposure of governmental mal-
functioning, and even though Feroze had not the least intention of
embarrassing his father-in-law, the result was in a sense unfortunate. In
the 1950s the Congress ruled by such an overwhelming majority that no
official opposition worth the name existed. Criticism when it came from
a party member seemed even more glaring.

If Feroze's satisfaction at achieving, almost overnight, a national stature
as a parliamentarian was soured by these reservations, his colleagues
now began to gather round him like bees drawn to honey. After question
hour in Parliament he would go to a corner, and like Rafi Ahmad Kidwai
before him, he would gather his cronies there. This was the very stuff of
his life, the wit and thrust of debate, the endless fascination of inner politics,
the easy dominance, the jokes, the affability, and, at last, the confidence.
Where he sat came to be known as Feroze's corner, and there was an air of
expectancy, mingled with nervousness for those who feared it, for what
might next come out of the Feroze lobby. There was light-hearted raillery
with an undercurrent of inside knowledge. He was meticulous about avoiding
any reference to his association with the prime minister. If it had been left
to him he would have felt more independent without it, but he could not
help being privy to certain possibilities. Once, sitting among fellow M.P.s
in the central hall, he saw Tarkeshwari Sinha, their ebullient young
woman colleague, wearing a blue sari. He laughingly called her a "blue
chip." It was prophetic. Within a week, like the blue chips of the stock
market, her value rose and she was appointed deputy minister of finance.
He had a sense of sportsmanship too. The day before his speech on the
railways he happened to run into Jagjivan Ram, then minister of railways,
and warned him good-humoredly what to expect. There was the bitter-

sweet pleasure of crossing swords with his father-in-law. None of the personal tension, or the political doubts he had, could take away his regard for the man. It was difficult not to admire him when he strode into Parliament with the air of a man who controlled it. A hush would settle as if only by his coming could the real business of the house begin. He was master of his subjects, he was head above them all in the sweep of his ideas, and he showed a concern not only for the niceties of parliamentary procedure but its colorful asides. When Feroze had brought in his strictures about the Bharat Insurance Company and Dalmia had been arrested, Shanti Prasad Jain, his son-in-law, had acted as his surety. When arguments raged over the case in Parliament subsequently, amidst the pointed interpellations that sought to question the propriety of some aspects, there was a clarification that Feroze insisted upon: "Will the prime minister be pleased to state the relationship of the surety to the accused?"

Nehru was irrepressible.

"The same as that of the questioner to the answerer," he replied, and the house roared with laughter.[64]

These were good moments indeed. But Feroze was apprehensive that his parliamentary exposures might be linked with a kind of sensationalism. He was determined to be corrective and constructive, and determined also to win the respect of "Jawaharlalji." His line was unequivocal. He was an ardent socialist. He was disturbed that the majority of congressmen seemed only to pay lip service to the ideal. To a friend, Jagdish Kodesia, he once defined three types of socialists: "One, like Allahabad guavas, white outside but red inside, another like beetroot, red both inside and outside, and the third like *vilayati mooli,* red outside but white inside."[65] The Congress, he thought, had more of the last category, "outward and showy." He himself had an instinctive sympathy for the common man and his ability to draw the confidence of taxi drivers, *panwallahs,* clerks, and peons gave him the feel of the public pulse. He urgently wanted the Congress leadership, particularly Nehru, to recapture the passion of their early commitment. Nehru, after all, had been the ideal of the revolutionary young.

But the more earnestly he plunged into politics, the more impossible did it become to work from Tin Murti. He confided in a friend: "As a member of Parliament all sorts of people come to me, some pro-government, some anti-government, as also many sufferers and dimwits.... It would be basically wrong for me to receive all these men at the prime minister's house."[66] His own house in Queen Victoria Road therefore became more and more a home. He had already made a point of receiving his constituents and entertaining his friends there. But his famous "cases" for Parliament involved extensive preparation and sometimes had him working far into the night, meeting people, making notes, and typing them, and he began to stay at the house some nights instead of going back to Tin Murti, especially if Indira happened to be out of Delhi with her father. Since he was permanently in Delhi himself, she could have stayed with him in their own house as well as acted as official hostess if she had wanted. By 1954 even the children were away in a boarding school at Dehra Dun. But Feroze's acceptance of the situation in that sense was total because his promise was categorical even before they got married, that they both would be responsible for Nehru.

"Too much has been made out of Feroze's other house," says Yunus. "It was a question of convenience. Apart from the politicians, many of his friends, even journalists, would feel uncomfortable visiting him at the P.M.'s house. They couldn't just walk in. They had to be checked at the gate and asked questions and all that. Besides, even for her, it became a place where she could meet their common friends more freely."

She preferred going at tea time with the children. Very few people knew when or how often she came and one person who remained absolutely tight-lipped was Jogeshwar, Feroze's loyal servant. Feroze, ebullient, even garrulous, seemingly casual otherwise, refused to talk about "Indu" under any circumstances with anyone. Only the photograph on the mantlepiece in which Indira in a black coat looked "soft, fragile and girlish" and to which friends noticed his eyes turned compellingly and often, bore mute testimony to his longings for more normal circumstances.

"But there were picnics often on sundays at Okhla," describes Yunus. "The boys played in the sand.... Feroze would fish, with his wife beside him, putting his catches in a bowl. If state formalities prevented her from accompanying them, he would feel sorry for her. 'Look at the fun she's missing,' he would say."[67]

"If I thought I could believe in reincarnation like you people," Feroze laughingly burst out to a Hindu friend once, "I would like, I think, to get married to an *amrud wali* in my next life."

"Good Heavens, why, Ferozebhai?" expostulated the surprised listener.

"Well, at least," and his eyes twinkled, "she would be there to press my feet when I came home in the evenings."[68]

But she says he could not hide the wistfulness in his voice.

Yunus gives the most exact and authentic interpretation: "The whole thing has been highly exaggerated. People, even family members, had not approved of this marriage, so they derived consolation from any minor sign of discord that you can find between any husband and wife. I remember a party at Tin Murti House once. Feroze and I were standing in a corner. Two society women, with their backs to us, were saying to each other: 'See, Feroze is not here. They have separated, so he doesn't even come here any more.' And there he was, right next to them! We had a good laugh."[69]

Had it been purely a question of acting as official hostess it might have been simpler. But Indira's attitude was compounded of four things—the weight of her role and the varied experience it provided her; the care she could bestow on her father; her increasing influence as intermediary; the enlargement of her sphere of interests and her growing political stature. Perhaps she might have sacrificed everything if she had been a different kind of person. But, as she says, she was just not cut out to be a mere housewife. Both she and Feroze were too headstrong for routine smoothness between them, their preoccupations were above the personal, and circumstances pushed them toward wider tasks.

On September 9, 1951, Nehru assumed the presidency of the Congress for yet another time, in addition to being prime minister, in a triumphant reassertion of organization will in party matters. The following year, in India's first general election, he exercised his influence on the campaign with such vigor that the Congress became synonymous with Nehru, and Nehru with the Congress. It became almost a one-man campaign, and the strain on Nehru was to tell.

He was sixty-two at the time. He went everywhere—by plane, car, train, horse, and on foot, addressed an estimated 30 million people, covered 30,000 miles of varied country in forty-three days, made an average nine speeches a day, and slept only five hours at night. Those nearest him began to voice their concern.

But there was Indira, daughter, companion and confidante who was there to devote herself completely to his comfort. 'Someone whose one concern in life became to take care of him, see that he got a hot cup of tea when he wanted it, five minutes' rest occasionally, and protect him from the hundreds of people he needed never to interview. It was all the inessential things he insisted on doing that drained him.'

"What I do mind," said Indira, "is that much of his time is taken by people's personal problems and by matters which could be dealt with by the people in charge of departments more directly concerned."[70] She thought he remained so accessible to people with genuine problems that they tended to flock to him with the feeling that they would get justice only from him. And there was a mistaken notion that the prime minister, like the kings of old, had only to mention something for it to be implemented. "Fortunately or unfortunately," she said, "democracy does not function in this way and each matter has to be referred through the proper channels to the right authority. This is a long business which depends on many officials." Her understanding was mixed with chagrin. "If the people were more considerate of my father's time, it would be possible for him to have a little leisure which is so essential."[71]

She could not stop the people, but she could stop him. She did it by substituting for him wherever possible. As a woman of influence, the role was implicit from the time that she set off as his emissary to Tagore in 1937, helped screen his appointments in Europe while she was there, assumed the responsibilities of Anand Bhawan, and tried to fill with companionable devotion the emotional void in her father's life. By 1942, even public institutions were beginning to attempt an approach to Nehru through Indira. The

Cawnpore Children's Association, for example, in urging Nehru to visit
their children's hall during one of his visits to Cawnpore, used what was
to become a familiar gambit. "Miss Indira Nehru," they stressed hopefully
in a letter to him, "was favorably impressed with the children's hall established by the association . . ."[72]

But the first time she took over some part of his public duties was in 1947
when she sat patiently in the P.M.'s house from 8 A.M. to 1.30 P.M. every
day interviewing hundreds of refugees and tried to save him from meeting
all but the most urgent cases. She was not prepared, however, to accept office.
She refused an offer to run for the constituent assembly before partition.
She refused again when Govind Vallabh Pant urged her to stand for election
to the U.P. Legislative Assembly. She refused to listen even when Pant
prevailed upon Gandhi to put in a word of persuasion. She said she had
her children to took after. She had a marriage to sustain. She had to
combine that with a minimum of tension, with her will to look after her
father. Yet it was not because of any lack of time that she hesitated. She
found time to work impossible hours during the riots, she had a myriad personal activities, and her deep interest in social welfare took her traveling
miles away from her family at frequent intervals. She made it coincide
with her children's attendance at school. She made it coincide as far as
possible with her father's trips away from Delhi so that she could be with
him when he was in the capital. But no rigid obligation to sacrifice herself
completely prevented her from doing what she wanted. Having a number
of interests, she declared, kept her young and she "did not mind her father
being busy." She could easily have scraped the time to be a politician if
she wanted.

It was not lack of ambition that prevented her. It was her sense of
occasion. In 1947, even her first work in social welfare and with women
lay ahead. To have accepted a nomination for office then would have
meant accepting it on the strength of being Nehru's daughter. She was
sensitive enough to want to prove her worth before enjoying its fruits.
She must have felt then the weight of the advice she gave to young people
later, to work so well that you cannot be overlooked. Besides, it could not
have appeared worth it to give up, for eight months of the year when Parliament or the assemblies are in session, and for the sake of the dubious distinction of being one of the multitudes of M.L.A.s or M.P.s, the constant
exhilaration of being near the center of power.

Nehru's election campaign from the Phulpur constituency in U.P. in
1952 was run by Mridula Sarabhai and Lal Bahadur Shastri. Nehru
himself was electioneering all over India. His name was a byword, his
election a certainty, but a minimum of organization was essential, especially
as it was the first time a general election was held in free India, and the electorate was largely uneducated. Above all, the very scale was dramatic: 3,800
seats that had to be filled, 17,000 candidates in the field, representing 59

parties, necessitating 2,500,00 ballot boxes, 600 million ballot papers, 133,000 polling stations, 196,000 polling booths, a voting population of 173 million, and a million men in charge of the election machinery under the supervision of an independent election commission. Indira took on some part of the intense excitement by opting to substitute for her father wherever required. Her first visit was to Chamba. It proved to be such a success that, as she says herself, "throughout the election I was, sort of, taken in. I mean I was made to travel, speak and so on, wherever my father couldn't go."[73]

In 1953 she reactivated the women's department of the AICC and both in regard to that and on behalf of the Social Welfare Board she began to tour the country in her own capacity. Her program schedule was tight, and demanding each time, but when her father happened to see the one laid out for her for a visit to Madhya Bharat in 1955, he was extremely upset, and yet in a dilemma. He felt that it was physically impossible for anyone to go through such a schedule but for Indu particularly it would be menacing for her health. He knew it was useless trying to persuade her to have the timings altered. He probably did not want to seem to be interfering; he knew how touchy she could be. So, like a typical father, he wrote to Mukul Banerjee. "Don't let Indu see this," he said, "but her program is too heavy, she will suffer in health."

"I never told her, not till this day, but I sent wires all over, canceling parts of that schedule," recalls Mrs Banerjee.[74] They were careful in the future.

By 1955, Indira's contacts were widespread, various, and irresistible. She had been to more places than almost any other politician, even places where there were no roads, and she had worked almost "at all levels" as she says herself. She had never been ignored, but now even her work could not be. The same year she was nominated for membership in the most powerful party executive, the Congress Working Committee, the body that had set the course of modern Indian history since its inception, the body that had in- cuded names which were already legend, and which had on its panel names that would become legend, and the body most of all, where she now sat as colleague with her father, the man who represented India's historic transformation from the old to the new. The same year, she acted as chairman of the special committee which arranged receptions for Soviet party boss Nikita S. Khrushchev and Premier Nikolai Bulganin during their tour of India. Once while accompanying them to Kashmir, in the plane, she spotted two journalists in summer clothes.

"Haven't you brought anything warm? You'll freeze," she told them.

Both of them were South Indians and unused to the idea of possible cold in Kashmir, so they had not brought suitable clothes. But there was nothing they could do, and they decided to suffer it.

"When we landed at Srinagar and reached the hotel—it took us much longer than the VIPs—we found two overcoats lying for us there," recalled E.K.

Ramaswamy. Mrs Gandhi had asked where they would be staying but they had not imagined she would not only remember their predicament but have something done about it.[75]

Indira first became a member of the Congress Working Committee repenting the women's section and youth affairs, but she was not a militant feminist. She just thought that women, having been repressed, must now be educated to learn to think and to do a job well. It was not necessary to deny one's womanliness, to do a man's job.

"I think there's a lot of the male and female in everyone," she said once in explaining her attitude. "If you are doing something you don't become any the less feminine for it."

"But that's how you feel," I said. "I mean—"

"It's not what I feel," she cut in sharply, "It's a fact."

She could go for that straight to the Hindu concept of the *Ardhangini*, the principle of equal and complementary virtues according to which the female is not derived from the male like Eve from Adam's rib, but holds the male in equal balance to form a whole. It was a concept that existed at the back of the minds of those who perhaps did not know its intellectual source, tradition being that miraculous alchemy which makes the knowledge of one century the instincts of another. But Indira recurrently returned to the sources of Hindu thought, to her association with India's spiritual leaders. Gandhi often referred to the "feminine side" of him and the "male side" of him and her own father talked along similar lines. It was an attitude that made it easier to delight in what you were, female and feminine, yet fight for all the manly rights, and encompass all the manly virtues.

Politically during the early 1950s, her ideas took shape around her belief that the primary purpose of any action should be the eradication of India's poverty. She even went to the extent of stating the controversial view that the need to remake the foundation of the country was so strong that she thought it was better not to have opposition parties, especially as "the people in the country were illiterate and . . . would be led away by slogans." If the people were influenced by opposition parties, she said, and were cut off from their moorings, they would drift toward destruction. Obviously, she thought the Congress was the only party then to offer sane goals. But the Congress was committed to parliamentary democracy which implied the acceptance of opposition. She clarified her ideas when her opinion was asked about the formation of the Swatantra party, which had come into being as a result of Rajagopalachari's reaction to the strong socialist bent resolved upon by the Congress at Nagpur. "I said that in our country the vast majority of the people are very poor. And all our programs and plans must be so arranged, so decided, that the good of the majority is always before us. If ever we move to the other side and try to look after the interests of any small group, then not only would we be finished as a party but there would be danger of chaos and revolution in the country."[76]

However, she was certain that it was not the fact of freedom but the way in which it was exercised that ultimately determined whether it would survive. Her faith in a democratic functioning of the people's will remained undaunted. "We have chosen the path of democracy," she affirmed, "and rightly so, because it is only through democracy that the individual has the maximum opportunity for growth and for participation in the affairs of the nation."[77]

She admitted that there was "dissatisfaction with the administration and irritation with the party." Remedies had to be sought. "As a nation we have many shortcomings," she said, but her natural optimism could not be contained. "If this were the whole of the story it would indeed be depressing. But as I travel around the country and have the opportunity of meeting people from all walks of life I see something else. Not perfection, of course, but many evidences of a difficult job well done. In the mass of our people there is perceptibly an awakening and a momentum that is gathering force."[78]

By the end of 1956, Indira was high in the hierarchy of Congress politics. She also assumed full charge of Nehru's election campaign for 1957. But when she was asked by Congress President U. N. Dhebar to take on an innocuous job like that of the presidency of the Allahabad City Congress Committee to bring some order into its faction-ridden affairs, she did not hesitate.

"No political leader of her stature would have touched a petty job like that with a pair of tongs," comments Uma Shankar Dixit, who was conducting Nehru's campaign with her at the time. "But she didn't mind at all. She was prepared to work with them, provided they all did too in the same spirit. She warned them that if there was no teamwork or if she detected any feuding or backbiting she would quit forthwith."[79] She stayed in Allahabad for two months, during which efforts were made to get the Samyukta Socialist Party candidate—who had come in place of the original Congress candidate on an election petition—rejected by the electorate in the by-election. Mrs Rajen Kumari Bajpai, who was secretary of the committee when Indira was president, recalls how strenuous was the door-to-door campaign conducted under Indira's guidance.

She also organized a meticulous coverage of her father's constituency. There were eleven hundred villages in all. She herself toured all of them on an average of ten or twelve a day until she was drawing an audience of 20,000 in some places. She showed a keen sense of propriety. As a modern woman she was not particularly fond of wearing bangles, which are an essential symbol of the married woman in traditional Hindu society. She also had short hair. She thought her bare arms would be taken as an affront by the mass of village women she would have to contact, so she would put on some bangles, cover her head in traditional style, and if she happened to be in a village on an auspicious day like Basant Panchami, on which custom enjoins the wearing of yellow, she would wear yellow.

When the election was over she went to Delhi, but wrote to suggest the names of the people to invite to a celebration party. When she returned to Allahabad for the party, Mrs Bajpai remembers that Indira's solicitousness did not fail in the smallest thing, not certainly in relation to her husband with whom rumor had begun to attach their mutual disenchantment. Feroze accompanied Indira to Allahabad, but he was late for the party. As soon as he came she went up to him and told him that his share of the ice cream had been kept for him and that he must have it.[80]

Mukul Banerjee says that in this respect, Indira's attitude to her husband was just like that of an ordinary devoted housewife. She remembers one morning when she went to see Indira. Feroze was hurrying out of the bedroom to go somewhere.

"Have you taken the pills?" Indira asked, for he had been ill.

"Oh, I forgot," replied Feroze casually, and made as if to leave.

Indira stopped him. "No, I won't let you go without that. I kept the water and pills in front of you. Excuse me, Mukul, I'll come in a minute," she said, and fetched the medicine and made Feroze take it.[81]

On another occasion, while a Congress session was on in Delhi, Mukul heard Feroze telling Indira that he was not feeling well and that he was going home. Indira felt his forehead, found he was feverish, and left the dais immediately and went home with him.[82]

"She is very pious," remarked Mrs Bajpai in a surprise analysis. "At Anand Bhawan, sometimes, when we went in the morning, the servant would say that she was doing *puja*. She doesn't do it the orthodox way perhaps. But in her own way. I've seen a *chandan* mark at the base of her throat at times, and on the forehead."[83]

It is this enigmatic mixture of old fashioned inclination—one cannot say belief—and a modern mind which places her at such an advantage in functioning in "the land of contradictions" as she calls India. She can meet its contradictions with her own, so that it becomes possible to temper expediency with understanding when it comes to allowing for the superstitions of village women, and to urge for a scientific outlook when spelling out an ideal for the young.

"Let our roots reach deep down into our heritage," she says in a typical exhortation, "but let us not keep looking backward or be bound down by traditions. Let us use them to help us to grow and face the clear sky of the future."[84]

She certainly made the women face it. For the 1957 elections the Congress allocated 10 per cent of the seats to women candidates, and at the end, Indira could point out proudly that there were 179 congresswomen in the state assemblies, and 24 in India's Parliament. "These elections have made it clear that women voters have tremendous power of influencing the course of our national life in terms of their political understanding and activity. True democracy can thrive only on an intelligent use of the vote and the capacity of the legislators to work in an enlightened and progressive manner," she emphasized. "It is not enough to have women members in the legislatures. We must see to it that they function efficiently and with knowledge of the subjects being discussed and the issues at stake."[85] She not only set in motion a scheme for the holding of seminars to train women legislators, but spelled out in detail what they must do to remain in touch and activate their respective constituencies. But she wished them to have no illusions. "It will need hard and intensive work," she said, "to spread new ideas among the people, to root out the old and deep-seated superstitions and to give them such a solid foundation of knowledge and enlightenment that they will not easily be led astray. Only this can gradually change the social outlook of the people and shape a new society."[86]

The point was that by 1957 congressmen began to see that Indira not only had keen organizational skill, but that she also had value as a vote-getter. Apart from dealing with her father's constituency she was eagerly invited on electioneering tours of other areas of India. One of the most critical requests came from the Gujarat Congress Pradesh Committee to visit Ahmedabad. The agitation for Mahagujarat State was on, the division question rested almost on the edge of a volcano. And again there was danger from possible mobs. But Indira told Kapoor, her energetic secretary, to write and tell the Gujarat P.C.C. that she was willing to go only on one condition. "I'll go in an open car," she said. "Nobody will throw stones. I'll travel in an open car not only from the place of residence to the meeting, but through the city."

The letter led to an emergency meeting of the P.C.C. in Ahmedabad. The older members advised each other that no risk should be taken. The younger ones said, no, if she is prepared, then let us do it.

In January, Indira landed, full of spirits.

"We traveled in two old cars, with their hoods off," describes Kapoor. "She sat in the front one with the P.C.C. president. There were tremendous crowds, and garlands. At one point, somebody plucked off my cap, but it was so packed with people around that it never fell on the ground. Some-body picked it off the top of the crowd and returned it to me. Again, it was lost, and again it came back to me somehow. Only at one place was there a demonstration by students who kept shouting, " 'We want Maha-gujarat, we want Mahagujarat'!"[87] Two small stones hit the two cars and disappeared amidst the flowers, the men, and a large number of women who looked upon Indira Behn as their own.

In 1957 she was also deputized by the powerful Central Election Com-mittee to the Assam Pradesh Election Committee to select candidates for that state, a job which immediately enlarged her political authority from women and youth affairs.

Offers to her of a Parliament seat to stand for the election came pouring

"Whatever the views of the Congress high command, the impression that one gathers from reports of the speeches of the Kerala Congress leaders is that their demand is not merely to present a chargesheet but that they are supporting a movement to pull down the legally established government there?"

"It may be," replied Nehru, "that in the excitement of the movement, some people may have delivered speeches of that type. But I am opposed to unconstitutional means at any time anyhow, because once you adopt them they would be justified in another context. You cannot judge things minus means."

He conceded that "the Communist party's normal tradition is not that of democracy" but that sometimes "as circumstances change these practices and ways also change." Nevertheless, he was asked specifically, "How do you think you are going to bring this government down outside the constitution? And, if you succeed in bringing it down or injure it, don't you anticipate repercussions in Congress-ruled states?"

And this time his answer was as specific. "So far as I am concerned, I do not propose, nor intend, nor look forward to, nor expect governments falling except through democratic processes."[21]

Nevertheless, on June 11, the Joint Standing Committee of the Congress (Kerala), the P.S.P., and the Muslim League decided to take "direct action" to end communist rule.

The same day in Delhi, Indira put it a little differently. "I am not saying the state government has to go, but if the people there feel aggrieved, something should be done about their grievances."

Here was a clear difference of opinion between father and daughter. And although Indira said that the situation in Kerala then did not call for president's rule she was certainly prepared to think along the lines of such an eventuality.

"The considerations that weighed with Nehru as P.M.," analyzed Sadiq Ali later, then one of the general secretaries of the Congress, "did not necessarily weigh with her. He had to be cautious. You must understand that the Congress did not create the 'vast upsurge.' But went along, yes. In the matter of joining up with the League, the all India body was against it, but the local Congress was all for it. Ultimately, local pressure prevailed. Mrs Gandhi had no compunction about this alliance with the League. She maintained that if one feels identically on a particular issue, then why reject an alliance, merely because of the feeling that 'Ah, that is the League!' "

"Were you pressurized by local politicians into encouraging the Kerala Congress to take part or did you agree that they should?" I asked her about the agitation.

"There was no such encouragement—I mean, even as congressmen they belonged to the Nairs or to the Christians. Besides, we couldn't have stopped the movement even if we had wanted to . . . ."

"Yes, but the Kerala Congress did, as a party, join hands with them? Did you support that?"

"Well," she answered quietly. "You can say that I didn't oppose that."[22] And that was putting it mildly.

"She studies a thing and then makes up her mind," said Sadiq Ali. "There are a lot of people who even after making up their minds seem to vacillate. She goes through with what she wants once she has decided."[23]

There was no question about what she wanted, had wanted, even as she said when she took over as Congress president—to win back Kerala for the Congress. The only doubt in her mind had been how, and circumstances and the communists themselves had to an extent played into her hands. She had decided that the situation was impossible when she went to Kerala herself, and thereafter it was only a question of finding a way. "The whole point is," she said then, "that here is an upsurge, and the Congress can't just stand by. In fact, it would be wrong for the Congress to stand and wait. By being in the movement, we thought we could guide it along non-violent lines. Our major concern in Kerala is that there should not be any trouble or anything which harms the state." As far as the communal elements were concerned, she thought, they were as much on the communist side as any other. To her it seemed almost an irrelevant factor. "It's no use bringing up the question now. The communists are making a whole issue out of it."[24]

"Did you discuss this with Mr Nehru?" I asked her.

"No. I just told him how I felt."

"He didn't try to dissuade you or persuade you?" I asked, particularly about the time when her attitude became more implacable about throwing the communists out.

"No. He didn't believe in interfering. And I can tell you that I don't brook any interference either."

"Perhaps it might have been different," I suggested, "if it hadn't been you who were Congress president. He might have tried to argue you out of it."

"Oh yes, I'm sure of that."

"He was against it, wasn't he? He wanted it to be democratic in that sense—no direct action and all that?"

She said impatiently, "He wasn't in touch. I had been touring Kerala myself, I knew what was going on."[25]

Perhaps one of the major reasons why she could take such a definite stand was that, as she had no compunction about an alliance with the League on grounds of tactical expediency, so she had no compunction about applying "undemocratic" methods to a party like the communists on the grounds that she did not have to be above applying a bit of their own medicine to them. She's been said to have been in a "bitter anti-communist phase" then, but how strongly she felt about it was revealed when she said, while inaugurating the Madras District Congress Political Conference, that she personally thought that the major danger for India was from communism. "Educated people realize this danger," she said and even analyzed rightist extremism against that context. "The danger from the rightist parties is that if their actions are not countered, they will throw the Indian people into the arms of the communists."[26]

Though the high command had told congressmen in Kerala to stop the agitation if there was any violence, she viewed the communist ministry with deep suspicion. When she was asked whether she expected violence there, she replied shortly. "The government can certainly provoke trouble."[27]

On June 12, she declared that she had no objection to "sitting round a table" with the communists to find a cure for Kerala's ills but she did not think "anything much could come out of it." She said there could be no solution if the communists did not put a stop to their own methods of violence and desisted from harassing workers of opposition parties.

The same day direct action began in Kerala with picketing of district collectors' offices all over "as a token," declared Shankar, Kerala P.C.C. president, "of the determination of the people not to tolerate the continuance of this government."

The general secretary of the Communist party of India, Ajoy Ghosh, reacted with sanguine hope. "If central intervention does not come—and I feel it will not—the struggle will peter out."

But the communists decided as a last resort to appeal to Nehru himself. The chief minister formally invited him to visit Kerala.

Humor still livened the tension. When Namboodiripad was asked by correspondents whether he thought Nehru would have any influence over the Communist party, he retorted: "All good men will have influence over the Communist party and Mr Nehru is a good man."

"What about his daughter?" came a swift interpolation.

"She is also a good lady," remarked the chief minister, amidst laughter.

But did the invitation to Nehru include his daughter, they all wanted to know. And this time, Namboodiripad replied gravely.

"I, the chief minister, have invited the prime minister of India because I find his visit will be useful. If I find his daughter's visit is useful I will invite her also. But please don't mix up the two. A formal invitation extended by the chief minister to the prime minister is one thing and the invitation of the Communist chief minister to the Congress president is another."[28]

The next three weeks were explosive. Police firing in a place called Ankamali inflamed the agitation. Clashes between crowds and the police began to be reported with increasing frequency. On June 16, Indira sent Sadiq Ali to assess the situation. On June 18, Dhebar also left for Kerala. On June 22, Dhebar returned saying that the demand for the resignation of the ministry was both "broad-based and overwhelming."

On June 22, Nehru arrived in Kerala, only to find the leader of the agitation, Padmanabhan, bent on its intensification "with or without the Congress." But Nehru's three-day visit yielded fruit—an agreement on a three-point formula: negotiations to discuss the specific charges against the ministry, suspension of the controversial sections of the Education Act, and a joint inquiry into the firings. The question of president's intervention in Kerala was apparently warded off, and Namboodiripad exuded an optimistic air. Nehru ruled out any action by the center but thought the best way out eventually would be to hold fresh elections in Kerala. He was very impressed by the popular unrest there and did not visualize the end of the agitation.

On June 27, the CPI executive rejected Nehru's suggestions for fresh elections.

At a meeting with the Congress parliamentary board on June 30 the Kerala leaders agreed to agitate for fresh elections rather than for a direct dismissal of the communist ministry but this was only a mild cover for the Congress president's real feelings. After one of the meetings held at Home Minister Pant's house because he was not well, when members were streaming out, the then *Hindu* correspondent, E.K. Ramaswami, related that he stopped Nehru with the loaded question, "Are you going to fight the communists or throw them out?"

"Throw them out? How? What do you mean? They've also been elected!" retorted Nehru.

But from behind him sharply came Indira's voice. "Papu, what are you telling them? You're talking as prime minister." She turned to Ramaswami and other correspondents, and said, "As Congress president I intend to fight them and throw them out."[29]

Mass picketing, mass demonstrations, and mass arrests kept mounting in Kerala and demands for central intervention began to pour in. "I smell it," said Govindan Nair, secretary of the Kerala Communist party. On July 4, hundreds of women in Kerala came out, in Gandhian style, to court arrest. Namboodiripad taunted the Congress for rejecting the P.M.'s formula by asking for election over and above the agreement reached in Kerala. But Nehru himself admitted that he had never before come across anything like the situation in Kerala. People were excited to the point of hysteria, and he had suggested fresh elections to lessen the tension. On July 6, Shankar arrived in Delhi to present the chargesheet against the Kerala government to the president of India. The communists countered with a move to make a representation to the president against Congress rule in West Bengal. The AICC meanwhile issued a fourteen-page statement warning people at large that democracy was in peril in Kerala. There was no official comment by Indira but her effort to pave the way for positive action by the central government was implicit in her approval of the statement which had been released after full consultation with her. On Friday, July

10, Shankar presented the chargesheet in the form of a memorandum to President Rajendra Prasad.

Both Indira and Nehru went for a brief spell to Simla. Namboodiripad followed them there, and had a three-hour discussion with Nehru. He had lunch with the prime minister, while Indira, with her two sons, looked stoical. Her silence was deceptive.

"She didn't say anything beyond discussing the weather," Nikhil Chakravarty recalls Namboodiripad telling him. "At that time he [Namboodiripad] was quite prepared to sign on the dotted line, but she didn't react."[30]

Namboodiripad, however, was again optimistic about the prime minister's attitude and reported that he did not fear central intervention. He in turn seemed to yield on the issue of midterm elections if, as he said, there was not this double threat of "direct action from below and intervention from above." In fact, he was believed to have promised elections if at least the Kerala Congress would withdraw from the agitation.

But the possibility of negotiations, the promise of compromise, and the prospects of a normal solution fell flat when the National Council of the Communist party rejected Namboodiripad's proposal, even censured him for suggesting it, advised negotiations between the communist ministry and the opposition as the only way out and threatened to launch an all India movement against any central action in Kerala. August 3 was planned as "Hands Off Kerala Day."

The next day the AICC released the text of the memorandum it had been withholding to avoid exacerbate the atmosphere. The CPI National Council's attitude made Congress high command circles feel that a showdown was imminent. Communist designs not only in Kerala but in other parts of the country, by using the Kerala issue as a garb to incite local discontent, spelled danger.

On July 17, opposition parties presented a memorandum against the Kerala ministry to the governor. On July 20, a team of three lawyers from Kerala reiterated the demand for its dismissal in a meeting with the president of India.

On July 20, the union cabinet met but discussed the Kerala issue only briefly. Nehru was still hesitant to suggest central intervention and seemed as if he were waiting for the matter to be discussed in the session of Parliament beginning on August 3. He also wanted to give Namboodiripad an opportunity to state his case in relation to his party's attitude.

Indira waited and fretted. She was particularly incensed by accounts of brutal beatings and lathi charges by the police and communist bands on women in Kerala. As a final palliative she sent Sucheta Kripalani, one of her general secretaries, to report on the matter. She was beginning to feel that the Congress organization had done all it could and that it was the duty of the central government, and her father, to act now.

Any vacillation and hesitation on the government's part, she and her colleagues realized, would aggravate the situation and encourage communist subversion of democratic procedures. The communists had to be tackled before they could spread disaffection in the country, while on a purely organizational level, the Congress party itself would lose face if its leadership did not act promptly.[31]

On July 25, Indira acted openly and vigorously, breaking her long official silence. She went directly to President Rajendra Prasad, formally communicated her views as head of the Congress party, and told waiting newsmen conclusively. "It is high time for the central government to act in Kerala. In fact, central action is long overdue in view of the hard facts of the situation." She explained that intervention was necessary not because there was a communist government in Kerala but "because of the actions of the state government which amount to the denial of fundamental rights and subversion of democracy."

She thought that when over a hundred thousand people had been arrested within one month in a small state like Kerala it showed that an extraordinary situation existed there and that the people must have intense feelings. But she was calm enough when she explained why, if the Congress party had felt so strongly about the issue, it had not gone directly to the central government with the advice to intervene.

"The position is somewhat complicated," and that was putting it mildly. "Personally, I do not think there is anything wrong in the Congress deciding the policy of the central government because it is a government of the party, but it is refraining from influencing the government. It becomes a little difficult to do so particularly when action has to be taken by the center in a state where the government is a non-Congress government."[32] She thought the center in its own right had to go by the facts of the situation.

But it was at a public meeting of women's organizations the same evening that she came out with her most trenchant statement. "The constitution is for the people, not the people for the constitution. And if the constitution stands in the way of meeting the people's grievances in Kerala it should be changed."[33]

She made three of the most telling points regarding her protracted involvement with the Kerala issue. She said she had foreseen the coming explosion when she visited Kerala. "I wanted the Congress to launch an agitation to protect the life and honor of the people, but it did not." She affirmed that she was a leftist, and had thought she could work with the communists if they were prepared to give up some of their "undesirable policies." But she had seen over the Tibetan affair that Indian communists' loyalties lay "elsewhere," that they had sided with China, and that they would never see anything wrong with Russia or the other communist countries. And the fact that they had eulogized Mao and Marx in textbooks in Kerala and avoided mention of Gandhi made her disillusionment with their antinational stance complete.

"I would be prepared to offer my life rather than see my boys given anti-national lessons."[34]

And when familiar agitationist, communist leader Bhupesh Gupta, berated her from the opposite camp for her "dangerous and provocative demand to amend the constitution," she made it clear in a statement that what she meant was that the constitution according to competent lawyers did actually include provisions to cover an emergency like Kerala's, but that if it did not the matter should be looked into.

"I am not pro and con any 'ism'," she added significantly, "but I do believe in certain principles and social and economic policies. Genuine cooperation from all those who agree with these basic programs will always be welcome, but surely the Congress cannot be expected to submit meekly when the Communist party is trying to undermine it?"

Her last sentence was biting.

"I do not believe that the communists or their sympathizers have a monopoly on the epithet 'progressive.' "

On July 31, Nehru and his colleagues decided to take action in Kerala. On August 1, the president signed a proclamation under which according to Article 356 of the Indian Constitution he was empowered to dismiss a ministry, abrogate an assembly, and assume full powers in a state if it was found to have been running counter to the provisions of the constitution. At seven-thirty in the evening, when the proclamation was issued, the communist ministry in Kerala ceased to exist.

It was Indira's moment of triumph. While Nehru tried to soften the blow by sending a courier to Kerala with a letter of explanation and "warm regards" for Namboodiripad, Indira felt no such compunction. She had vowed to get them out, and they were out. The next part of the program was to get the Congress back in. She stuck to the policy of an electoral arrangement with the Muslim League and other parties and conducted a vigorous campaign in Kerala in anticipation of the elections on the basis of a solid, united front against the communists. Crowds lined the routes wherever she went, they waited hours for her if she was delayed, and listened raptly to what she had to say. In February 1960, when the elections were held, the communists lost their majority to the anti-communist front led by the Congress and Indira's victory was complete.

She turned next to the vexing question of the division of Bombay state. The Congress had promised the linguistic reorganization of the states as far back as 1921. When independence came Nehru had second thoughts on the subject, fearing as he did that after the communal menace the thing that might balkanize India was regional differences. He was forced to start the ball rolling because of a dastardly act of political blackmail which led to the creation of Andhra Pradesh. But he wished to maintain the bilingual state of Bombay with its Maharashtrian and Gujarati speaking areas as the last bastion of inspiration for integration rather than disintegration. For two years after the two separatist organizations of Maharashtra and Gujarat ran on a communal platform and in the elections of 1957, Bombay had been beset by agitations and a rising demand for "separation." On August 24, the Congress led by Indira reopened the Bombay question. On September 6, the working committee authorized Indira to meet representatives of the various regional committees and give a report on the matter. By September 24, when the working committee met on the eve of the Chandigarh session of the AICC, she had had a chance to encounter representative opinion and had apparently come to the conclusion that Bombay should be divided. She promised an official decision in two months, saying significantly, "This state of uncertainty is not good."

"She is bold enough to make bold decisions, even unpopular ones," says K.K. Shah, who was then president of the Bombay Regional Congress Committee and got the impression that she would split the state. Indira herself stated that she needed a fuller assessment before giving a final verdict. Consequently, she decided to tour the Maharashtrian areas to balance her visit to the Gujarati side in 1957.

The Maharashtrian Regional Congress Committee eagerly submitted a tour program for her at Chandigarh and it was so heavy that Kapoor, her secretary, burst out on seeing it, "My God, they want to kill her!" In Chandigarh she announced the formation of a nine-man committee which would examine the Bombay issue. But back in Dehi after having conducted the AICC session with "great charm and dignity" as one report put it, she discussed the question with Home Minister Pant, and on October 9 the entire committee met and accepted the principle of the division of Bombay into the state of Gujarat and Maharashtra.

The next day she was scheduled to leave for a five-day tour of Maharashtra. She was interviewed by Paul Grimes, then *New York Times* correspondent in Delhi, just before leaving, but when he showed his curiosity about how she dealt with India's village folk, she said quietly, "Ask my secretary."

Kapoor interpolated, "Don't ask. Come and see."

What he saw was extraordinary.

The tour began in the morning of October 11 from the *chowk* of a town, upon which lanes converged from various directions. "There was a mountain of garlands in front," describes Kapoor, "and an organizer threw them up one by one. Her [Indira's] neck was scratched. Then she began taking them in her hands." [35] In the two days out of five that Grimes could suffer the pace, he counted her as having addressed "seven huge public meetings, laid five cornerstones, and opened three school buildings and cultural institutions." Her motorcade made more than seventy unscheduled "whistlestops" where villagers gathered at the roadside to welcome her. She was garlanded hundreds of times and her forehead had a blotch of smears where village women, as a gesture of goodwill, applied the *kumkum.* "From 7 A.M. until 11 P.M. Mrs Gandhi was almost constantly among her people, smiling gently, chatting softly, and flashing her dark brown eyes."[36]

She called it a "pilgrimage"[37] on which she had come to hear people's views. Her vocabulary, like the Maharashtrian saris she wore and the Maharashtrian dishes that she ate throughout the tour, was derived from a feel for the occasion. And because women also as usual formed a large part of her audiences, she talked in terms of the fundamentals that they understood. At Satara, she told a public meeting that the Congress considered it its "sacred duty"[38] to hear what the aspirations of the people were.

At Miraj, her meeting was arranged inside a gymnasium. A hundred thousand people were jammed inside while thousands strained to find a way in. There were cries of protest.

Nobody guessed as she spoke, smiled, and traveled at that hectic speed that she was suffering acute pain from a kidney ailment almost all through the tour. Boiled water had always been carried for her even before, but this time the doctor's instructions were that she should drink water every half-hour. So the faithful Kapoor followed her about with a flask in hand.

"Keep it in my car. I'll take it," she reassured him at one place.

"At one o'clock when we stopped for lunch, I thought I'd fill up the flask and found that she hadn't had any of the water. She'd been making short speeches of two or three minutes consistently apart from the major ones, but the pain had been so intense that she had been holding her stomach while talking to the public."[39]

Only at night could she indulge in the luxury of yielding to the pain. But her sense of humor kept her buoyant. At one place, she apparently saw that Kapoor's light was on in his room until late at night. The next morning she asked him lightly whether he was in the habit of sleeping with the light on. He told her self-consciously that he had been reading and had fallen asleep for he had found the book lying on the floor in the morning. "Ah," exclaimed Indira, "that means you are still young."[40]

Indira's tour was to last five days. Grimes left the party after two days. "I don't know how this lady stands it," he told Kapoor. "I'm tired and I'm going back."[41]

How did she stand it? The yoga that she learnt to practise from the example of her father, and handed down her sons? A mental equilibrium? The sheer excitement of being the cynosure of crowds? Or a feeling for Zen, that philosophy of concentration to which she refers with understanding?

"How do you ever relax?" I asked her.

"There's hardly any time. The only time I find I can relax is during work! But sometimes it happens in the oddest way," she smiled. She described the occasion of a three-week tour she undertook once of Vidarbha and Karnatak.

"When I arrived in Bombay I found a gruelling program awaiting me, starting from six in the morning. By the end of it I got dead tired, I was near collapsing. I even got a nervous tick in my cheek. The limit came when somebody dropped tea on my sari. Then I found I had to attend a formal reception amongst all those people in Bombay, be dressed up, and so on. Patil was PCC chief then. I told him I had to go home for ten minutes to change....He said all right, it didn't matter so much. When we reached the place he asked me to go to my room and lie down because I was looking so tired. But when I went in I felt like writing to my father. I realized I hadn't written to him during the whole of that trip. So I sat down and wrote to him, and I said how desperately tired I was and fed up. When there were only five minutes to go, they knocked to tell me—they thought I was sleeping—so that I could have a wash. I found that I no longer felt tired. I was relaxed, and when I came out of the room, Patil even remarked that I was looking very relaxed and had I slept?"

There were three reasons that prompted Indira's decisive stand on the division of Bombay. The genuine demand of the people there for separate states, the apprehension apparently confirmed by Bombay's then Chief Minister Y.B. Chavan, that a rigid attitude would lose the area for the Congress in the 1962 elections, and the feeling she always has about a problem, that if something has to be done it is better to do it at the earliest. She thought it illogical to deny one area what had been accepted as a principle for the rest of India and acted accordingly. The nine-man committee she had formed sent its recommendations to the working committee. This in turn confirmed the decision on December 4, 1959, ultimately sanctioned by parliament, to bring the states of Maharashtra and Gujarat into being.

In fact, Indira was guided mainly by a "robust common sense," as K.K. Shah describes it.[42] She liked to tackle a problem at the practical level and to meet the exigencies of a situation as they presented themselves. Within the broad framework of her belief in democracy, secularism, and socialism, her approach was flexible. In that sense she was more of a politician than her father, even to the point of indulging in "politicking" in the disparaging sense in which she referred to it later. She sincerely believed that the Congress party and her father's leadership were the two meaningful phenomena of India's re-emergence. Therefore the task was to execute their programs and if in order to do so the Congress had to be kept in power, she was not averse to finding ways to see that it was.

The distaste for power that she affirmed applied only to personal power, the fact that she herself was not greedy for it. But it did not apply to her feelings about the party. If she did not care to push herself into positions of importance, she was certainly anxious that the Congress should not slip away from them. The only quarrel she had with her father was not about policies, but about the pace at which they were being implemented. It was in this context that she allowed a Congress alliance with the feudal Ganatantra Parishad in Orissa in the first of her controversial acts as president of the Congress, and with the communal Muslim League in Kerala later. In Orissa, it was to ensure a certain stability for the Congress so it could remain in power and thus be able to give a spur to the developmental programs that she most cared about. In Kerala, of course, it was to ensure that democratic procedures would not be permanently endangered by the continuance of communist power. The decision to enter into a coalition ministry in Orissa signified a complete departure from previous policy, but both acts led her critics to utter disapproving cries about the bad precedents that they set, at the same time establishing her image as a decisive, if slightly unscrupulous politician with a mind very much her own.

"The world at large is not interested in excuses for failures," she once said. "This is very important. The world is interested in who wins. Very few care to find out why one has lost. It is success and victory which matter."[43]

It was not a soft philosophy, but it was a practical one. She also thought that if people in India put less emphasis on words and more on action it would change the shape of things. "We have tried to establish a more practical and down-to-earth trend in our functioning and to give more thought to detail," she said, in reviewing her own term of office. Set with the task of implementing the Nagpur resolutions for agrarian reform and introducing the controversial cooperative venture into India's rural pattern, she got down to brass tacks by having trained workers to not only explain the merits of the scheme, but also put forward the Congress view and counteract the propaganda of the newly formed Swatantra party that the Congress aim was totalitarian imposition. At the AICC session in May there was a long ovation when she rose to speak. She said ringingly that the Congress cooperative program "brooked no delay" and warned "vested interests" that ultimately it would be to their advantage to cooperate in "carrying the burden and responsibility" of introducing a new social order. But she also decided to choose a hundred workers to do publicity work as a first step toward extending the cooperative idea.

Shortly after, 110 persons were selected from all over India and a training camp was organized at Gandhigram in Madurai. She had no fixation that the idea was so good that the people must be forced to accept it. She was at pains to point out that to use force would not only be contrary to the principles of the Congress, but it would also, from a "practical point of view, be foolish for them to do so." She had toured ten of the states of India as president by then and thought she had found people generally responsive to the idea. Her enthusiasm did not prevent her from the perceptive realization later which made her say, "Absolute collectivism will never work in India. Our vast peasantry is much too individualistic. Our people are too tradition bound and very slow in accepting changes."[44] But she did not say it regretfully. For in spite of her impatience, the natural intolerance of the young, as she called it, she knew how difficult it was to fulfill a program or enforce a law when people were uneducated and unaware. " 'The ground of liberty,' " she quoted Thomas Jefferson with feeling, " 'is to be gained by inches. We must be content to secure what we can get, from time to time, and externally press for what is yet to get. It takes time to persuade men to do even that which is good for them.' "[45] Then again: "Obviously, it is easier to order than to persuade and we deliberately chose the more difficult path in the belief that it was the surer and better one and that it would educate and strengthen the people toward fuller political maturity. The jump from a bullock cart to a jet plane is not more dramatic than that of a feudal society to a modern democratic one."[46]

The planning subcommittee of the All India Congress Committee finalized its report on the third Five Year Plan while Indira was Congress president. The committee as she acknowledged was "Dhebarbhai's brain-child," and the planning seminar held at Ooty from May 30 to June 3, led by Nehru, was dominated by the Congress elite, including Indira. Her remarks, however, tried to set the deliberations on a down-to-earth level.

"We are all agreed," she said, "that the times call for hard work and austerity. But when we demand the sacrifice of the people, we must also give them some compensation. It is not only the bright future that they can expect in the distant years to come but they must have something in the near future, in fact, in the immediate present, which can give them hope and strength for the difficulties in working for [that] bright future. So, I hope that we will be able to fix some sort of priorities." She for one was certain what they must be. "The most important problem at the moment is the food problem and I personally feel that if we can ensure adequate food at reasonable prices, adequate education—these two, I think, are the main things—and some health programs, I think the nation will be behind us in anything we ask it to do."[47]

Her attitude toward foreign policy was similar to her father's. She was vehemently anticolonial and she believed in an Afro-Asian resurgence. She formed a National Committee for Algeria under Dhebar to popularize the Algerian cause and aid in their battle for freedom. She formed the National Council for Africa to express solidarity with those who suffered there, and to promote mutual understanding between India and the countries of Africa. She felt intensely about the Chinese invasion of Tibet and under her presidency the working committee fully endorsed the government of India's policy to grant asylum to the Dalai Lama and the hundreds of Tibetan refugees who streamed in. She formed an all-party Central Relief Committee for Tibetans with Acharya Kripalani as chairman. She thought the Chinese attack on Tibet sprang partly from their desire to "consolidate Tibet and their frontier with India." The furore over Chinese usurpation of 14,000 square miles of Indian territory was just beginning to shake Indian complacency, and though she had thought ever since her visit to China that "they might come when there might be conflict," both she and Nehru, she said, had hoped that it would never be "a fighting war."[48] Events were to prove them wrong in that sense, for even in 1959 there were fearful portents with repeated Chinese incursions into Indian territory and the killing of nine members of the Indian police patrol in Ladakh. Again, the working committee and the AICC took "serious note" of the whole situation although Nehru's approach in trying to build a strong industrial base and a workable economy before placing the same emphasis on military strength gave them an edge over predilections for defense preparedness.

Indira was hampered to an extent by being surrounded by her father's colleagues, a circumstance, however, which had not deterred her father when he had become Congress president in Lahore. There were the perils of being accepted "like our daughter." There was the occasion when she went to consult Pandit Pant on something vital, and he warded it off by steering her calmly to a room where his daughter could show her a new tea set they had bought. But this happened only rarely. As Rajen Bajpai says, "There was no consciousness among the top politicians about her being a woman. It was due to the fact that women worked jointly with men in the freedom struggle. We are not there on sufferance but because of our right." There was also the disadvantage of being accepted only as Nehru's protege. The day she took over, Dhebar said in his speech while referring to Nehru's attitude that "very few leaders would have had the courage to face the criticism that was bound to follow the election of his daughter as president" and that it was "equally creditable of Indira to have volunteered to undertake the task." But Nehru set the note for objectivity with his touching affirmation that he was proud of her as his daughter; proud of her as his comrade, and proud of her as his leader.

Nevertheless, they were both aware that certain conventions had to be set anew to make for smooth running, lack of embarrassment, and minimum criticism from outside. Nehru had no desire to impose his decisions on Indira, and Indira was definite that in her official capacity she must be free to exercise her will. It was another matter if heated discussions took place at home although there were times when they were both so busy that they could hardly meet, and at meals, as she said, "It makes one miserable if every time you sit down at the dinner table you discuss politics with your father. It robs the charm of family life."[49]

She let her father remain off the working committee, although he was invited to attend each time. She conducted meetings with impersonal discipline, pounding the gavel with as much determination if Nehru veered off the track as any other. She had the seating arrangements changed at the first AICC session she presided over in May. She introduced a traditional Indian style, with long rounded cushions and large bolsters and leaders squatting on the floor of the dais with an immaculate white spread over the *durry*, or carpet, instead of the high chairs and a table, and she had most of the leaders sitting in chairs in the hall instead of crowding rather pompously on the platform itself as they had done before. Her father, too, sat below. He mounted the dais only when the Congress president called upon "Jawaharlal Nehru"—simply and without frills—to speak on cooperatives. Everybody reacted to the obvious drama of the situation and there was "much applause mingled with laughter."[50]

Not as father but as leader of the Congress parliamentary party welcoming the new Congress president, Nehru said that she was "symbolic of a welcome change in the political atmosphere in the country just as the Nagpur decisions were symbolic of a change in a new direction...." He meant, of course, that she was young and had a modern outlook.

Indira's own approach was not only to absorb more young people into the organization but also more women. Her speeches during the pad yatra after she learned she had been chosen president and the advice she gave to individual workers indicated that she planned to give women a bigger say in Congress affairs. "At every village she advised women to elect their own representatives on mandal committees" observed a report. "Women reciprocated by turning out in large numbers to greet her together with their children."[51] She announced as soon as she took office that she would appoint a woman as one of the general secretaries to assist her, and took Sucheta Kripalani in that coveted job.

"Everywhere I was told," she herself observed with great satisfaction about her term, "that so many women had never been seen except at religious fairs and it was a surprise to the local people that women should be willing to suffer considerable inconvenience for the sake of coming to a political function."[52]

She concentrated steadily on drawing young people into schemes initiated by the Congress and making them members of mandal and district committees. The result was that youth became acceptable to old diehards within the Congress and made possible the appointment of thirty-eight-year-old D. Sanjivayya as chief minister of Andhra. In fact, Indira had suggested his name and was successful in having him succeed her as Congress president.

She tried to establish, as she had said, "a more practical and down-to-earth trend in our functioning and to give more thought to detail." This meant everything from curtailing election expenses for candidates for the assemblies and Parliament, appointing an adult team, setting up a central and permanent training institute for political workers, to studying a proposal for creating a Board of Social and National Integration. For in spite of the fact that she had herself worked out the division of Bombay because "it seemed invidious to make an exception in that one case," she believed that India's basic unity must also be stressed at the time. Though she gave a patient hearing to complaints about corruption or malpractices, it was party indiscipline which made her really indignant. But an indication of how subtle and complex her mind was came when she said that there was no need to take any obvious disciplinary action against members who publicly criticized the party because she would see to it that they would not be nominated to any party office or to the legislatures and would slowly be "weeded out of positions of importance."

She felt that one main disadvantage of being in power was that the people became self-conscious. "Until I became president," she said later, "the people would listen to me willingly and express themselves freely. Their attitude, however, changed considerably when I assumed that office."[53] To make up for that, perhaps, she became one of the first of the Congress presidents to make it a practice to meet the press every morning.

The significance of her eleven months as Congress president lay in what she had promised and her father had prophesied in the beginning: she was not out for spectacular changes in the working committee or elsewhere as she had said on her appointment. But she would "try and establish trends which it would be difficult to reverse." Not even her critics denied that she was successful.

Where had she sought inspiration or moral support?

"She acted only as our mouthpiece on Kerala," says Sucheta Kripalani now, in what appears to be an astonishing and the only observation of its kind but in keeping with her changed relations with Indira and quite opposite to what her colleague of that time, Sadiq Ali, says.

"I know for a fact," observes S.A. Dange, the communist leader, "that she was guided more by other congressmen than her father." But what he added showed that either he did not appreciate the fact that she gave very substantial reasons for her approach, or that he just refused to accept them. "In her speeches she made a stand against communism which was anti-communist you understand—anti-communist in the sense of being that only. That her father never was. She has no grounding in socialism at all."

The final decisions were always Indira's confirms a friend and gives a perfectly irrefutable reason. "That came from childhood and the pattern of individual thinking encouraged by Nehru himself. There were many occasions when she argued with him and didn't accept in toto what he said. After all, he never agreed with his father blindly either."

"When you were Congress president did you discuss relevant issues with your father?" I asked Mrs Gandhi.

"When I was Congress president," she replied firmly, "I made it a point to discuss nothing with him."

"Did you discuss things with Feroze?"

"Oh, yes."

"Did you take his advice when you were Congress president?"

"I took no one's advice when I was Congress president." Then, as if she realized that she had been too categorical, she added, "Of course, I discussed matters with people. . . . "

2. NOSTALGIA

There was a hint of sadness behind the achievement. She always felt that ultimately you must pay for what you get. And she had to pay dearly. Significantly, it was a political issue again over which there was an argumentative furore with Feroze. He was violently against her stand on Kerala. "Yes, she consulted him a number of times," a friend of Indira remarks. "She had great faith and confidence in him and knew that he would not give her advice which would harm her in any way."[1] But nothing he said on this issue would make her budge.

"He was so totally opposed to it," says Inder Malhotra, then political
correspondent of *The Statesman* and a good friend of Feroze, "that that
was the first and last time he undertook to volunteer information [about
how he felt about a situation involving Indira] to me and other friends, 'lest
you hear garbled versions,' he said, " 'that I have stopped going to the prime
minister's house.' "[2]

He felt that she had betrayed the leftist cause and was wrong on the ground
of constitutional impropriety. He was part of a group then as before, of
Krishna Menon, whom he personally did not like, and left thinking intellectuals Menon's attitude had been distinctly sympathetic toward the Kerala
government in the sense that he thought the central government should aid
the state government in maintaining law and order in face of the threatened
agitation. While these people were not communists, their enthusiastic socialism inclined them to a kind of sympathetic understanding of the whole leftist
bloc. Indira, as she admitted, had felt the same. But unlike her husband's
group, she had come to the conclusion that constitutional proprieties did
not work with people who themselves did not believe in them. In fact it was
a period of great disillusionment for her.

But Feroze's sense of humor remained irrepressible. Previously when
an official engagement would prevent Indira from joining in some personal fun decided upon by the family and friends, he would shake his
head and exclaim, "Never marry a prime minister's daughter, eh!"
When Indira herself became Congress president, his light banter was
reminiscent of the way Nehru was teased by his family when he first
became prominent in politics. Feroze would not say "Indu," but "this
is what the Congress president said," or, "this is what the
Congress president did," when any discussion demanded a reference!
"The differences between Indira and Feroze were of the surface only,"
insists a friend. "But like all men, his resentment expressed itself in a revolt
against a wife who was better known and his inability to accept a position
as secondary either to her or to her father. In fact, if he had been a man
of lesser caliber it would have been very smooth sailing."[3]

One doubts whether "being secondary to Nehru" whom he
had himself placed on a pedestal far above him, was at all a
reckonable factor with Feroze. He was intent upon his own achievement.
He had, in fact, begun to rely on his growing reputation in Parliament; he
had his hobbies; women paid court to him, and friends thronged his
house for chatter, warmth, and raillery. In proportion to the casualness
of his manner was the finickyness with which he kept house. Everything
always gleamed. The garden was a "fairyland of roses and gladioli," the
lawn was nothing short of a velvet carpet, the lacquered wood furniture,
made by him in his own workshop, was simple and tasteful in design. "In
appearance he was a typical 'U.P.-ite'," says another friend, "but in his

living very sophisticated."[4] You could become very conscious of your boorishness, and you felt the need to handle things with delicacy. *"Are bhai,"* his fellow M.P.s would exclaim when they came to see him and draw up their chairs to the veranda, "we'll put our chairs here—we are not fit to sit on that lawn!" And if you were sitting at the table having tea you had to be careful that you did not put the cup on its polished, burnished wood or your carelessness would immediately earn you a frown.

His own typing of his detailed "cases" for Parliament was so faultless and impressive that people became curious about who could have done it, and the copy was put away in a neat, docket file. He was extremely fastidious about the letterheads, the sort of typewriter, the quality of the ribbon, the stationery he used. Perhaps it was this neatness that was reflected in his mind. As Diwan Chaman Lall remarked, "Feroze was one of the most dynamic and clearheaded persons I have had the pleasure of meeting in my life."[5] In fact, there is a body of opinion which maintains that had Feroze and Indira been able to work together they could have provided leadership soon after Nehru that might have been practically unassailable. But although his colleagues and friends were constantly engaged in sympathetic or hostile speculation, both Indira and Feroze, and particularly Feroze, just would not talk about each other. Only, the first new gladioli that bloomed in Feroze's garden were specially cut and taken for Indira every morning.

Joachim Alva, another M.P., was driven by his admiration for Feroze to say that he was in one way like the young Pitt, a hero of Parliament. But Pitt "was the youngest who tasted all the sweets of office; not so Feroze who was overshadowed by his renowned father-in-law and in the course of time may be overshadowed by his distinguished wife."[6]

It was not a judgment. It was a prophecy. Shadows haunted that amiable countenance.

In 1958, he had a heart attack. Both Indira and Nehru had been away in Nepal. But illness and the feeling he had that he might not survive had broken his stoic reserve. To his sister Tehmina, who had come immediately from Allahabad, he kept repeating while they waited for Indira, "Where's Indu? Hasn't she arrived yet? When is the plane due?"[7] When Indira came she spared no effort to care for him. It might be argued that being more reserved than he was, she was less demonstrative in her love, but the devotion she showed made friends feel how deep was the essential communion between them. Perhaps a reiteration of that was what Feroze needed. Nehru came every morning and evening to see him, and a certain warmth began to pervade the room at the Willingdon Nursing Home.

Feroze recovered, and for a while his spirits seemed to recover, too. His illness had brought Indira closer to him, but events again swamped the personal. Indira became Congress president, and Feroze plunged back into work.

In January 1960, Indira decided not to seek re-election. She said that although for her, personally, "the year's work [had] been sometimes exhilarating, sometimes exasperating, but at all times worthwhile and interesting,"[8] the strain had also been enormous. She had had a chance to experience more acutely than before and certainly more directly, the pressures that govern a political organization, and she had made her own mark on it. But she felt she must give it up. There were three reasons. She was quite ill. Her kidney was so bad that she had to be operated upon. She also felt she had neglected her father because of the work, and she did not want that to continue. And Nehru was beginning to be affected by the criticism and did not want the fact that she was Congress president while he was prime minister to come in for comment.[9] Perhaps Feroze's attitude too had something to do with it.

In February Indira had the operation and "my jewel," as she had fascinatedly and with characteristic imagination begun to call her kindey, was removed. This time it was Feroze's turn to be concerned. During personal crises when extraneous issues did not cloud their involvement their underlying love seemed to rise to the surface. "They hurt each other terribly, those two," a friend of Feroze's remarked, "but he loved her to the last breath of his life."[10] The day Indira had her operation, Feroze's friends noticed he was in quite a state. One of them, for instance, when she visited him that day found him pacing up and down his room worriedly. When she asked him what was wrong, he kept repeating, "It is Indu's operation today."[11]

If Feroze was impulsive, susceptible, and had his minor diversions, he was also the more ardent of the two. "The love and dedication that went into her nursing of him paled into insignificance," says Inder Malhotra, "compared with the transparent love and exuberance he showed for her when she had this . . . kidney operation."

There were moments to relieve the early passion. In June 1960, they even went away to Kashmir, and for a change there had been just the four of them—Feroze, Indira, Rajiv, and Sanjay. Feroze had remarked a little wonderingly and inwardly pleased when they returned that it had felt strange that there had been no one else. But with illness his outward composure, so carefully maintained until then, began to falter. "On two or three occasions," says Inder Malhotra, "the man seemed under great stress and it seemed to me that he was greatly involved and that he felt his emotion was unrequited."[12]

Talking about Feroze's uninhibited laughter and his appreciation of "Allahabadi jokes," which he called "unique and without parallel," and the fact that Feroze always told his old friends in the city that he went there particularly to forget his worries, Kamla Prasad Mohiley remembers, "I must say, however, that during the last days of his life, whenever I met him I found him to be sometimes morose and sad, and I told him always to come to Allahabad to get over that mood. He always agreed, but regretted that pressure of work prevented him."[13]

He was happiest when his sons came home during the holidays, and although they were all caught up by life at Tin Murti he spent a great deal of time with them. He was very conscious of the Nehru shadow, the advantages and the privileges that accrued to them while living with their grandfather. On one son's birthday he remarked a trifle wistfully that he wondered what he could give him because there was nothing that they had already not been presented with. At times when friends asked him why he did not go away with his family for a holiday somewhere, Feroze would remark with his usual air of casualness, "*Are bhai, bachon ki ma saath mein to—tum nahin samajhte.*" (Ah, my friend, if only the children's mother could go too, then, but you wouldn't understand.)[14]

"The point to understand about their relationship," says Yunus, "is that long before their marriage they had both agreed that the first priority would have to be to look after Nehru. When Gandhiji pointed this out to Feroze, his reply was, 'In addition to a daughter, he'll also have me to look after him. I feel as deeply for him....' So he accepted the situation from the beginning. But both were strong personalities, with minds of their own. There were differences. But contrary to the impression people seek to emphasize, these differences did not create a gulf, they cemented their respect for each other, for the strength of opinion it implied. It made them more united. They had so much in common. That always remained. Two lovely kids. A hero, Jawaharlal Nehru. The tremendous love for the memory of Kamala Nehru, and, of course, the political field in which they continued to work, perhaps argue, yet suffer together."[15]

In September 1960 Feroze had a second heart attack. Again, Indira was away, this time attending a women's convention in far-off Ernakulam. Feroze had been feeling some pain, and his doctor had advised rest, but the day it became acute he telephoned the doctor and instead of waiting drove from Parliament House to the hospital. He even sat and discussed the matter with Dr Khosla, who had looked after him previously and was now a friend. Khosla ordered tea, but as it was being poured, Feroze collapsed. On hearing the news Indira rushed back to Delhi and went straight to the hospital from the airport. But this time Feroze was unconscious and the impatient calls for Indu must have echoed in his inner heart alone. He regained consciousness for a while, as Indira sat at his bedside throughout the night, and his spirits must have lifted to see her there. But suddenly at 7.45 in the morning he had a coughing spell. Indira immediately took his head in her hands, but before she could realize what was happening Feroze's countenance clouded over.

Indira cried bitterly over Feroze's death. The letter she wrote to a friend soon after, on September 22, 1960, revealed how imperative her need of Feroze had been till the very last:

I don't know what to write—I am feeling so utterly desolate and miserable. You know how much Feroze and I disagreed and quarrelled over the years and yet instead of separating or slackening the bond of friendship, we were closer than before. We had a wonderful holiday together—nearly a month in a houseboat in Srinagar—and we made so many plans for the future. The boys are of an age when they need a father more than a mother. I feel lost and empty and dead.

And yet life must go on. The word "dizzy" is flung at me from all sides and I realize that I must get hold of myself and do something but what is the use when one's heart is not in it?[16]

She had had vague ideas that she would commit herself totally to him after her father needed her no more. Feroze had even bought a piece of land, in Mehrauli, near Delhi to build a house. Perhaps if he had lived she might have become the wife of a great man as she was the daughter of a great man. Feroze had been only forty-eight, and at the peak of his career. According to friends and colleagues and his countrymen, the future belonged to him. But what of her, as a woman of talent and intelligence? Would she have been content being the wife of a great man? It had not been enough to be the daughter of Nehru. Something had driven her to strike out on her own. And that something would have doubtless driven her away from even a settled, domesticated life, away toward purely personal fulfilment. She was just not a housewife, as she said, and that had its own compulsions. So there was just the cold and awful realization that came to her again and again that "you had to pay for what you get." Pay even for what you are. Perhaps it was for that that she cried.

Even in 1958, when Indira's influence in national affairs had not found an obvious stamp, Michael Brecher noted, while writing Nehru's biography and listing his possible successors, that "her direct influence on the prime minister cannot be gauged accurately but in the nature of things must be considerable. She is, perhaps, the only person with whom Nehru can discuss most matters with ease, and the sheer amount of time which she spends in his company gives her a strategic position shared by no one else."[17] But he did not include her in his list of the power hierarchy after Nehru. Besides, Nehru was then in robust health, and the question was not urgent. Nevertheless, by 1959 she was president of the Congress. And even though she said before her term ended that she would not seek re-election and wished to "return to welfare work and her family," her strong tenure and the overwhelming support she had gathered from the masses made observers feel that the matter had been taken out of her hands.

"A big question, however, is whether the masses will let her [return]," Paul Grimes commented after seeing her function, particularly in the Maharashtrian tour, "for the humble, illiterate people of India's 800,000 villages, who up to now have universally known only two names among their leaders—Mahatma Gandhi and Jawaharlal Nehru—are gradually learning a third."[18]

She still managed to keep out of office although she began to play the role that Gandhi had enjoined upon Sarojini Naidu in the 1920's and Nehru upon Vijayalaxmi later, that of India's unofficial ambassador abroad. In 1960, she received Yale University's Howland Memorial Prize, and the Howland Memorial lecture she gave on that occasion revealed how strongly she supported her father's economic blueprint for India's development. Three-fourths of the lecture dealt with the economic situation, one-fourth with the historical background of the nationalist struggle. She avoided any mention of India's non-domestic entanglements. Her attention at the time was fixed, it seems, on vital priorities and everything else was secondary. She took pains to point out that India's planned economy was not indicative of a communist approach.

"Because only communist countries have had planned economies, there is an erroneous conception that only communist countries can plan successfully. But we in India," she reiterated, "are determined that our socialism should adhere to constitutional ways and democratic processes, and what is more, that it should have its roots in our culture and traditions."[19]

Socialism, according to her, had to be of an Indian variety suited to the genius of the Indian people. If, as an opposition leader remarked once, Indira was a "fellow traveler" except for the anti-communist phase as Congress president, this was "fellow traveling" with a rather dogged individualistic streak indeed. She went to the extent of specifying, even then, that "when and if state control goes beyond the limit of stimulating development and stifles private enterprise, adjustments in policy may be necessary and advisable."[20]

Nevertheless she was caught in the predicament of a well-meaning democrat. She knew the rate of growth to be aimed at had to be ambitious enough to pull the people out of their slough. "You cannot cross a chasm in two jumps," she said, and quoted Professor Kaldor: " 'To go slow on the plan is like asking a plane not to travel fast on the runway because that might be dangerous. The trouble is if it does not travel fast enough it will never leave the ground'." But she also felt that "much as one would like to concentrate all effort toward economic development, in point of fact in a democracy it is not possible to do so at the cost of the people."[21]

Consequently there was the effort to introduce labor amenities even if they ran ahead of productivity, heavy taxation of high incomes in the interests of equality, and the breaking up of large farms to help the landless. If, as the president of the World Bank, Eugene Black, advised India, these factors hampered economic development, Indira argued feelingly that they also led to "more equality, greater regional fairness and possibly fewer revolutions."[22] If the third plan impinged upon the liberty of the individual according to some who opposed the concept of planning as such, her answer was a rhetorical, "What about the poor? The only liberty they have had is the liberty to starve. And they are the majority."[23] But she was convinced that the only method to employ was the method of persuasion, and she pinpointed her philosophy of political graduality in a realistic affirmation: "One must give in to some demands," she said, "so as to be able to resist others."[24] For her, as for her father, and indeed even Gandhi before him, change had to be sought, not in a revolution through violence, but through a revolution in restraint.

In May 1961, Lyndon Johnson, then vice-president of the United States, and his wife Ladybird, visited India. Ladybird, who relied greatly on Indira, stated that if you really wanted to know India, you had to have Indira as guide. Indira's association with world figures began increasingly to result not only from being her father's official hostess, but also her father's unofficial representative. For later the same year, Nehru sent her off for the first time alone, to Africa.

It was more than a goodwill visit. In her twelve-day tour she conveyed Nehru's good wishes to the African leader Jomo Kenyatta, of whom she later said, "He is a wonderful person and although he is a very powerfully built man, he gives the impression of great gentleness, and understanding."[25] It was her task to extract an assurance from him that the Indians in a free Africa would be treated fairly. She also held talks with other African leaders, like Ronald Nagla and Masinde Muliro, president and vice-president respectively of the Kenya African Democratic Union. In Uganda, she held discussions with spokesmen of political parties, including Milton Obote, president of the Opposition Uganda People's Congress. She also called on the governor, Sir Frederick Cranford, the Kabaka of Buganda, the chief minister of Uganda, and met representatives of women's organizations and African students educated in India. In Zanzibar, she was received at the airport by Chief Minister Mohammad Shamte Hamadi and the Afro-Shirazi (opposition) party president. She lunched with the British president and met the sultan and sultana. The garden party given in her honor by the India Association was attended by the heir-apparent and all the political and social elite of Zanzibar. At Dar-es-Salaam, she was the guest of the government and was greeted at the airport by Prime Minister Julius Nyerere.

This was obviously not merely a social tribute to the daughter of Nehru, even though Nehru was held in great esteem at the time as an articulate symbol of the Afro-Asian conscience. It was an indication that Indira was beginning to be recognized abroad as the political arm of Nehru, sometimes as a kind of advance guard, testing the ground for reactions, sometimes clearing the air for deeper decisions, sometimes, of course, just as a substitute. working on a different level. As she herself once said, "I believe the best way of understanding is to meet at different levels. We stress the political level but actually there are many other levels which are just as important—social, cultural, and artistic levels."[26]

In Africa, in that first visit, what she defined as her political attitude towards her countrymen settled there was to remain consistent throughout
the years that African turbulence created a crisis in their affairs. She understood both the "uneasiness" amongst the Asians at increasing native belligerence as well as the resentment of the Africans as any people long suppressed must have against those better off. But she felt strongly that the
Indians who had made their homes in Africa "should accept their responsibility as citizens of the country they inhabit." Inflexibility of attitude
disturbed her there as much as at home.

"I have been really surprised to see," she said, "that very few of them
know the language of this country reasonably well. Very few have really
mixed well with the people here or cultivated friendship with them. Even
now although we hear their attitude has been changing, even so, that change
is only toward the few African leaders and not toward the common African
people."[27]

"Incidentally, have you picked up something of the Swahili language
here?" she was asked.

"Only two or three words . . . ."

"Which words?"

"*Jammbo-Pole, Pole!* [Long live freedom]," she announced gaily.[28]

In November 1961 she accompanied Nehru to the United States for his first
meeting with President John F. Kennedy. Early in 1962, Jacqueline Kennedy
visited India alone, and Indira, as well as India, took special pains to make
her welcome. In March 1962 Indira went to the United States again, this
time alone and on a lecture tour, and almost the first thing she said there
was that she thought women often made better ambassadors than men. "I
think it was a very good idea for Mrs Kennedy to come," she commented.
"Sometimes an unofficial person can attain more than an official person,
especially when she is as charming and attractive as Mrs Kennedy."[29] The
Americans on their part acknowledged Indira as a "goodwill ambassador
without portfolio" and thought she "exemplified her country's image as a
bridge between the traditions of the East and the culture of the West."[30]
They were not slow to comment that the same thing was exemplified even
by the way she dressed. She would let her natural vanity as a woman come
to the fore when she went abroad. Her short, wavy hair was fashionably
styled and she wore make-up. But as the *Post Intelligence* of Seattle noted
as she stepped from a plane at Tacoma International Airport, "she wore
open-toed sandals and a gray-and-gold sari. Over this decidedly Indian
costume she wore a knee-length mink coat which would be the pride of any
Park Avenue matron."[31]

But, as in 1960, she had largely defended India's domestic policies and
Nehru's concept of planning, so in 1962 she took up the question of India's
foreign relations and Nehru's controversial concept of nonalignment, and
the middle path. This was the first time she espoused the cause at any

length abroad and as one newspaper put it at the end of her month-long tour, "Madame Gandhi bowled over all the controversial wickets from Goa to Kashmir to Red China."[32]

By April 1963, when she went to New York as chairman of the Indian World Fair Committee for the groundbreaking ceremony for the Indian Pavilion, India had been through the crisis of a Chinese invasion, and Nehru was almost broken by the perfidy and the consequent crumbling of his grand design for a Sino-Indian stance in international politics. But he rallied to maintain that "the aggression and resulting emergency have vindicated and should strengthen rather than weaken our policy of nonalignment and our stand on peaceful coexistence—the fact of their betrayal of their Panchsheel agreement with us only exposes the Chinese as militarists and expansionists. It does not in any way reflect upon the principles or turn them into bad principles or questionable principles."[33] He refused to be hustled either by criticism at home or cunning maneuvers by Peking into abandoning his economic middle way between socialism and capitalism at home or his political middle way of nonalignment between the communist and the "free world" blocs in international relations. To his critics in India who, as he said, began to "raise a howl" that he should seek asylum in a Western military alliance, he made the wry rejoinder, "I do not know whether these gentlemen realize the simple truth that this is precisely what the Chinese wanted us to do, to shake us off our ideological moorings which were anathema to them, force us to abandon our nonaligned, socialist and democratic values, compromise our independence, and thereby demonstrate to the world that our middle way between communism and capitalism was a bogus one."[34]

China had its eye particularly on Southeast Asia, where it wanted to establish its supremacy. As Nehru affirmed, its belief in the inevitability of war between the communist and the non-communist powers as the only method of resolving the ideological dispute rested on the necessity of a world polarization of forces. India and other nonaligned countries constituted a stumbling block to that polarization and therefore had to be disgraced, humiliated, or destroyed. Hence, nonalignment as a concept took on added value as the only sane way out of an insane rush toward total belligerence.

Indira valiantly took up the cudgels on her father's behalf to convince the West that he was right. In a brisk evaluation during her eleven-day visit to America in April, she pointed out that nonalignment had not only stood the test of the Chinese invasion, but that it had weakened the communist bloc. Communism's appeal for the intellectual had been blunted and a rift had been created in the Communist party of India. She was convinced that the Chinese had launched the invasion to coincide it with American and Russian preoccupation with Cuba to humiliate the Indians in their own eyes as well as internationally, but "statesmanship and foresight changed the situation." India not only got promise of help from the United States, England, and Russia, but, as she said, "our national goals of removing social evils and retarding influences, of raising living and educational standards have not been abandoned. Rather they are emphasized. Our soldiers need assurance that all progresses at home, and that India is worth defending."[35] But in justifying India's cautious approach to China, she struck a typical note of common sense. "We knew," she said, referring to the time when she had visited China with her father, "that their ideology and ours were poles apart. But, when one has a tough neighbour, one does not go out of his way to start a fight."[36] The border problem, she insisted, did not come as a "tremendous shock," but what was unexpected was that the Chinese should have resorted to "a shooting war."[37]

She took time out to emphasize that in spite of being "faced with the serious problems of maintaining our freedom, democracy, and sense of values,"[38] India still considered participation in cultural exchange an invaluable aid to lasting friendship and hence they had gone through with their plans for the fair. Her presence at the fair itself induced Ambassador Richard C. Patterson, the Fair's protocol officer, to make a dramatic introduction, "Since the passing of the great Mahatma, Prime Minister Nehru has come to be accepted as the voice of India. Now an important part of that voice is the brilliant daughter of an eminent father, Indira Gandhi."[39]

This recognition abroad was indicative of what was becoming a factor to be reckoned with in India's political life. By 1963, when Welles Hangen wrote *After Nehru, Who?*, Indira was one of the eight Indian politicians he covered in detail who he thought might succeed Nehru.[40]

Hangen wrote:

She is different from any of the others sketched in this book, not only because she is a woman, but because her political potential is harder to measure. She has probably been involved in more top-level decisions than any other member of India's present ruling hierarchy except her father. Yet she bears official responsibility for none and can properly claim credit for none. Her power is vast, amorphous, and indefinable. No one doubts that she has easier and more frequent access to her father than any other Indian, but no one really knows the extent of her influence on him. No congressman dares defy her, yet none openly proclaims his allegiance to her. She holds no official position in the government but when she goes abroad, President Kennedy and other chiefs of state vie with one another for her favor. No public figure in India disclaims political ambition so insistently and none is more disbelieved.[41]

Hangen was only partly right. Indira's membership of the working committee since 1955 had put her in the orbit of power, not just influence. In 1961, she became a member of the Central Election Committee, the powerful body for the selection of party candidates for the 1962 general elections, which meant that she had a voice in making or marring the careers of congressmen. In fact, each candidate was approved by her in agreement with Nehru and Shastri and especially in regard to disputed cases. She also became a member of a seven-member sub-committee formed after the election to punish indisciplined party members; no wonder, therefore, that no congressmen "dared defy her." In fact, Ansar Harvani labels the year 1962 as marking the beginning of Indira's "active political phase," from which there was no looking back.[42] In early 1962, Nehru had his first serious illness. His kidney was affected and though he recovered, it was bad enough for him to acquire a permanent stoop and for observers to feel that he would probably "never be the same again." In any case he was seventy-two and even his demonic energy had to accept the claims of age. He was compelled to curtail his working hours from an exhausting seventeen to twelve hours a day, to follow a strict diet, and to rest a little in the afternoons. The less he could do, the more Indira had to do to see that he was not beleaguered by unnecessary details. Her role as an intermediary acquired added importance.

But there were moments of nostalgia. Sometimes any odd thing would set her off toward wanting to give it all up—"politics, I mean and so on"— as she would say. In 1962 or thereabouts, Rajen Bajpai remembers that a pamphlet maligning Indira suddenly appeared. It upset her a great deal, and while on other occasions opposition or slander would only stiffen her resolve to go her own way, this time although she suspected another woman politician to be at the back of it, she felt disgusted enough to cry out fretfully, "I'm not keen to remain in politics. Even Feroze didn't want me to, and I even said that after a while I'd give it up."[43] It made her nostalgic about Feroze, too. In the 1962 elections, while she was on a tour in a village called Lakshgriya in the U.P., she and her companions got off the jeep to walk along a mud track on a lovely moonlit night. In one of her sudden but rare outbursts of confidence, Indira began to talk to Rajen Bajpai about Feroze and ended up by recounting how she and Feroze had been stranded once, also on an identical road on an identical night, because they got a flat tire on the way to Dehra Dun and had no spare.

Most of the time, she allowed little familiarity. She felt most at ease with her colleagues, but there was a level of intimacy beyond which she would never go. She retained, of course, a special concern for the women's department of the AICC and its band of loyal devotees, while the vagaries of new women politicians raised odd and amusing problems. In 1962 Indira learned to her horror that all the women's organizations of Allahabad, nursing grievances about neglect, had banded together to pass a resolution that they would set up a woman candidate against each of the Congress male candidates! Indira frantically got hold of Mukul Banerjee and another worker, Krishna Dave, of the women's department and sped off to Allahabad to soothe their ruffled colleagues. Mukul Banerjee remembers a gem of an incident about their train journey. It is indicative of how subtly Indira manages to reconcile the common touch with her natural aristocracy of taste. Indira had acquired the habit of drinking non-sweetened tea from the time she had been in Europe during the war. But at Indian railway platforms a special kind of tea served in *kulhars* has a heavy flavor sweetened not just by sugar but by *gur*. Early in the morning when Mukul knocked at her coupe door and asked her if she would like some of that tea, Indira unhesitatingly replied, "yes, why not!" But she poured the tea from the kulhar into a lovely silver glass which she was carrying and sipped it delicately out of that.[44]

When communal riots broke out in Jabalpur in Madhya Pradesh that year, Indira showed that she had not lost her tendency to tackle a situation head on. She was the first to rush to the trouble spot. Though she did not go in any official capacity her prestige was sufficient to calm the fanatics and allay the fears of the minorities.

By October 1962, the Chinese occupation of 14,500 square miles of Indian territory, the surprise attack on two fronts in NEFA (Arunachal Pradesh) and Ladakh, and the military reverses that India suffered had created a crisis of confidence in the Nehru government. But Nehru was very much Nehru and even the humiliation of those months could not break his charismatic hold over the country. If his illness earlier in the year had caused Indira to pay more devoted attention to his needs, his agonized state of mind made her even more anxious. But this time he himself encouraged her to help mobilize the people for defense. On November 6, at the first meeting of the National Citizens Council of Defense, organized to meet the emergency, Indira was elected chairman. In this capacity, she organized a tireless campaign to raise morale. She visited the front, provided amenities, pacified the fears of the women and children, and instilled confidence in the local officials. Her most daring act came with the fall of Bomdi La in November, and the panic which led to the evacuation of civilians as well as the civil authorities from Tezpur in Assam. Unafraid, she went straight to Tezpur and was given a rousing welcome by about 20,000 people who had stuck on grimly while the others fled. "I saw with what fortitude the people... especially the younger generation and particularly those of the border areas, organized themselves," she recounted later. "In that extremely difficult situation, they did whatever they could to help to keep sanity and stability and to maintain law and order."[45] They were particularly angry about the ministers and officials who had left them in the lurch.

Indira was clever enough to realize that this was no time to let the image of government be tarnished so she convinced them that the ministers and officials could not afford to stay because if they were caught by the Chinese they might be used to form a puppet government! She spent the night at

Tezpur in spite of being warned by Shastri that it might be dangerous in view of its possible fall to the enemy, and early the next morning she drove another twenty miles to the frontlines to cheer the soldiers. She had had the foresight to carry a number of transistors, and when along with her words of encouragement, Kapoor who had accompanied her faithfully, began to hand out the transistors to the despondent soldiers, their spirits lifted, and they raised a cheer with gusto.

Hostilities were eventually suspended. If the Chinese thought they had succeeded in discrediting India's defenses, they failed entirely in creating government chaos by which they might have hoped to affect communist subversion. Militarily, an advance into the vast plains of India meant a long line of communication which they could not hope to maintain, while the promise of support India managed to get not only from the United States but the Soviet Union isolated China's expansionist adventurism. Above all, tne Chinese attack, contrary to their expectations, not only unified India's heterogeneous forces into a dedicated army but created a division even in the center of possible support, the Communist party of India.

Indira, while acknowledging India's gratitude to America, England, and Russia, when she visited the States in April 1963, pointed out that there was a "wonderful, healthy enthusiasm in India to prepare the whole nation for any future surprises."[46]

In fact, by August, 1963, Nehru, too, was back in the fighting and carried out one of the boldest acts of his career, the famous Kamaraj Plan. Initially conceived by K. Kamaraj Nadar, then chief minister of Madras, it was given an executive fillip by Nehru which changed the entire power hierarchy of the Congress. Its explicit aim was to revitalize the party organization, particularly after the dents in its popularity created by the Chinese invasion and an increasing anti-Congress stand that became apparent in the 1962 general elections. It enjoined senior party members to renounce their positions of authority in government and seek "to renew the party contacts with the people." It had the merit of boldness and simplicity. There was need both to make the union cabinet more ideologically cohesive, and the party organization stronger. Nehru did it in one stroke. He first sought permission to resign. There was an absolute outcry and Kamaraj said that he would withdraw the proposal if Nehru insisted on applying the plan to himself. On August 10, in an unprecedented political drama, scores of chief ministers and union ministers carried out the stipulation of "party before post" and not only submitted their resignations but left it to Nehru to choose whom to retain in government and whom to designate for party work.

Nehru had basically pure motives in proposing the Kamaraj Plan. They arose from a desire to have something done to revive the "hope-level" of the people by taking the party "back to the people" and relying on the spirit of "service, sacrifice, and idealism among Congressmen."[47] He was genuinely

impressed with the broad idea but it would be attributing too much naivete
to Nehru to argue that he did not also use it as a means to clean up the anti-
socialist content as well as the inefficient elements at the state and central
levels. As one report put it, "Mr Nehru apparently saw in it possibilities
that had escaped the originator."[48]   Six cabinet ministers and six chief
ministers were axed. Of the stalwarts at the center, the going of Morarji
Desai [finance] and S. K. Patil [food and agriculture], who represented the
right, and to some extent, Jagjivan Ram [transport and communication],
shifted the balance of power to the socialist-leaning Nanda. He became
home minister. With T. T. Krishnamachari, who came back to finance as the
most senior member of the cabinet and by putting Morarji out, it entirely
changed the complexion of a possible succession. Though the mildmannered
disciple of Nehru, Lal Bahadur Shastri went out with them, he was
brought back as minister without portfolio only a few months later. To
the interpretation that this was actually a Nehru plan to throw out unwanted
colleagues, Nehru himself made the vigorous reply, "Did I have to go about
such devious ways to get rid of anybody?" But the implications of its being
used partially as such could not be ignored. It was consistent with his
frustration that his "forward-looking policies" did not get the push from
some of his colleagues that he wanted. If all of them were socialists of one
kind or the other, as he himself said about his cabinet, it was he who also said
that there were differences of degree.

The Kamaraj Plan was at first approved by all the Congress leaders. Only
Patil came out with the statement that the plan was meant to get rid of certain
people though it was he who had seconded the resolution! Indira made
no comment at all. But *The Times* (London) reported that "some of Mr
Morarji Desai's supporters reduce the grand strategy of the Kamaraj Plan
to the dark outlines of a plot to get rid of the finance minister....Others
of the plot school go further and say that it has been master-minded by Mr
Nehru in order to clear all possible candidates for succession out of the
way so that it may be free for his heart's choice, Mrs Indira Gandhi, his
daughter."[49]

Not then, but a year later, Morarji himself expressed the same view, and
added that according to information given to him, Nehru had wanted the
party to endorse Indira for Congress president again in 1963.

Nehru's own reaction was forthright. "This is the most fantastic kind
of motive hunting I have ever come across. It arises from something like
a dynastic concept of succession which is altogether foreign to a
parliamentary democracy like ours besides being repulsive to my own
mind."[50]

Nevertheless, the issue was out in the open and events were shaping fast
toward a denouement. In December 1963, a sample public opinion survey
conducted in Bombay put the vital question, "After Nehru, who?" for the
first time to the average person in India.   In view of the fact that the survey

was local it was not surprising that Y. B. Chavan, then defense minister and a staunch Maharashtrian, should have polled the highest number of votes. But Morarji was there, as well as Jayaprakash Narayan, Lal Bahadur Shastri, and others, and, among the women, Indira Gandhi and Vijayalaxmi Pandit.

In the same month, Indira went to Kenya and Zanzibar to represent India officially at their independence celebrations. She also toured the rest of East and Central Africa and in twenty-three days of listening, learning, and speaking, she effectively counterbalanced the impact of Chou En-lai's and other Chinese leaders' tours at the same time of North Africa.

"Ours was a small delegation to Kenya and Zanzibar, but the Chinese delegation led by Mr Chen Yi alone consisted of fifty-one persons," she reported later. "They did a lot of propaganda. But they did not cut much ice there because of our old and consistent policy of friendship toward African countries."[51] Also because, as press assessments concluded, she did a sound public relations job herself and restored the image of India in African eyes. Her accomplishment was fourfold. First, by pointing out that Indian military reverses in the initial stages of the war with China were only due to the natural advantage that an aggressor has, that India's emphasis on economic development precluded diverting resources to an exaggerated military build-up; that once the threat came, the government and the people had had the courage to fight as one man, and that India emerged unscathed politically in the end. Second, she showed no bitterness or belligerence about African desire to seek economic help from Pakistan, and the "quiet dignity" with which she refrained from abusing either Peking or answering the diatribe against India made by the Pakistan ambassador to the U.A.R. earned her great respect. Third, she advised the Indians in Africa, as before, to shed their aloofness from the Africans and act instead as ambassadors of India in cementing goodwill between the two peoples. Fourth, her visit timed well with the newly gained independence of African countries, and those about to gain independence like Nyasaland and Northern Rhodesia, to explore possibilities of economic and technical collaboration.

"On paper, the visit was largely a goodwill one," acknowledged one newspaper report but labeled her mission a success and added, "It is certain to result in a new and more dynamic focus on Africa in New Delhi."[52]

It also gave Indira added status at a critical time in her country's history and led to the irresistible idea that in making her leader of the delegation with the external affairs deputy minister second in command, Nehru might have been anticipating a decision to make her full-fledged minister for external affairs, a burden he had thus far let no one carry but himself. But shortly thereafter, on the opening day of the January 1964 momentous session of the 68th Congress at Bhuvaneshwar, Nehru was struck by a mild paralytic stroke which prevented him from attending the rest of the proceedings. It led to a flurry of nervous private discussions about the future among his colleagues and a great, surging burst of national solicitude. He had constituted himself virtually as a one-man public relations machine for the Congress, traveling thousands of miles, lecturing, pleading, cajoling, arguing, and communicating in a magical equation with millions of his countrymen; he had worked eighteen hours a day for forty years almost without a break, with the burden of the knowledge that for the last seventeen years he had held the destiny of his country in his hands. He had again relapsed into mental fatigue after the bracing tonic of the Kamaraj Plan, but he had kept up his gruelling schedule, which would have broken a lesser or a younger man. All Indian newspapers played down the illness, although what was officially termed "a light weakness of the left limbs" by the medical bulletin two days later had been making front page headlines the world over from the first day.

Acknowledging Indira's role as the supreme arbiter of prime ministerial time, the *Times of India* came out with the touching editorial suggestion: "Mrs Indira Gandhi must really be more strict with him. Mr Nehru's temperament being what it is, he might feel that such advice is an intrusion on his privacy. But his health is quite plainly a public affair of vital importance."[53]

Nehru's recovery was swift and by the third day he was relaxed, read a lot, and received a few friends and colleagues. By the eleventh day Indira, worried and concerned until then, could state jokingly to a cheering plenary session that at least one good thing had happened. "He has been forced to listen to me and the doctors."

The same day it was announced that Nanda and Krishnamachari would jointly look after the prime minister's day-to-day work. Nehru, according to the doctors, would have to take complete rest for four to six weeks, but his condition was not serious enough to warrant a temporary retirement. It was obvious, however, that even if Nehru recovered fully he would not be able to maintain his former work pace. Therefore to whom would he delegate responsibility? At the Bhuvaneshwar congress, it was suggested that he recall Shastri, and there was also a "draft-Indira movement" to urge Nehru to give her foreign affairs, or even make her deputy prime minister. Nehru, recuperating back in Delhi, refused to be drawn into the succession wrangle. But by January 22, Shastri was back in the cabinet, this time as minister without portfolio. Two days later it was announced that he would assist the prime minister in all the departments under his charge, including foreign affairs, which seemed to rule out Indira automatically.

Unfortunately, talk of Indira's induction into the cabinet had become allied with the succession issue. If Nehru was a self-conscious democrat he was also a self-conscious father who hesitated giving his daughter obvious political encouragement because she was his daughter. He had no doubts about her political capability and recognized that she had "a strong independent will of her own." [54]

"He referred to her love of truth many times," recalls Sadiq Ali, "He had a high opinion of her and thought she could take any position of power."

"Even as P.M.?" I asked.

"Why not? If she could be Congress president then she could be prime minister also. The only thing is that he didn't want to show it too obviously. On the other hand, he didn't want her to suffer merely because she was his daughter, in not getting her due." Nehru was loath to do anything that might smack of giving an official stamp to any possible successor. He was convinced that a successor must emerge naturally from the democratic process itself. He also had the feeling, as he affirmed later, "If I nominated somebody as people seem to expect, that is the surest way of his not becoming prime minister. People would be jealous of him, dislike him."[55] He was perceptive enough to recognize that the party would in any case hesitate to accept another Nehru as his immediate successor. The dilemma in his mind, if any, was resolved by Indira's attitude. She firmly discountenanced the campaign which had been set in motion on her behalf.

In April 1964, when she went to New York for the opening of the World Fair, *Time* magazine regretted that Nehru cut her visit short by calling her back to India to be by his side for an important confrontation with Sheikh Abdullah, but also noted that "both Indira's visit to the U.S. as her country's representative and her abrupt recall as her father's aide define her importance." It discounted the probability of her succeeding Nehru but counted her becoming foreign minister a "serious prospect." She was introduced on NBC's "Meet the Press" as "the most important woman in India," but she played down the significance of her having taken on additional powers and work during Nehru's illness by saying, "I am doing just what I used to do before . . . partly work for the party, partly social welfare work." She was evasive and guarded when she was asked to name Nehru's possible successor. "I don't think it would be tactful for me to name anybody, but I think there are people, and the most important thing is they should work as a team."

She was categorical when there was a straight question: "Would you like to be prime minister of India?"

"I would not," she replied.

But she could not get away with it that easily.

"Would you refuse to run if you were nominated and if elected, would you refuse to serve?" Marguerite Higgins of *Newsday* persisted.

"Well, I am not a member of Parliament and in India you cannot be in the government without being a member of Parliament," Indira prevaricated.

"If the will of the people of India were such that you were clearly the wish of the majority, would you serve as prime minister?"

"I find it very difficult to believe that there will be such an overwhelming demand," Indira rejoined.

"But you aren't going to say that you would refuse to serve?"

"Well," said Indira at last, "shall I say that 90 per cent I would refuse."

Even Miss Higgins was impressed. "Ninety per cent. Well, that is a pretty high figure," she said.

Indira became more certain if anything.

Three weeks later when it was pointed out to her by Arnold Michaelis, interviewing her for American television from Delhi, that her father had said that it was unlikely that she would succeed him and that he was "not grooming her for anything," she remarked that he was right. She had "no such idea."

"I would not call it ambition, because to me that does not seem a good thing. Different types of people want different things and it is just not what I want for myself."

"Would it not be a question of who had the necessary equipment to shoulder such a responsibility?" insisted Michaelis. "I am sure you have it."

"Well, I am not conceited enough to think that I am the only person who has it even if I do," she answered. "But a lot of other things depend on who will succeed. I know that I will not enter into this at all."

"If it were thrust upon you, you could not shirk, and would not shirk responsibility, would you?"

"It can't be thrust upon me," she said flatly, "if I do not want it."

The reasons which had led her all through the years to refuse office were still, if not more, relevant. Her father needed even more care and she was not greedy for what she now had even more than before, a position of overwhelming influence. Besides, sensitively attuned as she was to the political scene, she knew that the time was not propitious.

"To some, she was the Mrs [Woodrow] Wilson of the Indian government during that period," observes Brecher. "The prime minister's schedule, his appointments, the papers to be shown him—all came under her scrutiny and control—she was an important element in the power structure, by virtue of her unique access to the prime minister, still the seat of ultimate decision."[56]

She was to remain so, until May 27, 1964, when both her personal and political worlds came crashing down, except that her grief was mingled with that of the whole of India. Nehru collapsed at 6.20 A.M., went into a coma, and was unbelievably dead by 2 P.M. It signified the end, not only of an era, but of a stage of heroism and high hopes in Indian history.

He had left a most moving will. Vijayalaxmi Pandit's voice broke when she read it out over the radio. It was a testament of love for a land and its people.

When I die, I should like my body to be cremated. If I die in a foreign country, my body should be cremated there and my ashes sent to Allahabad. A small handful of these ashes should be thrown into the Ganga, the major portion of my ashes should . . . be carried high up into the air in an aeroplane and scattered from the height over the fields where the peasants of India toil, so that they might mingle with the dust and soil of India and become an indistinguishable part of India.

Assessments of Nehru's genius and his contribution to world politics poured in from all corners of the world. But the most spontaneous tribute came from the thousands upon thousands of ordinary Indians who poured into Delhi to have their last *darshan* of their beloved Jawahar. There were unprecedented numbers, even more than for Gandhi's funeral, and the city's seams seemed to burst. A million and a half people lined the funeral procession route from Tin Murti to the spot next to Gandhi *samadhi* where the death flames consecrated Nehru to the future—and a place in history. The grieving multitudes broke out with the cry, "*Jawaharlal Nehru Amar Rahe!*" (May Jawaharlal Nehru remain immortal!)

Indira had covered her head quietly when her father died, and cried. But all the time his body lay in state, she had kept a stoic vigil by his side, dressed in a white sari, her face taut with sadness but her heart a mirror of all the past. He had been perfectly normal the night before. She had left him to his accustomed work after dinner and gone to her rooms. He had been in pain from 4 A.M. but he did not wake the servant until dawn—and she had not known. After that, it had been a long seven and a half hours' fight by six of India's leading doctors to save his life. She had insisted that they take her blood when they needed a transfusion. Nothing had helped. It was the suddenness which was unnerving. He had recovered so well, even if he had begun to look tired and a bit strained. Only the week before, at his press conference, when he had been asked the inevitable question about a successor, he had remarked smilingly, "My lifetime is not ending that soon." And the whole hardened group of newsmen had broken into a spontaneous cheer! Even the last thing he had done and the last thing he had said related to the passion that had driven him so long: work for an India he loved. "We are condemned to hard labor," he had warned when India became free, and he had condemned himself to it most of all. "I have disposed of all the files and papers," he had said the night before, and gone to sleep. How tempting it had been for him, she knew, to give up and live a private life and write and read. But he had felt he must ensure the invincibility of what he had fought for. It was not love of power which made him stay on, it was the desire to raise such a fortress of democratic functioning that nothing could destroy it. For that there had to be time and sane leadership and he had not been sure that he could pass it into safe hands. It was a sense of mission that had sustained his energy and idealism.

She had found what he had jotted down on a little pad which lay on his work table. Perhaps the temptation to relax and give in and drift into the leisurely areas of the mind and body had swept over him the night before, too, and he had thought of the Frost poem and written it down to bolster his dying will.

> The woods are lovely, dark and deep
> But I have promises to keep
> And miles to go before I sleep
> And miles to go before I sleep

Thank God, there were no promises for her to keep.
Or were there? She was too tired and stunned to think.

"She was suffering under intense shock as if the earth had slipped away under her feet," recalls Teji Bachchan, "but she . . . is so sincere and loyal and self-effacing that . . . she thinks of others even in the smallest detail. She was sitting in the room holding her dead father's hand, his body hadn't even grown cold; even so, she had this sense of the impersonal demand in the midst of despair . . . and she exclaimed to me 'Oh, Teji, see that a doctor is available when Padma *mausi* comes! And a little later asking me again to see that a 'flask of juice was put in *phupi's* room'."[57]

Soon after, when she saw the old servants looking woebegone and un-washed, she told them to go and shave and dress for that is how "Papu would have liked them to be."

The "sense of the impersonal demand" was the condition of public awareness. She had been trained in it too long to forget what the occasion demanded, even if it were as shattering an occasion as her father's death. She could not even brood alone. From the twenty-ninth of May onward dig-natories from all over the world who had arrived for the funeral began to pay her their condolences, and the gates of Tin Murti were thrown open for the thousands of her countrymen who wished to share their sorrow with her. There were 30,000 condolence messages from all over the world. But the most touching were innumerable ones from India's children for whom Nehru had been their beloved "*Chacha Nehru*," among them an incomparable one from five-year-old Vandana: "I like your father very much. Please do not cry. Otherwise I will also cry."[58]

Her face was softened with grief those days, her whole being cold to whisperings about the succession. But one decision that she had to make as the person most directly concerned on the nature of Nehru's funeral rites, soon proved quite controversial. Nehru had been against organized religion in life. He wanted none of it after death. He had stipulated in his will that there should be no religious ceremonies performed on his death. "I do not believe in any such ceremonies and to submit to them," he wrote, "even as a matter of form would be hypocrisy and an attempt to delude ourselves and others."[59] He made it clear that his desire to have his ashes immersed in the Ganga was not out of regard for the Hindu religious sanction attached to it, but because the Ganga represented to him the symbol of "India's age-long culture," and the river around which were interwined India's "racial memories, her hopes and fears, her songs of triumph, her victories and her defeats."[60]

Indira had to decide virtually between what Nehru might have meant by orthodox rites and what would be part of his cultural affinity with the past. In the first impact of his death the matter was almost taken out of her hands. There was a clamor by spiritual leaders of all the faiths that they be allowed to read from each of their scriptures, and sing their devotional songs by way of homage to him. It was a singular tribute to a man who had admitted himself to be an agnostic. It seemed to be so much more a human rather than a religious demand that she felt she would be going against the spirit of Nehru's own flexibilities if she refused. Besides, so many of them being there meant that not one was being singled out. It was a secular requiem that included bishops, *pandits* and *maulvis*, each arriving at a synthesis of spirit at that moment which was symbolized most by the man they mourned. A secular requiem to a secular man.

Half an hour before the funeral was to start however, recitations from the *Gita* and the *Vedas* were conducted, and again at the cremation ground, a ceremony was performed by the head priest of Delhi's Lakshmi Narain temple and three other priests. Vedic hymns were also chanted as the sandalwood pyre was lit and waves of fragrance mingled with the air. "Yes," wrote Krishna Hutheesing later, "despite my brother's wish, there were priests at the cremation. The government had made all the arrangements for a traditional ceremony. We had nothing to do with that. And besides, the only people who knew how it should be done—building the pyre and all other details—were the priests."[61]

The problem cropped up again the next morning. Again there was a demand by the Muslims, Hindus, Christians, Buddhists, and Jews to hold services during the period of official mourning. At first Indira said no, recalls Mrs Hutheesing, but she thought that that would hurt them, so it was decided to hold services every morning between six-thirty and seven-thirty. Indira apparently insisted that there should be no partiality for one faith or sect so the result was that in the back veranda of Tin Murti, there was an amazing example of heterogenous worship and devotional song. There was a continuous chanting of the *Gita* in Nehru's own bedroom but that seemed to be in keeping with his personal regard for it.

Indira, in fact, thought that she had not yielded at all to orthodox ritual. The decisions, contrary to Mrs Hutheesing's contention, were arrived at in consultation with Mrs Gandhi.

"When my father was ill," said Indira, "they wanted to know if there should be some religious ceremonies. I didn't know what to do. I knew that I didn't think it necessary. I knew that he didn't believe in it. But I didn't want people to say that I had not been thoughtful enough or . . . anyway, I asked Anandmayee what I should do and she said I must do what I believe in. Did my father believe in that, she asked. I said no. Did I believe in it? I said no. So I must do what I think is right within me, she said."[62]

But Indira herself was considered to be a devotee of Anandmayee. Was that not the result of a religious attitude? Where did she herself draw the line between the religious attitude and a rational one?

"I don't believe in her for the spirituality and all that," she hastened to say. "She's a very good friend. It's as a friend that I meet her. She was a great friend of my mother's. So I feel a bond. She's a very comforting person to be with, but there's nothing religious about it. At least, she's not like that with me. I don't know what she's like with other people."[63]

I asked her if she was superstitious about yellow as she seemed to wear it so often. She plunged into a little dissertation on how she reacted to colors, but the ultimate revelation turned out to be of a kind of mystical sensitivity that drives her reactions.

"Yellow has always been my favorite color. I am very particular about colors. I used to dislike blue. In Oxford my room was blue. I thought I'd go crazy. Don't like mauve at all, or purple. I never liked pink before, now I like it. But even in that there are shades. With yellow I like all shades. My room in Anand Bhawan was yellow." She tried to make it sound very casual. "In khadi you have very little choice, only blue or green, sometimes you find everything you can get is one color. When I began to wear colors again recently, I found I had nothing but yellow, that's all."

What did she mean, "when she began to wear colors again"?

She hesitated. There was a psychic connection.

"Color makes a difference to the mood," she said softly. "A year before my husband died, I stopped wanting to wear colors. I don't know why this was but it was so. I began to wear white after he died. Then gradually I felt like wearing grays and browns and blacks. I was just beginning to want to wear colors again when my father died."[64]

3. SHADOWS

On June 2, 1964, Lal Bahadur Shastri was unanimously elected leader of the Congress legislature party and prime minister-designate of India after Nehru.

"You may have to carry a large part of my heavy burden," Nehru had remarked to Shastri at Bhuvaneshwar when he fell suddenly ill.

"I am prepared to do my duty," Shastri had replied humbly.[1]

The smooth succession was a triumph for Nehru's faith in the security of the Indian democratic procedure. The prophets of doom were belied: instead of chaos, there was continuity. Shastri sought to carry it further by reaffirming that socialism was to be the government policy. And politically, in a voice choked with emotion, by affirming that "Mrs Gandhi's continued association with us will be a source of strength to us."[2]

Indira remained out of the race as she had said she would. Neither her own state of mind nor the party mood was sufficiently conducive to it. But Gulzarilal Nanda, who, as home minister, filled in for eight days as acting prime minister and had striven hard to have the party accept him as permanent, said that he would willingly serve under Indira. Shastri's first act on being chosen leader was to visit Indira and tell her again that he would step aside if she were willing to assume the burden. It might have been a matter of form, but sentiment was high enough in the immediate post-Nehru period to tune political egoism to a muted key. But when Indira also reacted true to form and automatically refused, Shastri got down to his real mission—to persuade her to become a member of his government.

"Don't forget what you owe to the Nehrus,"[3] Kamaraj, the rustic-faced but Machiavellian chief minister of Madras who had become Congress president at Bhuvaneshwar, apparently told Shastri before going with him to Indira. Not only sentiment but shrewdness dictated that Shastri should not forget. He knew he needed her not only as the symbol of continuity and as the inheritor of the Nehru charisma but also as the one national figure whose mass appeal cut across all regions.

Indira's first reactions, as in the past, was to refuse office. But Shastri was insistent, and the circumstances were different. She was on her own. Thenceforth her position was going to be determined only by what she would make of it. There was only a faint stirring of such thoughts, but in spite of the personal shock she was suffering, she was political enough to feel them and realize that she was at a crossroads and any decision would be vital. In spite of the initial hesitation, from habit or the tragic situation in which she found herself, it is significant that she accepted what she had vigorously rejected for seventeen years (except for those brief eleven months as Congress president)—a political office. Shastri seems to have offered her foreign affairs. She said she would prefer "a lighter charge," and took information and broadcasting. In spite of the "light charge" she was ranked number four in the cabinet, immediately after Shastri, Nanda [home], and Krishnamachari [finance]. Her political sense was revealed in her preference and the choice was remarked upon as being a "wise" one.

"She apparently feels," said political commentator Krishna Bhatia approvingly, "that she must establish herself by her own work and not merely let the present wave of sentimental homage to her father carry her to the top. External affairs is a coveted portfolio. Others with years of standing in the cabinet and a record of success in other ministries are eating their hearts out for it. If Mrs Gandhi had started with external affairs she would have evoked a measure of jealousy and resentment and the party's good-will and affection for her—enormous at present—would have eroded."[4]

She also got the chance to see how the government would shape up without being immediately committed to the controversial field of foreign affairs. She did not rule out a subsequent change as Bhatia implied, but it seems that the tenor of the Shastri-Indira relationship itself changed as both began to acquire greater political stature in the succeeding months. The strain she had been under was so strong, however, that by the third week of June she was suffering from exhaustion, and doctors advised a week's rest. Thus, it was on July 2, 1964, fourteen days after the rest of the cabinet, that she was sworn in by President Radhakrishnan as minister of information and broadcasting.

Contrasting sharply with the white sari she wore on the occasion was a rosary of black wooden beads around her neck.

Indira was only forty-six. She became the hope of India's young intellectuals. She seemed to represent in her person more than any other member of the cabinet the combination of liberalism and imagination that spelled excitement. No miracles were expected, particularly for All India Radio and India's neglected fields of mass communication. None were promised. But the approach was characteristically challenging. She called for a change in the "broad policy pattern of government" in her first official pronouncement as minister.

"I believe in making mistakes. Nothing in the world has happened without people making mistakes," she affirmed. "There is no harm in honest mistakes made in trying out new ideas and new experiments. One should not avoid doing things because risk is involved."[5]

She wanted the press, radio, and television to be used not merely for propaganda but for promoting "a richer and fuller life" for the people and she emphasized the desirability of the "personal approach" like that of her father—his link with the people was of a personal nature, she said—which could guide modern media of communication to reach the masses. She emphasized three other things: that broadcasting should have "original thinking" behind it and include "more controversy and discussion," that the television network should spread out more, and that there should be coordination of media. "Now people tend to work separately," she said. "In films and radio, for instance, we should work more closely with the Education Ministry with regard to school programs."[6]

It was the promise that All India Radio's tired intellectuals felt could revive their early excitement, while the films division and the rather nascent television organization could hope for even more. But Indira's usual determination for change was tempered again by administrative reality and the need to establish trends rather than create revolutionary situations.

"In India we expect miracles all the time," she pointed out, "that is why we always get disappointed. But the Government of India runs in parti-

cular ways or ruts.   There are rules and regulations."   And then, indicating
her essential philosophy: "It is impossible to change everything overnight.
All one can hope is to take certain steps, leading to other steps, which will
bring about other changes gradually."[7]

Though she began to attend office promptly from the very next day after
taking over "punctually at 10.30 A.M." as she said, and talked in terms of
long-term planning, there was a general apprehension that her appointment as information minister was a stopgap arrangement to enable her to
get the feel of government and that she would eventually be given foreign
affairs.   This seemed to be confirmed by the fact that Shastri chose her,
along with Krishnamachari, to represent India in his stead at the Commonwealth Prime Ministers' Conference at London in July.   Shastri was
scheduled to go himself but sudden illness forced him to change his plans,
and "the substitutes," as *The Statesman* commented, "are the best that
India could have chosen." Recognizing that Krishnamachari's participation in the conference would give India's economic stance an authoritative
frame, it also pointed out that "Mrs Gandhi will impart to the conference
a sense of continuity, an asset in the Commonwealth which owes not a
little of its content and character to her father who will be sorely missed."[8]

Again, she preferred to remain in the background.   By a mutual arrangement between her and Krishnamachari, it was decided that he should act
as leader of the delegation though, officially, it was accepted that the rank-
ing of the two at the conference would be more functional than hierarchical.
Krishnamachari would deal with politics and economics and Indira with
cultural and social relationships between member nations.   She also thought
she would take the opportunity to examine radio and television networks
in the United Kingdom.   But a great deal of her time in London was taken
up with receiving the Commonwealth leaders who came to condole her on
the loss of Nehru. She naturally kept out of the glittering social activity that
accompanies a conference and her public engagements were few.   Her
interest in the working conditions of Indian women led her to pay a visit
to the newly opened tea center in Oxford Street.   The one public engagement she did accept indicated her preferences.   She agreed to preside over
a Tagore Memorial Lecture by C. P. Snow on his controversial concept of
the two cultures.   She thought also that she would keep up a tradition set
by her father whenever he visited London, which was to talk unofficially to
Krishna Menon's India League.   Menon was out and discredited.[9] Indira
herself had once wished that her father would not be so much under his
influence.

Nevertheless, London brought a flood of old loyalties back, her trips
with her father there, her mother, Feroze, the others, and inevitably too,
Menon and the League and the early national passions.   London was
youth and the early spreading of political and emotional horizons. London
was nostalgia.   There was in fact nowhere in the world she could go with-

out knowing something of her father there, and missing him. All her old loneliness was back, and she felt "numb." She was withdrawn, diffident, perhaps generally unsure, with a naivete that was disarming, for when questioned about her work as information minister she said simply, "I am so new to the job."[10]

It was not long before developments at home brought the harsh realization that she could no longer take her political strength for granted. Whatever vague idea political analysts might have had that Shastri would wait for her to be ready to assume greater responsibility and keep foreign affairs pending for her was discountenanced within days after her departure for London. On July 18 he announced that he was appointing Sardar Swaran Singh, the pleasant faced Sikh who had been a minister in the union cabinet since 1952 and was now a strong supporter of Shastri, as the first foreign minister of India with an independent charge.[11] Indira said cooly in London that it was "a good decision." and that Swaran Singh was "a very good man."[12]

Shastri was careful enough to soothe possible resentment, and reconstituted the important National Defense Council so as to include Indira. But there was an unmistakable appreciation among political observers that he had effectively taken the larger choice out of Indira's hands. There were modulations in politics that could be understood. Shastri wanted her in the cabinet but not in a position of power.

Kuldip Nayar, a recipient of Shastri's confidence at the time, confirms that Shastri had misgivings about giving foreign affairs to Indira because he thought it might make her "too important."[13]

Back in Delhi on July 23, Indira set about the task of implementing her promises for change in the ministry under her charge. The I & B, as it is generally called, had had fluctuations of status depending on the minister who headed it. With Indira, a full cabinet minister, everybody at the ministry felt that at last there was someone who could take action. The feeling was especially predominant among All India Radio's staff artistes, the long-neglected tribe of "temporary" writers, musicians, and actors who were contracted to AIR on the basis of constant renewals, sometimes for as long as twenty years, without getting any of the benefits of the permanent staff.

"When she was about to take over the ministry," observed Mohan Singh Sengar, a well-known Hindi writer who had been associated with AIR for a long time, "there were lots of expectations that she would effect changes in staff. So we took a delegation of about forty male and female artistes to her. She immediately asked why we didn't form an association. We said we could do it at once. Everybody narrated their difficulties. She not only gave a patient hearing but noted down a few points."[14]

"I can't understand why you people can't get them [the benefits]," she exclaimed. "What is the hitch?"

"Please ask the D.G. [director general]," they replied sullenly.

The director general was not directly responsible but dependent on the ministry for sanction of money. His discretion lay in either fighting for that sanction or remaining indifferent. The D.G.'s until then were not, with one or two exceptions, broadcasting men. They were picked for their "artistic inclinations" from the top administrative cadres like the Indian Civil Service and they carried the marks of their severe bureaucratic training. There had been another handicap. Staff artist benefits implied an additional budget of around fifteen lakhs rupees. The demand had indeed been made to the finance ministry by I&B but it had been rejected as a matter of course each time. Even when a previous minister, B. V. Keskar, showed personal interest in the matter, he did not have the power or the prestige to get it through finance. Indira had no such problem. She could go to Krishnamachari direct, and have it done. In fact, within a short period of her taking over she announced that dearness allowance, city compensatory allowance, and all other amenities hitherto given to the permanent staff of AIR would thenceforth be extended to staff artistes.

When she had advised them to form an association, Sengar, who led the delegation, recalled that she also told them that she hoped that "it would not only work for the improvement of the service conditions of the staff, but the quality of programs." And the delegation, in its turn, presented itself in a manner most calculated to draw her interest. It is an amusing example of how concerned the people were with "Nehruana." "The beautiful women—the announcers—were in front," said Sengar, with his eyes twinkling, "and the old Muslim artistes on either side. You see, we knew how vulnerable the Nehru family was to beauty and the minorities."[15]

Indira's study of the working of television in Britain during her Commonwealth trip convinced her further that television was imperative for mass education in India. It was only the expense that had to be considered. Narayana Menon, the man she made director general, quotes her as having said that the question was "not whether developing countries can afford to have television but whether developing countries can afford not to have television."[16]

Accordingly she sought a new orientation in radio and television by calling for a general report, and set up the Chanda Committee to enquire into the workings of both. This had long been needed but both the government and the Congress party in Parliament had resisted the idea, the ministers because they feared criticism of their policies, and the party because it was interested in retaining its hold over the medium for propaganda purposes although the possibilities of turning All India Radio into a corporation on the lines of the British Broadcasting Corporation was written into the contracts of employees.

It was characteristic of Indira that she should have initiated what her predecessor had neither the boldness nor the imagination to do. The Chanda Committee came into being on December 4, 1964, and it was set with the task "to determine and define the role of the ministry of information and broadcasting in terms of government's responsibility and functioning in mass communications, to examine and evaluate the operations, policies, programs, and production of the various media units of the ministry; to examine and assess, in general terms, the current and projected activities of the other governmental agencies engaged in mass communications; to indicate the extent to which these operations, policies, etc., in each of the units meet the standards of an effectively functioning unit in terms of (a) the present objectives of the unit; (b) the objectives of such a unit as determined in terms of reference; and (c) to recommend appropriate changes, where necessary, to be made in the various media units; to determine the desirability and feasibility of instituting a system of coordinating all government activities in mass communications and specify what form such coordination should take; and to draft a specific practicable program of mass communications with detailed reference to the media, facilities, personnel, funds, and time required for implementation of the program."[17] The report came out finally in April 1966.

But Indira did not wait for the committee's findings to go ahead with institutionalizing a more creative approach to radio, films, and television as well as planning an effective expansion. In her fifteen months as minister of information and broadcasting from July 2, 1964 to January 19, 1966, she seemed to know what dimensions to add. She found she could set a new trend by overhauling the personnel, but her search for a new director general of All India Radio or for the director of Audio Visual Publicity was guided by the criterion, as she said that, "he should be a man who has a reputation to lose." She ultimately changed the heads of the posts from the secretary of the information ministry to the principal information officer of the Press Information Bureau. As director general she appointed a man from within the organization who was a musician, litterateur, and broadcaster, Narayana Menon.

AIR had become notorious both for an emphasis on Sanskritized Hindi and complacent programing. Indira thought that the purpose of AIR should not be to propagate but to educate, and to project the program not the language. It was more important she felt to first get an audience, and then teach them. Therefore she was in favor of AIR's light program called Vividh Bharati and had no stuffy ideas about ramming heavy doses of classicism, for the sake of classicism, down the throats of the unwilling. Similarly, she felt that Hindi did not have to be stiff for the sake of being stiff. She saw to it that adequate emphasis was also paid to Urdu and was keenly aware of the advantages of having an Urdu service which would also draw listeners in Pakistan within its sphere of impact. Narayana Menon, in an assessment of her achievements, says she was responsible for sponsoring an Urdu service and a general overseas service, rehabilitating staff artistes, extending broadcasting hours; beginning reasonable controversy over the air, attempting to use radio in the wider national interest and not in the narrow governmental sense, instituting daily television, instead of the twice weekly service available until then. "She was pretty convinced of the role that television could play," adds Menon, and her enthusiastic support evoked the adage in the capital that if Nehru was a visionary and Shastri a reactionary, Indira was a televisionary. "She was impatient with the dullness of AIR's programs," recalls another observer, "and in meetings repeatedly asked what could be done about programs, and why implementation was not carried out. During her tenure, opposition angles began to be projected more. She accepted the principle of the primacy of means, that it should be a successful media of news, but she also had considerable feeling toward using mass media as a means of teaching finer taste."[17]

"She herself was not a natural broadcaster," says Menon, "but she would change the text of her script considerably and work hard at it." Although she was informal, friendly, and spontaneous—once while she carefully rehearsed a script she burst out with, "I am very hungry. I am always hungry these days!"—her disposal of files in the ministry was quick and effective and her interviews short and to the point. If a person who came with a request or to advise her tended to go into a long preamble she would break into an impatient, "Yes, yes, I understand. Just give me the point, that's all."

She initiated a coordination committee within AIR and was eager to also have coordination between broadcasting and films and the education ministry in planning educational programs. In September 1965, when the strain of Indo-Pakistan relations finally erupted into an intensive twenty-one day war, a central committee of defense on border publicity with representatives from the defense, home, foreign affairs, and I & B ministries, as well as from the planning commission and the cabinet secretariat, was set up at her prodding. She was all for giving facilities to correspondents to go up to the front though the defense ministry's initial hesitation led to a virtual uproar. But her belief in the freedom of the press was tempered by the awareness of a greater need. "We have seen the press losing its freedom in the countries around us, one by one. We do not want this to happen in India. But there is something very much greater at stake than the freedom of the press and that is the freedom of the individual," she said. "If the press encroaches upon that freedom, I, for one, will fight for the freedom of the individual and not for that of the press. The fundamental right of an individual extends only as far as the fundamental right of another individual begins."[18]

Consistent with this approach was the piloting of a bill in Parliament by her deputy minister for the establishment of a press council, and her deep interest in seeing it through. She disliked irresponsible journalism as intensely as she disapproved of coercive restraints. A press council seemed the ideal answer, because as she said, "it is always better for the press to regulate itself rather than be regulated by an outside agency like the government." But she made no bones about what the alternative could be. "I must, however, issue a warning. Wherever the press had not regulated itself, it has had to be regulated. This is the choice before the press in this country."[19] If she believed that mass media should shed the vulgar for a comparatively educative approach and emphasize "finer taste" as such, it did not mean that she wished it to become puritan. In fact, she sought a certain liberalization of attitude in the film censor board by changing its membership. She was a discriminating film fan with an appreciation of both the classic and *avant garde* and had been associated with the All India Federation of Film Societies of which Satyajit Ray was president. She was conscious of the role that film could play and thought of having film theaters built throughout the country. Her main frustration was the lack of funds, the budgeting for information and broadcasting being traditionally and unimaginatively low. It was as the result of her inspiration that India had its first international film festival. She took interest in the selection of films and the standard of jury although the organizational problems got out of hand. One eminent film critic of international standing was impressed enough to exclaim that he had met many ministers at European film festival centers like Cannes, Venice, Karlovy Vary, and others but "Mrs Gandhi is the first minister I have ever met who really knows something about international cinema. She actually discussed with me the relative merits of Rossellini and Ingmar Bergman."[20]

It made her aware of the limitations of Indian cinema. "Our films have a tendency toward the obvious, leaving nothing to the imagination. There should be a conscientious effort to achieve authenticity," she advised. Years later, when she became prime minister, Harindranath Chattopadhya, Sarojini Naidu's brother, wrote to her to endorse his movement of a new cinema and she showed that she had not lost touch.

"Our films are in need of all that you have mentioned," she replied, "meaning, sincerity, real values. Yet the film world resists everything except temptation, and many are the temptations to which it is subjected— money, glamor, and quick fame! It is just possible that a movement which includes able and imaginative persons would bring about changes, especially if it could show works of true merit, shunning new catch phrases. This has happened in many countries of Europe, there is no reason why it should not happen here."[21]

She revealed her usual meticulousness in one way nevertheless. Mukul Banerjee recalls that though they had both worked so closely together in the women's department and Indira had implicit faith in her, yet when she once asked her to write the foreword for a pamphlet on kitchen gardens that she had written, Indira sent the pamphlet to the relevant expert in the food and agricultural ministry for technical approval before sponsoring the idea in the foreword! So even with regard to Harindranath Chattopadhya all her personal regard for him could not drive her to a blind promise.

"I wish well the young men you are encouraging," she added in the letter about the new cinema, "But I should like to wait and see their work before publicly endorsing them."[22]

Indira's pronouncements on socialism were as staunch as ever. "If there is at any time any attempt by the party to surrender its avowed aims of achieving democratic socialism," she declared at a Socialist Convention of Northern India Congress Workers, "I would not like to be in it."[23] Inaugurating an international conference of the junior chamber of commerce and industry she avowed that the people of India would not tolerate a shift away from socialism in policy. "They have taken to it knowing full well that the salvation of the country lies this way alone. The process," she added pointedly, "is sure but slow."[24] She rigorously defended the basic tenets of heavy industrialization and a planned economy. She told the junior chamber that if the organization wanted free enterprise at the cost of socialist planning she would be opposed to it. "I am against this sort of private enterprise," she said. "The private sector in India," she argued, "had not blossomed on its own;" the credit went to the government's encouragement of a mixed economy. The private and the public sectors should be considered complementary and not contradictory to each other so "we must keep it up." Planning, she affirmed, had given a new voice to a people who had been dumb for centuries. "But this is not enough. We have not been able to convey the message of socialism to every individual. It is necessary to do so to get their participation in planning."[25] But as envisaged in the prologue to India's First Five-Year Plan, the true impact of the whole concept, she was generally careful to point out, would be felt only after thirty years. Impatient about the pace and direction otherwise of the solutions for India's ills, she could view with comparative equanimity a time gap such as this because what it promised was not a temporary succor but a permanent change. "For achieving self-sufficiency in this country, it is essential that the economic roots be made strong first and progress in other spheres would be automatic."[26]

The more intensely she felt about implementation of Nehru's socialist dream, the more resentful she was of any indications of a contrary trend. She was familiar with the protracted struggle that Nehru had had to equate the official economically progressive stance of the Congress for which he was invariably the guiding force with the unwillingness of a section of congressmen to work it in reality. It was particularly frustrating when this parallelism manifested itself, as she told the Congress workers' convention, in the "petty factions that have crept into the Congress party at a time when the country is passing through such a critical period and the party's unity and strength are of such paramount importance for solving our major problems of food and unemployment."

The apprehension, the criticism, and the malaise were to become even more familiar angles of the political pattern, challenging Indira to the prime ministership, and then spelling danger to her authority. The battle lines within the party were drawn early enough. There were "black sheep within the party," she said even then, "who are responsible for creating many obstacles in the country's path of smooth progress."

Why were they not thrown out of the party then, she was asked at the Congress convention. "It is up to you, the workers, not to allow them to come up," she replied. And in that answer one could foresee an attitude that was also to become more familiar: her belief that authority and charisma were best derived not from the opportunist loyalties of party bosses but from the rank and file, the people of India. It was an unwelcome posture for her close rivals. It implied an appeal over and above the party and certainly over and above the factional commitments that gave them their hold.

Prime Minister Shastri came into power with a reputation as a supreme conciliator, a political rarity as a man with no enemies. He was able, competent, with a humble air, incredibly tiny, five-feet two, with a round, vulnerable baby face sharpened by a mouth that closed decisively over a firm chin. He had none of the Napoleonic aggression of the small man, but he was ambitious enough to have made it to the top. As a young boy he had to walk miles and wade across a river to reach school because he did not have the money for a bus; as a young man he was so poor that he had to see his baby daughter die of typhoid because he could not afford enough money for medicines, but if his ambition was tempered by gentility it took him through elective posts in party and government from secretary of the Allahabad Congress Committee to union home minister under Nehru, and eventually his successor. As Brecher notes, "he moved deftly and lightly, always self-effacing and soft spoken...yet in many circles he was known as an extremely tough, even ruthless, positive manipulator of his own group, and a man able to press his own interests as any other U.P. politician."[27]

It is naive to imagine that any politician can function otherwise, the question being only to what extent power is directed by public rather than personal good. Shastri was nurtured in the Nehru tradition, and like a great many of India's politically aware young men in pre-independence days, especially from the U.P., the Nehru home in Allahabad and the Nehru aura were the tangible intangibles that provided political sustenance. He was not a radical at heart like Nehru. There was an essential conservativeness of approach, but he was secular, democratic, personally loyal to Nehru, and had a political centerism that seemed reassuring to Nehru and to all those who wished a continuation of his basic policies. He was also a realist, a pragmatist, and a man sufficiently conscious of his due: his quality of self-effacement would by no means turn into the ardor of sacrificial martyrdom. There is evident credibility in the sentiments ascribed to him therefore in at least one particular.

Asked whom he thought Nehru wished to succeed him, Shastri is supposed to have replied unhesitatingly, "His daughter. But it would not be easy," he had added.

"People think you are such a staunch devotee of Nehru that you would yourself propose Indira Gandhi's name after his death," persisted his interviewer.

Shastri's reply was revealing, "I am not that much of a *sadhu*."[28]

Once he achieved power he wanted to consolidate it. He realized he must have Indira in his cabinet as a symbol of continuity with Nehru. She and Morarji Desai also represented the only valid rivals he might have to fear, she for her massive image outside the party, and he for his substantial support within the party. If sentiment or practicality decreed that he should not alienate Indira after Nehru's death but give her the option to choose her own ministry, his decisiveness was also evident in what Brecher calls "the subtle denial" of foreign affairs to Indira. "She may indeed have been given carte blanche to choose a portfolio for the sake of form . . . if so, it may well have happened that an informal emissary persuaded her that it would be unwise to accept either because external affairs would be too strenuous and/or because there would be sniping in Parliament at dynastic continuity, which her sensitivity could not easily bear. All this is speculation," adds Brecher, "but two facts stand out. Shastri took the portfolio himself and when illness compelled him to lighten his burden, he did not give the post to Mrs Gandhi, despite the urging and expectations of some colleagues. He chose Swaran Singh instead."[29]

If as it seems there was an attempt to subdue the political importance of Indira Gandhi at the time, the question of the by-election for Phulpur, the prestige constituency left vacant by Nehru's death became a part of this quiet drama. Indira was indeed too upset to campaign for election immediately after losing her father. But when she agreed to take a ministry in Shastri's cabinet the rules allowed a six-month period during which she could become a member of either the Rajya or the Lok Sabha. A seat in the Lok Sabha, especially that of Phulpur, was indisputably preferable to membership of the Rajya Sabha, made up of members selected by an electoral college of party legislators from the state assemblies. The Congress high command opted for a Rajya Sabha seat for Indira. Shortly thereafter, a prominent congressman of the Allahabad District Congress Committee said that the high command had been assured that Mrs Gandhi would have no difficulty in getting elected from Phulpur but that it had committed "the greatest blunder" in getting her elected to the Rajya Sabha.

The president of the Allahabad District Congress Committee, Mrs Kamala Bahuguna, came out with an open statement resenting this "backdoor election of Mrs Gandhi." She apparently told the party enclave of decision-makers that when it was understood that the constituency was being

nursed for one of the Nehru family members the high command's decision
to get Mrs Gandhi elected to the Rajya Sabha had taken them [the U.P.
leaders] by surprise.[30] U.P. congressmen thereafter demanded that Vijayalaxmi Pandit, who was then governor of Maharashtra, should be persuaded
to contest the by-election from Phulpur, but Mrs Gandhi's name continued
to be mentioned. In fact, when she visited Allahabad and addressed a
large meeting, Congress workers of Phulpur constituency appealed to her to
stand for the election, saying that the people of Phulpur wanted her to
represent them after her father's death. That the mental or physical strain
involved in an election no longer weighed with her was evident. When
pressed for a reply she said, amidst loud cheers, "It all depends on you
people."[31]

On October 11, Indira flew into London on her way to attend a meeting
of the executive board of UNESCO of which she had been a nember since
1960. The Uttar Pradesh Congress Committee remained dead-set on Indira
but on October 22 it was Vijayalaxmi Pandit who filed her nomination
papers to contest the election at Phulpur. Back in India, at a press conference on November 2, Indira confirmed that when the question was discussed as far back as July before she attended the Prime Ministers'
Commonwealth Conference, she had been conscious of the fact that apart
from the election there would also be the involvement in keeping up constituency work. "I did not feel able, emotionally or physically," she said,
"to take on something which was so strenuous because I was quite ill and
doctors thought that I should be in bed for some months."[32] But when
a correspondent provocatively suggested that she might have disdained the
contest at Phulpur to avoid a defeat, she retorted spiritedly, "I do not think
anybody thinks I would have lost the Phulpur seat. Even my worst
opponents would not say this."[33]

What was it then, she was asked, consideration for "someone dear to
her?" No sentiment governed this relationship, but Indira has grace.

She admitted, "My aunt did want to contest and I thought if she wanted
to, she should especially when I had a seat in the Rajya Sabha."[34] She
added that she thought it "extremely silly" to leave the Rajya Sabha after
only two or three months. Nobody asked her, and she did not explain
why she had in that case smiled and said, "It all depends on you people"
only a fortnight back to those who wanted her for Phulpur.

On October 16, 1964, the Labour party won the election in Britain and
Harold Wilson became prime minister. Indira, in Europe for the UNESCO
conference, became the first Indian minister to call on the new British
government. Shastri was clever enough to have the formal greetings of
the Indian government conveyed through her. He wished to give her due
importance, though only from time to time, while her long association
with Labour leaders whom she had been meeting when they were in the
opposition, was a factor to be taken advantage of. She discussed with

Wilson the question of an official visit to Britain by Shastri. On October 26 she went to Belgrade on a purely personal visit in response to an invitation by Marshal Tito, but on the twenty-eighth she arrived in Moscow for a four-day sojourn described by the Indian aide as "unofficial" but which turned out to have all the ramifications of a top-level exchange.

Khrushchev had been ousted in a dramatic turn in Soviet politics on October 4 and Indira again was one of the first to seek assurances on behalf of India that there would be no change in Russian policy particularly in regard to military aid and the Indo-China dispute. She gained an immediate entree to the new top Russian leaders, whom she had known over the years. She met the new Soviet premier, Alexei Kosygin, twice in two days in talks which were described typically as "very friendly, fruitful, frank, warm, and cordial."[35] She also met Foreign Minister Andrei Gromyko and Michael Suslov, the key man in the Khrushchev ouster.

In Moscow she declared tactfully, "We are grateful to the people of this country because of their interest in our struggle for freedom and also the help they are giving in building up our country. This support is not only moral but in other concrete ways as well. This has helped tide us over difficult times."[36] Back home after three weeks she stilled Indian fears with the report that the Russians had assured her that their desire to "smooth the sharp edges of their relationship with China would not develop into a policy of unfriendliness toward India. Contrary to speculation, Khrushchev's aid-to-India emphasis during the Indo-Chinese war was not one of the factors held against him, the Russians assured her, and even with regard to Kashmir there would be no change. Her sense of humor enlivened her account. Suslov had had a dig at the West in Moscow with the remark, "When I cough, the Western press magnifies it into thunder." Telling Indian correspondents in New Delhi that she found Suslov "looking quite normal" and pretty much the same as when she last met him sixteen months back, Indira added conspiratorially, "He had a cough, however."

The Moscow parleys were at her initiative. She said that the return via Moscow had been the shortest route back and while there the Indian ambassador in Moscow, T.N. Kaul, suggested that she might meet the Soviet leaders. It was her personal stature which lent the affair its significance, for Shastri had not added the weight of his authority as prime minister. In fact, a coolness between him and Indira was beginning to be perceptible. On November 23 Vijayalaxmi Pandit, whose aim had always been to come back to active politics—she had already had an enviable career as high commissioner in London, ambassador to Washington and Moscow, the first woman president of the UN General Assembly, and governor of the state of Maharashtra—won a resounding victory at Phulpur. In spite of Vijayalaxmi's hopes, the situation remained an embarrassing one. Toward the end of her stint abroad she had wanted to return to India, but Nehru had been as unwilling to give her an obvious position of authority—with her seniority it could only be a position in the cabinet—as he was to his daughter. She accepted second best as governor, but she was never happy. Under Shastri it was again embarrassing, this time because of Indira. It was an obvious case where being a Nehru was a disadvantage. With Indira already in the cabinet Shastri could hardly induct another Nehru. Therefore he subsequently began to give Vijayalaxmi semiofficial assignments abroad as his personal representative to Paris at one time and Japan at another and so on, which for her were simply palliatives. He did not, or the Congress as such did not, encourage her in the only equivalent prestige post to one in the cabinet, that of chief minister of a state, particularly U.P., in which she might have thought she could establish herself in no time. Whatever the personal resentments between Indira and Vijayalaxmi, Shastri seems to have worked out a balance in which he was not prepared to give either one of the Nehru women more than the basic minimum due to their position.

The question, for instance, of which ministry should handle the ministry of external affair's publicity within the country hung fire for a long time. When Indira became minister of information and broadcasting there were indications that she would also be granted external publicity in order to coordinate it better with internal policy. But Shastri again sought a compromise solution by inviting Indira's cooperation on an *ad hoc* basis. He asked her and her ministry to submit a report on the functioning of publicity abroad and suggest remedial measures for what had long been felt to be an inadequate representation of India's image abroad. Indira did it with her usual forthrightness. She pointed out that Indian information officers were out of touch with matters at home and that even China, which was severely anti-West, got more newspaper coverage than India. So, as opposed to Vijayalaxmi's dramatic moves for a political hold which ultimately left her nowhere, Indira worked with that detached assurance which kept her free of narrow loyalties for larger ones. Shastri gained stature with power. Indira confirmed her's.

There was an initial disappointment after the early promise of her involvement in her ministry. She was out of India a great deal for the first months but the change in policy she brought to the mass media ultimately resulted in definite measures. It was her national image that grew, her fearless arrivals time and again to each center of crisis well ahead of the others, earning her the encomium of being "the only 'man' in Shastri's cabinet." She was one of the first to reach Madras to make an instant study of the situation when fierce riots broke out over the adoption of Hindi as the national language stipulated from January 26, 1965 onward. A circular issued by her own ministry that thenceforth all correspondence with the department should be in Hindi had added fuel to the fire, but she had the courage to go up and face the hostile south Indian crowds, even the violence-prone students, and make an impassioned plea for rationality. Hindi had been accepted by the south and the north in a Congress resolution before independence as the future national language of India and had later been embodied in the constitution. What the south resented was the effort to hasten the switch-over in such a manner that the non-Hindi-knowing peoples were left at a disadvantage. She was no bigot. After meeting local Congress leaders and state ministers and assessing their feelings, she went so far as to say that if the objective of fostering and strengthening national integration was not achieved by making Hindi the official language, then there should be rethinking on the entire language issue as such.[37] "My interest in Hindi is that all Indians should be able to communicate with one another. I do not believe in forcing it on anybody." Shastri also gave an assurance in a radio broadcast.[38] The rioting ceased, but the resentments remained. In June the same year she confessed to her distress in a public meeting at Coimbatore:

> I think it is very sad that when I come to Tamilnadu my speeches have to be translated. My father was a far-sighted man. And when I was small I went to schools in different parts of the world, and in India I studied at a Gujarati school which was located in Maharashtra. Then I went to college in Bengal. Perhaps, if I had had the opportunity of finishing my college education, I might well have come to Madras to take my degree! Unfortunately our life was so uncertain in those days that this was not possible. But this experience showed me the importance of the regional language to the people of that area and also that these languages are beautiful, have ancient, good literatures, and that it is important to develop all of them. But the problem of communicating with each other in different states still remains. If India or Parliament could decide that Tamil would be the link language, I would be very happy.[39]

It was a style, approach, and sentiment best calculated to soften the resentments of those who considered themselves victims of fanatic northern *Hindiwallahs,* but at the same time she also strove to emphasize the practical for she added regretfully, "But it is not a question of my views. Because I have learned a number of languages, it is easier for me to learn other languages. And when we talk of communication between people, I do not mean a few educated people in towns and cities, I mean all the people, whether they live in the villages, in the rural areas, whether they work in factories or anywhere else." She made an appeal to the northerners as well. "The south Indians share the feeling with others," she told them, "that India must have a national language to serve as a link between people speaking different languages. Long before the country became independent the people of the south had started learning Hindi."[40] In an address to students she declared herself in favor of retaining English as an associate language to Hindi to maintain contact, but advised the Hindi-speaking younger generation to learn another Indian language besides Hindi or any south Indian language so that the people of the south should not feel that they would have to be the only ones to learn an additional language. They needed to feel that the north had sympathy for their difficulties, she said.[41]

She again landed in the midst of a crisis in Srinagar in August 1965. She knew as a member of the cabinet of the extensive infiltration of armed men from Pakistan along the cease-fire line in Jammu and Kashmir and along the international line at some points that had begun on August 5. The situation was so serious that Shastri had to hold a meeting of the Emergency Committee, of which she was a member, on August 8. It was clear to the government that the operation had been planned, organized, and equipped in Pakistan. "Most of them [the infiltrators] belong," it said, "to the Pakistan-occupied Kashmir forces, though in civilian clothes, and have been obviously sent out with arms and explosives to commit acts of sabotage and foment disturbances."[42] August 9 was scheduled by the breakaway Plebiscite Front of Kashmir as "Black Day" to mark the day of the imprisonment of Sheikh Abdullah. Pakistan evidently based its strategy of infiltration both on making use of some of the resentment expected to be unleashed on the occasion and on the hope of carrying out a revolution on the tide of what they anticipated would be a popular upsurge of the local population, given the impetus against India.

When Indira decided to fly to Kashmir on the crucial day of August 8, it could hardly be for the "holiday" that was given as the ostensible reason. The five days she spent there turned out to be tense and critical precursors of a bitter confrontation between India and Pakistan, portents of the first all-out war between the two countries since the 1948 cease-fire. She was received at the airport by Chief Minister Sadiq, the state Congress chief and other Congress workers. They were worried and anxious. There had been repeated clashes between the armed Pakistani infiltrators and Indian security forces. The Kashmir cabinet met in an urgent session to which Indira was also invited. But as tension mounted on the ninth for the so-called takeover of Srinagar, at least one minister gave in to panic. He had fought against the Pakistani invaders in 1947 and he felt that if they got hold of him now, they would destroy him. "I'm quitting," he is said to have told Indira. Her reply was short and brusque. He could leave, she said, but she was determined to stay and fight.[43] The poor fellow probably blushed to the roots of his hair. But he gave up all thought of running away. On the ninth itself large-scale security forces from Delhi were flown into Srinagar. Three encounters between well-equipped saboteurs and Indian army and police units took place in a village only a few miles from Srinagar. Indira stuck it out. She told a press conference the next day that the captured arms revealed Pakistani markings and some articles even had Chinese markings. In some cases the signs had been erased.

"The situation is the same as created by Pakistan in 1947," she commented, and also told a Kashmir Congress executive meeting that they must form "a clear picture of their role at this juncture when the infiltrators were active in Kashmir."[44]

She kept in touch with the prime minister and Home Minister Nanda and it was at this stage that she seems to have felt that Shastri should have taken bolder action. The "insurrection" expected by Pakistan did not happen, however. The local people ganged up against—instead of with—the infiltrators. "It bears repetition," reported a correspondent, "that in almost all cases the first information about the presence in the valley of the armed Pakistani intruders came from simple villagers and the like. This may not reflect credit on the intelligence service, but it is an undoubted tribute to the intelligence and patriotism of the Kashmiri people or certainly most of them."[45]

In many cases, false women's hair and other disguises used by the infiltrators to move about the area were discovered. Indira herself contributed her share with that mixture of romanticism and daring with which she seemed to meet such situations. She told Deputy Commissioner Banerjee in Srinagar, at the time that she would prefer to move about incognito and would not like to have any security guards trailing after her. She made a habit of strolling around the marketplace in the evenings, pretending to shop. Because her face was not so familiar to the people who did not recognize her she could sometimes even pretend that she was a Pakistani sympathizer. This is how she learned one day of a plan by the infiltrators to blow up a large petroleum dump near a vital bridge. She came back, informed the army commander and steps were immediately taken to prevent the sabotage. On all these excursions, the only person she allowed to accompany her was the faithful Kapoor, who loyally followed her but kept a few paces behind.[46]

On August 11, further fighting broke out on the outskirts of Srinagar and at Jaurian in the Chhamb sector in Jammu. Indira made a ringing speech at a Congress workers' rally and gave a warning that any attempt to change Kashmir's relationship with India would endanger world peace. Referring to Pakistan's flirtation with China in an attempt to put pressure on India, she pointed out that she thought the Pakistani infiltrators were even employing Chinese tactics.[47] On the twelfth, the fighting continued. In the Chhamb area, Indian troops encircled two companies of Pakistani army regulars of about 250 men. The same day, and at last, Home Minister Nanda arrived in Srinagar, and on the thirteenth Indira left for Delhi to report that the immediate crisis was over, that the Pakistani plot to create unrest had failed and that India was in control of the situation. Indian troops and police were on a hot chase, she said, to round up as many infiltrators as possible. She was full of praise for the Kashmiri people, who, she felt, had "stood as one man" against this insidious invasion. She even recalled the night of August 9, as being indicative of their characteristic strength. "We heard firing at night. But it was amazing to see life in the city normal the following morning."[48]

In fact, one of the foreign tourists who decided to fly into Srinagar on the thirteenth—"the scare about the fighting notwithstanding," as they said gaily—was impelled to remark as she saw the lush quiet of the Kashmir valley from the plane, "What, no rockets, not even smoke!" But a day in Srinagar, the closeness of the fighting, and the dangerousness of the situation soon had her wondering by the evening. "What a remarkable people. So much is happening, and there is no panic."[49]

But there was anxiety. The planning, the use of modern arms, and the scale of the infiltration portended a bigger action in the future on the part of Pakistan. "In the next few days," as columnist Krishan Bhatia pinned the problem in his notebook on political affairs on August 14, "the government will inevitably be faced with a hard decision. Should India raise its hand only in self-defense, as it has all these years, or should it also sometimes hit the aggressor in retaliation? Should India always play the game of defense at the aggressor's bidding and according to rules prescribed by it or should it occasionally frame its own rules and choose its own ground?"[50] In fact, the increasing deployment of Pakistani army reinforcements along the cease-fire line and intensive shelling of Indian defense positions by the eighteenth signified the anticipated shift in Pakistan's approach. On August 22, Indian security forces beat back two Pakistani attacks in the Chhamb sector and Indian Defense Minister Chavan told Parliament firmly that if it was found necessary to cross the cease fire line to defend Indian territory, "I have no doubt we will do that."[51]

On August 23, the Pak army made its first open thrust into Indian territory in the Mendhar sector, near Poonch, but was beaten back. Prime Minister Shastri declared in Parliament that the raiders' bases would not be spared. On August 25, Indian troops crossed the cease-fire line in Jammu and Kashmir and occupied two posts opposite Tithwal. The action, the defense minister pointed out, was taken "in order to push out all infiltrators and prevent further infiltration."[52] On August 30, Indian troops occupied the vital Haji Pir Pass cutting off thereby the main route by which the infiltrators came. Pakistani forces tried pushing across the cease-fire line in the Gurais sector in a massive attack but were pushed back after an initial advance. The same day Indira told Parliament that her publicity units had stepped up propaganda in the border regions of Darjeeling and Sikkim.[53]

On August 31, fresh Indian troops were sent to Uri to consolidate what were called the "spectacular gains" of the Indian army in the Uri-Poonch troops on the cease-fire line. And in New York, United Nations Secretary General U Thant's report to council members was understood to have held Pakistan responsible for guerrilla infiltration into Jammu and Kashmir and related Indian military operations to the resultant provocation. On September 1, Pakistan escalated the Kashmir fighting with an aggressive thrust across the international frontier in South Jammu with Patton tanks and a full army brigade. The Indian air force went into action and a war, though undeclared, was on.

Indira decided to have All India Radio interrupt its programs to make major announcements on the Kashmir situation.

On September 2, U Thant issued an appeal to Pakistan and India for a cease fire. On September 3, the diminutive, soft-spoken Shastri cried out forcefully, "India cannot simply go from one cease-fire to another and wait till Pakistan chooses to start hostilities again. A cease fire is not peace." Pakistan must undertake to withdraw the infiltrators and its armed forces from Indian territory first, and give an assurance that there would "no recurrence of such a situation," he said.[54] On September 5, Pakistani aircraft crossed the international frontier into Amritsar and fired rockets upon an Indian air force unit. On Monday, September 6, Indian troops took retaliatory action. They marched across the Punjab border into Pakistan in the Lahore sector.

"We are at war with India," declared Ayub in a special broadcast that afternoon. He had been taken by surprise by Indian initiative and had banked instead on its usual long-suffering patience. Besides, he was even supposed to have remarked contemptuously in an obvious allusion to the average Hindu, and particularly to Shastri who normally wore a *dhoti,* "How can a *dhotiwallah* fight?"

In the very midst of all this, not the dhoti but certainly the sari-clad Indira was found again defying danger. On September 4, she was in Srinagar crying out in an instant rapport with the masses, "We shall not give an inch of our territory to the aggressor." For fifteen years she said India had it tolerated Pakistan's bellicosity but this was the end of its patience. The hand of friendship had been taken as a sign of cowardice. "We were just patient and wanted peace but Pakistan mistook it; now Pakistan is imposing war on us and we shall face it with all our might. We are neither weak nor cowardly and Pakistan shall know it."[55]

"She said this in two separate meetings of the Citizens' Council," reported an admiring dispatch, "and was repeatedly cheered for her forceful speech."[56]

A few days later in Delhi she decided to make the rounds of the capital incognito with two old associates, M.P.s Anis Kidwai and Subhadra Joshi, to see if civil defense arrangements were working properly. So, on the night of September 11, the two women, led by Indira, drove around the city in a private car from point to point for three hours, and the only person they found who had been doing something similar was the deputy home minister who had been spending an hour after midnight for the previous three nights in the control room from where the civil defense arrangements were being directed. What she saw made her feel that more guards were required for certain important installations. So the next day she telephoned the minister and asked him to have the guards from her own house withdrawn so that they could be put "to some better use." It did not seem to occur to her that in a critical period her own position might be more vulnerable. Nehru's words, which were fixed in her consciousness at an impressionable age, were never far away. "Be brave and the rest follows." The bravery was tempestuous but it was allied to commitment and no one sensitive to her public posture could overlook the obvious: that she could never, in spite of her "detachment" as she called it, be a wholly private person. The woman who looked such an introvert was not only ready but invariably the first among her colleagues to undertake the most active role.

She was in Kashmir when hostilities began and then again when they erupted with full force. When the fighting turned to the Punjab side, she arrived there, too, inspecting bombed-out areas in a border tour in khaki camouflage. In Ferozepur on September 18 she saw the localities destroyed in the air attacks, visited the military hospitals, chatted with the soldiers, and felt her own spirits lifted with theirs. Abohar, Fazilka, Ambala, Amritsar, Gurdaspur, with people gathered to hear her even in the blackout. "Wherever she went," said a dispatch, "Mrs. Gandhi was greeted by enthusiastic crowds."[57]

"We have fought our battles and we have fought them well," she claimed proudly. "Now we shall live up to our traditions and fight for our principles. Nothing can deter us from our path."[58]

On September 23, the highly emotionally charged and bitter war came to an end. Both India and Pakistan accepted a call for a ceasefire from the United Nations. Too much had happened, and too much was undefined for there to be hopes of a permanent peace. But in spite of the personal tragedies of those who had lost their men in the war, all of India surged with pride and achievement. India had won the war. Not only had its armed forces proved superior, they had used Indian made planes—the tiny Gnat produced by Hindustan Aircraft—and armor to the effective disadvantage of Pakistan's imported Pattons and Sabre jets. Indira was quick to point out that her father's policy had paid off.

"The present conflict with Pakistan has shown that India could stand on her own feet," she exulted. "All weapons used ... had been manufactured in India. This also proved the correctness of India's industrial policy of setting up big factories."[59]

The sense of achievement remained, but the relief was shortlived. There were continuous violations of the cease fire by Pakistan which kept the tension alive. In fact, Shastri refused to withdraw Indian troops unilaterally and warned the country of harder days ahead. But to President Ayub Khan's earlier contention that for Pakistan "marching on Delhi would be like taking a stroll," Shastri could make the rejoinder with all the confident humor of the victor: if that was how the president looked at the issue, he declared, then he should not take it amiss if "we too had decided to take the stroll and reached the outskirts of Lahore."

There was nothing humorous, however, about the series of air attacks by Pakistan after the cease fire on the civilian population of Punjab towns like Amritsar and Chheherta and others. It was unwarranted, cruel and unnecessary, and it had Indira rushing there soon after with her usual public solicitude. At Chheherta she walked over the bombed-out sites, a quiet anger showing in her face, but feeling all the poignancy of such wasteful destruction. On September 27, for the third time in three weeks, she was in Kashmir, this time to hold out hope for the refugees from the Sialkot sector who were being looked after at Kathua, about fifty-seven miles from Jammu. She made a policy speech at a public meeting, addressed the refugees, and assured them that their rehabilitation would be considered at the national level, visited the military hospital, distributed gifts to the soldiers, told newsmen once and for all that "Kashmir's status was not negotiable," and then, the sole woman and certainly the first minister from the central government to do so, went up to the village of Palhalan in the Haji Peer Pass area distributing sweets to the children, and then to the isolated pass itself, to meet soldiers who had won there the first of many victories that finally demoralized the enemy.

"Now they [the men] qualify my position and my situation as being a woman's," she said disgustedly later as prime minister. "When I was put in jail and tortured for civil disobedience along with others, when they asked me to join the marches and the demonstrations, they never asked me if I was a man or a woman. And later, when I was sent to quell the riots and the disturbances in several towns, they never thought of me as a woman. In one town where there was a riot, no man dared to go. I was sent, and I pacified the people. At one time, I had to walk for twelve days because the place was so rocky even a donkey could not get there. The most difficult jobs were given to me, jobs where a man's physical strength was needed. They never considered my being a woman whenever I was sent out on a job. Now they want to bring it out because of my position."[60]

The whole question of becoming any the less feminine as a result of that according to her just does not arise. "For instance," she once said spiritedly, "I was the one to go to Tezpur during China's aggression. I went to Kashmir during the Pak war. I went because I thought I should. The others, to the others, it didn't occur to do so. They don't think along those lines. One doesn't have to be mannish to do such things. One does them....I did them because I am like that, I think like that. If tomorrow I had to take up a rifle and go along and fight, well, I would—what has being a woman got to do with all that?"[61]

One of the factors that embittered relations between Indira and Shastri was her fear that he was not sufficiently committed to the Nehru line.

Shastri apparently argued that if the aim to benefit the common man had not been achieved there must be something wrong somewhere. Indira felt firmly that full achievement must derive from full implementation, and it was wrong to blame the emphasis if you only talked about it. As early as September 1964 her disillusionment with Shastri was evident. In fact, in writing about the customary factional pattern within the Congress which involved various group alignments, *Hindustan Times* columnist Krishan Bhatia pointed out that the situation was in a state of "flux and confusion" and nobody seemed to know who stood with whom. "Mrs Gandhi has been bellowing angrily," he put it a trifle unkindly, "about some threat that she sees to Mr Nehru's policies...."[62]

Nehru's birthday, the first year after his death, was sentimentally commemorated. Shastri's broadcast to the nation on the occasion was impeccably loyal. "I should like to remind every young man and woman in the country," he exhorted, "that so many things which today they take for granted are in the nature of a legacy which Jawaharlal has left to the nation. He it was who in 1928 proclaimed that complete independence and not mere dominion status was the political goal of India. It was he who took the lead in putting forward the concept of planned development for India even before World War II broke out. It was Jawaharlal who evolved the doctrine of non-alignment and peaceful coexistence to which an ever-increasing number of countries in the world subscribe. And it was his wisdom and counsel which on many an occasion reduced the tensions which were building up and removed the threat of war. Yet it is not with his achievements alone, great as they were, that we should try to identify him," he continued in words that seemed to carry their own conviction, "we should rather identify him more with the forces which he generated throughout the country; forces which imparted a new dynamism. It is for us to keep the flame burning, the spirit alive."[63]

The commitment was explicit. But Indira was not convinced. In a foreword to a book, *Jawaharlal Nehru—Congressmen's Primer for Socialism,* brought out at the time of the Durgapur session of the Congress in January 1965, by H. D. Malaviya, editor of the AICC's *Economic Review* for a number of years and then editor of the *Socialist Congressman,* Indira stated that there was considerable confusion in the public mind, as well as within the Congress itself, about the Congress policy of socialism. While all were agreed upon the need to bring in a "socialist society in our lifetime" as Congress president Kamaraj put it in his Durgapur address, he himself argued against the large outlay envisaged in the Fourth Plan and thought that "prudence should guide our actions," while Prime Minister Shastri in a major speech the next day ruled out any pruning of the plan and thought that it represented an "irreducible minimum" in relation to the nation's needs. A resolution on social and economic policy moved by Jagjivan Ram, who argued that effective measures were needed to break monopolies and ensure a fair distribution of national wealth was passed uanimously. It was important enough to be accepted as a guideline for the Fourth Plan, and it called for a special emphasis on agriculture and agro-industries, dispersal of industries, setting up of processing industries in the cooperative sector, implementation of the Third Plan land reforms, and the establishment of banking institutions for the farmers to meet their credit requirements more fully. Yet the leftists, represented by K. D. Malaviya, suffered a defeat in the elections to the working committee and the only branch of the Congress that was refused permission to hold a meeting in Durgapur was the Socialist Forum, the group within the Congress that called for speedier implementation of its socialist policies.

"Under the circumstances," reported a commentator, "anxious to avoid an unseemly clash, Mr G. L. Nanda considered discretion the better part of political valor and canceled the Forum meeting. The Forum's discomfiture apart, another senior union minister was firmly chided at the working committee meeting for having publicly moaned about the country's slow progress toward socialism."[64] The commentator like the others was provoked into a wondering analysis, "Is the party moving toward socialism or retracing its steps? Is the Fourth Plan going to be bigger or smaller than its tentative size fixed recently? Who is 'left' and who is 'right' in the Congress?"[65]

Regardless of who was chided—although it seems likely that it may have been Nanda—in the working committee, it did not deter Indira from expressing her doubts about the possible future of the Durgapur deliberations a few days later. "All these years," she said, "resolutions and declarations were being made but the fact is that we have not been able to fully implement all the things we wanted to do."[66] She conceded that it was a difficult thing to do in a democracy like India where people generally had "no conception of the programs, no scientific outlook, and no understanding of the technological problems."[67] She was resentful that an atmosphere seemed to have been created conducive to denigration of the Nehru image. She had said in an address to the All India Newspapers Editors' Conference at Gauhati shortly before, that a certain section of the press was intent on blurring the image of the late prime minister. "I think everybody knows which section that is, and it makes no difference whether I name anybody or any paper. It was in the context of what is happening in the country. I am personally not bothered about it. . .[but] by their comments against Mr Nehru and his policies the papers concerned were striking at the self-confidence and self-respect of the Indian masses themselves. They have to have the faith to achieve things—even with incompetent officials—and my father was able to inject that faith in them."[68] Events were to prove Indira right. The Shastri period, marked with intentions toward centerism but dominated by Shastri's essentially prudent and conservative outlook, merged gradually into a subtle process of de-Nehruization evident in four things: a greater hold by the bureaucracy in the form of the prime minister's secretariat and a greater reliance as a whole on the civil servants; an increasing trend toward capitalism and the emergence of the business community into spheres of decision; a spirit of Hindu revivalism; and a comparative withdrawal from the international, and a preference for, domestic involvement.

Indira had naturally supported the social and economic policy resolution at Durgapur. But she enlivened it with a very personal and subtle appreciation of the immediate response his own language evokes in a Bengali.   It was a long way away from Shantiniketan, but she had learned not to throw away advantages. She chose to speak in Bengali to that largely Bengali crowd and the results were predictable. The applause came, warm and frequent at different turns of her speech. Her image among the people began to acquire deeper dimensions, but also within the power echelons, to elicit deeper envy.

Inder Gujral, later one of her staunchest supporters who was to become minister of state in the ministry of information and broadcasting, remembers wryly that Shastri, having known his father as a loyal worker in the pre-independence struggle, quite favorably envisaged a political future for him as well and was willing to support him for a seat in the Rajya Sabha. But as soon as he discovered that Gujral had Indira on his side also and could bank on her goodwill, Shastri turned cold and blankly withdrew into a shell of indifference. It did not improve matters when she saw herself a part of the subtle process of de-Nehruization. She felt bitter, angry, humiliated, and alone and was convinced, like political analysts of the period, that there was an attempt to isolate her from the centers of authority.

She was a member of the Cabinet Sub-Committee on Defense and therefore at least ostensibly in a position to have a say on a matter like, for instance, the political demands of Nagaland.   But in late 1964 when negotiations were caught in an impasse and she was asked if she could do something as member of the sub-committee, she exlaimed, *"Are bhai, koi pooche to kahun, koi poochta hi nahin.* It's all decided among L.K. Jha, Dharmavira and Shastriji."[69] She felt anyway that it was wrong to let the problem fall into the clutch of routine officials. But she did not generally speak in the cabinet and only the very minimum in Parliament and, as Brecher remarks, did not make a mark in either.[70] It sprang possibly from her self-conscious awareness that it would not help much to do so. Her effectiveness, she felt, was curtailed also through the plan priorities. She had worked out a Rs 100-crores plan for television expansion. But the money allocated to her ministry by the Planning Commission whose chairman, of course, was the prime minister, was only Rs 43 crores, out which Rs 8 crores was set aside for border publicity and the rest allocated for plan projects. The emergency after the Indo-Pak war necessitated a shift in priorities in the plan program but till November her ministry was not touched in so far as that was concerned.

By December she had to admit that inadequate financial resources made it necessary to shelve the plans she had had for a "dynamic publicity policy." In fact, there was a point when the coolness between Indira and Shastri even surfaced to the social level and at times personal invitations between Indira and Lalita, Shastri's wife, went unheeded.

Indira had left "the big house" as the Nehru residence was referred to by a close group of friends, politicians, and journalists, soon after her father died. Shastri's first reaction was to seek a house for himself away from the Nehru shadow; he also felt diffident of being able to match the aristocratic style and elegance with which Jawaharlal had lived in the sprawling cream-colored mansion for seventeen years. The house and Nehru could not be separated. And in fact on September 4, Shastri, Indira, and their colleagues decided that Tin Murti should be turned into a personalia museum with a library dedicated to the memory of Nehru. On November 14, 1964, it was formally inaugurated and from then on the people began to come in steady, silent, awed lines to see how Nehru had lived and worked even in those few hours he had outside the public gaze. And for Indira, too, it was as if seventeen years of her own life had been turned inside out. But there was also a deep satisfaction, for she was zealously protective of everything attached to her father, that no other presence should impinge too soon upon that house and those years, so inextricably a part of the Nehru legend.

There was another kind of compensation in shifting to the bungalow at 1 Safdarjang Road, not far from Tin Murti, which she was allotted as minister of information and broadcasting. For the first time she was absolutely on her own, with everything in her own right to make what she wanted out of it. But would she? And did she really want to? It was tempting to let leisure set the pace of her days. Tempting to just relax, savor time and idleness and poetry and music and reading. Time to drop in at friends casually, without being the prime minister's daughter, the prime minister's hostess, cool, reserved, haughty, with an image to uphold. She had her house done up tastefully, with curios, sculpture, paintings, and photographs of Feroze, her two sons, and her father, in front of which a rose kept nostalgic vigil. She had packed and sent off a number of her personal possessions from Tin Murti to Anand Bhawan. But she had kept some books, and these, alongwith those she kept buying, were in bookcases in the foyer or lined in long rows along the settees in her bedroom. They ranged from Jean-Paul Sartre to Arthur Schlesinger to Swami Vivekananda, displaying the same eclectic taste as her father, her curiosity ranging like his in a searching variety. She would take time out particularly to do the flower arrangements herself. She was fond of animals, but of the hectic menagerie of Tin Murti she had only the three favorite golden retrievers, Madhu, Papita, and Putli.

She had sent both her sons to England. Rajiv was already at Cambridge when his grandfather died and had barely made the journey back in time for

With John F. Kennedy, and Jacqueline Kennedy on visit to U.S.A. with Jawaharlal

Indira, Vijayalaxmi Pandit, Eleanor Roosevelt, and Jawaharlal Nehru on a visit to
Roosevelt home, 1949

With Nehru and the Eisenhowers

With Nehru and Pat and Richard Nixon

Visiting National Gallery of Art, Washington, 1961

As guest of Women's National Press Club, Washington, 1961

In Rome, after winning Italy's Isabella d'Este Prize for diplomacy in 1965

With Nehru and Shastri

In London, with T. T. Krishnamachari, to atten[d] Commonwealth Premiers Conference, 1964

With father   In Sikkim

With Nehru at Bhuvaneshwar session

Indira as Congress
president

With father, at a reception

In the lawns of Tin Murti, with Nehru →

With Nehru, Rajiv, and Sanjay in the prime minister's house

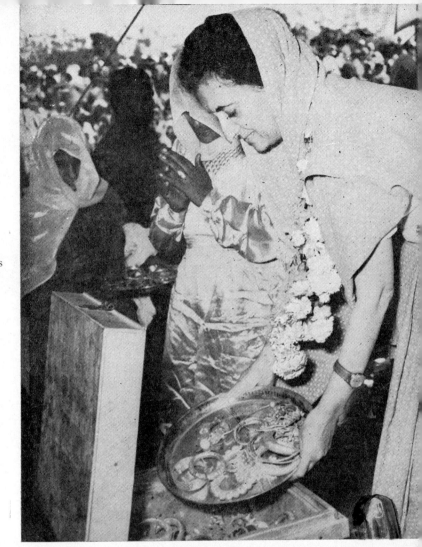

Accepting donations
of jewelery for the
defense fund, 1962

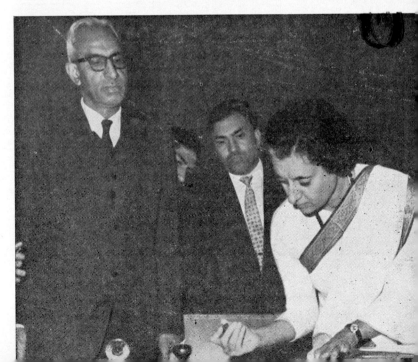

Indira as prime minister

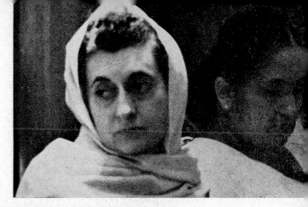

Indira, in mourning for father

Nehru's funeral
procession

the funeral. She sent Sanjay soon afterward to be an apprentice with Rolls-Royce. She was criticized a fair amount for this decision. Why, people argued, should she, Nehru's daughter, have found it necessary to send her sons abroad for education? When she was asked about this as prime minister her natural reaction was to burst out with, "I couldn't care less what people say. I thought it was necessary for my boys to go to England." But a moment later, as if she realized that she should learn to tailor her expression along more cautious lines, she added, "I am not saying I never care what people say. I am very concerned about the opinion of others and quite often they have been right and if they were I was quite willing to change what I had done or begun. In fact, I have changed things but, in this case, it wouldn't be right. It doesn't mean that I am criticizing education here in India or that I consider it better there, but I think young people ought to travel abroad."[71]

She was keen on keeping her sons away from the political environment instead of training them for it. "Here my sons wouldn't have a chance to be independent," she remarked. "If they did something good, it would be exaggerated and if they ever did something which people didn't consider good, that would also be exaggerated. I sent them away because they are my sons."[72]

Her personal life ran evenly, skirting obvious involvement. Rumor tried hard to read meaning in familiarity with colleagues, gossip fed eagerly on a stray remark, a vulnerable situation. But while her father was alive, her devotion to his care had affected one marriage, she could hardly be eager for another. When she became prime minister, she was "too busy" even generally as she said "to recall the past" or to create a more personal future. Passion seemed better tuned to an abstraction. During the brief period as minister of information she was comparatively free, but only comparatively more than before. Everything—leisure, music, reading, poetry, personal relationships—was secondary to one absolute: her public life. She seemed to have sublimated all ordinary desires into that essential fact of her being. The people still came devouring her hours, the issues still beckoned, smothering private wants. In 1965 she was forty-eight, and sensitive enough to resent that entire concentration of forces after her father's death which made her feel "left out" politically. She was unused to the shadows, and the reminders were too frequent.

Each occasion when she was the recipient of attention because of her father was an occasion that made her feel she owed a debt to the past, a memory, and its promises. If it was a documentary film made of her father like Russia's "To the Memory of a Great Son of India," it was she who officially received it from Russian Ambassador I.A. Benediktov. If it was a silk scroll embroidered with a part of Nehru's will, "a humble dedication to the champion of suffering mankind, the jewel of India," as it was termed by the artist, a well meaning, feudal maharani, it was Indira who was presented with it for the Nehru Museum. But she was interested in seeing her father's memory perpetuated in other, more practical ways, than by the statues that had begun to spring up all over India. She was forthright enough to declare at a function to unveil one that she thought this was wasteful expenditure and that the money would be better spent on working for the ideals Nehru had projected.[73] On the same trip typically, she inaugurated a massive waterworks and a building for a children's welfare organization.

On November 23, 1965, Indira was awarded Italy's Isabella d'Este Prize for "outstanding work in the field of diplomacy." She went to Rome to personally receive the prize, and came back five days later to hear encomiums from the Congress parliamentary party which met to felicitate her on the distinction. Shastri himself praised the two qualities that in private he recognized as being potentially competitive, that she was "exceedingly wise and tactful."

On December 31, 1965 Finance Minister Krishnamachari resigned owing to differences with Shastri. His replacement, Sachin Chaudhri, was ranked tenth in the cabinet. Indira's position, after the prime minister and Home Minister Nanda, rose to No. 3.

On January 3, 1966, Lal Bahadur Shastri left for Tashkent for summit talks with Ayub Khan of Pakistan as the result of Russia's first attempt to play a mediatory role between the two countries. Shastri determinedly took his ubiquitous dhoti to wear instead of the trousers or pantaloons suggested by Jan Sangh President Atal Bihari Vajpayee to be more suitable for the Tashkent cold. Shastri remembered Ayub's arrogant remark casting doubts about the capacity of a dhotiwallah to fight, and he would not have been human if he had not wanted to have an indirect dig at the Pakistan president by meeting him in that very dress, as victor. But he went in a spirit of peace. He hoped that Ayub would agree to eschew war as a means of solving problems between India and Pakistan. For three days personal cordiality fought with political rigidity. On January 7, there was a thaw. The following day saw a virtual deadlock because of Pakistan's insistence on including Kashmir in the discussion and India's vehement objection. On January 9, Premier Kosygin made personal efforts to save the talks. On January 10, Kosygin's "friendly persuasion" and compromise won out, and a nine-point pact was signed between Shastri and Ayub. In the evening they attended a state banquet given in their honor by Premier Kosygin.

"Khuda Hafiz [God be with you]," said Ayub to Shastri in farewell at the end.

"Khuda Hafiz," rejoined Shastri in the impeccable Urdu of a man from U.P. *"Acha hi ho gaya* [it was all to the good]," he added.

And Ayub replied: *"Khuda acha hi karega* [God will do only good]."[74]

The diminutive Indian was looking well at a moment in which his per-

sonal reputation as a man capable of fighting and a man capable of peace
was at its height.   Less than nine and a half hours later on January 11
Lal Bahadur Shastri was dead of heart failure.

The news reached Home Minister Nanda first. Indira had returned to
Delhi after another of her tours early on the tenth. At 1.30 the next
morning her secretary received a telephone call telling him that Shastri
had died, and that the home minister had gone to the home of the president.
He immediately informed Indira, who decided to join Nanda at Rashtrapati
Bhawan.   The only other minister to arrive there at the time was Sachin
Chaudhri. So around three in the morning Nanda as the seniormost minister
in the cabinet was sworn in as acting prime minister and Indira and Chaudhri
as part of the new council of ministers.   In spite of the shock and the
suddenness of Shastri's death, the process of succession was carried out
smoothly and without panic.   But the real succession was to begin once
again within a bare nineteen months.

This time there was no definable successor. The issue was an open one
between equals.   In the early cold pale hours of January 11, Indira knew
that she would not push herself forward, but if the future beckoned that
would be different.   Meanwhile, in spite of the recent bitterness, there was
the sorrow at losing yet another link with the past.   Shastri was one of
the few adults who had played with her as a child in her lonely hours at
Anand Bhawan.   He was the man she had sheltered in her house when the
police were after him in 1942. Politics destroyed so much of the personal.
She was sorry it had turned out that way. But now a flurry of thoughts
were charging the air with possibilities, political possibilities. She would not
let her mind rest on any one of them. She would be philosophic. She was
calm.   She would wait and see.

4. TRIUMPH

Gulzarilal Nanda, acting prime minister twice within two years was beginning to think that he deserved better than to serve as a substitute. He was the first to call Indira on the eleventh asking her if she intended to be a candidate. Her immediate impulse was to answer no. He then asked if she would support him. She got impatient and a little put off that he should have thought it necessary to have started canvassing so soon. She thought the question deserved wider participation and consideration in the context of the country's interest.[1] But Nanda cut almost a pitiful figure in his eagerness. She remembered how it had been even on the previous occasion, in 1964. "Nanda came to me and said he would like to continue for at least a month. He seemed so terribly keen that I made a special effort to wrench myself from the numbness that I felt and said to Kamaraj and the others, "Why not let him continue for a month or so, there can be no harm in this and he is so keen. They bawled me out for suggesting that sort of thing."[2] So this time she told him she would support him if the others also felt the same. It was a conditional offer, but the overeager Nanda took it as a promise. The same day Indira's supporters and workers among the all-important rank-and-file congressmen sought clarification and guidance from her in private. One of them, Vishwabandhu Gupta, editor of the Urdu daily *Tej* and son of the reputed nationalist, Deshbandhu Gupta, recalls that when they asked her that day if she would contest for the prime ministership, she replied, "If Kamaraj asks me, I will."

"So we decided to go ahead and start work anyway," says Gupta.[3]

Congress President Kamaraj was rushing back from Madras that morning. At the airport in Delhi when he was told of Nanda's conversation with Indira, he is supposed to have said, "Don't worry. Let's receive the body," adding significantly, "I have made up my mind."[4] Beyond that, he would say nothing. In the evening after the funeral, when Indira met him and conveyed her conditional support for Nanda he said, "Just leave things as they are; I will consult with many people."[5] His mind was made up in favor of Indira from the very beginning as he revealed later, but he preferred to work it out tactically to create a movement in that direction. He remembered, as he stated later, that Nehru had remarked to him when he came back from Bhuvaneshwar "I've great confidence in Shastri," and that he had rejoined with, "I've great confidence in your daughter." But Shastri was the more natural choice then, and Kamaraj was just as sure that it must be Indira now. "I believe in a certain amount of aristocracy in the background for a politician, most of them have no background," he is reported to have confided to some people during the second succession. "If anybody is worth the Indian crown as P.M. it is Mrs Gandhi."[6]

Discussions, feelers, and meetings on the eleventh and twelfth of January threw up no candidate for a consensus except Nanda. From the evening of the twelfth to the night of the thirteenth, there was a concerted bid by the party pressure group called the syndicate to induct Kamaraj as the best man "in the election year." To that Kamaraj's answer was a categorical no. On the afternoon of the eleventh Nanda had told Madhya Pradesh Chief Minister D. P. Mishra that if he himself could not continue as prime minister the only person he would agree to serve under would be Mrs Gandhi. On the afternoon of the twelfth after the funeral, West Bengal party boss Atulya Ghosh and the Rajasthan chief minister discussed the possibility of Mrs Gandhi being the second choice if Kamaraj refused to stand. She had made it clear that it was all up to the Congress leaders, which meant that she had declared herself available. To her supporters, of course, she had already said so. By Wednesday, Kamaraj's confabulations with chief ministers, state leaders, central ministers, and the ubiquitous syndicate made it apparent that candidate apart, the general consensus was in favor of unanimity.

Morarji Desai's categorical affirmation at the juncture that no matter who the other candidate was, he would stand and "take the contest to the open vote" did three things. The anti-Morarji feeling—due to Morarji's political and personal rigidity—was too strong for him to be chosen unanimously, so the ranks closed in against him. Desai's determination to stand removed Nanda as a possible contestant because of the realization that he was not strong enough to win in a straight contest against Desai in the Congress parliamentary party and certainly would not be able to carry the Congress image in the general elections set for 1967. Thus it was imperative to find a candidate who could. On Thursday afternoon, Chavan and Indira decided they would back each other in the event of either of them getting majority support, and the same day Indira apparently told D. P. Mishra: "If there is near unanimity and Kamaraj asks me, I would stand."[7] By Thursday night, Kamaraj was further convinced that it must be Indira because he found, led dexterously into this position by his own clever maneuvering, that most chief ministers were for her. Then he suggested to her himself that she should not meet anyone or make a statement for the next two days. "Then we knew" (that he wanted her) recalled a member of the press corps eagerly looking for signs of the Congress president's obvious preference.

On the fourteenth the working committee took merely forty-five minutes to decide upon the procedure regardless of candidates: election of the leader by the parliamentary party on January 19, 1965, would be by secret ballot. They still hoped for unanimity and instructed the Congress president to seek a consensus until the last. But with Morarji adamant, resolved to fight, and vetoing the very idea, nobody had much hope. Now it only remained for those who wished to keep him out to join forces against him. "Will it be smooth sailing?" The question was put to D. P. Mishra after the meeting. He forecast cleverly, "It will not be smooth sailing, it will be smooth selling."[8]

He had probably defined his own role in his mind. For on the same day, reportedly inspired by Kamaraj himself, Mishra seized the initiative and called a number of chief ministers together. The result was that eight chief ministers affirmed their support for Indira. By the morning of the fifteenth there were ten and then twelve, and "with this development," commented the *Hindustan Times*, "Mrs Gandhi's election as the Congress party leader and the country's prime minister should be considered assured," to which the other papers added the next day, when more chief ministers joined the popular momentum, "Indira Gandhi likely to be next prime minister" (*Times of India*); Argus in the *Indian Express*, "Bar the tumult and the shouting, it looks as if Indira is in." And halfway across the world *The Washington Post* recorded, "It now appears that Mrs Gandhi has become one candidate who promises to pull in enough party votes to stop one announced and most determined candidate Morarji Desai."[9] *The Baltimore Sun* saw even more in it and concluded that "in some ways the contest between Mrs Gandhi and Desai would be a clash between the left and the right wings of the Congress party—though both labels involve a considerable amount of oversimplification."[10]

In fact, although the issue did emerge as that in the final sense, the immediate considerations were various: for Kamaraj, with a comparatively leftist orientation then, it was also a choice in the party context, for as Congress president he had to have a perspective on the Congress chances in the general elections in 1967, for which he had to have a candidate with a "vote-getter" image. For the syndicate, normally considered a rightist group which therefore should have been on the side of Morarji, the question of power balances mattered more. They wanted someone malleable whom they could control, and rallied toward Indira only when they were presented with a *fait accompli* by Kamaraj and the chief ministers. The chief ministers, with a gradual power shift to the states since Nehru's time, were anxious to consolidate that equation: Morarji's authoritarianism spelled danger, Indira's cooler judgment, a promise.

The Congress parliamentary party, fearful and resentful that the high command, the syndicate, and the chief ministers were appropriating all the decision-making, was glad that a contest ensured that the ultimate choice would have to be its own. For all that, with Kamaraj setting the lead quietly and surely with a view perhaps to re-establishing also his own supremacy which he had lost in the previous six months during the prime ministership of Shastri, there was a difference. It was a choice between one generation and another, between one image and another. Morarji, seventy-one, had all the personal asceticism and political conservatism to go with his years. Indira, forty-eight, modern in outlook and cosmopolitan in taste, had the white-hot sympathy for the underprivileged which could make leadership in one-half of the world in the twentieth century meaningful.

Five groups, however, were involved thereafter in the canvassing for Indira. Apart from the chief ministers, there were the press, the local leaders, those associated with the Nehru family, Congress workers, and, of course, the Pradesh Congress Committees. What were the issues that had to be faced when electioneering for her? According to one of her workers: "One, that she was a woman. 'She may be intelligent, experienced and all that, but after all, she's a woman,' some of the people would say. But if you pursued the point further, they had nothing to add. Second, that she was the daughter of Nehru. That was a disadvantage as much as an advantage. People felt that that shouldn't automatically ensure her the election."[11]

But the fact of her being a woman did ensure her one thing—extra party support among fellow women parliamentarians. "I know of a number of women who in spite of their group affiliations [inside or outside the Congress party] voted for Indiraji," says Mukul Banerjee. "They said, 'We know how much she has done for women so we'll vote for her'."[12]

A lighter aspect of the traditionalist versus modernist conflict was an example given by veteran M.P. Ansar Harvani to the question of whether her being a woman came up as an issue in the election.

"No, nobody thought of it that way," he said. "The only member who objected was a Naga M.P. from Assam. When I told him that the first thing Morarji Desai would do would be to ban liquor, he decided to vote for Indira!"[13]

Though from the sixteenth onward, people began to pour into her home to congratulate Indira, the actual election still held all the promise of intense drama. The chief ministers might come out openly on her side, but the legislators were free to vote any way they liked, especially when it was to be by secret ballot. Morarji, after an initial period of cool aloofness, had plunged into active canvassing. His appeal to the members of the parliamentary party from various states not to be intimidated by the indirect pressure, as he called it, from above, could influence the trend of the voting to some extent. To counter this was the appreciation among observers from both sides, who were continuously counting and computing the probable alignments, that members would be unwilling to jeopardize their own chances of getting tickets for the next general elections by defying the declared leanings of their leaders. Kamaraj was taking no chances. He apparently told his supporters canvassing for Indira, "Even the aunt [Vijayalaxmi] may vote against her. Have to be careful about the rest. See that they are not bought over overnight."[14] He himself decided to meet Morarji for a last attempt to persuade him to withdraw only on the eve of the election. But he set in motion another campaign that was guaranteed to secure the chief ministers' stand. He encouraged the M.P.s from individual states to meet and adopt resolutions supporting Mrs Gandhi. It began on Sunday the sixteenth with the Punjab M.P.s. By Tuesday, there was a formidable list, extending into certain majority for Indira Gandhi the next day. It broke the back of Morarji's claim that he was "the M.P.s' candidate" and Mrs Gandhi only the "Congress president's candidate."

Even Vijayalaxmi, seething perhaps with ironic fury at a comparatively unknown niece staking so successfully a claim that a more famous aunt might have made, was led to say, "We Nehrus are very proud of our family. When a Nehru is chosen as prime minister the people will rejoice." And then about her niece's capacity, she agreed she had the ability. "Now she needs experience.   With a little experience she will make as fine a prime minister as we could wish for.   When she becomes prime minister a new younger leadership should emerge in India." But what she remarked further was by no means calculated to carve her a place in the future prime minister's heart any more than her attitudes had previously done in a niece, for Vijayalaxmi chose to pick on an aspect that Indira had long outgrown from her teens and disproved by her hectic political pace later, but which propaganda when it wanted to be adverse chose to emphasize.   "She is in very frail health indeed," said Vijayalaxmi, adding with what nobody could help seeing was vindictive sarcasm "but with the help of her colleagues she will manage."[15]

Of the record number of world television teams that were converging upon India's capital to cover a succession which they thought held even more interest than the one after Nehru, Dutch television began the same morning by commenting in an interview with Indira that it seemed she would be prime minister the following wednesday.

"It is too early to say," Indira was cautious.   Then came the question that was to be asked of her repeatedly wherever she went and whoever she met.

"What do you think of a woman becoming prime minister of 480 million people, the world's biggest democracy?"

And her answer, which was always to be as rational.   "It is a question of one being a human being, not a man or a woman."

And in spite of his diehardism in other matters, it was a revelation of the total political emancipation of attitude in India that when Morarji was asked the next day what his reaction would be if a woman became prime minister, he could reply simply, "I have no sex consideration in this matter."[16]

On the eighteenth a day before the crucial meeting in the central hall of India's Parliament, Morarji Desai personally contacted one by one, with single-minded determination, all the M.P.s who had gathered in Delhi by then.   It was an unprecedented involvement for a man who claimed to disdain the mechanics of politics.   But Indira kept herself in the background and relied on her workers for such obvious confrontations.   At 6 P.M. on the eighteenth Kamaraj called on Morarji at his house.   Asked immediately after the meeting what he had said, Kamaraj replied, "I told him, as far as I know, the majority of the members of Parliament were with Mrs Gandhi."

"What was Mr Desai's reply?"

"He said he had the majority."

"Did you formally ask Mr Desai to withdraw?"

"Yes, but he said he was going to contest."[17]

Desai put it differently. "The only thing he [Kamaraj] said was that we should work for unanimity and I said yes.   There can be unanimity but 'how' is the question.   Does that mean I should withdraw?   He silently conveyed that that may be so.   Then I said that I would like to know which of the two candidates was superior and who is the best candidate. What crime have I committed, I asked him."[18]

Kamaraj came away tight-lipped and grim. Later the same evening Desai issued a letter elaborating upon his commitments to all the members of Parliament gathered in Delhi asking them to support him in the contest the following day. But Indira merely said, "My beliefs and convictions are well known to my fellow party members. There is no need for reaffirmation on my part." She refused to comment on the letter. "I have served the country in my own humble way in various capacities and situations. It is for members to judge and decide. I can only say that I shall continue to serve the ideals we all cherish."[19]

Morarji was determined to fight. "I am doing the right thing in a democratic way," he said.[20]

"I am not afraid to lose, and I am not afraid to win," said Indira.[21]

The next morning by ten o'clock, the central hall was seething with expectancy. The crucial meeting of the Congress parliamentary party was scheduled for 11 A.M. and the corridors were beginning to spin with last-minute calculations and varying predictions of the voting pattern. The crowds, the newspapermen, the television teams, the people outside were caught in the drama of a contest for the prime ministership of a country of 480 million human beings, that one of these involved was a woman, and that she was the daughter of Nehru, the man who had laid the foundations of the country she might have to rule.

At 10.40, accompanied by Nanda and Subhadra Joshi, Indira arrived wearing a white sari and a brown shawl. She was presented with a bouquet, but Subhadra took one red rose and pinned it on her shawl, and the gesture took on a symbolic meaning. The red rose was Nehru's favorite flower, which he invariably wore in his buttonhole against a beige, black, or an immaculate white sherwani. He wore it out of aesthetic necessity, he explained once to an inquiring fan, to compensate for the drabness of khadi. The single red rose became in the last feverish pre-election moments a charismatic symbol of continuity. Indira was surrounded by people as she walked toward the hall. Five minutes later Morarji went in, and greeted everybody with folded hands. Indira, who had been detained outside by insistent photographers, walked in and immediately went up to Desai and shook hands with him. The members of the house, tuned to a high pitch of excitement, clapped at what they thought was another example of the Nehru style. The dais was packed, the galleries were full, and there was a record number of 526 of the total 550 Congress M.P.s in both houses present.

At 11 A.M. party president Kamaraj got up and made a few introductory remarks, and then, "I request you to propose the name of the candidates." Hanumanthaiya, a former chief minister of Mysore, went up to the dais and proposed Morarji's name. He was seconded by Rajasthan member Tikaram Paliwal. But it was acting Prime Minister Nanda, having hoped to achieve the honor himself but reconciled to the only other person he was willing to stand aside for, who came forward and proposed Indira's name. He was seconded by Sanjivya Reddy, the man who was to become the subject of a raging controversy between the syndicate and Indira later.

At this early point an effort was made by Rajya Sabha member Diwan Chaman Lal to make the first vote unanimous. He rushed up and called for unanimity for Indira, but from a section of the house, fiercely committed to each side, there came protests of no, no. The members were then called up. The votes began to be cast, and as the minutes began to tick slowly by, the tension began to rise, and outside, the crowds began to shift restlessly.

At 1 P.M. the voting ended, and the box which had been lying in front of Kamaraj was taken away for the counting to begin. Everybody waited. After a while Defense Minister Chavan jokingly asked the minister for parliamentary affairs, Satya Narain Sinha, to sing a song or relate an anecdote to break the suspense. Sinha answered wryly, *"Bhookey bhajan na hoye Kripala* [None can sing on an empty stomach, O merciful one]."[22] But just after three the returning officer, G.S. Pathak, was seen pushing toward the dias, and there was the absolute finality of the words, "I declare Mrs Indira Gandhi elected." The verdict was Indira 355 votes, Morarji Desai 169. She had won by a two-thirds majority, and the country was hers. For a moment she could not take it in as the towering lifesize portraits of India's national heroes, Mahatma Gandhi, Tilak, Gokhale, the flamboyant Motilal Nehru, and her father looked down from the circular walls of the hall. And she, to be a part of it! But then the applause broke, garlands were heaped around her neck, and a torrent of good wishes swirled in her ears. She made another but this time very traditional gesture. She went to Morarji, and as elder sought his blessing.

Outside an insistent screech rent the air: "Is it a girl or a boy?" "It's a girl," rang back Satya Narain Sinha's triumphant cry.

Serene, smiling, confident, and moved, Indira made her first speech as leader of her party and prime minister designate, first in Hindi then in English, from the platform that had been used for seventeen years by her father. At home she had her first confrontation with the press in her new capacity. The cameras kept clicking, people kept coming, garlands, bouquets and flowers invaded her house, and Indira on this day of her greatest certitude, still had her doubts.

"Have you read that poem of Robert Frost? Of the man who didn't want to be king?" she asked Narayana Menon when he went to congratulate her that evening, and she murmured the beginning, relieved to be able to make a literary reference to someone who could understand:

> *The King said to his son: Enough of this*
> *The kingdom's yours to finish as you please*
> *I'm getting out tonight. Here, take the crown;*

But the Prince drew away his hand in time
To avoid what he wasn't sure he wanted.

"I feel just like that," she added ruefully.[23]

It was a moment of withdrawal, like the eye of stillness in the center of a storm. But total involvement soon prevailed. She was alive to everything around, to things other than politics even at the moment of her greatest achievement. She remembered that she had been told that day that Krishna Kripalani, her old teacher at Shantiniketan and then secretary of the Sahitya Akademi, had been taken ill. She insisted that Narayana take him some flowers immediately on her behalf. "In fact," recalls Menon, "when I walked out of the room, people remarked that I was the only one who seemed to be taking flowers out rather than in!"[24]

There had been a moment, too, in the morning when this self-containment, this cool graciousness, this unflurried sophistication had deserted her. She had driven to *Shantivana* early, escaping the crowds, and then to Tin Murti before the museum's opening hours. She saw the rooms exactly as they had been, perpetuating the image of Nehru for that endless stream of people who came during the day. For her it was an image of the glittering, controversial, yet fruitful, years of her own life. She stood briefly near the certificate of Bharat Ratna (India's highest civil award) which had been given her father and the row of medallions which gleamed in remembrance. But in the bedroom near Jawaharlal Nehru's photograph, a man there gave her some *kafoor*. She lit it. The act of homage, remembrance, dedication, and love that it implied, the tension of the last few days, the power yet the enormity of the task that was to be hers, sheer sentimentality, whatever it was, or, like any daughter bemoaning a beloved father, Indira's eyes filled with tears. Rajen Bajpai, Indira's old co-worker from Allahabad who accompanied her there, was both moved and surprised. She had never seen Indira in that state, never certainly seen her cry, but the words of consolation she uttered happened to meet the refrain in the other woman's heart. "This is no time to cry," Indira heard her say. "You're doing what he had to do."[25]

Sentimental, even irrational, human, the other side of the reserved public face. Slightly superstitious. Susceptible to mystic symbols.

"Is my sari crumpled?" she asked Rajen Bajpai when she saw her in the morning.

"If you like you can change it," tactfully replied the other.

"I was wearing this the day I heard I had been chosen Congress president," Indira rejoined quietly, "so I am wearing this today also."[26]

It was a white sari with a black border. Round her neck was the string of black beads, another talisman, which was never missing, as part of her ensemble on a critical, significant occasion. The statue of Ganesh, the elephant god of the Hindu pantheon, the remover of all obstacles, stood at the entrance to the narrow hall of her house, and there was always an offering of flowers lying at the base. Soon after she was chosen leader and prospective prime minister she called on Lalita Shastri. It was a delicate gesture of formality from that part of her that was responsive to every subtle play in the practical world she knew so well. But the other part took her for benediction and succor to Jhoosi, across the Ganga, to a camp there for holy people—to Anandmayee—mother, saint, friend, and spiritual mentor.

In the summer of 1927, Motilal Nehru had written to Krishna, his daughter: "You seem to have turned into quite a little politician, but do not think being a girl will in any way be a handicap to you. Many women have taken as great a part in the uplift of their country as any man has done and some have distinguished themselves much more than men. It is all a question of one's feeling toward one's country and how seriously one applies oneself to the work of uplift. There is no bar of sex—on the contrary, a determined woman's influence is much greater than a man can ever sway. So there is every chance for you. You must remember that as a true politician patriotism is in your blood and unless you actively suppress it, it is bound to assert itself sooner or later."[27]

He might have said the same to Indira, his granddaughter. The former toyed with, the latter proved his contentions. But the important part is that those were the ideas that nourished the seeds of Indira's growth. No wonder then that when she became prime minister, she was irritated by the question about being a woman prime minister. Srimavo Bandaranaike, the only other woman in the world to have been prime minister before Indira, and significantly enough also of another Asian country, Ceylon, did not react the same way. When she was asked when she visited India in 1964 how she felt about being the only woman prime minister, she just smiled. "I have got used to it now, being among so many men. It was difficult in the beginning."[28]

Indira, on the other hand, would not admit the validity of the question itself. Her contention was brusque and simple. "I am a person with a job," she said.[29]

Her elaboration on this later was even more pointed. "I do not think a person who is head of state should think in terms of himself or herself as belonging to any group whether it is sex, religion, or caste. If the people accept you as leader of the nation, that is all that matters."[30]

Indian editorial comment, conditioned by then to accepting women in all kinds of high posts from ambassador to president of a shipping company to governor, confined its arguments to the ability, aside from considerations of sex, of the woman who was going to be prime minister of India. The people's reaction was varied but nobody could overlook the fact that the psychological climate in Indian society had made it possible for the populace to put its faith in a woman. The world was intrigued. Woven into its cool, political analysis was the appreciation that an exotic element had been added to the drama of politics. Women everywhere rejoiced. Mrs Patsy T. Mink, a congresswoman from Hawaii, affirmed in the U.S. House of Representatives that Mrs Gandhi's election made her and women generally feel "fully an inch taller."[31]

She thought it remarkable that Indira was chosen not merely by ordinary people, the masses, who might be expected to go by the glamor and charisma of a legendary name, but by political professionals like party bosses and seasoned parliamentarians who would have much harder criteria.

"It is nothing short of sensational that Asia, where women are still emerging from bondage, should have produced the modern world's first two women heads of government," cried the *New York Herald Tribune*.[32] "Woman with the toughest jobs of them all," said the *Washington Evening Star*.[33] "It is a great and unprecedented thing," remarked *Azang* of Iran[34] while Tunisia's *L'Action* stated: "The fact that she is a woman was not taken into consideration. It is a good example to the Third World, which is unfortunately inclined to believe in misogyny."[35] *The Economist* (Britain) predicted that she was a woman of strong will who would not be a "front woman of queen makers."[36] And *The New York Times*: "Mrs Indira Gandhi is going to be a very interesting and unusual prime minister of India. This is not simply because she is a woman and the daughter of Jawaharlal Nehru. She is very much a person in her own right with positive ideas that will not necessarily coincide with those of her father or her predecessor." Referring to the support of the political bosses and "king-maker" Kamaraj's virtual elevation of her to the prime ministership, it observed dryly, "But those who chose her are likely to find that they picked a master and not a servant."[37]

John Grigg in *The Guardian* [Britain] stated, "Probably no woman in history has assumed a heavier burden of responsibility and certainly no country of India's importance has ever before entrusted so much power to a woman under democratic conditions. She has a sharp mind, a strong will and a dedicated spirit. If she makes a success of the job she will deal what may be a knock-out blow to lingering notions of male superiority."[38] For *Pravda*, in Moscow, she was "daughter and comrade-in-arms of Jawaharlal Nehru," and as Premier Kosygin assured her in his congratulatory message, "In the Soviet Union you are greatly respected as India's prominent political figure and stateswoman and we are convinced that the government headed by you will follow along the road of Jawaharlal Nehru and realize his ideals." At home, one of India's most trenchant columnists, "S.M." in national affairs [*Hindustan Times*], always sharp, sardonic, sarcastic, and without illusions seemed on that occasion to break into a song of eulogy. "She is a positivist, a woman of action, impatient of delay and red tape. In everything she has said and done, there is a deep strand of humanism, the kind of humanism that looks for real improvement in terms of popular well-being and is not impressed by the doctrinaire application of theories that do not work.... The era that is now opening can well be the most exciting in India's recent history.... Her assumption of leadership is not merely a change of person; it is a change of generation, a change of quality, mood, and pace. She is old enough to have suffered and participated in the agonies and adventure of the generation who fought for independence but not old enough to be a stranger to the dreams and aspirations of the inheritors of the post-independence period. With her more than any other person who could have been thought of in the role of prime minister, the young generations of India will feel a sense of identity and partnership.'' It was a Kennedyian situation and the comparison was not slow in being taken.

The Nehru name, long political training, years of familiarity with international politics, a modern mind, dynamic and determined, with firm convictions of what India should be, she was in repeated political assessments recognized to have a distinct left-of-center bias. But the most perceptive comment from someone who obviously knew the intensively pragmatic, undogmatic, and therefore the challenging adjustments that could be met by what was also a practical mind came from Selig Harrison, writing in *The Washington Post:* "Most signs suggest that Mistress Gandhi is best judged not by the Western right-left standards but as an Asian nationalist in a hurry. This is a familiar type one usually associates with the stereotyped images of intense bespectacled young men carrying placards in the streets. Indira Gandhi with her regal good looks and cosmopolitan tastes, her searching eyes and almost flirtatious banter does not fit the conventional image. But behind the cool sophisticated facade there is a restless impatience to see India arrive."[39]

Just after 2 P.M. on January 24, 1966, Indira arrived at the oak-paneled Ashoka Room of Rashtrapati Bhawan for her investiture as head of government along with her new cabinet. There was a glittering assembly of onlookers. There were her two aunts, Krishna Hutheesing and Vijayalaxmi Pandit. Rancor was forgotten on the occasion, and she gave them both a spontaneous hug.

At 2.15 P.M. Indira Priyadarshini Nehru Gandhi was sworn in as prime minister of India.

She took the oath by the strictly neutral phrase, "I solemnly affirm," and not the religious one, "I swear by God." But modernity still blended with tradition. A cream-colored sari was draped around her with casual sophistication, but there was the auspicious vermilion mark on her forehead. And for luck, the string of black beads.

She had precisely thirteen months and twenty-four days to prove that her performance could match her promise. The general elections were scheduled for February 1967 and the new leader of the party would be chosen after that. If she failed in these thirteen months she would have the dubious satisfaction of having filled an innocuous page in Indian history. If she succeeded, if her leadership justified a more substantial and lasting mandate in 1967, she could perhaps mold the nation she had vowed to serve, and make history, the dream her father had instilled in her in childhood. She had to make a choice. She could give a radical spur to the policies she had been advocating and establish her image with such rapid force among the people that the entrenched elite or party diehards in the organization could either be overwhelmed into acquiescence, or be provoked into a hostility which could throw her out of power before she could do anything. The other alternative was to play everything in low key, soft-pedal controversy, compromise wherever it was absolutely essential, and use the interim period to so strengthen her support in the organization that it would guarantee her a free hand for what she wanted ultimately to do.

She had the advantage of taking over with a fund of goodwill: party bosses at home were satisfied that they had settled upon a candidate who would be amenable to reason and hopefully, as they thought, even pressure, while opinion abroad was prepared to go a long way to accommodate a liberal, Oxford-educated socialist, and essentially Western-oriented leader at the head of a democracy. She had a national image which could carry the Congress in the elections and a nonregional commitment which could still partisan fears within the party. Both at home and abroad, she was Nehru's daughter as well. But she had no illusions. The disadvantages, too, were palpable. The party coterie which had initiated support for her, including Kamaraj, would expect its pound of flesh in the form of advice given and loyalties demanded. The Nehru inheritance could rebound. Expectations would be greater and a comparison each time would not be with a lesser person than Nehru himself. The contest that gave her the victory marked for the first time an explicit division in Congress ranks. The conflicting claims, pressures and, yes, possibly threats and the constant vigilance and effort to maintain a balance would do the very things she hated, slow the pace she wished to accelerate, delay decision-making and perhaps force a nauseous status quo.

She had a taste of what was to come almost immediately. She had wanted to make a near clean sweep of the old cabinet, bring in new faces, fresh blood, stronger spirit to put sinew into sagging Congress intentions. She had wanted a cabinet bearing the stamp of a new direction. She wanted home, for instance, removed from Nanda's then frustrated image. She was prepared to let him be number two in the cabinet but as minister without portfolio. But he had gone running to Kamaraj, and Kamaraj had urged—it amounted to insistence—that there should be no big changes until after the elections! The others had enjoined upon the retention or the promotion of their favorites but what she had been able to do was to bring in Asoka Mehta, G.S. Pathak, Fakhruddin Ali Ahmed, and Jagjivan Ram, also comparatively old but who had become staunch allies toward the latter part of the succession drama, and new entrants in the second line as ministers of state and deputy ministers. She had dropped only two—A. K. Sen, law minister, and Humayun Kabir, minister for petroleum and chemicals. The major portfolios remained. Y.B. Chavan, defense; Swaran Singh, external affairs; Subramanian, food; and Sachin Chaudhri, finance.

"It is a pity," commiserated the *Hindustan Times*, "that Mrs Gandhi is not allowed to face the formidable task that lies ahead of her as India's new prime minister with a team entirely of her own choice deployed according to her own will." Nevertheless, it noted that continuity had not triumphed entirely at the cost of change. "There is enough new blood at all levels to indicate that a change is at work, a change principally of pace and style in both of which directions there was room for improvement. There is some shedding at all levels of what will be agreed was dead wood. Though the process could well have gone further, Mrs Gandhi's first cabinet has the appearance of being workmanlike." It added consolingly, "She must not allow the initial difficulties in the formation of her team to discourage her. Her great asset is the support she has in the country. It will ensure for her sufficient authority in the discharge of her onerous responsibilities."[40]

She was not the type to get discouraged. Problems were not likely to overawe her because she was conditioned by "having lived," as she said, "in the midst of crises from the earliest childhood." But her operational style was likely to be conditioned both by her impetuosity as well as her hardy common sense. For if she could say, "I prefer to take up difficulties head-on. I have done this since childhood. This is my nature," she could add at the same time, "As P.M. I cannot be foolhardy but we have to carry the people."

Her immediate tasks were indeed formidable. For one, the implementation of the Tashkent agreement in the face of mounting criticism at home for what certain people had already begun to call the "betrayal" by Shastri. In fact, a raging disillusionment over that part of the agreement which called for a withdrawal of forces to the pre-August 5 position and consequently the surrender of the hard-won Haji Pir Pass, had been stilled temporarily by the shock of Shastri's death. She would now have to bear the brunt of its implementation. Ram Manohar Lohia, the Samyukta Socialist party leader, old and vitriolic critic of the Nehrus, both father and daughter, had already issued a warning. "If Mrs Gandhi withdraws from Haji Pir, she must understand well that nobody will allow her to throw the responsibility on her predecessor. The praise or blame will be entirely hers."[41] She had made it clear in her first policy statement after being chosen leader she would implement the agreement. China's intermittent border irritants and the danger they spelled, however, would make it even more difficult to abandon a dominant military advantage gained on one side.

In addition there was the threat of famine, following a drought. The economy had been badly hurt by the strains imposed on it by the India-Pak war. America had suspended aid to both countries, and India, which got more economic than military help, was consequently at a greater disadvantage. As late as December 1965, when she had not yet become prime minister, Indira had made quite an emotional plea for creating conditions in the country which could make it possible to do without aid even if if it was aid as loan repayable with interest. "Unless this is done we cannot really be independent," she had affirmed. She thought India was at the crossroads and if in trying to solve its difficulties it joined hands with one country or the other, it would be weakened: nonalignment therefore was a guarantee of freedom.[42] Nothing had happened since then to make her change her mind. Just before she was elected leader, she was interviewed by the BBC for "Panorama." One pointed question was whether her "pronounced left-wing views" would affect relations with the United States. Her answer was more practical than idealistic:

"I don't see the world divided into left and right. I think most of us are in the center and in a country like India where the basic problem is one of poverty and of trying to convince the average man that we are on his side you have to be more or less in the center and try to keep as many people with you as possible."[43]

As to the question about the balance she would like to see struck between the U.S. and the Soviet Union the reply was consistent with the others: "We hope we will continue to be friendly with both."[44]

Nevertheless, there were nuances even within neutralism which made the course she would actually take as prime minister intriguing. "Never has the Western world so held its breath over the will and intentions of a woman as it now does over the new prime minister of India," cried out *The Washington Post* in suspense in the person of columnist William S. White. It was understood that the Shastri administration had been under pressure by America and the World Bank to liberalize its economic policies. It was also recognized that because Shastri had succumbed, agreed, or deferred to them—depending on how you looked at it—to some extent, Indira had become resentful and had begun to criticize this move away from the Nehru line. Shastri's "pro-U.S. tilt to neutralism" as it was called by Western observers and the "stronger private enterprise flavor to mix" had made Indira react angrily at one stage: "Where is non-alignment? Are our policies socialist? India has swerved from the right path!"[45]

What would she do when she had to meet the exigencies of problems head on? There was always a difference between arguing from inside or outside government. She was sensitive to throwing open the Indian economy to foreign private investment on terms which might contain a nonsocialistic bias. Yet she was "closely identified," as Selig Harrison pointed out, "with a group of modern-minded politicians and officials who have been chaffing at the cautious Shastri approach to programs for controlling the population, stepping up food production and streamlining administrative procedures, all high on the U.S. priority list."[46]

If her basic impulse was to be economically idealistic—"any sincere program to serve the people has necessarily to be socialistic"[47] —and proudly
national—"interdependence in the world was essential but India had learned
'the hard way' to stand on its feet"[48]—her approach was to be a hard
professional one, and it is reasonable to assume that she was guided at
the outset by what she reiterated later: "No mere 'ism' will help, not even
pragmatism.   We can succeed only if we have a basic faith in our people and
in our own abilities and if we have a clear view of the future.   In everything
we do we must ask two questions: Does it enlarge or narrow the inequalities in our society?   Does it make us more self-reliant or less?"[49]   It was
obvious that she would not be ideological at the cost of practical or
democratic necessity. Her first months as prime minister therefore confounded the leftists who expected a bias as it were in their favor as much as her
tenure as Congress president had confounded the rightists when she had
cracked down so ruthlessly on the communists.

   She soon came up against a harsh reality which hardly left her any option.
The day she was sworn in, the U.S. budget was presented by President
Johnson to Congress. Though there was provision for resumption of
assistance to both India and Pakistan on a scale which made them the biggest
beneficiaries of American foreign aid, there was a condition attached which
made it plain that aid would go faster to those who would plow it into schemes
for immediate relief of social ills like education, health, agriculture, and
social welfare, "the critical industry" as it was termed, rather than into huge
industrial complexes which would yield results much later. For Johnson,
the new priorities came as part of his "great society" concept of economic
development. For Indira it meant temporary relief but a setback in the
progress toward India's self-sufficiency. Comparatively minor welfare
projects could be undertaken, for instance, under the country's own financial
impetus. But it was for major industrial development, technical assistance,
and foreign credits and the like, that India had to look for resources outside.
The whole theme of Nehru's emphasis on heavy industrialization was the
theme of an effort toward a self-generating economy, to make India capable
of producing what it sought from outside, and free it ultimately from the
psychological and practical burdens of foreign dependency. It meant
imposing a restraint on the growth of the consumer society, but never a
complete denial even for a specified period. He had been too much of a
humanitarian for that. The result was that progress was slow in both the
spheres but certain values of human commitment remained.

   However, at this point drought, war, and insufficiency of food and financial
reserves upset that balance. The primary aim was to prepare for the threat
of famine and get the economy going again. The immediate task was to
to wring out the squelch from the Fourth Plan and give it a fresh resistance.
Almost the very first decision of Indira's government, as early as January 24
in fact, was to take a new look at the Fourth Plan. Her appointment of

Asoka Mehta as minister for planning indicated that she had every intention of giving planning—weak under Shastri—its old importance, but aid on a long-term basis was a factor that had to be adjusted to the internal realities of this emphasis. American wheat supplies had been comparatively regularized but India had to know how much and what else it was going to get, and on what terms. Indira as prime minister now felt the need to justify the role that aid-giving countries were playing in palliating India's scarcity ills.

"There is nothing wrong in accepting help," she stated in addressing her first mammoth public meeting in the capital as prime minister, "but to become complacent will be a serious mistake and can spell danger to the country's freedom."[50]

On March 27, she sallied forth as her country's pre-eminent representative to see if she could do the first and stave off the latter. She had written to President Johnson to say that she would like to visit America as soon as possible. It was understood that she had also made an urgent appeal for resumption of aid, pointing out that conditions did not allow a delay until her meeting with him. On February 16, Johnson called for the third of the meetings of diplomatic representatives of developed countries to discuss India's food crisis. Appreciative of the dimensions of the food shortage India was facing, he felt that a system of multilateral assistance from a consortium of countries should be worked. But Indira wanted to stop conjectures at home that she was going on a sellout to the United States. The visit was not linked with aid, she tried to say in Parliament before she left; it was a goodwill visit. But when Bhupesh Gupta persisted with arguments about possible American pressure through aid on India's stand on Vietnam, she said with dignity, "I shall not agree to anything which goes against our national interests."[51] "The whole misunderstanding arises," she reiterated in Parliament, "because the word 'aid' is a misleading word . . . foreign aid is by way of loans and we have been repaying the loan. The real objective of foreign aid is the ultimate elimination of aid."[52]

"I would rather prefer India to starve on her feet than live on her knees," rejoined the unbending Krishna Menon.[53] To this, Indira's reply seemed to be what she had already said to a less sophisticated audience at a civic reception held in her honor by the Delhi Municipal Corporation. "Whatever aid we received is being paid back. People should not get dispirited or lose heart. Only living and dynamic nations have difficulties," and then added her famous statement, "the dead alone have no problems."[54]

The immediate problem she had to face with Indo-U.S. relations was quite different from that her father found in 1961 when John Kennedy's vision transcended the cold war stance to understand Nehru's. Nehru's nonaligned role had significant relevance to a world then polarized into two warring forces: the emphasis in their talks was therefore on clarification of Indo-U.S. stands on foreign policy tender spots, Berlin, Laos,

Pakistan, nuclear testing. Economic aid was understood both by Nehru and Kennedy to be a spur to the growth of underdeveloped areas and not a political string to jerk puppets into line.   Nehru's stature and Kennedy's sympathy ensured India's utilization of the aid according to its own sights.

By 1966, the world situation had changed.   Moscow and Washington had drawn closer, China had rocked Indian calculations about independent defense, but India's increased dependence on the United States for food and economic viability did not deter it from consistently voicing a politically independent stand on Vietnam which hurt the United States at its most vulnerable point.   Shastri had played down the Vietnam issue.   In fact, before he died he supposedly urged the Russians to take a less lenient view of the Chinese stakes in Vietnam and give America credit for wanting the problem solved, but India consistently stood for a nonmilitary as against America's military solution for this explosive problem.   Official American opinion had therefore begun to harden against such "recipient" nations which meant that aid could no longer be considered an adventure in international cooperation but a force in power politics.   Consequently, there were unwritten expectations of some returns, not only to give aid but to see how it was used when American surpluses were diminishing and American fears about Indian complacency were rising.

Indira, never rigid when it came to practical necessity, seemed to realize within a month of taking over as prime minister that controls for the sake of controls was not something she would like to sponsor as a program for economic action.   If the measures needed to revitalize Indian economy turned out to be those that coincided with American insistence she was not going to shy away from them merely so as not to invite a cry from the left.   The problem was to relate these steps to Indian imperatives and not to external "interference."   New Delhi's willingness to implement some of the recommendations of the World Bank's Bell Commission of 1965 along these lines, providing that aid-giving countries should bear the burden of the heavy cost of foreign exchange involved, removed Western reservations about India's doctrinaire concepts at the same time as it threw responsibility back at them.   Nevertheless, the signs were too obvious to be missed that, for Indira, pragmatic "adjustments" of policy were to be the pace-setters. Even on Vietnam, the issue for her became a practical one.   "So many people have been trying [for a solution]," she said, "and not getting anywhere, and unless we can think of something new, I don't think it serves any purpose to repeat the same thing."[55]

The mood was indeed propitious for a meeting with Lyndon Johnson. Personally he was no stranger, and he had shown an eagerness to arrive at a direct understanding with the new prime minister.   A rather abrupt suggestion for a postponement of a scheduled Shastri visit to America earlier had embittered Indian feeling.   Perhaps to offset that reaction he had had Ambassador Chester Bowles call on Indira the day she was sworn in to invite her to the United States. In Washington he sent for Indian Ambassador B. K. Nehru within hours of the latter's return from India and was supposed to have repeated with Johnsonian exuberance that if he heard from her on a Saturday that she could come he would be ready to welcome her the next day. The dates were fixed. She decided to spend two days in Paris en route on March 25 and 26 meeting President Charles de Gaulle and Prime Minister Georges Pompidou. She was to make the subsequent transatlantic flight by a commercial airline but when by the twenty-third a strike disrupting air traffic threatened to continue, Johnson offered to send his own plane to fetch her from Paris. It set the tone for a political meeting which triumphed over protocol.

Indira arrived in Washington looking beautiful, fresh from a Parisian hairdresser, with her black hair upswept and back-combed, its streak of gray adding dignity, the angularities of her face softened and the slight make-up she invariably used when on a visit abroad giving warmth to the delicate pallor of her face. Everyone was curious about her style.

"The staggering novelty of her position and her difficulties would have recommended her itself," stated Mary McGrory in the *Washington Evening Star*. "But she was something more. She was the real thing. She was good looking and obviously sensible and she knew when to smile and when to be quiet. Her approach in this complicated capital was unnervingly uncluttered. She was neither strident nor gushy. She seemed willing to let her appearance and the facts speak for themselves. Half the town rushed to the Indian Embassy Monday evening to see her at the crowded reception. Reporters who had been bellowing at foreign visitors for years lowered their voices considerably so as not to startle the fine-grained visitor from the east."[56]

Without coquetry but with a Cleopatra-like perspicuity which even her colleagues at home found rather effective, she could react as the situation demanded and turn it to her advantage with a smile or a frown. She chose to be crisp, terse, and coolly feminine, and Americans who had wondered if she would be mushy or sentimental about India's needs or self-righteous about the rights of poor countries, responded gallantly. No one more so than the president, who was totally charmed by this "exotically efficient creature in her flowing saris."[57] She combined tact with womanliness. Johnson was moved into playing the knight. She cited specific needs but she also asked "as prettily as possible." Her aim was not to persuade Johnson to give aid but help him devise a rational pattern which would secure congressional and public support. She gave specific examples to emphasize comparisons between America's rich and India's poor and between the poor and the very poor, quoting an Indian proverb: "I complained that I had no shoes until I met a man who had no feet." She was tactful on Vietnam but made her tact more personal by being sympathetic about Johnson's predicament. At the White House banquet "the great monopolist monopolized her" said one senator who could not get a word in edgewise. The next day she met leaders of the American Congress. By Tuesday evening Johnson had called twenty senators and told them that they must help "this little lady" and that he was asking Congress for immediate food shipments to India and for approval of a new program to help India's food needs. The senators, eager to restore America's generous image, gave their assent.

Indira in turn became quite eloquent in her farewell address at Washington before going for two days to New York: "We always seek the closer understanding of friends. We have found such an understanding. It is spring in Washington. I trust there will always be a touch of spring in Indo-American relations and that the friendship and goodwill between our two countries will ever blossom in profusion and brilliance." She made a speech at the New York Economic Club to a gathering of eight hundred top American businessmen the same night to say that India would welcome increased foreign investment and that she would even be willing to relax its policy control. Even before she went to the U.S., her government had been thinking in terms of liberalizing industrial licensing policy, and had agreed to liberalize marketing controls on fertilizers in return for American participation in setting up sorely needed fertilizer plants. She felt that India was in urgent need of fertilizer and that the government should try to get it, as she said, "whatever way it could."[58] In a major enunciation of policy she told the Federation of Indian Chambers of Commerce and Industry on March 12 that she was quite willing to relax unnecessary controls, that her government had no desire to be rigid and suggested that a review might be made of the role and the manner of working of controls in general. It was consistent with her view that given an end, the means must be practical. Wherever controls were productive they should be enforced, wherever unnecessary they should be discarded. She pointed out that controls over food grains, for instance, could not go under the existing circumstances, "In conditions of scarcity controls become necessary and even unavoidable," she emphasized, adding nevertheless, "But we must be careful that controls are not administered in a manner which tends to perpetuate scarcity conditions in which they are born." She was anxious, she said, to seek advice on the methods by which a higher rate of growth in the economy could be achieved as well as a better performance in every sector of the activity with lower investment or input of resources in general.[59] It was the same flexibility of approach which won her such a resounding response in America.

"Qualitatively, it seems to me," she explained to the New York Economic Club, "that much of our present difficulties in regard to food and foreign exchange are in large part a reflection of the fact that the rising expectations of the Indian people have overtaken the progress so far achieved. [But] I do fully agree with the plea for a rationalization and simplification of procedures for operating controls. In this area wherever the supply situation has improved, such as in steel or cement, we have loosened allocation procedures. We have also taken a number of steps to streamline the approval mechanism. Ultimately, liberalization of controls is possible only with a greater inflow of foreign aid or foreign investment. We do not believe in controls for their own sake and with an additional supply of foreign resources, we shall certainly be prepared to relax many of them." She expected the Western countries in turn to open their markets much more than they had done so far. Her plea for help was characteristically couched in terms which made it a call to adventure. "In the last century," she told the makers of modern America, "you tamed the Wild West. My appeal to you today is that in the next few decades you should allow yourselves to be tamed by the developing East."[60]

The next night she was principal guest of New York's business and cultural elite at the Plaza Hotel. She spoke on aid and Indo-Pak relations but it was in regard to China that she made her most effective point: India's progress under strictly democratic conditions and her resistance to China on a two-thousand-mile Himalayan frontier constituted noteworthy attempts to prevent China from taking over the crucial Afro-Asian forum and turning it into a political launching pad and as a revolutionary substitute of the United Nations. "India had earned little notice of thanks for this," she pointed out, and added, "But I venture to suggest that this is a contribution of high significance since it has the unique distinction of meeting China's challenge on the ground and plane of Peking's own choosing."[61]

Politics apart, she was thoroughly pleased with the warmth of her reception in the United States. But it was the personal rapport she achieved with Lyndon Johnson that marked the high point of her visit. It became the talk of Washington. After the first formal talks, he described her as a "proud, able, gracious lady." But at the end of the visit, he was almost in raptures.

"He [Johnson] showed a protective affection for her—you could see that," recalls B. K. Nehru. "He called me and told me 'we must get her elected—you tell me what to do—send her food, attack her. I'll do whatever you say.'"[62] Some photographs had been taken at the White House by the famous Japanese photographer Okamoto. While showing them to Nehru the enthusiastic Johnson kept exclaiming, "Isn't she beautiful?" He was quite taken by what he thought was a great resemblance between Indira and Ladybird Johnson.[63]

Indira in turn was impressed with what she called Johnson's genuine sympathy, and his "genuine desire to do something [about the Indian problem]." "As you know perhaps better than I do," she told John Galbraith, former ambassador to India, during a television interview in New York, "he is a man of action and he doesn't believe in thinking about a thing and putting it on the shelf. He believes immediately in acting on it."

She thought he appreciated the Indian problem in relation to international affairs, the importance of her achieving an economic breakthrough, and "the necessity of having a stable, united India."

On stopping in Paris, on her way to the U.S., Indira had made it a point to speak in French not only with de Gaulle and Pompidou but to the press on subjects ranging from famine to Vietnam. But the French, however susceptible to the wife of a president, like Jacqueline Kennedy, had strong male reservations about a woman who was herself a prime minister and tended to react more to her saris than to her views. Nevertheless, she came back to India via a meeting in Britain with Prime Minister Wilson and Premier Kosygin in Moscow, on a crest of self-confidence.

She pointed out before setting forth on these series of visits abroad that her aim was not to seek anything but understanding of India's problems, aims, and basic policies. Even editorial opinion at home, normally chary of handing out kudos, remarked on the fact that she had proved herself highly successful. "She had not been away long before it became evident," remarked an important national daily, "that she was giving the visit an entirely new dimension. In her talks with President de Gaulle in Paris she left no doubt that she was more concerned to point out what this country stood for in international affairs than to explain why it needed or deserved aid. This became even more apparent in Washington and New York.... She maintained this line subsequently in London and Moscow. There can be no doubt that she was right in her approach. At the end [of the visits] it is possible to feel that the countries that have been most directly involved in India's progress see in clearer light not only her problems but her opportunities and her ability to use these to the best advantage."[64]

If Indira's first hundred days in power spelled a personal triumph for her in international affairs, they were matched by a vigorous attempt at shaping events at home. In fact, in the first three months as prime minister, she showed a verve in office that had been missing when she became minister of information and broadcasting. She was infected by a sense of urgency. "Time is not with India," she told the National Press Club in Washington, "but against it. With the increase in population we have to run to stand still."[65] But the apparent buoyancy which she was able to communicate to the people in those early months was due to her conviction that the crisis in India was "a crisis of development,"[66] and not of defeatism and that she was for the first time in a position of authority to be able to tackle it. The stoical contours of her face relaxed. There was an expansion of personality, a growing warmth, a relaxation which came from power. For the first time she alone was answerable and responsibility, added to previous influence, gave a mature beauty to the face. She seemed no longer aloof. She was able to accept the opportunists with no misgivings, the importunists with tolerance, and friends without suspicion. Her enthusiasm was joined with dedication.

The eradication of poverty remained the fundamental goal; against it she instinctively weighed the merit of an economic measure or of a political act. She was not an economist or a political theorist. She did not claim to be. But she was concerned with ideas and their implementation. And she was now in a position to tune the instruments of social change to a pitch higher than before. "It is not with caution and circumspection that we shall win the war against poverty," she said, "but by our capacity to take risks and to accept burdens and responsibilities."[67] Vision and duty must be combined. Both the technologists and the intellectuals must be drawn into the country's endeavor. The sights must be high but the means down to earth. The catchword was efficiency. It was too soon for the results to show but the trends she liked to initiate were unmistakable: imagination, efficiency, and an emphasis on youth.

She called for a "revolution in administration" in her first major speech in Parliament. The work of the already existing Department of Administrative Reforms was not spectacular according to her and implementation had also been slow, but she thought that if "the approach was developed and extended" it would yield solid results. Just as she had appealed for a cooperative effort above party affiliations to solve the country's problems when she became Congress president, so she did the same as prime minister. But this time she went one step further. She wanted this cooperation to be effective "not only among us politicians, but even among others like scientists, educationists, industrialists, workers, and peasants."[68] She made it also clear that she did not think it necessary that a politician be an expert, but that he must go by expert counsel and that it was the specialist who could most efficiently transcribe a politician's policy objectives into workable reality. It was the stress on efficiency and technological expertise, she said, which had been the most potent factor of progress in the countries that had achieved prosperity, whether they were socialist or capitalist. Talent and youth were the concomitants of this success. She said she was willing enough to seek guidance from those with "long experience in public work," but she was eager to invite "the cooperation of young men and women in shaping the future they will inherit."[69] She tried to invoke a less stereotyped response from her own party workers. A sharper sense of political purpose, she pointed out, must be strengthened by knowledge of economic and social trends, greater faith in the scientific quest and a sense of urgency.[70] Apart from emphasizing the need for discipline, constructive work in the constituencies, and giving the highest priority to the education of the voter as the routine preliminaries to the coming election which was already beginning to exercise the national—and international—mind, she again emphasized in evocative terms, "Democratic life perishes if a political career does not command respect and is not reinforced by the idealism of youth. To grow and flourish, the Congress must become the party of the builders of tomorrow."[71] This call for youth, intellect, and broader horizons was reminiscently Kennedyian, and in fact, the stir of enthusiasm it created in that community of people was seen to be so similar by political commentators that some of them began to call her "the Indian Kennedy."

Her first act to strike a nonpartisan attitude in national affairs was when she sought to prove her promises to the south on the language issue. She made her first Republic Day broadcast on January 26, in English only, a Hindi translation being read out after that by an AIR announcer. The Hindi belt rose up in arms but it acted like balm to the south, and together, whether out of curiosity, admiration, or satisfaction that a Nehru was again in the saddle, at the first Congress session after she took over, attendance of AICC members was greater than it had been in the past six years. Not more than four hundred AICC members had attended the sessions since 1960, but at the 70th Congress at Jaipur, in February 1966 there were 462 present out of the total of 726. Her crowd-drawing capacity was to remain the one dominant factor intimidating her opponents time and again into beating a hasty retreat. She had also the satisfaction of knowing that wherever she went she would be ensured of the support of at least one-half of the population. Women formed a more noticeable portion of the crowds at her meetings than ever before, and at Jaipur she received the traditional welcome from them—garlands upon garlands and the rush to apply *tilak*, the sacred red powder, on her forehead.

She was careful about forging these links with the people, and the first visit she made outside Delhi after becoming prime minister was to a place nobody had bothered about before, the Miri tribal enclave in Assam. She calmly donned a Miching woman's costume they brought for her and then addressed the annual conference of the Miri tribe at a village called Kulajan. She remembered the restless, scared, and angry crowds she had encountered in Assam during the tense days of the Chinese aggression in 1962. This time the welcome was bright and extravagant and "along the routes of her motor journey," said one report, "ceremonies were performed reminiscent of a daughter's homecoming."[72] She showed herself willing to meet with the rebel Nagas before her departure, and during the next eight months she used all her energy to try to solve the unhappy tribal problem. The state of Nagaland within the Indian union had been constituted in 1964, but it had not drawn the cooperation of the rebels wanting an independent Nagaland. Serious clashes between the underground Nagas and Indian army units intermittently created a security problem within as well as on the national border and threatened a breakdown of the ceasefire agreed upon earlier. On February 18, for the first time, an Indian prime minister and the leaders of the rebel Nagas met face to face. The Naga leader had insisted that he would talk only with the prime minister, and Indira had readily agreed. Though members of the Nagaland Peace Mission were present and all of the Naga underground delegation, Indira did without aides. No problems were solved, for Indira was firm on one condition, that a solution must be sought within the Indian union, and the Nagas obdurate on the other, that it could only be without. But the approach was such as to soften hostility and pave the way for quieter commitments.

She was neither a flashy speaker nor did she have the aura of her father. Nehru was no great orator, but he could always speak with the authority of being the father of modern India, the man responsible for setting a tradition of respect for parliamentary procedure, the man who gave to parliamentary democracy in India its first inviolabilities, and hence Parliament, its prestige. No wonder, then, that when he stood up to speak, so great was the attention paid to his words for hints of a new direction or a definition of policy that the manner was forgotten, and concentration, sometimes love but always respect, flowed out from opposition benches. For Indira, the years of nonofficial involvement in political affairs paid off in terms of earning her nonpartisan loyalties in the beginning, but the lack of parliamentary experience did much to sap her confidence. She spoke only when she had to, and she was good only when extreme provocation, as in Dublin years ago, spurred her to a fighting speech. Unlike her father, who would leap up to the defense of any of his ministers in trouble and do their work for them by answering difficult questions in Parliament, Indira let her ministers bear the brunt of the attacks themselves. Her claim was that she would rather they learned to take care of themselves and come better prepared, but by contrast, it made her own parliamentary presence less effective. It took her time to master the intricacies of parliamentary procedure and to insist upon ministerial discipline, but a general deterioration in parliamentary manners since her father's time made her unhappy, and she tended to look with silent horror or desperate disdain when a kind of raucous vulgarity was introduced, especially by her arch enemy, the deliberately offensive but exuberant Dr Lohia. However, this came later, for it took time even for the belligerent to get familiar.

She sought to establish a rapport with parliamentarians in a smaller forum, where she was always more at ease. For her own party members there were meetings of the Congress parliamentary board or the Congress parliamentary party, but she sought to continue Shastri's practice of gathering together opposition leaders in Parliament for informal meetings on current issues. Expecting a concerted attack in the budget session of Parliament beginning on February 15, on the government's food policy and the Tashkent agreement, particularly the surrender of Haji Pir, she decided to discuss these matters with the opposition in a pre-Parliament attempt at persuasiveness.

Unlike Shastri, who had a disastrous confrontation in his first press conference and gave up the idea of having regular meetings with the press, Indira took up the challenge right away and kept at it. She was moderately good, but utterly different from her father. From his dominant intellectual position he would use the stimulation of meeting sharp minds not only to inform but to expound, expose, and philosophize. An enunciation of

policy would turn often, with probing exchanges, into an analysis of political
theory or vice versa. Nehru's press conferences, when he was in top form
and before his illness, were unique experiences for Indian and foreign correspondents alike. Indira did not try to emulate Nehru. Her own manner
was terse, to the point and enlivened only occasionally by a barbed shot of
humor. She was more relaxed with foreign correspondents and seemed to
show far greater resistance and wit in such exchanges when abroad. At
home, she was liable to be tense, on guard, and had the feeling that she was
constantly being tested.

Nevertheless if she was in the right mood she could throw back a question
with a slow coquettish smile, a sparkle in her eyes, and with evident delight
at being feminine, and in power. She was quick to discern touchiness
and also quick to soothe it with tolerance. In her very first press conference,
a question put to her in Hindi provoked the ire of a correspondent from
the South. "We can't allow the press conference to become a deaf and dumb
show for those who don't know Hindi," he exclaimed excitedly. "You're
prime minister of India, not of North India!" Indira just smiled and offered
to render a translation herself. The next time when again a question came
up in Hindi, she turned to the South Indian correspondent before he could
say anything and calmed him. "Now, don't get excited. I'll translate it
myself." At the end of the press conference she promised to have transla-
tions provided in future, but she asked the same correspondent why he did
not learn Hindi. And again, before he could reply, her eyes twinkled.
"Well, I'll ask the other chaps to learn a South Indian language too."

From April onward, until electioneering upset the schedule, she held a
major press conference once a month. She also followed up her own
plea to harness the energies of the young and the talented by initiating
monthly meetings with young industrialists, and inviting artists, architects,
musicians, and the creative community in general to give their opinion on
relevant matters. In April she started to make what began to be called
"Person to Person," monthly broadcasts over AIR, through which she
hoped to communicate with the masses at large. These multilayered levels
of contact helped to offset her weakness in the party organization and her
growing differences with Congress chief Kamaraj. It was ironic, in the light
of subsequent events, that he should have been upset over the nonsocialist
bias that she had shown since assuming the prime ministership. He did
not think much of those on whom she relied for economic advice—Subramaniam, Asoka Mehta, and Pitamber Pant in the Planning Commission—
all of whom at the time stood, at least officially, for selective decontrol and
a comparative freeing of the economy. Kamaraj is said to have felt that
Mehta was merely a theoretician, that if he himself knew little of economics
Mehta knew even less! In a convocation address at Saugar University in
early February, Mehta spoke for an effective utilization of greater controls
even in the banking sector and when this raised a hue and cry among the

business community—FICCI President Kirloskar, who had cherished the hope that the "pragmatic" policies initiated by Shastri would be continued by the new government, said it had given a "jolt to business confidence"— he said he had not spoken in his official capacity as minister!

"Yes, I suppose you could call me a socialist," Indira ruminated in an interview, "but you have to understand what we mean by that term. Socialism, like democracy, covers such a wide range. It covers what is happening in Sweden, the Soviet Union, and China. We used the word because it came closest to what we wanted to do here—which is to eradicate poverty. You can call it socialism; but if by using that word we arouse controversy, I don't see why we should use it. I don't believe in words at all."[73]

"What do you think?" Kamaraj had asked Ramakrishna Iyer, a veteran colleague from the south with a reputation for refusing ministerships, the day Indira was elected prime minister-designate. "I've selected this lady. I hope she proves to be Nehru's daughter and not a mere lady."[74]

Where he went wrong was in estimating that she would be happy being merely Nehru's daughter. No doubt she worshipped, as people concluded, at her father's shrine, but she did not worship blindly. She was not doctrinaire and she genuinely believed at the time that the steps she was taking were the only practical steps to be taken in the nation's good. If there was a misunderstanding of motive between the two, there was also chagrin on Kamaraj's part that if on the one hand he had not found her to be Nehru's daughter, on the other he had found her to be nothing but that. She was too independent, sometimes too obstinate, but too conscious of the duty of her office to let gratitude for his role in making her prime minister make her spineless and subservient. Two occasions on which she came into a clash within the first three months with the other groups of supporters, the chief ministers—on the issue of dearness allowance for government employees and the question of forming food zones for effective procurement and distribution—made her realize that the logic of parliamentary governance demanded its own loyalty. Neither its convention nor her temperament provided for a party enclave to try to dominate (apart from policy directives which were agreed upon jointly) the actual business of government. She was caught in a "historical trap." Supported by a group who banked on her weakness to bolster its own strength, her attempts to reassert the position of the prime minister brought her immediately into a clash with the same group. To remain prime minister she had to count on their support, but to be effective she had to risk that support. If she could have had the loyalty of a strong party chief, her position and her capacity for work would have been considerably strengthened, but the motives that operated with the Congress president regarding this equation were identical with those of the chief ministers: the weaker the prime minister, the greater the influence that would accrue to or flow from them. "It is only as king-maker that Mr Kamaraj has shone," one political analyst observed. "He has failed completely to help the party revitalize itself to play a constructive role in the country's crisis....The prime minister can expect little help from him."[75]

She herself thought that "revitalization" included raising the whole party machine out of its lethargic slough, gearing it up for mass contacts in the countryside generally instead of only at the time of elections and, most important, identifying itself with its plans and programs so that it could serve as a bridge between the people and the government. That this was not being done, that there was this continual tension among its members, and that it sought to act like the government itself, instead of in cooperation with it, did not at the time lead her to the extreme view that a split along ideological lines was feasible or even desirable. She did not think the groups within the Congress were so defined as to split apart. But, and this is important, she did not think that an eventual split would spell any danger to democratic functioning in India, as a lot of people had already begun to argue.[76] The government's task at the time she viewed to be a practical rather than an ideological one, even in regard to the need for a sociological shake-up that she was always stressing.

"It is a question of, perhaps, giving greater encouragement to the people with a modern scientific outlook and people with more expert knowledge. I think different types of people are needed for different jobs. In many spheres they are in the right places, in some spheres they are not. So right now it is a problem of administration. It is not one of changing policies but of implementing those policies."[77] Even with regard to development programs, she told the Congress parliamentary party on the eve of the budget session of Parliament, urgent attention was required to be in hand. "This is not the time to initiate new programs," she insisted.[78]

Her major political act of implementation was the establishment of the Punjabi *suba,* or a Punjabi-speaking state, which had dragged on since her father's time. A simple reorganization along the lines of what had taken place throughout India was complicated in this instance by a communal issue. Punjabi Hindus even denied, in a census, that Punjabi was their language in order to avoid a Punjabi state which they feared would be dominated by the Sikhs, while the Sikhs, voicing their demand for a Sikh homeland seemed only to feed those fears. Indira decided, as she had about Maharashtra and Gujarat years back, that this unsavory situation should be settled as soon as possible. She had been a member of the cabinet subcommittee for the Punjabi suba in Shastri's time. A new subcommittee was formed on February 13, and only a week later there were indications that both the working committee and the government would make a final decision by the following month. Representations, however, began to pour in from the Hindi-speaking areas in the Punjab for a separate state of Haryana. Pressure for a three-regional division began to mount up from the Akalis, with Sant Fateh Singh declaring that he would go on a fast unto death if the suba was not conceded within four weeks. A controversy also arose over the scope and status of another parliamentary committee created by Kamaraj in addition to the one headed by Speaker Hukam Singh. On March 2, Indira decided to discuss the matter with opposition leaders. The confusion about the committees, Sant's threat, and the inherent difficulty of the problem could have overwhelmed both government and the organization.

"In any case," observed commentator Krishan Bhatia warningly, "the government should not adopt a posture of sternness toward the Akalis if later, under the pressure of events, it is going to give in to them sullenly. But if Delhi's past performances are an index, that is precisely what will happen."[79] He apparently did not bargain for a changed style at the top. For, precisely a week later, in a major policy announcement, the Congress conceded the demand for a Punjabi suba! Bhatia himself was led to comment, this time approvingly, "With its decision the Congress leadership has crossed a major mental hurdle....The latest decision... is a happy exception to the tendency in high places to live in a state of blissful ignorance and defer action till it is too late."[80]

When I asked her about her role in the matter, the prime minister shrugged. "Once the Hukam Singh Committee had been nominated, we had no choice... knowing the composition of the committee we knew what its decision would be. There was no way in which we could have gone against it."

Except to hurry it up, she might have added. In fact, the day the Congress Working Committee met, Rajen Bajpai, in town from Allahabad, who knew of the impending decision remarked, "So, you've decided to concede the demand for a Punjabi suba, Indiraji?"[81]

Indira's reply was almost expectedly characteristic. "If it has to be done ultimately, why not get it over with and face it?"

Once when she had been asked how she would explain the fact that she was sometimes personally attacked for her "dogmatic" views on socialism, she countered with, "Well, sometimes I am attacked for being the opposite. What can I do about it?"[82]

After her return from America, she was certainly attacked "for being the opposite." To Morarji and his group who sought every opportunity to play her down to pave the way for his possible comeback was added the disillusioned anger of the left who felt badly let down. Her economic policies seemed to them unpalatable. She had been too quiescent on Vietnam. But on top of that an agreement to establish an Indo-U.S. foundation "to promote progress in all fields of learning"[83] raised nightmares of CIA infiltration into Indian cultural life, and so strong was the uproar that she let the idea peter out eventually. Resentment within the old guard of party leadership also sprang from her tendency to rely for advice on the younger elements of her cabinet and even outside, especially when, like Asoka Mehta and Dinesh Singh—and Subramaniam to some extent—they happened to be, each, a political lone wolf, and had not much to show for a sound political base at the time.

What the congressmen dared not say in the open was voiced in Parliament by P.S.P. leader H. V. Kamath, who in an oblique reference to Dinesh Singh joined issue with the prime minister, among other things, for her elevation of a deputy minister to the rank of a minister of state but also investing him with "certain powers" by a presidential decree which made him "a virutal *de facto* assistant prime minister."[84] What angered her most, however, was the attempt, strangely enough from both right and left, to condemn her on the count that she was turning away from the Nehru line. There began a move within the party to mount a concerted attack on her at the AICC session scheduled for May in Bombay.

She had no illusions about the motives of some of her detractors. "Some people say I am a stopgap premier of an interim administration. All I can say is that some of these people obviously aspire to become prime minister themselves."[85] At the session, whatever hesitations of manner she had because of the burden of the problems on her were swept aside by the provocation to her feelings. She needed a challenge to bring out the best in her. Bombay provided both the occasion and the stimulus. Her speech defending her policies brought back what they called the Nehru fire to the political arena. She began with a sarcastic reference to those who were shouting against her in the name of Nehru.

"There are people who really respected him, but there are also some people who neither respected him nor his policies while he was alive," and she quoted the famous lines about Homer.

> *Nine cities claim Homer dead*
> *Through which the living Homer begged his bread.*

"We have a similar case here," she said.[86]

She emphasized the background of her own political association with her father. "Jawaharlal was the nation's leader, but he was my father, my companion. I had grown with his policies. I am familiar with every bit of his thought. Today, I am told that I do not know his views. Today his erstwhile critics have to tell me what his policies were." She pointed out that the three pillars of those policies were secularism, democracy, and socialism, but both Mahatma Gandhi as well as Nehru had insisted upon the mind remaining open to new ideas and not making a fetish of any principle.

"I am convinced," she added, "that I am not straying away from those principles [Nehru's]. But if it was needed for the sake of the country I will certainly do so. That however is not necessary. . . . My responsibility is to the whole nation. I will follow the path I consider right. You can remove me if you do not like the policies."[87]

Kamaraj was reportedly not happy with the interpretations that had been given to the fertilizer deal, foreign aid, and the educational foundation issues, and the nature of a personal crusade against the prime minister and each other that the ideological wrangles were taking in party discussions. At least that is what he tried to make clear in Bombay before the opening of the session.[88] He sought to give the impression that he had an open mind on economic issues and that he was all for "a realistic and impersonal appraisal of the government's policies." The agenda for the session was left formally undefined. The official resolution that was ultimately passed did avoid ideological controversy and called only for holding the price line and encouraging the agricultural sector. But a detailed note submitted by Asoka Mehta to the working committee was not even considered during discussions about the basis of the resolution.

The prime minister's speech, apart from throwing out a personal challenge—to remove her if she was not a acceptable—also contained a strong indictment of the party's lack of cooperation with the government.

"If the party had gone hand in hand with the government in the execution of various programs," she said, "the face of India would have been quite different."[89]

Two weeks later, on June 5, in a sudden, dramatic, and swift move, in its most major act of economic daring, Indira's government announced the devaluation of the rupee by 36.5 per cent.[90]

"The exchange rate is nothing more or nothing less than the price of foreign exchange. In this sense, it is like the price of anything else and is not a matter which should affect pride or raise emotion," declared Finance Minister Sachin Chaudri soothingly.[91]

But pride and policy rose up in arms. If the decision was hailed as a bold one on the one hand, it was decried as a sop to external pressure on the other. Chaudri did not deny that the International Monetary Fund had advised India to devaluate. "They have given us advice, and they must give us advice. But they have not said we must devalue to this extent nor have they said that unless we devalue they will do this or that," he said.[92]

At the crucial cabinet meeting called by Indira on the fifth, she put the question to her colleagues about the necessity for devaluation and then sat silent while they wrestled with emotion and practical economics. At the last she had said simply: "If we don't devalue, we don't get aid."[93] She had a habit of picking the basic point of a problem and felt it was no use evading its implications. The World Bank, the IMF, and American suggestions might not have allied the question to aid in strictly pressure terms but the implications were well enough understood by both sides.

The decision on devaluation came as the culmination of a six-month period in which Indira had shown her capacity for forceful action and independent thinking. She had realized the extent of the acute economic crisis facing India, and had gone about doing something about it. She had got aid flowing in again. She had shifted the emphasis in her travels abroad from international problems to more pertinent ones nearer home. She had tackled national issues with firmness as well as tolerance, with regard to Punjab, the Nagas, the Mizos, and she had made personal appearances and shown her concern at every trouble spot. Her spontaneous reactions endeared her to the source of her greatest support, the masses. When rice scarcity in Kerala turned into a major crisis, she tried to set an example to those who had plenty by surrendering her rice ration altogether and only those who knew how fond she was of rice realized what it meant to do without it. When drought conditions led to extreme privation in some areas, as in Madhya Pradesh, she went there herself, and found she could hardly control her tears. Her sympathy for the downtrodden was something real, acute, and personal. "Just as a mother loves her weakest child so should one love the poor," she said.

She had kept an open mind on foreign affairs. Some of the provisions of the Tashkent agreement, like exchange of prisoners and withdrawal of forces, had been carried out straightaway, but prospects of normalization had met with truculence at ministerial talks at Pindi. If she had a tendency to be a hardliner on Pakistan before she became prime minister, once in office she had shown patience and reserve but also an eagerness for economic cooperation between the two. She kept "the door open," as she said, for talks even with China. In fact, she began as a whole to try to shift the emphasis from the political to the economic, with greater involvement in countries nearer home, in Asia and Africa. Even in the party organization she had been able to establish herself with greater surety though the rift with Kamaraj created a constant tension. He was opposed to devaluation and thought she had done the wrong thing for party prospects in the elections then only six months away. Her contention was that national good must override party interests, and this was a decision in the national interest. She was irritated by its being referred to as part of her "adjustments of policy."

"It is an economic step which you take in a given situation. For instance, the Soviet Union took it, Yugoslavia took it. It has nothing to do with policy."[94]

By August when expectations of results from devaluation began to be aired, she countered with, "How can an objective prove successful during two or three months? It will take a year to know the results. Certain steps which should have been taken immediately afterwards have been taken. It is not possible, as some of the opposition parties said, that all preparation should be made beforehand. Some of them could have been but much could not have been done."[95]

Nevertheless, she was unnerved by three things: continuing criticism, virtual sabotaging of follow-up action to devaluation from within her own ministeries, and a realization that she had totally alienated the left. Her prime ministership in those thirteen months can be divided easily into pre-devaluation and postdevaluation phases. The first was marked by action, optimism, and a pragmatic lack of commitment that took her closer to the right.   The second phase found her almost on the rebound, a little dispirited, subjected to the intense pre-election propaganda from the opposition and frequent motions of no-confidence, a preoccupation with election issues rather than executive ones, and an effort to win back the left to the old equation.

"There was no grand design of policy, but any grand design, as far as India was concerned, could go either the communist or the capitalist way. She likes herself as *avant garde*. She is normally afraid of seeming to go against the left," observed B. K. Nehru. "Devaluation was the watershed. She fell back."[96]

"She's not on the side of the rightists," admitted communist leader Dange, "it's a sort of centrism, at the same time she doesn't know how to be against them."

"That means she wants to and can't?"

"Even if she just carries out her father's policy she'll make a room for herself in history. He did not allow India to be in the American camp, he emphasized heavy industry and built up the state sector, and he did not lay down a policy and leave it to the gods and you to carry it out. It is unjust to compare Indira with Nehru, but we did so expect that she should have inherited by association at least....I expected her to inherit something of the backbone of socialism. Nehru, even on the point of humanism, used to thunder against landlordism, the ills of the peasantry. But she doesn't take any sides..."[97]

Krishna Menon, smarting no doubt under the comparative disregard displayed by Indira toward him at the time, revealed the extent of disillusionment felt by the leftists. "How can somebody who is really progressive make a theory out of the center of the road policy? As I said, you're bound to get knocked down." And springing from his own commitment on the Vietnam issue and his chagrin at Indira's tactful silence in the early months, he added, "She hasn't a clue about international relations."[98]

How right she was about being attacked from both sides! If the leftists were indicting her for turning to the right, the rightists were not far behind in claiming the opposite. "She's fellow a traveler," said Minoo Masani, "both she and her father always were."[99]

In the second half of 1966 however, she tried to retrieve her leftist image. A visit to Moscow resulted in a communique that called for an immediate halt to American bombing, with both sides expressing concern about the explosive war danger and deterioration of international relations "as a result of aggressive actions of imperialist and other reactionary forces," sentiments she had carefully avoided expressing during her American visit.

"What made Mrs Gandhi move so far away from the postures she adopted in Washington in March is none too clear. Her anxiety to secure continued Russian support against Pakistan is understandable but cannot be all,"

commented *The Economist*. "Perhaps the stronger motive was her anxiety
to make a good impression at home. Devaluation and other measures
preceding it have left the impression of subservience to Washington that
she is keen to erase."[100]

There was even an attempt to establish a greater equation with East
Germany, but it resulted in nothing but a period of strained relations with
the western counterpart. In November, she got rid of home minister Nanda,
and appointed Chavan in his place. It made Lohia say admiringly, "*Mohre
jamane mein bohut tez hai*. [She's adept at placing her pawns]."[101] But she
did not get the Central Election Committee to give Menon a ticket for
north Bombay, a move opposed by S. K. Patil. She said she tried, but
from all counts it was a half-hearted attempt. "You can't blame Patil for
wanting to conserve his influence!" she said. Menon resigned from the
Congress and decided to stand as an Independent candidate in the elections.
The left was further alienated from her.

She had been almost a year in power. The frustrations remained,
although she still believed she could function within the democratic framework. But when she was asked why she let things slide toward the end of
that year, she replied, "W-w-ell, I got so involved in things of the moment.
When I wanted some changes, there was some tension on the border. And
everybody kept saying that I should wait till after the elections!"

"Do you think it would have been better if you had gone ahead and done
what you wanted to?"

She smiled ruefully, "It probably would have been better."[102]

PART III

LEADERSHIP

1. CAMPAIGN

On September 16, on an official tour of the U.P., Indira Gandhi visited
Saidabad, a small town in the Phulpur constituency. At a huge public
meeting that Indira was to address, Vijayalaxmi Pandit made a typically
florid gesture. She offered Phulpur to Indira. She said it would be an
honor both to the constituency and to the prime minister if Indira were
to agree to seek election from the place where Jawaharlal Nehru began
his political career."[1] Apart from the embarrassment Indira felt such

an acceptance would cause in view of the undercurrent of hostility that invariably ran through relations between aunt and niece—perhaps this was Vijayalaxmi Pandit's desperate bid to undo the past for the sake of a political rapprochement—Indira had another reason for politely declining the offer. She had already set her heart on the constituency that had been her husband's—Rae Bareli.

Rae Bareli seemed to stand for the half-finished aspirations of a man cut off at the peak. Feroze's death in 1960, at the age of 48, came at a crucial point in his career. He had worked tirelessly and imaginatively and gradually been able to evolve his own equations in the Indian political scene. To be Nehru's son-in-law or Nehru's daughter often meant patronization. Feroze had freed himself, but could she? Her image in the current context could derive its inspiration more suitably from the independent road to fulfillment struck by Feroze in Rae Bareli than from the inheritance of influence represented by Phulpur.

Yet, Rae Bareli was not totally cut off from the Nehru heritage. It fell within the orbit of influence exercised by Motilal in the days when he was only tentatively extending his political control over the whole of the United Provinces, as Uttar Pradesh was known in pre-independence days. Rae Bareli had been consistently and strongly nationalist, and was alongwith the adjoining districts of Faizabad and Partapgarh, the center of an agrarian upheaval in the early 1920's. Rae Bareli had sent an urgent telegram to Jawaharlal Nehru in January 1921, asking him to help them meet the threat of possible police action against the *kisans*. He had left for Rae Bareli immediately and found on arriving at the railroad station that some peasant leaders had been arrested and were in the local jail. Angry peasants from the surrounding area were agitating to lead a mass demonstration into the town. But the British government was determined to prevent them from doing so and had extra police and even the military called in to stand by. When the peasants began their march they were stopped at a small river. Jawaharlal went straight to the river but the peasants had already been fired upon by the police. The whole episode came to be known as the Munshiganj Bridge Firing case, and the kisans involved were later defended in court by Motilal. Rae Bareli, like the rest of India but more so, was soaked in the Nehru legend and there are people there still who recall Indira Gandhi as a child seated on her grandfather's lap.

Then there was Feroze, and the fact that he stood for election from Rae Bareli brought it immediately and directly within the Nehru fold. He was natural, uninhibited, and informal. He spoke with gusto and cheer and he was sensitive to the demands of the poor. For his election in 1952, he would visit their homes in the heart of his constituency incognito to find out the people's feelings about him. He was ready and fluent with the local dialect and there was one occasion when he was told by a family that they could not vote for Feroze Gandhi because they disapproved of "Indiraji" having married a "Muslim." "Now if it could be you," he was told, for his manners had won them over completely, "we'd vote for you straight-away." And with an irrepressible twinkle that was a part of him he stated, "But I am that Feroze. Will you vote for me?"

He charmed the entire constituency for he would always be available at a time of crisis and before making a major speech in Parliament he would make it a point to send copies of it to the local leaders. An old resident of Rae Bareli, Mohammad Zakir Khan, said that in 1952 when both Feroze and Indira had discussed election prospects with him, he had jokingly re-marked to Feroze that once people became M.P.s they forgot their consti-tuencies and never came back. "No, not I," Feroze had protested firmly. "I'll come." Although from 1952 to 1957, he was not as assiduous, devoted, or interested as he might have been, from 1957 onward he nursed his constituency carefully and the people of Rae Bareli remember him almost as one of them. So in his own way, he too left a legacy for his wife, and the terrifying intensity of their devotion made her realize that even as Nehru's daughter her life could not belong to herself alone. In contrast with an educated, hero-worshipping assembly the total, wondering, almost childlike trustfulness of the villagers drew a sense of responsibility that was infinitely moving. That is what her father had felt, and written about when he first came into contact with the rural poor of India: "They showered their affection on us and looked on us with loving and hopeful eyes, as if we were the bearers of good tidings, the guides who were to lead them to the promised land. And their faith in us, casual visitors from the distant city, embarrassed me and filled me with a new responsibility that frightened me."[2] Those villagers in Rae Bareli had been like that, and the seeds of a compulsive relationship between them and Indira Gandhi was formed straightaway. It was an experience like this that gave her the right to say years later as prime minister that she could go over and above the party to the people directly if she wanted and they would give her the sanctions.

Whatever it was, because she was Nehru's daughter, because they remem-bered Feroze with love, or whether they were awed by the fact that she was already prime minister, probably because all the three things had worked into their minds, when Indira visited Rae Bareli on her way to Allahabad she found a people who were only waiting to be granted the privilege of having her as their candidate. Congress party workers had planned to hold a meeting at the party office and afterward introduce the workers to Mrs Gandhi one by one. But on her arrival there was such a stampede particularly among the women to rush and throw themselves at her feet, that the organizers had to take her away hastily. Later, when they pressed her to make her decision because time was running short for beginning the election campaign, she told them, "I have decided I'll fight from Rae Bareli. You may go and start your work." This was unofficial, of course, until it could go through the entire procedural channels to its sanction by the Congress president, but it was unlikly that Kamaraj would offer any argument against her declared preference. As early as August 30 there was an indication that she had something of the sort in mind because Dinesh Singh, who had stood from Rae Bareli in the previous election, this time asked for a ticket for the adjoining Pratapgarh constituency.

Rae Bareli had never elected a non-Congress Member of Parliament in the three previous elections. But it had begun to feel left out. There was dissatisfaction with the party organization and execution of government plans and its people felt vaguely that perhaps it was its indeterminate location, "neither east nor west but between," as they say in U.P., that led to lack of official interest. So Rae Bareli had cogent reasons for wanting Mrs Gandhi as their representative. The constituency would gain an immediate importance, and with her as head of the executive branch they could indulge in a "renewed hope" for well-administered facilities. They wanted her obviously not merely as their candidate but as prime minister. And with the urgency that is typical of small-town demands, they told her during that tentative political sojourn of hers what she must get for Rae Bareli. It was Shiv Shankar Singh from the village of Dalman who articulated the need for the four things that were relevant to Rae Bareli and his area as well: tubewells and extensive canalizing; bridge over the Ganga at Dalman; replacement of the railway line from Rae Bareli to Dalman which had been dismantled during the 1965 India-Pak war; and perquisites, remuneration, and help for the widows of servicemen who had died during that war. It was the last request that elicited the first assurance from her that she would see that something was done at once through the Citizens' Council.[3]

"In the district of Rae Bareli," said Baij Nath Prasad Yadav, a member of the scheduled caste and secretary of an organization called the District Backward Classes, "over every brick you turn you could find a *Lalji*." Until 1957, Yadav said they had had to fight for recognition of the difficulties of the backward classes, but after that Feroze and the party began to pay more attention and it was then he said, that "the public turned toward the Congress."[4] In 1957, Yadav was elected to Parliament along with Feroze because Rae Bareli was then a double-member constituency. Feroze used to stay with him whenever he visited the area. Yadav expressed unmixed admiration for the brilliant leader who was so sensitive at heart. He also recalled that the unexpected simplicity and lack of air shown by Indira when she came to help electioneer for her husband in 1952 left its own impact. At a place called Nil Mathna, she addressed two long meetings, which had both been held at night. It had been a gruelling day and they were all tired out, but they were scheduled to spend the night at another village called Kunda. While driving they were stopped on the road by an old woman who mistook their car for a lorry. "Did you have to go somewhere particular?" asked Mrs Gandhi attempting to speak in the local dialect. The woman explained, and it turned out it was in the opposite direction. "Sit down with us," said Indira to her kindly. "No, no, no," said the old woman nervously. "I can't sit in the car." She was frightened of presuming too much and overreaching her place in the hierarchical fabric of society. So not only did Indira have to persuade her to overcome her inhibitions and sit with them in the car—the woman ultimately insisted on squatting below in the leg space—but she made everybody drive back along the way they had come, drop the old woman where she wanted, and then drive on again to their own destination.

At Kunda they stayed in a small school building with an encircling verandah. It was a bitter cold night of January, and the bare rooms seemed to freeze the breath. Mrs Gandhi, however, strode calmly into her room and went to sleep. But what really surprised her party was that in the morning, by the time they had hot water brought in, she had already had a bath—in cold water.[5]

Yadav's commitment to the Congress, however, was not all emotional, and he believed firmly in its democratic stand. He also had an interesting point to make on the indispensability of Indira's candidacy in 1967. According to the Kaka Kalelkar Commission set up by the government to inquire into the condition of the backward classes, women had been accepted in the category of the backward classes. "With Indiraji," declared the spirited Yadav, "we are very happy. She's a symbol of the backward classes, and it means that recognition has been given to them."[6] That was certainly one way of looking at it! But during an election this view was undoubtedly valid for 50 per cent of the population which was female.

At the inspection house bungalow where she was staying for the night Indira was visited by Mrs Zulfiquar Khan, the daughter-in-law of the land-lord mentioned earlier, who told her that the women of Rae Bareli wanted her to address a separate women's meeting the next time she visited them. The district's total population of 1,300,000 was almost evenly divided between men and women, and in the importance of its women's vote Rae Bareli anticipated the pattern that was to be set for the whole of India in the 1967 general elections. As a woman, Indira Gandhi could appeal to this half of the population as a right while they in their turn would deem it their duty to vote for her. Her candidacy was expected to act as a catalyst to bring more women into the political fray, either as workers or as voters, for they would be doubly inspired to come out for one of their own kind. This was immediately evident in Rae Bareli, for at the earlier public meeting, there were women who sat waiting in the hot sun for Mrs Gandhi, "though they were dying of it," as someone put it, who never had the interest or the courage to attend a public meeting before.

Mrs Zulfiquar Khan made a second request to Mrs Gandhi on behalf of the women, a request for grain. There had been no rain in the area for almost two years, the people were agriculturally backward, and the comparative scarcity, as always, hit the women and children worst. The opposition made capital out of these conditions and promptly laid the blame at the door of the Congress party as for rising prices. But the average Rae Bareli congressmen met the argument with the stoical reply that the drought was "nature's fault." Loyalties were in most cases traditional, sentimental, and personal and it was difficult to disentangle the national role of the Congress before independence from its increasingly disparate functioning as a political party after independence.

Rae Bareli in another sense represented the political pattern of the whole of India. It had a sizable Muslim minority consisting of 16 per cent of the total population and all the vexatious problems that arise out of the multireligious composition of India—the petty exploitation of the communal issue for political ends, the inherent tensions, or the happy everyday living that joins the residents ultimately in a common loyalty. For the Muslim women, most of whom were still in purdah, Indira's coming acted as a cathartic release and the more daring among them later cast aside their veils in the tempo of the election campaign.

Indira had flown to Rae Bareli by helicopter after making a forceful speech at Kanpur in which she reiterated the significant policy statement which created an uproar in the AICC session at Bombay soon after she began her first term as prime minister. She denied the charge that she was deviating from her father's policies. She in fact declared that they must be pursued with enthusiastic fervor, but she added pithily, as then, that if it was necessary, "I am quite capable of changing them." But in Rae Bareli, she took the opportunity to assure party workers on more personal grounds. She stated that the allegations made by some of the opposition resulted from the frustration that they all suffered at being unable to even entertain the hope of forming the government. They "talk sensibly," she said, only in Kerala, where they had support and knew that they might be in a position of authority one day. The opposition—she did not name any particular party—behaved as if it was their "right to make allegations and my duty to disprove them." Substantial proof was never forthcoming from their side. And in accordance with her oft-repeated contention that the Congress must close its ranks to this type of vilification, she asked her campaign workers to face the voters unitedly and boldly. By the time of the public meeting held in the town later, people came to know that she would choose Rae Bareli and the enthusiasm swelled the crowds to about an estimated 150,000. "We never had such a large meeting," remarked a townsman of Rae Bareli, "not even during Nehru." But for her it was a pattern. She took the masses who came to hear her almost for granted. She had never known it to be otherwise; the millions who thronged around Nehru when he was alive and she went with him or on behalf of him, and now when they came for her despite ideology. Previously, they knew only Gandhi, Nehru, and the Congress party, the three symbols of a struggle, and a victory. For long they remained the symbol of continuity too. It was only now, 20 years after independence, that the spell was breaking, but it was not enough to make them forget that Indira Gandhi was born a Nehru. Hence the loyalty, the curiosity, and the bond.

At the meeting, she gave a preview of what most of her early election speeches were going to be like. She turned particularly and pointedly toward the women who formed a sizable portion of the audience and said she appreciated what they had to suffer because of rising prices for "you have the responsibility of running the home," but she explained to the rest that the crisis had arisen because of the drought and the expenditure that the country's economy had to bear due to two wars, with the Chinese in 1962 and with Pakistan in 1965, within a mere five years. But she made it a point to emphasize that India had developed even faster than the U.S. and the U.S.S.R. had when they were struggling to evolve into modern, industrialist societies.

As far as India's foreign policy was concerned, she said she was criticized intermittently for being either pro-Russian or pro-American, but India, she said, continued to follow her old path of maintaining friendship with both. Among the opposition at home she explained that the communists wished for closer ties with Russia and the Swatantra party with America; and in order to encourage a sort of polarization of alignment, they tried to make convenient allegations. "This happens when one follows the middle path," she added wryly. That very day she laid the foundation stone of the Feroze Gandhi College, and there she took the opportunity to enunciate another pet theme that had also run through her father's speeches, that of advising students not only to study science, but also "to cultivate the scientific outlook."

She was presented addresses by the Zila Parishad (the district council), the Municipal Board, and the Krishak Samaj (the farmers' society) and at the end of it all, she was formally asked by Chief Minister Sucheta Kripalani and Pradesh Congress Committee Chief Kamlapati Tripathi, who had accompanied her to Rae Bareli, to stand from there. To the newsmen who insisted on knowing her mind, she gave a noncommittal reply. "But I have asked Mr Kamaraj to do the choosing for me."

She then flew to Allahabad, in what was her first trip to her home city after becoming prime minister, and drove to Anand Bhawan in an open car. The entire eight-mile route was lined by chanting crowds, arches, flags, and colored bunting. But later in the evening, in front of the historic compound which had resounded to the arguments, aspirations, and conflicts of the most famous of India's men of politics, there was a black flag demonstration by the Allahabad branch of the Samyukt Socialist party against high prices, consisting of several hundred people who kept chanting "Indira Gandhi, go back." The Congress, not to be outdone, gathered its own men, who shouted back "Indira Gandhi Zindabad" and "Congress Zindabad."

For a person who had always had to take opposition in her stride—to a French television company many days later when they asked if she did not get upset by opposition, "No," she said, "it stimulates me"—it must nevertheless have come as a shock that in Allahabad, sacrosanct for the Nehrus, it should have been possible to hold such a demonstration. A nagging doubt might have started in her mind, as such incidents against the Congress and established leaders steadily gathered in tempo, that the past was losing its aura. She was scheduled to address the students of Allahabad University the same evening, but there was such pandemonium—students were jampacked inside the Senate Hall, while numbers of them were crowding the place outside—that beyond saying that she was pleased at the "enthusiastic reception" she thought it would be better if she talked to them another time, and left abruptly.

But the first thing she did on the day after the fracas at the university was to address the women workers of the Congress at Swaraj Bhawan. She picked her topics carefully, and her examples with understanding. Fresh from her experience at the university and the wave of students' agitations that had been sweeping across parts of the country of late, she chose to warn the women that the damage done to government property in the process could only be made up through additional tax burdens on the people, and that they would be the ones to suffer from slow progress in general and soaring prices in particular. She put it to the women to prevent their men and their children from indulging in destructive violent activity. More spiritually vulnerable as the average Indian woman is, and knowing that, Mrs Gandhi cleverly brought in the reference that seldom fails: "I am extremely sorry that the people in India are ignoring the Gandhian principle of ahimsa and are taking to violence, whereas people in foreign countries are adopting this principle to achieve their objective."[7]

But the meeting consisted, after all, of political workers and there were issues that were of significance otherwise. She had been the first to come out with a statement, when she was minister of information and broadcasting, that the habit of picking faults with one's people or with one's government all the time was more demoralizing than constructive, and that one could look instead at the brighter side of things. This became the main theme of her optimistic posture regarding Indian failures as such. It is this that she chose to refer to again, because again India's image, she thought, was being vitiated by superficial personal allegations made against her and the tendency to denigrate the government as corrupt. It ruined the image of India both at home and abroad, she said, although as she talked it became apparent that she was quite indignant about having herself been brought into this sordid controversy.

"No one gave me any costly things except my father and grandfather. I do not have any large share in any concern except that left me by my father in the *National Herald*," she declared warmly.[8] Perhaps it was

natural to go on from this to the question of less wasteful expenditure, the
need to conserve foreign earnings, and the arguments on devaluation.

Soon after this she addressed all the Congress workers from Allahabad
district and the city. Here the emphasis was slightly different. She stressed
the need to resolve their own internal "petty quarrels" and "meet the challenge of the opposition parties." She insisted that India was going about
the right way to solve her difficulties even though the current year and the
next were going to be difficult. In spite of her optimistic predictions for the
future she quite willingly painted the present in stark terms and blamed
the opposition for trying to exploit these difficulties and urged the workers
to go to the masses so that they could act as liaison officers between the
government and the people.

Indira's next meeting was at Jasrah, about 14 miles from Allahabad,
in the heart of U.P.'s poorest and most drought-stricken area, where a crowd
of 50,000 waited in the blazing sun to hear her. On the way, at a village
called Gohona, her car met with another black flag demonstration of about
200 S.S.P. workers shouting "Indira Gandhi, go back." It was strange,
she thought, that they should do this when she had come to hear what the
people's grievances were, and at the meeting she said contemptuously,
"Those who ask me to go back do not understand politics. They should
go to school and learn."[9] But for the rest she concentrated on the immediate local problems. She promised more water development aid, irrigation
facilities, and employment opportunities, but she said that they themselves
must help in setting up village and cottage industries to bolster their rural
economy. As a congresswoman, she took the opportunity to condemn the
opposition—a natural election gambit—for raising superficial diversionary
issues which took people's minds off solid developmental work.

On September 16, Indira left on a tour of the eastern districts of U.P.
and in one day, in three whirlwind meetings at Gorakhpur, Maharajganj,
and Kushinagar, she addressed over a million people. Kushinagar had a
special importance. It was here 2,500 years ago that Gautama Buddha
attained spiritual fulfillment—Nirvana. The inspiration was too obvious
to miss, and in her meeting Indira emphasized the fact that the India of
today was following assiduously the same precepts of peace and nonviolence preached by the great saint and savant so many years ago. And
then, seeing the large number of women squatting on the ground with
babies in their arms and looking up at her with an uncomprehending
but worshipping look, she turned to them and told them that the time had
come for them to break the hold of silent suffering and work for their own
betterment. What evoked thunderous cheers from this audience of a comparatively undeveloped area was Mrs Gandhi's assurance that she would see
that the government made efforts to treat such regions on a different footing
than the others when it came to distributing economic parities. And back
in Delhi, the next morning, she declared that she had found the trip "satis-

factory" and had been "most impressed" by the public response.

This was, on the whole, just a skirmish in the election campaign. But Mrs Gandhi had utilized the opportunity not only to study the drought-hit, "undeveloped" areas as she said but to gauge the public pulse. Her programing showed, however, the three emphases that her electioneering would have later. There were again, first of all, the women. I think she was conscious from the very beginning of the enormous advantage she had in being able to appeal to half her electorate in a personal, intimate way—"I, too, have to run a home and look after children" sort of thing—that only another woman can. Then there were the villagers for whom the most basic issues had to be explained and somehow related to the sophisticated mechanism of political choice. Last, there was the urban audience—comparatively educated, critical, perceptive, conscious of world trends, conditioned to ideological onslaughts, and intellectually free of the male-female distinction in politics. Here she had to talk man to man with a sense of camaraderie and in the more modern context that was natural to her. Even so, she felt the limitations, for among them there was only a very small group with which it was possible to communicate. So she held back—although not from a political commitment—trying to feel with the majority and yet aware all the time, like her father, of wider, more contemporaneous criteria.

She knew what a gulf separated her from the masses. In spite of all their sacrifices to the cause of freedom, Motilal was notable to shed his aura of riches, nor Nehru his aura of aloofness, "I took to the crowd, and the crowd took to me, and yet I never lost myself in it; always I felt apart from it,"[10] said Nehru. But although Motilal dominated the great parliamentary debates of preindependent India against alien rule with flashing wit, heavy sarcasm, and unassailable logic, Jawaharlal talked to the poor and won their hearts. As far back as 1920, he realized "how cut off we were from our people and how we lived and worked and agitated in a little world apart from them."[11] In his first direct contact with the Indian peasantry on his visits to Pratapgarh in June 1920 his eyes were opened to a "hungery naked mass" which was to remain his mental picture of India. As a shy, young aristocrat, educated in England, he had become used to the complex nuances of the English language. He was frightened at the idea of speaking in public, especially, in Hindustani. But this very shyness found a cathartic release in a contact with India's common man. "How could I be shy of these poor, unsophisticated people," argued Nehru then. "I did not know the arts of oratory and so I spoke to them, man to man, and told them what I had in my mind and in my heart."[12] The result was nothing short of a mystic communion which soothed his doubts, enriched his confidence, and made it difficult for his opponents to detach even his mistakes from the intricate framework of idealism and practicality against which his life and work were placed.

Nonetheless, he set a trend in style, and his halting, conversational, intimate, introspective approach began to be employed more and more by the younger generation of politicians. His daughter also acquired some of his manner. There was an attempt, by those who oppose her, to dismiss her as a pale imitation of her father on the ground that she learned all she knew from him, that she was unduly influenced by him and had no opinions of her own. "But it is important to remember," said a colleague of hers animatedly, "that Nehru influenced the entire younger generation of Indians. We were all under his spell—why should she be singled out for being weak just for that?"[13] It is interesting to note that although she certainly learned how to tackle a mixed crowd from him, her style is still very different. She is comparatively brief, she seldom repeats herself in a speech, and she is concise, dramatic, and to the point. She is not a thinker like Nehru who could be provoked by an idea at the spot and take himself and his audience on an analytic tour of its origin, its implications, and its future application. She uses homely similes and restricts herself to the main themes that she chooses to speak upon. But although outwardly confident, there is an inner reserve which does not allow her to relax with the masses, as her father did.

"It may seem odd," he said once, "but I feel most comfortable in dealing with them [the masses] directly. I am fairly frank with them. With a large crowd I speak my intimate thoughts always more than in a small committee."[14] And with his daughter it is the opposite. The barriers only really fall, and then infrequently, with a small, limited circle of confidantes. The prime minister reveals her basic convictions and herself as a person only when she is alone with someone. She eschews the public projection of a personal image. But it also explains the passionate loyalties that she evokes from those who work closely with her and know her well.

As the campaign got into full stride Indira saw that her ability to draw crowds was unparalleled. Whereas other Congress or non-Congress leaders could get large audiences in areas where they had influence, she could get crowds anywhere in India at any time. On a visit to Bihar in September streams of people from the city and the nearby villages came to the airport to catch a glimpse of her. At Monghyr and Sadaqat Ashram in West Patna there was occasional hostile shouting from an anti-Congress section of the crowd, but there were half a million again who sat through and cheered her statement that India would steer herself through her bad days. "The Congress organization is as strong as before," she cried, "and it is the only organization which can keep the country together to meet the challenge of poverty."[15] Always, crowds, garlands, and a shower of flowers —people touching her *palloo*, falling at her feet, pledging loyalty, swearing sacrifice, evoking associations of her father, her husband, all the crowded past. There were always the garlands, the effusive smell of marigolds, jasmines and roses; the hands eager to help; the women with wistful looks;

and the shrill cries of restless children. She spoke to the Youth Congress leaders about her expectations of them: "All of them have not been fulfilled,"[16] she said, but she told them that courage and enthusiasm would elicit recognition from society. And then she pointed out, with all the assurance that was relevant to her own controversial entry into the field, "Nobody is given an invitation to join politics. You show your worth and you will get the place."[17]

By October 1, when she visited Kashmir, she was in a fighting mood. She looked like a bride as she drove in an open car from the airport to tour Srinagar; her head was covered with a thick, soft silk sari and she had a shy smile on her face as the flower petals rained down along the route and filled the car with their heady fragrance. But at the sports stadium, where 75,000 people were gathered in eager expectation, she began a speech in an aggressive vein. She said she admired the people of Kashmir for having gone through two wars in five years with Pakistan and China without turning a hair; she declared her willingness to be on good neighborly terms with both these countries but she cried spiritedly as the applause began to thunder in the valley, "India would never buy peace with dishonor."[18] She brought the same fury to her remarks about the economic war in which India was engaged and the fact that the discontinuance of foreign aid at a crucial point had hit industrial production. It is a lesson, she said, never to depend upon external aid. But "aid or not aid, we shall continue to advance," she affirmed, "nothing will be allowed to impede our progress."[19] Yet, because Kashmir was a largely Muslim majority area, she emphasized what most people tend to overlook, that India had the third largest Muslim population in the world, but was one of the few countries which had avowed to achieve democratic secularism. These were generalities carrying the weight of her other promises but they held her audience in thrall, so that her entire seventy-minute address was interspersed with resounding shouts: "Indira Gandhi Zindabad," "Azad Hindustan Zindabad," "Sadiq [Chief Minister of Kashmir] Government Zindabad." She did not forget the men who had fought in those wars—the jawans north in the Tithwal and Uri sectors. She went there and told them that they had defended India's frontiers with distinction.

But Mrs Gandhi's expansive, reminiscent, reflective mood while sitting under the trees outside the chief minister's residence later and talking to Congress legislators and workers, led her to make a statement that created apprehension in the hearts of some of her conservative opponents and particularly the free-wheeling Swatantra democrat, Minoo Masani. "Seven years ago," she said, "under this very tree I addressed a similar meeting and pleaded for the extension of the Congress to Jammu and Kashmir. My advice was not relished by some and they complained to my father how ill advised I had been in offering the suggestion."[20] But in relation to the revival of the National Conference she came out with the astounding statement that there was no need for an opposition party (to the Congress) in the present circumstances. She justified her contention by voicing her fear that it might lead to a scattering of nationalist forces with the other party itself "going astray." Her remark was meant to apply specifically to Kashmir. It is easy to see too much in it, of course, because it arose out of a momentary and consuming impatience. But Minoo Masani in a desperate moment of extremist reaction exclaimed on an occasion while referring particularly to this statement of Mrs Gandhi, "Like her father, I tell you, she's a Commie at heart."[21] This is a highly melodramatic misreading of her character. She is not rigid enough to be a communist or an anti-communist in the fanatic sense; she can be obstinate, but not one-sided. As far as the socialist tendencies of both father and daughter are concerned as for planning, an emphasis on heavy industry, equitable distribution—to each according to his need rather than to each according to his opportunity—a greater stake in the public sector than in private enterprise, the aspiration to a welfare state, the whole gamut rests on the foundations of Gandhian training in nonviolent means, persuasion rather than coercion, the belief in the sanctity of the individual, the conviction that a person can be slowly but effectively educated to fit into the framework of a parliamentary democracy. And as much as Gandhi's "spiritualization" of politics set an example for the later reactions and political attitudes of Jawaharlal Nehru, Motilal's deep and enduring belief in constitutional means did in another way. Indira Gandhi was therefore fed from the beginning on a revolution in restraint, that fantastic period in pre-independence history where all the revolutionary things were done, an alien power thrown out, a social conscience awakened, traditional prejudice broken, but all in the most improbable, unconventional, unrevolutionary way.

Again and again, Indira has returned to the theme of peaceful means. At her convocation address at the North Bengal University of Siliguri on October 10, she pleaded with the students not to resort to "the methods of the streets." "If our democracy is to prosper," she said, "we must learn to assert our right to orderly government....This country is yours, its future is what you make it...we have to build this new India....We have to give new life and new meaning to swadeshi, to nationalism, and to modernism."[22] The next day at Darjeeling, in the pure Himalayan air, she told her Congress colleagues of her fear that fascism might sweep over India in the garb of the current wave of hooliganism and the same "methods of the street." She hated the thought of democratic freedom being interpreted as license. This was surely not the voice of totalitarianism that Minoo Masani had talked about. It was the voice of humanism—perhaps the one "ism" that Indira represents best.

The Tripartite Conference, the beginnings of the "ban cow slaughter" agitation, the firing outside Parliament House, the Cabinet reshuffle, the increasingly critical food shortage, and the spate of foreign dignitaries visiting India one after the other kept Mrs Gandhi tied to Delhi for the latter part of October and for the whole of November. Marshal and Madam Tito and President Nasser were followed by Queen Frederika and Princess Irene of Greece on the sixteenth, and soon after, on the twentieth, President and Madame Novotny of Czechoslovakia. By the twenty-seventh there was the decision on denying Krishna Menon the north Bombay seat for Parliament.

There was her forty-ninth birthday on November 19 which she celebrated sentimentally, at Tin Murti. It was only rarely that she allowed herself a personal function such as this after becoming prime minister. Her staff managed to persuade her to have a party. They got a huge twenty-five pound cake covered with lemon frosling and trimmed with forty-nine red rose buds and distributed slices to the great variety of guests who came and were received by her. There was President Radhakrishnan who arrived with a bouquet of chrysanthemums and red roses, and a check for the U.P. and Bihar Drought Relief Fund, Vice-President Zakir Husain, Dr Karan Singh, Governor Padmaja Naidu, an old friend, all of whom also brought contributions. By the evening it was expected that there would be a round collection of Rs 100,000 at least—so really even a personal occasion had its uses for the national good. She wore a strawberry-pink sari with a design in yellow. And on her forehead someone had applied the black line of the auspicious *tilak*. The cake of course was light yellow, and there was more of yellow in the pattern of her clothes. Was she wearing yellow as an auspicious color for her first birthday as prime minister? The coincidence, as on other times, was too marked to be missed.

Meantime, the shadow of the coming election began to penetrate into remote corners of the country. The people began to talk. The parties began to deliberate. The politicians began to make promises. The 1967 general elections were to be the fourth five-yearly general elections that had taken place in the two decades of Indian independence. The number of voters had progressively increased. In 1952, it had been 73 million, in 1957, 93 million, in 1962, 218 million, and in 1967 it was expected to be 242 million. There was a new feature in the voters' composition this time. There were 20 million young people who had come on the voting list for the first time.

Out of the total of 242 million voters, 160 million were between 21 and 40, a generation which was absolutely cut off from the pre-independence struggle and would be expected to have a different criterion for its choice of party or candidate than the Congress-conditioned one of older times. Also, there had been a steadily increasing equalization of the ratio of men to women voters. In 1957 it was 55.75 men to 38.77 women. In 1962, it went up to 62 and 48, and in 1967 it came to 53.47, and with more literacy among women, it was also expected that they would exercise their franchise independently of the political opinion of their men. A majority of India's voting population was illiterate. But adult franchise had brought them to face issues of the most significant choice and despite some glaring inadequacies they had brought to bear on them constructive good sense, as earthy, practical, and realistic as the lessons they drew from the soil.

India's experiment in democracy was working backward. It had given an unlettered electorate the hard shocks of political argument when the foundations of academic perception had still to be laid, but the experiment had blundered through, wonderingly and inexorably to a definite shape. It had been undoubtedly bolstered by Nehru's consistent, inspiring, and unshakable faith. But it was just that which created a lingering doubt: could it survive without his towering influence?

If any country could be knit together by one man, it was India by Nehru from 1947 to 1964. While Nehru was there, no matter what the danger signals, there could be no disintegration of mass loyalty. The first major sign that there would be no panic even in the worst crisis, his death, came with the smooth and unanimous choice of his successor, Shastri. But the method, the mood, and the decision were related here to the small and exclusive group of members of Parliament. The masses still had to prove that they had grown with the system that Nehru had left them, and that could be seen only through a general election. The test was round the corner, only a few months away, and two factors began to create an atmosphere of extreme tension. Theoretically, there was the question of whether or not democracy had really taken root in India. Politically there was the desperate hope of opposition parties that Nehru's absence might portend a major Congress collapse. Apprehensions about the democratic system were largely voiced by international prophets of doom. In India itself, the ruling party was calm to the point of complacency. The opposition predicted chaos but only if the Congress party remained in power. Indira had the buoyant optimism of her father. The people of India, she believed, would always pull through.

The political seduction of the voter was initiated with the election manifestoes of the various parties which were first approved and then released one by one. The first party organ to sit in session was the All-India Congress Committee at Ernakulam on September 22, 1966. The manifesto they issued was in line with the preceding socialistic ones of 1952, 1957, and 1962, which had been drafted by Nehru. The 1967 manifesto was largely approved by his daughter. The most controversial clause dealt with the need for "social control of banks," but the controversy, except for one major opposing speech by Babubhai Chinai, centered on the ambiguous nature of the phrasing: why beat about the bush, the party left-wing asked, why not call it nationalization? The Congress they said had always affirmed its socialistic principles but never put them into practice. This "social control" seemed to be another one of those gambits calculated to pull wool over the eyes of the electorate. Surprisingly it was Krishna Menon, who was expected to demand nationalization, who defined the advantages of the milder term. According to him whatever the limited difference between social control and nationalization, the manifesto could be said to give the mandate to a future Congress government to socially control credit in the country for a social purpose, namely the removal of poverty. Regardless of the wording, it should be clear that the institutions should be made to subserve to a social purpose. "It is not merely ownership in the public sector but it is putting the institutions thus owned to effective social purposes. As such, if the banks are nationalized, the Reserve Bank should be first nationalized."

Indira later put it slightly differently: "What matters is how we interpret these words. Some institutions under government control are not functioning the way they were intended to. The job is to make the institutions function effectively in the interests of society." She was a member of the manifesto subcommittee along with Kamaraj, Jagjivan Ram, S.K. Patil, and Y.B. Chavan, which had the duty of preparing the final draft of the manifesto, but there was nothing to show that she had led the issue on bank nationalization. Yet the fact that a few days later the subcommittee came out with a consensus in favor of "social control of banks" with the proviso that the initiative be left to the government seems to suggest that she had, as prime minister, given an assurance on behalf of the government. At the working committee meeting on September 11, there was overwhelming support for a complete "bank takeover," but the "social control" concept was ultimately accepted probably with a view to making it less embarrassing for the government. The manifesto was passed unanimously.

On October 3, the Jan Sangh released its manifesto. On October 8, the general council of the Praja Socialist party adopted its manifesto. Two weeks later the Akali Dal (Sant group) and the Hindu Mahasabha released theirs. And then, of course, the S.S.P., the C.P.I. (Right), and the C.P.I. (Marxist), on December 15, the Swatantra party on December 13 and the D.M.K. on January 2. Except for the Swatantra party, all were in favor of the nationalization of banks. But the Jana Sangh and Hindu Mahasabha had no economic policy to speak of and concentrated mostly on the need for military preparedness on the part of India, specially in relation to Pakistan and China, while the P.S.P., whose aspirations and the methods advocated could hardly be distinguished from those of the Congress, differed in calling for self-sufficiency in both conventional and nuclear weapons.

The Jana Sangh stood against the policy of nonalignment as "a permanent creed" but advocated instead "bilateral alliances" of convenience which would make it possible, according to its thinking, to hunt with the hounds and run with the hare; like Pakistan, which could with impunity flirt with Communist China under the protective shadow of the U.S.A. Both the Jana Sangh and Hindu Mahasabha represented their particular brand of tough chauvinism with the former calling for "the ultimate reunification of India and Pakistan," and the latter for a revision of the Constitution to make India "a democratic Hindu State" which blitherly ignored the inherent contradiction in the concept of a "theocratic democracy." The major difference between the C.P.I. (Right) and the C.P.I. (Marxist) lay in the pro-Moscow "revisionist" line of the former and the extreme pro-Peking alignment of the latter. The Swatantra stood opposed to all the others. It advocated in essence "proper defense alliances with reliable powers," which was only another expression for a military pact with the West, free enterprise in trade, a system of proportional representation, that is, the number of seats in an assembly or Parliament that a party wins should be commensurate with the percentage of votes it gets within, of course, a democratic framework and a vague but high-sounding call for a restoration in the body-politic of "the Gandhian principle of giving first priority to the rule of dharma as the true basis for enduring moral progress and material prosperity."[23]

But whatever the ideological definitions of these parties, they were driven by only one fateful pre-election passion—to oust the Congress, anyhow, anywhere, everywhere, and in every way. For that they were prepared to go to any lengths, and form an electoral alliance with the most irreconcilable party as long as it was not the Congress. A communist spokesman could perorate: "To defeat the Congress in as many places, as many constituencies and as many legislatures as possible, that is the primary aim of our party, because we consider the Congress government as 'the main enemy of the people'."[24] A.B. Bajpayee, the general secretary of the Bharatiya Jana Sangh, gave a hyperbolic call. "The hour of decision has struck. The national general elections are nigh. The wrath of the people has rocked the thrones of [the] New Delhi nawabs. Now is the time for the people to exercise their sovereign right to change the government. Here is the opportunity to sweep away the Congress with all its follies and crimes and corruption."[25] Madhu Limaye, the fiery parliamentarian of the Samyukt Socialist party, gave a surprisingly balanced argument. "Most political parties are in a state of decomposition and decay. While there have been minor shifts and realignments, the pattern revealed by the first general election has drearily repeated itself in the second and third general elections, and threatens, in spite of the collapse of the government party's moral authority and reputation, to reproduce itself in the fourth, unless, in the meantime, the opposition parties bestir themselves, rise above their jealousies and hatreds and so adjust their election strategies as to avoid mutual contest, increase their own as well as other parties' legislative representation and help break the stranglehold of the Congress on the central and state administrations."[26]

But the Praja Socialist party struck a high-minded resolve: "A higher degree of mobilization and morale can be achieved if the forces of social transformation are brought into play, if socialism is taken forward. It is in this task that it wants supporters and allies: naturally, while it calls for cooperation among those who believe in this approach, in the ideals of the nation's defense, democracy, socialism, and national unity, it shuns any alliance with those who have basic differences with it."[27]   The Jan Sangh and the Swatantra parties ruled out any alliance, electoral or in government, with the left or right communists.   But the effort of the opposition parties as a whole was geared to form united fronts where necessary and break the advantage that a split vote automatically gave to the Congress party.   They also envisoned a different role than the one they had been playing so far.   As a disparate group of protest they had been able to ventilate the people's grievances in the assemblies and in Parliament on isolated issues, keep the government on its toes with effective criticism, and in some cases influence legislation.

But the Congress party in elections with Jawaharlal was one thing and the Congress party in elections without Jawaharlal was another.   As a combined organ of protest, the opposition now saw an opportunity to provide an alternative government.   They decided, however, that they would fight the elections on the basis of their individual programs and only afterward, if their combined strength came to more than that of the Congress party in any state or even at the center, would they decide on a common program by which to set up a government.   It was clear, however, that the election would not be fought on the level of political theory but on the regional, personal, and parochial levels that had prevailed in the past.   But the growing despair of the opposition this time made them steadily increase their use of the weapons of personal vilification and pre-election unrest. The *bandhs,* the gheraos, the student agitation, the cow slaughter ban movement were not necessarily begun with that end in view, but were certainly utilized by the opposition as an effective means of either embarrassing the government or discrediting it.   On the ruling party, however, this had an oddly unrealistic effect. The Congress thought it could safely assume that the opposition was behind various agitations. It tended to overlook the fact that the basis of this unrest might be a genuine grievance, that the people were seething with a new awareness of their power, and that half the electorate of India now consisted of a new generation that would not vote Congress because of sentiment for its past associations with the freedom struggle.   It preferred to rest on its laurels and its major link with the past, Indira.

The opposition sought to break that link and their "smear tactics" became virulent when they were directed against the person of the prime minister herself.   They could not attribute shady political deals to her as they did to some of her ministers, so they took up the most petty personal angle. They accused her of having accepted a mink coat as a present from the notorious Dharma Teja[28] at a time when her position as Nehru's daughter enjoined upon her, they said, a semi-official sense of responsibility. They said she had bought shares in concerns by using the advantages of her position.   She of course made a spirited denial. But the manner of her reaction confirmed her as a decent person who felt revolted by the tawdry level on which politics could be played rather than as a seasoned parliamentarian. She gave the rebuttal, not in the Rajya Sabha where it was made, but at the meeting of the Congress parliamentary party later, where she denounced the allegations as "false and baseless."

She later explained that the irritation she had felt made her want to get up and answer the allegations there and then in the Rajya Sabha, but she had been "advised not to" because it would have provoked other Congress members and the opposition into a prolonged, bitter, and more unseemly personal wrangle. The point of the matter is that had she had enough parliamentary experience, she could have used this as an opportunity to expose the opposition's rather childish preoccupation with inanities when there were bigger issues at stake, and to chastize them for lowering the criteria of political dialogue. This is where her steady refusals in the past to stand for parliament took their toll, for if she had been able to combine parliamentary experience with the enviable background she already had she could turn it into a formidable weapon of leadership. However, there is the question of style. Her style is essentially personal, involving quiet and effective working behind the scenes, and the slow building of a trend.

The first major demonstration organized in the capital and directed particularly against the "Indira government" was that of the right communists on September 1. About 50,000 people marched from the Red Fort, the imposing Mughal structure bridging old and New Delhi, and wound their way through Connaught Circus to Parliament House, carrying banners that said, "Indira Government Must Resign."   In a speech to the rally, Chairman S.A. Dange said that "this would be the last march of the party." He thundered, "No more will we come to Parliament House and demonstrate. If you [the government] don't mend your policies, we will find some other ways....This is the last and final warning."[29]

But this was actually the beginning. Shortly afterward the Jana Sangh organized demonstrations against the government's economic policies in the three states of Uttar Pradesh, Rajasthan, and Madhya Pradesh, significantly the three states in which it hoped to win the elections.   Student riots erupted in Madhya Pradesh and spread over the country.   In Uttar Pradesh, Congress Chief Minister Mrs Sucheta Kripalani explained carefully to a puzzled audience in a village that student violence was the result of the dangerous schemes of the left communists to upset the socio-economic equilibrium. Nevertheless, the discontent could not be attributed to a pre-election up-surge and Kamaraj put it in a nutshell when he said, "There was a growing lack of communication between the student community, the academic authorities, and public men who are charged with the duty of interpreting to the new generation the meaning of the new, free, equal, and democratic society we are engaged in building up."[30] But just how confused was the thinking and how befogged were the leaders of party rivalries became apparent when the Jana Sangh came out with an assessment that this was a revolt of "volatile" youth against their living conditions, while another opposition spokesman, Dr Harekrushna Mahatab (formerly a Congress chief minister of Orissa) blamed the Congress for fomenting this lawlessness. And at the U.P. Congress political conference at Muzaffarnagar which the prime minister attended, Kamlapati Tripathi admitted the party had failed in inspiring the younger generation but added that history would not forgive them for spelling danger to democracy by their use of violent methods. Mrs Gandhi put it more soberly: "While efforts to solve these [the students'] difficulties would be made within our limited means, it must be understood that agitations and bandhs harm society and weaken the country."[31]

On November 2, the Jana Sangh moved a motion of no-confidence against the Congress government in Parliament. On the same day, troops were flown to Visakhapatnam in Andhra Pradesh to help civil authorities meet the violent turn taken by a widespread agitation demanding the location of the fifth steel plant in Andhra. There was a curious background to this. It seemed from all accounts that regional congressmen were themselves involved in the agitation as a way of pressuring the government into granting Andhra this steel plant. They had apparently turned the national agitational mood to their own limited parochial account. Mrs Gandhi was furious. When Andhra Chief Minister Brahmananda Reddy flew to Delhi to ask her to agree to have the plant located there she answered with a flat "no". She told other members of the Congress parliamentary party concerned, "I believe in diversification of industry in states which are without them.... When we have the resources perhaps we can think of setting up all of them. But today it is not possible. We are short of resources. What resources we have are being diverted to programs like irrigation."[32]

By October 31 the agitation for a ban on cow slaughter had gathered force, which made Mrs Gandhi say that any decision taken under pressure would lead to the interpretation that it was not an independent, well-considered one. She said she realized that the issue had a strong sentimental tenor but it nevertheless existed within an economic and constitutional framework that had to be taken into consideration. But on November 1, 280 sadhus, the saffron-robed order of religious wanderers who represent on the one hand the apex of the Hindu search for individual spiritual salvation and on the other, the most decadent ritual conservatism, were arrested in the precincts of Parliament House when they defied a prohibitory order banning the assembly of more than four persons, and forced their way in to demand a ban on cow slaughter.

On November 2, Mrs Gandhi presided over the executive committee of the Congress parliamentary party which unanimously approved an effective ban to be promulgated all over the country. The same day, the Congress Working Committee met, considered the executive committee resolution and decided that it would ask the various states to fall in with the decision. But it gave the major portion of its time to the increasingly critical food situation. The opposition, however, was out to exploit this very dilemma. On November 7, a massive procession of supporters of the ban swelled in the streets of Delhi, converged from three directions on the Minto Bridge leading to Connaught Place and emerged outside Parliament House. It was an overwhelming amalgam of sadhus, politicians, and hooligans welded together by an impractical goal and provoked into creating a crisis which was to boomerang on them. For the violence that erupted immediately alienated the sympathy of the common man.

While the procession was winding its way, until then peacefully, toward Parliament House, Mrs Gandhi was waiting in a crowded Lok Sabha to give her reply to the debate on the third motion of no-confidence against her government since she came to power. Early in the day the speaker had to adjourn the house for half an hour when it became impossible to control the effusions of the tall, hefty Jana Sangh member, the saffron-robed Swami Rameshwaranand, on the issue of the cow-slaughter ban. He was finally suspended for ten days. But the mood of the house remained tense, angry, frustrated, and bitterly critical as one member of the opposition after another rose to chastise the government on various points, but principally on its inability to check rising lawlessness. Just before 2.00 P.M., when Mrs Gandhi was to speak, a short, burly-looking man rushed down the aisle into the central hall, threw up his hands and shouted, "Atrocities are being committed outside while you people sit calmly here. The police are firing and innocent people are being killed." The man was obviously dramatizing himself. "I was there, I saw," he screamed. The house was in an uproar. Mrs Gandhi hurriedly consulted a member of her staff and apparently sent one of them out to report on what was happening.

When the procession reached the gates of Parliament House the expelled Swami Rameshwaranand climbed up to a makeshift rostrum and made an inflammatory speech in which he urged the demonstrators to surround Parliament House and not let the ministers come out. A peaceful crowd turned into an unruly mob, and tried to swarm the gates. The police lathicharged, then fired tear-gas shells, and finally bullets; some people were killed. On their frenzied run back along the route they burned buildings, destroyed private cars, vehicles, buses and, in an unprecedented impulse, set fire to the houses of K. Raghuramaiah, minister for technical development, and of Congress President Kamaraj.

When Mrs Gandhi rose to speak in the house, she was shouted down. She shrugged her shoulders disgustedly and sat down until there was comparative calm. Some members of the opposition walked out. She was then heard in silence: "What was happening outside was an attack on our way of life, on our values, and the traditions we have so long cherished." She made it clear that she thought the atmosphere of lawlessness in the country had been encouraged. "Whether it is among students or among other sections of the people there is a very deliberate attempt to incite them to violence...the opposition has an important role to play in a democracy and we want to give the views of the opposition full consideration. We do it. But I submit that they sometimes take advantage of this and it is because of this that we witness some of the things which we are witnessing outside."[33]

She spoke slowly and clearly but in a low voice. She looked small and unprepared amid the vast lot of sullen M.P.s and the courageous words of her speech were lost in her timid stance and the schoolgirlish inflexion of her voice, which is particularly prominent when she speaks in English. It was surprising that in the pandemonium that preceded her speech she did not get up and rebuke the others into silence as her father definitely would have done. She seemed reluctant to assert her authority over her arrogant colleagues and to that extent her performance was disappointing. The Lok Sabha, however, rejected the motion of no-confidence by 235 votes to 36 with three abstentions.

Late that night, after a curfew had been promulgated in the affected area, Mrs Gandhi drove through the streets examining the damage, while Home Minister Nanda did the same separately. She had not wanted Nanda in her cabinet from the very beginning, but she had kept him under pressure from the Congress president. She now saw an ideal opportunity to replace him with someone of her own choice. At the cabinet meeting earlier in the evening members had been vociferous in their criticism of the way the problem of law and order, which was under the jurisdiction of the home ministry, had been handled. Mrs Gandhi had remained silent, which Nanda rightly took as a sign of her lack of confidence in him. He offered to resign. But on November 8, a flabbergasted Lok Sabha first heard the home minister give the exact sequence of events that led to the shocking violence the day before culminating with the attack on Kamaraj's house. The prime minister suggested to Defense Minister Chavan, who had just returned from Bombay after an operation, that he take over as home minister. On the thirteenth this was officially confirmed, and Nanda was finally out. But the government's ineptitude in controlling lawlessness in the states or at the center invited derisive comment. "Mrs Gandhi's government," sneered Frank Moraes in the *Indian Express,* "has been the target of both concentrated and dispersed criticism over the past many weeks if not months, not only from her avowed opponents but by the more dangerous and subversive elements who masquerade as her friends. It matters little to us whether her government survives or not but it matters or should matter greatly to every Indian that our country should be so exposed to the obloquy and shame that our irresponsible Minutemen, holy and unholy, rightist and leftist, young and old, have now reduced it to....Monday's events were the climax to a weak-kneed erosion of its authority by the government and to a surrender of their responsibility by the people."[34]

The *Hindustan Times* tried hard to be understanding. "Mrs Gandhi, required to make party points at the expense of the opposition in reply to the no-confidence debate, could not be expected to be entirely fair in her analysis of the situation. That some of the opposition parties have scant respect for constitutional methods and have taken advantage of the opportunities offered for generating violence and the law of the street is of course true. The whole truth, however, is somewhat different. It is that Congress governments at the center and in the states have, by running away from their duty to preserve law and order, brought about an atmosphere in the country where the use of force is not only unchecked but is seen to pay."[35]

But the irony was that if what a commentator called "the pre-election paralysis" seemed to mark governmental activity or rather inactivity at this period, a monumental confusion seemed to prevail in the Congress organization. The date fixed for the final selection of candidates became far overdue. Principles were thrown overboard in the race for the ticket. Personal rivalries imposed their own prejudiced, partial criteria in the choice of candidates. Even the AICC seemed to have no time to plan tours for the prime minister or anyone else. Mrs Gandhi's program was outlined by her own staff after sifting the requests received from various states.

The Congress was to pay dearly for its laxity and what the *Hindustan Times* called "its mistaken analysis" that "the general unrest [was] not only to be expected but welcomed as denoting some kind of a revolutionary *elan*." The next few weeks preceeding the elections saw an intensification of angry reaction against authority, which by now meant the Congress and its leaders, the idealistic awe in which the organization had so long been held having been broken by the cow-slaughter agitators when they burnt the Congress president's house and made him flee for safety. Henceforth, the Congress would not be immune to the pre-election tensions and the election uncertainties that beset any political party. In fact, as congressmen began to move out to their constituencies for the election campaign there were an increasing number of incidents where their meetings were disrupted and the speakers heckled, booed, and sometimes run off the platform by volleys of shoes, and, what was more serious, stones.

2. PATTERN

The first of the stone-throwing incidents took place on January 2, while Morarji Desai was addressing a meeting at a small town called Dhrangadhra on the first day of his election tour of Saurashtra. At his meeting in Surendranagar two days later, the trouble began when a procession of about 150 women shouting "Ban cow slaughter" and "Bring down cost of living" reached the scene. This provoked the audience, and in the confusion some members of the crowd began to pelt stones onto the platform.[1] Again, at

Jaipur, on January 8, it was a Desai meeting that provided the occasion for unruly violence. But this time it was apparently the result of an organized attempt by opposition parties.

On January 9 and 10, it was the redoubtable D.P. Mishra who became a victim of this brand of political humiliation. Most of the public meetings he addressed while touring the two districts of Ratlam and Mandsaur in Madhya Pradesh were disturbed, beginning with the chanting of hostile political slogans and ending with the throwing of stones. In some cases, the police officials and members of the audience were injured. On January 12, a meeting organized in Ajmer to launch the Congress election campaign with Chief Minister Mohanlal Sukhadia as chief speaker had to be abandoned because of persistent heckling and the chief minister, the finance minister, B.K. Kaul, and the deputy education minister, Prabha Mishra, had to leave under protective police escort. On January 14, another meeting of Morarji Desai's, this time in Monghyr in Assam, erupted into violence and an order had to be promulgated banning meetings, processions, and the carrying of arms. He was again unable to speak at Dhanbad, so at a press conference at Durgapur on January 15, he accused the opposition parties of having created the trouble.

On January 15, it was Allahabad which showed a hostile face. Twelve miles away, at Lawain Kalan village, a crowd broke up a meeting which was to have been addressed by Kamla Bahuguna, president of the Allahabad District Congress Committee, and stoned her car. And on January 20, Allahabad finally cast sentiment out by stoning the car of Vijayalaxmi Pandit while she was driving along the road named after her sister-in-law, Kamala Nehru. It was at the height of the U.P. employees' strike and when she saw a procession consisting of part of this disgruntled force coming in front, she asked her driver to turn into a by-lane. But the by-lane was too narrow, so the car had to be abandoned to the stoning that followed while Mrs Pandit stepped hastily into a rickshaw which took her straight to Anand Bhawan, where she was staying. On January 22, while Union Labor Minister Jagjivan Ram was on his way to address a meeting at Buxar in Bihar, his car was stoned by students along with other vehicles and jeeps that were following him. The meeting was canceled. Before that, the students had made a bonfire of Congress flags and khadi caps. But it was U.P.'s increasingly anti-Congress face that provided the real surprise because that was the home of the Nehrus, and you could, if you wanted to, read the most inexorable protest in that. In and around Lucknow, for instance, there were alarming incidents in which people snatched away the Congress party flag from vehicles, forced Congress workers to take off their badges, and prevented a Congress meeting from being held at all. It was Allahabad again which provided the drama, because of its past affiliations, of the supreme example of ritual protest. On January 24, a group of young men removed the white caps worn by Congress workers and burned them as symbols of what they regarded as a dead era. There was no doubt that opposition parties took a hand in these hostile demonstrations against the Congress and even sponsored, abetted, and encouraged them, but they found a readier public than ever before, a public which felt resentment and needed only a spur. One could deduce three perceptible stages of intensity in this show of hostility. At the first, it was directed at the ordinary congressman or the local spokesman or candidate. At the second, it turned upon Congress leaders of national stature like the chief minister, the party bosses, or members of the union cabinet. At the third, it denied the Nehru charisma itself by not sparing those most intimately related to him, like his sister, Vijaya-laxmi, and ultimately his daughter, the prime minister herself.

It was against the shape of these coming events that a forty-day election campaign was ultimately planned for the prime minister in which she was expected to cover all the states in the union. Those who thought that the frantic efforts of candidates to get the prime minister to visit their consti-tuencies was a feature only of the Nehru era were mistaken. The same eagerness became apparent, but the delay in the Central Election Commit-tee's choice of candidates did not leave her time to assuage these pleas. Indira Gandhi's first official foray into the campaign proved her the crowd-getter that she was. Though it was anticipated that the two states of Gujarat and Maharashtra would probably be free of the pre-election violence that marked the other areas, it still came as a surprise when Indira's election tour of Gujarat caused unending and totally receptive crowds to roll out. It was even more surprising because Gujarat was Morarji Desai's home state and it was presumed that their long rivalry, stemming from the election contest in 1966, would result in a cool reception to her. But the crowds were so large and so responsive—the general reaction was such that even Nehru might have been pleasantly taken aback—that a correspondent covering the tour was impelled to ask Mrs Gandhi herself as to what she attributed these crowds, and this apparent fascination. She answered with a simple claim: they had always come like that, during Nehru's lifetime, and even after his death. She picked a random example of the year before when she was not even P.M. to illustrate this. She had gone for the opening of the Mankama bridge in Bihar and the local leader insisted that she address a meeting the next evening. Because she was due to leave for Bengal in the morning she told him she might be able to fit in a meeting just before that. When the leader was asked how many people they expected would turn up, he said, "About 30,000 in the morning, but five lakhs in the evening, guaranteed." But when she went to the meeting the next morning, said Mrs Gandhi, there were two lakhs people already assembled. She reacted sharply to the suggestion that this might be only because she is Nehru's daughter—she feels strongly and believes sincerely that her relation-ship with the Indian masses springs from her long years of work amongst them. The opposition however insisted on three reasons. One, that she was the prime minister. Two, that she was a woman prime minister. Three, that she was Nehru's daughter. And then, they said in snide remarks: *"Kya hai, film star hai.* (She behaves like a film star.) That's what they come to see."

The theme of her speeches was a call for cooperation and unity in the country. "We make mistakes," she said, "tell us what they are, help us, and we'll do something." Yet she did not ask directly for a vote for the Congress, and the opposition maintained that it was because she did not dare to. When the cow-slaughter issue threatened to overshadow the political ones, some supporters of the ban thought up a novel gambit to exploit the fact that the prime minister was a woman. They decided to pit the women against her, and avowed that they would get 100,000 women dressed in black saris to demonstrate against the government's policy on this matter at the public meeting organized by the city congress committee at the Kankaria football field in Ahmedabad on the twelfth. Supporters of the ban, however, could muster up only fourteen women to march to the field and they were taken into custody before they could reach the prime minister! But in the audience a large number of women followers of the religious leaders who had begun protest fasts to precipitate a ban stood up, waved black ribbons, and shouted a few slogans when Mrs Gandhi began to speak. This provoked the prime minister into declaring in a ringing voice that the government would not even consider the issue if there was any attempt at intimidation.

Later, the Mahila Congress (women's congress) and about forty women's organizations and welfare bodies gave her a mammoth reception. In a short address she asked them to pause to consider the reasons for the comparative disfavor in which the Congress found itself and then attempt to do something about it. She particularly advised them to seek greater representation in elected bodies commensurate with the equal rights that they enjoyed with men. And all the while, watching the wealth of feeling generated in his home state for the woman who had been, and would be again, his rival, was the stoical Morarji Desai.

But what was seen to be significant, apart from the size of the crowds that Mrs Gandhi drew, was their composition. There were three obvious elements—the women, the younger people, and the villagers and mill workers. The reason for the comparative absence of white collar workers was that the rising cost of living had hit the urban middle and lower middle class the hardest, while the farmer was happy that he was getting more for his produce than ever before. The Congress was going to survive on the basis of its rural vote, for there the current disillusionment with the party met with a setback against persistent sentiment but also increasing well-being.

Indira Gandhi's election campaign, which brought her every moment into the public eye, disproved once and for all the stories about her ill health. Under a slender exterior the woman had a kind of steely energy with which it was difficult for those accompanying her to keep pace. She wore no make-up or "what little there was," said one of her party, "probably came off in the course of the hectic touring of about eight hours a day and at the end of it she didn't seem tired as we were."[2] This was, mind you, without the strain of having to make the speeches she did, the main ones, the small ones, the wayside ones, the right ones, the careful ones, the forceful ones, the private ones, and the endless capsulizing of a dream into terms of communicable reality.

On December 23, the shy, thin, scrawny-looking seventeen-year-old who had left Shantiniketan to be by the side of her dying mother, went back to lay the foundation stone of a new building for the university library. It brought back nostalgic memories. She had arrived during the Paus winter festival that celebrates the rice harvest. Its celebration had begun with the recital of Vedic hymns and the singing of devotional songs under the unforgettable Chhatim tree. And yet, she could barely recognize her old university, it had grown so much in space and character. "We cannot stop it," she commented. "The whole world is changing, and so is Shantiniketan." But what did she feel coming back, she was asked. "A sense of fulfillment," she answered. And then went on to make a stirring convocation address the next day.

"The major task of our educationists is to stress the creative aspect of university life," she said, "but this sense of common intellectual endeavor is conspicuously lacking in many of our universities. It is sometimes said that universities reflect the situation which exists in the rest of society. This may be partly true but if it is true, it is unfortunate, for it is from universities that the higher values flow, and they are or should be the source of idealism." And then, perhaps because it was Christmas Eve or because she was affected by the world vision of culture that the poet Tagore had sought to instill in his extraordinary university, she quoted the Bible to illustrate her point. "'If the salt hath lost its flavor wherewith shall it be salted?' We cannot escape from our responsibility to ourselves or to others. We cannot shape our environment or control events. But we can control our behavior and our own reaction to it. In that sense we shape our destiny."[3] They must not, she reiterated, fall into the habit of an "easy negativism."

Earlier, at an election meeting at Bolpur, the tiny station town from where it is a three-mile route by road to Shantiniketan, she referred ironically to the fact that when India was backward many people "befriended" India, but now that it was progressing fast, criticism had taken the place of the earlier warmth. Obviously there was fear that a strong India would make its impact felt all over the world. The best thing to do, she said, was to rely upon oneself, and not be discouraged by adverse opinion. And it was here that she reiterated the Congress pledge to ensure what the P.S.P. leader had advocated so earnestly as his own party slogan, "democracy, socialism, and secularism."[4]

On December 25, Mrs Gandhi was back in Delhi. The next day, it was officially and finally announced that the prime minister would stand as a candidate from Rae Bareli. On December 27, she went to Shillong to assuage the feelings of the hill leaders about their demand for reorganization of the state of Assam. The president of the Jana Sangh, Balraj Madhok, declared that his party would support every opposition attempt to pit a common, "worthy" candidate against the prime minister. For the new year, starting January 1, 1967, Mrs Gandhi went to Rae Bareli, now officially her constituency, to open her election campaign. Again there were the crowds, and again the flowers and the garlands, the roses and the marigolds and the very heady smell of politics itself, drawing her inexorably and inevitably into its vortex. She had reached the point from where she knew she could never go back to an apolitical anonymity.

The large Jana Sangh element in Rae Bareli which was against cow slaughter made campaigning there dependent on this issue. In fact, it was to be the issue that was to provoke the prime minister the most in her speeches in the northern states, and form the main ground for the opposition attempt to disrupt her meetings. At Rae Bareli, some Jana Sangh demonstrations tried a silly irritant. They turned their own loudspeaker toward her meeting. She stood obstinately and accused them of violating the code of election conduct. The demonstrators were shamed into ineffectuality. But she pointed out the illogical nature of the agitation: Why, she asked, is there such a demand in states which already have a ban (the northern states) and why not one where there isn't? And why, she asked, was everything quiet all the years that she nursed her father's constituency and why did this agitation erupt only before the elections? The Jana Sangh had no program worth the name; it indulged in a lot of sloganizing, and in the name of religion abused the Congress. When someone remarked to her after the meeting that the intensity with which she spoke would act as a strain on her ultimately, she shrugged helplessly, "What am I to do? I get angry, they want to besmear the Congress, that's all."

She was in Rae Bareli only for New Year's Day. On January 3 she went to Hyderabad for a whirlwind tour of three districts in Telengana, where she had to again face the cow issue. "It is not a question of votes," she said while referring to the government's attitude to the ban, "the question has to be viewed in its entirety."[5] But that is not how the slogan-shouting audience at the public meeting she addressed later regarded it. There was persistent attempt to disrupt the prime minister's speech. She was clever enough to start off by tackling the subject of controversy. This confused the agitators although they kept up a slow chorus of dissent. But she seemed to thrive on each wave of interruption for her voice would ring out intensely with even greater indignation and contempt. Hyderabad, significantly, was supposed to be a Congress stronghold, but the next day, leaving at dawn, Indira covered 300 miles of the rural districts of Telengana, where she was heard in rapt silence by vast crowds even though there were some areas which had returned opposition members in the previous election. It was precisely for this reason Mrs Gandhi had been scheduled to go there. This was in line with the decision of the AICC to send its prominent leaders to "problem states" or problem areas, a policy which later resulted in an ironic twist. For many of these prominent leaders themselves lost in their constituencies while they were busy campaigning for others.

Indira's case, of course, was different. As prime minister, she had to campaign with a national conscience, project a national image of the Congress, and concentrate on national causes. Oddly, it was for this very reason that it was difficult to judge whether the crowds that thronged around her in an area signified a possible change of alignment or whether they came due to the appeal which rose above the regional considerations that otherwise came to the fore at the polls.

In Telengana a curious aftermath to the previous election was that most of the candidates who had stood as independents later rejoined, if they were dissidents, or joined, the Congress. This time a large section was again expected to fight the election not only on an independent stand but as favorites of rival groups within the Congress itself. This is what made Indira repeat that while "the functioning of different parties is understandable, the independents represent none but themselves. Their election will not help the country or the people." She did not, however, visit the communist pockets of Nalgonda and Warangal. She was particular about referring to regional problems within the broad national content of her addresses, and she made a definite and very obvious effort to appeal to the women wherever she went, especially in the rural areas. As always, she was sensitive to regional languages. In Telengana, the language was Telegu. So at a place called Kamareddy she learned a phrase and began by addressing the audience as Sahodri and Sahodarulava (sisters and brothers) after which she remarked that that was all the Telegu she could muster, and continued in Hindi. At another meeting, she ended her speech with an exhortation in Telegu, "Congressku otu evala" which is Telegu for "vote for Congress."[6] At Karimnagar, she drew a simile that she knew would appeal to the agricultural background of the people. She made no sophisticated attempt to explain the theoretical base of the Congress party, but said simply about its lapses that if a tree did not bear fruit in abundance it did not mean it should be cut off at its root but that it should be nourished further to enable it to give a better yield.

The undisturbed nature of these rural meetings, and the obvious receptivity of her audience sitting patiently in the burning sun, gave her an opportunity to tell them what her party had been able to do, and to impress the people of this backward region with the socialist aims of the Congress with such attractive phrases as "equality of opportunity," "equitable distribution," and "increased production." All along the route she was welcomed with garlands and the ritual of *aarti* which had first moved her so much when she went with Feroze to Rae Bareli.   Women offered her the auspicious coconut water and there were Muslim women in burqua delighting in such rigid Hindu customs as applying *kumkum* on her forehead! She in her turn would get down from her car, accept this homage in the traditional Hindu way with folded hands, and give garlands and bouquets to the children.   There were flowered arches, bunting, roses and marigolds, and the Congress bosses, whose hearts had begun to doubt the infallibility of Indira Gandhi when they saw the heckling and the disturbance at the meeting in Hyderabad, took heart and felt anew they were right in having placed their faith in her as the biggest vote catcher the Congress had. Besides, they repeated hopefully, it was in the rural as opposed to urban areas that the Congress traditionally had its strongest support.

On her flight to Madras on January 7 to launch the Congress election campaign in the southern states, Mrs Gandhi relaxed and talked to the correspondents accompanying her and was filmed by a West German television unit.   While she was talking to one of the members of the team the coffee arrived.   As soon as she it sipped she made a wry face, and sent it back with the order that it should be brewed better.   The second time it was brought in carefully by a member of her staff, and served in a beautifully laid out silver coffee set.   The incident was cited as typical of the vast difference in approach and style between the late Prime Minister Shastri and Mrs Gandhi.   Shastri, it was said, would never have dreamed of sending the coffee back.   He would have taken whatever there was and probably not even noticed the flavor.   But Indira, like her father, grew up with the precepts of discrimination of her grandfather.

At a students' meeting at Madras later, in exhorting them to fight for princi- ples, she gave an example out of the crowded diary of her grandfather's life in his battle with the British.   At one time, she said, no Indian was allowed to use the Nainital lake to swim or to sail, and it was kept apart exclusively for the ruling British community.   Any Indian contravening this convention was fined Rs 50.   Motilal Nehru took up the challenge.   Each day he would set sail in his boat on the Nainital lake and each day he would pay the exorbitant fine.   Ultimately he won his point for the British authorities gave up in despair and were shamed into abandoning the rule.   She was criti- cized for giving this particular example which showed so glaringly the contrast between what one man could afford and what the majority of Indians could not.   There were people in the country who did not even earn Rs 50 a month, and there she was talking about Motilal throwing it away in a day!

But nobody who knows Indira Gandhi can accuse her of lack of taste.   If you ask her what she hates most she will say simply "vulgarity." But there is a pride.   The pride of a family who had everything, and had something more: the power and the sensitivity to sacrifice it.   A recurrent theme in Indian society, and therefore in its politics, is renunciation and she is very much a part of it. For her it seems more meaningful to give up things you have as it takes more moral strength to renounce them after having known their fateful fascination than if you have never known them at all. In its deeper significance it parallels the tenet of Hinduism which enjoins that you must face experience, transcend the supremely sensual before you can find fulfillment in the silent, imageless sanctum of the inner heart, and that the value of finding fulfillment is the greater for having first seen, known, and then overcome temptation.

Mrs Gandhi won over the students in any event. They had been in the forefront of the agitation for the retention of English as the official language of India. When she addressed them, she was greeted with determined chants like "Down with Hindi imperialism." She countered this by an accommodating tone and the spirited exhortation to think in terms of an "up, up attitude" instead of a down this and down that one. She did not go into the details of the Hindi-English controversy beyond saying that English had to be maintained "since we cannot afford to lose this link with the outside world."[7] There was a tinge of wistfulness when she remarked that she would not offer any advice or analyze what lay behind their fanatical approach because she realized that they would not accept it. But she could not help defining her attitude. "I undertook what is admittedly the toughest job in the world today. I took it without fear, because I count on the support of young people who have the courage to face problems."[8]

Mrs Gandhi visited six major cities in her three-day tour of Tamilnadu: Madras, Coimbatore, Ooty, Madurai, Tiruchi, and Tanjore. She traveled by car, by plane, and by helicopter, and the rice paddy lushness of the southern landscape was matched by the effusiveness of the crowds. At Madurai, the famous temple town, they seemed to come swarming from every corner, street and hutment, a warm, eager half million of them; at Ooty, the "queen of summer hill resorts," where she went to open the Hindustan Photo Films plant, before her helicopter touched ground, she could see the hillside almost flooded over by a sea of human beings, and while driving from Tiruchinapalli to Tanjore the crowd of men, women, and children broke through the cordons at a village stop and surrounded her car. What color! Sometimes women outnumbered men, which seemed part of the spirit of development in the area where new heavy industries defied the centuries' old agricultural pattern. The women really held the future of the country in their hands, she thought; it would depend on how they brought up the children. She was so glad that they now formed an electoral force with which the party would have to reckon. It was becoming clear that the fact of her being a woman prime minister was opening the eyes of avaricious party bosses to her appeal to this new, sizable electorate.

The Tamilnadu tour was a dramatic one, for she was accompanied by

Congress President Kamaraj and on at least two occasions, at Madras and Madurai, the people had a chance to hear them from the same platform. Against rumors of a rift between Indira and him, and against rumors of Kamaraj's stirrings for his own candidature for prime ministership, this became an eager exercise in comparison. He was thick-set, dark and swart like a big black beetle, with piercing black eyes under glowering eyebrows, a full wide mouth turning occasionally into a half-smile, a ready, rural, terse wit, the easy affability, the telling sarcasm, and the local cunning of a village headman. He spoke swiftly and gutterally in colloquial Tamil rich with innuendo. He established an instant rapport with his audiences. Indira Gandhi was small, slender, and sophisticated and spoke earnestly in smooth, careful English. Her appeal was to the people direct, in mass meetings. Kamaraj tackled them effectively at the organizational, personal, back-slapping level. In his speeches he hit out at the opposition front of nine parties formed against the Congress. "Can nine lame men by tying themselves with each other hope to run faster than a normal and healthy man?"[9] he would ask, or "Who will be able to digest nine dishes mixed together?"[10]

Mrs Gandhi would not name the parties but talked at length about the "negativism" of opposition alliances or the "one party"—meaning the communist—which according to her seemed to want to participate in the democratic process only to destroy it from within. She got what Kamaraj called a "queen's welcome" in Madras and in spite of her taciturn demeanor and her sudden withdrawals, she displayed a superb showmanship. Although her style of speaking was quite different from her father's she showed the same delight in communicating with a crowd; standing up in an open jeep on village roads or in a sleek convertible on the main streets of cities and acknowledging with folded hands or a wave the cry of the multitudes; throwing garlands and bouquets to eager, scrambling hands; fondling a child, saying a word to the women; stopping the car and getting out for a wayside group and accepting their garlands and flowers, all with an untiring, receptive, slow smile of obvious pleasure. In fact, these were the crowds that went to her head. It were they that made her say in a controversial interview with a news agency on December 25, 1966, that even though there might be differences within the party, her "position among the people was uncontested,"[11] a statement, her party colleagues argued, which implied her desire to go above and beyond the party mandate. The fact is that it was India's millions who gave sanction to the tremendous authority of Nehru over the party organization. As popularity with the crowds was a major factor in her ascendency to the prime ministership, his daughter thought, then it was reasonable to derive repeated sustenance from that continuingly loyal source, and as far as possible strengthen it.

The question had become imperative with the increasingly frequent clashes between her and Kamaraj, for although she was grateful to him for his unqualified support for her candidacy in 1966 she was not prepared to forever grant him the veto in government or Congress affairs. After all, it was she who was the prime minister. But to maintain at least a facade of the unity she thought was necessary, she demurred when faced with the question. "There are no differences really. Of course there are bound to be divergent viewpoints on candidates."[12] The difference anyway had not resulted in any diminishment in the way she was welcomed in the Kamaraj area. She had always received an enthusiastic response in the south, she remembered, and even in Kerala, only six months before, Communist black-flag demonstrations against her had been swept away completely in the tide of support for her. Madurai had been the focal point this time in Tamilnadu with its surging crowds. She had been very moved. Perhaps it was that which impelled her to make an unscheduled, slightly sentimental, impulsive visit to the Meenakshi temple. She had been accorded temple honors, and it seemed fitting that she should worship there, a little, quietly, and so she did.

Then, the round began again. In her three-day tour of Mysore State, she covered six districts, traveled 600 miles, and made twenty-two public speeches. It was good to inaugurate the Tungabhadra canal project, undertaken jointly by the states of Mysore and Andhra Pradesh; even the completion of the first stage of the project was going to make a radical difference to the drought-stricken areas of Rayallaseema, and a total of 450,000 acres would ultimately be irrigated in the two states.

A big country needed big plans, big decisions. It was projects like Tungabhadra which replenished her faith and made her reaffirm at the meeting in Bangalore and on other occasions that the center was keen on sponsoring as ambitious a Fourth Plan as possible because "the country's needs were great." According to her, if the people of India felt chary of assuming the burdens of defense and development now, they would not be able to do so later. It was not a single revolution that they were going through, but a revolution at all levels—economic, technological, social, intellectual, psychological, and aesthetic—and "to be creatively alive," as she said in her convocation address to the students of Bangalore university, "it [India] must mold the future out of its own experience and also recognize differences between assimilation and mere imitation. The conflict in India was not primarily one of ideology as such, but a clash between those who clung to old ways of thought and those who wanted India to understand the changes occurring all over the world and adapt herself to the needs of the second half of the 20th century."[13]

That it was doing so, albeit slowly, was evident for at all her meetings in Mysore State there were more women than men. It was ironic to find the past so modern, for at the small historical town of Kittor she found herself in the environments of the great woman fighter, Rani Chennamma, who 150 years back had led her soldiers to battle against the British armies in defense of her tiny kingdom and her country. It hit Indira forcefully each time, this seemingly absurd, outwardly improbable, but inherent juxtaposition of backwardness and daring in India's women. Its legends and its history abounded in examples of this contrast throughout the centuries and ended in the present with such opposites as a woman in purdah, and a woman as prime minister. It was imperative that there should be a dialogue between the two and Indira Gandhi, representing the apex of political consciousness, strove valiantly to light the spark in the other one. If Indian women had taken to the sword in the past, she said to the women of Kittor, they had to take up the sword of the mind to fight another battle, a battle against poverty and illiteracy. But the military tradition personified by Chennamma remained. Mrs Gandhi officially opened a military school for girls in Kittor while a guard of honor consisting of 200 descendants of Chennemma's army stood by.

Although her speeches were full of rhetorical repetition and great sentimental appeal, their actual impact was indefinable. It nevertheless made the D.M.K. leader Annadurai, himself a fluent orator, say her Madras speeches were "poor" and that if Mrs Gandhi was going to speak in Madras in such a "lackluster" manner why did she come at all? This was part of an opposition campaign to try to denigrate her image, and local congressmen, perceptive enough to understand, countered the criticism with the sly remarks that Annadurai would not have been so concerned if the speeches had indeed fallen flat.

There was, however, a comparative disenchantment in the country with Indira. The beginning of her term had been far too full of promise and raised far too many expectations to let the pitch of enthusiasm or achievement remain consistently level. Besides, she had faltered. It was not that she was not going in the expected direction but that she was going too slowly—the very fault about which she had so vehemently argued with her father. In places where urban consciousness was dominant, such as Kerala, and where a rival party had made deep inroads into the popular base of the Congress, she found a palpable stiffening of public response. In other states an odd meeting or two was disturbed, but the crowds were invariably huge. In Kerala, they had been like that when she had visited it six months back. They were not as large on January 13 and 14 but they did listen to her. She could not help hitting out at her old enemies, the communists, whom she had ousted in 1959. At Calicut she charged them with spreading dissension in emphasizing in their election manifesto the differences of pay and facilities between the ordinary soldiers and the officers. India was proud of her army, she stated, and any attempt to create a rift would be "dangerous."

On January 15 Indira was back in Rae Bareli, her constituency. The next day she traveled 90 miles over bad, dusty roads and bumpy paths in the interior areas of this backward region. It was what one report described as a "tour of victory." Rae Bareli was special and it gave her a special

welcome. The opposition was as yet nowhere in sight; there had been
only a stray Jana Sangh banner hung aloft the Congress welcome arch at
Harchandpur, where Indira had made her first stop the previous day. No
one was sure of the number of opposition candidates. There were two
so far. A millionaire jewel merchant, Bishan Seth, a member of the fanatical
Hindu Mahasabha party, who had been promised support in Rae Bareli
by both the Jana Sangh and the Samyukt Socialist party, and Dr Gope Gurbax,
an independent. While Seth's main plank was the cow slaughter issue,
he mentioned some other "fundamentals" that he did not think worth
dilating on. The doctor banked on resurrecting the old romantic theory
that Subhas Chandra Bose was still alive and had been living as Swami
Seradhanand in the ashram of Shoulmari. Dr Gurbax thought he would
be able to win votes if he could promise his electorate an appearance by
the militant leader. On Friday, January 17, Mrs Gandhi filed her nomination
papers before the assistant returning officer who was the collector and
district magistrate of Rae Bareli, J.P. Singh. Here she signed an affirmation
of her "true faith and allegiance to the Constitution of India as by law
established," and pledging to "uphold the sovereignty and integrity of
India."[14]

The integrity of India, sixteen states.[15] Sixteen languages...1,652 dialects.
People, customs, and places more varied than the whole of Europe put
together. Princes, and the poor. A feudal order fighting with democratic
aspirations. Four major religions. A minority as big as the population of
England. A birth every minute. A yearly increase of twelve million. Having
to run to stand still. The necessity for aid. The imperatives of defiant
self-respect. The will to move fighting with the lethargy of centuries.
India at the crossroads. The ideals of two men, Nehru and Gandhi, both
necessary, but mutually contradictory. A legacy of dilemmas. Against
all this a fierce, continuing, consuming desire for unity on the part of those
who understood, and those who cherished an entity that was, indeed, India,
one nation, one people. That was the slogan she presented at Ernakulam,
at the Congress session. One nation, one people. One party, too. She
did not think of the Congress as one party in the dictatorial sense. It was
an amalgamation. If the concept of unity had driven her father to some
early compromises, it had also made Gandhi say that the nation was safe in
Jawahar's hands. She was going to see that it was safe in hers too, through
the same concept, "unity in diversity," and allow for the flowering of local
genius.

There was the conflict in Goa, for instance. There was the Maharashtra-
wadi Gomantak which had been compaigning for the merger of Goa with
neighboring Maharashtra, while the anti-Merger Front and United Goans
wanted it to remain independent Union territory, with its own legislature
and state government. She decided to settle the issue by having an
opinion poll there. The idea met with instant popularity and there was

an unprecedented rush on voting. Even here, it was fantastic really, the women were expected to influence the outcome of the poll because they had constituted nearly 65 per cent of the electorate, and they had participated in the voting proportionately. The decision to hold the poll had a salutary effect in general.

The ludicrous aftermath of the cow slaughter agitation, however, still persisted and was agitating the average Hindu. The Jagadguru Shankaracharya of Puri was on the fifty-ninth day of his fast to protest cow slaughter and there were no signs of his letting up. She was not going to give in either. But the issue had a terrible nuisance value and was going to arise at every election meeting especially in areas where the Jana Sangh was making substantial gains, such as Rajasthan, Madhya Pradesh, and Maharashtra. The people had been incited. In West Bengal, the communists were strong. They would not dare play up the cow issue for fear of tarnishing their "progressive" image, although they realized its vote-catching value well enough to remain silent when it was expected, again in line with their "progressive" image, that they would vehemently oppose the postulates of the agitation.

Indira Gandhi's spirits were high, nevertheless. On the plane from Delhi to Jaipur on the cold, bracing morning of January 18, she looked down at the bare sandy landscape of Rajasthan occasionally brightened by a flaring red, green, blue, or orange *ghagra* and a multihued veil, and remarked chattily, "Isn't it strange how nature compensates—there [in Kerala] it's so lush and green, so people wear white mostly. Here, the landscape is barren and dry and the clothes are so colorful."[16] There were four of us sitting in the special enclosure reserved for the prime minister: Mrs Gandhi, a minister of the Rajasthan cabinet, a member of Mrs Gandhi's personal staff, and myself. The talk turned to the southern beaches and Mrs Gandhi began to tell of the time when she and her father were traveling in Kerala, and all at once she began to get frantic trunk calls from Homi J. Bhaba, India's leading scientist who was later killed in an aircrash. Each time the call would just miss her, for it would come through soon after they would leave a place, or before they reached their next stop. She began to wonder what the urgency was when at last a call caught her at the airport. "And you know what he had to say," she laughed, "he said I must take my father for a dip in a particular bay, because it was absolutely lovely! We did go and swim there, in fact." Her gaeity was undiminished. When we were about to land at Kotah, the first stop, I asked her if I could sit and talk with her at some length in the next two days. She smiled, for her throat was hoarse, "Certainly. But I think we'll have to talk in sign language by then!"

As soon as Mrs Gandhi stepped down the ladder at Kotah, she was garlanded by local leaders and surrounded by an assortment of politicians, officials, and admirers. It was a small landing strip, and just outside the barrier a colorful awning had been set up under which a row of chairs had

been arranged.   In the front was a line of sofas and Mrs Gandhi was escorted
there.   We were all to have tea before going on to the meeting in the town.
The tea came, silver teaset and all.   A local gentleman began to pour it
out while standing, and at the same time Indira murmured, "I'll make the
tea myself." He continued pouring it and filled the cup to the brim, at which
she could not help exclaiming with a sort of controlled irritation in her voice,
"Ap to dal te hi chale jate hain." (You are going on and on filling it up.)   So
another politician quickly suggested, "Make another cup.   Give the P.M.
another cup." But Indira took the teapot and made the tea for herself as well
as for the others.   She sat chatting for some time, and then assured a venerable looking Muslim gentleman that contrary to some reports which were
evidently exercising his mind, the government had no intention of changing
the Muslim personal law.

"There are lovely tales of old Rajasthan," she said in Rajasthan thereafter, "but the tales of new India are also lovely."[17] And then, as people
crowded on to house tops and balconies and trees surrounding the teaming
grounds, she spoke simply, earnestly, unfalteringly in Hindi and explained
in absurdly clear terms to an audience of near-illiterates the cause and
effect of the industrial revolution in England and the political revolution
in India.   In the West, she said, affluence came first: education was imparted to the people because the moneyed exploiters wanted workers for
their factories.   With education came enlightenment, then the demands.
But the means had evolved by then to meet those demands.   Here, in
India, it was the exact opposite.   Political awareness came first, then the
demands.   But the economic condition was not equal to them.   Hence the
tremendous gap between demand and supply.   "But now," she said, "we
must eradicate poverty regardless of class or creed.   Like a child in the
family, if he is ill, he must be cured, otherwise it's a burden to the rest.
So, to government, all of the classes of people are like its children."[18]   Or,
about the need to take advantage of the scientific process: "In the olden
days, people used to be frightened of lightning, they thought the gods were
angry.   But now we not only recognize it but can exploit it.   So knowledge
doesn't mean knowledge from outside alone, but a realization of truth
and science."[19]   About adult franchise: "A long time back, I went to
U.P. I went to speak in a village.   An old man told me that a day earlier a
member of an opposition party had also spoken.   'Have you told the truth
or he?' asked the old man.   I told him, 'If you ask me I'll definitely say
that it's I who am telling the truth, if you ask him, he'll say he is telling
the truth.   The meaning of franchise is that the listener should be able to
decide on his own who between us is telling the truth.'   But the old man
insisted, 'If you think he's not telling the truth, why don't you prevent him
from speaking?' It took me a long time indeed," said Indira Gandhi, "to
explain to him the implications of free choice!"[20]   Her recurrent theme was
the inherent problems of change: "We know no miracle to solve India's

problems. That is why a thirty-year plan was envisaged. Of this only fifteen years have passed. These are the present difficulties, pangs of development, signs of change and as the child grows, his clothes become smaller."[21]

"We have not discarded the old policies of the Congress," she said, "Not because we must hang on to them but because they are still relevant. But there are instances like that of food production where the emphasis has to be greater. America no longer has that much surplus as before, either. No matter what we have to suffer, we must be able to stand on our own feet."[22] And again, there was the homely simile, the patient exposition about the national propensity toward extreme self-criticism: "This repeated decrying of our own achievements leads to loss of self-confidence. If there's a patient and someone goes to him and tells him everyday that he'll die, its quite likely that he would die. But ask any doctor, if that same man is told that he'll be well it's quite likely again that he would get well!"[23]

At Chittor, that historic rampart town, which even against the fiery tradition of Rajasthani bravery, shines with a special brilliance, she seemed inspired. "I've always wanted to see Chittorgarh," she said. "In fact, when we had to fix a meeting with regard to women in the earlier days, we tried to do it in Chittor. Here is a city where the stone walls cry out with valor, where the blood of courage runs through every vein."[24] So she was equally fearless. "We have made mistakes, yes," she said, "but I believe that you cannot progress without mistakes," and she believed firmly too, that the progress was palpably discernible. "I don't want that everybody should become the same, but that each problem should be related to the country as a whole....At the time of Pakistan's aggression we saw how unity could be established....Without unity, we can achieve nothing. One of our mistakes has been that we were hesitant of learning anything from outside—but now, on the one hand, we are fighting poverty, on the other, our young people are going out."[25]

And then, of course, about the women. "Whenever I go out, I'm invariably asked how women in India, so backward, can hold so much responsibility. I feel this is because of Mahatma Gandhi, who brought them out into the political field, and earlier, even if there was general backwardness, there were always a few women who shone like 'a handful of stars' as examples. But it's no use if an odd woman achieves status and importance. The point is to accord that status to the average women."[26]

At Ajmer, sitting on the balcony of the Circuit House overlooking the lake, she talked to some of us accompanying her, on other matters of topical interest, but it was Warren Unna of *The Washington Post* who, being struck by the fact that she had been making a special appeal to women, asked her if she had found any change. "Well," said Mrs Gandhi, "they come in larger numbers now. I've been told that this is the first time they have come out like this. Once, when I was here before, I made a woman take a vow in front of me that she would give up purdah. The next time I found out that her father, mother, and the whole family had been turned out of their village for that!"[27]

Obviously, the change was there. Not only were the women out, they were unveiled. At Chittor the officials said they had to increase the number of the women's enclosures at the public meeting from one to three to accommodate the unprecedented enthusiasm with which they had come. At Nasirabad in the midst of her speech from up the twenty-foot high rostrum, Indira looked at the women and smiled, and at the end, overcome suddenly by an idea, she came to the women's side and walked down one length distributing the garlands she had in her hands. The women stretched out their hands to touch her and one old woman cried out ecstatically, "We remember your father—he did a lot for us."[28] A woman candidate for the Rajasthan Assembly at the same place told me earnestly that all the women were "solidly" behind Mrs Gandhi because they feel that its "the rule of women now!"

Indira spent the night of January 18 at a place called Banswara. It had been a gruelling day but she did not show it. Presiding over the dinner table, flanked by political leaders of the state on either side and the rest of her party, she smiled, chatted, and reacted with pleasure to the merry bantering that went on about the cow issue. I thought provincial minds would be more conservative and reserved, especially on such an emotional question, but there they were, bringing up points about Hindus having taken contracts for selling beef during the war, and that a member of the Shankaracharya of Puri's own family had come and said to one of them that the Acharya had been trapped into an irreconcilable position by his followers, and nothing else. It went on and on in this strain, with twinkling eyes, chuckles, and even open laughter, and that indeed was the most revealing aspect. In fact, when I asked Mrs Gandhi later how she could reconcile her faith in a growing modernism to the fanatical preoccupation of the country with the cow slaughter ban, she referred to this very occasion. "Look," she said, "you wouldn't have heard the sort of conversation you did at dinner if there hadn't been a change."

But while she was in Rajasthan, the tension was at a high pitch, and publicly at least she had to accept that as an important challenge. Her steadfast rationality earned her the reluctant approbation of even as caustic an enemy as Minoo Masani, who said to me on a later occasion that he admired her for her outspokenness. "I must say if I were in her place I might not have been able to be so firm."

Jaipur was the last stop on the way back to Delhi of a tumultuous election tour of Rajasthan. It had been crowds and colors right through from Kotah, Bhilwara, Banswara, Udaipur, Ajmer, and Chittor. But Jaipur was a prestige opposition stronghold. This was the area from where Gayatri Devi, the maharani of Jaipur, had won in the last elections on the Swatantra party ticket and where the traditional awe for the ruling house of Jaipur

With President Lyndon Johnson on visit to the United States, 1966

With Ladybird Johnson, 1966

With UN Secretary General U Thant at the UN Headquarters New York

With late author, Pearl S. Buck, New York, 1966

With Mayor Lindsay and Mrs Lindsay, New York, 1966

With Lawrence E. Spivak in NBC Television program, "Meet the Press"

With B. K. Nehru and Lyndon Johnson, Washington, 1966

At Philharmomic Hall, Lincoln Center, New York, 1966

With President Charles de Gaulle, Paris, 1966

With British Premier, Harold Wilson, London, 1966

With Soviet Premier Alexei
Kosygin, Moscow, 1966

Against a portrait of
Nehru, Nasser, and Tito
—as prime minister

With Khan Abdul Ghaffar Khan before his departure for Kabul, 1969

With Kamaraj

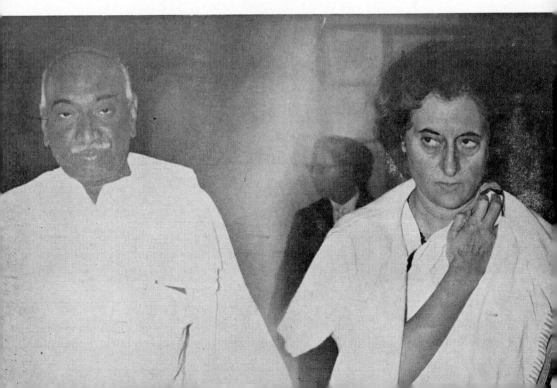

With President
Radhakrishnan at
Willingdon Nursing Home
New Delhi, after her nose
injury in the election tour
in Orissa

Driving home with Rajiv
from the hospital

At an AICC session at Delhi

At a special AICC session during
the Congress split in 1969

At home in 1, Safdarjang Road

As prime minister, January 24, 1966

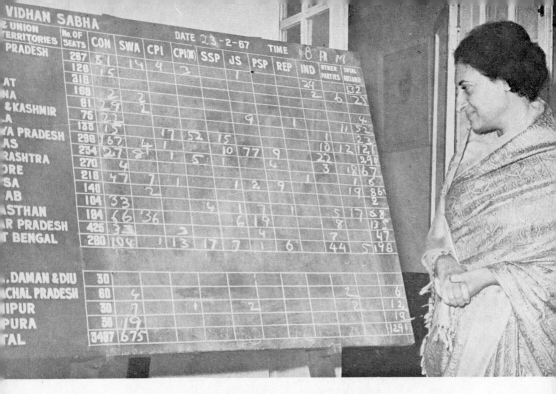

Studying election results, 1967

Being garlanded
by Morarji Desai,
1967

Eating corn

In the lawns of her house at Safdarjang Road, at a press conference after re-election, 1967

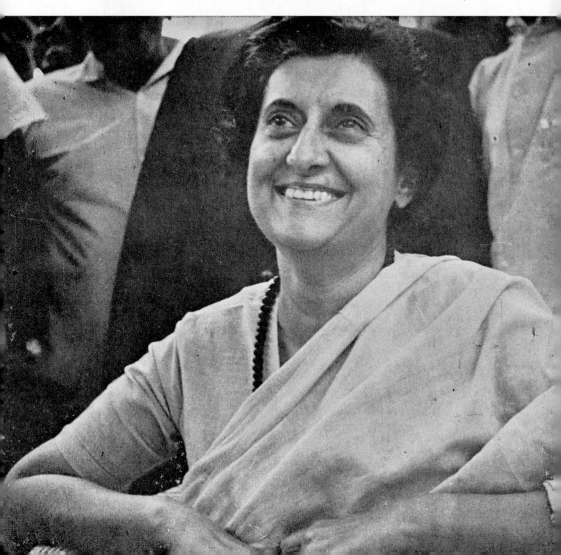

Cutting her bir
day cake, New
Delhi, 1969

At the feet of
Anandmayee

Taking the salute

Among hill people

In Kinnaur, H. P.

With son Sanjay

In Rajasthan, 1967

Acknowledging congratulations of college students for banks nationalization, 1969

At Patna, addressing a meeting after the nose injury, 1967

At Bal Sahyog Bhawan

Indira, a study

With Rajasthani folk dancers

still held the electorate. So much so that the maharani's own campaign seemed like an act of condescension to democracy.

In contrast to Mrs Gandhi's personal reserve, the maharani's aloofness suggested an aristocratic disdain. In contrast also to Indira's apparent simplicity Gayatri Devi adopted the grand manner. She traveled in a sleek station wagon driven by a liveried chauffeur, and carried her own loudspeaker. In her energy she proved almost equal to the prime minister. She could cover 200 miles in a day over dusty, unmade village tracks into the remote areas of Jaipur, make twenty main speeches and attend a number of wayside receptions along the route. For a women who only five years before knew only luxury this was indeed an achievement. She had in addition learned all the tricks of a campaign speech. She said she had been forced to plunge into politics because she could not bear to see the poor suffer. What had the Congress done for them, she asked. "Don't you have to pay a bribe every time you go to the police or officials to get anything done?" The time had come, she said, when instead of aiming to act merely as a break to the swelling ego of the Congress party the opposition must make a bid for the levers of power. Her party, she claimed, was the party of peasants, workers, traders, and the people, and the promise was for abolishing land revenue, ending the permit-licence raj[29] and finding more money for more irrigation and electricity for the benefit of the villagers.

The fact, however, was that Gayatri Devi represented in the Swatantra party the ex-rulers and princes of India, the big moneyed landlords and industrial tycoons and the policies generally associated with the conservative right. In person, she stood as a strong rival image to the prime minister. She was a woman. She was beautiful. She had the aura of aristocracy. And she could rely on the idolatrous crowds whose awareness of new equalities had not dimmed their memory of the time when the court of Jaipur demanding unquestioned obeisance. But she was not as seasoned a politician as Indira Gandhi and although there was no occasion ever for a personal clash between them, Indira was challenged at Jaipur into showing that she could nullify all the appeal symbolized by the maharani.

There was a rumor that the opposition parties had been planning to hold a meeting at the same time as the one scheduled by the state's Congress committee (the Rajasthan Pradesh Congress Committee) for Mrs Gandhi, but had then thought better of it. As it was they could not stop the outflow of people toward the spacious grounds of the Medical College, the place set for the prime minister's address. By 6.30 in the evening, the entire city of Jaipur seemed to be converging on this one point. By seven, when she drove into Jaipur straight to the meeting, she saw spread out before her a gathering of about 100,000 people. The members of her party were tense. She had had a surging reception thus far. Was Jaipur going to turn the tide the other way? Was that immense crowd going to applaud or to jeer? She looked slender but undaunted in a green, printed cotton sari, a gray shawl covering her head and embroidered flat Indian *juttis,* merging into, yet dominating the native scene, presenting an image quite different from the sophisticated, fashionably coiffured woman who goes as India's prime minister to the far countries of the East and West. It was the usual high rostrum but draped all round in the three colors of the Indian flag—white, green, and saffron—and under the numerous yellow and neon lights, she could see immediately in front of her in the first semi-circular enclosure, the women and children with eager, attentive faces. It was unthinkable that they should jeer Nehru's daughter. It was unthinkable that anyone should; it was if there was a limit beyond which political chicanery should not go. It was all right to decry the party, but a personal affront to Indira Gandhi— no. That was how the thoughts of those with her went and it did not help to recall that Nehru himself had had to face great hostility from his own people in his time, and it had taken a grave enough form. There was also the background of the current political scene. The withering away, or so it seemed, of the Congress party. The shedding of awe of its leaders. The spate of incidents relating to the breaking-up of Congress election meetings, and the humiliation that some of its eminent men had suffered. The proportion of the times that they were jeered, booed, or hooted was minuscule compared to the number of times that they were heard, but against the enormous prestige that the Congress had wielded in the past and its great sentimental hold on the people, even that came as a shock, the shock of change. Only Indira could stem the tide because she would be or must be inviolable.

The trouble began when the local Congress leader got up to speak before Mrs Gandhi. A well-rehearsed section of the crowd composed mostly of students, or so it seemed particularly toward the left side, began to scream loudly, "Ban cow slaughter, ban cow slaughter, ban cow slaughter?" The cry was loud and persistent and it made the rest of the people restive. Hearing those slogans and sensing that it was an organized political stunt to disrupt the meeting under the garb of a so-called religious call, something seemed to snap in Indira. She forgot the months of studied restraint, the tedious disciplining in political tact and the severe electioneering routine required of her since December with a curbing of her natural forthrightness.

She strode up to the microphone, caught hold of its stem, and turned forcefully to the group that was jeering. "You can yell as much as you like, you're not going to stop me from saying what I wish to say. How much will you yell? And do you know what you are yelling? Are you aware that this is the twentieth century? Or do you want to go back to the 5th or the 6th? Have you no libraries? Do you read no books, no newspapers, no magazines? Don't you see how ashamed we must feel in the eyes of the world? Are these the issues that must guide our choice?"[30]

She made no bones about the kind of people she thought were behind the cow slaughter agitation—"people who used to take contracts for the supply of beef during the war," she cried, "and I can tell you, they were

not Muslims.'' She said that it was the Hindu Mahasabha and the Jana
Sangh and others of a similiar orientation who were responsible for the
partition. She told them it was the communal, sectarian parties who used
to abuse Jawaharlal Nehru who were now doing the same to her. She
included the princes. She asked the crowd who it was that fought the
British, "We who risked our lives, went to jail, wrecked our homes, or the
rajas and maharajas who stayed in their palaces and entertained the foreign
rulers? They are the ones who wanted the British to stay. Perhaps it
was our mistake that we did not deal with them more harshly. We needn't
have agreed to give them such munificent privy purses. We could still
take them away. But we don't want to do any injustice. They are welcome to their palaces as long as they don't stand in the way of India's
development.''[31]

She spoke in Hindi with her customary clear enunciation, her hands
resting behind her on her back, palms raised outward or holding the mike
in front. Her stance was reserved, but her voice, always slightly high-
piched, had become strident and sharp and the classic lines of her face
with the dark, big eyes, usually impassive in public, were vibrant with anger.
She had changed since the time she had once campaigned for her father in
Allahabad and almost cried because she could not bear the personal
abuse of the opposition. Now, if there were tears, they would be of anger.
Besides, she had learned to control the masses from no less a person than her
charismatic father. Suddenly, she found that the crowd had fallen silent
and was listening. Each time the slogan-mongers grew restive, she would
bring up an unassailable point: meet their emotionalism with an emotionalism
that made them shift with unease. She maintained this high oratorical
tenor for a full forty-five minutes and by the end of it she had the crowd
in her hands. The sloganizing became desultory and half-hearted and when
she asked them all to join her in her usual end-of-speech call three times,
"Jai Hind, Jai Hind, Jai Hind" (Hail India), the cheering was unequivocal.
This was, as Inder Malhotra of The Statesman once wrote, an unfailing
device to make a call for unity on the one hand and put the crowd in good
humor on the other. The next morning the newspapers cried nostalgically
that Mrs Gandhi had at last shown the Nehru temper.

The cow issue remained a live one during Indira's subsequent campaigning in the states of Maharashtra and Madhya Pradesh, but her diatribe
against the princes gathered added momentum in the latter state where there
is one of the thickest conglomerations of ex-rulers in India, including the
famed, historical ones of Gwalior and Indore. At a meeting in Bhopal,
she stated that there were rajas and maharajas in the Congress party, but
the Congress was attempting something which had not been done in 200
years: making the princes think of serving the people! It was typical of
the conditioned response of the majority that when Mrs Gandhi drove out
of this mammoth meeting at Bhopal—such crowds had not been seen they

said since Nehru—after having lashed out at the rajas and maharajas, the
cry that was spontaneously raised in her honor by an old man and some
women outside was, *"Indira maharani ki jai"* (Hail Indira.) At another
place a woman was heard saying in awe, "The maharani of Hindustan is
coming."

The concept of ruler was contained for the ignorant in the word maharani
or maharaja rather than in the unfamiliar, modern title of prime minister.
The monarchial affiliation is still pervasive in India's masses and it partially
explains the unquestioned authority they granted to one man, Nehru, in
the twentieth century, which approximated the supreme authority of the
ruler of old. This was true of course only of the rural majority, because
the greater spread of education and political awareness at the same time,
was leading to a gradual but definite breaking of idols. Mrs Gandhi, because she was not only an inheritor of power but the inheritor of a myth, and
because she had maintained constant contact over the years with "her
people," remained largely untouched by this iconoclastic mood.

Jaipur marked a turning point. It proved without doubt that Indira
Gandhi could tackle and win over a hostile crowd, but it proved also that
she was vulnerable to that hostility in the first place, and that the myth no
longer held. The wrath against the Congress which was evincing itself all
over the country was gradually getting dangerously near the prime minister
and after Jaipur a barrier was down. For though Mrs Gandhi was listened
to with respect, the crowds made no bones about their dislike of the congressmen accompanying her and more often than not shouted them down. But
after Maharashtra and Madhya Pradesh, and another trip to Rae Bareli,
there was West Bengal. Again there were the spilling numbers that came,
again the spirited speech and with only another eleven days left for the
campaign to end it seemed as if the prime minister had carried it off without
blemish. But then, there was Orissa—and Bhuvaneshwar.

"Personally, the moment we drove into the meeting, I had a feeling something was wrong," recalls I.L. Kapur, Press Trust of India correspondent.
He had been accompanying Mrs Gandhi on her trips throughout the
campaign, as he had done to cover Nehru for sixteen years, and apparently
was the only man from among the rest of the party, aside from the
security guards, who remained close enough to follow the details of the
incident that then took place. "The crowd was tense and I was all
attention. I have never been so alert as there. We drove in straight to
the back of the rostrum. I went and stood on a cement platform on the
right, down below, while the others went up. As soon as Biju Patnaik,
chief minister of Orissa, went to the mike, the hooting started. I was
standing and watching the crowd. The restive ones were in the two front
enclosures. There were some on the sides, too, but the ones in front were
more vociferous."[32]

On the rostrum were Mrs Gandhi, Patnaik, the local Congress candidate,

Education Minister Mahanty, and the president of the state Congress Committee, Pani. The two guards stood apart. There were three chairs placed in a row, and one slightly forward nearer the mike. But there was a fair gap between the mike and the chairs and the speaker, whoever it had to be, had to walk some distance up to the mike. With Patnaik there, the crowd was shouting, in Oriya, "Stop. We've heard enough of you. We know you." They did not allow him to speak. So he came back and sat in one of the chairs. Then the P.C.C. president walked up to the mike. He too was hooted down, so he came back and sat in the same row. It was a determined, organized, and prepared crowd. As soon as Mrs Gandhi appeared at the mike the hooting began again. There were jeering, catcalls, oooohs and aaahs, persistent and offensive. For a while she stuck to her usual theme of development and solidarity, but as the hooting showed no sign of abating she switched to the way she spoke at Jaipur.

By that time it was dark, the lights had come on, and some people were jumping and waving their hands and shouting "go back." It was at this stage that Kapur thought he would be able to see better from the rostrum itself so he climbed up and stood near a wooden plank draped in khadi which was supporting the canopy on the right. That is when the first stone came and hit him on the knee. "There was no cry from anywhere, so I presumed nobody else was hurt, but I went down and warned a senior security officer that the stones were coming. He had already seen that some pebbles had swung from across the rostrum and hit the roof of Mrs Gandhi's car which was parked close behind, so steel-helmeted police with lathis moved into the enclosures and formed a human barricade between the crowd in the two front enclosures and the rostrum."[33] The security officer was extremely agitated and upset, and the chief of police, to whom Kapur spoke, suggested that the P.M. should wind up her speech and come down. Two security men had gone up to her and were trying to keep her protected under outstretched hands. But she would not hear of finishing her speech and leaving.

One of the guards was hit on the forehead, he began to groan and left the rostrum. Some advice was passed to her at one stage that the trouble-makers could be broken up by force but she rejected the suggestion outright. The officials claimed that that made them helpless because this was an election tour and the decision had to be a political one. There were only two alternatives, either to use force or to withdraw from the meeting, but Mrs Gandhi would not agree to either. She seemed to be as determined as the crowd and alternately talked in her speech of wider questions and the behavior of the people.

Kapur says that after warning the persons below that some stones were reaching up to the rostrum and had even hit him, he decided to go back to the rostrum for he knew "as a newsman that that's where the story was."[34] But until then it seemed the stoning was occasional and sporadic with a stray stone coming in. Mrs Gandhi finally concluded her speech to the relief of all and walked safely back to one of the chairs in the front row. The immediate crisis seemed over and had it not been for her own impulsive action later it might never have turned into a major one. After Indira's speech it was the local candidate Mahanty's turn, and it was then that the stoning started in earnest although it never turned into a "shower" as it was reported later. There were big and small stones, hitting the planks with great thuds, but they came one or two at a time, though in quick succession. Mahanty kept speaking, and Indira could not stop herself; she rushed to Mahanty's rescue, and cried angrily to the crowd. "What insolence is this! Is this the way you're going to build the country?" Her throat was caught again, she turned aside and exclaimed helplessly. "My throat is hoarse. I can't even speak."[35]

She asked for some water which an aide ran and brought for her in a glass covered scrupulously with a napkin. She drank half the water and with the glass still in her hand turned again to the crowd and exclaimed, "I ask you, are these the sort of people you're going to vote for?" meaning obviously that the opposition was responsible for going to this extent in trying to disturb a Congress meeting. That is when three or four stones came together and one of them hit her. She put the glass of water on the ground, covered her face with both hands, bent a little, came back and sat in her chair. She was calm, cool, unruffled, and made no cry, so nobody realized quite what had happened. Then somebody yelled *"pani."* Kapur saw the man who had brought the water for Mrs Gandhi going down the steps, so he repeated, *"Pani lao"* (bring some water), and ran up to Mrs Gandhi. She said, "Water won't help, it's ice I need." So Kapur shouted down the steps, "Bring some ice." But even while the security man from below shouted back agitatedly, "But there's no ice available, sir," Mrs Gandhi began to walk down the steps. She was holding her nose with a handkerchief which was soaked in blood. That's when the rest of the journalists who had been sitting below began to shout, "She's been hit, she's been hit on the nose," and there was pandemonium. A woman jumped out of the enclosure in front and began shouting at the others, "Aren't you ashamed hitting a woman? What sort of men are you? Hit me then."[36]

Mrs Gandhi got quietly into her car and drove to Raj Bhawan, and while the doctors were being summoned she kept applying the ice to her profusely bleeding nose and wiping it with the handkerchief. The injury as analyzed later consisted of "a minute crack on the nasal spine but with no displacement while a tooth on the left side of the upper jaw had become loose." Her nose was immediately bandaged and plaster streched across the ridge. She had dinner alone in her room. "And when I went to Raj Bhawan," remarked Kapur, "I was reminded of the days when Nehru was struck by paralysis—the same drawing room furniture, the same people and three years later the irony of his daughter lying in the same room."[37]

Next morning, the country awoke to a sense of shocked shame. While messages of concern poured in from even such declared "enemies" as her rival candidate Bishan Seth in Rae Bareli and the redoubtable Rajagopala-chari, the Swatantra leader, who said that he was "not only disturbed politically over it but personally also," Mrs Gandhi showed a spirited public face.

She insisted on going on to her next scheduled stop at Patna in spite of the doctor's injunction for rest and in spite of the arrangements that had been automatically made for her to fly straight to Delhi. There was also the apprehension that Patna would prove risky. In this trip across West Bengal and Orissa that is where the trouble had been originally expected from an agitated student community. Against almost unanimous advice urging her not to go, there was only one aide of hers who suggested that she should go if she did not want to be misunderstood, and it was his advice that she chose to take. Nathu, her personal servant, relates that when he kept saying worriedly to her *"Bibi, mat jao, mat jao"* (Madame, don't go, don't go), even as he did the packing for her, her reply to him was full of ironic good humor, *"Abhi to aur pathar khane hain, Nathu, too ek hi pathar se dar gaya."* (Nathu, many more stones have yet to be faced, you've got scared with just one stone.) And on the plane to Patna, with her sari covering her head and the lower portion of the face up to the nose with only her eyes twinkling above, she remarked softly, "Now I know what it feels like to be a *purdah nashin."* (A woman in veil.)

Soon after the stone-throwing incident, a prominent ex-congressman, Mahamaya Prasad Sinha, who had become the leader of another breakaway splinter group from the Congress called the Jana Kranti Dal, made a singularly sentimental appeal to the people of Patna. He exhorted them "to show due respect and courtesy to the great daughter of Jawaharlal Nehru, and not to do anything that might even remotely be construed to be disrespectful or discourteous." The general mood was subdued and the crowd at Patna heard Mrs Gandhi in pin drop silence, She thought she would make a token appearance but she spoke instead for half an hour and did not even deign to mention the nefarious incident.

"Whatever the shortcomings of the government's reaction in the face of such undemocratic challenges," wrote the *Hindustan Times* that day in relation to what it called the government's "readiness to yield to pressure," "Mrs Gandhi has shown an example of personal courage that will win her admiration throughout the country."[38] On the way back to Delhi when a member of her party commiserated with her about the incident she shrugged, "This is part of life." But when some concern was expressed about the extent of the injury she laughed ruefully, "I have a long nose, but I certainly don't want to have a crooked one in the bargain."[39] And at Palam airport she was relaxed with those who went to greet her and said, in answer to queries, "I am as tough as ever."[40]

3. OPPOSITION

There was no way of gauging how far the mood of guilty atonement in the country was going to help the Congress but for a time at least there was a feeling that there might be a landside toward old loyalties because of the incident relating to the prime minister. It was as if people were conscious that the limits of decency had been crossed and a reaction to make up for it would be natural. Though Mrs Gandhi had not used the incident to shame the public at Patna, the party organization had no such compunctions.

It printed scores of leaflets in which they showed the picture of the prime minister with her plastered nose, and had them air-dropped as an election gambit later in Orissa, particularly Bhuvaneshwar. (Significantly, the Congress candidate to Parliament from Bhubaneshwar lost the election.) Mrs Gandhi's personal stock had risen greatly but the opportunity to exploit the sentiment was curtailed when the doctors advised hospitalization for a day, and no electioneering after that. This time Indira did not demur.

There were three questions that now began to exercise the minds of the political analysts. That Mrs Gandhi would be elected to Parliament was taken for granted, but there was the question, first, whether the Congress party would come back to power, second, what its majority would be if it did, and third, what the chances were of Mrs Gandhi again being chosen as leader of the party and consequently remaining prime minister of India. She was fighting the election as prime minister, of course, but the party's platform did not rest on the assurance that she would remain so. The question of the leadership had been shelved to a post-general election period, and the Congress appeal to the electorate was strictly on the basis of party tenets.

The Congress faced an initial disadvantage in its poll prospects. It was the only party to have ruled independent India and it stood alone as absolute and final arbiter of the nation's well-being. It could usurp all the encomiums for the good that had accrued under its guidance but it could point to no other leaders barring its own and no other organization barring its own, for the weakness that dogged the footsteps of its vision. The three major factors leading to public disenchantment were corruption, lack of essential commodities, and high prices. "The future of the country is dark for many other reasons," wrote S.M. Morosely in his column, "National Affairs," "all of them directly attributable to nineteen years of Congress rule...."[1] Second, there were serious dissensions within the party which had filtered down to the district and village level so that in almost every state there was a parallel "dissident" group of congressmen who could sabotage the chances of the party's official candidates out of personal rancor. When this took a more open and, according to "loyalists," therefore a safer form, it led to defections. By the first week of January, these dissident, defecting congressmen had formed their own version of the Congress under names like Jana Congress in Orissa, the Bangla Congress in Bengal, the Jana Congress in Assam, the Jana Pakha in Mysore, and so on, in at least twelve of the then sixteen states of the Indian union.

In spite of Mrs Gandhi's optimistic assertion that these defections were a recurrent feature of every pre-general election period, this time the scale on which these defections had taken place and the importance of some of the men who quit were significant. There were Ajoy Mukerjee and Humayun Kabir in West Bengal, Takhtmal Jain and Mahant Laxmi Narain Das in Madhya Pradesh, Kumbharam Arya in Rajasthan, Dr Mahatab and

Pabita Mohan Pradhan in Orissa along with a hundred less important congressmen. Congress supporters went back to the 1950's for a parallel example when socialists like Jayaprakash Narayan, Ram Manohar Lohia, and Asoka Mehta had left the Congress, and when Acharya Kripalani broke away to form the Kisan Mazdoor Praja Party without seriously affecting the great monolith. But between then and now was the vital factor of Nehru. His towering stature had in itself been a unifier of the Indian people and his absence correspondingly gave release to simmering discontents.

While this meant a growing maturity for the democratic process, it posed an immediate and critical threat to the party in the first elections without him. In addition there was a paucity of election funds. Compared with the Rs 8.8 million that the party had managed to collect from industry in the 1962 election, it now had less than a million. Four factors had affected the collection for the central party coffers: the new directive, which seemed to bear Mrs Gandhi's zeal for establishing sound precedents, to raise the money from members and small contributors instead of from big business firms as of old; the new policy of some of these business firms to offer their own candidates; the lack of someone like Vallabhbhai Patel, the organizational chief of the fifties who had raised funds with overriding determination; and the tendency of the states this time to hang on to their individual collections, instead of sending them to a central pool, with the far-reaching implication that they could exercise much more control over the fate of local candidates, resulting ultimately in a subtle but nevertheless palpable erosion in central authority.

The Congress party's chances in the election came within the running assessment of the political shape of things to come made by Eric da Costa, head of the Institute of Public Opinion, on the basis of a sample opinion poll conducted by his organization, and statistical evidence from past elections. These were the factor of "turnout," the number of candidates put up against the Congress, and the working of what da Costa had evolved to be "the Congress multiplier," that is, the ratio between the percentage of popular vote for the party and the percentage of seats that it obtained in the past, and, on the basis of that, what it could therefore be predicted to get this time.

In the first three elections in 1952, 1957, and 1962, the Congress percentage of popular vote for the Lok Sabha had been 45.02, 47.78, and 45.06 respectively, while the seats it had obtained were out of all proportion, 72.40, 70.50, and 73.02 per cent.

The ratio da Costa obtained by dividing the percentage of seats by the percentage of valid votes polled and this he called the Congress multiplier, which in 1952 turned out to be 1.65, in 1957, 1.47, and in 1962, 1.62. The greater the approximation between the popular votes and the number of seats won, the smaller the multiplier, as was evident in the case of the 1957 elections. In 1962, the popular vote was down by three per cent but the seats were as high as 73.20 per cent. The reason for this brings up the question of the number of candidates per seat. In 1952 there were 1,892 contestants for the Lok Sabha; in 1957, 1,594; and in 1962 as high as 1,984 contestants. The increase in contestants splits the opposition vote and helps the Congress. But for the 1967 elections there were strong prospects of electoral alliances between opposition parties and even if that yielded only one candidate less per seat—three per seat against four per seat as in 1962— the Congress multiplier would be down to 1.4. According to these surveys, the Congress popular vote had come down everywhere by about five per cent stabilizing at around 41 per cent. If this downward trend continued until February and brought it to only 40 per cent, coupled with the Congress multiplier being as low as 1.4, the prediction was that the Congress would be able to secure only 56 per cent of the 520 Lok Sabha seats, that is, 292 seats as against the overwhelming existing majority of 364 that it had.

An analysis of the turnout apparently revealed that there was substantial increase in the valid number of votes polled from 1957 to 1962. In fact, the figures were a total electorate of 193.7 million in 1957 out of which the Congress secured 47.8 per cent of the approximately 90 million valid votes polled. In 1962, the electorate rose to 216.4 million and the Congress got 44.7 per cent of the 115 million valid votes polled. It was calculated by the Institute of Public Opinion that in 1962 two out of every three additional valid votes polled went to the opposition. If the same trends were made applicable to the expected figure of 245 million valid votes for the 1967 elections, it meant that the popular Congress vote would be down to 42.5 per cent. Further, if the shift away from past affiliations and therefore from the Congress of the younger generation and the neoliterates were to be taken into account, the Congress popular vote could conceivably drop even below 41 per cent.

As da Costa expressed it rather dramatically, "The young, the less educated, and particularly the illiterates, the minorities and, most unpredictable of all, the lowest income groups, are all rewriting their basic loyalties. To the candidates this is, perhaps, a struggle for power. To a political scientist it is, as nearly half a century ago, the beginning of a break with the past. It is by no means yet a revolt; but it may be in time a revolution."[2] But the restraint was again implicit. The Indian voter had been a bipartisan voter with different allegiances at the states and central level. And the Congress popular vote for the center had always remained higher than its vote in the states. It was in the cards that the electorate, even if it denied the Congress an overall majority in the states, would still give it a mandate at the center. This then was the hope.

For the opposition the prospect of power in three or four states was exhilarating, but it began to sponsor a cry for a central coalition government after the election, while relentlessly prophesying the disintegration of Congress central authority. According to Ram Manohar Lohia, the Congress was finished in the Hindi region, and if it came back to power there would be anarchy. But he slipped badly on the issue of methods. He affirmed his commitment to non-violence as a result of years of Gandhian influence but at the same time stated that a people had the right to overthrow a government by all possible means if it had lost its rationale to exist.[3]

Acharya Kripalani, another disenchanted congressman turned independent, advocated a "government of all talents" after the elections and while arguing that any government would get corrupt if it remained too long in power also added: "I welcome any revolt in the Congress."[4] Jayaprakash Narayan, the Sarvodaya leader, also an ex-congressman who had left the party in protest against what he and others deemed Nehru's reluctant socialism but whom Nehru himself at one time called his natural successor as prime minister, argued that a minority party such as the Congress, if it came back to power, should have the "humility" to invite outside participation resulting not necessarily in an all-party government but a "broad based national" one.[5] But the most damning strictures came from Chakravarti Rajagopalachari, ex-congressman, ex-chief minister of Madras, founder of the Swatantra party, first Indian governor general of independent India, scholar, and caustic wit, who declared at the party convention in Delhi on December 12, "The country is disgusted with Congress rule and congressmen are downhearted.... Money-bought shows, illegitimate advantages accruing from holding office and even borrowed ship-loads of grain bullied out of American resources will not help the Congress this time. Mrs Gandhi's words of encouragement recently given to her party members only show that they stood in need of such encouragement." He was bitterly opposed to the communists when he was chief minister of Madras state for two years (April 1952 - March 1954) and called them his public Enemy No. 1. But he now turned his acid judgment against his own former party. After saying about the communists that he had "tamed them through parliamentary methods" and that "a few communists coming into Parliament or state legislatures will not constitute any danger now, but remember, even one congressman added to the phalanx is bad," suggested that the electorate should not be daunted from voting the Congress out of office by the fear of a possible political vacuum. He took the plea that the Indian Constitution was flexible enough for any contingency, that the president could do what he deemed best in the event of there being no viable alternative to the Congress, even if it was voted out for the sake of being voted out, and that he (the president) would be "entitled to exercise his judgment with the assistance, if necessary, of the advice of the chief justice of India."

A lot of "filth and dirt" had seeped into the Congress, admitted a leading congressman and transport minister in the union cabinet, Sanjeeva Reddy. It would help the party to be in the opposition for some time, he said, and following the logic that power corrupts he hoped that that filth and dirt would then besmear the party in power while the Congress would get a chance to revitalize its image. But to the charges that the Congress had no ideology the party's general secretary, Sadiq Ali, made the countercharge that an amalgamation of ideologies that the opposition was offering through its "united fronts" could hardly be called a constructive alternative. In fact, the P.S.P., while deciding to stand aloof from these arrangements, said much the same thing: "A few ounces of Swatantraism, some dictatorship of the proletariat, a little of the Jana Sangh's militant Hindu nationalism with a dash of democratic socialism may bring in a few more votes, but it will be as great a fraud as is the Congress." There was no doubt that the Congress posture for stability and continuity would weigh heavily in its favor against the loss of Nehru, the economic crisis, and the defections. Among congressmen therefore there was a basic optimism. S.K. Patil, the railway minister, predicted that the Congress would lose 25 per cent of its seats at the center but none of the others seriously doubted, the pessimists among them, that the Congress would win at least 300 or 325 seats in an enlarged Lok Sabha of 521 members.

Where did this place Indira Gandhi's chances of being re-elected leader of the party and prime minister? Would the choice be determined by the decisive group of party bosses called the syndicate which aspired to such importance the last time? Would it lie instead with the party rank and file? And would there be a decision by consensus or by contest? There was a major difference since the 1966 crisis. There was no political vacuum to be filled such as the death of a prime minister and concomitantly, there could be no stopgap arrangement this time but a deliberate, well thought out mandate for a full term of five years. There were initial advantages in favor of a prime minister already in office. Within the party the feelings of those inclined toward a full term for Indira Gandhi were summed up best by West Bengal party boss Atulya Ghosh's rather vague and amorphous tone of commitment in the confused pre-election period. About whom he would like as the next prime minister, he was clever enough to give a reply which left loopholes for possible contingencies in the future.

"I may like some but they may not be willing to contest. If the present prime minister wants to continue she'll get my support. But I do not know whether she will offer [her candidature]. That is up to her. I must know from her that she is willing. But that is after the elections. That question does not arise now."[6] He maintained, of course, that the Congress was fighting the elections on the basis of her leadership and that they had absolute confidence in her. "Nothing has come to my knowledge that we are going to change her. At the time of the elections, what will happen, nobody knows."[7] Mrs Gandhi had indicated as far back as December 21 that she was willing to run for a second term. She had declared this at a press conference in Delhi and even said, in view of Morarji Desai's reported statement that he would be a candidate, that she "may" contest. Atulya Ghosh's interpretation of her readiness probably centered on a show of eagerness on her part to have him organize support for her. For that she was willing to wait a while. But a string of possible contestants began to be bruited around in party circles. With no one as dominant as Jawaharlal Nehru, there was a feeling among aspirants that they were at least equal to his daughter.

When Kamaraj was asked whether he had aspirations to the prime ministership he replied brusquely, "Do not ask that question."[8] But his posture in the previous few months suggested that he was not going to automatically opt out as he had the last time. He was disillusioned with Indira's intractability and felt that a direct affirmation of his own strength might tilt the balance against her and for him. His trip to Moscow in July 1966, when he was invited by the Communist party chief in his capacity as the Congress chief, was an experiment in dealing with the international scene, an area in which his parochial genius and his lack of style had so far placed him at a disadvantage.

There was S.K. Patil. About his view on Mrs Gandhi continuing in office after the elections he commented, "This is a question which one should not discuss now. It is not a question to be settled before the elections. It does not help. It embarrasses even the person named."[9] But would he himself be a candidate in 1967? "I have never projected myself as a candidate. But I surely do not say that I am not fully qualified. I am second to none in qualifications to be prime minister...in a democratic setup, and in a cabinet which takes decisions by consensus, anyone can be prime minister." If members of the party wanted him, would he decline the offer? "Not at all," he affirmed. "You can positively say that I am not fighting the election with the expectation of becoming a candidate for the prime ministership. But surely I would have a positive voice in a decision on who should be the next prime minister of India...."[10]

There was Jagjivan Ram, sitting on the fence, representative of the scheduled castes, union minister of labor, employment, and rehabilitation, confident in the support of a solid block of votes in Parliament which even if it could not win him the first job in the land gave him the power to sway opinion. He would not rule himself out. He had been mentioned as a "compromise candidate" for prime ministership in 1967. "I have not heard this," he said hopefully, "but I am in politics." Was he committed to anybody? "No, no one has approached me."[11]

There was Y.B. Chavan, then home minister, with a finger on the pulse of every state in India, rough-hewn and clever, with a reputation for ruthlessness and a background of youthful idealism. He was the unpredictable new factor in whom the long-standing and obvious controversies of the pro-Indira or the pro-Morarji stands might find a unanimous outlet. He was the one in view when the prime minister was asked whether she envisaged the possibility of there being a "third formidable candidate" (in addition to her and Morarji) in the contest for leadership to which she replied non-chalantly, "why not?"[12] But Chavan stilled all rumor when he stated categorically, "My position is very clear. I think the present prime minister should continue. She has provided leadership for the country. She has the capacity to make decisions and I think the interests of the country and our party are safe in her hands...." Did that mean he would support her in 1967? "I have no doubt about this in my mind."[13]

Morarji himself was being circumspect and cagey about his own intentions but very frank about his opinion of Indira Gandhi. "If I felt the same way as Mr Chavan, I would not have contested last year."[14]

"Mr Desai does not have a philosophy of democracy, and in fact, no relation with it, if he becomes prime minister, it would be disastrous," said the right communist party chairman, S.A. Dange, on January 9. He added significantly that Desai was a "champion of the worst kind of vested interest" and therefore he would prefer Mrs Gandhi. He had no illusions about her socialist enthusiasms. She had forgotten what Jawaharlal Nehru had taught her about socialism, he said.[15] But in an interview he gave to the United News of India, on February 10, a week before the election, he seemed to have been further disillusioned with her. "There is no question of our party supporting this or that individual belonging to the Congress on the so-called theory of the lesser evil. Ours is a party of consistent struggle against the Congress."[16]

S.S.P. firebrand Ram Manohar Lohia came out with a typically unique solution as a palliative for the "false bitterness" created in the non-Hindi areas. A Hindi prime minister "must be banished" for the next two years, he said. This got a unanimously adverse reaction from leading congressmen like Chavan, Patil, Jagjivan Ram, Morarji Desai, and others, including, of course, the prime minister herself, who remarked pithily, "To me an Indian is an Indian. I do not see him as a south Indian, north Indian, or a Hindu or a Muslim. I think the sooner we get rid of this feeling the better it would be...."[17] It was natural to grant her, therefore, a basic, popular, national image as Minoo Masani did, with the proviso that that would make her the most suitable choice as head even of a coalition government.

That was in November. By February 9, the ebullient Rajagopalachari affirmed, along with his challenging invitation to the electorate to throw out the Congress regardless of consequences, that he would be in favor of the formation of a "national government" under the leadership of a non-party man like Jayaprakash Narayan. This did not prevent him from also repeating what he had said on Mrs Gandhi's election as prime minister earlier in 1966 that he had "no objection to her becoming the prime minister [again] if the Swatantra were returned to power at the center....If there was no other person available." That sounded terrible but he added sincerely enough that, "Mrs Gandhi had in some matters done even better than her

father."[18]   This was no tongue-in-cheek remark.   Repetition must be assumed to give substance to intention.   But this peculiar fusion of political an-
tagonism and personal involvement was a unique facet of the breakaway,
splinter groups that now formed opposition parties to the parent Congress.

There was a past held in common, particularly the sharing of the struggle
for independence, which with its idealistic fervor which cut across caste,
creed, region, and sex generated strong personal loyalties, above ideological
argument.   That was the strength in the beginning of the Congress, for
loyalty allowed no divisiveness.   That became its weakness, for it could
no longer support itself on its concept of being a national "movement"
and had to act according to the logic of a political party: its unity became
an imposition on its members rather than the natural outcome of like
opinions.   Jawaharlal Nehru placed this unity above everything else even
if it meant compromising with the pace or the emphasis of his political
policy. Indira Gandhi, his daughter, seemed to be imbued with the same
concern.   So, when she became prime minister, she plumbed for heterogeneity
within an equally amorphous area of agreement, resisting with the typically
infectious Nehru smile, the clash of personalities within.   That made her
the most acceptable candidate.   On the eve of polling beginning on February
15, she was poised for almost certain re-election as leader of her party, but
with the Congress obtaining a majority of 300 in the Lok Sabha as the acid
test. With that number of seats she could be presumed to have led the party
through the elections with comparative success.   Less than that would
project an image of failure, hence afford a chance to those opposed to her
within the party to sponsor an alternative.

Her personal campaign in Rae Bareli meanwhile had gathered color,
momentum, and supremacy. Dr Gope Gurbax almost disappeared from
the scene after trying to persuade the electorate that they should give him
votes "with a view to bringing home to the Congress the importance of
ethics, religion, sadhus, Shankaracharyas, pandits, priests, *maulanas* and
maulvis."[19]   A.J. Faridi of the Majlis-e-Mushawarat of Lucknow aspired
only to offering "symbolic opposition" to Mrs Gandhi and C.P.I. right
members said of their own party candidate for Parliament that he was
bound to lose his deposit.   Even Bishan Chandra Seth, the Hindu Maha-
sabhaite who was a sitting M.P. and who had the added support of the
Jana Sangh and the S.S.P., displayed a flippancy about his motivations that
seemed to go ill with the grave intent of his purpose.   To the question why
he had decided to contest the Rae Bareli seat particularly he made the
frivolous answer "To seek publicity. My wish to contest her father was
never fulfilled."   Opinion in favor of Mrs Gandhi had been further whipped
up by a fervent reaction to the stone throwing incident.   An unprecedented
procession of women, nearly five hundred of them, had been led through
the town by Mrs Zulfiquar Ali Khan, Mrs Sheela Kaul, and Mrs Shirrajwati
Nehru, the last two relatives of Indira's from Lucknow, social workers, and

aspiring politicians of Rae Bareli. When Mrs Zulfiquar asked for permission from the district magistrate and the police to hold the procession they said they could not undertake the responsibility for the safety of so many. Mrs Zulfiquar felt emotional enough to exclaim with the rather exaggerated sentiments that the incident had evoked generally, "If Indiraji could withstand a brick we don't care if we have to suffer bullets."[20]

She described how they shouted themselves hoarse during the procession and how her mother-in-law, who was eighty years old, walked with them through the entire town. A young Muslim woman who had never been out of purdah before and who was a relative of Mrs Zulfiquar told me, "From our house to *Bhabi's* which is next door we used to have to go in a rickshaw. We never saw the light of the sun but now we have got blisters on our feet. [From walking and electioneering.]" Rae Bareli resounded to the cry that they had raised then in the form of a couplet: *"Bacha bacha kare pukar, Indiraji ki chote hammar."* (Even the children cry out, Indira's hurt is our hurt.)

Earlier a great deal of fuss and ceremony attended the conversion of a prominent young member of the Socialist party to the Congress camp. Atop the large, sprawling, brick building that was his house where the socialist flag used to fly, the Congress emblem began to wave. The high tea that he gave to mark the occasion of his change of faith was attended by the leading campaigners for the prime minister. There was Ram Kripal, the *mithaiwala,* a white mostached, short, benevolent-looking fellow who had proudly stuck a huge Congress placard on the facade of his building which dominated the town square.

The C.P.I. fixed a loudspeaker on a chair in the parapet of its office and blared forth the tenets of their creed. At one of the offices set up by Bishen Seth above a jeweler's shop, a loudspeaker broadcast political *bhajans,* and at the nearby Congress office, another loudspeaker mouthed exhortations in prose. The building itself sported a clay figure of a congressman holding a red torch, while the campaign jeep wove in and out and around the town bedecked with gay paper garlands and flowers. The workers drew up charts, mapped out their areas, and set out early in the mornings for the mass contacts that made this one of the best organized campaigns in the 1967 election. It was well imagined, well planned, and well executed, with running good humor, a dash of sentiment and a fervent loyalty.[21] The onus was put on the electorate. To the workers, it was: "There she is electioneering for others, but you have the privilege of electioneering for her."[22] And to the voters: "Imagine, you have been granted the honor of being able to vote for her directly."[23] But the greatest disadvantage that they suffered was in having to carry with them the Congress candidates for the assembly seats. The selection had been unpopular and the reaction generally was, "We'll vote for Indiraji of course, but the others...."[24] And to this, too, the Congress camp made the retort, "There is not much point in voting the general [Mrs Gandhi] in if you vote the army [the Congress assembly candidates] out."[25]

By February 15, election day, excitement was at fever pitch in all the country. By the evening of the twenty-first, six days after, the fourth general elections in India came to an end. And area of 1,200,000 square miles had been covered, a cost of 600 million had been incurred, an estimated 270 million people had cast their votes, peacefully and efficiently, and the Indian democratic process could be seen to have come of age. "The prophets of doom have been falsified,"[26] declared the Election Commissioner K.V.K. Sundaram. There were astonishing election sidelights which showed how challenging had been the condition that his commission had to deal with and even the perils that the election officers had to face in organizing the poll in the varied physical and cultural landscape of India. A pair of pigeons, for example, brought the happy tidings of the safe arrival of a polling party in the Digtoli village of Morena district, known as a hideout of robbers and highwaymen, in Madhya Pradesh! The pigeons, they say, flew back to Bhopal in ten minutes. In North Arcot district women with babies in their arms were given priority for voting by the poll officers. This led to a scramble for babies and even unmarried women managed to get precedence on the strength of borrowed babies!

In Barmer and Gudamalani, sandy areas in Rajasthan, the people went to polling booths in camel carts with rubber wheels. Voters in Coimbatore district in the south had to be ferried across the turbulent Bhavani river to enable them to reach polling stations which were inaccessible by any other means of transport. There were tigers encountered in the jungles of Madhya Pradesh, sub zero temperatures, rain, sleet, and snow for the people of Himachal Pradesh who thronged nevertheless to the 1,300 polling stations. The aboriginal tribes of Girasiya came in groups to the beat of drums and musical instruments to exercise their franchise. The women voters outnumbered the men in many places and in the Keonghar tribal district of Orissa 64 per cent of the voters were women.

A polling officer in Raipur got an unusual request from an illiterate voter whose wife had just been delivered of a baby. Since she was very anxious to vote, would the officer go to their house and take her vote? At a polling station in Punjab, voters asked a 102-year-old man to jump the queue if he liked and vote first. "I can stand here till the next election," he rebuffed them. In Rae Bareli, in the four dominantly Muslim villages of Chatonuna, Barwallia, Gachpati Khera, and Tal Katela, the women had never voted before. But this time they told Mrs Zulfiquar, "You've come. You're a relation. And then it's a question of Indira Gandhi—so we'll vote."[27] The result was that out of the total vote of 511 there, 211 were women!

But a near revolution was in the offing. By the twenty-second, results began to pour in. Three Congress chief ministers were returned, including the redoubtable D.P. Mishra. The maharani of Jaipur lost her assembly seat to Damodar Vyas, Congress health minister in Rajasthan, but she still had her parliamentary constituency with which to possibly reaffirm her shaken prestige. But the Congress was routed in Kerala, and cutting into Congress stakes in the capital city of Delhi was the Jana Sangh lead in six out of seven parliamentary constituencies and nineteen out of twenty-eight declared for the metropolitan council. There were shocks in the Punjab and several other states where even ministers who had been tipped as future chief ministers lost their seats. By the next day, a debacle was declared for the Congress in Madras, Bihar, and Delhi. Three union cabinet ministers had been unseated, some others were trailing behind, and, most shocking of all, Congress President Kamaraj was in difficulties. Mrs Gandhi was leading Bishan Seth by 52,800 votes.

By the twenty-fourth, Kerala, Madras, Punjab, Rajasthan, Orissa, and West Bengal had voted the Congress out of power, and half the union cabinet was itself out. Though Indira had been thinking that a few shocks would do the Congress good, she now began to feel slightly anxious. Hour by hour, the scoreboard at her residence ticked off more and more reverses for the Congress in assembly and parliamentary constituencies. But two factors emerged strongly, nevertheless. Her own personal victory of 91,000 votes over Bishan Seth and the fact that she had been able to carry even the rest of the reluctantly accepted congressmen in the area. In fact, Rae Bareli was like a pocket of light. Second, there was the rout of the syndicate which could have an undeniable impact on the leadership issue. Out of the generally accepted inside group of pressure makers, consisting of Kamaraj, Patil, Atulya Ghosh, Siddhavanahalli Nijalingappa, and Sanjeeva Reddy, the first three had lost ignominiously. But the problem facing the Congress and the prime minister now was whether and how much would be its majority at the center in the Lok Sabha. Till then, out of 132 results declared, the Congress had got 63, the Jana Sangh 20, and the C.P.I. (M) and the Swatantra 10 each.

By February 24, the Congress had got 189 out of the 359 seats declared. It needed 72 more seats for an absolute majority in the Lok Sabha. It had lost Bihar and Orissa, but it had obtained a majority in Madhya Pradesh, Assam, and four other states. The prime minister put a brave face on it and bearded the lion's den: she went to inspect the munificent election news room set up at Hyderabad House by the Press Information Bureau, and made some pithy, self-assured comments on the election trends to the foreign and Indian correspondents who crowded around her, and tried to pin her to embarrassing commitments. She talked to them while having tea with them under a multicolored *shamiana* and then in groups while she moved around on the lawns, with the reporters and the television cameras following. Only those nearest her could follow the exchange of comments and an American journalist remarked that the occasion reminded him of "President Johnson's famous strolls round the White House lawns, minus bourbon and soda!"[28]

From the instant repartee and casual observations the most significant points to emerge were Indira's pleasure in the fact that elections had been fair and free, pointing to a vitally alive democracy—she was proud of the people of India, she said, because they had exercised their franchise with discrimination—and her anxiety as a party member for the fate of some of her colleagues.   She looked slightly harassed and her lips were dry with strain but there was only a trace left on her nose and lip of the Bhuvaneshwar injury, and her answers were buoyant enough.   But when she saw the London *Times* man who had been the most alarmist of the prophets-of-gloom group, she turned witheringly to him and asked, "Do you see democracy collapsing around you?"

"No," he fumbled.   "This has been an exciting experiment in democracy. But what people want is good government."

"You will never think we have a good government no matter what we do," and before the bewildered journalist could answer, Mrs Gandhi added, with a sense apparently of the lingering drama of Indo-British relations, "You have been saying these things not lately but for twenty years."[29]

But her humor still did not desert her.   On February 26, she saw that the Congress had lost eight out of sixteen states in India that it had dominated so far, and the personality rout was further confirmed by the resounding defeat of Biju Patnaik. For the Lok Sabha, out of the 468 results declared by midnight of February 25, the Congress had won 254 seats. But it needed seven more for a majority.   The driblets in which it was adding to its score was unnerving.   So she laughed when she saw a cartoon that morning in a daily depicting her reaction to the election results.   In one panel, her hair had been sketched like it was, black with a streak of silver grey. In the other, the eyes were sunken, the lips were drawn, and most amusing of all, the hair was white and only the streak black. "I thought it was rather good," she remarked delightedly to her secretariat official Natwar Singh as he drove with her to one of her engagements of the day.[30]

4. CONTINUITY

By 2.30 A.M. on February 27 came the news that the Congress party had won
the vital seat to give it the majority in the Lok Sabha. It could now form the
government at the center. But first it had to choose its leader. The question
became alive, dominant and tricky. Could it be Indira Gandhi again, or
would the wrath of Congress defeats in state elections make her the scapegoat?
The majority was short, for her, of the advantageous 300. But many of the
powerful figures of the day had fallen. If this was a slap in the face of the

popular image of the government, it was also a slap in the face of party "bossism"—the force that Indira genuinely believed stood in the way of creating the image she wanted. Her opinion was strengthened by the pattern of defeat and victory. The Congress party lost its majority in eight of the sixteen states it had ruled for two decades. But it had been returned to power at the center. It was obvious that the Indian electorate, instinctively perceptive, in spite of its illiteracy, had attempted to chasten rather than destroy the party. Even the opposition was shocked. When the results in the Delhi elections to the metropolitan council, the corporation, and the Lok Sabha swept the Jana Sangh to victory, one of its leaders is reported to have remarked ruefully, "All our candidates were selected to act as an effective opposition. We never thought we'd need them for office!"

The Congress had two alternatives. It could rely on Mrs Gandhi as the one who had steered the party through the elections and promise her the support she needed for the critical period ahead. Or, it could take the shattered political strength of the Congress as a reason to change its leadership. The alternative, it knew, could only be Morarji Desai. Still influential and hovering on the fringes of absolute power since Nehru's death he turned up each time as a rival candidate. In the first succession after Nehru, it was he who stood as a possible threat to Lal Bahadur Shastri. It was he who had to be placated before they could arrive at a consensus. It was Morarji again who contested against Indira Gandhi after Shastri died. And it was Morarji now who loomed like a shadow between Indira and the absolute mandate she sought. On the other occasion she had hesitated, wondered about the political feasibility of her decision to undertake a responsibility she had hardly imagined would be hers one day. This time, she felt secure, confident and cheerful and she made it clear to D. P. Mishra as early as February 24 that she would stand for re-election.

Both Indira Gandhi and Morarji Desai did not officially declare their intentions. But while Indira's bid for re-election was expected the speculation about a contest arose from Morarji's nature. He had contested last time. Why would he not this time? This was his last chance. He was 71. But he had reason to believe that it was his hasty, eager candidacy earlier which earned him a certain disapprobation. There was a psychology about the Indian mind. It admired aloofness, a not too obvious thrust for power, the pretentions to renunciation. He had not understood it then. He was being careful now. Then, of course, there were the sheer mechanics of it. Last time, the alignments within the members of the Congress parliamentary party could be forseen. The loyalties were implicit. The elections had brought them out—335 for Indira, 169 for him. This time, a new assessment would be necessary. How many of the old guard would stand, how many of the new, risk with him, a defeat? It would not be easy to tempt them to vote against a prime minister entrenched in office.

Nevertheless, Morarji could take solace, comfort, and perhaps inspiration from a theory he propounded earlier when I met him. He analyzed the reasons for his varying postures in his other two bids for power. But the major cause for optimism in 1967, he said, was the fact that it would take place after the general elections. That is, the members of Parliament would have no reasons to be "pressurized," as he called it, into voting the way their bosses directed because of the scramble for the ubiquitous ticket that created a periodic havoc in pre-election party allegiances. "The M.P.s will not be dependant as they were last time, when they had only a year to go before the elections," he said. "This time [1967] the tickets have been distributed already. The M.P.s will have a clear five years and they won't be afraid. . . ."

Morarji was presuming here that the "unpressurized" support would automatically go to him. He went even as far back as the first succession in 1964 to say that "everybody knew if I had contested that time I could have won by seven or eight votes, or Shastri could have won by seven or eight votes." He gave three reasons for his having agreed to Shastri as a unanimous choice. "It was soon after Nehru. Everywhere I went abroad, for instance, before he died, I found that people were prophesying chaos, saying that the Congress would disintegrate and that democracy would be no more in India. So we *were* keen that the process of election should be smooth. Secondly, I didn't want to divide the party into factions. Also, I would have had half of them always against me and I wouldn't have been able to function the way I might have wished to. Thirdly, I felt it didn't matter so much, that Shastri could carry on the government." There were three reasons again, which led him to a contest against Indira Gandhi in 1966. He was not so sure that she could run the government, there was no longer any fear of chaos, or the need to prove "the prophets of gloom" wrong, and, he felt he could win. "I really might have if some of them had not forsaken their earlier stand—they'll lose by it, you'll see, not I. They were afraid that with me the center would be strong, and they'd have to go straight." As if realizing that this might be taken as an expression of personal resentment, he took the discussion back to a statement of theory. "I don't think there should be a law unless all agree to it. . . ." He was indirectly answering the criticism that had cost him his support then: that he was high-handed, rigid and autocratic, and that his concern for parliamentary decision was not sincere. Nevertheless he was proud of the democratic values of the 1966 contest. "I believe I have done great service to the country by withdrawing the first time and contesting the second time. Now they won't be able to use the same methods again—the maneuvering that went on—they've been exposed."

For all the cold, withdrawn, puritanical image that he had created for himself, he was evidently not above a bit of common involvement. I pointed out that he himself had contacted people in 1966 and tried to solicit support.

"Ah, but that was straight canvassing. I rang up the M.P.s and sent them notes saying they must exercise their independent judgment, that they must think whether I'd be able to do the job or whoever they thought could do the job, and vote without fear. I didn't tell them that they must vote for me, but they shouldn't be pressurized. I didn't promise them anything in return."

"You mean there was no bargaining?"

"Exactly."

When I asked him if he thought it was Mrs Gandhi who had been directly involved in this maneuvering then, or just the people behind her, he replied quietly, "If I asked somebody to commit murder and he did it, could I absolve myself from the responsibility?"

He began by asserting that he did not want to even verbally harm Mrs Gandhi or the party. He ended by saying that he did not think one should seek power, but accept it if it comes. No harm in wanting power if you have ideas you want to put into practice, I said. "Oh, I have strong ideas, but I don't feel I have a mission to perform. I am not vain enough to think that way. In fact, many times I've wanted to go away, especially in 1957 after I came to Delhi. I've never known such a murky atmosphere. But there again I felt I shouldn't run away from responsibility either. . . a sense of duty." He became reflective. "One is touched, being in power. I thought I wasn't, but during the last three years I have realized that I too was affected by it. One cannot be immune. People flatter you all the time, you begin to feel you're a different being! I think I am a nicer person since being out of power. . . more mellow. I realize better how things are, what people want."

"This implies you lost contact with the common man while in power?"

"No, but it's easier, better when you are out."

"Wouldn't you apply that to the Congress party too? That it would be revitalized if it were out of power?"

"Oh, certainly, certainly," he exclaimed. "But then what would you have in its place?" And he smiled gently.

In the gathering tensions of the hour, however, and within the party the date to be fixed for the election of the leader acquired dramatic significance. Till then there had been almost a unanimous agreement that the question should be settled in early April, after the "lame-duck session" of the outgoing Parliament. Now the voter had shown that the Samsonic symphony of Congress power was beginning to fall on deaf ears, the giant body was sagging, the heart listless. To let it drift for even a month and a half without a political leader would further strain its morale. An early election of the new prime minister, top Congress leaders were reported to feel at that stage, "was essential to remove any feeling of political uncertainty as well as to prevent dissension and disunity within the Congress ranks, especially so soon after the major electoral reverses."[1] Supporters of Mrs Gandhi had an additional and vested reason in encouraging this view. An early election, they thought, would help her cash in on, first, the immediate nervous reaction to the staggering collapse of party stalwarts in the party organization and, second, on the wilted aggressiveness of these stalwarts which would prevent them from aspiring to their earlier role of power-makers. Later she would not only have to contend with a possible resurgence of spirit amongst the defeated and a possible renewal, shifting of stands, bargaining, and politicking that had made politics a game rather than a concern, but also with the tarnished image that a badly-mauled cabinet might present even in the lame-duck session. In the expected contest therefore, with the stoical Morarji, she would have to begin from a position of weakness rather than strength. He, on the other hand, having been out of the government for four years but trying desperately to build a base for himself within the party, could dilate upon the failings of one and the inspirations of the other with impunity.

The preliminaries to the historic day for decision were tackled with "remarkable promptness" and "unusual speed." The Congress Parliamentary Board met at 10 A.M. on the twenty-seventh in the library of the All-India Congress Committee office at 7, Jantar Mantar Road, New Delhi. The members were Mrs Gandhi, Morarji, Dhebar, Kamaraj, and Fakhruddin Ali Ahmed. By 11.30 A.M. the decision had been made for the election of the leader on March 12 and before the lame-duck session. The first round had gone to the delicate-looking woman who was already prime minister. She had stuck to her point firmly in spite of Morarji's cogent attempts to emphasize the possible anomaly of a situation in which if she were not re-elected, she would still have to carry Parliament through the lame-duck session as a defeated one. This might be embarrassing, suggested Morarji. "Not for me," replied Mrs Gandhi, "I'll not be embarrassed." He also suggested that a postponement would help settle the "election dust." But this again was countered by the argument that, instead, it might gather more dust.

It was at the working committee meeting, held the same evening, that an analysis of election reverses was expected to be followed by a firm, unambiguous, and constructive stand on the choice of leader of the party. Instead the working committee evaded the question altogether and began "the biggest exercise in belly-aching" that, as a member described later, he had ever seen. There was a bitter apportioning of blame for the Congress failures in the elections, and those who were looking for hints about the alignments that would determine the choice of the next prime minister found them in the extent to which the responsibility was held to be that of the government, or the organization: policy as against execution, Mrs Gandhi as against the party.

Among the nineteen participants in this tense national drama were the nine members of the parliamentary board and the strong men of the party who had themselves been defeated at the polls—S. K. Patil, Atulya Ghosh, Sanjeeva Reddy, Biju Patnaik, and Kamaraj himself. It was too early to tell how far the resultant loss of prestige had led to a decline in influence, but on the surface they had retained the minimum control of votes to justify their postures of power. But so delicate, personal, and non-political were the motives behind the line-up that when it was noticed, after the working committee gave over at 7.45, that Patil had driven off with Morarji and Dhebar with Mrs Gandhi, there was an immediate attempt by the political analysts on the scene to construe some meaning out of it! Morarji, whom I saw later that night, laughed if off: "Patil was coming to see me, so we came together, that is all!" I had been told of an instance about Atulya which seemed to confirm how from this sometimes touching, but wholly idiosyncratic inspiration the power blocs within the Congress organization had begun to emerge. Atulya had fractured his foot. His short, flabby, fat body put an unequal strain on his foot which made him nervous and careful. On one occasion during that period, after they had attended a meeting together, he was about to fall when Mrs Gandhi immediately put her arm under his and helped him along. The exaggerated fear of another injury, the instinctive concern shown about him, and that it was Mrs Gandhi who had shown it, made him blubber childishly with pleasure later. "It was Indiraji who saved me," he kept repeating to a confidant. "If it hadn't been for her, I would be laid up in bed again." A phone call later enquiring about the possible damage to his foot won him over completely.

There were some in the party who turned against Indira because they felt she has been acting arrogantly, especially since her father died. Perhaps Atulya had been one of those. Only at the last minute in the last election had he thrown his weight behind the syndicate when he had realized that Kamaraj and the group of chief ministers would sway the votes in her favor. Indira herself disliked his peremptory presumptions to act as party boss. But while she was in the process of forming her cabinet after the election, she had softened towards Atulya and made him feel all the illusions of power by asking him to remain nearby for consultations. But after keeping a tortuous vigil in an ante-room while the interminable balancing went on in the next one till the early hours of the morning, he told an aide, "I'm tired and sleepy. Tell Indiraji that whatever she does will be right," and limped into his car at 2 A.M. This time he was committed from the beginning.

The night of the twenty-seventh set the pace, mood, and intensity of the days till the moment of decision. A feverish exchange of views took place at the climactic level, allegiances were drawn that would decide the fate of a nation, and there was no sleep, only excitement in the air, in the silent, shaded streets leading to those lighted pockets of alertness where the top leaders confabulated, confided but dared not, as yet, confirm.

Atulya talked with comparative frankness. When I met him that night he said, "The situation is fluid still. On the surface, Mrs Gandhi has 60 per cent support, but this time what is on the surface is not necessarily what is underneath." He seemed oddly circumspect. He explained that even Mrs Gandhi's own camp had begun to feel that she might not be able to manage it alone. "They've asked me to suggest to Morarji to join in as deputy prime minister. But he can as well turn to me and say, why not her as No. 2, eh? What answer would I give then?"

I thought it was obvious. He could state categorically that it must be her as No. 1, because they supported her and because she was thought to be the superior choice.   Did Atulya Ghosh find he had to be apologetic to Morarji Desai, I wondered?   It seemed so.   At that moment, the phone rang.   A drunken voice asked inquisitively: "Mr Ghosh, is it h-her or is it h-him?" "Who is speaking?" "Who are *you*," remonstrated the voice. "I want Mr-er-Ghosh." "Mr Ghosh is not available," said the man who had picked up the phone and put down the receiver.   A minute later, the phone rang again.   The same voice repeated plaintively, "Mr Ghosh, is it him or is it her?" "Sounds like a foreigner," helplessly replied the man who held the phone. "Must be a journalist," laughed the others.   Atulya Ghosh smiled. "The general desire is for unanimity," he explained, the phone forgotten. The point was who would be the one to compromise.   If not, a contest was inevitable.

"Would you say there are 60 per cent in favor of Mrs Gandhi and 40 per cent for Mr Desai?" Biju Patnaik was aked earlier in the evening.   "I think that's about the correct estimate," he answered, lounging back in his armchair.[2]   Patnaik was another of the giants that had fallen, for the rumblings of fury which had shown such a truant and unfortunate form at Bhuvaneshwar resulted in a major electoral defeat for him.   Six feet, three inches, dressed in dhoti and kurta with a shawl thrown elegantly across his shoulders, this one time blue-eyed boy of Nehru with a reputation for efficiency, ruthlessness, and personal greed might have made it right to the top echelons of Mrs Gandhi's own advisory circle, had not an overweening ambition, combined with a gambler's daring, made him forget that the processes to power must be tactfully nurtured.   He talked with a blase air, in broken sentences, offering to give information yet holding back, skirting around an obvious commitment.   His large, munificent drawing room was furnished in impeccable taste.   His wife, a Punjabi, was there, ordering snacks with the typical spontaneity of a generous hostess.   His daughter, in jeans, a short, langourous cut of hair, and a young son were sitting around, laughing with daddy at his description of his own election discomfiture.   "I'm at the bottom now, couldn't go lower," he shrugged casually.   He was however still a member of the powerful working committee.

It became clear that Patil voiced the strongest protest against the government.   His own position was hardly viable in the party ranks after his thumping defeat, what *Blitz* rather picturesquely called the defeat of "Patil's Rotten Rump."   But it was possible that he still controlled enough votes to be able to give substance to protest.   Patil, when I saw him that night, was surly and upset.   He was sprucely dressed in a beige raw silk sherwani and cream colored pants.   His blotched complexion with tints of dark and light, the quick snake-like tongue which darted out to lick his lips on either side as he talked, and his small, wary eyes in a heavy-jowled face made one uncomfortable.   He was suave, smooth, and indulged with self-evident ego in a bright

turn of phrase. He had been India's food minister at one time, so he presumed for himself a certain commitment on the subject. About the leadership
issue, he exclaimed: "I might have lost, but I have my men." From his attack
on Mrs Gandhi's so-called "kitchen cabinet" it seemed he held her
responsible and would vote against her. But a few moments later, he began
to talk of age limits, and that he was the one to have originally offered the
suggestion that ambition should draw the line at 65. He was ruthless in his
analogies and so pointed was his sarcasm that one felt it was an indirect
indictment of the 71-year-old Desai.

As we turned after that into 7, Tyagaraja Marg, stopped the car near the
porch and entered the bare, cold, carpetless ante-room, I felt only the shock
of an uncompromising atmosphere. The taste in furniture, whatever little
there was, was plebian and dry, and everything had a hard defiant look.
A short, stumpy, thin little man was getting agitatedy into a car. It was C.B.
Gupta, aspiring chief minister of Uttar Pradesh, Mrs Gandhi's home state.
Gupta was a Morarji man, but pre-election adjustments, the distribution of
tickets, and Mrs Gandhi's changing attitude about his role in U.P. politics had
pointed the way toward a reconciliation between them. Last time he had
voted for Desai. This time he was expected to vote for Mrs Gandhi. What
was he doing at Desai's house then? U.P.'s bloc-vote was substantial: why was
Gupta angry? "I might as well not be in Delhi for all the notice they take
of me," he cried. "They invited D. P. Mishra to the meeting [the working committee meeting] because he happened to be in Delhi. Why not me,
eh? I don't know anything. Why don't you ask Morarji Desai?" Desai,
coming along from some inner sanctum, added bitterly, "Ask them," he said,
"they have the power and the means, there's nothing I can tell you."[3]

His tone was no longer that of philosophic detachment, nor indeed did he
exhibit the superior, stoic, mental reserve, which he always tried to project
in his political image. Later in his sitting room arranged in the Indian way
with a wide mattress covered with a white sheet spread across half the room,
and white bolsters to rest one's arms or back on, Morarji sat against the wall
on the side on the floor, and dexterously avoided a commitment. But he
smiled softly, and prevaricated cleverly on the questions of the day. What
had happened at the working committee? Who had blamed the government?
Who had blamed the organization? What was Patil's stand? And what
would be Kamaraj's position? Was the leadership issue discussed? Would
there be a contest? Was there a possibility of a third candidate?

I referred to his contention that he had avoided a contest after Nehru's
death because he did not want to risk splitting the party in a time of crisis.
"Wouldn't you say that the Congress, after suffering heavy losses in the
elections this time, is facing another kind of crisis? So the same assessment
can hold good now and that therefore you shouldn't stand?" I asked him.
"I don't think a contest would weaken the party. Besides, why should
unanimity be achieved only at my cost? The other side can also step down."

"Does that mean you will contest?"

"What's the hurry? I can even decide on the morning of the eleventh."
The point was: would he win? And why?

It was apparent at the end of the day that the working committee session
was an explosive one. Chavan, the home minister, stood unreservedly
for government, confirming his stand in favor of Mrs Gandhi's re-election as
prime minister. "The blame cannot be put on government," he said. Patil
criticized the government for the party reverses. "Its [government's] policies
have not stood the test," he cried. Kamaraj too roundly condemned government, and took up the issue with regard to what happened in Madras.
"It was strange that the supply of rice was stopped three weeks before polling." Nanda, the ex-home minister, feeling pathetically the ignominy of
being an outsider, blamed government policy in the morning at the parliamentary board meeting and in the evening, turned upon the organization. Both
times he was ticked off. Mrs Gandhi and Morarji were comparatively quiet.
Morarji said briefly that "the government must share the blame for not
paying attention to the needs of the people," while Mrs Gandhi pointed
out that "it was not fair to apportion blame without a proper assessment of
the causes underlying the party's unsatisfactory performance!"[4]

"They were fighting each other, trying to cut each other's tails," Patnaik
put it succinctly later. "How can there be any reconciliation between the
haves and the havenots?"[5]

It was late at night when some of us saw Kamaraj. By then it was obvious
that the center of ultimate influence was shifting to him again, as in 1964.
He was lying in bed, reading the papers. The man was affable, yet withdrawn, not frank but direct; he would not say anything but would say it
unequivocally, and yet you felt oddly that political wile was second here to a
basic directness of heart. His knowledge of English was economical but
always to the point.

"What have you decided about the leadership issue?"

"Nothing, nothing. Wait and see."

"Do you foresee a contest?"

"Can't say."

"Whom will *you* support?"

"I'll see how everybody feels."

"Last time you took the initiative."

"Last time was different," said Kamaraj tersely.[6]

Two things were clear at the very outset. Kamaraj could not be taken to be
an unqualified supporter of Indira Gandhi like last time. And the entire
syndicate, that pressure group comprising Atulya Ghosh, S. K. Patil, Sanjeeva
Reddy, and Kamaraj himself, though ignominiously defeated at the polls,
did not seem to be broken in spirit: it was waiting again for an opportunity
to secure the areas of influence to determine the choice of the next prime
minister.

In the tense, dramatic, and stirring struggle for leadership that resulted in
a win for Indira Gandhi in 1966, the one person, who had initiated an active
commitment in her favor in nine out of sixteen chief ministers, even before the
contest took place, and which was considered to be a tactical and brilliant
move to catch the election on a rising tide of enthusiasm for her, was Dwarka
Prasad Mishra, the then chief minister of Madhya Pradesh.   This time again,
he was obviously the most committed amongst the powerful clique of party
bosses and government heads who were gathered in Delhi, apart from
Kamaraj. So with the trust that his earlier role had evoked Mrs Gandhi
called a "triumphant Mishra" to Delhi on February 24 (he had won a thumping victory for the Congress in Madhya Pradesh) and told him she was standing for election.   He, in turn, declared his support for her.   On the personal
level, Mishra felt he owed a debt of gratitude to Indira Gandhi.   On the
political level, he was perfectly capable of arguing that her comparative
inexperience, and his advocacy of her candidature would make her reliance
on him imperative and give him the necessary lever of power at the center.
Morarji Desai had analyzed with cynical perspicacity that one of the reasons
"they" didn't want him as prime minister was because they feared he would
be too strong and that he would make them "go straight."   It is ironic that a
year and three months later, when the time came for another and final trial
of strength between Mrs Gandhi and Morarji—it was now or never obviously
for Desai in 1967—it was "they" again who got nervous about *her*.   Her
public support, in spite of a year of bitter travail, was undisputed and they
feared that if in addition she won in a straight contest, her power would become
absolute.   To some political analysts therefore, the move to include Desai
in the cabinet as deputy prime minister and evolve a solution through unanimity was the only way to dilute the possible might of Indira who would
come in this time not as an interim prime minister but for a full and impatiently awaited term of five years.   On the other hand, Atulya Ghosh had
remarked, on the night after the first session of the working committee, that
"even members of the prime minister's own camp felt that in the context of
the Congress debacle in the elections, she might not be able to carry the burden
of government alone"[7] and that therefore Morarji should be asked to come in
as her deputy.   The prime minister's "own camp" included Mishra.   On
February 26 even he seemed cautious. He declared that he had an "open
mind" on the issue of leadership and that anyone wanting to become prime
minister "must first convince himself that he will be able to cope with the
present situation."[8] He thought work on the organizational level was "more
important than who becomes prime minister" and he added that he favored
an uncontested choice for prime minister.   But it was he who persistently
mooted the idea of a unanimity move on the basis of drafting Morarji into an
Indira cabinet.   He was the first to suggest it from the moment the question
of leadership came up, but up to February 27, "while he had talked to a number of leaders, the one man be did not discuss the matter with was Mr Desai,"

Ironically both Indira and Morarji disclaimed all knowledge of any direct feelers from either side and continued to act as if the decision or the solution was going to be arrived at individually.

The "sides" however were "itching for a fight" as another hawk in the P. M.'s camp put it. It was in this context that the unanimity moves of the Congress president began to draw the center of activity to that bare-looking bed-room with the green shaded windows, dark, cool, intimidating, where the walls began to reverberate again to the stormy accents of a few men and one woman of history. In a brilliant cartoon in the *Hindustan Times* only a few days before, Kamaraj had been shown immediately after his defeat in the elections, slumped in a waste paper basket with the withering caption, "Whom shall I make prime minister now?" It was a biting parody of a man who had been shorn of his authority as kingmaker, the reputation he had acquired after the last election. But it was obvious during the crises of decision later that his defeat had finally stifled the hum about his own candidature for prime ministership which had been gathering increasing resonance during the last months before the elections and to which his "differences" with Mrs Gandhi had added conviction. Yet he could rely upon his especial genuius for balancing, bargaining, and a solution by consensus to give him again an emphatic say in shaping the image of the country, the party, and the leader- · ship for the next five years. It was a measure of Mrs Gandhi's weakness that she allowed the initiative to slip back to "that rustic" as she had once being provoked to call Kamaraj in a private conversation (and which had promptly been reported to him). But like her father, she was not averse to achieving a show of unity if it could be done with minimum surrender. After all, the fight was only within the clan, and the clan, in the ultimate, must stick together.

On February 28, when Atulya went to Morarji with the unanimity formula, Morarji, I'm told, asked him: "Why shouldn't she be No. 2?" It was what Atulya had feared. But Morarji, on a personal and vulnerable level, is also reported to have suggested a compromise formula of his own, which militated against his public image and presaged the final weakening. "Let me be prime minister for two years then. She can come after then. She is young. She can afford to wait."[9] Was that really the last throw of the coin of an aging gambler? Or an astute challenge on the part of a tired politician? He might have agreed at that moment with those political analysts who predicted that in the context of its election reverses and in its razor's edge balance with six opposition governments in the states, the Congress party would have only another two years lease of life and that elections would have to be held again soon after that period? Outwardly, but unofficially, Morarji retained his inflexible posture. He was for prime ministership or nothing, and threw hints about an eventual contest. "We hope there is a contest" repeated the circle close to the prime minister. She herself was well prepared for it. A contest, if she won it, as the indications were that she would, could give her absolute authority as the elected choice of the party rank and file and the right to keep Morarji out of the cabinet altogether as she had done after she had won in 1966. But why did she still want to keep him out?

First, there was the clash of personality: it was fierce and irreducible. Second, the continuous hostility toward Desai was implicit because, in essence, she was her father's political child too. If Desai was associated with the rightists, Indira Gandhi was to the left of center and in 1958, even showed sympathy with the Ginger Group in the Congress party which attacked the party for "lethargy and failure to carry out its stated policies."[10] Mrs Gandhi herself told me much later that her disagreement with her father was only about the pace at which things were going, rather than about any glaring ideological difference. She was certainly progressive, broadminded, secular, and basically contemporary. Like her father, but unlike Morarji, she could view with fascination rather than disapproval the modern scientific rationale of the twentieth century.

In 1966, the different stands of the two contestants were obvious. By 1967, the alignments were less ideological, and more personal. Indira Gandhi's year and three months as interim prime minister blunted the edge of her idealism by presenting her continuously with the challenging mechanics of remaining in power. She proved herself equal to the task, but in the process her image as a rebel changed. The existing structure of the Congress party made compromise imperative. The existing situation in the country made pragmatism the need of the hour. At the time that she stood poised for re-election, the slate had been wiped clean. If her rightist rivals had lost in the elections, so too had her old leftist allies, and the break, at least outwardly, was complete. What remained of her commitments basically was the emphasis on youth. Even here, the pertinent fact was that she was the youngest of the old generation and not a member of the new. One could say that this made her the trust representative of transitional India: a country caught between the values of the past and the compulsions of the present. A country so old at one point, so young at another, and in terms of political concretization yet in the process of emerging. But was it enough that she should merely reflect the image?

"Unfortunately," said the *Hindustan Times* on the morning of February 28 after the working committee meeting, "the question that most obsesses congressmen is not what is going to happen to the party but what is to happen to them while the going is good. A strong leader could alter the situation. If the electoral verdict could impart such strength, Mrs Gandhi could be that strong leader. She could be the instrument of the transformation of the party—and of the country. But has she the will and the vision?"[11] The point straightaway arose: had any of the others? In a hardened, casual, cynical appraisment of the hectic pre-election politiking, Atulya Ghosh at one point laid bare the truth: "Ideology? Nobody has bothered about ideology."[12]

I went to see Mrs Gandhi on the twenty-eighth. Her house at No. 1, Safdarjang Road, with its makeshift arrangements for seating visitors, was already seething with people. Members of Parliament from all over India were beginning to come in to affirm their loyalty to her, offer their services for canvassing, act as emissaries, and partake from the very beginning of the high political drama that was to be played during the next ten days. Fourteen of them sat in the beige and grey ante-room and presented in face and dress the fascinating diversity of religious belief and regional difference that is found in India. There were groups knotted in whispers, and from snatches of conversation that flew across the room, it was obvious that the atmosphere was alive to only one dominant question: would Indira Gandhi be re-elected leader of the party and prime minister? When Mrs Gandhi came out of the house into the verandah, she spoke to each person softly, smiled and looked utterly and absolutely relaxed: the tension from the scene vanished. This was no woman fighting for power, but some one calm, confident and opti- mistic. There was only a slight nagging in one's mind that this face of calm might be, in the ultimate, the face of unconcern. But then her manner rarely revealed what her thoughts were, her reserves were as ever the reserves of the lonely. When I asked her, "Do you think there is any ideological base in the approach to the choice of leader?" the answer came simply and cogently without embarrassment, "No," and then added, "I see it as a conflict between the forces of change and the forces of continuity."

"And the election results?"

"If you will notice" she said, "there have been very selective defeats—I don't mean that some good people have not gone, but generally it has been selective."

There was a smile of impish pleasure. She seemed quite pleased. After all, the ones who had "gone" could no longer stand in her way and she could now, if re-elected, invest daringly in the very "forces of change" she so evidently approved of.

The next few days saw activity shift from discussion, bargaining, and turn of alignment among the top leaders and party bosses to the inner working circles of the two sides. They began to enquire into the background, ideas, known affiliations and likely change of attitude in the newly elected group of members of Parliament gradually converging upon Delhi in a steady driblet from all corners of India. On Morarji's behalf, there was his son Kanti, whose controversial image had done much to damage that of his father but who now stuck close to him in protective regard and sympathy and almost stood guard over him to the hour of decision. With Indira were the old loyalist campaigner from Lucknow, Uma Shankar Dixit, Dinesh Singh, then minister of state for external affairs, Inder Gujral, M.P., and, of course, Y. P. R. Kapoor, Mrs Gandhi's private secretary for fourteen years. They worked out that the support of 150 Congress members of the Rajya Sabha was evenly divided between Indira and Morarji. This gave Indira roughly seventy-five there. But of a total of 280 seats that the Congress had won in the Lok Sabha, the Desai camp was apparently relying only upon a solid block of 121. The Indira camp was magnanimous enough to concede even 135 to the rival side. "That still leaves us with a majority in the event of a contest," they explained, "and mind you, we are giving them a wide margin, even allowing for a sudden shift in loyalty of those whom we would otherwise count for Indiraji."[13]   A break-up of the assessment in the Lok Sabha was thought to be somewhat like this:

Out of the eleven seats that the Congress party won from Gujarat, the majority would be for Morarji and only two or three for Indira.

From the thirty-four members from Bihar, seven were supposed to be with Morarji, led by Tarkeshwari Sinha, twelve were for Kamaraj consisting of L. N. Mishra and others, and of the remaining fifteen, ten were for Indira, led by Binodanand Jha, and five absolutely non-committed.

In U. P., out of the total of forty-seven, at least twenty were with Tripathi, seven with Dinesh Singh, consisting of the Rajput group, and the remaining twenty owing allegiance to Gupta, though Gupta himself claimed about thirty-seven.   West Bengal's fourteen members consisted of twelve of Atulya Ghosh's followers who were "prone" toward Indira, and two independent, uncommitted ones.

Out of Assam's ten, seven were straightaway for Chaliha, the chief minister who was for Kamaraj in whatever decision he would take, and three with Deokant Barua whom Indira was sponsoring at one stage as a replacement for Chaliha, and who would naturally support her.

Madhya Pradesh worked out to twenty out of a total of twenty-four, dominated by D. P. Mishra who of course was all for Indira, and only four possibly voting for Morarji.

Out of Haryana's seven, Bhagwat Dayal Sharma, then chief minister, controlled five, which were expected to be for Morarji, while the two remaining ones could possibly go to Indira.

The five from Jammu and Kashmir were straightaway counted for Indira. Kerala's solitary member was for Kamaraj, as well as Madras's total of three.

Out of Maharashtra's thirty-seven, Indira could rely upon a solid thirty, with a few of the rest voting possibly for Morarji, while the others would be uncommitted.

Mysore's eighteen were on the surface for Indira, for fifteen were controlled by Nijalingappa.   It was argued that Nijalingappa would go along with Kamaraj, but not if Kamaraj were to support Chavan.   Only three here could be counted for Morarji.

In Orissa, four out of six were held by Biju Patnaik who would have supported any syndicate decision, but the prediliction was for Morarji.

Punjab's nine were wholly for Indira, but of Rajasthan's ten, the majority was expected to side with Morarji under Sukhadia's influence who was apparently nursing a grievance against Indira for accepting the support of the Birlas when they were zealously sabotaging the prospect of his candidates in Rajasthan.   Goa, Tripura, and Himachal Pradesh were to go to the polls later in the month.

It was clear that the prime minister had nothing to lose and everything to gain by contesting. She had an added advantage—she had declared to D. P. Mishra as early as the third week of February, and that is what had brought him to Delhi, that she was ready to stand for re-election. She could therefore set in motion the whole machinery of gathering support with no holds barred. Morarji, on the other hand, had not officially declared his candidacy. Therefore, the actual canvassing from his side had to be in a subdued and indefinite key. He was certainly not going to risk losing this time, and it seemed even on February 28, that his show of rigidity was calculated to obtain at least the second best. His decision to contest or not depended upon a counting of lists which had already begun. Her decision to contest, if necessary, was explicit, so her canvassing had begun. She was one step ahead from the start. Mrs Gandhi's program for the day consequently underwent a change. Instead of staying at office from ten in the morning to about 6 P.M., which was the normal routine, she began to come home for lunch at 1.30 and stayed on to receive the flood of visitors that came throughout the afternoon and the evening till it would peter down, to the last, to an intimate group that left late at night.

By the evening of February 28, three things had happened. Atulya Ghosh had publicly indicated that a fresh contest between Mrs Gandhi and Morarji was inevitable. D. P. Mishra had met with an impasse in trying to have Desai included in Mrs Gandhi's future government as deputy prime minister, and Kamaraj maintained that he would strive for unanimity, refused to divulge if he had any preferences, and said cooly, "All are my candidates." The same day a number of leaders left Delhi including Atulya for Calcutta, Morarji for Ahmedabad, and Patil for Bombay, in order to make their presence felt on the regional leadership issues in their home states.

Meanwhile a move to scuttle the "lame-duck session" of Parliament (due to meet on March 18) came up from the opposition spokesman, Praja Socialist party leader, Nath Pai, who met Dr Radhakrishnan, then president of India, and argued for an early session of the new Parliament on the grounds that it would be a "constitutional monstrosity" for the old Lok Sabha to meet when a new one had been elected, especially when the people had voted so substantially against the majority party. He later sent the president a letter incorporating the need for an ordinance that would make this possible and pointed out that the last session should more appropriately be named the "dead duck" session. Chatterjee, another M.P., endorsed this view in another letter and added colorfully that since "many of the old bosses of the ruling party have figured prominently in the list of trounced leaders . . . the contour of the new House will be radically different and it is only proper that national issues should be tackled by the newly elected legislatures."[14] An ordinance was necessary to amend the Representation of the People's Act which empowers the Election Commission to notify the constitution of the new Lok

Sabha only after polling has been completed in each part of the country. There were constituencies in Himachal Pradesh and Goa where polling was scheduled to be held as late as March 31, so conventionally the new Parliament could meet only after April 1, and not in time to "vote appropriations," before the end of the financial year which also fell on March 31. Hence a lame-duck session of the old parliamentarians was to meet and pass a vote on account while the latest results came in. But the major voting patterns had been confirmed already, so the lame-duck session would have been quite anamolous. Nath Pai shot off copies of his letters to the president, to Mrs Gandhi, and to the speaker of the Lok Sabha.

At first Mrs Gandhi had wanted to abandon the session and have the new Lok Sabha called in earlier because of the uncertainty about the election of the leader. When the date for that was fixed for March 12 and her party could view the prospect of facing the lame-duck session with the authority of a newly confirmed leader, she lost interest in its being rescinded. But within a day and a night, with Mrs Gandhi favorably disposed to the opposition initiative, the government changed its mind. Home Minister Y. B. Chavan ascertained the views of opposition leaders in various states with urgent long distance calls, and by the evening of the twenty-eighth itself it had been decided to call off the lame-duck session.

The next day President Radhakrishnan signed the ordinance. The third day it was decided that the new Lok Sabha should be convened on March 16, so that the swearing-in of new members, the election of the speaker and the deputy speaker, and the president's address should be over by March 18. This would leave two days for discussion on the president's address, and a clear week for the lower house to pass a vote on account to be taken on the twenty-third and to pass the three ordinances which were pending including the one about the lame-duck session. On the fourth day, a short, pointed notification signed by the president dissolved the third Lok Sabha six weeks before it completed its five-year span. Mrs Gandhi immediately called on the president and discussed the question of the continuance of her cabinet. The president asked her to carry on till the election of the leader on March 12. As Mrs Gandhi did not offer her resignation, there was again a minor uproar amongst her critics. But it was pointed out with naive authority, that her father, Jawaharlal Nehru, had never done so either after the 1957 or 1962 elections. He had waited till after the election of the leader of the Congress parliamentary party each time.

The whole lame-duck affair offered another instance when no delay was allowed between deliberation and decision by the Indira government. But the government's motives were guided by an awareness of the advantages it would gain. By calling off the anachronistic session it saved itself the possible discomfort of having to meet, with its own depleted ranks, a near triumphant opposition. "With nearly half her colleagues thrown off the ministerial benches by the electorate's earthshaking verdict," said a trenchant editorial in the *Hindustan Times* of March 2, 1967, "Mrs Gandhi would, indeed, have had to face rough weather . . . the axed ministers would have been quite incapable of meeting the opposition's attack with any confidence when the electorate itself had so decisively demonstrated that they had forfeited its confidence. Ad hoc replacements in a reconstituted government would have been just as ineffective." It added, "With the question of the party's leadership as yet unsettled, the abrogated lame-duck session could easily have run into a situation of unprecedented political piquancy." In a stinging resume of the cabinet's initial bungling about the "lame duck" affair, Inder Malhotra pointed out that "the dubious decision to hold this session was taken as far back as in December, by a committee of senior secretaries to the union government. The reasons which have now prompted the government to go to the extent of passing an ordinance to cancel the session that should have been summoned were then brushed aside with a flippant wave of the hand. . . the secretaries made only a recommendation. It was the cabinet which accepted their recommendations without devoting even a modicum of thought to the matter."[15] Bureaucracy was to blame for having joined with law experts in encouraging the cabinet in its folly. "That the same gentleman did a complete about-turn in less than 24 hours [three months later] only shows how fragile is the stuff the 'abominable no-men' of the administration are made of," added the *Statesman* correspondent, and then threw the ultimate responsibility back to the political tribe. "The best of bureaucracies," according to him, was bound to "go astray" without political guidance. "The politician must be in the driving seat, and the impetus must come from the top. That is why March 12, when the Congress parliamentary party has to elect its leader, has become such an important date from the point of view of the country's future."[16]

But the bosses continued to prevaricate and the horse-trading went on. A cartoon by "Abu" in the *Indian Express* epitomised the party malaise. Three ships were shown in receding order. In front was one called "Indira," behind it, "Morarji," and a third further back called "Chavan." Some people in Congress caps were shown floundering in the water. But there were two stalwarts, seated on a raft having lost even their clothes, who continued to confess worriedly to each other, "I can't decide which one to board." Increasing support however was indicated for Mrs Gandhi. There were reports that S. K. Patil had decided to back her candidature. The Haryana members of Parliament met former Home Minister Nanda (who had become the super-ego of the Congress party in Haryana) and decided also to back her. Kamaraj maintained an official calm, privately viewed Mrs Gandhi as unsuitable but thought that unless there was a spontaneous demand for a change, he would not suggest anybody. "I'd say, carry on." He is even supposed to have told Morarji's supporters when they blamed the government for Congress losses that he, having lost himself, was in no position to offer advice. He had concluded that there was no difference in ideological emphasis between Indira and Morarji and argued cynically that on the previous occasion foreigners wanted Morarji in power because they wished to see the country go to the dogs, and they wanted Indira this time for the same reason![17] On the second, however, he conveyed to Indira that he would support her as a unanimous choice. He was for continuity because he believed that "any contest now will weaken the party." On the third, Morarji returned to the capital. He contented himself with an optimistic analysis of the election results: they were not a "prelude to weakness, chaos, and disintegration," he said, but "the natural expression of the popular will in a complex nation of diverse modes and manners."[18] But while a number of Rajya Sabha and Lok Sabha members called on the prime minister and assured her of their allegiance, amongst the fourteen M.P.s who saw Morarji was Indira Gandhi's own aunt and smouldering critic, Vijayalaxmi Pandit. Bitterness, it seems, was running deep enough to defy long years of shared memory.

On the surface of it, it seemed that all Mrs Gandhi had to do was to decide that she would face a contest if there was to be one, and if she genuinely felt that a contest would do no good, then try to achieve a compromise with Morarji. She was foiled in both by one of the cleverest political gambits in political maneuvering seen in recent times in India. This was the ambitious determination of the syndicate to prove its power once again: to tell its erstwhile supporters that the syndicate's defeat in the elections did not reflect upon its strength at the centers of decision. One way was to control the issue of leadership and come in again as a pressure group. So it mobilized a bid for unanimity which ensured for itself a continuing powerful role as a go-between and peacemaker, and by making that unanimity the condition for support of either of the two contestants, confirm its influence over both. Though his supporters claimed that Kamaraj's neutrality arose sincerely from a self-conscious awareness that he had no *locus standi* anymore, he was, and remained, the natural leader of the syndicate. A fascinating development took place under the very nose of Kamaraj when another parallel syndicate was formed. This had D. P. Mishra, C. B. Gupta, and Nijalingappa (the Mysore chief minister) as its nucleus. At first, Mishra, and later Gupta and Mishra together, aspired to be king-makers. While the old syndicate was anti-Morarji because it feared his authoritarianism, and anti-Indira, because she had not proved to be as malleable as they had expected, the new syndicate was purely and simply anti-Chavan. The old syndicate wanted unanimity to tie the hands of both Morarji and Indira by pitting their irreconcilable personalities against each other in the same government so as to make them lean on the syndicate as a balancing force. The new syndicate wanted Morarji to balance Chavan's increasing influence with the prime minister. There was a third center of influence this time. In 1966, Indira Gandhi was no longer a Kamaraj protege and formed a close knit "resistance group" of her own with Chavan, Asoka Mehta, Subramaniam, and Dinesh Singh. Brecher had written about Chavan and Indira in connection with their role in the earlier succession that among all Congress leaders, there was a "known affinity between these two in policy outlook, indeed, along with Subramaniam and Asoka Mehta, they have been meeting informally together since early 1956 and may be regarded as a "new force" in all-India politics, a counter weight to the caucus."[19]   At that time, however, the separate identity of this new force had not crystallized for they had the total backing of Kamaraj and he was taking in his quiet efficient way all the initiatives.   This time Morarji was an anti-force and they were on their own.   This time the activity was triangular, so the terrific pressure, pace and passion of this pre-election leadership phase can well be imagined.   Even though she did not lose her buoyancy at any time, the endless pattern of earnest tete-a-tete in which Cleopatran guile had to compete with sympathetic earnestness, depending on who had to be won over and who inspired, the long hours of discussion, the office, the diplomatic engagements, the international issues, the opposition on the warpath, the sheer lack of sleep really, left dark circles under her eyes.   The tiredness was held by grit and only briefly did the uncertain look of her youth sweep across her face.

5. CHALLENGE

In the first week of March, alongside the Congress party's search for its leader and India's prime minister, various opposition and Congress governments began to be sworn in. The Congress was comfortably set in the nine states of Maharashtra, Gujarat, Mysore, Andhra, Himachal Pradesh, Madhya Pradesh, Assam, Haryana, Jammu and Kashmir, but so used had it become to total dominance over the last twenty years that one non-Congress ministry taking over after another in the other states reinforced the state of shock created in the party by its personality debacle earlier in the elections. The first of these was West Bengal, where a former congressman had become leader of the United Front and now chief minister of a coalition of no less than thirteen parties. The entire opposition had united to build a majority of 153 as against 127 of the Congress in an assembly of 280 members. Though the latter was the largest single party, the local Congress unit had shown a disinclination to even try and form a government with the help of some independents or defectors or otherwise, a decision which was hailed as a realistic one for their having seen presumably "the writing on the wall." On March 5, a 14-man non-Congress Bihar ministry was sworn in. Here again, the Congress formed the largest block with 128 members in a house of 318. The newly elected leader of the Congress legislature party, Sinha, declared that he had been urged to try and form a government with the help of 60 independents and "like-minded members," but had decided not to as that would have meant "circumventing the process of democracy." This first non-Congress ministry in Bihar since independence was sworn in amidst riotous public enthusiasm, so perhaps Sinha was only being cautious. On March 6, two more non-Congress ministries took office. They were in Kerala where Marxist C.P.I. leader E.M.S. Namboodiripad again became chief minister and Madras, where C. N. Annadurai, the ebullient orator of the Dravida Munnetra Kazagham party replaced inexplicably, irrevocably, and with thunderous majority, a Congress government which had been administratively beyond reproach. Annadurai explained later that there should be no confusion between administration and government. The administration was run by a cadre of professionals, what the people had revolted against was the vagueness of Congress policy. In both these states, the question of Congress magnanimity did not arise—it had been swept off the board. On March 7, the *Hindustan Times* declared forlornly: "New governments in Madras, Kerala; E.M.S. heads 13-man U.F. ministry." The *Statesman*, however, conservative and restrained, put the announcement mercifully on the back page in a single-column staid headline: "Kerala coalition ministry assumes office." This was one state where the communists were kept out of power by two periods of president's rule. One, during Mrs Gandhi's presidentship of the Congress when she was greatly responsible for it, from June 1960, and then again from March 24, 1965 to March 6, 1967. But the prime minister, irrepressibly spontaneous, conscious of her impartial office, and sensitive to the niceties of human relationships rang up Annadurai at Madras that very evening and offered him her congratulations. On March 8, another non-Congress government, a Swatantra-Jana Congress coalition was installed in Orissa. Here, again, it was a straight solution. The Swatantra had the largest block of forty-nine members in a house of 140 and the Jana Congress twenty-six. The Congress had only thirty members. Coalition with any other party was ruled out according to a policy directive, and the independents, with whom a dialogue was possible, constituted a pitiful group of three.

"Up to and through the elections," said the *Hindustan Times* on these coalitions, "many of these [parties] were more divided against each other than united in their opposition to the Congress. . . yet, despite everything, the omens may be confounded and the expedient and uneasy coalitions called upon to wield power in the various states may well develop a resilient will for survival." The principal failing of the Congress it attributed to "the electorate's disenchantment with it and the distance that it had allowed to be created between itself and the people it was supposed to serve."[1]   There was a mixed reaction: of elation at the change in the political configuration of the country and of nostalgia for the only party (the Congress) that had the historic names of the freedom struggle associated with it.   A *Statesman* editorial took the example of the united front in West Bengal to point out that opposition governments were "invested with the special responsibility of proving to the electorate that in cautiously moving away from the Congress in some states, it has not acted unwisely.   The onus is on all those who can so far only be described as non-Congress; they have accepted a challenge and must be equal to it."[2]

But while Congress ministries too were being installed in Gujarat, Andhra, Himachal Pradesh, and so on, there were some problem states where the balance between the opposition and the Congress was so precarious that while the Congress was loath to let go the initiative, the opposition, seeing power so close, felt justified in indulging in the same political horse-trading for which they had accused the Congress.   Here, the independents held the veto and were receptive to blandishments from either side; but such was the mood of the country, reiterated in statements by opposition spokesmen, that the Congress was expected to willingly step aside and "give a chance," as they demanded "to the opposition."   This was anathema to the Congress. It had suffered in the elections, but it retained its political stakes, and the logic of that implied automatically the fundamental will to power wherever possible.   In Madras, Kerala, and perhaps Orissa where the majorities were totally against it, it had to accept outright defeat.   In West Bengal, the local Congress leadership was not keen even to try for office.   In U.P. and Bihar, the Congress formed the single largest group but was far smaller than the combined strength of the opposition.   It was only in Punjab and Rajasthan that its strength was evenly matched with the total strength of the opposition, so the impulse to form a ministry proved tempting.

In Rajasthan, for instance, on March 2, it was reported that in a house of 183 members, the Congress could command 92 seats and the United Opposition Front (consisting of eight parties), 91.   Congress leader and ex-chief minister Mohanlal Sukhadia assessed his own support to be 93, while the opposition he said had only 89.   The Congress was no doubt the largest single party.   Its total strength of 88 was almost equal to the joint strength of the eight other parties.   It needed only four independents, which it said it had, to get an absolute majority. The Congress had lost its absolute majority in some states, but not the elections. Its sustained dominance even after its apparent debacle infuriated the opposition and made it desperate, while it continued to give the Congress the same delusions of strength that had led to its downfall in the first place. Hence the air of comic unreality: of an opposition that was not an opposition and of a party that went on trying so hard to remain one. It led to the drama of shifting allegiances. A Congress M.L.A. (member of the legislative assembly) switched over to the opposition and the result was that the opposition and the Congress reached a critical parity leaving a solitary communist M.L.A. the option to give either of them the majority. Amongst the opposition parties, the Swatantra claimed back the allegiance of an M.L.A. whom the Congress had termed neutral. And on the basis of a common minimum program agreed upon by all the opposition parties, it was expected that the communist legislator would fall in behind the opposition and not the Congress party. Soon after he actually did! This gave the United Opposition Front 92 seats and left the Congress with only 91!

Meantime Sukhadia had raised the point with the governor that the party which formed the single largest unit should get preference over an amalgamation of parties like the opposition for being asked to carry the responsibility of government. Congress President Kamaraj from Delhi expressed a similar view and declared in a press conference that this should be established as a convention: only if the largest single party is unsuccessful in forming the government should the others be invited to try. Indira Gandhi apparently held a different view—not with regard to the principle but about the situation in Rajasthan in particular. This arose from her instinctive sensitivity to, and almost sympathy with, the mood of public opinion after the general election. She was known to have said that she was in favor of letting the opposition form governments wherever possible. There was a background to this. A definition of Congress policy had been laid down with regard to the formation of governments in states where it had the majority and in states where it did not. With the concurrence of both Mrs Gandhi and Kamaraj, a set of rules had been almost unanimously approved. It was felt that where the party had a majority it should not be in a hurry to form the government, and where it did not, it should not make an alliance or coalition. Third, no rebels who had left the party should be re-admitted on the grounds of political expediency or otherwise. As usual, Congress pronouncements sounded disciplined and well-intentioned, but the inevitable loophole was there for the members to act differently. That is where Sukhadia took his cue, dropped his idea of accepting expelled congressmen into the fold, but went ahead with trying to win over independent members to get an edge over the opposition and push the Congress back into executive authority. That made the opposition wild. To be so close to the fruits of power and yet have to see it slipping away was not the reward they had hoped for after twenty hard years of waiting. Exasperation, anger, resentment, frustration, helplessness, and dependence on the governor's decision who had to call either of the parties to form the government, according to his assessment of their strength, made one independent member of the opposition exclaim petulantly after they were coming away from a meeting with him that he hoped that "the governor would be impartial in taking a final decision." The governor was unperturbed and declared the next day that he was inviting Sukhadia to form the government.

He took three factors into account: that the Congress party was the largest single party with 88 members while the combined opposition had only 80; he left the independents out because they did not form a solid block and did not represent any policy or program; and, he did not want to dissolve the assembly or recommend president's rule because he felt that "a fair trial should be given to the democratic forum." He was guided to an extent by the Madras precedent where in 1952 T. Prakasam had formed a United party of various opposition groups but the governor had asked C. Rajagopalachari, then leader of the Madras Congress legislature party, to form the government because his was the largest single party. Governor Sampurnanand opined further that "precedents may not be relevant but every governor has to take a decision in the light of the specific conditions obtaining in his state and the past does provide help in arriving at decisions."[3]

Kamaraj in Delhi had already given the Madras example as a guide to his own thinking. After the governor's decision, he observed that if the opposition had reason to differ in each case of this nature, it should ask the governor to summon the assembly and "put to test the respective strength of the parties."

The opposition did not see it this way. They were up in arms and described the governor's stand unconstitutional, undemocratic, and one-sided and the manner in which it was dramatically announced seemed to them "to smack of a pre-conceived conspiracy and an axis between the governor and Sukhadia." There was the complaint that "by a single stroke the governor had converted a minority group into a majority party and had acted arbitrarily in depriving the opposition of its constitutional right to form the government."[4] A procession carrying black flags went through the city, shouting, "Down with the Congress, down with the governor." Some shops were closed, some buildings damaged, stones were thrown at buses, and an effigy of the governor and the chief minister carried through the streets and burnt. Eight people were arrested. In the evening the opposition held a dramatic mammoth meeting and asked the people to defy the prohibitory order, protest against the governor's decision, and organize a black flag demonstration the next day to Raj Bhawan (Government House). The Maharani of Jaipur declared vehemently, "I will not sit idle till the Congress goes, whether in a week or two or a month," and then added heroically that she would not hesitate to invite arrest if necessary but would seek her husband's permission (oh, shades of submission) to do so. In Delhi, the Jana Sangh party, in a typical inflammatory reaction, declared that it would organize a nation-wide agitation against the political handling of the Rajasthan issue and advise extensive hartal in the state itself.

The next day, the entire city went on strike in sympathy with the opposition. A procession of 50,000 people carrying black flags marched toward Raj Bhawan in defiance of the ban, and six opposition leaders, including their leader, the Maharawal of Dungarpur, were arrested. Tear gas shells dispelled the crowds. They were not allowed to see the governor.

Congress leaders in Delhi maintained that instead of resorting to violence, the opposition, if it was so sure of its ground, could have waited till March 20 when the assembly was to be convened. The opposition conceded that the governor had followed the "letter" but not the spirit of the constitution because though the Congress formed the largest single unit the fact that it had not been elected in an absolute majority demonstrated conclusively the electoral swing against the Congress. Maharaja Karni Singh of Bikaner, an independent member of Parliament, criticized the ruling powers sharply: "The recent announcement by the prime minister that the elections have proved India's firm faith in democracy has been belied . . . the horse-trading that has been going on in a bid to win over members of the opposition by hook or by crook has surprised every fair-minded citizen and set him thinking whether the Congress party really believes in real democracy as it professes to do...."[5] Maharani Gayatri Devi called for intervention by the center to restore law and order in Rajasthan and made the allegation, in telegrams to President Radhakrishnan, Prime Minister Indira Gandhi, Home Minister Chavan, and Rajagopalachari, that opposition leaders were being detained to prevent them from attending the coming session of the Rajasthan Assembly. She challenged the governor to advance the date for calling the assembly if a trial of strength had to prove anything. There was a persistent feeling that the assembly was not being convened earlier to enable the Congress to win over some independents and make its "present minority into a workable majority."

The matter hinged basically upon the position, relevance, and importance of the independents and the governor gave valid reasons for discounting their, and the loyalties of members of various parties. First, he said, he had been told that some controversial M.L.A.s were kept in detention and were not even allowed to see their friends and relatives. "Such means," he said, "have no place in democracy and to promote them is to demolish this philosophy."[6] There were instances where a group of M.L.A.s met him, declared their support for a particular side in writing and changed their minds within the next twenty-four hours. There was one member who described how he had been threatened at the point of a pistol and made to promise his allegiance to one side, but when the other side exerted similar pressures, he changed over to them. "I really don't know what value can be attached to the words of such people," said the governor and pointed out that this in itself had made him entertain the idea of dissolving the assembly or asking for president's rule. The *Hindustan Times* came out strongly in favor of the governor's action in emphazising that he had acted strictly in accordance with "democratic conventions." But it chastised the ruling party for its impatience. "It would have of course been in the Congress party's own interest, in the delicate balance of opposite forces resulting from the electorate's verdict, to postpone its claim to be re-installed in power . . . the opposition could well have been allowed to put its makeshift unity to the test."[7] It was the prime minister's own feeling, according to reports of what she said to some people then, that this is precisely what should have been done. But Sukhadia had been persistent and she had shrugged her shoulders later and said, "What can I do!" It is conceivable that it was not weakness that made her yield but that she had the leadership issue in mind and felt that she would rather not thwart the ambition of the Rajasthan leader at such a critical juncture; her instincts led her to anticipate the probability of the power-hungry cooking their own goose, an appreciation which had been borne out in the general elections and the "drubbing" that the presumptuous had received.

Events in Rajasthan slowly mounted to a constitutional crisis. There were fresh clashes in the city of Jaipur and fifty-four people were arrested in connection with what was described as "a three-hour stone throwing game of hide-and-seek between the people and the police." A delegation of opposition M.P.s and members of the new Rajasthan Assembly rushed to Delhi to see President Radhakrishnan. They pleaded with him to advise Governor Sampurnanand not to swear in a new Congress government into power. They reiterated in a memorandum which they submitted to him that the United Opposition party or the Samyukta Dal, as it had been named, had the support of 92 members, which gave it a clear majority and the right to form the government. They attached with this a statement signed by 91 members of the Rajasthan Assembly. They suggested that the appointment of governor should no longer remain the exclusive right of the center when "more than half of the people of the country had voted Congress ministries out of power." The leader of the opposition in the Lok Sabha, Nath Pai of the P.S.P., declared he would move an amendment to the constitution to the effect that the appointment of governor should be subjected to ratification by Parliament. "With non-Congress governments functioning in some parts of the country, an arithmetical authority at the center should no longer distribute patronage of governorship to persons found difficult to deal with or defeated at the polls,"[8] he said. Maharaja Karni Singh, in his usually scrupulous appraisal of things, wrote letters to the president and the prime minister in which he urged them to see that the "principles of democracy" were upheld and that "whichever side, the united opposition front or the Congress has the majority, gets the first opportunity to form the government."[9] Gurnam Singh, leader of the United Front of opposition parties in the Punjab, cried out from there, "Congress leaders in Rajasthan are laying the foundation of their government on shifting sands . . . "[10]

But while President Radhakrishnan promised to discuss the matter with the prime minister, the government in Rajasthan, led by Sukhadia in the interim period before being formally sworn in again, sought to placate the opposition by withdrawing the ban on meetings and processions and promising to release the rest of their leaders, the two demands made by the Maharani of Jaipur when she met Dr Radhakrishnan and Chavan in Delhi on March 7 and by the Maharaja of Jaipur when he met Sukhadia in Jaipur. Chavan even declared that the state assembly could be summoned earlier, on March 14, instead of March 20. The lifting of the prohibitory order in Jaipur had a contrary effect, and before government could release the opposition leaders, there was an outbreak of further violent protest in the city. In Johri Bazar, a busy market center, tense "guerilla warfare" went on between the people and the police all day long: it resulted finally in a frenzied mob attack on a police party. The police opened fire, seven people were reportedly killed and forty wounded, and the army was called in for patrolling the streets. A verbal outcry was followed by a chain of allegations, and accusations against the ruling party in Delhi and a request to the president, again by Maharaja Karni Singh, "to exercise powers vested in him to restore peace and amity in Rajasthan." The president as well as central leaders in government seemed to hold the view that the governor's decision had been taken within the constitutional discretion, so "nothing could be done about it." But the purely human angle of the trouble evoked from Mrs Gandhi the usual feelingful response: "I am most deeply distressed at the happenings in Jaipur in the course of which lives have been lost. . . . I appeal to the people and leaders of all parties and sections to help restore peaceful conditions."[11]

Sukhadia rushed to Delhi on March 8, had a meeting with Mrs Gandhi, Chavan, and Kamaraj, and that very night, got a heart attack and was admitted to hospital. For two days he was immobilized at this critical juncture, but his resolve to form the government did not falter. The swearing-in was scheduled for March 14, so party members toyed with the idea of electing a temporary substitute leader. On the morning of March 11, Sukhadia left for Rajasthan. The same day Governor Sampurnanand came to Delhi to discuss matters with the prime minister. Meanwhile, the curfew, which had been imposed on Jaipur after the violence on the seventh, was still in force, and odd demonstrations kept erupting. Speculation about Sukhadia's new ministry engaged his party colleagues and a disgruntled opposition. Congress General Secretary, Sadiq Ali, went to Jaipur to find out whether the Congress party had the requisite majority to form a stable government and whether Sukhadia would be fit enough to lead it. Sukhadia said he *was* fit enough. Accordingly, the swearing-in ceremony was fixed for 7.30 A. M. on March 14.

But on the night of March 12 Sukhadia wrote a letter to the governor declining his invitation to form the government. He explained that the shadow of recent events in Jaipur was repulsive to his conscience and "the emotions that they [the opposition leaders] had built up in bloodshed" which had "pained him beyond words" had never occurred throughout his twelve years as chief minister.   He said that the desire of the opposition to discredit him, the accompanying threats to peace and order, and the suffering that would entail for "innocent citizens," in fact, the whole warring, irrational web in which the issue of government had been cast, made him want to "step down."[12]   The next day president's rule was imposed on the state of Rajasthan by a presidential proclamation.

The political drama in Rajasthan has been dealt with in detail because it took place at the same time when a more momentous one was being played in the capital.   Each issue as it came up in Delhi or elsewhere and the way it was handled immediately formed an excuse, for those who opposed her re-election, to put the blame on Mrs Gandhi if it turned out badly, and exultation for those who supported her, if it turned out well.   The Rajasthan affair elicited a mixed reaction.   If the Congress did nothing to alter the image it had acquired as a party wishing to retain power at any cost, the opposition did nothing to dispel the idea that it wanted power at any cost.   By resorting to an agitational approach when it had a constitutional one at hand it earned the encomium of a desperate amateur, and there was at least one opposition M. P. from there who declared later that president's rule had come as a life-saver and that they would have found it difficult to form the government any-way.   As far as Mrs Gandhi was concerned her instinctual good sense automatically led her to the view that the Congress party should have abstain-ed from the power struggle.   But there were three things which had prompted a decision otherwise; Sukhadia had argued for a Congress government with the authority of twelve years of leadership, good administration, and experi-ence behind him: there was need to offset the psychological impact of so many opposition governments coming into power one by one by proving that the Congress could still wield the upper hand in many, and there was the political imperative to get Sukhadia, if possible, on her side in the leadership struggle in which she herself was involved, and during which she had to tell herself again and again that she would have to let valor yield to discretion.

Even as the Rajasthan crisis found a temporary solution in president's rule, comparable trouble was brewing in the Punjab on the north-eastern side.   Here again, the Congress party and the opposition were criti-cally balanced.   In a house of 104 members the Congress had won forty-eight seats, five short of an absolute majority while the rest of the parties, including nine independents, added up to fifty-six.   But the opposition was not united, and a vital element had entered the scene in the form of Maharaja Yadavendra Singh of Patiala. He had resigned as India's ambassa-dor to Rome in order to fill what he had sensed was a "political vacuum" in the affairs of his home state of Patiala.   He had been the undisputed ruler before the amalgamation of the princely states into the Indian Union in

1956, then Raj Pramukh (equivalent to governor) of *Pepsu*, and later an impartial observer and non-party influence in the tensions of Punjab politics. He was a tall, good-looking Sikh who exuded an air of majestic bearing and personal dignity.

Before the elections he had sought the Congress ticket, but met with a chilling reaction even though his decision to enter politics had "the blessing of the Congress high command." He had decided to fight as an independent. The Congress then had dreams of an undisputed majority and thought it could afford to overlook the Maharaja. After the elections, he held the key, and he set a condition; he would support the Congress with the help of the eight other independents, provided he was accepted as leader and chief minister. It was in this connection that as early as February 23, he met the outgoing Congress chief minister Giani Gurmukh Singh Musafir. The next day a group of prominent congressmen at Chandigarh wanted him to join and "strengthen" the Congress party. He then met the Punjab Pradesh Congress Chief, Zail Singh. There were two factions of opinion within the Congress, those who wanted a ministry to be formed anyhow, either with the help of the Maharaja or with the help of any other group of independents, and those who thought that the opposition could be allowed to have a try. The former opinion was encouraged by Union Defense Minister Swaran Singh who, even from the center held the whip in Punjab and who believed that the Congress should "go ahead and form a cabinet." But another section in the party believed with Zail Singh that they should let the opposition try first, if it showed the capacity or the inclination to do so. They thought that would expose its weakness in a short while for "it has no magic wand either to reduce prices or resolve the other difficult problems." This seemed suspiciously like the prime minister's own attitude. Zail Singh was actually consulting prominent party colleagues "at the instance of the prime minister." This proves that as early as February 24, even before the final results had come in, the prime minister was showing none of the "unseemingly haste" in grabbing ministries that some political commentators criticized her for later with reference to the Rajasthan episode. They even said that the government had learnt a lesson from Rajasthan and was therefore acting differently in Punjab. But it was obvious from the kind of attitude that the prime minister was sponsoring in Punjab even earlier than the rumblings of the Rajasthan affair that she was not hustled into any sort of decision.

The Congress bid for power in Punjab was stalled on two counts, and both from within the party. First, there was no agreement about the acceptability of the Maharaja of Patiala as chief minister. Second, an inordinate delay over choosing its leader resulted in the initiative to form the government passing into the hands of the opposition. But before this ran a dramatic sequence of doubts and dreams of power. On February 24 Swaran Singh arrived in Chandigarh. He found two groups of congressmen. Those who wanted Musafir back as leader if he would fight a mid-term by-election, and were so anti-Patiala that they threatened to resign if he were brought in as chief minister. They claimed that their experience of him when they were *praja mandal* workers was that he was a "reactionary." The pro-Patiala group said that he would bring in fifteen members and be able to raise the Congress strength to sixty-three. The Jana Sangh had a group of nine in the assembly as against the sixty-eight of the Congress and the thirty-six of the Leftist-Akali alliance (which had fought the election on a joint front). It was not prepared to side with the Congress or with the communists, but it could facilitate the fall of both. On February 25, when Punjab leaders converged upon Delhi to discuss the matter with Kamaraj and Mrs Gandhi, three opinions were voiced; that the Maharaja was welcome to join the Congress, but unconditionally; that it was not possible for a non-party man to be accepted as leader of the Punjab Congress as chief minister, in fact they would have Swaran Singh (also a Sikh) as chief minister if he could be spared; and that either the Congress should form a government on its own, with the help of a few independents or form a coalition with the Akali Dal, the Sikh communal party in the Punjab. As far as an alliance with the Akali Dal was concerned, here again there were two blocs within the Congress composed of those who could be tolerant of the communal texture of the Akali party, and those who would have "no truck with communalism."

By February 27, the opposition was making moves for a joint non-Congress front. The Leftist-Akali alliance, which was rigidly anti-Patiala, sought to keep him out by asking another independent, Major-General Sparrow, to lead them in the hope that some congressmen would cross over to them later. Seven leaders of the Akali Dal, which by itself commanded a membership of twenty-four in the assembly, met in Ludhiana and after an exhaustive comparison of notes lasting three hours declared that the opposition parties were in a position to form the government.

By February 28, a Congress coalition with the Sant Akali Dal was ruled out. The Maharaja of Patiala met Mrs Gandhi and Kamaraj and "offered his services" to lead the Congress government in Punjab. He was told that he must first join the Congress unconditionally. Swaran Singh came out with a statement that the Congress was in no hurry. Musafir held consultations with colleagues and even with the leader of the opposition, Gurnam Singh, in order "to assess the situation." "Should these efforts fail," said the *Statesman* omniously, "and in the absence of an alternative arrangement, the imposition of president's rule will become inevitable."[13] Meanwhile, the date for the election of the Congress legislature party was set for March 6.

Overnight there was further crystallization. The Maharaja of Patiala was out. The opposition parties had failed to come together and because they were not in favor of president's rule, it was left to the Congress to form the government. This it decided to do on the assumption that it could rely on six independents and some members of the Sant Akali Dal to join the Congress. Gurnam Singh met the chief minister twice to discuss the latter possibility but the only thing Musafir said was "whatever we talked was for the good of the state." It was pointed out that Swaran Singh's pre-election blue print was based on such a Congress-Akali coalition and that this was not the first time in the political history of Punjab that the Akalis would be making a deal with the Congress for the advantages of office. This time, of course, there was the added incentive for the anti-Patiala sections in both the parties to jointly plan a strategy that would keep him out. These parleys with the Congress, however, did not prevent the Akali Dal from trying to further their original aim to form a united opposition front. Even the Communist party (right) had agreed to cooperate as also the other extreme party of the right, the Jana Sangh. The Akalis and the Jana Sangh had decided upon a minimum common program. All three agreed that they could have the independent member, Major-General Sparrow, as the common candidate for leadership. The Congress party on the other hand had decided that it would have only a party man as leader, and that too, an elected party man. But in order to avoid the usual "unseemly controversy"—a phrase which became a cover for the lack of personal stake and political commitment—it was suggested that the choice of leader be left to Swaran Singh and Gurmukh Singh Musafir.

On the morning of March 3, congressmen vitally concerned with the issue unexpectedly decided upon a near unanimous choice for leader, Hukum Singh, the erstwhile speaker of the Lok Sabha and controversial mediator between government and the Sant during that fantastic fast undertaken by the Akali leader and his threats of self-immolation. In fact, Hukum Singh was even acceptable to the Akalis. The earlier condition to have an elected leader was forgotten, for Hukum Singh had not contested the elections. Here, the Congress argument was that "elected leader" meant a man who had stood for elections and won, as against one who had lost, and this had no reference to a man who had just not fought the elections.

The Maharaja of Patiala, rebuffed by the Congress party, presided over a meeting of the nine independents and quietly told Gulzari Lal Nanda, who had gone to Chandigarh for the Haryana leadership issue, that the independents were now "prone to side with the opposition." Some other independents and members of the Republican party, who had promised to support the Congress party in forming the government, began to have second thoughts because of "the race for leadership in the state, the Punjab triumvirate's (Gurnam Singh, Zail Singh, and Gurmukh Singh Musafir) eagerness to put into the saddle someone of its own choice, and the delay caused by the prolonged debate on the subject, all of which tended to show that the Congress had little prospect of forming a government."[14] Obviously, the fruits of office hung temptingly in front of the legislators' eyes.

At a conference of the United Front at Ludhiana the next day an attempt was to be made to coordinate its strength against the Congress. The vacillating group of independents, it was felt, might decide finally to join the opposition if it could make a resolute choice of leader and muster up the requisite force. To prevent this contingency, Congress leaders began to try frantically for a reconciliatory arrangement between their party and the Maharaja which would give them an upper hand again. The idea was to elicit the Maharaja's support on the basis of having Gian Singh Rarewala, his uncle, and to whom he was "favorably disposed" as the leader of the Punjab Congress party and chief minister. But the Maharaja was not available and when he did meet Swaran Singh late at night he promised, it seems, nothing.

When the parties met for the momentous conference six out of the nine independents over whom the Maharaja had influence and who would have acted under his advice even the other way turned the scales in favor of an opposition majority. The opposition acted swiftly. Within two hours, six parties agreed upon an 11-point program, left the controversial Chandigarh and Punjabi suba issues out of the argument and elected Gurnam Singh, the leader of the Sant Akali Dal, as the leader of the People's United Front. Ironically for the Congress, it was the attitude of the independents led by General Sparrow that clinched the matter. But credit for such unanimity or lack of principles was due to the maneuverability of the communists, that they could forge an alliance with the Akalis in the first place; the vulnerability of the Jana Sangh which could, contrary to its otherwise declared hostility to them, combine with the communists; the Tara Singh group's willingness to join with the rival following of Fateh Singh in the Akali Dal; and of course, the ability of the independents to merge with all. The People's United Front acquired an effective majority of fifty-three in the House of 104 and could therefore form the government. Gurnam Singh, other representatives of the parties, and the independents left immediately for Chandigarh to meet the governor to convince him of their majority and invite them to form another one of the chain of what were significantly called by the negative appellation of "non-Congress" governments. They had taken too long, vacillated too much, and were now on a losing wicket. On March 6, however, the Punjab Congress party elected Rarewala as its leader, which meant that even within the Congress ranks, the Maharaja's influence was weighty. But the Congress refused to accept the opposition figure of fifty-three. They said they had four independents and one Republican to support them which gave them the option on the same number. They informed the governor about their choice of leader, a procedure adopted by a party that expects to be in a ruling position and wishes to be noted as the largest single party. Here, the prime minister's stand became ambiguous. Contrary to her earlier plea that the opposition could be allowed the first initiatives wherever possible, she told a congressman who argued that the Congress should sit in the opposition in Punjab, that on principle the largest single party should be allowed to form the government. It seems that at this stage, the prime minister reiterated the theory in defense of the governor in Rajasthan rather than as an indication of her inner belief. She had not been in favor of the Congress attempt to force the government in Punjab till the twenty-fourth. But after their meeting with her, congressmen were jubilantly saying, "Now we will form our government." The governor's appointment with the opposition leader Gurnam Singh for the next day at 12.30 A.M. did not give the Congress much time.

The morning of the seventh dawned in Chandigarh with all the promise of high drama. The factors involved were volatile: the Punjabi character which is intense, single-tracked, and inflammable; the precarious majority to which the opposition laid claim which needed only an impulsive change of heart of three people to bring in the Congress instead; the flirtations of the independents; and the whole dynamism of change in the first post-Nehru election scene in India. But in view of the Rajasthan governor's misgivings about the claims to majority of the Rajasthan opposition, the People's United Front in the Punjab felt it could take no risks. It decided to take fifty-three legislators in person to Governor Dharma Vira at Raj Bhawan and present him with a *fait accompli*. The drama began at the Legislators' hostel when congressmen literally saw their majority being snatched away in jeeploads to power. The independents' attitude proved galling. The pique, resentment, and fury of a congressman had to be seen to be believed when an independent who had dinner with him the night before and promised support to his party would clamber up an opposition jeep the next morning! This *volte face* so infuriated some congressmen and even one minister that they bodily lifted two such independents from a jeep to prevent them from taking a "traitorous" path! Violence, crudity, and passion notwithstanding, the democratic spirit was at work in the most basic way. When the governor declared himself convinced that the opposition had the majority and invited them to form the government, outgoing Congress chief minister Musafir accepted the verdict in good spirit. He stated that if the united front could provide sound government, they would offer it their total cooperation and then added fervently: "We shall serve Punjab wherever we are, whether we are in government or out of it."[15]

During this period the *Hindustan Times* came out with a scathing attack on Congress yearnings for power. "Congress bosses in some states," it said, "seem like the Bourbons, to have learnt nothing and forgotten nothing." It pointed out that there was nothing wrong constitutionally for the Congress to woo the independents except that in most cases these independents were disgruntled ex-congressmen, who had been refused nominations as party candidates. "To woo or entice them back into the party would be to set a premium on indiscipline." A broader issue to be taken into account was the electorate's "strong negative vote against the Congress which must be regarded against the background of earlier electoral behavior as a decisive rejection of the party so long in power...the Congress party owes it to the health of democracy in this country to put them [the opposition] through the educative process of wielding power and shouldering responsibility. A spell out of office for congressmen is likely to do them a world of good."[16] But if the first requisite of politics is the thrust for power, then it is illogical to expect those who have it to relinquish it.   No ordinary congressman was willing for what he thought would spell political suicide.   There was an apprehension that if the reins were allowed to slip the psychological landslide against the party might gather so much momentum that in the five years to the next general elections it might be blotted out from the face of India altogether. Mrs Gandhi's opinion was only a variant.   She did not feel that the Congress should give the opposition a chance, like an elder brother teaching the younger to shoulder the family responsibility, but so that it should be proved inefficient. If it was to help a new generation in an awareness of the burdens of power, then the Congress as a political party would rather do it for the younger members of its own ranks as part of the approach toward "giving youth a representation" which was the prime minister's pet theme.

One thing was clear.   The prime minister genuinely believed that the Congress should behave with restraint, decorum and detachment, and re-establish its image as a party with a program.   This meant desisting from the temptation to play for power, and because of the immediate need after the election setback, to revitalize its soul.   But the regional pressures did not work that way.   She herself was subject to them for their possible effect upon the leadership issue, so her stand was diluted.   In Rajasthan she did not think it expedient to impose her belief, because Sukhadia was obstinate, and she needed him.   In the Punjab there was no one in authority, like Sukhadia in Rajasthan, with a conflicting stake in power, and whose support she might have thought worth winning.   The Congress chief minister, Gurmukh Singh Musafir, had been defeated in the elections, and the regional Punjab Pradesh Congress (the state Congress unit) had yet to choose the new leader of the Congress Punjab legislature party.   In both cases her political motivation can be surmised to be the same—the possible effect on the leadership issue— but the outcome was dependant on whose support she thought it worth making a compromise for.

There were plots, sub-plots, and counter-plots in the election drama in the U.P.   The demoralising loss suffered by the Congress in this "nursery of Indian prime ministers and eminent politicians," as this state was called, was largely due to the infamous history of the Gupta-Tripathi rivalry within the party.   Mrs Gandhi had to deal with the warring demands of these two equally ambitious, equally unscrupulous, and till then equally influential party men even when she was Congress president.   C.B. Gupta's alignment with the Desai group, and Tripathi's with "socialist-minded" congressmen had encouraged Mrs Gandhi to look with comparative favor upon the latter.   But Gupta's aim to again be chief minister of U.P. and Tripathi's to become one, however, kept U.P. politics in a continued state of frenzy; during the latter part of Indira Gandhi's tenure as interim prime minister. The elaborate U.P. government employees' strike which disrupted to a large extent the administration of the entire state was said, at times, to be encouraged by the Gupta faction to bring the then chief minister, Mrs Sucheta Kripalani into disrepute and clear the ground for Gupta himself. This it did to a degree. When tickets were apportioned to candidates in the general elections, Mrs Kripalani was given the Parliamentary constituency of Gonda for the Lok Sabha, and not for the state assembly. This meant that her claim thenceforth, after becoming a member of Parliament, would be to the union cabinet and not to the state cabinet. Apart from the personal downfall that this spelt for Sucheta Kripalani it was still the most obvious yet tactful method of getting her out of the way. It was also an indirect recognition of Gupta's strength. In fact, while the fate-decreeing Central Election Committee sat and debated upon the U.P. list for candidates, Gupta was given an assurance that if the Congress returned to power he would receive the backing of the high command. December was near enough to the elections to make Indira Gandhi increasingly sensitive of her position and Gupta's support in return was not to be an insignificant factor. Mrs Gandhi's pre-election strategy was definitely to acquire a sound, regional base in some state to sharpen the valuable but diffused image of her cosmopolitanism and general acceptability. It was natural to choose Uttar Pradesh for emotional and political reasons. The Nehrus were not only born and brought up there but had contributed a substantial part of their working life to that area. U.P. continued to dominate the Indian political scene after independence. But to woo U.P. meant wooing the stronger of the two factions in the Congress first, casting aside personal and even ideological preferences and only later maneuver them back to advantage. A compromise between Tripathi and Gupta made it possible to promise Gupta the chief ministership. But in the distribution of tickets, the effort of both was to get weightage in their own favor, that is, the group behind the individual leader was urged to be considered as a whole, with some candidates sponsored amongst Gupta's men and some from the Tripathi side. The larger group, if successful in the elections, would automatically dominate the affairs of the party. It is important to realize that all this politiking was for a play of power within the party and not against it. So unassailable was the strength of the Congress party in India since independence that the party bosses could not afford, or so they thought, to forget the possible effects of this rivalry upon the cores of loyalty in the parent body. Anyway, in keeping with the promise of leadership to Gupta, the Central Election Committee's decisions on the U.P. list gave a slight edge to the Gupta group. Even Tripathi and his associates admitted that the Gupta faction had attained an advantage of about thirty to forty candidates over them. But, and here I suppose Mrs Gandhi's other basic allegiances were at work, parity was sought to be maintained in another way. The Gupta men were given more tickets, but Tripathi's men got easier constituencies where the popularity of the Congress would ensure the election of its candidates. Tripathi was bitter. During the C.E.C.'s meetings in Delhi, he was confident of his continuing influence in U.P. politics and he certainly did not appear to be disenchanted with Mrs Gandhi's role. He said two things which showed the extent to which he appreciated her position. First, that she had to weigh the issues as well as the pressures that mount up in a case like this, and second, that he was sure that she would do things the way she wanted to only after she came in on a sure wicket as prime minister in 1967.

Mrs Gandhi's conflicting purposes were resolved dramatically by the election results. Tripathi lost and Gupta won by a margin of only seventy votes over his nearest rival and his group suffered heavily. Not only did he see his staunch lieutenants topple but chunks of territory torn out of the reach of his influence. This threw open the question of leadership. It was calculated that of the 198 elected congressmen and the 105 who were sitting members the known Gupta men among them amounted to fifty-three: forty-three were "dissidents" (Tripathi group) and nine uncommitted. Of the new Congress members, forty-one were said to belong to the Gupta faction, thirty-six "dissidents" and fourteen uncommitted. The total therefore came to ninety-four supporters for Gupta, seventy-nine "dissident," and twenty-five uncommitted members. The Congress party was left with a majority of only 198 in a house of 431 members whereas previously it had a total of 275 seats. It could not even form the government without outside support and the morale was as low as a bitter defeat can make it.

From the twenty-fifth onwards the opposition sought to unite and destroy the tottering Congress empire. What they found galling was that the Congress remained the biggest single party in the legislature. They had two alternatives. They could either fall in behind a single opposition party to form the government or unite into a coalition with a minimum common program. But as early as March 1, the leaders of the Jana Sangh and the S.S.P. with their respective strength of 98 and 44, met Governor Biswanath Das to convince him of their right to form the government. In the Congress camp, Tripathi, as president of the state Congress committee, began to initiate moves for a unanimous choice of leader, but the seeds of conflict were sown by a section which urged the former forests and local government minister, Charan Singh, to contest.

Meanwhile, fourteen of the thirty-seven independents elected to the assembly, organized themselves into a group. Out of these were a majority of the twelve "rebel congressmen" who fought and won the elections as independents, but who were supposed to be actually committed not only to the Congress party, but to the Gupta faction within it. It is likely that this was a pre-election strategy to strengthen Gupta's membership by helping to cut away votes from the official Congress nominee who might have been a Tripathi man, on the assumption that after their election they would be welcomed back into the Congress fold. "The disappointed Congress candidates can be divided into two categories," wrote S. Nihal Singh in his "Report on the Campaign," concerning the U. P. scene on the eve of elections, "those who decided to

contest against official candidates and those who stayed on in the organization, remaining content with working against official candidates—some
members of each of the two factions are reported to have arrived at an informal
understanding with opposition candidates to divide the winning and losing
seats with an eye on reducing the other group's strength in the legislature."[17]
This odious in-fighting tore at the vitals of the Congress monolith in the
elections, but it indirectly threw up a body of independents to hold the
balance; a characteristic feature of the 1967 general elections for the whole of
India, representing a much more solid third force in Indian politics than there
had been before and which could keep both the Congress and the opposition
in a perpetual state of tension, if either of the two should be in power.

But as Congress efforts to win the independents began to intensify, the
opposition became anxious and urged the governor to do away with the lame-
duck session of the local assembly so that the new assembly could be constituted at once and the opposition establish its stakes. "Keep the people's verdict
in mind," cried the opposition in a desparate appeal to the independents,
"and help bring about a change in government."[18] But while power parities
were being worked out, rumors of an inevitable struggle within the Congress
burst into the open with an announcement by Charan Singh that he would
contest the election to its leadership. The drama that was to unfold during
the next few days centered round the unique image of this man alone.

Charan Singh's loyalties to the Congress were supposed to be invincible.
He had been in the Congress government in U. P. without a break, but his
reputation for personal incorruptibility was unstained. There was such
unanimous regard for him that he had been the only congressman in the entire
general elections who had not been opposed by any of the opposition parties,
and he had won his election (from Chaprauli in Meerut district) by the largest
majority of any candidate in a state assembly in India—52,188 votes. "A
storm may break over our heads any day," he announced, "I offer myself as
a candidate because I believe I can meet this challenge successfully." When
it was suggested to him that in the event of a stalemate within the party, he
might join with the opposition on the condition that he would act as leader, he
denied it vehemently. His decision to contest threw both the Gupta and
Tripathi factions into disarray. For Gupta he was a dangerous rival. Although
Gupta could depend upon the support of a majority of the sixty-six Congress
members of the Upper House, and on the known loyalties of some of
the 105 sitting Congress members of the Lower House who had been elected,
the possible allegiances of the new Congress members were uncertain; in fact,
they were expected to be hostile. For Tripathi, who had been accepted
as the dissident leader within the party, Charan Singh could henceforth stand
as a rival rallying point for the anti-Gupta forces. As far as the formalities
were concerned, Gupta declared that he would stand for election as leader if
he were nominated by the high command. Charan Singh said that he was
not aware of any "directive" from the high command for the need for a

unanimous selection which should prevent him from contesting and added categorically that he would not withdraw his candidature under any circumstances. But both on the fourth and the fifth Tripathi, as president of the U. P. Congress Committee, declared in two statements which sounded only weakly hopeful that he was striving for a unanimous choice.

Meanwhile, seven opposition parties got together and formed a joint legislature party called the Samyukta Vidhayak Dal, and with the alleged support of twenty-seven out of thirty-seven independents elected to the assembly claimed a majority of 215 in the new house of 425 members. The twenty-seven independents were the ones who had earlier combined into a separate group. The parties consisted of the Swatantra, the Jana Sangh, the S.S.P., the P.S.P., the Republicans, and the two Communist parties. But how varying were the stands and their set of emphases was reflected in their approach to the question of government. The C.P.I. and the Jana Sangh said they would join any government that would be formed, the P.S.P. said it would join the Dal but not its government, the Swatantra and the Republicans made their joining the government conditional upon permission to be obtained from their national party executive, while the S.S.P. said it was prepared to join any government of the Dal. But the whole affair assumed again an unnatural air of desparate politics. It was said on behalf of the entire Dal that there was no decision yet on whether it would remain a combined force in the event of its not being able to form a government! A committee, appointed to advise upon the selection of leader of the Dal, recommended the name of an ex-congressman, Ram Chandra Vikal, now an independent who had resigned from the Congress party just before the elections because he had been refused a "ticket"! It was difficult to escape from the shadow of the Congress. In the actual Congress camp, Gupta had not declared his candidature, but it was certain that he would do so, and Tripathi denied an earlier intention to make "an appeal" to party men after obtaining a consensus. On March 7, when the Congress Legislature party was to meet to elect its leader, Mrs Gandhi's redoubtable twosome, Dinesh Singh and Uma Shankar Dixit (Dixit had also managed Mrs Gandhi's election campaign as manager), flew to Lucknow to persuade Charan Singh to withdraw. He in turn tried to convince them of his authority by calling a meeting of his principal supporters to show them the confidence and authority that he commanded in the party. But only a few of the supporters turned up! Feeling piqued, let down, and cheated out of his resolution to power, Charan Singh took the first step toward an opportunist compromise that was going to ultimately land him in the opposition camp. He agreed to withdraw, said a contest would weaken the party, and himself sponsored the name of Gupta for leader. Outwardly, that seemed to put the Congress house in order, and with as staunch an opponent as Tripathi now backing him fully, Gupta could make a bid for chief ministership. That very day, in fact, the Congress claimed 225 members as its supporters from the new assembly.

But a chain of switchovers began. An independent member who had been a vociferous Dal man joined the Congress from which he had been expelled five years back. The Congress was jubilant about defections from the Dal. The Dal assured itself cooly that a number of dissident congressmen were bound to leave the party after the election of the controversial Gupta as leader. The governor calmly received the lists submitted to him and kept his opinions to himself, though there were, again, twelve names common to both lists.

"The battle for the thirty-seven independents" and other party members became "hotter". The Dal got nervous. Leader Vikal sent a telegram to President Radhakrishnan to urge Governor Das to hasten his decision so that efforts could not be made to "corrupt legislators!" The Dal felt that with a total bigger than the Congress, it had a stronger claim to government than the Congress. The Congress, it said, must otherwise announce a coalition or a merger. In this scramble for presenting a bigger majority, there were no holds barred, and a "scared independent," said to be on both lists submitted to the governor, was produced at a Dal press conference for a gruelling examination by the press where he confessed that he was with the Dal—naturally. Meantime, Mrs Kripalani submitted the resignation of the old Congress government.

On the ninth when the national leadership issue itself was poised for a climactic solution, Gupta was told in Delhi, by both Mrs Gandhi and Kamaraj, that he should go ahead with his plans to form the government if the Dal could not. Mrs Gandhi was taking no chances apparently with Gupta's commitment to her. She needed him for her own election, and she needed the solid block of seats that her home state controlled in Parliament, and over which Gupta's influence would be considerable. The only reservation that was laid upon Gupta was that no rebel congressmen who had got elected as independents should be allowed to rejoin the Congress, though their support could be accepted. By the ninth evening itself, Gupta was confident of getting a Congress majority and expected the call from the governor to form the government. It was the Congress contention that the group of twenty-four independents had promised to side with the Congress on the assumption they themselves held that that would be the only way to ensure a stable government in the state. When the governor heard arguments from both the sides, the Dal representative told him that the increasingly bigger list that the Congress seemed to be able to present was due to the compulsion that it exercised upon individual legislators. Otherwise how could one explain the fact, asked the opposition spokesman, that whereas the day before only seven members had been listed by the governor as being common to both lists, that day, their number had risen to ten? To settle the question directly though in a somewhat unorthodox way, the governor even considered the idea of meeting all the newly elected members face to face and checking their allegiances. On the tenth, the Dal wanted twenty-four hours to produce more "seceders" from the Congress. On the eleventh the new leader of the Dal, the erstwhile Congressman, R.C. Vikal, declared that if the Dal was not called upon to form the government, it would keep fighting in the legislature. At the same time, the secretary of the Jana Sangh, Nanaji Deshmukh, who had generally done much to bring the opposition parties together, made a statement in which he questioned the bonafides of the U.P. governor, predicted a threat to the "security, peace, and progress of the state" if the Congress were allowed to return to power, pointed out that it had 198 members but it had polled only thirty per cent of the votes and said that "to ignore the wishes of seventy per cent of the people who had voted the Congress out of office would be a reprehensible act."[19]

The next day Governor Das asked Gupta to form the government. He said simply that the Dal had not been able to produce before him any independent members (other than their leader) or even signed statements in writing of any such members. He had taken constitutional and legal advice, but if there were any lapses, such as there must be in any human decision, there was always the assembly where each party could prove its strength. "The strength of democracy lies in devising a machinery for resolving differences as a substitute for force and violence," he said. "The machinery devised in this case is that of the governor. I have accordingly tried in my humble way to ascertain the respective positions of the contending parties. . . . Under the circumstances, let me wish and hope that the distinguished and honorable members constituting the contending parties will not fail to strengthen democracy and will follow the democratic and enlightened methods open to them under the law and convention."[20]

There was an outcry amongst the opposition. There were threats of hartal, meetings, and demonstrations and some members of the Dal went so far as to pass a resolution in which they accused the governor of an indulgence in "legal trickery" to favor the Congress, and asked the president of India to dismiss the governor. But unlike Rajasthan, the threats did not lead to a movement to disrupt the functioning of the future government, and Gupta got busy conferring with colleagues about his cabinet. Moreover, the opposition was not solid enough to start an agitation. But the methods to seek a majority were similar to the ones employed by both the opposition and Congress parties in Rajasthan. The stake was immediate. No matter what the governor said about a final and irrevocable confrontation in the assembly, the fact was that once a party was in power and holding office, it had the advantage, particularly in being able to tempt floating loyalties into its fold.

I have chosen to describe what happened in the three states of Rajasthan, Punjab, and U.P. on the question of leadership, and the Congress having had for the first time to deal with sizable oppositions because it threw up for the first time in India's post-independence history the constitutional confusion arising from the appointment of a governor by one party alone and its implications in the choice of the president of India, and, in the relevance of this elective process to the major ones of choosing a leader of the Congress party on the national level, thereby the prime minister of India, and the kind of confrontation possible between a party in power and the opposition, at the center.

6. AFFIRMATION

What was happening in Delhi at the same time was Rajasthan, Punjab, and U.P. enlarged to national proportions. If ever there was doubt that Indira Gandhi was indifferent to the challenges of power, it was cleared now. "There's something about the Nehrus," a member of the family had opined once, "the greater the opposition the more determined they become."[1] The issue was the gruelling mechanics of a power struggle, and Indira seemed to have vowed that she could be as equal in that as any. The arduous preoccupation with talks, the balancing of forces and the assessment of loyalties, the almost total replacement of the personal by the political became an acceptable and natural fact in her daily routine. She was no longer afraid of showing her involvement, and in that sense I think one could see the emergence at last of a mature political affirmation of herself. The conflict was over. The stake was clear. She wanted to be prime minister again. The first twelve days of March when the issue had to be decided were the test of her will, endurance and much more than on the previous occasion when she had stood apart and let others, notably Kamaraj, guide the choice, her direct attempt to ensure for herself the majority she needed for her re-election.

She was not vigilant enough however. And her disinclination to personally bargain with Morarji Desai, coupled with the inflexibility that he displayed when two of her emissaries met him as far back as the beginning of March, the growing pressure from within her own camp for the need for unanimity, consistently and forcefully argued by D. P. Mishra, and of course the syndicate's own efforts to rehabilitate itself were the unwelcome reasons that made her fall back again upon the wily, mediating powers of the Congress president. His emergence again along with his other defeated colleagues, his participation in a momentous national decision such as the choice of leader of the party and prime minister, in the context of his own shattered political face, drew one of the most vitriolic comments of those twelve days, from Frank Moraes, editor of the *Indian Express*: "With their heads chopped off by the electorate, the Congress high command comprising Messrs Kamaraj, Atulya Ghosh and S.K. Patil are running in circles like headless chickens round a barnyard. Cocks have been known to crow from dunghills. It is from no Mount of Sinai that Delhi's headless wonders, bereft of their voices, flap their wings signalling to all and sundry that now is the time to come to the aid of the party. . . .Who are these headless wonders to attempt to decide at this moment not only who should be prime minister but the central government of a country which has decisively repudiated them and bundled them out of political existence?"[2] In his "Political Commentary," Inder Malhotra said much the same thing: "Hurt to the quick by the suggestion that rather than strut about the political stage in the capital, they should have the political decency to retire at least temporarily, some of the defeated stalwarts have been saying that their party continues to have full faith in them. Could there be a more lurid confession of the dictum: party before people and self before party?"[3]

So strong was the anti-syndicate feeling among the political intellectuals in the capital, commensurate with its popular rejection, that it created an undercurrent of sympathy for Mrs Gandhi. It was understood pretty soon that she had the strongest chance of winning. The attempt on the part of some of the party bosses to fetter, bamboozle and condition her to a course of action aroused on the one hand, a certain contempt for a political inadequacy that had made her so vulnerable, and on the other, a kind of protective regard. This sprang from the realization that political inadequacy was in proportion to a strong, inviolable, ingrained base of personal decency. Her determination they would interpret as obstinacy, but I think there was always a point beyond which her growing ambition would not stake decorum, self-respect and an integrity of purpose. In the very ultimate then, she could sanguinely throw up the office and its honor. In that lay her strength: in the resolution to go through with a thing if she thought herself right to the point of risking her political future, and in the loyalty that this evoked from the average congressman.

After March 4 soon after Morarji Desai returned to the capital from his trip to Gujarat, the curtain went up on a drama in which the raw theme was nothing less than the fate of a nation, but whose level was not beyond the tensions of a bitter family quarrel. The Congress parliamentary party office began to prepare for the eventuality of a contest, so it issued invitations to the new Congress members of Parliament inviting them to the meeting scheduled for March 12. There was the checking of lists of Congress members, both of the Rajya Sabha and Lok Sabha, and the preparing of ballot papers, which had to be signed by the secretary. The election was to be by secret ballot, and Asoka Sen, a former law minister, had been appointed to act as returning officer. On the fourth itself the first concerted bid to resolve the leadership issue was made when Kamaraj met President Radhakrishnan for one long hour. His main purpose was to find out what the president's own opinion was and then to ask him to try and persuade Indira to accept Morarji in her cabinet.[4] This confirmed the impression that Kamaraj had already decided that the best thing was for Indira to remain prime minister. It was only the question of accommodating Desai that stood as a bone of contention. President Radhakrishnan also thought Mrs Gandhi would be the most acceptable candidate to the country with the added advantage that the now sizable opposition also would find it more congenial to deal with her rather than with Desai. President Radhakrishnan presumably conveyed his opinion to the prime minister herself when she met him later. There were top level confabulations again when Mrs Gandhi called at the Congress president's house where she met Atulya Ghosh and Jagjivan Ram. Desai refused to formally declare his candidature and said he would do so only after the working committee meeting on March 9. But the idea of his being No. 2 in an Indira cabinet had been put to him, reportedly through Mishra's offices, with the argument that if by chance she should fail he could automatically take over. To this Desai apparently replied that he thought his image would be better outside the government. Mishra felt that it would be no use talking personally with Desai for he was already annoyed that they should not have opted for him straightaway: "I'll catch him when he's not in an angry mood," Mishra remarked at that stage, "and make him see reason."[5] According to the assessment Mishra is reported to have made then, there was overwhelming support for Mrs Gandhi in the party and there was no question of her not winning in a contest. The same day Atulya Ghosh made an identical point by saying that there was no alternative to Indira. He added categorically that there would be no contest either,[6] which obviously meant that Desai was going to use his inflexibility only as a lever to extract the maximum possible advantage without actually staking his claim to the prime ministership. Meanwhile, a statement was issued on behalf of the top executive core of the Congress—the high command—that the working committee had no intention of usurping the right of the parliamentary party by trying to make them accept any particular name for leadership, but that it would only offer some advice generally.

On the fifth, the syndicate met for dinner at Patil's house and for the first time articulated the conclusion that there was no other choice than Indira. But it was apprehensive of her power and felt that, elected for the second time and for a full term, she would be far too independent unless Desai could be brought in. Patil took the initiative to talk to Desai. His aim was to neutralize Chavan, with whom the rivalry for influence in Bombay politics had changed to antipathy. Patil believed that his election rout had been stage-managed in order to destroy his base. Patil told Desai that he should not accept anything less than the home portfolio. At this point, I think, Mrs Gandhi became aware of the need to meet Morarji personally before letting the movement toward unanimity gather momentum. But she held back when she was "advised" that her going to Morarji's house or taking the initiative in calling him to hers might be construed as a sign of weakness. The question of the image here had to be weighed against political expediency.

On the seventh, Mysore Chief Minister Nijalingappa came on the scene when he also met Morarji with the same resolution in mind, that *Chavan must not be in.* Later in the evening, the question about a third candidate (Chavan again) was put to Kamaraj, and the dialogue ran typically:

Who is the third person? I do not know.
Does it mean a third person is ruled out?
How can I say? I will tell you when I want [to tell]. Therefore you wait.
And then a question with an unmistakable Indian flavor:
"Has a third person approached you for his blessing?"
At this the enigmatic Kamaraj only laughed.[7]

Desai later told newsmen in an informal meeting that he would announce his decision to contest or not after the working committee met on the ninth. But it was apparent that the real issue was not to center on a contest but on unanimity under certain conditions. There was unanimity about the need for unanimity. That much had been achieved. But both Mrs Gandhi and Morarji wanted that unanimity on the basis of being No. 1. Two procedural methods to resolve the issue were that Kamaraj could repeat the consensus experiment of 1964, when he personally ascertained the views of the parliamentary members and then declared that the majority was for Shastri: this way he could even specify who should be second in command. Or, an informal ballot could be conducted, the loser would propose the name of the winner, the voting strength would remain undisclosed, with perhaps a guarantee for the loser that he or she would automatically be accepted as No. 2.

On the eighth, for the first time, Kamaraj suggested to Mrs Gandhi the formula of a joint Gandhi-Desai team in which Indira would be prime minister and Desai, not merely in the position of No. 2, but with the status and dignity of the office of deputy prime minister. Mrs Gandhi's reaction was immediate. According to her, to make her selection as leader of the party conditional upon whom she should have in her cabinet and in what position, would straightaway place her in the position of a weakened prime minister saddled with an executive which would not be of her choice. Kamaraj conveyed the idea to Desai but could not make an actual offer because of Mrs Gandhi's reservations. Desai therefore called the whole affair "hypothetical" and repeated his cynical observation that unanimity was all very well, but "unanimity on what and on whom?" He is believed to have said that he would agree to a directive for unanimity from the working committe if it came, but on this issue, as a member of working committee himself, his own dissenting voice could act as veto against it. Mrs Gandhi asserted that she would welcome his "co-operation" but she was opposed to the idea of being forced to accept him in a pre-determined position. In fact, a compromise with Desai was threatening to become a symbol of her weakness as her resistance to him had become one of strength, although after their separate meetings with Kamaraj, Desai indicated an obvious shift in attitude by pointing out the value of an un-contested election in contrast to his repeated assertions that a contest would not be harmful to the party. Mrs Gandhi was totally uncommunicative. When pressed hard by reporters to say something to prevent needless speculation, she merely quipped: "I thought you enjoyed speculating."[8]

The persons closest to her, like Chavan, Dinesh, Subramaniam, and Asoka Mehta, were all in favor of a trial by the ballot in which they were confident she would emerge an undisputed victor. By the ninth, when the working committee met again and Kamaraj reiterated his "unanimity formula," there was no doubt that the parliamentary party was substantially behind Indira. Of the combined strength of 437 Congress members in the Lok Sabha and the Rajya Sabha, Mrs Gandhi's side was confidently claiming at least 282 votes, which left Desai only a 150. It was significant of course that though the Desai camp was optimistic in its general statements, it was holding back about actual figures. This contrasted sharply with the previous occasions when they had measured the possibilities down to the last vote, as Desai's own remark about the 1964 leadership debate showed. In view of Kamaraj's attempts to find a solution, the working committee decided not to discuss the question. In fact, when an argument about center-state relations came up— a subject which was going to be the dominant headache of the new government —Patil said that it was irrelevant to discuss it before deciding upon the new leadership.   By the evening it seemed that the issue centered on, not a contest, not even whether Morarji would be in the cabinet or not, but the status that he would have. Indira Gandhi was willing to have him in the position of No. 2, but she would not revive the post of deputy prime minister which Nehru had abolished after the death of Sardar Patel, the only person to have held it. Desai was equally set on it.   It was a tense conflict of wills and chaffing under the strain, angry that she should have been placed in a situation like this, she exclaimed spiritedly in confidence on the ninth that it was unthinkable that they should expect her to agree.   Morarji wanted deputy prime ministership and the home portfolio, Indira Gandhi was willing to give him the No. 2 position and the finance ministry.   The question of the deputy prime ministership raised the concept of "duality of authority," specially if it were joined with a powerful home minister and the influence he wields over the various states of the union. Desai realized that the deputy prime ministership by itself would only have the dignity and not the substance of power.   An earlier attempt to ally it with a right in cabinet formation and the evolution of policy met with outright rejection by Mrs Gandhi.   On the ninth, sitting in brooding isolation in his house but constantly called for advice by Mrs Gandhi, former Food Minister Subramaniam affirmed his apprehension about any government based on divided source-areas of powers.

Desai's earlier intention to declare his candidature at 10 P.M. after the meeting on the ninth was thwarted—hopefully for him—by Kamaraj who succeeded in getting both Mrs Gandhi and Desai to agree to meet at his house the next morning at 10 A.M.   But while Desai told an eager Indian and world press gathering at his house of his decision, therefore, to postpone the announcement, he exuded an air of tremendous assurance.   He seemed to be fully aware of his worth and within the limits of the demand he had set, confident that he would get what he wanted.   "What is the delay in decision?" he was asked.   "Indecision," he replied.   "I'm like Hamlet today."   But when someone said that this vacillation was not characteristic of him, he remarked quietly, "Please remember, I'm also human."[9] I wanted him to commit himself on what he thougnt was the fundamental issue.   "Is it on the issue of government efficiency alone that you wish to fight Mrs Gandhi or on the point of certain differences in ideological emphasis?"

"Ask me that tomorrow," he said to me, "I'll tell you."[10]

It seemed almost as if a discussion of ideological theory were an irrelevant thing, but Desai was being careful.   If he did not contest he would be directly committed to the image, policy and emphasis of the government of Mrs Gandhi.   If he criticized it he would not find the justification to join it soon after.

On the fateful morning of March 10 Mrs Gandhi dressed early, and with rather typical spontaneity told an aide (Kapoor) that it would be a good idea to call on Morarji at his house before going on to No. 4, Jantar Mantar, the residence of the Congress president.   So they drove off.   The meeting

lasted twenty minutes.   In the car on the way to Kamaraj's, again to meet
Morarji, Mrs Gandhi gave a hint to Kapoor that it had not worked.   At
Kamaraj's house while the meeting was taking place the atmosphere was
electric.   At first the newsmen were spread around in clusters in front of the
house and on the lawns on the sides, exchanging notes, prophesying an outcome, wondering. . . . As soon as someone signaled the end of the meeting,
there was a desperate scramble to line up in the verandah on either side of
the door, leading into the corridor from where the three controversial figures
of the day were to emerge.   Mrs Gandhi was the first.   The well intentioned
line broke up and the reporters and correspondents converged upon her.
"I have nothing to say," she told them.   As she came down the steps toward her car, I was almost carried off my feet towards her by the battling
crowd of eager newsmen.   I was the only woman among them.   Mrs Gandhi
stopped, shrugged off all queries, looked extremely concerned at my plight
and warned me with a smile: "Be careful.   Don't get crushed."   That
was all.   The human touch in the midst of strain.

At noon the same day, at a crowded press conference in the lawns of his
house at Tyagaraja Marg,   Desai declared that he was going to contest the
election.   He sat on a chair under a pipal tree: on one side behind him was
his son Kanti and significantly for those who look for symbolic mean-
ings, on the other side stood Maniben Patel, the daughter of Sardar Patel.
In a flamboyant assertion which went ill with the mantle of humility that is
his intellectual safeguard, he declared that he was contesting because he
considered it his duty.   "It is not merely a duty, I consider it in the country's
interest rather than in the party's interest."[11]   He said he thought he could
provide better, more competent leadership, but again he avoided the questions
on policy and promised an outline "at the proper time."   Again one could
not help but feel that he was leaving a necessary loophole, for to commit
himself on actual issues would be to block a possible negotiated comeback.
He would not say, for instance, that he stood for a stronger implementation
of Congress party resolutions, controversial as they were within the party
itself, or the ones never put into practice, or about which a lot of noise was
made like prohibition.

Mrs Gandhi did not have to define herself again: her pronouncements in
her year and three months as prime minister indicated the lines along which
she would proceed.   But primarily of course, the choice between Mrs Gandhi
and Desai for the country at large and for the M.P.s in particular meant a
choice of personality.   Desai gave the entire question, incurably, a spiritual
twist.   When he was asked who was responsible for the eventuality of a
contest he replied, "Destiny."

And was he confident of success?

"Well, success is always in God's hands."

"Not in the hand of the M.P.s?" he was asked again with ruthless logic.

"Members of Parliament, certainly," agreed the unruffled Desai, "but God ultimately."[12]

From her office in South Block, atop the sprawling sun-struck avenue of New Delhi's loveliest expanse, Vijay Chowk, Mrs Gandhi, in a green cotton saree declared her own stand. She was forthright, down to earth and un-ambiguous. "I am the leader of the Congress parliamentary party and I am the prime minister. I continue to be a leader unless a vote of no-confidence is brought against me."[13]

It was obvious that Desai's gamble had not paid off. He thought Indira would yield him the home portfolio, but she made it clear that she saw no reason why she should do so. She said, soon after Desai's declaration that he would contest, that she was prepared to give him No. 2 position and an "important" portfolio, presumably finance, but she had "learnt later" that he wanted home with the expectation of being the deputy prime minister. She said she was not prepared to waive the right to allocate the portfolios as she chose and she could not be constricted by any pre-condition, that was all. The morning meeting at Kamaraj's house, with the two incumbents sitting on either side of him on a sofa in a small drawing room, had broken off entirely on this issue. Desai insisted that he himself had made no offer, the offers had only been made to him. Anyhow, he would not agree to Mrs Gandhi's suggestion and as she remarked he probably thought that his stewardship of any ministry other than home would be unacceptable. In spite of Kamaraj's persistent efforts, therefore, and after him, D. P. Mishra's frantic running to and fro among all the three—Mrs Gandhi, Morarji, and Kamaraj—to find a base for unanimity, a stage had arrived to make both the contestants implacably obstinate. The entire atmosphere had been vitiated, tempers had risen, and a kind of shallow smouldering war between rival camps finally erupted in callous assessments of each other's leaders. The time was ripe for action, and the emotions suitably charged for a dramatic denouement two days later. The capital, and the country were on tenter-hooks.

But the tenth of March had a few surprises left. At the working committee meeting that evening, Kamaraj admitted that his efforts had failed: he chastised Morarji for insisting on the home portfolio when there was already a person in charge of it, and pointed out that there was such a thin line between "No. 2" and deputy prime ministership that it admitted of a possible adjustment. He told both Mrs Gandhi and Morarji to try once more to arrive at an agreement, and to the considerable astonishment of those who were gripped by the details of the turn of events, from professional, political, or objective reasons, all the three drove down together to the Congress president's house for another meeting. Some progress was made there to the extent that Mrs Gandhi agreed to let Desai be called the deputy prime minister, but she specified that that would mean nothing more than No. 2, what Nanda had been in fact, without the right to have a say in the formation of the cabinet and without of course the home portfolio, and only that portfolio which the prime minister may name expressly at the appropriate time. But Desai continued to play it hard and after the meeting announced, "I am still contesting." He planned to send out an appeal to all members of Parliament, setting forth the issues constituting his platform and asking them to support him, and he said he intended to release it at 9 A.M. that night.

This was in the evening at about 6.30 P.M. In spite of the seemingly unequivocal stand that he took Morarji said about his second meeting with Mrs Gandhi that "Nothing was broken up at the meeting. It was not choked off."[14] Kamaraj took this up apparently as a provocation for continuing his efforts at unity, but nobody could tell exactly what would happen. At 8 P.M. that evening the home minister, Y. B. Chavan, sat in a corner of his L-shaped drawing room, the furniture as heavily comfortable as his own frame, exuding like him the same air of tranquil modernity, and commented: "A people ought to know what is their government and the government ought to know who is its leader."[15] He thought a duality of authority dangerous and had misgivings about the adaptability of a temperament like Morarji's. He knew him well and had worked under him in Bombay in the fifties and his personality he thought would be an alien one within the inner circles close to the prime minister, including himself. Besides, he had a "vested interest" in keeping Morarji out. Normally, the rank, influence and status of the home minister is second only to the prime minister. The addition of a deputy prime minister would make this clear-cut hierarchy vague. On the other hand, Chavan had the advantage of being in the confidence of the prime minister, which Morarji, even as No. 2 and deputy prime minister, could hardly hope to be. So the contest was still very much in the air.

Yet events were overtaking intentions. C. B. Gupta, that fiery politico from the U.P., entered the picture effectively enough again to make the situation fluid. He met Mrs Gandhi in the evening and joined with Kamaraj in his blandishments for a softer, pliable attitude, but there was an implicit threat which no politician, even Mrs Gandhi, could ignore. He conveyed the impression that he was all for her election as leader, provided the choice were unanimous. As Mrs Gandhi, under no circumstances, even these, was prepared to take the home portfolio away from Chavan and as she had already agreed to allow the post of deputy prime minister to Morarji, the only thing left now, on which a compromise could be worked out was to name a specific portfolio. She had avoided doing that because it meant that her right to form her cabinet would be conditional. But it was obvious that the choice would have to be from the three most important home, finance or external affairs, and talk had already centered round finance. So the explicit offer from Mrs Gandhi on the evening of the tenth could only be for deputy prime ministership with finance. For Desai it meant climbing down from his original demand for home and settling for a comparatively lesser though important ministry. But C. B. Gupta put it to him clearly enough: that he should agree in view of the fact that he could not bank on a majority, including Gupta and his men, to vote for him in a contest.

At the prime minister's house the atmosphere was tense, anxious and dramatic. A long, sleek car would drive up the porch, disgorge a grave looking cabinet member or leader from time to time and park on one side. One of Mrs Gandhi's aides would come rushing to greet the person, usher him in, and earnest confabulations would go on in an ante-room to the left of the drawing room. A hawk-like group of top newspaper correspondents coming and going, or just waiting for further developments would argue, if they saw Swaran Singh, Jagjivan Ram, D. P. Mishra and Atulya Ghosh taking a dominant and prolonged part in the discussions that there would be a compromise, and if it were Chavan, Subramaniam and Asoka Mehta, that it would mean a fight. But in the midst of these momentous goings on, Mrs Gandhi took time off to brief the press directly, either by meeting the correspondents one by one for a minute or two, or seeing them together. At about 8.30 P.M. she came and sat down with a few of them in the room next to the porch facing the main house. She was visibly strained. She had decided not to say anything because the negotiations were at such a delicate stage that any statement could be misunderstood. As it was, her affirmation in the morning that she was the leader and prime minister and therefore did not have to declare her candidature had been quoted against her for its supposedly arrogant tilt. She would not talk about the actual conditions that were being bandied back and forth. Her replies were tense but softened by a rather helpless accompanying smile. She admitted of course that the issue again was open and the way she referred to Kamaraj's initiative in the matter showed a distinct appreciation of his authority as Congress president. She made no bones about the fact that it was on his advice that she had decided to refrain from defining the situation so that whatever possibilities it offered could still be explored. She said clearly: "Mr Kamaraj rightly feels we should have unity in the party. We have to see how that unity can be achieved . . . an avoidance of a contest will help towards it, that it why *he is trying* to avoid a contest."[16] (Italics mine.) With regard to Morarji's contention that he would provide more competent leadership, she merely remarked that that would be for the members of Parliament to decide, but her concept of government centered round more on dynamism and youth.

At 9 o'clock, as Mrs Gandhi herself said later, she got an indication from Morarji's side that he was "willing to consider a compromise." At the same time Morarji's appeal to the M.P.s which had been released to newspaper offices was swiftly withdrawn. The press correspondents gathered at his house at that time in accordance with his earlier promise but were told to come at 10 P.M. Desai said he was withholding the release of the appeal at the behest of the Congress president. But actually, it was Gupta who had made a dash to the prime minister's house with Morarji's offer of compromise. Morarji was expecting a phone any moment from her signifying her acquiescence. He allowed an hour for that, but till 10 P.M. when there was still no news and the correspondents were pressing him he just had nothing to say. He could not even say that he was waiting and would not admit that he had climbed down from his earlier demand, and the uncertainty, the latent fear that Mrs Gandhi might have decided to have a contest at any cost which he knew he would lose, therefore the delay affected his habitual aplomb. If Mrs Gandhi had been visibly strained earlier, Desai was visibly wilted by 10 P.M. and to the discerning it seemed obvious that he felt he had lost the battle.[17] Even if Mrs Gandhi agreed, Desai's image as a strong, implacable man of principle standing detachedly for the cause of efficient government could no longer excite the imagination of his supporters and impel the awe of his detractors, for he was clearly waiting and earnestly hoping now for the call of office. He called the press again at 11 P.M.

At the prime minister's house, there was a hitch. The woman some people thought weak had dug her heels in and would not budge on the question of the role of a deputy prime minister. She was initially averse to recreating the post but after that there was the question of its significance. She was adament that it should mean no more than "No. 2" with no extra powers. The conference that took place to resolve the issue was a high powered one, for in addition to the prime minister herself, there were the chief ministers of Madhya Pradesh (D. P. Mishra), Maharashtra (V. P. Naik), Andhra (Brahmananda Reddy), Mysore (Nijalingappa) and Chavan, Jagjivan Ram, Atulya Ghosh and Dinesh Singh. As more and more people arrived on the scene of final decision, M.P.s, journalists, and members of her publicity staff, the place assumed almost a theatrical air. R. K. Narayan, the famous novelist, who happened to step in briefly to talk to someone, sat down for a minute, looked absorbedly around at the feverish activity and murmured: "One could write a play on this. . . ."[18] Mrs Gandhi herself, on one of her trips out to the front room, looked around quizzically and remarked, "We'll soon have to get some extra beds, I think."[19]

At 11 P.M., again at Desai's, there was only an air of expectancy. By now he looked, acted and spoke with a mixture of bravado and wilful piquancy. He admitted he was acting under the directive of the Congress president. "The Congress president says that he is continuing his talks and I must not issue that thing to you just now," he explained. "That thing," of course, was the copy of his intended appeal to the M.P.s. He made it clear that the situation had neither "improved nor worsened" and when he was asked if he stood by his morning statement about contesting, he was clever enough to put a counter question: "The morning statement stands. How can it disappear?" He didn't deny that there was a chance of his meeting the prime minister or the Congress president the next day. By this time it was nearing 11.30, and apparently the call was not coming. But when somebody asked him if he was going to issue the appeal, Desai passed it off by remarking: "How can we send it now? Who will receive it? They will all be asleep?"[20] Shortly after that, unable to prevent the shadows of disappointment flitting across his face, he said he was going to sleep. And he did. At least officially.

But the close conferring at the prime minister's house went on. The long wait, the excited discussions among the newsmen and others, the genial hospitality of the prime minister's household in the little office room in front made it a vivid, receptive center of the news or impressions that trickled in from the inner room. There was Kapoor, effervescent, efficient and insistent host, and Nathu, the old servant with the chubby dark looks, offering cold drinks and *laddoos* with the solicitous air of a man who feels he belongs. The people who remained behind had special reasons for doing so, and even among the newsmen, it were mostly those who were generally considered pro-Mrs Gandhi and whose relations with her inner circle were especially cordial. At midnight, we were even served dinner, informally but hastily got up. *Tandoori* chicken with *naan* and butter chicken and *kababs*, at the long dining table in the room behind the two rooms in front, and it made one wonder whether Mrs Gandhi herself had had the time to sit at that table for a meal that day. However, hardly was there a chance to feel guilty by eating with zest what she might have swallowed in haste between marathon sessions of deliberation when we learnt that the meeting had ended.

There was a tremor of excitement. Was it to be a compromise or a fight? "She's agreed, she's agreed. They're going to tell Kamaraj," someone said. Indeed, the majority of those who had been confabulating inside began to get into their cars one by one to go to the president's house. D. P. Mishra, Atulya Ghosh, Jagjivan Ram, Nijalingappa, Brahmananda Reddy, C. B. Gupta, and—there seems to be some controversy about this but I am sure I saw Chavan at Kamaraj's—Y. B. Chavan . It was 1 A.M. The Congress president was kept informed on the phone about the trend of developments. He was waiting. He was told that Mrs Gandhi had agreed. When the leaders came out of his room, again one by one, almost all of them had a smile on their faces, and Gupta was positively beaming. "Everything's all right," he exclaimed, and then added proudly, "Wherever I am, agreeement must come."[21] I was told later that he went straight to Morarji and woke him up to tell him that he would be deputy prime minister, with an unofficial promise for the finance portfolio.

Back at the prime minister's residence at 1.30 A.M. there was a short and significant meeting with that loyal and patient group of pressmen who were still waiting, when Mrs Gandhi personally announced that she had accepted the inclusion of Desai on the above basis. She added smilingly that the formality would be complete only when Morarji was informed, but that he had gone to sleep. She was looking slightly tired, but by no means disspirited, and she took pains to point out, even at that stage, that for her the role of deputy prime minister could only mean the No. 2 position and no more, "with the right" she explained "to preside over cabinet meetings in the absence of the prime minister, as Nandaji did."[22] She was speaking warily however and what was disturbing was the obvious attempt of one of her senior publicity officers from outside the P.M.'s secretariat, who seemed to have taken upon himself the right to act as Mrs Gandhi's right hand man all of a sudden for that day, to try and censor her expression. He did not dare interrupt her, but he would try and stop her with a warning gesture or put in a phrase at a critical moment. It was surprising that Mrs Gandhi showed no impatience and went on to talk almost docilely of the events leading up to the latest decision, as if she was not aware that it was going to ensure for her again, the highest, the most difficult, and the most significant honor that a country and a people can give to one of its citizens.

She may be a "born optimist" as she described herself later on one occasion, but she was cautious and she was not the type to take anything for granted. Her attitude, in the early hours of the eleventh morning of March, showed that it was this inherent carefulness which made her play down her own possible excitement, and so she communicated the same feeling of caution to others. Perhaps she still had some reservations. That her caution was not misplaced was proved when she found later that morning that the hawks in her camp had organized a meeting of M.P.s at the home minister's house expressing their resentment at the compromise formula. But when they went to Kamaraj led by a younger group of vociferous leaders, they met with a rebuff that extended later to protestations by Asoka Mehta and Chavan himself. The resentment had been so intense that Mrs Gandhi had gone to the extent of asking Kamaraj to desist from finalising anything with Morarji till she had another talk with him. Secondly, on being told of her agreeability to the compromise formula Desai did indeed come straight to her house, but when he was given the definition of deputy prime minister, he almost walked out of the meeting. He resented the presence of her other cabinet colleagues who, he thought, had been called to be "witnesses," but it was Mrs Gandhi's contention that the point required a proper understanding by those who would be vitally concerned. It was apparent that the persons present at that meeting would form a part of her new cabinet too, hence the need for their appreciation of what a deputy prime minister would stand for in the daily counsels of government. The tension was seemingly endless. Morarji had a scowl on his face. So it was only as late as 1.30 in the afternoon that Mrs Gandhi made the momentous pronouncement that agreement had been reached, and that the choice of leader of the party and therefore of the prime minister would be unanimous.

How complete would be the acceptance of her authority was shown in an exposition given by Morarji himself in another of those press conferences based on wit, repartee, and pungent good humor. He had turned overnight, as one account put it, from Mrs Gandhi's "most fierce combatant to her most disciplined lieutenant,"[23] and he came out in an unashamed, frank assessment of the limitations of being a deputy. About the factors that made him decide not to contest he reiterated: "Interests of the country and the interest of the party."

"Yesterday you said that in the interest of the party you wanted to contest?"

"Yesterday was yesterday."

"Yesterday you said you would make a better leader?"

"A deputy prime minister cannot consider himself better than the prime minister," he said calmly.

"Will there be duality of authority?"

"How can that be? Authority can be with only one person."

Again and again he emphasized the absolute supremacy of the prime minister.

"The deputy prime minister is included in the prime minister. How can there be duality of power?"

"Would you also be deputy leader of the party?"

"That does not follow from the deputy prime ministership."

"Will you be leader of the House?"

"The prime minister is normally the leader of the House, unless she chooses to ask someone else."

"Will there be special functions and responsibilities for the deputy prime minister?"

"Whatever function is assigned by the prime minister will be the special responsibility."

"How do you define the functions of the deputy prime minister?"

"I refuse to be drawn into this type of controversy."

"Is there any demarcation between the areas of functions of the prime minister and deputy prime minister?"

A slight irritation did appear on his face, but he would not be provoked into expressing a sense of frustration. He knew he was being pressed deliberately upon this issue, and even though it might have felt like salt in a wound, his discipline overode his pride.

"I do not see what prompts you to ask that question. I will do whatever I am asked to do."

"Will the deputy prime minister have some of the functions enjoyed by Sardar Patel?"

"Do not go twenty years back,"[24] said the deputy prime minister-designate succinctly and in that, I think, he anticipated with the clear perception of those who have decided to follow when they know they are not in a position to lead, the mood of his leader and the future governance of India.

"Who won the battle, you think?" Desai was asked curiously at the end of it all.

"I do not think in terms of victory," he replied shortly.[25]

But a victory it was, for Indira Gandhi. It was nothing less than that she had bowed the indomitable Desai to her will, a man who was twice her age, a man who had been her father's contemporary and a man who had aimed for the highest of goals much before she dreamt of it. If one considered the opinion Desai held of Indira's government, during its thirteen-month tenure, his climb down becomes all the more significant, not so much for its opportunism but for its admission of helplessness against a woman who proved to be more than a match. He had won to the extent that he could call himself a deputy prime minister. But she had held fast to her contention that its substance would not be commensurate with its status, and that in the formation of her cabinet and in the ultimate sanction of policy her voice would be supreme and inalienable. "The lady has guts," Ariel in the *Indian Express* put it sharply in his column the day after the long, bitter and "hot-paced" struggle for leadership. "Mrs Gandhi has been described as weak," he continued. "If anything she is inclined to be assertive as her bearing throughout the hard fought tussle for the prime ministership demonstrated. Her moral fibre is tougher than most people think...."[26] This was certainly a change from the time when people would trace elements of similarity with Ceylon's Mrs Bandaranaike in that both were women, and that both were inheritors of power, one from her husband and the other from her father.

Indira Gandhi was far beyond such comparisons now. Her re-election as leader of the Congress parliamentary party and continuing prime minister gave her a new status. The first time, a party and an electorate could make a mistake or be swayed excessively by sentiment. It would repeat that mistake only if it were devoid of all political intelligence. The later election had shown that the Indian electorate had matured beyond expectation, while the Congress party, having suffered a setback earlier, could not afford to make another mistake or rely only on sentiment. Here, its choice of leader had perforce to be a hard, relentless, political one. That it fell again upon Mrs Gandhi showed that it respected her for possessing a basic talent for leadership, independent of her exalted inheritance, and for having so effectively consolidated her position in the party organization, that she could withstand successfully a challenge from so opposite, rigorous and long standing a rival as Morarji Desai.

There was another startling and pointed change. She was no longer, indeed not even once, referred to as Nehru's daughter. "Mrs Indira Gandhi" by itself was deemed enough. Second, in all that feverish debate during the leadership struggle, not once did anyone talk, write or argue that Mrs Gandhi could not do the job because she was a woman or that she could do the job because she was a woman. Whatever curiosity the fact of her being a woman in such high office had raised in the minds of many before, the retrogressive resentment that it created in the minds of the hidebound, the charm of pure femininity that those who know and work with her feel at every step, all this receded completely, totally, and permanently into the background against the appreciation that woman or man this person was, and was going to be, the prime minister of India.

Sunday, the twelfth of March, dawned cool, exciting and cloudy. Around four o'clock in the morning, three were a few drops of rain, and till nine, the clouds swung lazily across the skies. It was as if the bitter heat of controversy had risen high and sought its own cure. Rain, according to the Indian tradition, is an auspicious omen. Indira as usual got up early and was dressed by eight. She had a light breakfast and it was expected that she would drive down to Rajghat and Shanti Vana, the two hallowed spots commemorating the two men who had created the nation that she now had to rear—Mahatma Gandhi and Jawaharlal Nehru, her father. She had gone to pay her homage and to "seek inspiration," as they all put it, the other time in January 1966 before going to Parliament house for the acid test of strength that resulted in her victory against Morarji Desai. So the "pilots" were ready and waiting this time too, as well as the light beige cadillac, with its shaded glass and curtained rear window, and its loyal driver. But she did not go. She went briefly to the house at Tin Murti, then to her office, worked there for about an hour and met a few people. It was as if she had decided to concede to herself only the minimum of sentiment, no more. It was too big a burden to carry to wonder all the time what she would have been if she had not been her father's daughter. Like her father nevertheless she wore that day across the shoulder but over her muted salmon pink silk saree, with slightly heavier shaded pink flowers, a salmon pink rose. It was the Nehru symbol, coolly recognizable, suggestive and full of romantic authority.

At exactly two minutes to eleven, Indira Gandhi drove up to Parliament and entered the historic central hall, with its high vaulted ceiling and its long semi-circular row of immense, life-sized oil portraits of India's past heroes, men and women who had lifted her out of her political and cultural thraldom and renewed her dormant freedoms. There was Nehru himself at one end, then Rajendra Prasad, Maulana Azad, Lajpat Rai, Tilak, Gokhale, Sarojini Naidu, Rabindranath Tagore and, of course, Mahatma Gandhi. Twice to the same place, twice to be elected prime minister. And all within a year and a half. She remembered the previous occasion. The tension, the drama, the memories of a father, the thrill of following in his footsteps to such tremendous honor. It was something to which no human being could be immune. And yet, there had been the feel of something temporary, impermanent and elusive about the satisfaction then, a stopgap feeling, a sense of uncertainty. But this time, her achievement was real and palpable to the touch. She had made it on her own, alone, without father, mother, husband, sister or brother, and even the two sons seven thousand miles away. She had made it the hard way, fought the politicians on their own terms, stood fast on certain principles, established a very personal image, and was now all set to find a line for the nation to take. She did not know how, that would have to be worked out, but she knew where it must go. Toward a total elimination of physical and mental poverty, where she would never have to see the faces of ill-nourished children with that empty, unhappy, unkempt look on their faces. To her the image of a prosperous India lay in the image of the happy, healthy and courageous face of a young child.

The central hall was packed with Congress members of Parliament both of the Rajya and the Lok Sabha. All the 521 seats were occupied, 430 of them with the new ones and the rest with the ones who had been defeated in the elections but had been invited nevertheless. The election of leader may have been a mere formality in view of the agreement that had been reached, but the actual ceremony retained its magical aura. So the visitors' galleries spilled over even into the jealous precincts of the press gallery. As one reporter put it churlishly afterwards, "it was impossible to function because the [press] gallery was invaded by a large number of other visitors, including political hangers-on, society ladies and plain busy bodies." Near the platform and the microphones down below there were the dozens of television cameras and the national and international team of photographers, hustling each other for vantage positions, silently, ruthlessly edging their way to the front and unconcernedly blocking the view of the rest. Among party men there was constant cross talk which turned to a rousing cheer when Morarji Desai came in with folded hands, accompanied by Maniben Patel. There was even louder acclaim when the Congress president walked in. But the loudest roar went up when they all saw Indira, who came in last. She was garlanded with red roses. Red roses for a Nehru. So it was again the Nehru refrain, but in a muted key.

Indira Gandhi sat on the lightly raised platform facing that teeming hall with Kamaraj on her right and next to him, Morarji Desai. He had sat with the M. P.s on the other two occasions, but was invited this time, significantly, to take a position of honor. Some other members of the Congress parliamentary executive were also seated with them in a line, and at one end, near the mikes on the left toward the side of the main entrance door, was A. K. Sen. He had been selected to act as the chief returning officer for the contest, but his duties now were to conduct proceedings relevant to a unanimous decision. The meeting opened with Kamaraj's typical and theatrical economy of word. He strode to the mike and said succinctly: "We have assembled here to unanimously elect Mrs Gandhi as leader of the parliamentary party."[27] There were thunderous claps. But so relaxed was the atmosphere after the gruelling conflicts of the preceding days, that the rest of the formal procedure took a bare three minutes. Sen got up and called for nominations. There was a quickening of interest when it was Desai, Mrs Gandhi's rigid opponent of not so long back, who himself came to the microphone. Dressed in spotless white, with white dhoti, white kurta, white jacket, white cap and white jutties with the clean, dignified, scrubbed look that he always has, he said firmly, "I propose Indira Behn." He was followed by Jagjivan Ram, who looked such a contrast with his burnt chocolate complexion, his full mouth and hefty body, but who was dressed also in the same impeccable white. "I second the proposal," he said. "Any other nomination?" reverberated Sen's voice in that suddenly expectant, hushed moment. "No, no...no," the cry went up from the members in front. "In that case," affirmed Sen, "I declare Mrs Indira Gandhi..." and here, there was such enthusiastic table thumping that I'm sure nobody heard but just understood the last two words, ...duly elected."[28]

Soon after the party meeting was over, Indira Gandhi drove to Rashtrapati Bhavan and submitted the resignation of her government to President Radhakrishnan. He asked her to carry on till the new council of ministers was appointed. "The president," said the official communique from Rashtrapati Bhavan, "has requested Mrs Gandhi to form the new government and recommend to him the names of the other members of the new council of ministers."

That night she sat in one long session till 1.30 in the morning and made her choice of cabinet. There was no hesitation, no unnecessary consultations, and by 10.30 in the morning she had the list ready. Fifteen minutes later she was again at Rashtrapati Bhavan for the swearing-in ceremony....

March the thirteenth, at eleven o'clock, in the glittering Ashoka Hall, with its intricately painted ceiling, its tall marble pillars, lush carpet and a long shining table with rows of chairs with coral colored covers and the presidential crest in gold on the back, Indira Gandhi stood by the side of President Radhakrishnan, took the oath and repeated it after him....[29]

Twice to the same place, twice to be sworn in as prime minister. She looked around at her team of cabinet ministers, this time all chosen by her. She had not consulted even Kamaraj. She had shown him the list only that morning. He had been a little annoyed because she had dropped one of his proteges, Sanjeeva Reddy, a member of the syndicate. She had included a number of party unknowns. She was not going to repeat her mistake of last time and be saddled with a cabinet she did not want. It was time to do things her way now. Time to act. To "open a new page" as she had said after her election. She could not help thinking that her faith in the Indian people, in the country she was born in, could not be misplaced. "Let us look at that bright side, and I am sure we shall be able to show not only by our talk, not only by the decisions we take, not only by the resolutions we pass," she had cried feelingly the day before, "but by our achievements and our performances, that the Congress is a party that is alive, that is undaunted by defeat or setback, that it will always march forward for the welfare of the country and the people of India."[30] Well, she had meant it. The Congress was not merely a party to her, but a historic association which had given shape to an India her father and her grandfather had dreamed about. It was up to her to further that vision. She had a clear five years, and she was determined to try.

One watched this pale, slender, sophisticated, somewhat vulnerable looking modern woman carry her covetous destiny with a shy smile and an impassive calm through the swearing-in ceremony: afterwards, in light, relaxed and good humored conversation over tea with the president of India, her colleagues, and other guests. But there was also a saffron robed swami, grave, silent, unobtrusive yet inexplicably there. Between him as the symbol of a tradition, the *mala* worn for luck by the prime minister, and her mystic sensitivity there seemed to be an unbroken line from India's past to its present intent upon the future. And then she walked away.

PART IV

IMAGE

1. TRENDS

When Indira Gandhi was asked in 1967 what she thought had been her most major achievement to date, she had answered swiftly, "Setting trends toward modernity."[1]

When asked in 1970, after she had been prime minister for four years in what manner she thought she had been able to give practical shape to that concept of modernity, she looked as if the question were irrelevant; "But it's not in any one thing. It's part of my life, the way I took at things, whatever I do."[2]

The two answers encompass a span in her own development that has brought her sharply from a vision of social welfare to the hard realities of power politics. She has managed not to lose her spontaneity. She has gained a political image. The Indian National Congress, too, has emerged from its stand of battling idealism that made it an organization for liberation, and has recognized the exigencies of a political party.

The inter-relationship of Indira Gandhi and the Congress has been the major factor in the mood, achievement, and failures of Mrs Gandhi's years of leadership. History itself would have decreed a change of form for the Congress, but Indira acted as a catalytic agent, with careful deliberation and impassioned involvement and to that extent made a positive, not a negative impact upon the times. The Congress split during highly emotional circumstances on November 2, 1969, into a left: owing allegiance to the daughter of Nehru, and a right: including Morarji Desai, S.K. Patil, and others, around Congress President Siddhavanahalli Nijalingappa. When the question of unity could still be broached, Nijalingappa could say, "Unity, compromise, all these things are always possible. Let us think about it."[3]

But the prime minister was categorical. "If we feel strongly that impediments are being created in achieving our goal we should not be afraid of seeking a new way. It is absurd to suggest that in order to maintain discipline one must not forge ahead. We may not win. But to give up because of this fear will be nothing short of cowardice."[4]

How and why did this great monolith of political pressure that had humbled even the British empire break? And why did Indira, who owed such loyalty to an organization nurtured by her father and grandfather, not only allow, but single-mindedly work for its split?

The Congress could survive in its old form, only if it maintained the status quo. Indira could survive, as a political power, only if she broke up the status quo. So delicate was the balance of ideologies and personal rivalry within the Congress, carrying as it did the dying aims of pre-independence days, that its unity could be preserved only at the expense of change. The 1967 election results had shown that the sleeping electorate of the past had awakened to a new realization of its rights. Indira was one of the first to understand that the old reference points of the Congress no longer held good. Even as the general election results were pouring in state by state, her analysis of each defeat, according to those who had the opportunity to appreciate her immediate reaction, was "sharp, pointed, and detailed."[5] She obviously knew exactly what factors operated, so differently, but substantially to one end, in inflicting a crushing blow to her party. They were bossism, the attempt to rule by coterie, the unwillingness to give a different shape to party candidature, and the inability of her older colleagues to judge what must be for a politician a primary requisite, the mood of the times.

The conflict of views in the Congress came to be symbolized by the executive head, the prime minister, on the one hand, and the organizational chief, the Congress president, on the other. In fact, what happened in 1968 and 1969 was implicit in what had happened in 1966-67, the only difference being that the conflicts became steadily more and more obvious. There was the distinct attempt, carried over from Shastri's time to establish a pattern of rule by consensus, or group rule by collective leadership, whereas the modern trend is toward concentrating executive power in the hands of the prime minister.

It was Indira's desire to have a homogenous, closely knit party organization functioning as a "liaison" between the government and the public, playing an interpretative role, preparing the masses and creating the right climate for any sociological, political, or legislative reform planned by the government, in fact, a party which, having enunciated policy, plays an active part in helping government to execute it. This the old Congress would not do. It was content to pass resolutions, then sit back and see the government chastised for not putting into practice what diehards in the organization and within the cabinet did not really want to see put into practice. The aim was twofold: to prevent the economic policies favored by the radicals in the Congress from being effected and to weaken the image of Indira Gandhi.

For example, it was generally understood that the endorsement of the ten-point program at the Jubbulpore Congress in April 1967 and the chalking out of a definite and practicable program of implementation was largely due to many months of work by the prime minister and her close colleagues. The issues were as controversial as the nationalization of banks, the ceiling on ownership of urban property, land reforms, abolition of privy purses of the princes, and the development of the public sector. S. K. Patil, former member of the government, party treasurer, and an old stalwart who had been rejected by the electorate in the general elections, made no secret of his opposition to some of these measures and did not hesitate to voice that opposition in non-party circles. Morarji Desai, vehemently opposed to bank nationalization, was against abolishing the privy purses and giving the public sector (industries controlled by government) in industry a greater stake. As finance minister he was in a position to block, dilute, or oppose any proposals favoring the other point of view. Atulya Ghosh, defeated West Bengal party boss, and Biju Patnaik, defeated Orissa party boss, tended to play opportunist politics. That left Y. B. Chavan ideologically on her side. A big potential rival, Jagjivan Ram, was an inscrutable entity, and former Congress President Kamaraj, defeated in the elections, carried the burden of a broken image. Kamaraj, a socialist and rural progressive, with a regional reputation that had developed into a national one as "king-maker" was caught ultimately by a personal ambition that proved too high for him. The power conflict with the prime minister, any prime minister, was an inherent one and he could not accept being in second place. His ideological stance became irrelevant, and he opted for power regardless of policy.

At a later date when she could take a comparative look at three Congress presidents she had to deal with as prime minister, Kamaraj, Nijalingappa, and Jagjivan Ram, Indira said of the relative roles of the prime minister and party president, "The prime minister, it is true, has to have a national point of view. The organizational chief is more concerned about the party. This is what happened with me, for instance, about devaluation. I was told that I should make the decisions after the election so that nothing should hurt the party's prospects. But if he has a political stake he has to have the same stake [as the prime minister]. The clash of personality really is secondary. The basic difficulty is that politics here is separated from the grass roots—there is a tendency for us, as a nation, that if something is good, you go into super- latives and if it is bad, you plunge into despair. The party must act as a 'bridge' between the government and the people." She did not think conflict was inevitable. "It was clearly defined for instance," she said, "between my father and me."[6]

In 1968 and 1969, Indira Gandhi was a frustrated leader. She was not strong enough to defy the organization and not rash enough to quit. She was prepared to sit in the opposition provided a sizable core that made such a play about being radical was prepared to do likewise. Her invariable retort to those who came to pledge their support to her was, "Yes, come with me, if you are not afraid to sit with me in the opposition." Very few, when it came to the point, were willing to risk the possible political oblivion that a shedding of political office entailed in the current Indian context.

Nevertheless, the tests were not slow in coming. Almost the first issue on which Indira Gandhi sought to assert her leadership was the Congress party's nomination for the office of president of India on the expiration of Dr Sarvapalli Radhakrishnan's term. She wished a natural accession to the office, and Vice-President Zakir Husain to be accepted, as Vice-President Radhakri- shnan had been previously. She saw no reason why it should not be so and many reasons why it should be so. Dr Zakir Husain, like Dr Radhakrishnan, was a scholar and a non-controversial figure. The former was a philosopher, the latter an educator. He had the additional advantage of a record of dedi- cated service in pre-liberation India. His personal reputation was unimpea- chable, and she thought, to have a Muslim as head of state, would be good for India both nationally and internationally.

Kamaraj had no personal objection to sponsoring Zakir Husain's candidacy on behalf of the Congress party, but he wanted to play safe. He thought that a group of communally minded congressmen could sabotage the choice by vot- ing against Zakir Husain because they did not favor having a Muslim as pre- sident of India. It was an undoubted risk, but to Indira a risk worth taking. She allied herself with her choice determinedly. It became a prestige issue, to the point where the people began to say that her own party's rejection of Zakir Husain's candidacy would amount to an expression of no-confidence in the leadership of Indira Gandhi. She herself later played down the signi- ficance of the tensions.

"Some people disagreed," she said casually, "we had several meetings . . . before it was decided."[7]

But that she was upset and not so sure of the outcome was revealed in a letter she wrote to a colleague who had expressed his sympathy about her predicament.

"It is good of you to say kind words about me. I wish I deserved them. The situation is an extraordinarily difficult one. Unfortunately from the beginning there has been lack of cooperation all along the line. The coming period will be even more difficult.

"I fully agree with you about Dr Zakir Husain and have already spoken about him and others. It is probably the group in our own party which stands so strongly for Hindi who will oppose him. If he is not elected president I doubt if he will want to remain as vice-president and that will damage us internationally."[8]

The communal issue was compounded by a fear on the part of some syndicate sympathizers, instilled into their minds by opposition arguments, that Zakir Husain would be a mere rubber stamp to the prime minister's wishes. Hence the wider divergence of the internal party conflict. But the world loves a fighter, and any party a vigorous stand. Indira's positive canvassing won over the majority. Not only was Zakir Husain nominated by the Congress but he also won the election to the presidency of India. It was acknowledged as a personal victory for the prime minister, but the pattern of voting anticipated the alignments that would affect the far more dramatic and irrevocable election two years later of V. V. Giri, to the presidency of India. Both times it was calculated that a dissenting core of congressmen voted against the popular trend. Both times the hidden votes of the opposition strengthened the final result, presaging a vague kind of polarization that was seen to be cutting across official party commitments. In fact, if the Congress was going through the throes of disintegration and possible rebirth, so indeed were the other parties. The talk, the plans about, and the concept of ideological alignment began to stir political thought in India. But both the courage and the vision were lacking until then to give it tangible form.

The internal contradictions in the Congress continued to cast their shadow over events, or were actually responsible for giving events their particular shape. All the drama was latent, all the conflicts were undercurrents, and the widening fissures in the party given a patched-up public face. The giant, swaying on its feet, continued to stand, and Indira, despite constant prognostications to the contrary, continued to survive. Each session of Parliament was envisaged to be her last one, and yet she was there for the next, chastened but wiser, acquiring increasing support within her party, slowly but inexorably, developing the experience as a parliamentarian that turned her from the shy, timid speaker who read, with her eyes cast down, from the text, to an eloquent protagonist of her government, marking time with compro-

mise and shrewd tactics until she became invulnerable enough to strike out
over basic policy issues. This was the period in which she emerged as a
pragmatic strategist above all, placating wherever necessary, being angry or
tactful wherever necessary, but keeping what she had in mind very much to
herself. She initiated a style of decision-making in which she consulted everyone, confided in no one, and arrived at a decision in the quiet solitudes of
her own mind. She remained the inscrutable madonna, with a faint smile on
the lips, a hint of sadness in the eyes, but a sense of purpose and an accessi-
bility that communicated itself to the rank and file of her party men.

"What main political lessons did you learn from your father?" she was
once asked.

"It's difficult to separate political and other lessons. The one important
lesson I learnt is to be sincere and to be oneself."

"But about staying in the [his] shadow?" the questioner asked further.

"I was glad to be in the shadow."[9]

She was glad, no doubt, to be in the shadow, but only in the shadow when
Jawaharlal Nehru was there. Not anyone close, nor those who knew her
then subscribe even to that interpretation. All the characteristics of her
personality that were so marked as prime minister, a determination tinged by
ruthlessness, a sense of political timing, an appreciation of statecraft, an
involvement with the masses, a concern for practical policy, a sense of urgency,
an urge to ready means and the tendency to take politics at its simplest level,
whatever promised the best to the most, an impatience, but an impatience
tethered to restraint, held back until it got people on the move, all this was
there much before, except that the limelight fell on it only after Nehru's
death.

What is surprising is that the old Congress leadership should have mis-
calculated so badly. When what they had hoped to get was a puppet, they
got a woman who, if the occasion demanded, was prepared to manipulate the
strings just as well. They had planned to go along with her only until the
general elections, to use her name and background to bolster the party
votes, and then drop her. But the electorate, as she had expected, dropped
them first. Yet many of her older colleagues who remain even in her own
cabinet tended not to take her seriously in the beginning. Cabinet ministers
would sometimes stroll in late at meetings, offer a perfunctory apology, and
sometimes even leave early. The attitude was paternalistic and complacent,
she could be taken for granted as Indu, the daughter of "Panditji." This
was thought to be a significant disadvantage under which she had to function.

"Did you feel this inhibition?" I asked her. "Did you feel at a disadvantage in having to deal with older people who were your father's colleagues and who perhaps you could not scold, or tell off, as you might have with
your own age group?"

"I had no reservation. I was used to dealing with them as Congress
president, you forget. Besides," she added, her eyes lighting up humorously,

"I never scold anyone."[10]

Her increasing strength made the old clique nervous, and her obvious preference for relying on an unofficial group of younger advisers, made them resentful. It effectively undermined the influence of the diehards, but they made much of the one very obvious weakness in her armor—that the people around her had no organizational base in the party. The "kitchen cabinet" as it came to be called came in for a lot of snide comment but nobody could stop a clever move on her part to shift the centers of power away from the traditional ones. By the end of 1968 even Kamaraj was out. His term had ended, but he hoped that at least a lack of unanimity in the beginning about a possible alternative would get him re-elected. Indira managed to prevent it but she was outmaneuvered by the syndicate on the next choice. The man put up, without leaving her room to argue, was Nijalingappa, chief minister of Mysore, known in closed circles to be "Kamaraj's man." Indira did the only thing possible; she played a shrewd game of timing and before Kamaraj could say so, she announced Nijalingappa as her nominee. The move had only psychological value, for her relationship with the organizational side threatened to remain tense except for that initial "closer cooperation" that a new personality on the scene might bring—Nijalingappa was new as Congress president, but he was an old tactician and a member of the syndicate.

At the 71st session of the Congress at Hyderabad in February 1968 with Nijalingappa presiding, the Congress resolution again gave a call for action: "The main result of the election for our organization is that while the people have gained confidence in the ballot box to bring about changes in the governance of the country, they are also increasingly impatient for the speedier and more effective solution of the problems."[11] There again she knew that the trap was as insidious as ever. She said feelingly on one occasion that everywhere one could see that all other things could be built up, "but vision if lost, is not easy to recover and a people without vision must perish."[12] How had her own blueprint for India worked out, despite the limitations? She had said when she had first been elected prime minister that she was not afraid of changing previous policies—which automatically meant her father's policies —if the good of the country demanded it. The change was interpreted to mean a possible shift away from the Nehruian posture, therefore, a non-socialist one. In 1969 when she was asked whether she had noticed any weakness in her father's politics, she replied, "The situation that he faced and that I face are entirely different. He had to dig the foundations. I have only to build on them."[13]

By 1970, the "change" was interpreted to have the opposite meaning, that she could be more socialistic than Nehru, not less. Her persistence was apparent in some key areas. When the draft for the fourth five-year plan was being prepared in 1966 she was one of the strongest protagonists of a big plan, "overruling," as Minoo Masani exclaimed indignantly one time, "those against it among the officers, the members of the planning commission, her own colleagues, everybody."[14] For two years after that, however, she was forced to a "plan holiday" with only yearly plans being devised because aid uncertainties and other factors made an overall adjustment difficult. It was a temporary and commonsense measure and did not reflect a move on her part away from a firm belief in the concept of planned development. In fact, by 1969 she was being quite sarcastic about those who advocated a continuation of the holiday pattern.

"It is indeed surprising that my honorable friend opposite, Professor Ranga, is still harping on a plan holiday," she retorted in the Lok Sabha to the criticisms made by the Swatantra leader, "especially since the very captains of industry on whose behalf his party speaks are urging the government to increase their investment. There can be no holiday for the nation —not so long as this party is in charge of the government of this country, not so long as there are hungry millions seeking social justice."[15] Her enthusiasm for the public sector industries controlled by government was undimmed in spite of prolonged inefficiencies. "It is very easy for people to ask, why is the public sector not giving profit. The answer is simple. It is because it is busy building a base."[16] In 1970, when the fourth plan was formulated the public sector was given a major share.

Second, she took the issue of the nationalization of banks to the point where the ideological divergence within her party could not help coming out in the open. Until the time that she felt she could substantiate her own point of view with the majority in the party, she was careful. She compromised. Nationalization was watered down to "social control of banks," the only extent to which Morarji Desai, in the vital position of finance minister, was prepared to go.

As far back as December 14, 1967, in the Lok Sabha, Desai "not only outlined the various structural and other reforms proposed but provided a powerful justification for rejecting nationalization advocated by many, including, reportedly, some members of the central cabinet."[17] On December 23, the bill [the Banking Law (Amendment) Bill] to bring banking institutions in the country under effective social control was introduced in Parliament. Thereafter there was an uneasy peace. It was agreed that "social control" could be tried out for two years to give it a fair chance. The radicals in the party would not let the controversy die, however, and tension was recurrent in meetings of the working committee. In 1969 the prime minister decided to force the issue herself. Illness compelled her to delay her departure for the AICC session scheduled at Bangalore for July 10, 11 and 12—a session that was to set off other momentous events—but she sent a note on economic issues for consideration of the working committee, the style, timing, and content of which set the old leaders on fire.

It contained a new set of economic guidelines which approximated the demands put forth earlier by party radicals. It suggested the nationalization of "the top five or six banks," or, alternately, the raising of bank investments in government securities by about 50 per cent—yielding 200 crores—for the benefit of the public sector, reorientation of financial institutions, appointment of a monopolies commission, government ownership of consumer industries, investment by foreign capital, and legislation which could help enforce the retirement of "former industrialist chairmen from private bank boards of directors."[18] The timing of the note's presentation was highly dramatic and seemed calculated to take the working committee by surprise and change the direction of discussion. The draft was "unveiled," as one report called it, by Fakhruddin Ali Ahmed only toward the end of the meeting of the working committee. "These are just some stray thoughts rather hurriedly dictated," the prime minister had written at the end of the draft; but the issues were too far-reaching not to have earned some hard thinking beforehand, and nobody had any illusions.

S. K. Patil, as expected, was one of those who objected strongly to the attempt to revive the suggestion for the nationalization of banks. Morarji Desai was equally hostile, legislation to enforce social control was barely six months old, he said, and to reopen the issue would create confusion in the public mind. The next day Indira arrived in Bangalore. A climate of controversy was already existent. The Congress Parliamentary Board meeting of the presidential nominee set the seal on conflict. Indira returned to Delhi on the thirteenth. Three days later she stripped Morarji Desai of the finance portfolio. Desai resigned, and she herself took over finance. She let him know that she was prepared to keep him on only as deputy prime minister. During the next two days there was another attempt to reconcile the two rivals. Morarji was prepared to withdraw his resignation if he was given finance back, the office that meant power, not just prestige. Indira was adamant. She refused. On July 19, in an overnight move, with an ordinance signed by the president, Mrs Gandhi announced the nationalization of fourteen major banks in the country. It gave the government, she said with satisfaction in a broadcast the same night, control over "the commanding heights of the economy."[19]

Her third socialistic posture was in her indirect sympathy with the equivalent of the old ginger group, the fiercely committed band of angry intellectuals who have been termed the Young Turks. They talked big, they were impatient, they were impractical, but they conformed to a convention which is almost as old as the Congress party itself—that of a pressure group that is an irritant, but nevertheless a stimulus to change. The issues earlier were different, but the pattern the same. The Swarajist party of Motilal Nehru and C. R. Das represented a stand almost in direct opposition to one-half of the Congress but ultimately it became "the party within the party." Jawaharlal Nehru's India for Independence League was meant to exercise influence in favor of a Congress demand for total independence. A socialist group eventually broke out of the Congress, but even in Jawaharlal's time there was the impatient left—the ginger group—whose manifesto Indira and Feroze, as she says, did not sign, but with whose commitments she was in sympathy. Nothing changed in her mentality to make her oppose, for quite sometime while in official authority, the emergence of such pressures. If she did not actively encourage them, and even if she clashed at times with their angry attitudes, she could certainly use them as a weapon to beat old ideas with; using one extreme to paralyze the other and then finding a safe but progressive and feasible way.   It was a strategy that to an extent, paid off.

Fourth, she inducted men for key positions in government and the semi-autonomous corporations who were socially commited. She called for a committed administration.

"By this I do not mean an administration committed to one ideology or the other," she hastened to point out, "but to the policies of the government, to work them sincerely and with a sense of purpose, to feel a stake in the country."[20]   Obviously, if the government has a socialistic stance, the administration should work toward its implementation, but in the current Indian political scene with governments of varying complexions in different states, this is impossible.   In fact, the administrative revolution she sought, like her father before her, has not come about.

"The only way to effect a change is to gradually get the right man for the right job. Look what happened when we tried to send one senior official back to his state," she shrugs helplessly, referring to a case in which the central government's initial zeal was brought up short by a bland wall of legalities, "He went to court and nothing could be done! It has to be a slow process, that's all."[21] But as long as her government is in power, the criteria of choice for the men and women around her, whether they are officials or politicians, will include a preference for those with a leftist orientation; to that extent the image may change.

Fifth, she has carried on an increasing and virtually a verbal war of propaganda in favor of socialist ideals.   There is a perceptible shift in emphasis from Nehru's time.   The Indian public is still susceptible to an "education from above"—the method Nehru used as a short cut to a change in vision that might ordinarily take two generations of literacy and education to achieve.   "His task was almost solitary," says Indira, "in emphasizing science and a rational approach."[22] The fact that she can talk, almost continuously, in every speech, in a village, township or the cities, to every kind of audience, specially, even to the ignorant rural masses, of the concepts of socialism, suggests the change in understanding that has been wrought.   But it is only another furtherance of Nehru's goals.   This is what she maintained when she said that he had to dig the foundations, while she had to build on them. Her biggest achievement in 1969-70 was to raise the expectations of the masses. She struck out with such concern, such emphasis, and such promises for the poor and the underprivileged that she not only raised the criteria for other political parties but she made it impossible for them to exist in a political vacuum.

Acknowledging greetings of party members on Yahya's acceptance of ceasefire, 1971

Being awarded the Bharat Ratna by President V.V. Giri,
January 26, 1972

With President Giri, 1973

Greeting
Mujibur
Rahman,
Palam
airport,
New Delhi,
1972

With President Giri and Mujibur Rahman, 1972

With the Nixons, 1971

With Madame Tito

Addressing party members after re-election,
Central Hall, Parliament, 1967

With Canadian Premier Trudeau

Greeting Zulfikar Ali Bhutto of Pakistan, Simla, 1972

At a conference with Indian princes

With Swaran Singh and Alexei Kosygin

With President Giri, before the opening
of budget session

With Henry Kissinger

With Emperor Haile Selassie of Ethiopia
With Britain's Edward Heath

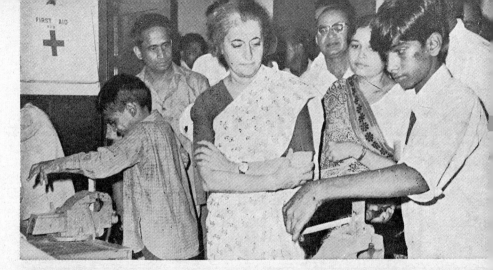

aking the
dependence
edge with party
lleagues

residing over
ood ministers'
onference

ith colleagues

eft, bottom)
residing over a
eeting

(top) At Bal Sahyog Bhavan

(middle) With American astronauts

With a Japanese visitor

At Simla

Visiting a jawan in
Ambala hospital, 1971

Addressing a
morning meeting,
at home, grandson
Rahul standing
behind her

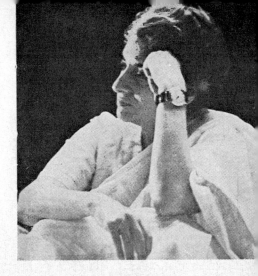

In a pensive mood

← Visiting the Hall of Nations at the Third Asian International Trade Fair, New Delhi, accompanied by Chairman, Steering Committee, M. Yunus

←
At Gandhi Samadhi

At Rajghat, on Mahatma Gandhi's birth anniversary, 1970

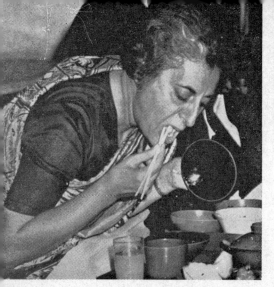

Eating with Chopsticks in Soji Temple,
Yokohama, Japan, 1969

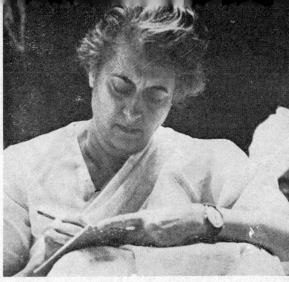

At an AICC session

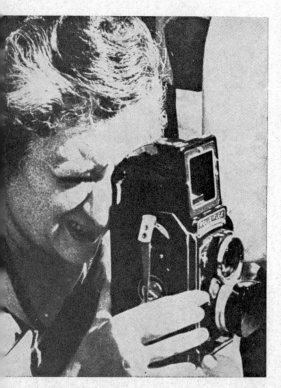

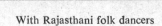

With Rajasthani folk dancers

(middle, left) Photographing the
photographers, 1970

With sons, Rajiv and Sanjay Gandhi

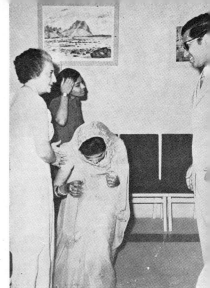

Blessing a newly married couple

With Rajiv, at his wedding. Extreme right is Sanjay.

With sons Rajiv and Sanjay and daughter-in-law, Sonia

Congratulating the three service chiefs, Army chief S.H.F.J. Manekshaw, Admiral Nanda, and Air Marshal P. C. Lal, on winning the war, 1972

A crown of flowers, for Bangladesh victory   With pet dog

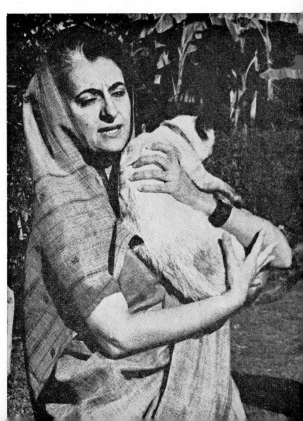

Taking the salute at Red Fort, Independence Day

↓ Visiting the front   ↑ Addressing jawans in a forward area

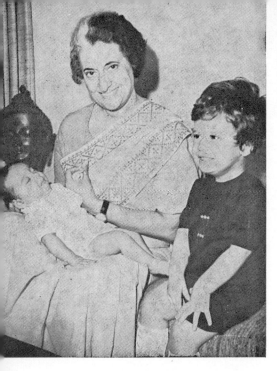

With grandson Rahul and
grand daughter Priyanka

With grandson Rahul

Garlands for triumph

Mass enthusiasm became apparent soon after the nationalization of banks; the issue was reduced to its simplest terms as a measure for the common man and as a rebuff to big business which had used bank monies to reinvest in their own future. There were constant rallies outside her house, groups of people of all kinds, from teachers to *tongawallas* joining in a massive show of support. They would insist on her coming out and speaking to them; she would do so, each time, tired but elated. She made two points clear: that the nationalization of banks had been a party plank, that she had just put it into effect, and that nobody should expect miracles to happen overnight. But the link between her and the decision was too immediate and the hopes generated too high. In fact, the syndicate leaders, still part of a Congress that was now limping but whole, reeling under the impact of this fresh link between Indira Gandhi and the masses, began also to fear that this feverish rise in the hopes of the people might recoil on the party, obviously a possibility that could be admitted only in the contest of a party that would prefer a status quo, not otherwise. It was as if events were being built up to hurry them. It marked a shift to the other side of the power sources of pressure.

There was an element of irony no doubt in the spectacle of laundrymen, taxi drivers, or vast groups of the comparatively uneducated shouting slogans about the social benefits of nationalization, and the opposition within and without the Congress sneered at what they called a populist trend in politics, and the exploitation of the ignorant. Indira's answer reduced the matter to the fundamental: "Many people say that the rickshaw pullers, cobblers, and others who came to my residence do not know anything about banks or nationalization. What I would like to know is that when we go out and seek their votes do we say that they do not know anything about democracy?"[23]

In January 1969, when Indira Gandhi completed three years in office, Frank Moraes, the leading political journalist not generally in sympathy with her, was drawn into unwilling admiration of a quality that was impinging more and more on public consciousness: "The lady has not emerged unscathed from the ordeal, but she comes out of it tougher in body and mind. In the political in-fighting which seethes in the Congress at all levels, Mrs Gandhi has shown that she is well able to take care of herself. Like the denizens of a jungle, politicians on the prowl acquire a protective alertness and cunning... in three years... the prime minister appears to have veered away from the airy generalities which affect a considerable section of her party. Both in the domestic and foreign field she has grown increasingly pragmatic and practical minded."[24] According to another: "Much of the criticism may have been justified, but even her opponents could not have been happy over the sweeping denunciation of her government and its handling of national problems. Hardly ever has she been given credit for the systematic and sustained efforts she has made to give a clear direction to policies and to transform the administrative machinery into a smoothly working organization." The next sentence was significant. "She also belongs to the fast dwindling group of congressmen who have both faith in and loyalty to their party. Others' attitudes and even motives may at times be doubted, but she is steadfast in her belief in secularism, socialism, and democracy."[25]

"Mrs Gandhi, it is true, has been the harbinger of change," commented another political analyst a year later. "She has stirred up the Congress party before events entirely overtook the aged, declining giant. One would have had admiration for the prime minister for doing so if it were not for her motives."[26]

What motives indeed did she, a loyal party worker, as she was considered to be on one hand and a "harbinger of change" as she was on the other, actually have in eventually accepting the challenge of the syndicate to such a point that it made a split in the Congress inevitable? It is interesting to note what her reactions were as far back as February 1966, when she first became prime minister. A leading question was put to her. "It seems in forming your cabinet, you had to take into account various tendencies in the Congress party . . . you concede that one has to keep together such a cumbrous organization . . . because a split would put democracy in danger in India?"

"I do not know," she replied, disagreeing, "if it could put democracy in danger."[27]

Nevertheless she did not stake her political future on such a gamble. In 1969, she did. It was both—the battle for power and the battle for an economic policy—that led to a confrontation between her and the old men in the party. Her strategy for three years had been to try to make her hold on the organization secure and work a revolution from within. Hence, the compromises. But a series of by-election victories brought both Kamaraj and S. K. Patil back to national politics with renewed zest and the syndicate, maimed and disheartened earlier, took heart. Chavan became the key man, his own ambitions creating a conflict of alignment. So strong was the talk of a rift between him and Mrs Gandhi that they had to deny it officially. "We have been functioning effectively and unitedly in the last two years or so," Indira tried to sound convincing. "In any cabinet which has able persons, there is bound to be creative discussion."[28]

Chavan was even contemptuous. "Some people seem completely divorced from reality and want to thrive on gossip. The government is pulling in one direction with one mind, and that is the feeling among people at large."[29] But things were not so smooth a year later, and Chavan's commitment could tip the scales one way or the other. However, while the tensions were brewing in July 1969, Chavan maintained a careful silence and the moves were tried out by the syndicate. One of the first obvious hints that they wanted Indira out from the center of political authority was a suggestion by Kamaraj that she be nominated for president of India, a post that it was vital to fill due to the sudden death of Dr Zakir Husain in May. Indira had no intention of falling into such a trap, but it was a challenge she could not overlook. In fact, the Congress choice of presidential candidate became a test case for power alignments in the parliamentary board which was to decide the matter at Bangalore. Even before Bangalore, the syndicate's preference was linked with Sanjeeva Reddy, former union minister who was speaker of the Lok Sabha, and Mrs Gandhi's, in spite of her denials, with V.V. Giri, a former cabinet minister and governor who was the incumbent vice-president of India. The ideological lines were sharply drawn. Sanjeeva Reddy was a member of the syndicate, with all the associations of big business and vested interests that it had come to signify. V.V. Giri had been a labor union leader and an ardent advocate of the rights of the common man.

Before the meeting of the board, made up of Congress President Nijalinga-ppa, Mrs Gandhi, Morarji Desai, Y.B. Chavan, Fakhruddin Ali Ahmed, and Kamaraj, Mrs Gandhi, relying on the support of Chavan and another special confidant, Ahmed, was fairly confident of avoiding an embarrassing denoue-ment. There was no agreement at the meeting. She even suggested a compromise by putting forth Jagjivan Ram, who as a Harijan leader, could be considered an appropriate choice in what was then being celebrated as Mahatma Gandhi's centenary year. She also suggested postponement of the decision so that the matter could be sorted out with less bitterness later. A unanimous decision on such issues was the criterion generally adhered to by the Congress until then. But Nijalingappa had come prepared. Regardless of the prime minister's suggestions he put the matter to a vote. Indira found herself outvoted by four to two with Chavan voting with the other side. She went back to Delhi shocked, angry, and further upset by newspaper re-ports describing her humiliation.

Her subsequent actions in depriving Desai of finance, his resignation, her taking over his portfolio, and then nationalizing the banks were seen as a reaction to her assessment that the Bangalore events were part of a plan to squeeze her out of power. There was little doubt that Mrs Gandhi would make some move in retaliation against the Congress Parliamentary Board's success in forcing Sanjeeva Reddy's candidature on her, in spite of her objections, as a political correspondent said, adding, "Most political observers were left a little breathless by Mrs Gandhi's action."

"We had decided as early as January to do it [nationalization]," Mrs Gandhi later stated, "so it had nothing to do with the board's decisions really."[30]

She explained to a Congress workers' meeting later: "In Bangalore some of the people were saying that I am using Morarji as an excuse not to go through with nationalization—I had decided in my mind even then that I would go back to Delhi and relieve him. So it wasn't because of what happened about the presidential issue."[31]

But the timing was important, and it took the wind out of the syndicate's sails. Some of her colleagues describe how quietly she took the decision. They had met together at her house and urged her to take the step immediately. She had listened to all of them, but said nothing. They had barely got back to their respective houses for lunch when they received copies of the letter she had sent meanwhile to Morarji, and they rushed back to congratulate her!

The internal contradictions in the Congress were such that even the opposition took more note of them than of their own need to settle upon a common candidate. Early in July, the Communist M.P.s, Hiren Mukerjee, S. M. Banerjee, and Jyotirmoy Basu took strong exception to Reddy's candidature from a non-party angle. "It will be a bad day for parliamentary government in this country," they said, "when speakers are not content with their assignment but look avidly for pastures new."[32] On July 10, another four opposition parties in Parliament, the Swatantra, the Jana Sangh, the Bhartiya Kranti Dal, and the Dravida Munnetra Kazhagam called for a "free, unfettered vote"[33] in the presidential election.

On July 13, Nijalingappa formally announced the Congress decision to nominate Sanjeeva Reddy for president. The same day Giri who had hoped to get the verdict in his favor announced his candidature as an independent acting as he said according to "the dictates of my conscience and duty to the nation."[34]

On August 2, Mrs Gandhi herself filed the nomination papers of Sanjeeva Reddy for president, but turned down a suggestion for issuing a joint appeal with Nijalingappa asking congressmen to vote for Reddy. It was clear that she felt compelled to go along with the official decision but that she had her doubts. The question of issuing a party whip in view of the growing fear in syndicate circles of possible cross voting in the election, began to be raised by Congress leaders in the state legislatures. At the center it could be done only by Mrs Gandhi as the leader of the Congress parliamentary party. The meeting of the C.P.P. therefore became a crucial one. Would Indira Gandhi issue a whip which would make it mandatory for congressmen to vote according to the party dictate, and wou'd the C.P.P. as a whole stand by her? There was speculation that it might even state its lack of confidence in her leadership. When the meeting actually took place, the lid flew off and a full battle ensued. A member stood up, waved some papers in the air, and pointed out that he had some articles by Mrs Tarkeshwari Sinha, who was pro-syndicate, in which she had outlined the syndicate's strategy for eventually throwing out Mrs Gandhi. If it could not be done any other way, she had said, there was the possibility that syndicate Congress members in Parliament would get the support of the Swatantra and Jana Sangh and vote her out of power. There was absolute pandemonium. Mrs Gandhi herself described the events over the months beginning with the presidential issue in the simplest terms:

"I had kept on asking them who they had in mind, and they kept putting it off. We met four or five times, but nothing came of it. Suddenly they put forward a name at Bangalore. I was very hurt. Two of us had a different opinion. In the past too if a decision was not unanimous we would meet again and try and find a way. But they wouldn't agree to that, and announced the result straightaway. The next day the papers came out with reports that the prime minister had been humiliated. Now that's something I couldn't accept—it's a question apart from who is prime minister. It matters that it is the prime minister whose prestige is lowered. Even then I said all right, if they have decided, then I will accept it. But at the parliamentary party meeting it came—someone had written articles—in which it was stated clearly that this was only the first step of a strategy to throw the government out, and in which it was stated clearly that even if a percentage of Congressmen do not go with that group, they would align themselves with the Swatantra and Jana Sangh and form the government themselves."[35]

In the next few days two basic points emerged from what began to be called Mrs Gandhi's camp, the "indicate," as opposed to the syndicate, that the syndicate had betrayed the confidence of the party by having "parleys" with a "reactionary" party like the Swatantra and one with a communal stance, like the Jana Sangh, and that the syndicate's choice of presidential nominee was part of a larger design to oust the Congress government even with the help of the opposition: hence the prime minister's endorsement of the decision could be withdrawn in view of the "changed circumstances." It became clear that from the prime minister's point of view, thenceforth, congressmen were not to feel bound to vote for the official nominee. Leaders of Congress parties in the state legislatures had to do some hard thinking. An issue of the whip would commit them irrevocably to the syndicate, not to do so would place them on the side of Indira. The choice was inescapable. In addition to this was a feeling of genuine predicament: to go against the official nominee meant violating party discipline, to go against the unspoken stand of the prime minister meant going against the one Congress leader who commanded mass support. Nobody dared think that issues had gone far beyond party discipline. Nevertheless, the momentum of the coming election was too strong to brook delay. As each state Congress unit got a whip it was notched up as a victory for the syndicate, and as each state Congress unit was left free, there was jubilation among Indira's supporters. By August 15 eleven leaders of state legislatures had issued the whip, six had not.

This was still no indication. What mattered was whether congressmen, even after getting the whip, would vote for the official nominee or not. The election of Reddy in the circumstances would signify a complete triumph for the syndicate. The opposition had put up a candidate, former finance minister in Nehru's government and a member of the Indian Civil Service, C. D. Deshmukh. Indira had no candidate as such, but it was clear that congressmen on her side could demonstrate loyalty only by voting for Giri, the independent candidate. The opposition's alignments became obvious in their official stand on how each party should give its second preference votes, to Reddy or Giri. Going by these indications, Indira had a slight edge over the syndicate. A movement for a "free vote," irrespective of party commitments, was gaining ground as the most democratic method for choice of president, an office that too must have a non-party image. But most congressmen who supported Indira were waiting for some clear indication from the prime minister what they should do. The responsibility was too great for them to feel confident without a lead. The poll date was August 16. By August 15, with Indira still silent, the tension was almost unbearable. That evening, I asked one of the many congressmen waiting thus, who he was going to vote for. He shrugged worriedly, "We are waiting for the call."

Late that night, beautifully timed to appear in all the papers of the country the next morning and in time for the peak listening news broadcasts of early morning so that the country would almost wake to the momentous decision, Indira Gandhi issued her historic statement: "Vote according to conscience."

For three days discussion ranged throughout the country on the prime minister's stand and even the mass of the people from politicians and administrators to the man on the street were talking in terms of being pro-Indira or pro-syndicate. She was condemned for cutting through the roots of party discipline and building a personality cult around her, and she was supported for her courage in calling the bluff of the party bosses and staking her future on the issue of cleaning the Congress of anti-socialist forces. There were no doubts. In the circumstances, eventually either she or they would have to be out.

On August 20, the verdict came, "Giri for president." Delhi went wild. Crowds thronged the prime minister's and the president-designate's houses. Giri was acknowledged as "The people's choice." "Our stand has been vindicated,"[36] exclaimed Mrs Giri when Indira went to their house to congratulate them.

> Who will carry the corpse of the syndicate?
> No one, no one!
> Brave as a tigress, long live Indira Gandhi![37]

All through the night the chants rent the air outside the prime minister's house, and as on the day of bank nationalization, she would be called out again and again, and she would come, dead tired, this time with dark circles under her eyes but looking, as one supporter sighed ardently, "ethereal in her loveliness." But there was nothing ethereal about what she said. It was as brief, pointed, and challenging as ever as she stood on a makeshift platform outside the gate: "You call me the offspring of a tiger. One daughter of a tiger can't do anything. You have all got to be sons of tigers!"[38]

Even before the election results were announced, however, Mrs Gandhi and Jagjivan Ram and Fakhruddin Ali Ahmed, the two men who had come to be associated with all her moves during that period, got official notices from the Congress president asking them to explain their attitude. The day after the results came in, the syndicate began to press even more strongly for disciplinary action against the prime minister. On August 25, the Congress Working Committee met but a crisis was avoided. A unity resolution was passed and what was called a "patchwork peace" achieved. The papers announced: "CWC Battle won by P.M.!" It was more appropriately an explosive peace: anything could touch it off. A controversy over the locale for the next session of the AICC, the scheduling of the session, the attempt of Nijalingappa to drop pro-Indira members from the Congress Working Committee, the demand by the Indira group for an early meeting of the AICC to either endorse or reject the Congress president's stands, finally resulted in a deadly confrontation between the two groups by October 30.

On October 31, Nijalingappa dropped Fakhruddin and disqualified Subramaniam from the Congress Working Committee. The prime minister's supporters went to Nijalingappa to officially call for a special AICC session. He refused. Mrs Gandhi decided to boycott the meeting of the working committee scheduled for the next morning. On November 1, the rupture was complete. Nijalingappa's working committee met at the old headquarters of the Congress party, and the remaining members with the prime minister at her house. Nijalingappa and his supporters ruled out of order the request by as many as 405 AICC members for the special AICC session to seek election of a new Congress president, and decided to hold the session as before, at Gujarat in December. Mrs Gandhi and her group were less strident but equally determined. They passed a resolution asking the Congress president to withdraw the order dropping Fakhruddin and Subramaniam, and decided to hold a special session on November 22 and 23.

"With two parallel AICC sessions in the offing the only thing that remained today to put the official seal on the split," commented a political observer, "was last night's decision of Mrs Gandhi and her advisers that they should refrain from calling this morning's parallel meeting of her supporters a 'working committee meeting'."[39]

The country was flabbergasted yet full of expectations. "A split within the Congress right and the Congress left might be good for the country," commented Jaya Prakash Narayan, seeing through all the extraneous factors of the struggle.

On November 3, Mrs Gandhi was presented a massive chargesheet by the Congress president for following "the ways of intrigue and disruption." On November 4, she dropped a pro-syndicate member of her cabinet. On November 7, a luncheon meeting between her and Nijalingappa failed to find any agreement. By November 11, the impossible was being expected. On November 12, the headlines in the papers screamed again, "Mrs Gandhi expelled." The reaction was immediate: How had a minority the right to expel the majority? Who was the Congress? Whose was the Indian National Congress now? On November 13, it was clear. Three hundred and ten Congress members of Parliament out of a total of 429 stood by Indira Gandhi in a meeting of the Congress parliamentary party chaired by her. On

November 22, the special session of the AICC was held in New Delhi and 446 AICC members comprising the majority were reported to have come to attend it. The syndicate's rout was complete. But amidst the idealistic fervor of the speeches, for there was exuberance and a feeling that now, at last, the Congress could go the way it wanted, Indira Gandhi's voice rang out stirringly, until she came to the point of mentioning her whole family's involvement with the Congress: how their lives had been sacrificed for it, and her's, who had been in it from childhood, with her father, mother, grandmother, grandfather, and all the aunts and uncles and cousins that made up a part of that generation of earnest nationalists. "And then," she said, the enormity of the idea overwhelming her, "they even expelled me, me, from the Congress," and her voice broke, and the tears stood precariously close to her eyes, while the audience watched her, heavy with sentiment. But the spell broke. The determined politician took over. There was frantic clapping while she cried out, "No one whose heart and mind is in the Congress can be expelled from it."[10]

Judging from this culmination of events it is easy to understand the pulls and contradictions that made an effective functioning of not only day-to-day government but the implementation of major policies painfully slow and sometimes impossible. Indira may not have done what the syndicate wanted, but the overall pressure of constant dissent certainly prevented her from doing what she wanted at least for a time. Her greatest lapse was in education. Barring a firmly stated belief in the three language formula on Hindi, English, and a regional language as compulsory learning for all students and an attempt to palliate the south on the spread of Hindi as the national language, she has done nothing to remove the immediate ills of the Indian educational system or change the nefarious criteria by which only an arts degree opens the way to employment. On other matters, even if she has pleaded inability of action due to a paucity of resources or the requisite cooperation, she has carried on almost relentless propaganda through her own speeches: on communalism, for instance, on growing more food, on democracy, on national unity, on a scientific application, and family planning, but she has seldom stressed the need for an overhauling of the educational system or gone into its devastating ramifications which contribute a little to literacy, no doubt, but almost nothing to education.

Two years of drought and the aftermath of the short Indo-Pak hostilities threw economic priorities awry, but even in 1967, Indira Gandhi was asking rhetorically of countrymen, "I ask you, honestly, has there been no change? It is true that food and milk and sugar were cheaper in the old days. The middle-class people in the town could engage servants on a low wage. But what about the conditions of the servants themselves? Were their children going to school? How many of them could hope for better days? Prices were low in the cities but what was the fate of the farmer in the countryside? What was he getting and what was he eating? How many children in the villages went to school? Did they travel by bus or bicycle? How many could survive the epidemics? How high was the rate of infant diseases?"[41] The answers she gave were a statistical record of improvement, with the average age of the Indian increased by 20 years.   By 1968, "the clouds were beginning to lift," as Dr Zakir Husain said in his presidential address to the budget session of Parliament that year, by 1970 the Green Revolution was on the way, and there were expectations that India would be self-sufficient in food by 1974. Gloom remained centered on the old middle class, the salaried administrator, and big business.   The farmer and a new middle class of small entrepreneurs and professional men were the main beneficiaries.   "What is impressive," wrote a British commentator in January 1970, who returned to India after a gap of five years, "is less the concrete achievements, frequent though they are, than the mood.   Once people waited for the *mabap sarkar* .... Now they want to do things for themselves, to experiment, to take risks, to create. What they ask of the government is that it should help, not hinder, and that if it cannot help it should lay off, leaving the people to do it."[42]

An emphasis on domestic preoccupation kept India's involvement in international affairs minimal under Mrs Gandhi, a major shift from previous years. Her stand on Vietnam and West Asia remained the same, nonalignment is as valid to her as ever, while she did some tightrope walking on the Czechoslovak crisis, "lauding the Czechs," as a correspondent described it, "while refraining from blaming the Soviets."[43]   On China she told Alexei Kosygin when he visited India in January 1968 that India was willing to follow the path set by the Taskent declaration, but added, "We have a saying that we cannot clap with one hand."[44]   One positive step she has taken in the international field is in cooperating more closely with smaller countries and in increasing the areas of economic cooperation.   Her visits to New Zealand and Australia, and the countries of Southeast Asia were taken particularly with this in view, and she was the first Indian prime minister to visit South America. She has advocated a "global strategy" for prosperity and economic cooperation guided by some moral purpose.

Soon after the Congress split in the organization became irrevocable, a hard core of the syndicate group in Parliament asked for a reallocation of seats separate from the ruling Congress of Mrs Gandhi. This group consisted of about 60 members and for the first time in India's history since independence, an official opposition party which began to be called the Congress Organization came into being. No party before this, including the Swatantra party which had been the largest opposition group so far, had the requisite 50 members in Parliament to merit being called the offical opposition, and it was ironic that in this, too, the Congress had provided the lead, in creating its own enemy.   Dr Ram Subhag Singh, Indira's former minister of railways, became the leader of the opposition, with Morarji Desai given the rather empty privilege of being the chairman of the parliamentary wing. Sentiment soon got into political stride when two months later, replying to the debate on the president's address for 1970, Indira made one of the most forceful speeches of her career, mixing irony with wit, and anger with passion, and deflating further the perceptibly wilted old Congress leaders by remarking how sorry she was to see that they had not even provided an effective opposition. Apart from anything else, this speech marked the coming of age of Indira Gandhi, as one parliamentary correspondent enthusiastically reported, as a parliamentarian. A month later, she presented the central budget and successfully piloted the finance bill, item by item, through Parliament.

The most exacting domestic hurdles she faced at the time were the rut of political self-seeking set off by the Congress loss of power in 1967, the precarious balance of coalition governments in the states which made every member of a state assembly feel that he was an important entity in the game of toppling, so that a shift in party loyalties has become a chronic disease, the loss of majority that Indira suffered when the syndicate left in a group and her dependence, to a considerable extent, on some "like-minded" and other parties, each with its own stakes, like the P.S.P., the Akalis, the D.M.K., the Muslim League, and the Communist party. Her parliamentary victories remained quite impressive. Within her own ruling Congress, there were remnants of old leadership, too, but a vital change in position became discernible. Whereas she was sought to be used as an advantage by the old guard once, she was in a position to use them to her advantage now.

She was criticized severely for the "conscience clause" in the voting for the presidential election which was taken as the main cause by her detractors of the lack of party morality that became visible on the scene. But the fact that a near split came in almost every party after the Congress one, from the Swatantra to the Jana Sangh and the Communists, showed that the long-awaited polarization of forces was slowly taking place. It was characteristic of the compulsive critics that they condemned Nehru for not having had the courage to risk a split in the Congress and they condemned Indira for bringing it about.

Organizationally, her timing and tactics were faultless. She took action when the pulse of the people was with her. It has basically been a "better late than never" approach based on the astute appreciation that it is power which provides the opportunity, not political wilderness. If she had felt that "political wilderness" could provide the opportunity, she might have used that alternative. But she knows the Indian masses, and she knows their psychology too well to let her practical vision turn to visionary lines. The public reaction on bank nationalization and the Giri election showed that a strong stand inevitably wins the masses. But would it have earned the same reaction a year earlier, or when she first became prime minister? Only the reminiscing perspectives of history can judge that. We are for too near the times. What marked the situation was that she did not lose the masses in the years that she has been in power, and she retained all the confidence. As a correspondent remarked, "It has been the return of the rose, but more and more people are discovering that the rose is of a new variety, perhaps harder than its parent and containing new properties."[45]

Indira Gandhi herself has no regrets.

When I asked her the old question she had been asked in 1966 about the possible threat to democratic functioning caused by the Congress split and the so-called breaking of party discipline, she maintained spiritedly that party discipline in this case meant the imposition of the few over the many. She was enthusiastic about the presidential election.

"Democracy involves the participation of the people. It doesn't merely mean voting every three or four years. In this case the average citizen, even in the early stages, became a part of it. I was told of a story by an M.P. that when the count was taking place he had gone to visit a professor friend of his for tea. Suddenly, the servant there rushed into the room and exclaimed, '*Hazoor, ham jeet rahe hain.*' He said *we* are winning, that's how he felt!"[46]

According to her the very fact that every party in India had begun to think earnestly about the criteria of political behavior was a good enough sign. It signified a healthy "shaking up" of what had been stagnating for so long. And thenceforth?

"The future has no precedents," said Indira Gandhi.[47]

It was a phrase that was to prove significant. There was no precedent for what the Indian political scene comprised for the next year, or the triumphant denouement at the end which enabled the common masses of India to shake off the past and throw out a challenge to the present—and to Indira, whom they made the symbol of change.

2. CHARISMA

Having rid herself of the recurrent menace of ideological sabotage within her own party Indira Gandhi found she had to lean for support in Parliament in the period November 1969-February 1971 on a potentially dangerous ally—the Communist party of India and the regional Dravida Munnetra Kazagham; two strains, one representing the supra-national one, and the other, an insular one, both of which went against the grain of her own commitment. This was a fact that few realized. An arrangement of expediency in no way signified a trend in her thinking or in her purpose. It only indicated which of the lesser evils she would opt for if it had to be a choice between two evils. Events and her own statements showed that she preferred even left adventurism to right orthodoxy. It had always been so. But this time preference could join with opportunity to build an image—for power. Power through popularity. A charisma to charm the people. The role was clear. A leftist road to communion with the masses. This was the base for the great split. This became the base for action for the year following.

Indira had to take practical steps to show that her posture was not an opportunist one. The challenge was spelled out clearly as early as November 26. "With most of the old party bosses out, the government can no longer complain that they are breathing down its neck," warned political columnist and editor Sham Lal in trenchant tones. "But with its hold-all character it is still not free from group pressures. And when these come from different directions it will have to try hard to find a point of equilibrium and keep its balance. The consensus between Mr Gaekwad and Mr Yadav will not be any easier to work out than one between Mr Desai and Mr Menon." If there was understanding about possible inner party convulsions even in the new Congress, there was also impatience. "If it does not make haste its encounter with socialism will turn into a cramped love affair."[1]

She had to work out also an organizational strategy that would give her party all the advantages. There was need to set up parallel parties in the states where the existing units had opted for the other Congress faction, there was the need to win back former congressmen who had left in disgust with the old party bosses to strengthen her side, and there was the need to establish the image of the Congress led by her as the real inheritor of the past and as the true harbinger of a political future.

"Immediately after the split it became clear that the people's mandate would be necessary," recalls H.N. Bahuguna, who became one of the general secretaries of the New Congress as the party led by Indira Gandhi came to be generally known, as against the Old Congress which retained the hard core of the party bosses. "There were many of us who urged Indiraji to go in for a poll immediately but her strategy was to give time to the opposition to expose itself. Substantially, the rank and file of the Congress was with us, but there were still some doubting Thomases around. At the Ahmedabad session, for instance, the Congress(O) tried to show they were the real revolutionaries; it could have misguided a lot of party workers and made confusion worse confounded. But like the shrewd politician she is, she knew that time would show them in such light that no explanations on their part would be able to deceive the people. . . . And, in fact, as time passed, the Congress(O) in the Lok Sabha began to bid goodbye gradually to the policies of the united Congress."[2]

Mrs Gandhi missed no opportunity to point out the contradictions in the old Congress. For instance, while it supported the Jana Sangh, and the form. It should certainly NOT be a fad or imitation.

It is a state of mind, a sense of direction, knowing what to reject & also how to build. No one can be a superficial rebel. You must think & feel deeply.

Needless to say it is belittling the word & the thought to associate it with petty grievances or personal frustration.

INDIRA'S DEFINITION OF A REBEL

Swatantra party in the Lok Sabha on the Monopolies and Restrictive Trade
Practices Bill on the ground that it would lead to governmental monopoly, Dr
Ram Subhag Singh who was chosen leader of the Congress(O) party in Parliament wrote a letter to Mrs Gandhi demanding the abolition of privy purses
and the privileges of ex-rulers.   There was also a consensus in the Congress(O)
executive meeting for a ceiling on the ownership of urban property.   Both
these plans formed the ideological base of the Congress led by Mrs Gandhi.
In fact, these were the identical reforms proposed at the executive committee
meeting of her own Congress parliamentary party.   But in an "obvious dig
at members of the opposition Congress," as a report delightedly put it, she
said that the imposition of ceiling on urban property had been opposed by the
very people now sitting on the opposition benches.   "But we stand by our
commitment,"[3] she exclaimed.

"The crucial test will come not when the government at last makes up its
mind on what to do about the privy purses—the odds against the princes are
very heavy indeed—but when it gets down to doing something about land
reforms," warned Shamlal again.[4]   Three days later, Mrs Gandhi in fact
inaugurated a chief ministers' conference on land reforms, where what she
said seemed almost like an answer.   "We must act now when there is still
time and hope—what needs to be done is fairly well known but the crucial
question is how to do it."[5]

The pattern of promise by the new Congress, and villification by the
opposition, specially the old Congress, was set immediately after the split
and gained momentum through the year.   If Indira Gandhi came to epitomise
the struggle for social and economic reform for the masses, for the opposition she was an anti-democratic force, guilty of indiscipline.   Even the
generally cool Morarji Desai was led into haranguing Mrs Gandhi for misleading people with "dangerous illusions and delusions," and then the near
abusive: "we will soon know whether the prime minister is a tigress or a she-
goat."[6]   The Jana Sangh extremist, Balraj Madhok, described her alliance with
leftist forces as "unholy," her socialism "communist-oriented, undemocratic
and a step towards state monopoly and state capitalism," which also meant
"an equal distribution of poverty."[7]   And at the Ahmedabad session called
by the Congress(O) to determine its hold on the percentage of congressmen
loyal to it—a week before the new Congress was to hold another at Bombay
with the same end in view—President Nijalingappa set the tone for an election
campaign that was to become so personal that it showed how bitter the taste
of defeat was in their mouths.

The first salvo was fired with a sixteen-page note issued by the Gujarat
Pradesh Congress Committee called "Bangalore and After" in which the
language and the sentiments revealed chagrin and anger, but also an indirect
acknowledgment of Mrs Gandhi's superior tactics.   "She appears to have
full confidence in her ability to outsmart everybody.   That she has been able
to outsmart her colleagues in the Congress is something we may accept.   But

we should also observe that the colleagues she decided to outsmart were persons inhibited by considerations of truth and fair play, feelings and respect for her father's memory. They took from her much that they would not have taken from anybody else. They were hit below the belt all the time."[8] Most of what Nijalingappa said in a 8,000-word address 'read like a charge sheet in which Mrs Gandhi figured as the principal accused'.[9] "She could not be entrusted with the governance of the country," he said. "Her technique was clear. Through the nationalization of banks, she drew to herself an aura of radicalism. She allowed simple, poor people to interpret the move in fantastic terms of immediate benefits to themselves. She stirred up the politics of mass hysteria. She cynically exploited the government media of mass communication for her own ends. It was a brazen faced assertion of the personality cult organized with the full panoply of her vast authority in the government." You could almost hear the screams of frustration in his praise. He declared that "her dilatoriness in decision-making, her formulation, her inability to evolve a framework of policies, her aversion to a precise schedule of priorities, her propensity to please all and seek scapegoats for her failures," had all resulted in slowing down the tempo of development. "Her professed radicalism is not meant for a thrust forward but to hide her inadequacies and incompetence."[10]

"Save Democracy" became the slogan of the opposition against Indira.

"Quit Poverty," urged Indira's Congress in a bold bid for a positive image.

Within the Congress party, matters had been moving toward a confrontation for a long time. Even if President Zakir Husain's death had not made alignments in the choice of successor imperative, other factors would have provided the reason for a break. In 1966, Mrs Gandhi said that she could appeal to the people above the party. By 1967, she realized that if "she had to be a real weilder of power there would have to be a parting of ways and she decided to play one against the other, balancing Kamaraj against Morarji," as political observer Inder Malhotra put it.[11] But what emerged later, apart from the clash of individual personalities, was the clash between a modern and conservative outlook. "In everything," emphasized Inder Malhotra, "in dress, taste, tolerance, liberalism, in making you feel at ease if you are smoking, for instance, while with an older party boss you feel the generational gap in values, she is modern; she is modern even in the leftist commitments that she advocates because after all leftism is essentially a *modern* ideology."[12]

Although between 1969 and 1971, the ideological clash was not the only cause of the split, it was used by Mrs Gandhi and her colleagues as a powerful weapon for creating a new image for the Congress. It not only identified her party with a forward intellectual thrust, but it obliged the opposition parties to support the new or the old Congress, and thus determine their own image. So strong were the feelings generated by this issue that these parties were further divided into the pro-Indira or the anti-Indira factions. The group within the Socialist party led by Raj Narain was anti-Congress(N),

that led by Joshi for it.   The C.P.I. was for, the C.P.I.(M) against, the Praja
Socialist party's Dwivedi held one view, and his colleagues another.   Even
the rigidly rightist Swatantra party showed signs of disunity.   To that extent,
it set a significant trend toward a polarization of forces.   It also created a
socialistic momentum.   No party could hope to get anywhere any longer
without discarding its feudal hangovers and subscribing to a minimum program for the benefit of the underprivileged.   An indirect acknowledgment
of this came from Morarji Desai himself when he sought to justify the growing
kinship of the Congress(O) with the Swatantra and the Jana Sangh.   When
he was asked about possible electoral alliances, he explained: "The policies
of other parties are also changing.   The Jana Sangh is having second thoughts.
They are now going in for very progressive economic programs, even if
they do not call them socialist.   Even Mr Masani said the other day that
they alone could not remain outside, they had to think in terms of such programs if they wanted to remain politically efficient and active."[13]

The three main points of criticism that the opposition made against Indira
Gandhi during this period were: an encouragement to indiscipline, the building up of a personality cult, and the tendency to think communist.   She
answered with another three points of her own.   She accused the Jana Sangh
of communalism, the Swatantra of feudal commitments, and the Congress(O)
of a continuing stake in a status quo.   "Is it a coincidence," she asked spiritedly in Parliament soon after communal frenzy had wrought havoc in a place
called Bhiwandi in May, "that when people who belong to the RSS or the
Jana Sangh go somewhere, there is a riot there soon afterwards?"   And then,
"I am not criticizing Shri Vajpayee's party as a party but merely two aspects
of it: the communal aspect and the second, which is even more dangerous,
their deliberate distortion of history."[14]   To the Swatantra and the Congress(O)
both, she gave the example of a society which was like a child with new
clothes: it outgrows them, they begin to hurt, he keeps crying that they don't
fit, but nobody changes them till they rip apart: "That's when we get to the
stage of violence."   As she began to tour the country, thousands of people
thronged to her meetings.   She would say in homespun Hindustani, in an
easy manner, confidingly, "Why not change the clothes in time, eh?   Why
not get new ones, why not make them ourselves before we are compelled to
do so?   You can't cling to something old when it is no longer relevant!"[15]

The momentum grew.   There was an attempt to widen the base of the
Congress(N) and in Bombay, before the power-testing plenary session, the
preparatory committee of the Bombay Citizens' Convention announced that
500 "intellectuals" wished to join the new Congress.   Mohan Dharia, an
articulate Young Turk, addressing what was called a "progressive group" in
Bombay gave the cry for "the politics of commitment" as against "the politics
of convenience."[16]   Some members of the Praja Socialist Party who had
joined the new Congress asserted worriedly that the "intellectuals" were those
whose past connected them in some way or the other with communism or

communist organizations.[17] The opposition continued charging the new Congress with communist sympathies. Humor still enlivened this intense vituperation campaign, and the allies of the prime minister came in for their share of raillery. A Jana Sangh member, for instance, took a dig at the Communist party of India in the Lok Sabha on one occasion and said that it was no longer the Communist party of India but the "Congress party of Indira"! But the prime minister was serious. "We were never communists. We are not communists," she affirmed categorically. "We shall never be communists."[18]

Nevertheless, the accusations took their toll. Although earnest pleas were made for "the forces of change" as against "the forces of status quo" at Bombay, the economic policy resolution was toned to a muted radical key, in order to disprove the opposition and to still the fears within those sections in the new Congress which preferred a less extreme commitment. At the same time, some basic steps like nationalization of general insurance, a new credit policy, the abolition of privy purses and fiscal measures to reduce disparities in income and property in the urban areas were promised. These had the advantage of being mild enough for effective implementation and strong enough to establish the credibility of government intentions.

By December, events were warming up. Radicals within Indira's own party were unhappy because implementation was not fast enough; the rise in steel prices and the grant of permission to the big business interests of the House of Tatas to set up the Goa fertilizer plant brought further dissent. One major ally in Parliament, the C.P.I., thought the economic policies spelled out by the Congress at Bombay were not radical enough; another ally, the D.M.K., was quiet, but a smaller faction supporting Mrs Gandhi, the regional Akali Dal from the Punjab, was waiting only for a decision on Chandigarh to settle its political alignments. The budget session of Parliament due in February in which Mrs Gandhi was to present the budget—again the first woman ever to do so—as her own finance minister (she had not replaced Morarji Desai) began to look like a crucial one. In fact, the Congress(O) began to work toward an alliance with the Swatantra and the Jana Sangh to defeat Mrs Gandhi on a cut motion on defense demands during this budget session, to force her to resign and not give her the option to ask for a dissolution of Parliament and a mid-term poll. It was becoming clearer that as a minority government in power, her hands were severely tied. She had no alternative but to go to the polls. All she could do was to choose the timing, and the manner, the two weapons in her political moves which continued to confound her opponents and her colleagues.

Indira sought to consolidate her personal hold within her party by acquiring a solid individual base in the two Hindi states of U.P. and Bihar, to match that of the only two strong men out of the party bosses left on her side, Y. B. Chavan, who could pride himself on his control over Maharashtra, and Jagjivan Ram, who commanded solid Harijan support. Politics in both

Bihar and U.P. from then on were conditioned by this factor. From the party's point of view, she had to see that as many states as possible in India should be in the hands of the Congress(N) or under president's rule to give her the maximum advantage at the time that she might call for a mid-term election. Moves were also initiated or circumstances created to make it possible for the merger of many splinter groups like the Janta Congress in Orissa, Bangla Congress in West Bengal, the Bharatiya Kranti Dal in U.P., and others with the Congress(N). Last, the immediate precursor to the announcement of a possible poll would have to be a step that would fire the imagination and draw the participation of the people.

In January, Mrs Gandhi, who had been given the right to arbitrate on the issue by both sides, announced her decision on Chandigarh. She left it as the capital of the Punjab but awarded other prestigious areas to Haryana. This was accepted as the most logical solution of the problem. But in January itself, she began to consider the question of the abolition of privy purses of the princes of India—all that galaxy of the proud, rich, and the idle which symbolized privilege. On February 20, the budget session began on a high note for the Congress(N) because the party had secured a vantage hold in both Bihar and U.P. When the session ended, the opposition was in disarray. Mrs Gandhi's budget turned out to be a miracle of such balance that it offended no one and satisfied every opinion. Even the Congress(O) conceded that it combined social content with a minimum risk to investment or growth. Admiration was unmixed from the press. "Mrs Gandhi has apparently perfected the art of divining popular reaction and immediately adjusting her policy stance to suit it," wrote political diarist, C. S. Pandit. "She goes a step further and exploits popular policy issues to her best political advantage. She did that with bank nationalization; she did it again by asking Mr Nanda to withdraw all unpopular freight and fare increases before the opposition could exploit them on the floor of the House. But her master stroke was her budget. . . ."[19]

Also, Indira had matured as a parliamentarian. The change from the shy, hesitant speaker who read from the text with her eyes cast down to a woman with poise, wit and the confidence of power, was complete. According to C. S. Pandit, this budget session witnessed the emergence of the prime minister not only as a master strategist, but also as an effective parliamentarian able to attack the weakest links in the opposition. "Without losing her composure even for a second, she was devastating in repartee during her reply to the debate on the president's address in the Lok Sabha."[20]

Although the prime minister, her colleagues and her party were keeping everyone guessing about a mid-term election, speculation began to acquire substance by June 1970. The opposition had turned from its old attitude of anti-Congressism to one of anti-Indiraism, and a "grand alliance" of the Congress(O), the Swatantra, and the Jana Sangh was in the offing. The Congress(N) could boast of two advantages. Of the 34 by-elections that had taken place since the split, Mrs Gandhi's party had contested 26, and won 20. It also got 46.9 per cent of the votes as against only 42.9 per cent obtained by the united Congress in the same constituencies. "Their trend is quite clear,"[21] observed Mrs Gandhi herself. On the other hand, she had so succeeded in pinning the Jana Sangh to its communalistic stance that there were attempts even within the Congress(O) to emphasize its secular character, rather than its identification with an ally like that. In fact, the call of the Congress(O) for "the consolidation of national democratic forces to repel the threat of communist subversion and communal virus" evoked such an avid chain of reaction from the Jana Sangh and the Swatantra that it became embarrassing for some of its leaders. There was a scramble therefore to seek the association of the Samyukt Socialist party to balance the rightist tilt. But the constant branding of the three as a reactionary group took its toll of their image, specially of the Congress(O). By July these parties had formed themselves into a united opposition; its working was intended to be limited to Parliament and its specific aim was to replace Indira Gandhi's government with a coalition. At the same time, in order to forestall any surprise move by the prime minister, the opposition began to call for a mid-term poll. With the monsoon session of Parliament beginning on July 27, however, the initiative was back in Indira Gandhi's hands. The Congress(O) backed out of the proposed united opposition and a motion of no-confidence against the government failed miserably.

Meantime, Mrs Gandhi reshuffled her cabinet in a major move to emerge as the undisputed power. Chavan as home minister had an influential place in governmental hierarchy, and the right to exercise political leverage. She tactfully suggested and then insisted that he should take up finance instead. Surprisingly, Chavan made only a gesture of revolt and then agreed meekly. One of the factors which helped him in this decision was that the prime minister had decided to take away Appointments, the Central Intelligence Bureau and the Central Bureau of Investigation from the home ministry and put them under her own charge, which meant that real power would vest in her. As it was, she retained home for herself and took the Bureau of Revenue Intelligence from the finance ministry to add to this powerful complex of departments for effective coordination. "In other words," analyzed a political observer, "the prime minister will have direct charge of all those important limbs of government which have a direct bearing not only on the functioning of all the ministries but also on the functioning of the entire administration including the state governments. Mrs Gandhi had to undertake this exercise not only to consolidate her own position within the party but also to project her image in the country as the strong leader, probably with an eye to the coming elections. It was a challenge to her to see that she was able to enforce her will on her senior colleagues like Mr Chavan, Mr Jagjivan Ram, and Mr Fakhruddin Ali Ahmed."[22]

On September 1, Indira took the one major step that was to associate her in the eyes of India's deprived millions with the slogan that had already come from her party, "Quit Poverty." She introduced the Constitution (Twenty-Fourth) Amendment Bill in Parliament which she said "represents the momentum of social change in our country," by which the government could discontinue the privy purses, abolish or restrict privileges, and abolish the concept of rulership. "History is replete with instances of customs, practices and enactments which were regarded as sacrosanct in one age and inhuman in the other. It will be for the house, irrespective of party affiliations, to show a sense of history," she said challengingly, "and to consider whether a princely order with attendant rights and privileges should continue indefinitely in a society striving for equality and social justice."[23]

Again, Indira Gandhi had taken a calculated risk by staking her political prestige on an issue. Again, the rightist alliance of the Jana Sangh, the Swatantra and the Congress(O) came together. And again, the opposition hoped to throw out her government on this crucial issue. In fact, the Congress(O) forgot its previous commitments in deciding to vote against the bill and Kamaraj went to the extent of saying that there should be only a "one-point programme," to throw out Mrs Gandhi. Until then, he said, the "ten-point programme" which the Congress(O) claimed to inherit from its united days, could wait.[24]

But the Lok Sabha did have a sense of history and the people did not want to wait. The bill was passed to the thunderous cheers of a record-breaking attendance. It had to get through the Rajya Sabha, the Upper House, also to become law, but the mood that the Lok Sabha victory generated was victory enough for Indira Gandhi. "It is now immaterial from her point of view whether the purses are abolished or not," observed a political analyst. "What is important, and she has ensured it beyond doubt, is that she tried her best to push through another of the important items of the ten-point programme."[25]

"She has become like a goddess for us—she's *Shakti*," exclaimed the taxi driver who drove us back from Parliament House that day. "Look what she has done. She has finished them [the princes] at one stroke. She's got more guts than her father!"[26]

A fraction of a vote less than the two thirds majority in the Rajya Sabha however blocked the bill. Mrs Gandhi got a presidential order obtained which de-recognized the princes. The princes took the issue to the Supreme Court of India. The Supreme Court, having passed an adverse judgment on bank nationalization, now declared the presidential order illegal. It looked like a defeat for Indira Gandhi. But with characteristic perspicacity, she turned it to her advantage. She used it as another example to tell the people that any progressive step initiated by her and her party was vitiated by some circumstance, vested interest or reactionary force. On December 27, she made the dramatic announcement that had the country and the opposition on its toes. She advised the president to dissolve Parliament, then called for a mid-term poll to get a fresh mandate from the people.

"Why did we do this," she asked in a broadcast that night, "when it is conceded on all sides that our government could have continued in power for another 14 months?   It is because we are concerned not merely with remaining in power, but with using that power to ensure a better life to the vast majority of our people and to satisfy their aspirations for a just social order. In the present situation, we feel we cannot go ahead with our proclaimed programme and keep our pledges to our people."[27]

On March 1, the country went to the polls.   On March 10, the results began to come in.   The Congress(N) was in the lead.   People began to speculate, to place fantastic bets on whether Indira Gandhi would be able to surpass the figure of 220 which she had in Parliament before the dissolution, or, whether she would get the majority with the figure of 261.   Those who thought she would get even less than what she had before were as convinced as the ones who were optimistic in her favor.   Soon, the question was no longer whether she would get the majority, but how big it would be.   Her own party men had predicted optimistically the figure of 280.   By March 13, the Congress(N) had crossed the majority.   Still the results came pouring in with a monotony that itself became exciting.

It was like a political juggernaut across the whole country, sweeping over all opposition.   By then, nobody wondered whether Indira Gandhi would attain a simple or a large majority, but whether she would get the two-thirds majority in Parliament—over the 350 figure, out of a house of 515 members—the two-thirds majority that would give her party the supreme liberty and the unquestioned power to change the Constitution.

On March 13, the papers were shouting: "Congress(N) heading towards landslide victory," "The Congress(N) sweeps the polls."   On March 14, the fantastic had happened.   The Congress had won the two-thirds majority. It was a result that stunned even Indira's own colleagues.   The party had won by her image, and the victory was a personal one for the prime minister. Her authority could thence be unchallenged, her powers, if she wished, dictatorial, and her charisma matching, and according to some, even surpassing that of her father.   The final gamble had paid off.

But Indira Gandhi, on the morning after her brilliant success, with good humor but unruffled calm, smiled quietly and said, "I have never gambled. And I do not intend to gamble in the future."[28]

Nobody believed her.

EPILOGUE

All that happened after March 1971 was an affirmation of Indira Gandhi's dominance in national affairs. Her values, style, and functioning did not change. She got the added opportunity, because of her tremendous mandate, to shape events at home, and to give India a voice abroad. The momentum of triumph was maintained up to the stunning Indian victory over Pakistan in December 1971 and the emergence of Bangladesh. This created a new equation in the Indian subcontinent, resulting in a hostile frontier made friendly on the one side, and the neutralization of Pakistan on the other. An internal, less obvious war, saw the virtual neutralization of the Indian communist.

But Indira Gandhi's persistent theme that "you have to pay the price" had relevance both to national affairs and her own image. She had warned people of the economic aftermath of the Bangladesh victory. But one of the worst droughts in India in thirty years, further brought home the lesson of "price" in more ways than one. The one gamble the prime minister lost was on the state takeover of wheat.

The Indira government's supersession of three supreme court judges raised a howl of protest from the protagonists of liberty that she was turning into a dictator. But if she allows for the processes of law to come to the aid of the citizen before he can be declared guilty and is therefore slow in punishing the allegedly corrupt, she is belabored for lack of firmness. These are isolated issues. Basically there is a choice before the Indian people at this moment. Should they be patient with "the almost unprecedented task of using democratic methods to bring about a social transformation in her country" which Indira Gandhi is trying? Or should they encourage the alternate of dictatorship which might bring quick relief in some fields, but would doubtless initiate a prolonged agony in others?

There is a chance for democracy in India. No other system can work in such a heterogenous nation. If that conclusion is valid, then it is also valid to say that no other person is more suitably poised to work it than Indira Gandhi. The existing situation, with increasing lawlessness, runaway prices, black marketing, and the non-involvement of the privileged in the deprivations of the poor calls not for dictatorship, but certainly dictatorial firmness.

There are provisions within parliamentary democracy itself to reward efficiency with such effect and to punish corruption with such force that no one should dare risk the former for the temptations of the latter. It is up to the people to call for that kind of firmness. They can do it with confidence. With Indira Gandhi, there is an overriding advantage. You can be sure that the compulsion to be firm will not be used as an excuse to dictate. She does not have to resist the blandishments of dictatorship. She just does not want it. Like Jawaharlal Nehru in the 'fifties with his massive magic with the masses, Indira Gandhi after 1971, with her massive mandate from the people, refused to institutionalize the individuality of power.

The following, very comprehensive replies that Mrs Gandhi gave to some questions by me on September 25, 1973, bring events and reactions right up to the present in this book.

What would you say were the gains that accrued politically to you, your party, and the country because of the split in the Congress in 1969?

When one fights for a cause—to defend a country's freedom or to save a party —one does not think of gain: one thinks of values. In 1969 the nation's premier political party had to be saved—because the objectives for which it stood were the only objectives by which India could live and grow, and no other party was capable of holding the country together. The Congress was reborn in 1969. There was a great upsurge of national confidence and hope. The people rediscovered their power and an important lesson was drawn by Congress—indeed by all parties—that our people would not tolerate cabal politics.

Did you have a definite strategy in mind after the split to project the image of your party?

This expression "projecting the image" comes from advertising jargon, which I don't like. The question was not of image but of reality. What I wanted and worked for, then as now, is the reality of a Congress whose allegiance to secularism and socialism would be uncompromising and a Congress which drew continuous sustenance from the people, by reflecting their true urges and always keeping the interests of the people as a whole above those of any particular class.

The united Congress had a curious amalgamation of rightists, leftists, and centrists due to the circumstances in which it grew. How is the Congress now, under you, different?

The Congress is a broad-spectrum party. Its strength over half a century lies in the fact that it comprised and represented all sections of our people and all regions of the country. It has never subscribed to the harmful theory that only some people are people and others are not. Under Gandhiji and Jawaharlal Nehru, it rejected the doctrine of class war. While being a party of the poor—especially of kisans and workers—and while being stoutly opposed to vested interests, whether feudal or economic, it firmly believed in bringing about equality through non-violent, constitutional means. The Congress has not been a party of ideological priests who propound the doctrine and excommunicate nonconformists. But there is no place in our party for anyone who works against secularism and socialism or lacks faith in our basic outlook.

Do you find that the internal party pressures are not there or are they different to the ones you had to face before?

There will always be pressures in any party or in any group of people. There will be personal ambitions and conflicts between narrow and larger loyalties (especially in a large country like ours, with its diversity of language and religion). The federal nature of our political system gives rise to certain tensions although it also contributes to the basic strength of our nation by providing safety valves for smaller loyalties. The question is not "Are there internal party pressures?" but "Is the party walking in step with the people and steadily towards its objectives?" The party's record in this regard is much better now than before the split.

In view of what I would call the revolution in restraint that you have set in motion, how do you propose to deal with extreme radicalism inside and outside your party?

I do not have to deal with it unaided. The people will do so. It is the people's basic faith and good sense that prevented the growth of Naxalism on the one hand and extreme religious fanaticism on the other. But we cannot relax our vigil. Violent radicalism can be prevented only by convincing the people through our actions that we are removing glaring economic and social injustice and deprivation.

How do you propose to give a more modern direction to party functioning?

I am afraid our performance is disappointing. The party continues to function in a rather flabby way. It devotes too much attention to elections at the cost of the solid fieldwork which alone builds the party's base. It lacks the apparatus which could enable it to do systematic work amongst young and rural people, industrial labor and other workers, women and the intelligentsia. Although we have trained some people, we do not seem to have enthused any band of people to make a deep study of national and international trends and to educate party workers. This is the aspect of politics which interests me most.

Do you see a polarization of ideologies in India in the near future?

Most opposition parties are trying to combine to fight the Congress. But they have inner contradictions and personality conflicts. A grand alliance of sorts was forged but it was not very grand in size or in its hold on the people. Polarization implies a sort of parity in strength between the two poles. I doubt if there will be such a situation for a long time to come unless the Congress acts with unbelievable ineptitude. What is true of parties is also true of ideologies.

Would you say that there was a deliberate effort on your part to isolate the Marxists in West Bengal and Kerala on the one hand, and the Jana Sangh on the other, as part of the strategy toward winning the elections? Or did you react to each issue as it came along? In fact, here it comes to a matter of style. Is your style of functioning instinctive or deliberate?

Answering the second part of your question first, it is for others to judge whether I act out of instinct or deliberation. I have neither the time nor the inclination for public self-analysis. I suppose I make as calm and dispassionate an appraisal of forces as anybody. I have never felt any conflict between intellect and emotion. Once you have a framework of belief, you naturally treat each issue in its own setting—separating the peripheral from the basic. What enables me to act decisively, I suppose, is that I am not unduly perturbed by reverses, so long as I am satisfied that I have put my best into the effort. As regards my attitude toward the Communist party (Marxists) and the Jana Sangh, I am convinced that their coming into power will not be in the best interests of the country because they both pursue policies which will aggravate tensions in the country. It has been a revelation that parties with such widely differing ideologies and policies should join hands for narrow party ends!

In view of your very committed stand against communalism, how do you explain your alliance with communal or regional parties like the Muslim League and the the Akali Dal except on the basis of expedient alliance-making?

The Kerala alliance was made long before our party split and the decision was taken by all the then leaders of the undivided Congress. At that time the Kerala Muslim League did not indulge in communal politics in Kerala nor did it function outside the state. At the present time there is a coalition in

Kerala in which the Kerala Muslim League and we are participating. It is
to be considered whether we shall serve the state and the country better by
ensuring the functioning of an effective government there or by throwing the
state into chaos. I do not think that any communalism was involved in the
working arrangements with the Akali Dal which at that time had offered to
function from the larger point of view. At any rate, today we have no understanding of any kind with the Akali Dal.

*Would you say that the elections of 1971 were different from the earlier ones?
That they marked a watershed in India's political consciousness?*

Surely the answer is obvious.

During the four earlier general elections to Parliament opponents of
Congress were not so confident of their chances. But in the 1971 elections a
determined attempt was made by a combination of communal, monoplist,
and extremist parties to pull down the Congress. In fact many spokesmen
of the opposition, in their public speeches and through writings in the big
press, predicted the rout of the Congress, giving our party a mere 150 to 180
seats in the Lok Sabha! (I am told that the grand alliance had even
formed a cabinet and allocated portfolios.) But they happened to count
without the people.

The major events of 1969—the Bangalore AICC, bank nationalization,
President Giri's election, the syndicate's refusal to call an AICC meeting and
their decision, instead, to expel me from the Congress, and finally the split—
all these had generated intense public interest and educated the people in the
motives and methods of parties. So they knew where their true interest lay
and who could serve them best. That is why they gave us such a decisive
mandate. The 1971 election was the high-water mark of our political evolution in the first quarter century of freedom. But it was not a watershed,
because that would imply that politics took a different direction, whereas our
policies are a continuation (in the same direction) of the policies of the
Congress and the country under Jawaharlal Nehru.

*Would you say, specially in relation to the year after these elections, that you
worked toward "power for a purpose" as a justifiable aim? That the politics
of expediency are a necessary corollary to pragmatic idealism?*

I resent the insinuation in this question. Power is always for a purpose.
The question is whether the purpose is a large one or a narrow one. The aim
of our national movement has always been that the power of the party and the
power of the state should be used to enlarge freedom and welfare and remove
all forms of discrimination. The word pragmatism has been given so many
shades of meaning that it is distrusted in our country. Idealism is not
necessarily impractical. Nations are built and saved, and history redeemed

only by practical idealists. I have not and do not now work for power nor can any action of mine be called one of expediency. To me the function of politics is to make possible the desirable.

Would you agree for instance that you are much less sentimental than your father? Particularly in your political dealings?

Comparisons are unfair. But to call my father sentimental shows little understanding of his nature. What others term softness was his effort to prove that politics need not coarsen one or rob life of its grace.

In view of the resounding majority you won and the stability that was expected as a result of it, did your mind turn more toward international affairs at the time? Or did you wish to tackle problems at home? What is your priority of interest?

There are no "priorities" in such matters. An effective foreign policy can be conducted only from a sound base of domestic policy. At no time can any country afford to ignore the international situation—for, as Nehru used to say, the world impinges on us all the time. What was the situation immediately after the 1971 elections? We were engrossed in the excitement of the elections—and were looking forward to speeding up our programs of development, and undertaking special measures to narrow social disparities. Hardly a week had passed after Parliament assembled, when the Bangladesh situation exploded. An internal issue of another country overflowed across our borders and became the number one problem for us—at once a domestic and a foreign policy question. Even now our economy carries the impact of the events of that year. Priorities often are simultaneous, not *in seriatim.*

The prime minister not only runs the country, shapes its future but also has to hold the country together—in short, what is the lesson for India, of Bangladesh?

The country cannot be run nor the future shaped unless the country is held together. The prime minister's office, as it has evolved in our country, must fulfill all these functions. We cannot have status quo prime ministers. Nor can we have a prime minister who does not treat all regions of the country and people of all religions, especially the minorities, with a sense of equality. It is true that the constitution guarantees equality to all sections of the people. But a constitution cannot enforce itself. There must be constant effort to generate the political will through Parliament, through political parties and non-official institutions, through executive and judicial action, to ensure that statutory guarantees become real.

What are your views on the workability of the federal structure in India?

We are a society with diversities. Indian tradition proves that diversity can become a source of strength. The experience of other countries shows that efforts to foist uniformity whether of language, religion or a so-called unitary administrative system has often led to tensions and even breakdowns. As I said in reply to one of your earlier questions, a democratic system provides safety valves and in a country of such diversity, the expedient of federalism allows regional loyalties to find expression within the general range of a national culture.

When our constitution was drafted, the political unity of India was itself rather new and many forces were at work to weaken us. Our federal system had to include provisions to safeguard our unity in emergencies or in the event of constitutional deadlocks. Hence the provision for central rule. Some constitutional experts call our system a qualified federalism. Political institutions and conventions are not made to prove theories but to find practical solutions to complex problems. On the whole, our federal system has worked well. It suits the genius of our people. No region feels constrained. That is why groups, which began to champion secession, have come round to swearing by the political inviolability of India. Movements for greater autonomy have failed to gain momentum. In fact, there is a demand that for greater progress and effective functioning of government, some subjects now in the State List should be transferred to the Union List.

Do you feel that certain state subjects, like education and medicine, for instance, might be dealt with more imaginatively and to more constructive purpose if they were directly in the hands of the Center?

That would certainly help. But it is not the constitutional position which is blocking progress, so much as our inability to adopt bold new methods of work.

What priority would you give to the question of population control? Have you a list of priorities in your mind with regard to what you have said is your first aim, the removal of poverty? Do you think that effective population control would enable the benefits of development to reach a wider mass of people in a shorter time, and therefore it requires to be tackled urgently, or do you think this priority should go to another area?

There seems to be confused and contradictory thinking about population control. It is true that a lowering of the rate of growth of population is essential for faster economic development. This is why we have adopted this as one of our national objectives and we are one of the few countries to have accepted family planning as an official program. At the same time, one should also remember that we cannot employ compulsion but have to rely wholly upon persuasion. We have to convince every couple that by having fewer children they can give each of them a better chance in life. We must provide facilities to those who wish to practise family planning. The advantage of compact families is appreciated where some development has already taken place. The poorest and the illiterate, especially those who live in villages, need it most to plan their families. But it is those who have already begun moving up the development escalator, the educated and the urban, who are able to practise family planning. This is our dilemma. Propaganda alone will not help much. Our experience is that wherever there is a dedicated worker, the results have been good, but if the worker regards his work as just a livelihood, the program makes no impact in spite of the money spent. The increase in the growth of population is not due to a higher birth rate but to the progressive decrease in the death rate. Science, which enabled our public health program to succeed and to cut the death rate, must now come up with drugs for reducing the birth rate and devices which are far more effective than those now available. It should also be appreciated that the spread of education and industrialization have a direct impact on family planning.

What constitutional changes would you like to bring about further to give a more socialistic orientation to thinking in the country?

No major amendments to the constitution are now on the anvil. We have very recently gained a few notable constitutional victories: the first was the recognition by the court of Parliament's right to make laws even in regard to fundamental rights. Earlier, another hurdle to progress was removed when the amount payable when property was taken over was left, by amendment of the constitution, to the discretion of Parliament.

Do you view the Marxists or the anarchists as the major threat to India? How do you propose to deal with this?

Whom do you mean by Marxists? The Naxalites claim to be Marxist-Leninists. The C.P.I.(M) claims to be Marxists. The C.P.I. also swears by Marx. Some socialists believe in Marx. In theory Marxist parties are opposed to anarchism. But judged by the way some Marxist groups have functioned in our country, their objective seems to be to create anarchy. They seem to hope that the people, disgusted with the government's inability to improve the situation, will turn to them. Anybody who is opposed to peaceful change and constitutional government is obviously a threat to the country's future. Your question ignores the communal fanatics and the groups which are hostile to change. The danger is not only from the extreme leftist groups and anarchists, but equally from the extreme rightist groups and communal forces.

Whatever the policies instituted by government it is the administration which has to execute them. How do you propose to make the administrator in India not only "expert" but "efficient"? Are there not some drastic methods required to change the habits of complacency by something more than trying to create the right atmosphere?

We should have changed our administrative and educational systems when we achieved freedom. However the first months brought all kinds of upheavals. The old system was largely retained. The range of administrative functions has increased vastly. I doubt if the oft-heard remark that efficiency has gone down is really true. More likely it comes out of the habit of romanticising the past. That our colonial rulers allowed millions to die during the Bengal famine is hardly a tribute to their efficiency. There are countless other examples. In those days nobody dared speak up. Efficiency is important but it cannot ignore the human cost. The administration must be responsive to the needs of the people and have unqualified faith in the national objectives of social equality and secularism. When this self-evident truth is expressed, I am accused of wanting to set up a dictatorial or communist state. My whole record has been one of fighting against a police state, against a social system which tries to thrust conformism on all people.

We do need an administration which is better trained for the numerous and increasing demands of society. The system must be less hierarchical and rigid and should care for the individual. Our financial and accounting procedures have to change. There should be greater flexibility in recognizing merit and reprimanding slackness. Initiative should not be throttled and allowance must be made for risk-taking. Without risk there can be no innovation nor any real improvement. It is difficult to have a cut and dried solution but I am continuously thinking about the problem. Some small steps have been taken but I know that they do not adequately meet the needs of our times.

There is a feeling prevalent in the country that the average Indian is seldom motivated by a sense of national commitment, whether it is the administrator, educationist, trader or the politician. It has become a career-oriented society in which few are prepared to sacrifice the personal for the general good. What are your views in the matter, and how do you think this pride can be awakened and sustained, apart from the usual trick of resorting to military adventures as some countries do?

There should certainly be greater pride in our work and in our country. But even now this is far more widespread than your question implies.

You said in your address to the Federation of Indian Chambers of Commerce and Industry in March 1973: "My faith in man's higher nature does not allow me to accept the adequacy of the profit motive as an effective dynamic for growth and progress. . ." Is that not being very idealistic? What do you think spurs a man to work hard? Someone has remarked that there is so much poverty in India and you see so much of it around that even the rich have not yet lost the subconscious fear of it, hence their tendency to hoard what they make. Would you agree with that? That a community has to lose its subconscious fear of poverty to be able to give fearlessly?

In a society of wide inequalities, there is a greater tendency to hoard, to profit, and to make vulgar display of wealth. A family's status is judged by the amount of food, or electric bulbs! Perhaps it is true that owners of large properties fear the envy and hostility of the "have-not" masses. But to suggest that prosperity will bring fearlessness is, to my mind, a fallacy.

Are you thinking in terms of some time-targets for fulfilling your promises?

Frankly, we are still in a stage when we should stress the direction of our advance: it is only after much more has been achieved that we can speak of time targets to fulfill promises. Our people do not suffer from the luxury of cynicism. They know that we do not yet have the resources to give everyone a job, a house, medical aid, and adequate quantities of nutritious food. But they do not call into question the objective of "Garibi Hatao." They realize that the longest journey has to be covered in short steps.

After the grand elections, as one cannot help calling them, of 1971, there was an attempt by opposition parties to form an alliance against you. Now again there is the same kind of talk. Yet, there is this question of the merger of the old Congress and the new. Don't you think this would be a retrograde step? Like taking events back to 1969?

There is no question of merger. I have made my views clear on different occasions. All those who believe as we do that, in today's circumstances, only the Congress can keep real unity and bring progress to the country, all those who believe in socialism and secularism are welcome to join us or to help from outside. I see no evidence of a 1969 situation.

In another field too, one would think one were back in another era. There is again a preoccupation with communal politics. There is again talk of Hindu-Muslim relations as something apart from the problems faced by the citizens of a country. Why do you think this is so? Would you say that the minority leadership is not enlightened? There is widespread criticism among Muslims one meets that even your ministers, your Muslim ministers, do not have the courage to tell you what the situation really is like, that they are so afraid of being branded communalists that they refuse to even hear the grievances of their community. Is the return of Sheikh Abdullah a step in the direction

*of getting people near you who can speak out on this problem?   Would you
think in terms of getting a more modern minded and confident set of persons
to represent this community now?*

It is unfortunately true that Hindu-Muslim tensions have not disappeared.
When riots occur, they appear to be more carefully planned.   Unfortunately
Hindu communalists and Muslim communalists are active and exploit communal feelings for political ends.   Lack of enlightenment is not a prerogative
of minority leadership.   People in the communal organizations of Hindus
are equally unenlightened.   In any economic crisis it is the poorest who
suffer.   Among these are Muslims as well as Adivasis and Harijans.   But it
would be wrong to say that Muslim ministers or Muslim congressmen are
afraid to speak their mind.

   I am trying to ensure that greater opportunities are given to Muslims and
other minorities in our party and in our administration.   Special instructions
have been issued with regard to language and employment, so that they are
not denied their rights under the Constitution.

*Would you say that 1973 has been the worst year of your tenure so far as prime
minister?*

"Best year" and "worst year" are journalistic expressions with no historical
significance.   Prices did rise to an unprecedented extent—they have done
so in almost all countries.   I do not think there was any decline in the country's
capacity to meet these challenges.

*It seems to me that from 1969 to 1972 when things were going well, the credit
was sought to be taken by or given to the advisers you were supposed to have at
the time.   Now when the times are bad, nobody talks of the advisers and the
blame is attached to you alone.   Does that make you cynical?*

I don't know how you form your impression.   In Parliament between 1969
and 1971 and in the 1971 elections, there was no dearth of people who
attacked me.   One heard the constant refrain that everything had failed and
so I must be removed.   Even after the 1971 election when we had to deal
with the Bangladesh crisis I was continuously accused of misjudgment and
inaction.

   In modern government, a prime minister or president has to deal with a vast
range of problems and no individual can be an expert about all of them.
The prime minister seeks and takes advice, but the ultimate responsibility
remains his or hers.

*What is your reaction to the criticism of the Maruti project?   Do you feel it is
personally directed or is it a part of the opposition to the indigenous small car
idea as such?*

It is obvious that some people are opposing my son's project and attributing all kinds of irregularities to it merely to malign me. Although the opposition went all out to find something wrong they were unable to do so. In fact nothing irregular has been done and no favor shown to the project. I would not countenance any violation of rules and procedures. There is nothing wrong in a young man proving his capacity. His product will have to stand the test of the public who are the users.

One point that has to be understood is that this is not the usual licence which is given to businessmen who use it to make money through the work of others. Here a young man has been working with singleness of purpose for a number of years in the most difficult circumstances and with no encouragement or help. Whatever he built up was done with his own hands. It was only when the base was ready that the question of putting up a factory arose. I admire his spirit and his endeavor. I know that there are many young people in the country who wish to get into industry but not so many who are willing to work with their hands. It is also true that our system gives little encouragement to such individual effort.

Has politics affected your relationship with your family?

No, why should it? We have always been close yet independent, with widely differing tastes and aptitudes. A common sense of humor binds us.

You have been in politics for a long time. But being in power is different. Has it changed you in any way? Do you still have your moments of detachment?

Any worthwhile person changes and grows all the time imperceptibly or visibly because one cannot remain unaffected by one's experiences. But I do not think the prime minister's office has changed me in any basic way—except that I get much more done than before. When one works at greater speed one must organize one's time more efficiently and when one's faculties are exercised to the full, one has a greater sense of fulfillment. I have always tried to follow the old teaching that one must learn to be still in the midst of activity and be vibrantly alive in the midst of calm!

After this spell of supreme power, what would you do if you were to give it all up?

The power of a truly democratic prime minister in India is far from supreme. So far as commitment to the larger good of the Indian people is concerned, there is no giving up. As long as there are mountains, they must be climbed!

The rest, too, is history.

NOTES

PART I: LIFE

1. AFFLUENCE

[1] Sir Geoge Rainey, quoted in B. R. Nanda, *The Nehrus*, p. 227.

[2] D. E. Dhanabala, "A Great Fighter," *Motilal Nehru Centenary Souvenir*, 1961, p. 147.

[3] Indira Gandhi, "The Story of Swaraj Bhawan," *Motilal Nehru Centenary Souvenir*, 1961, p. 73.

[4] Diwan Chaman Lal, "A Giant among Leaders," *Motilal Nehru Centenary Souvenir*, p. 93.

[5] Mohan Lal Saxena, "Some Anecdotes," *Motilal Nehru Centenary Souvenir*, p. 34.

[6] B. R. Nanda, "A Biographical Sketch," *Motilal Nehru Centenary Souvenir*, p. 69.

[7] Vijayalakshmi Pandit, "Swarup Rani Nehru," *Motilal Nehru Centenary Souvenir*, p. 97.

[8] Named after her mother, but after her marriage known as Vijayalakshmi Pandit.

[9] Vijayalakshmi Pandit, "Swarup Rani Nehru," *Motilal Nehru Centenary Souvenir*, p. 98.

[10] Sri Prakasa, "Some Reminiscences," *Motilal Nehru Centenary Souvenir*, p. 55.

[11] B. R. Nanda, *The Nehrus*, p. 343.

[12] C. F. Andrews, "A Maker of Modern India," *Motilal Nehru Centenary Souvenir*, p. 41.

[13] According to S. Radhakrishnan (later President of India), Jawaharlal mentioned this to Gandhi and Radhakrishnan referred to this in his speech as vice-president of India while inaugurating the centenary celebrations at Agra on April 6, 1961. There is no evidence that Jawaharlal denied this.

[14] Nehru, *Autobiography*, p. 5.

[15] Pattabhi Sitaramayya, *The History of the Indian National Congress*, vol. I, p. 99.

[16] Nanda, *op. cit.*, p. 85.

[17] *Ibid.*, p. 86.

[18] Nanda, *op. cit.*, p. 107.

[19] *Ibid.*, p. 86.

[20] Krishna Hutheesing, *We Nehrus*, p. 8.

[21] Shyam Kumari Khan, a cousin of Indira, to author.

[22] Krishna Hutheesing, *op. cit.*, p. 10.

[23] *Ibid.*, p. 12.

[24] Nanda, *op. cit.*, p. 178.

[25] Indira Gandhi: Montessori School magazine, untitled, November 1957. Courtesy, prime minister's secretariat.

2. PLUNGE

[1] In July, Jawaharlal wrote to his father to let him go to Oxford instead of to London to

study law. "Law and Science are all very well in their way," he opined, "but no man, however great a lawyer he may be, will or should be excused for his want of knowledge in certain other subjects. I would much rather risk my success at the Bar than go through life as a mere lawyer with no interest in anything, save the technicalities and trivialities of the law." Motilal's reply was duly ironic. "I am not dense enough not to be able to guess what that branch of knowledge is to which an unfortunate lawyer is or should be a stranger. I may, however, tell you that a mere lawyer has not yet been known to succeed in his own profession, and that the lawyers who have succeeded and will succeed have generally something more than mere law to draw upon. Please do not judge the profession by the bad example of your father who is not even well versed in law."

[2] Nehru, *Autobiography*, p. 35.
[3] Pattabhi Sitaramayya, *The History of the Indian National Congress*, vol. I, p. 119.
[4] Nehru, *op. cit.*, p. 15.
[5] *Ibid.*, p. 15.
[6] Pattabhi Sitaramayya, n. 3, p. 134.
[7] *Ibid.*
[8] *Ibid.*, p. 130.
[9] Nehru, *op. cit.*, p. 31.
[10] *Ibid.*, p. 562.
[11] B. Nehru, cousin of Indira, later Indian ambassador to the United States. In an interview with the author.
[12] Shyam Kumari Khan in an interview with the author.
[13] Indira Gandhi to author.
[14] B. R. Nanda, *The Nehrus*, p. 148.
[15] Nehru, *op. cit.*, p. 40.
[16] Nanda, n. 14, p. 157.
[17] Sitaramayya, n. 3, p. 166.

3. CATALYST

[1] Shyam Kumari Khan in an interview with the author.
[2] Indira Gandhi, Montessori school magazine, untitled, November 1957. Courtesy, prime minister's secretariat.
[3] *Ibid.*
[4] Shyam Kumari Khan to author.
[5] Nehru, *Autobiography*, p. 77.
[6] *Ibid.*, p. 73-75.
[7] B. R. Nanda, *The Nehrus*, p. 196.
[8] *Ibid.*, p. 196.
[9] Nehru, *Autobiography*, p. 79.
[10] *Ibid.*, p. 79.
[11] Krishna Hutheesing, *We Nehrus*, p. 45.
[12] *Ibid.*, p. 52.
[13] Nehru, *Autobiography*, p. 96.
[14] Indira Gandhi, "My Reminiscences of Bapu," *Gandhi Marg*, vol. I, no. 3, July 1959.
[15] In a conversation with the author.
[16] Indira Gandhi, n. 14.
[17] Nehru, *Autobiography*, p. 129.
[18] Pattabhi Sitaramayya, *The History of the Indian National Congress*, vol. I, p. 225.
[19] *Ibid.*, p. 235.

[20] Nehru, *Autobiography*, p. 82.

[21] Quoted in Nehru, *Autobiography*, p. 83, from an article by Mahatma Gandhi on the "Doctrine of the Sword," 1920.

[22] Nanda, n. 7, p. 202.

[23] Nehru, *Autobiography*, p. 88.

[24] Padmini Sengupta, *Sarojini Naidu—A Biography*, p. 169.

[25] *Ibid.*, p. 169.

[26] Nehru, *Autobiography*, p. 88.

[27] Nanda, n. 7, p. 214.

[28] *Ibid.*, p. 214.

[29] *Ibid.*

[30] In an interview with the author.

[31] Nehru, *Autobiography*, pp. 105-6.

[32] Nehru Papers: Unpublished. Courtesy, Nehru Memorial Museum and Library, New Delhi.

[33] Nehru, *Autobiography*, p. 12.

[34] Nehru, *A Bunch of Old Letters*, Romain Rolland to Nehru, May 11, 1926, p. 49.

[35] Krishna Hutheesing, *We Nehrus*, p. 68.

[36] Nehru, *A Bunch of Old Letters*, Sarojini Naidu to Nehru, October 15, 1936, p. 50.

[37] Nehru Papers: Unpublished.

[38] Nehru, *Autobiography*, p. 159.

[39] Nehru, n. 34, Motilal to Nehru, December 2, 1926, p. 51.

[40] *Ibid.*, p. 55.

[41] Pattabhi Sitaramayya, n. 18, p. 305.

[42] Nehru to Gandhi, Nehru Papers: Unpublished. Courtesy, Nehru Museum.

[43] To the author.

[44] Sitaramayya, n. 18, 316.

[45] *Ibid.*

[46] B. K. Nehru to the author.

[47] Indira Gandhi, "Women, Children and Youth Welfare," *Sur*, December 1956.

[48] Indira Gandhi, "On Being a Mother." Courtesy, prime minister's secretariat.

[49] Interview with Winston Burdett, *CBS*, February 18, 1966.

[50] *Ibid.*

[51] Interview with Arnold Michaelis, *McCalls*, April 1966.

4. PRECEPT

[1] Nehru, *Autobiography*, p. 170.

[2] *Ibid.*, p. 180.

[3] Nehru, *A Bunch of Old Letters*, Gandhi to Nehru, December 3, 1928, p. 70.

[4] Indira Gandhi, "On Being a Mother." Courtesy, prime minister's secretariat.

[5] Nehru, n. 3, Gandhi to Nehru, July 29, 1929, p. 74.

[6] Nehru, *Letters from a Father to His Daughter*, p. 10.

[7] *Ibid.*, p. 28.

[8] Nanda, *The Nehrus*, p. 291.

[9] Nehru, *Autobiography*, p. 68.

[10] Nehru, n. 3, Motilal to M.A. Ansari, February 17, 1930, p. 85.

[11] Nanda, *The Nehrus*, p. 273.

[12] Nehru, n. 3, Gandhi to Nehru, May 20, 1927, p. 57.

[13] Nehru, n. 3, Motilal to Gandhi, July 11, 1928, p. 61.

[14] Nehru, n. 3, J. M. Sengupta to Motilal, July 17, 1928, p. 61.

15 Nehru, n. 3, Motilal to Subhas Bose and Sengupta, July 19, 1928, p. 63.
16 Nanda, *The Nehrus*, p. 312.
17 *Ibid.*, p. 313.
18 Nehru, n. 3, Gandhi to Nehru, November 8, 1929, p. 80.
19 Pattabhi Sitaramayya, *The History of the Indian National Congress*, vol. I, pp. 349-50.
20 *Ibid.*, pp. 350-51.
21 *Ibid.*, pp. 351-52.
22 Nehru, n. 3, Nehru to Gandhi, November 4, 1929, p. 77.
23 *Ibid.*
24 Interview with Arnold Michaelis.
25 Pattabhi Sitaramayya, n. 19, p. 354.
26 Nehru, n. 3, Sarojini Naidu to Nehru, September 29, 1929, p. 75.
27 R. K. Karanjia, *The Philosophy of Mr. Nehru*, pp. 140-41.
28 Indira Gandhi, in a conversation with the author.
29 Indira Gandhi, "My Sixteenth Year," *Roshni*, November 4, 1953.
30 Krishna Hutheesing, *We Nehrus*, p. 55.
31 Winston Burdett, *CBS*, February 18, 1968.
32 Arnold Michaelis, *McCalls*, April 1966.
33 Shiv Dutt Upadhyaya to the author.
34 Nanda, *The Nehrus*, p. 332.
35 Arnold Michaelis, *McCalls*, April 1966.
36 Shyam Kumari Khan in an interview with the author.
37 Nehru, *Autobiography*, Appendix 'A', p. 612.
38 Nehru, n. 3, Gandhi to Nehru, March 11, 1930, p. 86.
39 *Ibid.*, p. 87.
40 Nehru, n. 3, Motilal to M.A. Ansari, February 17, 1930, p. 85.
41 Nanda, *The Nehrus*, p. 328.
42 Welles Hangen, *After Nehru, Who?*, p. 166.
43 Krishna Hutheesing, *We Nehrus*, p. 142.
44 Related to author by D. N. Singh, who was then in Allahabad, later with Nehru's own paper, *The National Herald*, in Lucknow.
45 Nehru Papers, unpublished. Courtesy, Nehru Museum. Translated from the original in Hindi by author.

The whole letter is interesting because it indicates the tensions in the family and the manner in which Vijayalakshmi and even her husband, according to Kamala, misrepresented her to Jawaharlal: "The day of your release is approaching but I can hardly hope that you will actually be out. Even if you were to be released you'd soon be thrown in again, but I'm not worried really. I am now prepared for everything." She was particularly upset that both Swarup (Vijaylakshmi) and Ranjit who had come from Calcutta to take part in the movement were misrepresenting her to Jawahar. She tells him that she had put Ranjit in charge of the hospital but that he did not do any work and instead put the blame on her. "I have so often wanted to talk to you, about so many things but there's never any opportunity and it all remains in my heart. So much is happening here that you should know both sides of the picture. So far you get to know only what Ranjit and Swarup tell you—it has become impossible to continue with my work here—It keeps occurring to me everyday that it would be a good thing if both I and Uma bhabi were also to be arrested. Those who think that we are afraid of going to jail and spoil everything, let them go through it themselves—the ones who throughout the summer have *khas tattis* and fans to keep them happy and don't even stir out of their homes, they have the nerve to talk about us. I did not really want to write this but I am so pained that people should spread such talk and that many others should believe it.

I wish I were arrested before you come out, though I have very little hope. Luck has to be added to sacrifice to give one the reward of jail."

[46] Interview with *Forward*, Calcutta, March 1, 1936.

[47] *Ibid.*

[48] Nehru, n. 3, Motilal to Nehru, November 11, 1930, pp. 92-3.

[49] Nehru, *Autobiography*, p. 240.

[50] Nehru, *Glimpses of World History*, p. 5.

[51] Nehru, *Autobiography*, p. 240.

[52] *Ibid.*, p. 207.

[53] Rattan Karaka, *Current*, Bombay, January 1, 1956.

[54] Nehru, *Glimpses of World History*, Nehru to Indira, October 26, 1930, p. 3. According to the Gregorian calendar on November 19, but Jawaharlal had gone by the Samvat era, according to which it fell on October 26.

[55] Krishna Hutheesing, *We Nehrus*, p. 138.

Kamala herself was in good spirits. She described her routine in jail and wrote to her husband, as always in Devnagri script, but in a language that freely used both Hindi and Urdu, and addressing him simply as 'Jawahar,' "There are 21 or 22 other women here, for 2 or 3 days I did not take my walk, but now every morning after tea I walk about a mile or a mile and a half. Then we have prayer, after that a bath and all, and then I read. At 10.30 I have my lunch, at 3 o' clock another cup of tea, 6 o' clock dinner and after that we are locked in for the night. At ten we sleep. I wake up at 5 but get up at about 6.30 or 7."

She resolves to set up a more constructive routine and then confides in him : "When I was arrested I was quite worried about Induji—I wondered what she would do by herself; but now I am feeling quite confident that she is capable of looking after herself. She promised me that she would keep happy and look after herself...."

In the same letter, she added a paragraph for Indira

Induji, Lovei
You must write to me what you do with yourself the whole day.

Get the reports from your master and the pandit and send them to your Papu every 15 days.

I hope you will keep in mind what I told you before I came away. I think of you specially when I take my walks here alone. You too must keep up with them, and then when I am released we shall again go together. There are six months to go, but you will see, six months will be as nothing for you as for me.

I shall write you a much longer letter next time. So far time goes mostly by default, but I am determined to chart out a proper programme. With much love.

Yours
Ammi

Indira followed this up faithfully with her usual newsy style. On 20 January from Allahabad, she wrote:

Papu Darling
Mummie's letter arrived here today just now. And Dadu told us to write to you so that we could send you all the letters together this evening.

Dadu spent a sleepless night yesterday. He coughed most of the time and this morning his face is all swollen up.

I study Sanskrit and English regularly now. I also go to the convent for French and violin lessons.

Raj Chachi phones everyday to let us know how mummie is.

I have read a lot of the books in the library at least all that I could understand. Could you suggest some more that I could read.   You can tell me when I come at your next interview.

Please give my love to Phupha and keep lots for yourself.

Yours loving
Indu

56 Upadhyaya in an interview with the author.

57 Nehru, n. 3, Motilal to Nehru, Januray 20, 1931, p. 96.

58 Nehru, n. 54, p. 39.

59 C. Andrews, "A Maker of Modern India," *Motilal Nehru Centenary Souvenir*, p. 44.

60 Krishna Hutheesing, *Nehru's Letters to His Sister*, p. 19.

61 Arnold Michaelis, *McCalls*, April 1966.

62 Nehru, *Autobiography*, p.562.

63 Nehru, *Glimpses of World History*, p. 31.

64 *Ibid.*, p. 38.

65 *Ibid.*, p. 4.

68 Nehru, *Autobiography*, p. 274.

5. INDIRA DIDI

1 Nehru, *Autobiography*, pp. 255-60.

2 B. C. Roy to Nehru, Nehru Papers : Unpublished.

3 In an interview with Coonverbai Vakil.

4 *Ibid.*

5 Indira Gandhi in an interview with the author.

6 Now a professor in the Sardar Patel Vidyalaya, New Delhi.   In an interview with the author.

7 In an interview with the author.

8 Shanta Gandhi, who was with her in school, in an interview with the author.

9 In an interview with C. Vakil.

10 Shanta Gandhi in an interview with the author.

11 Naik to author.

12 Indira Gandhi to Chanchal Mitra, Leader, Nandadevi, East Expedition, August 29, 1967. Courtesy, prime minister's secretariat.

13 Indira Gandhi in an interview with the author.

14 C. Vakil to author.

15 Indira Gandhi to author.

16 Nehru, *Letters from a Father to His Daughter*, p. 36.

17 Naik in an interview with the author.

18 *Ibid.*

19 B. R. Nanda, *The Nehrus*, p. 150.

20 Pattabhi Sitaramayya, *The History of the Indian National Congress*, vol. I, p. 67.

21 *Ibid.*, p. 466.

22 *Ibid.*, p. 468.

23 *Ibid.*, p. 480.

24 *Ibid.*, p. 481.

25 *Ibid.*, p. 472.

26 *Ibid.*, p. 489.

27 Letter from M. Gandhi to Home Secretary, H. Emerson, Simla, August 27, 1931. Sitaramayya, n. 20, p. 490.

[28] Nehru, *A Bunch of Old Letters*, Roger Baldwin to J. Nehru, April 29, 1931, p. 99.

[29] Nehru, *Autobiography*, p.293.

[30] Gandhi at Minorities Committee, Round Table Conference, London, 1931. Sitaramayya, n. 20, p. 495.

[31] Sitaramayya, n. 20, p. 496.

[32] C. Vakil in an interview with the author.

[33] Indira Gandhi in a conversation with the author.

[34] C. Vakil, in an interview with the author.

[35] Sitaramayya, n. 20, pp. 516-17.

[36] *Ibid.*, p. 521.

[37] Nehru, *Autobiography*, p. 344.

[38] Nehru, *Glimpses of World History*, Nehru to Indira, January 9, 1931, p. 11.

[39] Krishna Hutheesing, *With No Regrets*, p. 77.

[40] Nehru to Indira, April 23, 1932. Nehru, *Glimpses of World History*, p. 87.

[41] C. Vakil in an interview with the author.

[42] Nehru, *A Bunch of Old Letters*, p. 110.

[43] Quoted in Sitaramayya, n. 20, p. 543.

[44] *Ibid.*, p. 543.

[45] *Ibid.*, p. 545.

[46] *Ibid.*, p. 547.

[47] C. Vakil in an interview with the author.

[48] Mrs Gandhi in an interview with the author.

[49] Nehru, *Autobiography*, p. 371.

[50] Gandhi's statement to Bombay government, September 15, 1932. Sitaramayya, n. 20, p. 547.

[51] Gandhi to Ramsay MacDonald, September 9, 1932. Sitaramayya, n. 20, p. 546.

[52] Sitaramayya, n. 20, p. 558.

[53] Nehru, *Autobiography*, p. 373.

[54] B. Roy to Nehru, Nehru Papers : Unpublished.

[55] Nehru to Indira, July 22, 1932. Nehru, *Glimpses of World History*, p. 266.

[56] Indira's letter to Kamala, Nehru Papers : Unpublished.

[57] Nehru, *Glimpses of World History*, p. 57.

[58] Indira Gandhi to Elizabeth Burrel, December 2, 1966. Courtesy, prime minister's secretariat.

[59] Nehru, *Glimpses of World History*, Nehru to Indira, March 28, 1932, p. 59.

[60] Nehru, *Glimpses of World History*, Nehru to Indira, August 4, 1932. p. 274.

[61] Nehru, *Glimpses of World History*, p. 548.

[62] C. Vakil in an interview with the author.

[63] Jehangir Vakil to Nehru, February 28, 1936. Nehru Papers : Unpublished.

6. SHANTINIKETAN

[1] Nehru, *Autobiography*, p. 479.

[2] Krishna Kripalani, *Rabindranath Tagore: A Biography*, Nehru to Krishna Kripalani, August 7, 1941, p. 399.

[3] Nehru to Anil Chanda. Quoted in Anil Chanda, "The Beloved Leader," *Visva Bharti* quarterly, vol.XXIX, nos. 2 and 3, 1963-64, J. Nehru Number.

[4] *Ibid.*

[5] Indira Gandhi, "My Sixteenth Year," *Roshni*, November 4, 1959.

[6] *Ibid.*

7 *Ibid.*
8 Indira Gandhi to J. Fancher, August 7, 1967.   Courtesy, prime minister's secretariat.
9 Indira Gandhi in an interview with the author.
10 Indira Gandhi, n. 5.
11 Hungarian wife of B. K. Nehru.   From an interview with Dorothy McCardde.   *The Washington Post*, January 20, 1966.
12 Nehru, *Autobiography*, p. 386.
13 Neville Chamberlain, quoted by Nehru, *Autobiography*, p. 386.
14 Pattabhi Sitaramayya, *The History of the Indian National Congress*, vol. I, p. 568.
15 *Ibid*, p. 569.
16 Nehru, *Autobiography*, p. 506.
17 *Ibid.*, p. 490.
18 Nehru to Anil Chanda, April 27, 1934, n. 3.
19 Nehru Papers: Courtesy, Nehru Museum.
20 C. Vakil to author.
21 Kamla Nehru to Anil Chanda, n. 3.
22 Indira Gandhi, "Reminiscences of Tagore," *Women on the March*, January 1961.
23 *Ibid.*
24 Anil Chanda in an interview with the author.
25 *Ibid.*
26 In an interview with the author.
27 *Ibid.*
28 Anil Chanda, n. 3.
29 In an interview with the author.
30 In an interview with the author.
31 Indira Gandhi, n. 22.
32 Anil Chanda to author.
33 Nehru, *A Bunch of Old Letters*, Tagore to Nehru, April 20, 1935, p. 122.

7. OXFORD

1 Nehru, *Autobiography*, p. 567.
2 *Ibid.*, p. 567.
3 Nehru's report on Kamala. Nehru Papers: Courtesy, Nehru Museum.
4 Krishna Hutheesing, *We Nehrus*, p. 123.
5 Krishna Hutheesing, *With No Regrets*, p. 119.
6 *Ibid.*, p. 119.
7 Amiya Kumar Sen, "Jawaharlal and Shantiniketan," *Visva Bharti Quarterly*. J. Nehru Number, 1963-64.
8 Nehru to Agatha Harrison, Nehru Papers: Courtesy, Nehru Museum.
9 Nehru, *Discovery of India*, p. 26.
10 *Ibid.*, p. 29.
11 Nehru, *A Bunch of Old Letters*, Gandhi to Nehru, October 3, 1935, p. 123.
12 *Ibid.*
13 Nehru Papers. Courtesy, Nehru Museum.
14 Nehru, n. 11, Tagore to Nehru, October 9, 1935, p. 125.
15 Nehru Papers: Courtesy, Nehru Museum.
16 *Ibid.*
17 K.N. Katin to Nehru, March 13, 1936.   Nehru Papers: Courtesy, Nehru Museum.
18 *Amrita Bazar Patrika*, March 2, 1936.   Courtesy, Nehru Museum.

[19] *Ibid.*, March 3, 1936.   Courtesy, Nehru Museum.

[20] Letter from Mahatma Gandhi to Indira, March 30, 1936.   Translated from the original in Hindi by the author.   Courtesy, Nehru Museum.

[21] C. F. Andrews to Nehru, February 29, 1936. Nehru Papers: Courtesy, Nehru Museum.

[22] Nehru Papers: Courtesy, Nehru Museum.

[23] Princes Aristarchie to Nehru, August 6, 1936. Nehru Papers: Courtesy, Nehru Museum.

[24] Indira Gandhi to the author.

[25] Nehru to Agatha Harrison, July 15, 1936. Nehru Papers: Courtesy, Nehru Museum.

[26] Shiela Grant Duff to Nehru, August 14, 1936. Courtesy, Nehru Museum.

[27] Nehru to Agatha Harrison, February 22, 1937. Nehru Papers: Courtesy, Nehru Museum.

[28] Nehru to Agatha Harrison, February 22, 1937. Nehru Papers: Unpublished.

[29] Welles Hangen, *After Nehru, Who?*, pp. 166-67.

[30] Bhupesh Gupta in an interview with the author.

[31] Indira Gandhi in an interview with the author.

[32] *Ibid.*

[33] Bhupesh Gupta in an interview with the author.

[34] Feroze Gandhi to Nehru. Nehru Papers: Courtesy, Nehru Museum.

[35] Nehru to Feroze Gandhi. Nehru Papers: Courtesy, Nehru Museum.

[36] Rajni Patel to Nehru, December 16, 1936. Nehru Papers: Courtesy, Nehru Museum.

[37] Nehru Papers: Courtesy, Nehru Museum.

[38] Nehru, n. 11, Tagore to Nehru, December 31, 1936, p. 221.

[39] Nayantara Sahgal, *Prison and Chocolate Cake*, pp. 71-72.

[40] Sitaramayya, *The History of the Indian National Congress*, vol. II, p. 34.

[41] Nehru, *Discovery of India*, p. 369.

[42] Sitaramayya, *op. cit.*, p. 32.

[43] *Ibid.*, p. 41.

[44] Nehru, n. 11, Tagore to Nehru, March 28, 1937,   p. 225.

[45] Nehru to Tagore, April 13, 1937.   Nehru Papers: Courtesy, Nehru Museum.

[46] Indira Gandhi to Dawn McBride, June 16, 1958. Courtesy, prime minister's secretariat.

[47] Nehru to Agatha Harrison, June 24, 1937. Nehru Papers: Courtesy, Nehru Museum.

[48] Nehru to Agatha Harrison, August 30, 1937. Nehru Papers: Courtesy, Nehru Museum.

[49] Indira Gandhi, "Women, Children and Youth Welfare," Argentinian Journal, *Sur*, December 1, 1956.

[50] K.A. Abbas, *The Return of the Red Rose*, p. 77.

[51] Nikhil Chakravarty (Editor, *Mainstream*, New Delhi) to author.

[52] Indira Gandhi to the author.

[53] Bhupesh Gupta in an interview with the author.

[54] Nehru, n. 11, Christine Toller to Nehru, August 27, 1936, p. 206.

[55] Nehru to Agatha Harrison, February 2, 1938. Nehru Papers: Courtesy, Nehru Museum.

[56] Nehru, n. 11, Lord Lothian to Nehru, December 6, 1935, p. 129.

[57] Nehru to Agatha Harrison, May 9, 1938. Nehru Papers: Courtesy, Nehru Museum.

[58] Nehru Papers: Courtesy, Nehru Museum.

[59] Nehru, n. 11, Lord Lothian to Nehru, June 24, 1938, p. 287.

[60] Nehru, *Autobiography*, p. 605.

[61] *Ibid.*

[62] Naik in an interview with the author.

[63] Helen Darbyshire to Nehru, September 12, 1938. Nehru Papers: Courtesy, Nehru Museum.

[64] Helen Darbyshire to Nehru, September 17, 1938. Nehru Papers: Courtesy, Nehru Museum.

[65] Nehru Papers: Courtesy, Nehru Museum.

[66] M. Nahas to Nehru, December 12, 1938. Nehru Papers: Unpublished.

[67] Nehru Papers: Courtesy, Nehru Museum.

[68] *Ibid.*

[69] *Ibid.*

[70] *Ibid.*

[71] Indira Gandhi to the author.

[72] Nehru to A. Harrison, October 21, 1939. Nehru Papers: Courtesy, Nehru Museum.

[73] Nehru to A. Harrison, November 16, 1939. Nehru Papers: Unpublished.

[74] Nehru, n. 11, Nehru to Edward Thompson, January 5, 1940, p. 420.

[75] Nehru to Agatha Harrison, March 4, 1940. Nehru Papers: Unpublished.

[76] *Ibid.*

[77] Nehru to Madan Atal, May 16, 1940. Nehru Papers: Unpublished.

[78] Krishna Hutheesing, *With No Regrets*, p. 123.

[79] Krishna Hutheesing, *Nehru's Letters to His Sister*, p. 66.

[80] Indira Gandhi to Ratan Karaka, *Current*, January 11, 1956.

[81] Bhupesh Gupta in an interview with the author.

[82] Welles Hangen, *After Nehru, Who?*, p. 167.

[83] Nehru, n. 11, Purnima Bannerji to Nehru, May 7, 1941, p. 457.

8. FOCUS

[1] Vijayalakshmi Pandit, *So I Became a Minister*, p. 19.

[2] Nehru, *A Bunch of Old Letters*, Nehru to Govind Pant, November 25, 1937, p. 263.

[3] Nehru, n. 2, Govind Pant to Nehru, March 23, 1938, p. 281.

[4] Maulana Azad, *India Wins Freedom*, p. 22.

[5] *Ibid.*

[6] Nehru, n. 2, Jinnah to Nehru, March 17, 1938, p. 278.

[7] *Ibid.*

[8] Nehru, *Discovery of India*, p. 397.

[9] *Ibid.*, p. 429.

[10] *Ibid.*, p. 432.

[11] Pattabhi Sitaramayya, *The History of the Indian National Congress*, vol. II, p. 132.

[12] *Ibid.*, p. 136

[13] *Ibid.*, pp. 136-37.

[14] *Ibid.*, p. 139

[15] *Ibid.*, p. 141.

[16] *Ibid.*, p. 151.

[17] *Ibid.*, pp. 169-70.

[18] *Ibid.*, pp. 174-75.

[19] Azad, *op. cit.*, p. 34.

[20] Sitaramayya, *op. cit.*, pp. 192-93.

[21] Nehru, *Autobiography*, p. 610.

[22] Nehru, n. 2, Jayaprakash Narain to Nehru, July 20, 1940, p. 446.

[23] Azad, *op. cit.*, p. 35.

[24] Sitaramayya, *op. cit.*, p. 206.

[25] *Ibid.*, p. 219.

[26] B. R. Nanda, *Mahatma Gandhi*, p. 221.

[27] Nehru, *Autobiography*, p. 451.

[28] *The Socialist Congressman*, Feroze Gandhi Memorial Number, September 15, 1961.

[29] Anand Mohan, *Indira Gandhi*, p. 136.

[30] In an interview with the author.

[31] Krishna Hutheesing, *Nehru's Letters to His Sister*, April 6, 1941, p. 77.

[32] Krishna Hutheesing, *We Nehrus*, pp. 141-42.

[33] *Ibid.*, p. 143.

[34] *Ibid.*

[35] Nehru Papers: Courtesy, Nehru Museum.

[36] B.K. Nehru in an iterview with the author.

[37] Ansar Harwani in an interview with the author.

[38] Nehru, *Glimpses of World History*, Nehru to Indira, October 26, 1930, p. 3.

[39] *The Leader*, February, 26, 1942.

[40] Nehru Papers: Courtesy, Nehru Museum.

[41] Nehru, n. 2, Gandhi to Nehru, March 4, 1942, p. 474.

[42] Gandhi to Nehru, March 4, 1942. Gandhi Papers: Courtesy, Gandhi Smarak Nidhi.

[43] Gandhi Papers: Courtesy, Gandhi Smarak Nidhi.

[44] Mrs Gandhi in an interview with Arnold Michaelis, *McCalls*, April 1966.

[45] Nayantara Sahgal, *Prison and Chocolate Cake*, p. 104.

[46] Nehru, n. 2, Gandhi to Nehru, March 4, 1942, p. 474.

[47] Interview with Arnold Michaelis, *McCalls*, April, 1966.

[48] Krishna Hutheesing, *With No Regrets*, p. 153.

[49] In an interview with the author.

[50] Uma Bajaj in an interview with the author. Uma Bajaj is popularly referred to as "Om".

[51] D. N. Singh in an interview with the author.

[52] Chalapathi Rau in *The Socialist Congressman*, Feroze Gandhi Memorial number, September 25, 1963.

[53] Sahgal, *op. cit.*, p. 147.

[54] In an interview with the author.

[55] K.A. Abbas, *The Return of the Red Rose*, pp. 88-89.

[56] Nehru Papers: Courtesy, Nehru Museum.

It is interesting to note that even a slight change in program made Indira wire to her father in Delhi.

> Darling my thoughts have been with you going Lucknow fifth night returning seventh Kashmir departure slightly delayed much love Indu

There was a constant exchange of advice between father and daughter, all through her honeymoon. "Give my love to Liddermat and Kolhahor," wired Jawaharlal on April 12, soon after they reached, adding with concern, "Avoid tiring excursions." On July 11, he wired again after hearing from Indira how much they had enjoyed Kolhahor. "Don't hurry back, live in beauty while you may." At the same time he suggested that they visit the North West Frontier Province on their way back. But five days later he was saying, "Visit to Frontier Province inadvisable owing to great heat, suggest your returning Allahabad before month end."

[57] Anand Mohan, *Indira Gandhi*, p. 157.

9. JAIL

[1] Winston Churchill, *The Hinge of Fate*, p. 214.

[2] Maulana Azad, *India Wins Freedom*, p. 50.

[3] In its resolution at Lahore, 1940.

[4] Nehru, *Discovery of India*, pp. 466-68.

[5] B. R. Nanda, *Mahatma Gandhi*, p. 226.

[6] *Ibid.*

[7] *Ibid.*, p. 229.

[8] Sitaramayya, *The History of the Indian National Congress*, vol. II, p. 237.

[9] *Ibid.*, p. 333.

[10] *Ibid.*, p. 334.

[11] Azad, *op. cit.*, p. 73.

[12] Sitaramayya, *op. cit.*, p. 335.

[13] *Ibid.*, p. 341.

[14] Nehru, *Discovery of India*, pp. 456-57.

[15] In an interview with Arnold Michaelis, *McCalls*, April 1966.

[16] Nehru, *Discovery of India*, p. 486.

[17] Sitaramayya, *op. cit.*, p. 345.

[18] *Ibid.*, p. 349.

[19] Krishna Hutheesing, *We Nehrus*, p. 156.

[20] Indira Gandhi, "A Page from the Book of Memory," *Women on the March*, September 1963.

[21] Vijayalakshmi Pandit, *Prison Days*, p. 1.

[22] *Ibid.*, p. 3.

[23] Kamala Prasad Mohiley, *The Socialist Congressman*, Feroze Gandhi Memorial Number, September 25, 1963.

[24] In an interview with Michaelis.

[25] K.A. Abbas, *The Return of the Red Rose*, p. 92.

[26] Indira Gandhi, n. 20.

[27] This happened to be Raja Rao, the writer, himself a participant in the 1942 struggle. In a conversation with the author.

[28] *The Socialist Congressman*, Feroze Gandhi Memorial Number, September 25, 1963.

[29] Indira Gandhi, n. 26.

[30] Vijayalakshmi Pandit, *Prison Days*, p. 20.

[31] Krishna Hutheesing, *Nehru's Letters to His Sister*, p. 92.

[32] Indira Gandhi, n. 20.

[33] *Ibid.*

[34] Vijayalakshmi Pandit, *Prison Days*, p. 72.

[35] *Ibid.*, p. 98.

[36] *Ibid.*

[37] Indira Gandhi, n. 20.

[38] Krishna Hutheesing, *Nehru's Letters to His Sister*, p. 102.

[39] *Ibid.*, p. 110.

[40] *Ibid.*, p. 112.

[41] *Ibid.*, p. 114

[42] *Ibid.*, 120.

[43] Vijayalakshmi Pandit, *Prison Days*, p. 116.

[44] *Ibid.*, p. 117

[45] *Ibid.*, p. 112.

[46] *Ibid.*, p. 123.

[47] Arnold Michaelis, *McCalls*, April 1966.

[48] Indira Gandhi, n. 20.

[49] Mrs Gandhi in an interview with Palsule, Multi Language Press Service of India, November 1967. Courtesy, prime minister's secretariat.

50 Krishna Hutheesing, *We Nehrus*, p. 167.

51 Vijyalakshmi Pandit, *Prison Days*, pp. 119-20.

52 Krishna Hutheesing, *Nehru's Letters to His Sister*, p. 162.

53 Anand Mohan, *Indira Gandhi*, p. 264.

54 Krishna Hutheesing, *Nehru's Letters to His Sister*, p. 162.

55 *Ibid.*, pp. 162-63.

56 *Ibid.*, p. 167.

57 Teji Bachchan to author.

58 Indira Gandhi, "On Being a Hostess at Tin Murti," *The International*, Bombay, August 1957.

59 Nehru Papers : Courtesy, Nehru Museum.

60 B.R. Nanda, *Mahatma Gandhi*, p. 241.

61 Congress Working Committee Resolution, Delhi, March, 1942.   Sitaramayya, n. 8.

62 Mahatma Gandhi, *Harijan*, April 6, 1948.

63 Nanda, *op. cit.*, p. 238.

64 Maulana Azad, *India Wins Freedom*, p. 140.

65 Michael Brecher, *Nehru : A Political Biography*, p. 316.

66 Allan Campbell-Johnson, *Mission with Mountbatten*, p. 35.

67 *Ibid.*, p. 139.

68 Arnold Michaelis, *McCalls*, April 1966.

69 Nanda, *op. cit.*, p. 250.

70 Welles Hangen, *After Nehru, Who?*, p. 169.

71 Krishna Hutheesing, *We Nehrus*, p. 193.

72 Hangen, *op. cit.*, p. 159.

73 Chalapathi Rao, "Indira : A Portrait in Outline," *Indira Priyadarshni*, p. 15.

74 Campbell-Johnson, *op. cit.*, p. 46.

75 Krishna Hutheesing, *Nehru's Letters to His Sister*, p. 186.

76 Nanda, *op. cit.*, p. 261.

77 In an interview with the author.

78 Mrs Gandhi's speech at a meeting of the Council for Promotion of Communal Harmony, May 23, 1965.   Courtesy, prime minister's secretariat.

79 Francis Watson, "A Story of Courage under Fire," *Guardian*, March 15, 1967.

80 *Ibid.*

81 *Ibid.*

82 Indira Gandhi, "My Reminiscences of Bapu," *Gandhi Marg*, vol. II, n. 3, July 3, 1967.

83 n. 78.

84 Watson, *op. cit.*

85 Subhadra Joshi in an interview with the author.

86 Watson, *op. cit.*

87 In an interview with the author.

88 n. 78.

89 In an interview with the author.

90 Indira Gandhi, n. 82.

91 *Ibid.*

92 R.K. Prabhu, *This is Bapu*, p. 1.

93 Nayantara Sahgal, *Prison and Chocolate Cake*, p. 220.

94 n. 78.

95 *Nehru's Speeches*, vol. 1 (September 1946-May 1949), Publications Division, New Delhi, Government of India, p. 25.

96 Arnold Michaelis, *McCalls*, April 1966.

97 Indira Gandhi to William J. Cook, *Newsweek*, February 25, 1966, and in an interview with the author.

[98] Sahgal, *op. cit.*

[99] Indira Gandhi to author.

[100] Vimla Sindhi to the author.

[101] Indira Gandhi in an interview with the author.

10. INFLUENCE

[1] Nayantara Sahgal, *Prison and Chocolate Cake*, p. 77.

[2] Indira Gandhi, "On Being a Mother."   Courtesy, prime minister's secretariat.

[3] Indira Gandhi, "On Being a Hostess at Tin Murti," *The International*, August 1957.

[4] *Ibid.*

[5] *Ibid.*

[6] *Ibid.*

[7] *Ibid.*

[8] *Ibid.*

[9] *Ibid.*

[10] Related to author by Inder Kapoor, PTI correspondent, who covered Nehru's visits for several years.

[11] Broadcast over All India Radio, August 22, 1956.   Courtesy, prime minister's secretariat.

[12] Nehru, *Autobiography*, p. 226.

[13] Michael Brecher, *A Political Biography*, p. 418.

[14] *Ibid.*, p. 420.

[15] James Cameron, "India's First Lady : Indira," *Envoy*, London, June 1966.

[16] *Ibid.*

[17] R. K. Karanjia, *The Philosophy of Mr Nehru*, p. 53.

[18] *Ibid.* p. 63.

[19] Welles Hangen, *After Nehru, Who?*, p. 171. B. K. Nehru recalls that when Jawaharlal was on the point of sending off a telegram to the Chinese government on hearing the rumor that the Chinese delegation had perished in a plane crash, it was Indira, who again restrained him with the advice : "First check whether the information is correct or not."

[20] Arnold Michaelis, *McCalls*, April 1966.

[21] K. P. S. Menon, *Russian Panorama*, p. 41.

[22] *Ibid.*, p. 42.

[23] Indira Gandhi to Mrs Deanah Salakhoba, July 30, 1967.   Courtesy, prime minister's secretariat.

[24] Indira Gandhi, n. 3.

[25] Teji Bachchan to author.

[26] Indira Gandhi, n. 2.

[27] In an interview with the author.

[28] *Ibid.*

[29] Broadcast over All India Radio, August 22, 1956.   Courtesy, prime minister's secretariat.

[30] *Ibid.*

[31] USIS Report, January 4, 1957.   Courtesy, USIS, New Delhi.

[32] Indira Gandhi, n. 3.

[33] Anand Mohan, *Indira Gandhi*, p. 255.

[34] To a group of Child Welfare Experts, New York, December 22, 1956.

[35] Address : Youth Convention, Baroda, November 21, 1958.   Courtesy, prime minister's secretariat.

[36] *Ibid.*

[37] *Ibid.*

[38] *Ibid.*

[39] Sitaramayya, *The History of the Indian National Congress*, vol. I.

[40] Mridula Sarabhai to Nehru, February 24, 1940. Nehru Papers: Courtesy, Nehru Museum.

[41] Maulana Azad to Nehru, March 3, 1942. Nehru Papers: Courtesy, Nehru Museum.

[42] Nehru to Azad, March 5, 1942. Nehru Papers: Courtesy, Nehru Museum.

[43] Mukul Banerjee to author.

[44] *Ibid.*

[45] Indira Gandhi in a foreward to the pamphlet, *Women and Elections*, published by the Women's Department of the Congress Party, August 1956.

[46] Indira Gandhi in a foreword to the pamphlet, *Women's Role in National Savings Campaign*, published by the Women's Department of the Congress Party, June 27, 1958.

[47] In a foreword to the pamphlet, *Task Before the Congress Women Workers*, published by the Women's Department of the Congress party.

[48] Related to author by Nikhil Chakravarty.

[49] Mukul Banerjee to author.

[50] Uma Agarwal to the author.

[51] Indira Gandhi to the author.

[52] Fory Nehru in an interview with Dorothy McCardde of the *Washington Post*, January 20, 1966.

[53] Walles Hangen, *After Nehru, Who?*, p. 160.

[54] Related by Vimla Sindhi to author.

[55] Related to author by E.K. Ramaswamy, then special correspondent of *The Hindu*.

[56] Related to author by Raj Thapar, wife of journalist and commentator, Romesh Thapar. The second woman she recalled to be Rajen Nehru, wife of R. K. Nehru, diplomat, administrator, and a cousin of Indira.

[57] Related to author by Prema Mandi, a friend of Feroze Gandhi.

[58] Chalapathi Rau, *The Socialist Congressman*, Feroze Gandhi Memorial Number, September 25, 1963.

[59] Related to author by Mohammad Yunus.

[60] Y. P. R. Kapoor to author.

[61] Chalapathi Rau, n. 58.

[62] *Lok Sabha Debates*, vol. X, December 9 to 21, 1957.

[63] *Ibid.*

[64] Related by Jagdish Kodesia in the *Socialist Congressman*, September 25, 1963.

[65] *Ibid.*

[66] *Ibid.*

[67] Mohammad Yunus to author.

[68] Prema Mandi to author.

[69] Mohammad Yunus to author.

[70] Article by Indira Gandhi in *Current Events*, quoted in the *Tribune*, November 5, 1957.

[71] *Ibid.*

[72] Nehru Papers: Courtesy, Nehru Museum.

[73] Anand Mohan, *Indira Gandhi*, p. 219.

[74] Mukul Banerjee to the author.

[75] E. K. Ramaswami to the author.

[76] Speech at a public meeting, Coimbatore, Madras, June 20, 1965. Courtesy, prime minister's secretariat.

[77] Address: Youth Convention, Baroda, November 21, 1958,

[78] *Ibid.*

79 Anand Mohan, *Indira Gandhi*, p. 221.
80 Related to author by Rajendra Kumari Bajpai.
81 Related to author by Mukul Banerjee.
82 *Ibid.*
83 Rajendra Kumari Bajpai to the author.
84 Speech inaugurating the Indira Music University, Khairagarh, October 14, 1956. Courtesy, prime minister's secretariat.
85 Indira Gandhi, "Women's Role in Shaping New Society," *Women on the March*, June 1957.
86 *Ibid.*
87 Related by Y.P.R. Kapoor to the author.
88 *Ibid.*
89 Ansar Harvani to the author.
90 Rajendra Kumari Bajpai to the author.
91 *Ibid.*
92 B. K. Nehru to the author.
93 Anand Mohan, *Indira Gandhi*, p. 225.
94 Krishna Menon to the author.
95 Dr Ram Manohar Lohia to the author.
96 Sadiq Ali to the author.
97 *New York Herald Tribune*, January 16, 1959.
98 Related by Y.P.R. Kapoor to the author.
99 *Ibid.*
100 Related by Inder Gujral to the author.

PART II: POWER

1. REALISM

1 Convocation Address, Bangalore University, January 8, 1967. Courtesy, prime minister's secretariat.
2 To the author.
3 Press Conference, Allahabad, February 7, 1959. *Asian Recorder*, February 7-14, 1959, p. 2490.
4 *The National Herald*, February 9, 1959.
5 *Asian Recorder*, February 14-20, 1959, p. 2502.
6 Address on taking over office, February 8, 1959. *The Hindustan Times*, February 9, 1959.
7 Press Conference at the AICC office. *The Hindustan Times*, February 10, 1959.
8 Anand Mohan, *Indira Gandhi*, p. 224.
9 Press Conference, February 7, 1959. *Asian Recorder*, February 14-20, 1959, p. 2503.
10 Howland Memorial Lecture, Yale University, 1960.
11 Elvira Marquis, *Christian Science Monitor*, March 6, 1960.
12 *Ibid.*
13 Paul Grimes, "The Most Important Woman in India," *New York Times*, January 11, 1959.
14 *Ibid.*
15 Quoted in Hangen, *After Nehru Who?*, p. 174.

16 Kerala Education Bill, April 17, 1959.

17 *The Kerala Situation*, pamphlet, issued by the All-India Congress Committee, July 17, 1959.

18 *The Statesman*, New Delhi, May 21, 1959.

19 Statement by D.K. Henry Austin, General Secretary, Kerala Pradesh Congress Committee, June 1, 1959.

20 Statement in Trivandrum, *The Statesman*, New Delhi, June 6, 1959.

21 *The Statesman*, New Delhi, June 12, 1959.

22 Mrs Gandhi to author.

23 Sadiq Ali to author.

24 *The Statesman*, New Delhi, June 12, 1959.

25 In an interview with the author.

26 Speech inaugurating Madras District Congress Political Conference, June 7, 1959. *Statesman*, June 8, 1959.

27 To correspondents, June 11, 1959. *The Statesman*, New Delhi, June 12, 1959.

28 To correspondents at Trivandrum. *The Statesman*, New Delhi, June 14, 1959.

29 Related by E.K. Ramaswami to author.

30 Related by Nikhil Chakravorty to author.

31 *The Hindustan Times*, July 26, 1959.

32 *Ibid.*

33 *The Statesman*, New Delhi, July 27, 1959.

34 *The Hindustan Times*, July 27, 1959.

35 Related by Y.P.R. Kapoor to author.

36 Grimes, n. 13.

37 *The Hindustan Times*, October 13, 1959.

38 *Ibid.*

39 Related by Kapoor to author.

40 *Ibid.*

41 *Ibid.*

42 K.K. Shah to author.

43 Inaugural address to All-India Students' Convention, New Delhi, July 1961. Courtesy, prime minister's secretariat.

44 Marquis, *op. cit.*

45 Convocation Address, Andhra University, December 7, 1963. Courtesy, prime minister's secretariat.

46 Speech at Women's Press Club, Washington, November 7, 1961.

47 *AICC Economic Review*, the magazine of the Congress party, July 22, 1959.

48 Speech at a public meeting, Coimbatore, June 20, 1965. Courtesy, prime minister's secretariat.

49 Grimes, n. 13.

50 *The Hindustan Times*, May 11, 1959.

51 *The Statesman*, New Delhi, February 5, 1969.

52 Speech at Bangalore, January 12, 1960. Courtesy, prime minister's secretariat.

53 Marquis, *op. cit.*

2. NOSTALGIA

1 Teji Bachchan to author.

2 Inder Malhotra to author.

3 Teji Bachchan to author,

[4] Prema Mandi, a friend of Feroze, to author.

[5] Quoted in *The Socialist Congressman*, Feroze Gandhi Memorial Number, 1961.

[6] *Ibid.*

[7] Anand Mohan, *Indira Gandhi*, p. 213.

[8] Speech at Bangalore, January 12, 1960.   Courtesy, prime minister's secretariat.

[9] Related by Rajendra Kumari Bajpai to author.

[10] Prema Mandi to author.

[11] *Ibid.*

[12] Inder Malhotra to author.

[13] *The Socialist Congressman*, Feroze Gandhi Memorial Number, 1961.

[14] Inder Malhotra to author.

[15] Mohammad Yunus to author.

[16] Indira to a friend who wishes to remain anonymous, September 22, 1960.

[17] Michael Brecher, *Nehru: A Political Biography*, p. 613.

[18] Grimes, "The Most Important Woman in India," *New York Times*, January 11, 1959.

[19] Howland Memorial Lecture, Yale University, 1960.

[20] *Ibid.*

[21] *Ibid.*

[22] *Ibid.*

[23] *Ibid.*

[24] *Ibid.*

[25] To Indian newsmen at Palam airport, New Delhi, on return to India. *Indian Express*, September 6, 1961.

[26] Interview in Washington, December 18, 1956.

[27] In an interview with Arvinda Dave for Asian National Program, Kenya Broadcasting Service, September 1961.

[28] *Ibid.*

[29] "Post Intelligence," Seatle, Washington, March 30, 1962.

[30] *Ibid.*

[31] *Ibid.*

[32] Press Release.   Courtesy, USIS, New Delhi.

[33] R.K. Karanjia, *The Philosophy of Mr Nehru*, p. 118.

[34] *Ibid.*, p. 118.

[35] Address to the University of Notre Dame, South Bend, Indiana, April 4, 1963. Courtesy, prime minister's secretariat.

[36] *Ibid.*

[37] In an address, "The Role of India in the 60's," to Mount Holyoke College, South Hadley, Massachusetts.   April 10, 1963.   Courtesy, prime minister's secretariat.

[38] Speech at the New York World Fair, April 8, 1963.   Courtesy, USIS, New Delhi.

[39] Richard C. Patterson, Speech at the New York World Fair, April 8, 1963.   Courtesy, USIS.

[40] The rest were Morarji Desai, Lal Bahadur Shastri, Y.B. Chavan, Jayaprakash Narayan, Krishna Menon, S.K. Patil, and General B.M. Kaul.   Out of these the first three, and of course Indira Gandhi, proved the validity of Hangen's possible power hierarchy.   But he was completely off the track with the general who nowhere emerged even as a "stop gap" in politics.

[41] Welles Hangen, *After Nehru, Who?*, p. 159.

[42] Ansar Harvani, former Member of Parliament, to author.

[43] Rajendra Kumari Bajpai to author.

[44] Related by Mukul Bannerjee to author.

[45] Inaugural address, Gauhati session of All-India Newspaper Editors' Meet, Gauhati, December 20, 1964.   Courtesy, prime minister's secretariat.

[46] On the N.B.C. television show "Today," New York, April 8, 1963.

[47] R.K. Karanjia, *op. cit.*, p. 134.

[48] Nandan B. Kagal, "The Year of the K. Plan," *The Times of India*, New Delhi, January 1, 1964.

[49] From *The Times*, London. Quoted in R.K. Karanjia, *op. cit.*, p. 136.

[50] R.K. Karanjia, *op. cit.*, p. 136.

[51] Speech at the plenary session, Gopabandhu Nagar, Bhuvaneshwar, January 10, 1964. *The Times of India*, New Delhi, January 12, 1964.

[52] D.B. McMahon, *The Times of India*, New Delhi, January 2, 1964.

[53] *The Times of India*, New Delhi, January 9, 1964.

[54] Sadiq Ali to author.

[55] Arnold Michaelis "The Essential Nehru," National Educational Television Program, New York, May 18, 1964.

[56] Michael Brecher, *Succession in India*, p. 25.

[57] Teji Bachchan to author.

[58] Letter to Mrs Gandhi from a girl named Vandana. *The Hindustan Times*, June 2, 1964.

[59] *The Times of India*, New Delhi, June 4, 1964.

[60] *Ibid.*

[61] Krishna Hutheesing, *We Nehrus*, p. 296.

[62] Indira Gandhi to author.

[63] *Ibid.*

[64] *Ibid.*

3. SHADOWS

[1] *The Hindustan Times*, June 3, 1964.

[2] Address to the Congress parliamentary party, June 2, 1964, reported in *The Times of India*, New Delhi, June 3, 1964.

[3] Related by E. K. Ramaswami to author.

[4] Krishnan Bhatia, "Political Notebook," *The Hindustan Times*, June 11, 1964.

[5] Address to Press Information Bureau officers, Akashvani Bhavan, July 2, 1964. Quoted in *The Statesman*, New Delhi, July 3, 1964.

[6] *The Statesman*, New Delhi, July 3, 1964.

[7] *Ibid.*

[8] *Ibid.*, July 2, 1964.

[9] Nehru was compelled to let Menon resign in 1962 as India's defense minister after a public outcry in face of the Chinese attack and India's military unpreparedness. See Welles Hangen, *After Nehru, Who?*, p. 177.

[10] *The Statesman*, New Delhi, July 20, 1964.

[11] Nehru had been his own minister for external affairs.

[12] *The Statesman*, New Delhi, July 19, 1964.

[13] Kuldip Nayar, *Between the Lines*, p. 14.

[14] Mohan Singh Sengar to author.

[15] *Ibid.*

[16] Narayana K. Menon to author.

[17] Romesh Thapar, editor of *Seminar*, to author.

[18] Inaugural Address, All-India Newspapers Editors' Meet, Gauhati, December, 1964. Courtesy, Press Information Bureau, Government of India.

[19] *Ibid.*

20 K.A. Abbas, *The Return of the Red Rose*, p. 134.

21 Indira Gandhi to Harindranath Chattopadhyaya, April 23, 1968. Unpublished. Courtesy, prime minister's secretariat.

22 *Ibid.*

23 *The Hindustan Times*, September 7, 1964.

24 Address to the International Conference of the Junior Chamber, New Delhi, September 24, 1964. Courtesy, prime minister's secretariat.

25 *Ibid.*

26 Address to the Socialist Convention of Northern India Congress Workers, *The Hindustan Times*, September 7, 1964.

27 Michael Brecher, *Succession in India*, p. 92.

28 Nayar, *op. cit.*, p. 9.

29 Brecher, *op. cit.*, p. 107.

30 *The Hindustan Times*, September 11, 1964.

31 *Ibid.*, October 8, 1964.

32 *Ibid.*, November 3, 1964.

33 *Ibid.*

34 *Ibid.*

35 *Ibid.*, November 1, 1964.

36 *Ibid.*

37 *Ibid.*, February 14, 1965.

38 *Ibid.*, February 12, 1965.

39 Speech at a public meeting, Coimbatore, Madras, June 20, 1965. Courtesy, prime minister's secretariat.

40 Address at a public meeting, Patna, February 19, 1965. Quoted in *The Hindustan Times*, February 20, 1965.

41 Address to a Students' Meeting, Patna, February 20, 1965. Quoted in *The Hindustan Times*, February 21, 1965.

42 *The Times of India*, New Delhi, August 9, 1965.

43 Anand Mohan, *Indira Gandhi*, p. 252.

44 Press Conference, Srinagar, August 10, 1965. *The Hindustan Times*, August 11, 1965.

45 *The Statesman*, August 15, 1965.

46 Related to author by B. K. Tiwari, Special Correspondent, *Indian Express*, New Delhi.

47 *The Hindustan Times*, August 12, 1965.

48 *Ibid.*, August 14, 1965.

49 *The Statesman*, New Delhi, August 15, 1965.

50 Krishan Bhatia, "Political Notebook," *The Hindustan Times*, August 13, 1965.

51 *The Hindustan Times*, August 24, 1965.

52 *Ibid.*, August 26, 1965.

53 *Ibid.*, August 31, 1965.

54 *Ibid.*, September 4, 1965.

55 *Ibid.*, September 5, 1965.

56 *Ibid.*

57 *The Hindustan Times*, September 20, 1965.

58 To a rally of women's voluntary organizations, New Delhi, September 21, 1965, *The Hindustan Times*, September 22, 1965.

59 At Jammu, September 27, 1965. Quoted in *The Hindustan Times*, September 28, 1965.

60 Indira Gandhi in an interview with the Phillipines Free Press, April 2, 1968. Courtesy, prime minister's secretariat.

61 Indira Gandhi to author.

[62] Krishan Bhatia, "Political Notebook," *The Hindustan Times*, September 18, 1964.

[63] *The Hindustan Times*, September 15, 1964.

[64] Krishan Bhatia, "Political Notebook," *The Hindustan Times*, January 15, 1965.

[65] *Ibid.*

[66] Indira Gandhi in an interview with the United News of India. Quoted in *The Times of India*, New Delhi, January 22, 1965.

[67] *Ibid.*

[68] *Ibid.*

[69] Related by Harish Chandola, then correspondent of *The Times of India*, New Delhi, to the author.

[70] Brecher, *op. cit.*, p. 113.

[71] Marion Woolfson, "The Woman in Charge," *Evening Times*, London, February 13, 1967.

[72] *Ibid.*

[73] At Chirawa, Rajasthan, March 20, 1965. Quoted in *The Hindustan Times*, March 22, 1965.

[74] *The Hindustan Times*, January 11, 1966.

4. TRIUMPH

[1] To author.

[2] Brecher, *Succession in India*, p. 256.

[3] Vishwabandhu Gupta to author.

[4] Related by E. K. Ramaswami to the author.

[5] Brecher, *op. cit.*, p. 193.

[6] Related by E. K. Ramaswami to the author.

[7] Brecher, *op. cit.*, p. 202.

[8] *The Hindustan Times*, January 14, 1966.

[9] *The Washington Post*, January 16, 1966.

[10] *The Baltimore Sun*, January 16, 1966.

[11] Vishwabandhu Gupta to author.

[12] Mukul Bannerjee to author.

[13] Ansar Harvani to author.

[14] E. K. Ramaswami to author.

[15] *The Hindustan Times*, January 19, 1966.

[16] In an interview with the *Daily Express*, London, and Granada Television, January 18, 1966. Reported in *The Hindustan Times*, January 19, 1966.

[17] *The Hindustan Times*, January 19, 1966.

[18] *The Hindustan Times*, January 19, 1966.

[19] *Ibid.*

[20] In an interview with the *Daily Express*, London, and Granada Television, January 18, 1966.

[21] *The Hindustan Times*, January 18, 1966.

[22] K. A. Abbas, *The Return of the Red Rose*, p. 10.

[23] Narayana Menon to author.

[24] Related by Narayana Menon to author.

[25] Rajendra Kumari Bajpai to author.

[26] *Ibid.*

[27] Motilal Nehru to Krishna. Quoted in Krishna Hutheesing, *With No Regrets*, p. 45.

[28] "As It Happens," *The Hindustan Times*, October 27, 1964.

[29] *The Hindustan Times*, January 20, 1966.

[30] *Look* magazine, April 1968.

[31] Courtesy, USIS, New Delhi.

[32] *New York Herald Tribune*, January 1966.

[33] *Washington Evening Star*, January 1966.

[34] *Azang*, January 1966.

[35] *L' Action*, January 1966.

[36] *The Economist*, January 1966.

[37] *The New York Times*, January 1966.

[38] *The Guardian*, January, 1966.

[39] Selig Harrison, *The Washington Post*, January, 1966.

[40] *The Hindustan Times*, January 25, 1966.

[41] Lohia also said in the Lok Sabha (*Indian Express*, February 24, 1966) that he was convinced that tension between India and Pakistan would persist as long as they remained separate states.

[42] Address to the Students' Union, Delhi University. See *The Hindustan Times*, December 24, 1965.

[43] Quoted in the *Financial Times*, London, January 18, 1966.

[44] *Ibid.*

[45] Interview with Kuldip Nayar, November 11, 1965. Quoted in his book, *Between the Lines*, p. 14.

[46] Selig Harrison, *The Washington Post*, January 20, 1966.

[47] Address to Indian Merchants Chamber, December 9, 1967. Courtesy, prime minister's secretariat.

[48] Address to the Students' Union, Delhi University. Quoted in *The Hindustan Times*, December 24, 1965.

[49] n. 47.

[50] *The Hindustan Times*, January 31, 1966.

[51] Rajya Sabha, February 15, 1966. *The Hindustan Times*, February 16, 1966.

[52] Lok Sabha, March 1, 1966. *The Hindustan Times*, March 2, 1966.

[53] Address at Kurukshetra University, March 11, 1966. *The Hindustan Times*, March 12, 1966.

[54] *The Hindustan Times*, February 27, 1966.

[55] Interview in ABC's "Issues and Answers," March 14, 1966.

[56] Mary McGrory, *Washington Evening Star*, April 3, 1966.

[57] *Ibid.*

[58] At a reception by the Press Association, New Delhi, March 12, 1966. Reported in *The Hindustan Times*, March 13, 1966.

[59] Speech, inaugurating the 39th annual session of the Federation of Indian Chambers of Commerce and Industry, New Delhi, March 12, 1966. Courtesy, prime minister's secretariat.

[60] Speech at New York Economic Club. Courtesy, USIS, New Delhi.

[61] April 1, 1966. Press Release, USIS, New Delhi.

[62] B.K. Nehru to author.

[63] *Ibid.*

[64] *The Hindustan Times*, April 4, 1966.

[65] Address to the National Press Club, Washington, March 29, 1966. Courtesy, prime minister's secretariat.

[66] *Ibid.*

[67] Reply to the debate on the president's address. Lok Sabha, March 1, 1966. Courtesy, prime minister's secretariat.

[68] *Ibid.*

[69] *Ibid.*

[70] Message to the *Economic Review*, February 1966. Quoted in *The Hindustan Times*, February 8, 1966.

[71] *Ibid.*

[72] *The Hindustan Times*, February 6, 1966.

[73] J. Anthony Lucas, "She Stands Remarkably Alone," *New York Times Magazine*, March 27, 1966.

[74] E.K. Ramaswami, in whose presence the conversation took place, to author.

[75] "Mrs Gandhi's First 100 Days," *The Times*, London, May 3, 1966.

[76] Interview with Jean Witz, *Le Monde*, February 8, 1966.

[77] *Ibid.*

[78] *The Hindustan Times*, February 14, 1966.

[79] Krishan Bhatia, "Political Notebook," *The Hindustan Times*, March 4, 1966.

[80] *Ibid.*, March 11, 1966.

[81] Rajendra Kumari Bajpai to the author.

[82] Interview with Jean Witz, *Le Monde*, February 8, 1966.

[83] Joint US-Indian Communique Washington, March 29, 1966.

[84] Lok Sabha, February 23, 1966. *The Hindustan Times*, February 24, 1966.

[85] Interview in *Christian Science Monitor*, March 15, 1966.

[86] From official translation from the original in Hindi. Courtesy, prime minister's secretariat.

[87] *The Hindustan Times*, May 21, 1966.

[88] *Ibid.*

[89] Official translation from the original speech in Hindi. Courtesy, prime minister's secretariat.

[90] Rs 7.5 to one US dollar against the previous 4.76.

[91] Finance minister Sachin Chaudhri's broadcast over A.I.R., June 5, 1966.

[92] Press Conference, New Delhi, June 6, 1966.

[93] Interview with R.K. Karanjia, *Blitz*, August 18, 1966.

[94] Interview with R.K. Karanjia, August 16, 1966. Courtesy, prime minister's secretariat.

[95] *Ibid.*

[96] B.K. Nehru to author.

[97] S.A. Dange to author.

[98] Krishna Menon to author.

[99] Minoo Masani to author.

[100] *The Economist*, July 23, 1966.

[101] Ram Manohar Lohia to author.

[102] Indira Gandhi to author.

PART III : LEADERSHIP

1. CAMPAIGN

[1] *Indian Express*, New Delhi, September 17, 1966.

[2] Nehru, *Autobiography*, p. 52.

[3] Related by Shiv Shankar Singh of Rae Bareli to author.

[4] Baij Nath Prasad Yadav to author.

[5] *Ibid.*

[6] *Ibid.*

[7] *Patriot*, New Delhi, September 16, 1966. She presumably meant the adoption of the philosophy and methods of non-violence by the Negro leader Martin Luther King in his efforts to achieve racial equality in the U.S.A.

[8] *Patriot*, New Delhi, September 16, 1966.

[9] *Ibid.*

[10] Nehru, *Autobiography*, p. 77.

[11] *Ibid.*, p. 55.

[12] *Ibid.*, p. 57.

[13] Inder Kumar Gujral (now minister in Mrs Gandhi's cabinet) to author.

[14] Tibor Mende, *Conversations with Mr. Nehru*, pp. 38-39.

[15] *Indian Express*, New Delhi, September 20, 1966.

[16] *Ibid.*

[17] *Ibid.*

[18] *Ibid.*, September 30, 1966.

[19] *Ibid.*

[20] *Ibid.*, October 2, 1966

[21] Minoo Masani to author.

[22] Convocation Address, North Bengal University, Siliguri. Courtesy, prime minister's secretariat.

[23] The Swatantra party manifesto, 1967.

[24] A.P. Chatterjee, "The Election Strategy of the Left Communists," *General Elections in India*, edited by M. Pattabhiram, p. 71.

[25] Atal Behari Bajpayee, "The Bharatiya Jana Sangh," *op. cit.*, p. 73.

[26] Madhu Limaye, "S.S.P. Perspective," *op. cit.*, p. 59.

[27] Surendra Nath Dwivedy, "P.S.P. in Indian Politics," *op. cit.*, p. 57.

[28] Dharam Teja, Chairman, Jayanti Shipping Company, who was later prosecuted and sentenced for misappropriation of the company's funds.

[29] *The Hindustan Times*, September 2, 1966.

[30] *Indian Express*, New Delhi, October 11, 1966.

[31] *Ibid.*, October 16, 1966.

[32] *The Hindustan Times*, November 1, 1966.

[33] *Ibid.*, November 8, 1966.

[34] *Indian Express*, New Delhi, November 8, 1966.

[35] *The Hindustan Times*, November 8, 1966.

2. PATTERN

[1] *The Hindustan Times*, November 9, 1966.

[2] B.K. Tiwari to author.

[3] *The Statesman*, New Delhi, December 25, 1966.

[4] Surendra Nath Dwivedy, "P.S.P. in Indian Politics," *General Elections in India*, edited by M. Pattabhiram.

[5] This device invariably ensured her instant rapport with the masses.

[6] *The Hindustan Times*, January 5, 1967.

[7] *Ibid.*, January 7, 1967.

[8] *Ibid.*

[9] *The Hindustan Times*, January 10, 1967.

[10] *Ibid.*

[11] "You see, there is the question of whom the party wants, and whom the people want. My position amongst the people is uncontested." In an interview with the United News of India. Quoted in *The Hindustan Times*, December 26, 1967.

[12] *The Hindustan Times*, January 9, 1967.

[13] Convocation address, Bangalore University, January 8, 1967. Courtesy, prime minister's secretariat.

[14] *The Hindustan Times*, January 18, 1967.

[15] Since 1967 five more states have come into being: Meghalaya, Arunachal Pradesh, Manipur, Himachal Pradesh, and Tripura.

[16] In the presence of the author.

[17] At a town called Bhilwara in Rajasthan. The translation from the original Hindi into English of all of Mrs Gandhi's speeches in Rajasthan are by the author who attended the meetings.

[18] At Bhanswara.

[19] *Ibid.*

[20] At Ajmer.

[21] *The Hindustan Times*, January 19, 1967.

[22] At Bhilwara, in the presence of the author.

[23] At Chittor.

[24] *Ibid.*

[25] At Bhanswara.

[26] At Bhilwara and Bhanswara.

[27] In the presence of the author.

[28] *Ibid.*

[29] The phrase coined by Rajagopalachari to denote the rule of government control through permits.

[30] In the presence of the author. Speech translated into English by the author.

[31] *Ibid.*

[32] I. L. Kapur to author.

[33] *Ibid.*

[34] *Ibid.*

[35] *Ibid.*

[36] *Ibid.*

[37] Related by I. L. Kapur to author.

[38] *The Hindustan Times*, February 9, 1967.

[39] Related to the author by a member of the prime minister's party who wishes to remain anonymous.

[40] *The Hindustan Times*, February 10, 1967.

3. OPPOSITION

[1] *The Hindustan Times*, November 2, 1966.

[2] *The Times of India*, New Delhi, January 30, 1967.

[3] At a Press Club of India luncheon, December 21, 1966. Quoted in *Indian Express*, New Delhi, December 22, 1966.

[4] *The Hindustan Times*, December 15, 1966.

[5] *Ibid.*, January 29, 1967.

[6] *The Hindustan Times Weekly*, January 30, 1967.

[7] *Ibid.*

[8] *Ibid.*, December 18, 1966.

⁹ Interview with the UNI. *The Statesman*, January 15, 1967.

¹⁰ *Ibid.*

¹¹ *Indian Express*, New Delhi, January 30, 1967.

¹² At a Press conference, December 21, 1966. Quoted in *Indian Express*, New Delhi, December 22, 1966.

¹³ Interview with the UNI. Reported in *Indian Express*, New Delhi, January 9, 1967.

¹⁴ *The Hindustan Times*, New Delhi, January 12, 1967.

¹⁵ *Ibid.*, January 10, 1967.

¹⁶ *Ibid.*, February 11, 1967.

¹⁷ Interview with the UNI. Reported in *Indian Express*, New Delhi, December 26, 1966.

¹⁸ *The Hindustan Times*, February 10, 1967.

¹⁹ *The Times of India*, New Delhi, January 21, 1967.

²⁰ Mrs Zulfiquar to author.

²¹ The author was present in Rae Bareli.

²² From author's interviews with people in Rae Bareli.

²³ *Ibid.*

²⁴ *Ibid.*

²⁵ S. Nihal Singh, "Confidence in Rae Bareli Camp," *The Statesman*, New Delhi, February 14, 1967.

²⁶ *The Statesman*, February 21, 1967.

²⁷ Related by Mrs Zulfiquar to author.

²⁸ *The Statesman*, New Delhi, February 25, 1967.

²⁹ The author was present.

³⁰ Related by K. Natwar Singh to author.

4. CONTINUITY

¹ *The Statesman*, New Delhi, February 28, 1967.

² In the presence of the author.

³ *Ibid.*

⁴ *The Hindustan Times*, February 28, 1967.

⁵ In the presence of the author.

⁶ *Ibid.*

⁷ To author, and others present.

⁸ *Indian Express*, New Delhi, February 27, 1967.

⁹ Atulya Ghosh to author.

¹⁰ Welles Hangen, *After Nehru, Who?*, p. 172.

¹¹ *The Hindustan Times*, February 28, 1967.

¹² To author.

¹³ Various campaign supporters of Mrs Gandhi to author.

¹⁴ *The Statesman*, March 1, 1967.

¹⁵ Inder Malhotra, "Political Commentary," *The Statesman*, New Delhi, March 4, 1967.

¹⁶ *Ibid.*

¹⁷ Related by E. K. Ramaswami to author.

¹⁸ *The Statesman*, New Delhi, March 5, 1967.

¹⁹ Michael Brecher, *Succession in India*, p. 202.

5. CHALLENGE

[1] *The Hindustan Times*, March 9, 1967.
[2] *The Statesman*, New Delhi, March 2, 1967.
[3] *Ibid.*, March 5, 1967.
[4] *Ibid.*
[5] *Ibid.*, March 6, 1967.
[6] *The Sunday Standard*, New Delhi, March 5, 1967.
[7] *The Hindustan Times*, March 6, 1967.
[8] *The Hindustan Times*, March 7, 1967.
[9] *Indian Express*, New Delhi, March 7, 1967.
[10] *Ibid.*
[11] *The Statesman*, New Delhi, March 8, 1967.
[12] *Ibid.*, March 14, 1967.
[13] *The Statesman*, New Delhi, March 1, 1967.
[14] *Ibid.*, March 5, 1967.
[15] *Ibid.*, March 8, 1967.
[16] *The Hindustan Times*, February 28, 1967.
[17] S. Nihal Singh, "Report on the Campaign," *The Statesman*, February 15, 1967.
[18] Appeal by Trilok Singh, then State Chairman of the P. S. P., *The Statesman*, March 4, 1967.
[19] *The Sunday Standard*, New Delhi, March 12, 1967.
[20] *Ibid.*

6. AFFIRMATION

[1] Shyam Kumari Khan to author.
[2] Frank Moraes, "Delhi's Headless Wonders," *The Indian Express*, New Delhi, March 10, 1967.
[3] Inder Malhotra, "Political Commentary," *The Statesman*, March 11, 1967.
[4] C. S. Pandit to author.
[5] E. K. Ramaswami to author.
[6] C. S. Pandit to author.
[7] *The Statesman*, New Delhi, March 9, 1967.
[8] *Indian Express*, New Delhi, March 9, 1967.
[9] At a press conference, attended by the author.
[10] To author, March 10, 1967.
[11] *Indian Express*, New Delhi, March 11, 1967.
[12] *Ibid.*
[13] *Ibid.*
[14] In the presence of the author.
[15] Y.B. Chavan to author.
[16] Mrs Gandhi to author, and other members of the press.
[17] The author was a witness.
[18] *Ibid.*
[19] *Ibid.*
[20] *Ibid.*
[21] *Ibid.*
[22] To author, and other pressmen.

23 *The Statesman*, New Delhi, March 13, 1967.
24 *Ibid.*
25 *Ibid.*
26 Ariel, *Indian Express*, New Delhi, March 12, 1967.
27 The author was present.
28 *Ibid.*
29 *Ibid.*
30 Official text. Courtesy, prime minister's secretariat.

PART IV : IMAGE

1. TRENDS

1 To the author.
2 *Ibid.*
3 *The Statesman*, New Delhi, November 3, 1969.
4 Speech at Nirankari Mission Convention, Ram Lila Grounds, New Delhi, November 12, 1969. Quoted in *The Statesman*, New Delhi, November 3, 1969.
5 Related by M. L. Bhardwaj (then principal information officer, Government of India) to author.
6 In an interview with the author.
7 *Ibid.*
8 Courtesy, prime minister's secretariat.
9 Mrs Gandhi in an interview with Dr Gunter Gans, German Television, February 14, 1969.
10 Mrs Gandhi to author.
11 *The Asian Recorder*, February 5-11, 1968, p. 8157.
12 Speech in Rajya Sabha during motion of thanks on president's address, February 24, 1969. Courtesy, Press Information Bureau, Government of India.
13 n. 9.
14 Minoo Masani to author.
15 Speech in the Rajya Sabha during motion of thanks on the president's address, February 24, 1969.
16 *Ibid.*
17 *The Asian Recorder*, January 8-14, 1968, p. 8111.
18 *The Statesman*, New Delhi, July 11, 1969.
19 Broadcast over All India Radio, July 19, 1969. Courtesy, Press Information Bureau, Government of India.
20 Mrs Gandhi to author.
21 *Ibid.*
22 n. 9.
23 At a public meeting (Delhi, September 9) attended by the author.
24 Ariel, "Men, Matters, and Memories," *The Sunday Standard*, New Delhi, January 26, 1969.
25 D. N. Kalhan, *Indira Gandhi : Three Years as Prime Minister*.
26 S. Nihal Singh, *The Statesman*, New Delhi, January 1, 1970.
27 Jean Witz, *Le Monde*, February 8, 1966.
28 At a meeting of the Congress parliamentary party, April 1, 1969. Quoted in *The Asian Recorder*, April 22-28, 1968, p. 8286.

29 *Ibid.*

30 In an interview with the author.

31 At a Congress workers' meeting, Ujjain, 1970. The translation from the Hindi into English is by the author who was present on the occasion.

32 *The Statesman*, New Delhi, July 11, 1969.

33 *Ibid.*

34 *Ibid.*, July 14, 1969.

35 n. 31.

36 *The Statesman*, New Delhi, August 21, 1969. Those with Mrs Gandhi were jubilant. Jagjivan Ram said: "Our stand has been amply vindicated and it has been demonstrated that the country is with us."

37 Related to author by L.K. Malhotra.

38 *Ibid.*

39 *The Statesman*, New Delhi, November 2, 1969.

40 The author was a witness to the proceedings on both days of this AICC session.

41 Speech on August 15, 1967. Courtesy, prime minister's secretariat.

42 Taya Zinkin, "India Revisited: II," *The Statesman*, New Delhi, January 31, 1970.

43 S. Nihal Singh, "Political Commentary," *The Statesman*, New Delhi, January 30, 1970.

44 *The Asian Recorder*, February 12-18, 1968, p. 8169.

45 S. Nihal Singh, "Political Commentary," *The Statesman*, New Delhi, January 30, 1970.

46 Mrs Gandhi to author.

47 Mrs Gandhi's address to the Third Annual Convocation of the Indian Institute of Management, Ahmedabad, April 13, 1968. Courtesy, prime minister's secretariat.

2. CHARISMA

1 Sham Lal, "The National Scene," *The Times of India*, New Delhi, November 26, 1969. The references are made to the Maharaja of Gaekwad (who had opted for the Congress led by Mrs Gandhi), Morarji Desai, Krishna Menon, and Chandrajeet Yadav.

2 H. N. Bahuguna to author.

3 *The Times of India*, New Delhi, December 6, 1969.

4 Sham Lal, n. 1.

5 *The Times of India*, New Delhi, November 29, 1969.

6 *Ibid.*, December 8, 1969.

7 *Ibid.*, December 19, 1969.

8 "Bangalore and After," pamphlet, issued by the Gujarat Pradesh Congress Committee.

9 *Indian Express*, December 22, 1969.

10 *Ibid.*

11 Inder Malhotra to author.

12 *Ibid.*

13 *The Times of India*, New Delhi, December 19, 1969.

14 Speech in the debate on the communal situation in the country in the Lok Sabha, May 14, 1970. Courtesy, prime minister's secretariat.

15 From a speech in Hindi at Chandni Chowk, Delhi, June 22, 1970. Translated into English by the author who was present on the occasion.

16 *The Times of India*, New Delhi, December 20, 1969.

17 *Ibid.*

18 At a public meeting at Allahabad, December 6, 1969. Quoted in *The Times of India*, New Delhi, December 7, 1969.

19 C. S. Pandit, "New Delhi Diary," *The Sunday Standard*, New Delhi, March 8, 1970.

20 *Ibid.*

21 In an interview with R. K. Karanjia, *Blitz*, February 20, 1971.

22 C. S. Pandit, "New Delhi Diary," *The Sunday Standard*, New Delhi, June 28, 1970.

23 Speech, Lok Sabha, September 1, 1969. Courtesy, Press Information Bureau, Government of India.

24 C. S. Pandit, "Purses Bill in Parliament," *The Sunday Standard*, New Delhi, September 6, 1970.

25 *Ibid.*

26 To the author.

27 Broadcast to the nation, December 27, 1970. Courtesy, prime minister's secretariat.

28 At a meeting with the press, March 11, 1971. The author was present.

BIBLIOGRAPHY

ABBAS, K.A., *Indira Gandhi: The Return of the Red Rose*, Bombay, Popular Prakashan, 1966.
———, *That Woman: Indira's Seven Years in Power*, New Delhi, Indian Book Company, 1973.
AZAD, ABUL KALAM, *India Wins Freedom*, Bombay, Orient Longmans Pvt. Ltd., 1959.
BRECHER, MICHAEL, *Nehru: A Political Biography*, London, Oxford University Press, 1959.
———, *Succession in India*, London, Oxford University Press, 1966.
CHURCHILL, WINSTON S., *History of the Second World War: The Hinge of Fate*, London, Castle.
CROCKER, WALTER, *A Contemporary's Estimate*, London, George Allen & Unwin, 1966.
GEORGE T. J. S., *Krishna Menon: A Biography*, Bombay, Jaico Publishing House, 1964.
HANGEN, WELLES, *After Nehru, Who?*, London, Rupert Hart-Davis, 1963.
HUTHEESING, KRISHNA NEHRU, *Nehru's Letters to His Sister*, London, Faber & Faber, 1963.
———, *With No Regrets*, Bombay, Padma Publications, 1946; The John Day Company, 1945.
———, *We Nehrus*, Bombay, Patel Publications Pvt. Ltd., 1967.
JOHNSON, ALLAN-CAMPBELL, *Mission With Mountbatten*, Bombay, Jaico Publishing House, 1951.
KALHAN, D.N., *Indira Gandhi: Three Years as Prime Minister*, Delhi, Radhakrishna Prakashan, 1969.
KARANJIA, R.K., *The Philosophy of Mr. Nehru*, London, George Allen & Unwin Ltd., 1966.
MENDE, TIBOR, *Conversations With Nehru*, London, Secker & Warburg.
MENON, K.P.S., *Russian Panorama*, Bombay, Oxford University Press, 1962.
MOHAN ANAND, *Indira Gandhi: A Personal and Political Biography*, New York, Meredith Press, 1967.
MONTAGU EDWIN, *An Indian Diary*, London, William Heinemann Ltd., 1930.
NANDA, B.R., *The Nehrus: Motilal and Jawaharlal*, London, George Allen & Unwin, 1962; New York, The John Day Company, 1963.
———, *Mahatma Gandhi: A Biography*, London, George Allen & Unwin, 1948.
NAYAR, KULDIP, *Between the Lines*, New Delhi, Allied Publishers, 1969.
NEHRU, JAWAHARLAL, *An Autobiography*, London, The Bodley Head, 1942; New York, The John Day Company, 1941.
———, *Glimpses of World History*, London, Lindsay Drummond, 1934; New York, The John day Company, 1942.
———, *Letters from a Father to His Daughter*, Calcutta, Oxford University Press, 1945.
———, *A Bunch of Old Letters*, Bombay, Asia Publishing House, 1958.
———, *Speeches: 1946-1949*, vol. II, New Delhi, Publications Division, Ministry of Information and Broadcasting, 1949.
———, *Discovery of India*, London, Meridian Books Limited, 1960.
PANDIT, VIJAYALAKSHMI, *So I Became A Minister*, Allahabad, Kitabistan, 1939.
———, *Prison Days*, Calcutta, Signet Press, 1945.

PATTABHIRAM, M., *General Elections in India*, New Delhi, Allied Publishers.

PRABHU, R.K., *This is Bapu*, Navajivan Publishing House, Allahabad.

PRASHER, UMA, *Indira Priyadarshini*, New Delhi, Popular Book Services, 1966.

PYARELAL, *Mahatma Gandhi: The Last Phase*, vol. I, Ahmedabad, Navajivan Press, 1956.

SAHAGAL, NAYANTARA, *Prison and Chocolate Cake*, London, Victor Gollancz Ltd., 1954.

———, *From Fear Set Free*, London, Victor Gollancz Ltd., 1962.

SAXENA MOHANLAL, *Motilal Nehru Centenary Souvenir*, Delhi, Motilal Nehru Centenary Committee, 1961.

SEN GUPTA, PADMINI, *Sarojini Naidu: A Biography*, Asia Publishing House.

SITARAMAYYA B. PATTABHI, *History of the Indian National Congress*, New Delhi, S. Chand & Co., 1935.

TENDULKAR, D.G., *Mahatma*, vol. VI, New Delhi, Publications Division, Ministry of Information and Broadcasting, Government of India, 1953.

GLOSSARY

AARTI : A religious ritual in which the devotee holds a salver bearing fruit, flowers, and an earthen lamp on the palm of the hand and swings it in a slow, propitiatory motion in front of the deity to the chanting of prayers

ABHAYA : Fearlessness

ACHKAN : High-necked, knee-length coat

ALPANA : The art of decorating with colored powder; such a decoration

AMRUD WALI : A woman who sells guavas

ASHRAM : A hermitage, a place of retreat for a religious group

ASSAN : Small mat or carpet

ATTA : Wheat flour

BANDH : A massive organized protest, characterized by processions and the closing of shops and institutions

BHABHI : Elder brother's wife

BHAJANS : Religious hymns

BHAI : Brother

CHANDAN : Sandalwood powder; considered sacred

CHOLI : A blouse covering the front leaving the back and midriff bare

CHURIDAR : Tight, close-fitting trousers

CHUNI : A long piece of cloth used by girls to cover the front

DARSHAN : Homage

DEEPAKS : Tiny earthen lamps

DHOTI : A long piece of cloth worn around the waist and between the legs so that it forms baggy gathers around each leg

DHOTIWALLAH : One who wears dhoti

DIWAN : Prime Minister

DIDI : Elder sister

FATWA : Command

GHAGRA : A heavy, flared petticoat

GHAR JAMAI : Son-in-law who lives with his in-laws

GURUDEV : Lord of teachers

HINDIWALLAHS : Indians whose mother tongue is Hindi

JAGIR : Estate

JUTTIES : Flat, semi-closed, decorative shoes with an upturned toe

KAFOOR : Camphor; considered sacred

KANYA DAN : One of the essential rites in the Hindu marriage connoting "offering of a virgin."

KATORIES : Small, deep saucers

KISANS : Peasants

KOTWAL : Superintendent of police
KULHARS : Clay tumblers
KUM KUM : A vermilion mark used on the forehead by women
KURTA : Loose, knee-length shirt
LAGAN PATRIKA : Wedding card
LATHI : Baton
LEHNGA : A flared skirt
MAHILA VIBHAG : Women's wing
MAMU : Mother's brother
MANDAP : Platform
MANTRA : Vedic hymn or prayer
MAHAMANTRI : Prime Minister
MAULANA : A Mohammedan learned in theology and law
MAULVI : Muslim spiritual leader
MAUSI : Mother's sister
MITHAIWALA : Sweet vender
MOHALLA : A block of houses built around a courtyard; a neighborhood
MULAQUAT KA DIN : The day of meeting
NAHAR : Canal
NAMASKAR : Joining both hands in greeting; a Hindu custom
PAD YATRA : Pilgrimage on foot
PALLO : The end of the sari that hangs lose over the shoulder
PANDIT : One who is learned in the religion of India, any learned man
PANI : Water
PANWALLAHS : Betel-leaf sellers
PHUPHI : Father's sister
PUJA : Worship, prayer
PURIS : Indian style pancakes
PURNA SWARAJ : Complete independence
RAM NAUMI : A Hindu festival observed to celebrate Lord Rama's birthday
SADHU : Saint, holy man
SAMADHI : The final place of rest
SHAMIANA : Awning
SHEHNAI : A wind instrument
SHERWANI : High-necked, knee-length coat
SHLOKAS : Sanskrit verses
SWADESHI : Indigenous
SWARAJ : Self-government, independence
TEHSIL : District
THALIS : Platters
TILAK : A red vermilion mark put on the forehead; considered sacred
VILAYATI MOOLI : Horseradish
VIVAHA : Marriage
ZENANA : Women's section

INDEX

578

INDIRA GANDHI

Chinai, Babubhai, 391
Chintamani, C.Y., 20
Churchill, Winston, 123
Civil disobedience, 40, 74, 82, 181
Coalition ministries, in states, 457, 458
Commissariat, Dr S.A., Feroze's aunt, 161, 164
Commonwealth Prime Ministers' Conference, 226, 227, 314, 323
Communal Award, 92, 123
Communal riots, 45, 152, 211-14; in Bengal and Bihar, 204; in Kanpur, 74
Communalism, 200; seeds of, 18
C.P.I., election manifesto of, 392, 393
Congress cooperative programme, 283
Congress-League scheme, 21
Congress ministeries, 134, 150, 151, 155
Constituent Assembly, 217
Cow slaughter agitation, 389, 390, 396-99, 413
Cranford, Sir Frederick, 295
Criminal Law Amendment Act, 36
Cripps, Sir Stafford, 131, 175, 179
Cripps Mission, 177
Curzon, Lord, 9

Dalai Lama, 224; grant of political asylum to, 284
Dandi March, 62
Dange, S.A., 187, 395, 431
Darbyshire, Helen, 140
Das, Biswanath, 472, 475
Dass, C.R., 15, 27, 40, 45, 46
Datta, S.K., 85
De Gaulle, Charles, 358, 361
Defections, phenomenon of, 459
Defense of India Act, 17
Delhi Manifesto, 56, 57
Delhi Pact, 82, 83
Democracy, experiment of, 391; role of the opposition parties in, 398; danger to, 396
Desai, Bhulabhai, 123
Desai, Mahadev, 85
Desai, Morarji, 322, 342, 438, 439-41
Dhebar, U.N., 257, 258, 441
Dinesh Singh, 449, 450, 454, 477
Direct Action Day, 204
Dixit, Uma Shankar, 197, 449, 474
Dominion status, concept of, 56
D.M.K., election manifesto of, 392
Duff, Sheila Grant, 127

Einstein, Albert, 44
Election campaign, 381-87, 433, 434
Election of 1967, 390-91, 394, 434, 435
Electoral alliance, 393
Extremists, aim of, 9

Fateh Singh, 367
Fiji, agitation against the oppression of Indian workers in, 17

Gandhi, Feroze, 64, 105, 106, 129, 161, 209; ardent socialist, 248; arrest of, 187; career in London; 129; death of, 292, 378; elected to Parliament for three years 1952-55, 245; equations between Mrs Gandhi and, 243-45; family background of, 161; general manager of the *Indian Express* in Delhi in 1953, 243; illness, 290, 292; maiden speech in Parliament, 245; managing director of the *National Herald* (Lucknow), 208-10; on corruption in the Life Insurance Corporation of India (Mundhra affairs), 246, 247; qualities of, 162, 290
Gandhi, Indira, aide and confidante of Jawaharlal, 223; approach to land reforms, 267, 268; attitude to politics, 59; birth of, 4, 14; central election committee, member of, 299; Congress president, 259, 264, 265; Menon and, 147; decision to contest the election from Rae Bareli, 380; differences with Kamaraj, 365; education, 75, 76, 109, 111, 112, 116, 126, 139, 140; election meeting in Orissa, 421; elected to the Rajya Sabha, 322, 323; Feroze Gandhi and, 131, 243-45, 292; hostess in the prime minister's house (Tin Murti), 243; illness, 95, 140-145; information and broadcasting minister, 312-20; influence of Jawaharlal, 257, Gandhiji, 103, Tagore, 115; marriage, 106, 147, 163-67; Morarji Desai and, 347, 437-55; on foreign aid, 388; on foreign policy, 383; on Hinduism, 39, 40; on mixed economy, 320; on nonalignment, 354; on planning, 320; on socialism, 320; re-elected prime minister in 1967, 449-55; sworn in as prime minister, 351; visit to Europe, 43, to Moscow, 228, 229, 324, to USA, 296, 356, 357